Financial Remedies Handbook

Ninth Edition

Financial Remedies Handbook

Ninth Edition

Roger Bird LLB, Solicitor
Former District Judge

Andy King MA
District Judge, Aldershot and Farnham County Court

Family Law

Published by Family Law
A publishing imprint of Jordan Publishing Limited
21 St Thomas Street
Bristol BS1 6JS

British Library Cataloguing-in-Publication Data

A catalogue record for this book is available from the British Library.

ISBN 978 1 84661 710 2

Typeset by Letterpart Limited, Caterham on the Hill, Surrey CR3 5XL
Printed in Great Britain by CPI Antony Rowe, Chippenham and Eastbourne

PREFACE

In this edition, some of the issues that were mentioned in the last edition as being susceptible of development have indeed been developed by the courts. The weight to be placed on agreements has been considered at some length and it has become clear that *Radmacher v Granatino* was by no means the last word on this subject. At the same time, the definition of 'marital' and 'non-marital' assets has been scrutinised in a way that would not have been anticipated some years ago and the law relating to inherited or pre-acquired wealth is constantly being modified. These are all issues that will not go away and add to the pressure for some radical reconsideration, perhaps even codification, of the law relating to financial relief.

These issues normally assume importance only where the parties enjoy considerable wealth. However, it should not be forgotten that the majority of cases dealt with by district judges up and down the country involve comparatively modest assets, and the now complete abolition of legal aid for such cases has created new problems. Parties of average income cannot afford the fees that solicitors have to charge but are at a loss when any non-standard issue arises in their case. District judges are forced to improvise to ensure that justice is done but there are limits on how far a judge can go to help parties in a system of rules devised for adversarial litigation. This inevitably leads to inconsistency between courts and injustice for some parties.

The time has surely come for the amendment of the rules to provide for something like a small claims track for financial relief cases. This would empower, and indeed require, district judges at the First Directions Appointment to adopt an inquisitorial approach and to identify issues that might be important, but which the parties had not identified. Orders could then be made to produce the evidence required. This would be a rule change that would have to be carefully drafted but there is no doubt that it is possible and indeed necessary.

As with the last edition, I am very grateful to District Judge Andy King for his contributions to this book.

The law given is as at the date below.

Roger Bird
24 June 2013

CONTENTS

TABLE OF CASES

References are to paragraph numbers.

TABLE OF STATUTES

References are to paragraph numbers.

TABLE OF STATUTORY INSTRUMENTS

References are to paragraph numbers.

TABLE OF EUROPEAN MATERIALS

References are to paragraph numbers.

TABLE OF ABBREVIATIONS

CCA 1984	County Courts Act 1984
CCR	County Court Rules 1981
CE	cash equivalent
CETV	cash equivalent transfer value
CJJA 1982/1991	Civil Jurisdiction and Judgments Act 1982/1991
CMOPA 2008	Child Maintenance and Other Payments Act 2008
the Commission	Child Maintenance and Enforcement Commission
the Convention	European Convention for the Protection of Human Rights and Fundamental Freedoms 1950
CPI	Consumer Prices Index
CPR	Civil Procedure Rules 1998
CSA 1991	Child Support Act 1991
CS(MASC) Regs 1992	Child Support (Maintenance Assessments and Special Cases) Regulations 1992
CSPSSA 2000	Child Support, Pensions and Social Security Act 2000
DPMCA 1978	Domestic Proceedings and Magistrates' Courts Act 1978
ECHR	European Court of Human Rights
EFTA	European Free Trade Association
FA	first appointment
FDR	financial dispute resolution
FLA 1996	Family Law Act 1996
FPR 1991	Family Proceedings Rules 1991
FPR 2010	Family Procedure Rules 2010
HMRC	Her Majesty's Revenue and Customs
HRA 1998	Human Rights Act 1998
IA 1986	Insolvency Act 1986
Information Regulations 2000	Pensions on Divorce etc (Provision of Information) Regulations 2000
I(PFD)A 1975	Inheritance (Provision for Family and Dependants) Act 1975
LPA 1925	Law of Property Act 1925
MCA 1973	Matrimonial Causes Act 1973
MFPA 1984	Matrimonial and Family Proceedings Act 1984
MO(RE)A 1972	Maintenance Order (Reciprocal Enforcement) Act 1972
NCIS	National Criminal Intelligence Service
NRP	non-resident parent

PCAO	pension compensation attachment order
PCSO	pension compensation sharing order
Pensions Regulations 2000	Divorce etc (Pensions) Regulations 2000, SI 2000/1123
POCA 2002	Proceeds of Crime Act 2002
PPF	Pension Protection Fund
PWC	parent with care
RPI	Retail Prices Index
RSC	Rules of the Supreme Court 1965, SI 1965/1776
SCA 1981	Supreme Court Act 1981
SERPS	State Earnings Related Pensions Scheme
SJE	single joint expert
the 1999 Rules	Family Proceedings Rules 1991, SI 1991/1247, as amended by Family Proceedings (Amendment No 2) Rules 1999, SI 1999/3491
the 2008 Regulations	Occupational Pension Schemes (Transfer Values) (Amendment) Regulations 2008, SI 2008/1050
TLATA 1996	Trusts of Land and Appointment of Trustees Act 1996
WRPA 1999	Welfare Reform and Pensions Act 1999

Chapter 1

INTRODUCTION TO FINANCIAL REMEDIES

SCOPE OF THIS CHAPTER

1.1   Financial remedies comprise those orders of a financial nature which the court may make in proceedings for divorce, judicial separation or nullity of marriage. In this chapter, the range of possible orders is set out and the general principles on which orders are made are considered. In later chapters, each type of order (eg periodical payments orders) is examined in detail; in this chapter, certain matters common to all such orders are considered, although where any individual factor merits more detailed examination it is the subject of a chapter in its own right.

This book also deals with one type of remedy which does not depend on the issue of proceedings for divorce etc, namely, applications for neglect to maintain under s 27 of the Matrimonial Causes Act 1973 (MCA 1973). The principles applicable to such applications are considered in Chapter 14.

Many readers were more familiar with the term 'ancillary relief' than 'financial remedy'. The change in nomenclature has been brought about by the Family Procedure Rules 2010 (hereafter FPR 2010) which came into force on 6 April 2011. Not only the names have changed; while the procedural reforms introduced originally as the pilot scheme and then as standard from June 2000 have survived more or less unscathed, the numbering is different and, as will be seen, there are a few changes of substance.

1.2   It would be unusual for the court to consider making one type of order only. That might in fact be the result of a particular case, but the court must have regard to the overall position, and the result of most applications is that a combination of orders is made. The court must take an overview of the whole case.

DEFINITIONS

1.3   'Financial remedy' is defined by the FPR 2010[1] as:

'(a)   a financial order;'

---

[1]   Rule 2.3(1).

This is the class of remedies with which this book will principally be concerned. However, the term encompasses a number of other remedies such as:

- an order under Schedule 1 to the Children Act 1989 (orders for children);

- an order under Part 3 of the Matrimonial and Family Proceedings 1984 (relief after overseas divorce);

- an order under section 27 of the MCA 1973 (failure to maintain).

A complete list will be found in the rules at Appendix B.

'Financial order' is defined as:

> '(a)   an avoidance of disposition order;
> (b)   an order for maintenance pending suit;
> (c)   an order for maintenance pending outcome of proceedings;
> (d)   an order for periodical payments or lump sum provision as mentioned in section 21(1) of the 1973 Act, except an order under section 27(6) of that Act;
> (e)   an order for periodical payments or lump sum provision as mentioned in paragraph 2(1) of Schedule 5 to the 2004 Act, made under Part 1 of Schedule 5 to that Act;
> (f)   a property adjustment order;
> (g)   a variation order;
> (h)   a pension sharing order; or
> (i)   a pension compensation sharing order;'

("variation order", "pension compensation sharing order" and "pension sharing order" are defined in rule 9.3.)' [and will be considered in more detail in Chapter 10].

THE PRINCIPLES GOVERNING THE EXERCISE OF THE COURT'S DISCRETION

1.4   Before embarking on a detailed consideration of the individual factors in s 25(2), the court's overall approach will be considered. This must involve consideration of the issues of equality and fairness, which have assumed greater significance over recent years.

Section 25 of MCA 1973 contains the matters to which the court is to have regard in deciding how to exercise its powers under ss 23, 24 and 24A. It has frequently been said[2] that the statutory 'guidelines' must be the principal determining factors for the court; decided cases showing how the court's discretion has been exercised on other occasions are of limited relevance although, clearly, guidance from appellate courts as to occasions on which courts have misdirected themselves are valuable.

---

[2]   Notably, first in *Sharpe v Sharpe* (1981) Fam Law 121, (1981) *The Times*, 7 February.

In a leading case,[3] Butler–Sloss LJ, as she then was, stated the position as follows:

> 'There is a danger that practitioners in the field of family law attempt to apply too rigidly the decisions of this court and of the Family Division, without sufficiently recognising that each case involving a family has to be decided upon broad principles adapted to the facts of the individual case. Ancillary relief applications are governed by the statutory framework set out in the Matrimonial Causes Act 1973 as amended in 1984. Sections 25 and 25A provide the guidelines and require the court to have regard to all the circumstances of the individual case and to exercise the discretion of the court to do justice between the parties.'

Although *White v White*, from which these words are taken, was subsequently the subject of appeal to the House of Lords (and will be frequently mentioned in the following pages), the guidance given in this extract remains compelling law. Indeed, as will be seen, the House of Lords reinforced the principle that the provisions of the statute are pre-eminent.

Each case will turn on its own facts, and reference to the statutory criteria is therefore always essential. However, this point needs reinforcing in view of the attention given to leading cases which have reached the House of Lords and Supreme Court in recent years and which must be analysed in some detail. The point which will be made, and which perhaps needs to be made now so that it may be borne in mind when the reader considers decisions of any of the highest courts, is that, notwithstanding the valuable guidance given in the speeches or judgments, authority for any proposition must ultimately be derived from the statute and not from any judicial gloss thereon.

EQUALITY AND FAIRNESS

1.5　Although s 25 prescribes the matters to which the court must have regard, it does not suggest or recommend any starting point, tariff or formula for deciding what proportion of the assets of the parties each should receive. This is in contrast to other jurisdictions, many of which contain prescriptions as to percentages to be awarded to each party, often depending on the length of the marriage. It is frequently argued by practitioners and academic commentators that the law of England and Wales should be amended to contain such guidelines. However, judges have continued to emphasise that such prescription is not possible within the terms of the statute, and that each case must be considered on its own merits against the background of consideration of the s 25 factors. What has been described as 'the search for principle' continues.

---

[3]　*White v White* [1998] 2 FLR 310, CA.

Having said that, guidance was given in the two decisions of the House of Lords which are about to be considered, and it will be seen that, save in one important area (as to which see **1.41**), there was general agreement as to certain important principles.

Neither the words 'fairness' nor 'equality' appear in the Matrimonial Causes Act. However, in *White v White*, Lord Nicholls, after recording the self-evident proposition that the court must act in a just and non-discriminatory way, set out the important principle that this means that the court must be fair, and that fairness implies equality. The 6 years which elapsed between the decision of their Lordships' House in *White v White* (*White*) and *Miller v Miller* and *McFarlane v McFarlane* (*Miller/McFarlane*) saw much discussion on the part of practitioners and judges as to what this meant in various classes of case.

Before analysing the statutory factors therefore, we will consider the following:

(1)   the significance of *White v White*;

(2)   *Miller/McFarlane*; and

(3)   developments post *Miller/McFarlane*, in particular *Charman v Charman*.

White v White

1.6   Very few cases relating to financial relief reached the House of Lords or now reach the Supreme Court. Family cases which get that far usually relate to children, particularly public law issues. When the financial dispute between Mr and Mrs White reached their Lordships in 2000[4] it was thought that this would be the final word on these matters for some considerable time. *White* set out guidelines for the determination of such cases which may be summarised as follows:

- The court must be fair. There can be no discrimination between husband and wife in their respective roles. Whatever the division of labour, fairness dictates that this should not prejudice either party when considering the statutory factors. There should be no bias in favour of the breadwinner as against the homemaker and child-carer.

- When carrying out the statutory exercise, the judge should always check his tentative views against the 'yardstick of equality of division'. Equality should only be departed from if, and to the extent that, there is good reason for doing so. This does not mean that there is a starting point or presumption of equality.

- The concept of reasonable requirements is erroneous. The statute refers to 'needs' but this is only one of the statutory factors.

---

[4]   *White v White* [2001] 1 AC 596.

However, this was not to be the last word and certain issues remained to trouble the courts, including the Court of Appeal. These issues may be summarised as essentially the search for fairness, and what fairness means. Given that the court must be fair, and given that the yardstick of equality is overriding but does not amount to a rigid regime of equality, what are the circumstances in which the court may be fair and at the same time depart from equal shares? Would this be appropriate where, for example, the marriage was short; if so, what constitutes a short marriage? Would it be appropriate where one party had created the wealth enjoyed by the couple by his or her exceptional contributions? If so, how exceptional would the contributions have to be? It would be inappropriate to recite here the cases in which these issues were discussed and sometimes contradictory answers given.[5] Running parallel with all this was academic criticism of the whole approach of the law of England and Wales.[6] This law is based on a discretionary approach, and even in recent times judges in the Court of Appeal have gone out of their way to emphasise that there is no formula which will apply to all cases; these matters have to be considered on a case-by-case basis.[7] The criticism made is that even on that basis, analysis of the cases reveals no rational pattern, and further, that this unpredictable case-by-case approach is unfair, since parties who wish to settle their disputes are given uncertain guidance and often have to risk large sums of money to achieve a result.

The combined appeals of *Miller v Miller* and *McFarlane v McFarlane* which were decided by the House in May 2006 therefore attracted widespread interest, both among family lawyers and in the popular press.

Miller and *McFarlane*

1.7   The House of Lords heard the appeals in *Miller v Miller* and *McFarlane v Macfarlane* (*Miller/McFarlane*) together because they clearly raised similar issues. Both were 'big money' cases, and both dealt with the issues arising out of *White* which are briefly outlined above. The facts in both cases need not be described here;[8] rather, the principles established or affirmed will be considered.

White v White re-affirmed

1.8   The two most important speeches were those of Lord Nicholls and Baroness Hale, who tried to set out a clear list of principles to be followed. They began with some fairly obvious but nonetheless important points; the

---

[5]   For a detailed analysis see R Bird 'Dividing Marital Assets after Lambert' [2003] Fam Law 534. However, two decisions of Coleridge J repay careful reading, namely *H-J v H-J (Financial Provision: Equality)* [2002] 1 FLR 415, and *G v G (Financial Provision: Equal Division)* [2002] EWHC 1339 (Fam), [2002] 2 FLR 1143. In *Lambert v Lambert* [2002] EWCA Civ 1685, [2003] 1 FLR 139, CA Thorpe LJ said that Coleridge J was not wrong (ie he was right!) to find that '50/50 resonates with fairness' [para 38].

[6]   See e g R Bailey-Harris [2003] Fam Law 386, and J Eekelar [2003] Fam Law 828.

[7]   See e g Wall LJ in *Miller v Miller* [para 88].

[8]   For more detail see R Bird *Miller and McFarlane: The implications for Family Lawyers* (Family Law, 2006).

court must be fair, and the statutory first consideration of the welfare of the children must be observed. The principles of *White v White*, such as fairness, non-discrimination and the yardstick of equality, were repeated and remain of the first importance.

Three principles: meeting needs, compensation and sharing

The House underlined the fact that financial relief is not a matter of taking from one party to give to the other, but is rather a matter of a proper and fair sharing of assets which both of them, in their interdependent and joint lives, have acquired.

The three principles which this case established and/or confirmd as being the rationale for financial provision contained in the 1973 Act may be summarised as follows:

(1) *Meeting the needs of the parties*
     Lord Nicholls said that mutual dependence begets mutual obligations of support. Fairness requires that the assets of the parties should be divided so as to meet their housing and financial needs.
     Baroness Hale said that the most common rationale for redistribution is that the relationship has generated needs which it is right that the other party should meet. Needs may arise as a result of one party having been a homemaker and childcarer, and needs generated by such a choice are 'a perfectly sound rationale for adjusting the parties respective resources in compensation'.

(2) *Compensation*
     Lord Nicholls said that compensation is aimed at redressing any significant prospective disparity between the parties arising from the way they conducted their marriage. Baroness Hale described this as compensation for relationship-generated disadvantage, which goes beyond need.

(3) *Sharing*
     Lord Nicholls saw sharing as derived from the basic concept of equality permeating a marriage. Husband and wife are equal partners in marriage.
     Baroness Hale described this as the sharing of the fruits of the matrimonial partnership.

These three principles may be taken as the foundation for any intellectual approach to the task of awarding financial provision. However, both Lord Nicholls and Baroness Hale made it clear that these are general principles and that they must be adapted to suit the requirements of a particular case. In particular, Lord Nicholls emphasised that equality applies 'unless there is good reason to the contrary. The yardstick of equality is to be applied as an aid, not a rule'.

Legitimate expectations and standard of living

1.9   The judge at first instance, and the Court of Appeal, had approved the concept of 'legitimate expectations'. The House strongly disapproved this concept; this could play no part in the decision-making process.

However, the importance of the standard of living of the parties during the marriage was affirmed, and this was one of the statutory factors prayed in aid by Lord Nicholls to justify the *Miller* award. For obvious reasons, it will only be important in cases where assets exceed needs, but this is an important reminder of the need to consider all the s 25 factors.

Application to smaller money cases

1.10   One of the problems with discussing decisions of the higher courts is that they normally involve very large amounts of money and rich parties. Many practitioners will be more interested in whether or not they apply to the normal run of cases.

It must first be said that the *White v White* principles of fairness, non-discrimination and the yardstick of equality apply to all cases, big or small and regardless of the length of the marriage. However, Lord Nicholls makes it clear that while the approach has to be the same, the result will be different in cases where the needs exceed the assets because the funds are not available to take the matter further. It is worth repeating his words:

> 'When the marriage ends fairness requires that the assets of the parties should be divided primarily so as to make provision for the parties' housing and financial needs, taking into account a wide range of matters such as the parties' ages, their future earning capacity, the family's standard of living, and any disability of either party. Most of these needs will have been generated by the marriage, but not all of them. Needs arising from age or disability are instances of the latter.
>
> In most cases the search for fairness largely begins and ends at this stage. In most cases the available assets are insufficient to provide adequately for the needs of two homes. The court seeks to stretch modest finite resources so far as possible to meet the parties' needs. Especially where children are involved it may be necessary to augment the available assets by having recourse to the future earnings of the money-earner, by way of an order for periodical payments.'

Baroness Hale expressed similar views. An equal partnership does not always dictate equal sharing of the assets. (One could interject there the view that, in lower value cases, it almost never does.) As Baroness Hale, said, equal division may have to give way to the needs of one party or the children.

> 'Too strict an adherence to equal sharing and the clean break can lead to a rapid decrease in the primary carer's standard of living and a rapid increase in the breadwinner's. The breadwinner's unimpaired and unimpeded earning capacity is a powerful resource which can frequently repair any loss of capital after an unequal distribution.'

Baroness Hale adds that recognising this is one reason why English law has been successful in retaining a home for the children.

Other issues were discussed in this case, but they will be considered under their separate subject-matter headings, see:

- 'Duration of marriage' at **1.32**;

- 'Contributions' at **1.38**; and

- 'Conduct' at **1.50**.

Charman v Charman

1.11   After the decision of the House of Lords in *Miller/McFarlane*, the courts were not idle. The first significant development was the decision of the Court of Appeal in *Charman v Charman* to which reference must now be made. In its judgment in *Charman*, the court dealt with several issues of considerable importance.[9]

The first of these issues was how the yardstick of equality should be approached. In the course of argument, there had been debate as to whether a judge should begin with some notion of equality and then, as it were, depart from it where appropriate, or whether the various s 25 factors should be considered with no preconceptions and then the provisional result compared with the yardstick of equality. The court dealt with this by reference to the new concept of 'sharing' introduced in *Miller*, and it is worth quoting the passage from the judgment of the court in full. This begins at para [64] where it is said that:

> '"The yardstick of equality of division", first identified by Lord Nicholls in *White* at p 605G, filled the vacuum which resulted from the abandonment in that decision of the criterion of "reasonable requirements". The origins of the yardstick lay in s 25(2) of the Act, specifically in s 25(2)(f), which refers to the parties' contributions: see the preceding argument of Lord Nicholls at p 605D–E. The yardstick reflected a modern, non-discriminatory conclusion that the proper evaluation under s 5(2)(f) of the parties' different contributions to the welfare of the family should generally lead to an equal division of their property unless there was good reason for the division to be unequal. It also tallied with the overarching objective: a fair result.
>
> [65] Although in *White* the majority of the House agreed with the speech of Lord Nicholls and thus with his description of equality as a "yardstick" against which tentative views should be "checked", Lord Cooke, at p 615D, doubted whether use of the words "yardstick" or "check" would produce a result different

---

[9]   It is worth noting that this was a particularly strong court, consisting of the President, and Thorpe and Wilson LJJ. It would be difficult to conceive a greater concentration of expertise in this field. Moreover, the judgment was the judgment of the court, so there are no differences of opinion to be analysed.

from that of the words "guideline" or "starting point". In *Miller* the House clearly moved towards the position of Lord Cooke. Thus Lord Nicholls, at [20] and [29], referred to the "equal sharing principle" and to the "sharing entitlement"; those phrases describe more than a yardstick for use as a check. Baroness Hale put the matter beyond doubt when, referring to remarks by Lord Nicholls at [29], she said, at [144],

> "I agree that there cannot be a hard and fast rule about whether one starts with equal sharing and departs if need or compensation supply a reason to do so, or whether one starts with need and compensation and shares the balance."

It is clear that the court's consideration of the sharing principle is no longer required to be postponed until the end of the statutory exercise. We should add that, since we take the "the sharing principle" to mean that property should be shared in equal proportions unless there is good reason to depart from such proportions, departure is not from the principle but takes place within the principle.'

It might seem from this, therefore, that sharing, which means equality and equal shares, is now more of a starting point than a yardstick.

The court then amplified this to guidance to 'flesh out'[10] what the concepts of 'sharing', 'need' and 'compensation' set out in *Miller* actually meant. First, on the issue of what property falls to be shared, and whether there should be a category of 'matrimonial property', the court said:

> '[66] ... We consider, however, the answer to be that, subject to the exceptions identified in *Miller* ... the principle applies to all the parties' property but, to the extent that their property is non-matrimonial, there is likely to be better reason for departure from equality. It is clear that both in *White* at p 605 F–G and in *Miller* at [24] and [26] Lord Nicholls approached the matter in that way; and there was no express suggestion in *Miller*, even on the part of Baroness Hale, that in *White* the House had set too widely the general application of what was then a yardstick.'

The court then dealt with the three principles enunciated in *Miller* as follows:

> '[70] Thus the principle of **need** requires consideration of the financial needs, obligations and responsibilities of the parties (s 25(2)(b)); of the standard of living enjoyed by the family before the breakdown of the marriage (s 25(2)(c)); of the age of each party (half of s 25(2)(d)); and of any physical or mental disability of either of them (s 25(2)(e)).

> [71] The principle of **compensation** relates to prospective financial disadvantage which upon divorce some parties face as a result of decisions which they took for the benefit of the family during the marriage, for example in sacrificing or not pursuing a career: per Lord Nicholls in *Miller* at [13], Lord Hope at [117] and Baroness Hale at [140]. But the principle goes wider than that. As long ago as 1976 this court decided that, where the marriage was short, it was relevant to consider

---

[10]   The author's term, not the court's.

whether a party had suffered financial disadvantage arising out of entry into it: see *S v S* [1977] Fam 127 at 134C, albeit that the consideration was there directed to restriction rather than augmentation of the award. Equally, in respect of disadvantage arising out of exit from the marriage, s 25(2)(h) requires the court to consider any loss of possible pension rights consequent upon its dissolution. Even disadvantage of the type to which reference was made in the speeches in *Miller*, i.e. that stemming from decisions taken during the marriage, had been held in this court to be relevant before it became the driver for a principle of compensation: per Hale J (as she then was) in *SRJ v DWJ (Financial Provision)* [1999] 2 FLR 176 at 182E and per Thorpe LJ in *Lambert v Lambert* [2003] Fam 103 at 122G. In cases in which it arises, application of the principle of compensation is an appropriate contribution to the fair result.

[72] The enquiry required by the principle of **sharing** is, as we have shown, dictated by reference to the contributions of each party to the welfare of the family (s 25(2)(f)); and, as we make clear in paragraph 85 below, the duration of the marriage (the other half of s 25(2)(d)) here falls to be considered. Also conveniently assigned to the sharing principle, no doubt dictating departure from equality, is the conduct of a party in the exceptional case in which it would be inequitable to disregard it (s 25(2)(g)). [The husband's counsel] argued to the judge that the husband's generation of substantial wealth was not only a special contribution on his part to the welfare of the family but conduct which it would be inequitable to disregard. We think, however, that it is as unnecessarily confusing to present a case of contribution as a positive type of conduct as it is to present a case of conduct as a negative or nil type of contribution: see *W v W* (2001) 31 Family Law 656.'

In this case there was also considerable analysis of the issue of contributions. This is considered in more detail at the paragraph dealing with that topic at **1.41**.

Case-law since *Charman*

1.12 Since the decisions in these leading cases have been handed down there has been a natural tendency on the part of practitioners to refer to them as if they and not the statute were the primary source of authority. The High Court has been at pains to try to refute this view as will be seen by the comments in a few leading decisions.

In *RP v RP*[11] Coleridge J said that care must be taken not to elevate passages from the speeches to some kind of quasi-statutory amendment. In particular, it was not possible or desirable to break up ancillary relief claims into separate 'heads of claim' like a personal injury matter. His Lordship also doubted whether 'compensation' added anything to 'financial obligations and responsibilities'.

---

[11]   [2007] 1 FLR 2105.

In *CR v CR*[12] Bodey J repeated these points; it was important that the terms 'sharing', 'compensation' and 'need' were not elevated into separate 'heads of claim' or 'loss' independent of the words of the statute. Otherwise, there could be a danger of double counting.

In *B v B (No 2)*[13] it was said that the reported authorities did not establish the proposition that equal division was the starting point in all cases. This remains the financial position of the parties and s 25 of the MCA 1973. In all cases the objective was fairness and avoidance of discrimination. The outcome of the s 25 exercise must always be tested against the yardstick of equality, which should be departed from only if and to the extent that there was some good reason for doing so.

Similar points are made in *P v P*,[14] *H v H*[15] (Charles J), *H v H*[16] (Moylan J), and *C v C*,[17] in which it was said that a formulaic approach should be resisted; the proper approach was to consider the s 25 factors and then to consider the principles of needs and sharing (and also compensation where appropriate, which was not the case here). In this case the judge added that, after a long marriage, factors of substance had to justify a departure from an equal division of assets.

One issue which remains difficult is that of wealth acquired by one party after separation. In *B v B*[18] Moylan J held that to award the wife half of the wealth existing at the date of trial would give insufficient weight to the fact that a substantial part of the husband's wealth had accrued directly as a result of his efforts since separation. Nor could such an award be justified on the basis of the wife's needs. As a general proposition, absent needs or compensation, the sharing principle should end at the end of the marital partnership.

For a recent case where departure from equality was justified on the ground of the parties' modest means, see *A v L (Departure from Equality: Needs)*.[19]

For further discussion of the proper treatment of inherited wealth, see the section on 'Contributions' at **1.38** et seq.

With some trepidation therefore, one might summarise the proper approach as follows. First, the s 25 factors must be considered in turn, always bearing in mind the need for fairness and absence of discrimination when considering each factor. (As to the relative importance of the factors in relation to each other, see **1.18** where this is considered in more detail.) In so doing, the

---

[12]   [2008] 1 FLR 323.
[13]   [2008] EWCA Civ 483.
[14]   [2008] 2 FLR 1135.
[15]   [2007] 2 FLR 548.
[16]   [2008] EWHC 935, [2008] 2 FLR 2092.
[17]   [2008] EWHC 2033 (Fam), [2009] 1 FLR 8.
[18]   [2010] EWHC 193 (Fam), [2010] 2 FLR 1214.
[19]   [2011] EWHC 3150 (Fam).

principles of needs, sharing and compensation should be borne in mind. Finally, the provisional result of this exercise must be compared with what would be the result of equal division of assets, and if it falls short of this yardstick of equality some good reason identified by the court and founded on the evidence must be available to allow the provisional result to remain un-amended.

Equality and periodical payments

The impact of the cases cited above on periodical payments will be considered in more detail in Chapter 2.

ALL THE CIRCUMSTANCES OF THE CASE

1.13   In deciding whether to exercise its powers under ss 23 to 24A, and, if so, in what manner, it is the duty of the court to 'have regard to all the circumstances of the case'.[20] The section goes on to set out particular factors, but the term 'all the circumstances' must be taken to mean what it says. It is in wide terms, and it has been held that the court must not confine itself to the specified factors.[21] It is necessary to consider all other circumstances, whether past, present or future. For example, the remarriage of one of the parties is not specifically referred to as one of the statutory factors, but it has been held that it is one of the circumstances into which the court may properly enquire.[22] Another circumstance which is not specifically set out in the statute but which is nonetheless important is the existence of an agreement between the parties. This is considered in more detail at **1.56**.

In *A v T (Ancillary Relief: Cultural Factors)*,[23] a case where the cultural values of both parties were not those of this country, it was held that in such a case and where the parties had only a secondary attachment to the English jurisdiction, the court should give due weight to the primary cultural factors and not ignore the differential between what one party might anticipate from determination here as opposed to another jurisdiction.[24]

As has been seen when considering the decisions of the House of Lords in *White v White*[25] and succeeding cases above two further extra-statutory principles, 'the yardstick of equality' and 'fairness', must now be borne in mind at all times.

---

[20]   MCA 1973, s 25(1).
[21]   See e g *Kokosinski v Kokosinski* [1980] Fam 72 at 183; *Trippas v Trippas* [1973] Fam 134 at 144.
[22]   *H v H* [1975] Fam 9; *Jackson v Jackson* [1973] Fam 99 at 104. However, prospects of remarriage are not a 'guessing game' and findings must be supported by some reasonable evidence: *Wachtel v Wachtel* [1973] Fam 72 at 86. A spouse is under a duty to be frank and give complete disclosure.
[23]   [2004] 1 FLR 977.
[24]   For another example see *G v G (Matrimonial Property: Rights of Extended Family)* [2005] EWHC 1560 (Admin), [2006] 1 FLR 62.
[25]   [2000] 2 FLR 981, HL.

FIRST CONSIDERATION THE WELFARE OF CHILDREN

1.14 It is provided that 'the first consideration' of the court must be given to[26] '... the welfare while a minor of any child of the family who has not attained the age of eighteen.' This requirement is therefore limited to children of the family, 'child of the family' being defined as any child who has been treated by both of the parties to the marriage as a child of their family.[27] It includes stepchildren and, where the parties have lived together with a child, it is difficult to imagine circumstances in which a stepchild would not be a child of the family.[28]

The child must be under 18 years of age, and the scope of the court's duty under this provision is limited to the period ending with the child's eighteenth birthday. This is not to say that the court may or should not have regard to dependent children who are over 18,[29] but such consideration would arise from one of the other factors such as the financial obligations or responsibilities of the parties, or as one of the circumstances of the case, and would not be the first consideration of the court.

1.15 As to the meaning of 'the first consideration', it has been held that this is not the same as the paramount consideration.[30] The welfare of a child is not to be regarded as taking precedence over all other matters but is the first matter to which the court should direct itself (see **1.18**).

NO ONE FACTOR MORE IMPORTANT THAN OTHERS

1.16 The statute sets out a list of matters to be considered, first when making orders as between the parties to the marriage and secondly when making orders in relation to children. The court is directed to have regard to all the matters contained in the subsection, and there is nothing in the Act to indicate that any one factor shall be more important than any other. Clearly, in some cases, consideration of one factor (e g discrepancies in age, or the length of the marriage) will occupy more of the time of the court than the others, and it may be that, in the circumstances of a particular case, one factor will prove to be more important than the others. In principle, however, there is no intrinsic reason why one factor should outweigh the importance of the others.[31]

---

[26] MCA 1973, s 25(1).

[27] MCA 1973, s 52(1).

[28] See e g *Teeling v Teeling* [1984] FLR 808, CA.

[29] *Lilford (Lord) v Glyn* [1979] 1 WLR 78.

[30] *Suter v Suter and Jones* [1987] Fam 111, CA. In that case, it was held that the judge had been wrong to elevate the children's interests so as to control the outcome of the case. However, see also *R v R* [1988] 1 FLR 89, CA, where it was said that, broadly speaking, a person having an obligation to maintain his children has an obligation to order his financial affairs with due regard to his responsibility to pay reasonable maintenance for them and to meet his reasonable financial obligations.

[31] It used to be argued, for example, that if significant conduct were proved, this might be the major determining factor in the case. This is not, and never has been, so. See also *Piglowska v Piglowski* [1999] 2 FLR 763, HL.

In one case,[32] Thorpe LJ, after considering the historical evolution of s 25, and the deletion in 1984 of the statutory duty to attempt to place the parties in the financial position in which they would have been had the marriage not broken down, observed that even prior to that amendment the Court of Appeal[33] had defined the judge's ultimate aim as being to do that which is fair, just and reasonable between the parties, and that had continued to be the judicial interpretation of the objective of the section. Parliament had not chosen to lay any emphasis on any one of the eight specific factors above any other.[34] He continued:

> 'Although there is no ranking of the criteria to be found in the statute, there is as it were a magnetism that draws the individual case to attach to one, two, or several factors as having a decisive influence on its determination … That said there is, if not a priority, certainly a particular importance attaching to s 25(2)(a).'

The reasons for that priority will be considered further below. Thorpe LJ concluded this part of his judgment as follows:

> 'It has often been said, and cannot be too often repeated, that each case depends on its own unique facts and those facts must determine which of the eight factors is to be given particular prominence in determination.'

In *Charman v Charman*[35] the Court of Appeal gave guidance on a further difficult question, namely how to resolve any irreconcilable conflict between the result suggested by one principle and that suggested by another. At para [73] of the judgment of the court, Sir Mark Potter P said:

> 'Often conflict can be reconciled by recourse to an order for periodical payments: as for example in *McFarlane*, per Baroness Hale at [154]. Ultimately, however, in cases in which it is irreconcilable, the criterion of fairness must supply the answer. It is clear that, when the result suggested by the needs principle is an award of property greater than the result suggested by the sharing principle, the former result should in principle prevail: per Baroness Hale in *Miller* at [142] and [144]. At least in applying the needs principle the court will have focussed upon the needs of both parties; analogous focus on the respondent is not present in the compensation principle and we leave for another occasion the proper treatment of irreconcilable conflict between that principle and one of the others. It is also clear that, when the result suggested by the needs principle is an award of property less than the result suggested by the sharing principle, the latter result should in principle prevail.'

The developing law as to pre-nuptial and other agreements provides a good example of how one issue (in these cases, the significance of an agreement) should be considered. These cases are considered in more detail at **1.60**.

---

[32] *White v White* [1998] 2 FLR 310, CA.
[33] In *Page v Page* (1981) 2 FLR 198, CA, at 206.
[34] See also *Smith v Smith* [1991] 2 FLR 432, CA, per Butler-Sloss LJ.
[35] [2007] EWCA Civ 503, [2007] All ER (D) 425 (May).

FINANCIAL RESOURCES

1.17 The financial resources of the parties are crucial to any application for ancillary relief. It is only when the court has all the evidence as to the resources of the parties that it can decide whether, and if so, how, to redistribute them. As Coleridge J put it in *Charman v Charman* at first instance,[36] 'the obvious starting point for all these applications is the financial position of the parties now'.

The court must have regard to:[37]

> '... the income, earning capacity, property and other financial resources which each of the parties to the marriage has or is likely to have in the foreseeable future, including in the case of earning capacity any increase in that capacity which it would in the opinion of the court be reasonable to expect a party to the marriage to take steps to acquire.'

In *White v White*, referred to in **1.8**, in the Court of Appeal, Thorpe LJ underlined the importance of this factor by saying that, in almost every case, it is logically necessary to determine what is available before considering how it should be allocated, and repeated his opinion, first expressed in *H v H (Financial Provision: Capital Allowance)*,[38] that the discretionary powers of the court to adjust capital shares between spouses should not be exercised unless there was a manifest need for intervention upon the application of the s 25 criteria.

It has to be said that the second part of that statement cannot survive unscathed the decisions of the House of Lords in *White v White* and of the Court of Appeal in *Lambert v Lambert*. It is certainly still the case that the court has to fulfil a fact-finding role but even then some caution must be exercised. In *Parra v Parra*[39] Thorpe LJ was concerned that the judge had examined the financial position of the parties at very great length and in extraordinary detail and gave the following guidance: 'The outcome of ancillary relief cases depends upon the exercise of a singularly broad judgment that obviates the need for the investigation of minute detail and equally the need to make findings on minor issues in dispute.' The task of the judge in ancillary relief litigation was different from that of the judge in the civil justice system; on the one hand, his quasi-inquisitorial role gave him a certain independence from the arguments of the parties but, on the other, he had an obligation to eschew over-elaboration and to: '... endeavour to paint the canvas of his judgment with a broad brush rather than with a fine sable. Judgments in this field need to be simple in structure and simply explained.'

---

[36] Approved by the CA at para [59] of its judgment.
[37] MCA 1973, s 25(2)(a).
[38] [1993] 2 FLR 335 at 347.
[39] [2003] 1 FLR 942, CA.

The issue of what are 'matrimonial assets' and 'non-matrimonial assets' was raised in *Jones v Jones*.[40] Here, the Court of Appeal held that for the purpose of the sharing principle it was appropriate to divide assets into non-matrimonial and matrimonial. The matrimonial assets were £16m and the non-matrimonial £9m. It was held that there was no reason to depart from an equal division of the matrimonial assets. However, it was also held that the trial judge had erred in ascribing a capital value to the earning capacity of the husband and treating it as a non-matrimonial asset. For further comment on this case see **1.43** below.

The duty of full disclosure

1.18   The exercise by the court of its statutory powers will be frustrated if one or other party is less than frank. The parties are therefore under an obligation to make full and frank disclosure of all relevant circumstances.[41] It is not appropriate to give partial disclosure, nor to wait for the other party to demand certain information. The information must be given voluntarily and completely. Failure to give full disclosure may result in the court exercising its powers to make interlocutory orders, for example for disclosure and production of documents,[42] will probably lead to the offender being condemned in costs, and, in extreme cases, may be regarded as conduct of a financial nature which it would be inequitable to disregard.[43] Readers are referred to the protocol that is discussed in Chapter 16. For a recent detailed summary of the case-law on non-disclosure see the judgment of Mostyn J in *NG v SG*.[44]

A related issue is the extent to which disclosure of potentially incriminating documents or evidence is privileged. In *S v S (Inland Revenue: Tax Evasion)*[45] Wilson J dismissed an application by the Revenue to keep a transcript which had irregularly come into its possession and to inspect affidavits and documents, on the ground that the public interest in encouraging full and frank disclosure in ancillary relief proceedings outweighed the interest in countering tax evasion. However, in *R v R (Disclosure to Revenue)*,[46] he permitted the Revenue to retain a transcript because it contained explicit findings as to evasion which had already resulted in action by the Revenue.

In *A v A; B v B*,[47] Charles J went further. A party to ancillary relief proceedings should be aware that if he or she does not claim protection against self-incrimination, the court may make or authorise disclosure in the overall public interest to a prosecuting or other public authority. The risk of serious

---

[40]   [2011] EWCA Civ 41.
[41]   *Livesey (Formerly Jenkins) v Jenkins* [1985] AC 424, HL.
[42]   See FPR 2010, r 9.15(2)(b).
[43]   *P v P (Financial Relief: Non-disclosure)* [1994] 2 FLR 381; *B v B (Real Property: Assessment of Interests)* [1988] 2 FLR 490. See also *Minwalla v Minwalla* [2004] EWHC 2823 (Fam), [2005] 1 FLR 771; where the court finds that a party has set out to conceal resources and to obstruct proper investigation it may draw adverse inferences and reflect such conduct in costs.
[44]   [2011] EWHC 3270 (Fam).
[45]   [1997] 2 FLR 774.
[46]   [1998] 1 FLR 922.
[47]   [2000] 1 FLR 701.

harm being done to the administration of justice does not outweigh the public interest in the payment of all sums lawfully due to the Revenue. Where a court is satisfied that there has been illegal or unlawful conduct it should generally report the relevant material to the relevant authority. Advisers and courts should be alert to warning parties of their privilege against self-incrimination, but the fact that such a party may have assumptions made against him or her that result in a high award is not something that founds a public interest that disclosure should not be made.

Since those decisions the position has become yet more difficult for practitioners with the coming into force of the Proceeds of Crime Act 2002 (as to which, see Chapter 21).

Income and earning capacity

1.19 Further consideration will be given to this matter in the section on periodical payments at **2.9**. Here it may be noted that the court will make an order on the basis of what the parties may reasonably be expected to receive if their opportunities are fully exploited. A party who chooses not to work when he or she could do so, or who chooses not to take advantage of opportunities to earn or to receive funds which are available to him or her, will find that the court draws adverse inferences from such unwillingness.[48] This is referred to as earning capacity, as opposed to earning potential.

The income to be taken into account does not normally include welfare benefits, so that it would be unusual, to say the least, to make a periodical payments order against a person whose only income was income support.[49] Nevertheless, the availability of welfare benefits to one party may be a source of comfort to a court which feels unable to make an order in favour of that party.

Earning potential

1.20 Slightly different considerations arise when the court considers any increase in earning capacity which it might be reasonable to expect a party to take steps to acquire, and the subsection recognises this by making it a separate matter. This wording was added to the statute by the Matrimonial and Family Proceedings Act 1984 (MFPA 1984), and must be read together with s 25A which is considered at **2.24** et seq.

Property

1.21 Property includes all real and personal property owned by a party or in which he or she has an interest. It therefore may include beneficial interests

---

[48] See e g *Hardy v Hardy* (1981) 2 FLR 321. But, for a contrary decision in a 'big money' case, see *A v A (Financial Provision)* [1998] 2 FLR 180.

[49] *Barnes v Barnes* [1972] 3 All ER 872; *Stockford v Stockford* (1982) 3 FLR 58, CA; *Fletcher v Fletcher* [1985] Fam 92 at 100.

under trusts.[50] The law relating to trusts was considered at length by Munby J in *A v A* and *St Georges Trustees and others*.[51] It was held that a spouse who seeks to extend an ancillary relief claim to assets which appear to be in the hands of a third party has to identify, by reference to some established principle, some proper basis for doing so. The determination of a dispute as to ownership between a spouse and a third party is completely different from the usual discretionary exercise between spouses and must be approached on exactly the same legal basis as if it were being determined in the Chancery Division.

Further guidance was given by Moylan J in *B v B (Ancillary Relief)*.[52] A two-stage process is required. First, it is necessary to determine whether trust assets are resources in which a spouse has any present or potential interest. Secondly, if he had, it is necessary to determine what (if any) legitimate expectation he has and, accordingly, the extent of resources likely to be available to him in the foreseeable future.[53]

In *Whaley v Whaley*[54] the trial judge had found that although £7m of the total assets of £10m were held in a Jersey trust, the trustees of that trust would do whatever the husband asked, and accordingly those resources were available to him. The Court of Appeal dismissed an appeal against the judge's order.

For a detailed review of the Family Division's various approaches to trusts in the exercise of its jurisdiction see the judgment of Mostyn J in *BJ v MJ (Financial Orders: Overseas Trust)*.[55]

Property also includes land, shares in public or private companies, partnership assets, business stock, choses in action, money, jewellery, chattels, and so on. Nothing of value which is within the control of the party concerned should be excluded.[56]

However, care must be taken not to breach the principle that a person and a company in which he may have an interest are separate legal entities. In *Gowers*

---

[50] For the position as to a discretionary trust, see e g *Charman v Charman* (above); the husband had appealed against the decision of Coleridge J to the effect that the assets which were in a Bermudan discretionary trust (a very sizeable proportion of the total) were to be regarded as assets over which he had control. The CA rejected the appeal.

[51] [2007] EWHC 99 (Fam).

[52] [2009] EWHC 3422 (Fam), [2010] 2 FLR 887.

[53] For other examples see *Thomas v Thomas* [1995] 2 FLR 668, CA and *SR v CR (Ancillary Relief: Family Trusts)* [2008] EWHC 2329, [2009] 2 FLR 1083 (Singer J).

[54] [2011] EWCA Civ 617.

[55] [2011] EWHC 2708 (Fam).

[56] See *Donaldson v Donaldson* [1958] 2 All ER 660 (husband derived his living, food and accommodation from running a farm, and his only other source of income was a pension. He was ordered to pay an equivalent sum to the whole of the pension to his wife and children). However, where a spouse receives income under a discretionary trust over which he or she genuinely has no control, the court should only take account of the actual income received (this would not apply where the spouse had de facto control): *Howard v Howard* [1945] P 1; see also *B v B (Financial Provision)* (1982) 3 FLR 298, CA.

v Gowers[57] a district judge had found that the husband 'was the company' in the sense that he appeared able to deal with the company finances and ordered that £500,000 which had been paid into court but which was in fact company money should be paid to the wife. On appeal Holman J said that the court had no jurisdiction to make such an order; the company was not a party to the marriage and the court could not pierce the corporate veil.

This issue has now received some guidance from the highest level in the decision of the Supreme Court in *Prest v Petrodel Resources Ltd*.[58] In this case the husband had placed certain assets in the names of various companies (the respondents to the appeal). The judge at first instance ordered the husband to procure the transfer of the seven UK properties legally owned by the companies to the wife in partial satisfaction of a lump sum order. He also directed the companies to execute such documents as might be necessary to give effect to the transfer of the matrimonial home and seven properties. In addition he awarded costs to the wife, and directed that the companies should be jointly and severally liable with the husband for 10% of those costs. The husband had been less than frank in his disclosure and appeared to be trying to mislead the court.

The judge concluded that there was no general principle of law that entitled him to reach the companies' assets by piercing the corporate veil. This was because the authorities showed that the separate legal personality of the company could not be disregarded unless it was being abused for a purpose that was in some relevant respect improper. He held that there was no relevant impropriety. He nevertheless concluded that in applications for financial relief ancillary to a divorce, a wider jurisdiction to pierce the corporate veil was available under s 24 of the Matrimonial Causes Act.

The companies appealed and the Court of Appeal allowed the appeal (Thorpe LJ dissenting). The wife appealed to the Supreme Court.

Giving the lead judgment of the Court, Lord Sumption said that there were three possible legal bases on which the assets of the companies might be available to satisfy the lump sum order against the husband, namely:

(1) It might be said that this was a case in which, exceptionally, a court was at liberty to disregard the corporate veil in order to give effective relief.

(2) Section 24 of the Matrimonial Causes Act might be regarded as conferring a distinct power to disregard the corporate veil in matrimonial cases.

---

[57] [2011] EWHC 3485 (Fam).
[58] [2013] UKSC 34.

(3)   The companies might be regarded as holding the properties on trust for the husband, not by virtue of his status as their sole shareholder and controller, but in the particular circumstances of the case.

After lengthy analysis he concluded that the first two bases did not exist and that the only basis on which the companies can be ordered to convey the seven disputed properties to the wife would be the third, namely that they belonged beneficially to the husband, by virtue of the particular circumstances in which the properties came to be vested in them (namely that the companies held the properties on resulting trusts for the husband). Only then would they constitute property to which the husband was 'entitled, either in possession or reversion'. His conclusion, with which the court unanimously agreed, was that this was such a case and that the order of the judge should be restored (albeit on different grounds).

The sanctity of the corporate veil has therefore been preserved, but, in cases where the evidence shows that a party has provided all the funds for the acquisition of properties that are then vested in a company, the court may regard those properties as beneficially owned by that party and therefore available for distribution.

In *White v White*,[59] the husband and wife had traded in a farming partnership for many years. This was a genuine, working partnership and not a mere tax vehicle. The assets were between £4.4m and £4.8m, and the judge found that the wife should, prima facie, have £1.5m. Nevertheless, he awarded her a lump sum of £800,000 on *Duxbury* principles.[60] The Court of Appeal allowed the wife's appeal and increased the lump sum to £1.5m. Thorpe LJ said that the first fundamental issue was what was the financial worth of each of the parties as if on the immediate dissolution of the farm partnership. Although, as was seen above, the reasoning of the Court of Appeal was subsequently criticised by the House of Lords, the need to establish the means (and contributions) of the parties remains an integral part of the court's duty.

The position as to property acquired after the separation remains in doubt. In *Charman v Charman* the Court of Appeal[61] considered that a bonus generated by work done 14 months after separation was clearly an asset of the husband, but that the way the court should treat such an asset (eg by applying different percentages for 'sharing') was a 'grey area which this court may need to survey upon a suitable appeal'. However, in *B v B*[62] Moylan J sought to bring some clarity to this (see **1.12**).

See also **1.38** as to contributions.

---

[59]   [1998] 2 FLR 310.
[60]   See **4.14**.
[61]   [2007] EWCA Civ 503, [2007] All ER (D) 425 (May) at [104].
[62]   [2010] EWHC 193 (Fam), [2010] 2 FLR 1214.

An entitlement under a pension scheme is frequently a valuable asset and, were it not for s 25B, would have to be considered in detail here. However, that section makes separate provision for pensions, and so pensions will be considered in detail in Chapter 10.

Dissipated assets

1.22 A party who recklessly or irresponsibly wastes or dissipates assets will not escape unscathed, because it has been held that it is a proper exercise of the court's discretion to 'add back' or notionally attribute such wasted assets to the party responsible for the dissipation when considering the overall position as to the means of the parties. In *Norris v Norris*[63] Bennett J said that it is only fair to add back into a spouse's assets the amount by which he or she has recklessly depleted the assets and thus potentially disadvantaged the other spouse.[64]

However, this is not a principle to be applied rigidly. In another case[65] Wilson LJ said that a notional re-attribution has to be conducted very cautiously by reference only to clear evidence of dissipation (in which there is a wanton element).

Expectations

1.23 The court must have regard to income, property etc which a party has or is likely to have in the foreseeable future. This does not include pensions, which are dealt with separately.

The most common example of a financial expectation is where one party is, or is likely to be, a beneficiary under a will or an intestacy. However, here the court must recognise that wills may be changed and that testators may outlive beneficiaries. The court also has problems of evidence, since it cannot compel a potential benefactor to disclose his or her intentions nor can it always accurately estimate the size of the potential inheritance.

What is the foreseeable future may also be debatable. In one case, it was held that the prospects of a 64-year-old woman inheriting from her mother who was in poor health should be disregarded.[66] In another, where the husband was indefeasibly entitled under German law to a substantial inheritance from his father, and the parties had always made their financial arrangements on that basis, the wife's application was adjourned until the death of the father.[67]

---

[63] [2003] 1 FLR 1142.
[64] For further authority see *Martin v Martin* [1976] Fam 335, and *Vaughan v Vaughan* [2008] 1 FLR 1721, CA.
[65] *Vaughan v Vaughan* [2008] 1 FLR 1721, CA.
[66] *Michael v Michael* [1986] 2 FLR 389.
[67] *MT v MT (Financial Provision: Lump Sum)* [1992] 1 FLR 362.

When *Miller v Miller* was decided by the Court of Appeal,[68] it was held that when she married a rich man the wife had a 'legitimate expectation' to be maintained thereafter as the wife of a rich man. As has been seen (see **1.11**), the House of Lords rejected this finding (while re-emphasising the importance of s 25(2)(c) (standard of living) – see **1.29**).

1.24 Before the coming into force of s 25B of MCA 1973 in 1996, there were authorities to the effect that the entitlement of a serviceman to a lump sum on retirement cannot be taken into account because of the provisions of the Army Act 1955 and similar statutes. It was also held that expectations which were more than a few years away were to be disregarded.[69]

These decisions have been reversed by s 25B, which is considered in Chapter 10.

1.25 Another common example of a financial expectation is a claim for personal injuries.[70] For this to be relevant, the court would have to be satisfied as to the likelihood of success, and the amount likely to be recovered. It should also be said that since, in serious cases, the award of damages would be intended to compensate a party for past and future loss, the damages would fall into a different category than, say, investments acquired during the marriage or a windfall inheritance.

In *D v D (Lump Sum Order: Adjournment of Application)*,[71] it was held that a court which decides to adjourn a lump sum application is doing no more than exercising the discretion vested in it, albeit that this step should be taken only rarely, where justice to the parties could not otherwise be done. One such circumstance was the real possibility of capital from a specific source becoming available in the near future.

In another somewhat unusual case[72] after a short marriage which ended 21 years ago a claim for a lump sum had been adjourned generally to allow the wife to apply again when the husband received an inheritance and the judge made the order for a lump sum many years later. The needs of the children were said to be the most important factor.

Financial needs, obligations and responsibilities

1.26 The court is directed to have regard to:[73]

---

[68] [2005] EWCA Civ 984, [2006] 1 FLR 151.
[69] *Roberts v Roberts* [1986] 2 FLR 152; see also *Priest v Priest* (1980) 1 FLR 189 and *Happe v Happe* [1991] 4 All ER 527.
[70] *Daubney v Daubney* [1976] Fam 267; *Roche v Roche* (1981) Fam Law 243, CA; *Wagstaff v Wagstaff* [1992] 1 All ER 275, CA; *C v C (Financial Provision: Personal Damages)* [1995] 2 FLR 171, FD.
[71] [2001] 1 FLR 633, Connell J.
[72] *Re G (Financial Provision: Liberty to Restore Application for Lump Sum)* [2004] EWHC 88 (Fam), [2004] 1 FLR 997, Wilson J.
[73] MCA 1973, s 25(2)(b).

'... the financial needs, obligations and responsibilities which each of the parties to the marriage has or is likely to have in the foreseeable future.'

In most cases, the task of the court will be to calculate the reasonable needs of the parties, in particular the needs of a parent who is caring for the children of the family, and to make a decision as to whether there should be a transfer between the parties of assets or income to meet those needs. In such a case, it is also necessary to ensure that the 'paying party' is left with sufficient to meet his or her reasonable needs.[74]

In average income cases, the subsistence level indicated by benefit rates, together with the cost of housing is frequently regarded as a minimum figure for needs.[75]

1.27   What constitutes obligations and responsibilities may be more debatable. Legal obligations assumed by one party from which it would be impossible to withdraw will normally be accepted.[76] The cost of maintaining a second family is clearly frequently contentious, particularly where the result is that that party is rendered unable to afford to maintain the first family. However, the court must be realistic, and must recognise that a second family which is being maintained by a person of average income will not have access to State benefits, whereas the first family might. There is nothing which the court can do to stop someone from establishing a second union and assuming the responsibility for children.

Where assets are surplus to needs it may be that a different approach will be adopted.[77]

Where there are children, the liability of either party under the Child Support Act 1991 (CSA 1991) is an obligation to be taken into account.

It has been held that the court should make a distinction between 'hard debts' such as debts to banks, and 'soft debts' such as money borrowed from relatives.[78]

---

[74]   *Allen v Allen* [1986] 2 FLR 265, CA.

[75]   Ibid; but see *Freeman v Swatridge* [1984] FLR 762.

[76]   See eg *Stockford v Stockford* (1982) 3 FLR 58, CA, where a husband had left his wife and first family in the former matrimonial home and bought a new house for his own occupation with the aid of a large mortgage. The court decided not to make an order against him since to do so would mean that he could not service the mortgage. Contrast *Slater v Slater and Another* (1982) 3 FLR 364 where the court thought that the husband had been extravagant in deciding to live in a country house with heavy expenses, and took no account of the unreasonable expenses. See also *Campbell v Campbell* [1998] 1 FLR 828, CA.

[77]   For two different approaches in relatively big money cases see *Norris v Norris* [2002] EWHC 2996 (Fam), [2003] 1 FLR 1142 (new children ignored) and *H-J v H-J (Financial Provision: Equality)* [2002] 1 FLR 415 (account taken of new responsibilities).

[78]   *M v B (Ancillary Proceedings: Lump Sum)* [1998] 1 FLR 53, CA, at 56 and 60.

1.28 It was once the case that different considerations applied to 'big money cases' where the parties enjoy considerable affluence. This is the subject of a separate section in Chapter 4, where it will be seen that, until the decision of the House of Lords in *White v White*, the concept of 'reasonable requirements' was used in place of that of needs. It has now been established that reasonable requirements were an unwarranted judicial gloss on the words of the statute and that consideration of the needs of the parties is all that the statute permits (although an award will not necessarily be limited to a party's needs).

STANDARD OF LIVING DURING MARRIAGE

1.29 Before the changes introduced by the 1984 Act, the court was directed to put the parties in the position in which they would have been if the marriage had not broken down. That was frequently impossible, and is no longer one of the concerns of the court. However, the court is still directed to have regard to 'the standard of living enjoyed by the family before the breakdown of the marriage'.[79] This was upheld by the House of Lords in the conjoined appeals of *Miller v Miller* and *McFarlane v McFarlane*[80] (see **1.11**).

It is perhaps important to note that the subsection refers to 'the family' and not to the parties; taken with the 'first consideration', this might entitle the court to take steps to ensure that the children of the family suffered as little as possible, even at the expense of one of the parents.

In most cases, the concern of the court will be to ensure that the standard of life of one party does not deteriorate to a greater extent than that of the other.[81]

1.30 Separate considerations may arise in cases of a short marriage and in big money cases. These are considered in more detail at **1.36** and Chapter 4, respectively. However, it may be helpful to note here that it has been held that, where there has been a high degree of affluence in the marriage, it is not necessary to ensure that the same high degree of affluence is maintained for both parties.[82]

Ages of parties and duration of marriage: age

1.31 The next factor in the s 25 checklist is 'the age of each party to the marriage and the duration of the marriage'.[83] The age of the parties is normally relevant in relation to their earning capacity. Subject to the needs of young

---

[79] MCA 1973, s 25(2)(c).
[80] [2006] 1 FLR 1186, HL.
[81] See generally *M v M (Financial Provision)* [1987] 2 FLR 1; *Leadbeater v Leadbeater* [1985] FLR 789; *P v P (Financial Relief: Non-disclosure)* [1994] 2 FLR 381.
[82] See eg *F v F (Ancillary Relief: Substantial Assets)* [1995] 2 FLR 45.
[83] MCA 1973, s 25(2)(d).

children, a young wife will normally be taken to have an earning potential, and the provisions of s 25A will apply (see Chapter 2).

Very different considerations apply to a woman aged over 50 who has not worked for many years. The court will take the age of such a person into account when deciding whether she has an earning potential.[84]

Duration of marriage: short marriage

1.32 When a marriage has subsisted for more than the average number of years, the significance of its duration is not normally an important factor; the usual guidelines apply and there is no separate point to be made about the length of the marriage. Duration is really only significant in the case of a short marriage, which is a topic which must now be considered.

The duration of a short marriage is not, of course, an isolated factor; associated with a short marriage are normally such other important factors as contributions (or lack of contributions), children, and earning potential. For example, when all the capital contributions have come from one party, and the marriage ends after a short period, in the absence of other factors the non-contributing party could not expect a substantial redistribution of assets.

The proper approach to a short marriage has now been considered by the House of Lords in the conjoined appeals of *Miller v Miller* and *McFarlane v McFarlane*.[85] It may be helpful first to summarise the leading pre-*Miller/ McFarlane* cases and then to contrast these with the House of Lords guidance.

Pre-Miller/McFarlane cases

1.33 In *Attar v Attar (No 2)*,[86] the marriage had lasted for only 6 months and the actual cohabitation only 7 weeks. It was held that because of those facts it was impossible to have regard to all the usual s 25 factors; the only proper approach was to have regard to the effect on the parties of the marriage and its dissolution. There were no children, the husband was very wealthy, and the order was for a limited term of periodical payments to enable the wife to readjust.

In *C v C (Financial Relief: Short Marriage)*,[87] the facts of the case were described as 'highly unusual' with features that made it 'unique'. There was, however, a child of the marriage. The judge had ordered periodical payments with no term, and this was upheld by the Court of Appeal. Ward LJ said that the appropriateness of a term order depended on all the s 25 checklist criteria,

---

[84] See the cases cited in Chapter 2 on 'Periodical payments', in particular 'The clean break' at **2.21** et seq.

[85] [2006] 1 FLR 1186, HL.

[86] [1985] FLR 653.

[87] [1997] 2 FLR 26, CA.

including the welfare of any child; it was not appropriate simply to presume the imposition of a term whenever there was a short-term marriage.

In *Hedges v Hedges*,[88] the marriage had lasted 4½ years; there were no children, and the wife had continued to work. She was awarded half the husband's liquid assets to help deal with her housing needs, and periodical payments for 18 months to help her to readjust. This was upheld by the Court of Appeal.

In *Hobhouse v Hobhouse*,[89] the parties divorced after 4 years of marriage; there were no children. The wife had inherited £0.5m and expected to inherit a further £1.5m on her mother's death. The husband's wealth was indicated by the fact that he pleaded the 'millionaire's defence'.[90] The wife was likely to return to Australia and her family home there within 3 to 5 years. The judge awarded her a lump sum of £175,000. The wife's appeal was dismissed. The marriage was childless and brief; the wife had not sacrificed any financial advantage; she had been allowed 3 to 5 years to rebuild her life. There was no obvious bracket, and the award was well within the judge's discretion.

In *G v G (Financial Provision: Separation Agreement)*,[91] the marriage lasted 4½ years. The wife brought into the marriage her two children from a previous marriage and they enjoyed a luxurious lifestyle. It was held that the short duration of the marriage was only one factor; both parties had made significant contributions to the welfare of the family and were likely to continue to do so. The husband's total wealth exceeded £4.5m; the wife earned £11,500 per annum and had a house (purchased for her by the husband) worth £250,000. She was awarded a lump sum of £240,000.

For an example of a more recent decision involving substantial assets see *K v K (Ancillary Relief: Pre-nuptial Agreement)* which is discussed at greater length at **1.52**. The most interesting point to emerge from that case in this context is that, after dealing with the capital claims of the wife, the judge dealt with the needs of the child of the family almost as a discrete issue and as if it were an application under Sch 1 to the Children Act 1989. The husband was ordered to provide a home and furnishings for the child at a cost of £1.2m, to revert to him eventually.[92]

In *Foster v Foster*[93] the Court of Appeal allowed an appeal from a circuit judge and restored the order of a district judge awarding a wife 61% of the assets after a very short marriage where she had introduced the bulk of the capital. The district judge had sought to give the parties back what they had brought

---

[88]   [1991] 1 FLR 196, CA.
[89]   [1999] 1 FLR 961, CA.
[90]   See **4.12**.
[91]   [2000] 2 FLR 18, Connell J.
[92]   For an even more generous order in favour of a child made under Sch 1 see *Re P (Child: Financial Provision)* [2003] EWCA Civ 837, [2003] 2 FLR 865 and **11.25**.
[93]   [2003] 2 FLR 299.

into the marriage at the value it held at that date, and that was not unfair. That was the only possible reason to depart from equality in this case. As will be seen below, this case is probably the most important of the pre-2006 cases.

In *B v B (Mesher Order)*[94] the marriage had lasted 10 months and there was one child. The district judge found the wife needed £220,000 to rehouse herself and awarded her a lump sum of £175,000 and periodical payments. The husband appealed and argued, inter alia, that there should have been a *Mesher* order. This was rejected on the ground that, given the wife's continuing contributions to bringing up the child, her prospects of being able to generate capital were small whereas the husband's were good. A *Mesher* order would therefore produce inequality of outcome. It was also held that a term order for periodical payments for the wife was not appropriate in view of the uncertainty and that the proper approach was to impose no term and to leave it to the payee to seek variation.

1.34 Perhaps the best way to summarise these decisions would be to reaffirm the importance of considering all the s 25 factors without preconceptions, while recognising that many of those factors will have little relevance in many cases of a short marriage. It was important to consider what had been the effect of the marriage on the parties, and, perhaps, to ask what they had lost in financial terms.

Where there is a child, it cannot be denied that this will have a significant effect on the parent caring for the child, and this would seem to make it prima facie inappropriate to impose a term on periodical payments.[95]

Miller/McFarlane guidance

1.35 The House held that, if it were not clear before *Foster v Foster*, it must now be clear that the old law relating to short marriages was swept away by *White v White*. The old principle of trying to restore one party, normally the wife, to her position before the marriage, was no longer applicable.

The principles of *White*, particularly the yardstick of equality and the concept of sharing, apply as much to short as to long marriages. *Foster v Foster* had made clear that all the s 25 guidelines must be applied in such a case. Having said that, in his speech Lord Nicholls also made clear that the application of these principles will not necessarily result in equal division. When he said that the length of the marriage 'will affect the quantum of the financial fruits of the

---

[94] [2003] 2 FLR 285, [2003] Fam Law 462.

[95] See also *Re G (Financial Provision: Liberty to Restore Application for Lump Sum)* [2004] EWHC 88 (Fam), [2004] 1 FLR 997, where after a short marriage a claim for a lump sum was adjourned generally with liberty to restore to enable the wife to apply in the event of the husband's inheritance; it was said that the interests of the children changed the perception of fairness.

partnership' he can only mean that the court must look at what the partnership produced during the term of the relationship, and that will be one of the factors to be considered.

Unsurprisingly, Baroness Hale agreed with the approval of her judgment in *Foster*. Referring to *Foster*, she said that:

> '... [a]lthough one party had earned more and thus contributed more in purely financial terms to the acquisition of those assets, both contributed what they could, and the fair result was to divide the product of their joint endeavours equally.'

1.36 A post-*Miller/McFarlane* case dealing with a short marriage but where the assets were large was *McCartney v Mills McCartney*.[96] This case attracted enormous public interest out of proportion to its legal significance because of the notoriety of the parties, but it does provide a useful example of how the courts may approach such a case. The marriage was a short one, but there was one child. The husband's assets exceeded £400m, but had almost entirely been earned by the exceptional talents of the husband many years before the marriage. The wife's assets were £8m. The wife was awarded £16.5m, and provision for the child.

An issue associated with the length of the marriage may be the significance which the court should give to cohabitation outside marriage. As to pre-marital cohabitation, the law seemed reasonably clear; the court may have regard only to the period between the marriage and the breakdown when considering the length of the marriage.[97] The same applies to post-marital cohabitation.[98]

However, perhaps a more contemporary approach can be derived from *GW v RW (Financial Provision: Departure from Equality)*[99] where it was held that where a marriage moved seamlessly from cohabitation to marriage it was

---

[96] [2008] 1 FLR 1508, Bennett J.

[97] *Foley v Foley* [1981] Fam 160; *Campbell v Campbell* [1976] Fam 347.

[98] *Hill v Hill* [1997] 1 FLR 730, an unusual case which turned on other issues, e g whether an order made in 1969 could be set aside on the ground of 25 years' cohabitation after dissolution. 'Under English law, a relationship of cohabitation no matter how long nor how great the dependence does not give the wife any right to claim nor power in the court to order either maintenance or discretionary capital provision', per Holman J. See also *Hewitson v Hewitson* [1995] 1 FLR 241, CA. See also *CO v CO* [2004] EWHC 287 (Fam), [2004] 1 FLR 1095, where Coleridge J held that committed settled relationships which endure for years outside marriage must be regarded as every bit as valid as marriage; where such an arrangement existed and seamlessly preceded the marriage it is as capable of being as important a non-financial circumstance as any other.

[99] *GW v RW (Financial Provision: Departure from Equality)* [2003] EWHC 611 (Fam), [2003] 2 FLR 108, Nicholas Mostyn QC. See also *S v S (Financial Provision) (Post-Divorce Cohabitation)* [1994] 2 FLR 228; another unusual case, involving cohabitation of six years before, eight years during and 15 years after marriage. Douglas Brown J held that it was necessary to have regard to all the circumstances and awarded the wife a lump sum of £185,000 out of the husband's free capital of £400,000 plus £100,000 in respect of her interest in the home. However, caution is required; in *Hewitson* (above), 'grave reservations' were expressed as to this decision.

unrealistic and artificial to treat the periods differently. However, it was equally unrealistic to treat the period of estrangement conducted under the umbrella of a divorce petition as part of the duration of the marriage.

Cohabitation of the party who applies for financial relief after divorce will be considered in more detail at **2.10**.

DISABILITY

1.37 The court must have regard to 'any physical or mental disability of either of the parties to the marriage'.[100] This is another factor which overlaps with earning capacity or potential, and the position of disabled parties would be no different if this provision did not exist. There seems to be no other way in which disability has ever been regarded as a factor in itself.

CONTRIBUTIONS

1.38 The next s 25 factor is:[101] '... the contributions which each of the parties has made or is likely in the foreseeable future to make to the welfare of the family, including any contribution by looking after the home or caring for the family.' The purpose of this subsection is, clearly, to try to reflect the value of each of the parties to the whole marriage, which is not an easy task. This factor may be subdivided into several categories.

Financial contributions

1.39 Contributions of a financial nature will include the earnings of both parties over the course of the marriage, any capital sums provided by them, for example for the acquisition of a house, and any inheritances which they have received from which the family has benefited. It also includes the value of a discounted purchase price for a former council house under the 'right to buy' scheme.

The court has a duty to make findings of fact where there is a dispute as to any financial contributions made by either party; any decision as to how available capital is to be divided to give effect to the s 25 criteria must start from an accurate assessment of what the parties' respective proprietary interests are.[102]

As to 'negative contributions', see **1.26**.

In *White v White* the relevance of inherited wealth as a contribution was mentioned and for a time it was thought by some that this class of asset might

---

[100] MCA 1973, s 25(2)(e).
[101] MCA 1973, s 25(2)(f).
[102] *M v B (Ancillary Proceedings: Lump Sum)* [1998] 1 FLR 53, CA, per Thorpe J at 58. See also *White v White* [1998] 2 FLR 310, and *A v A (Elderly Applicant: Lump Sum)* [1999] 2 FLR 969.

fall outside the ambit of the normal division of assets. However, in *Norris v Norris*[103] Bennett J held that Lord Nicholls had not enunciated a guideline that inherited contributions should not be included in the pool of assets for division. In theory, a spouse could claim more than half for this reason, but only in very limited and quite exceptional circumstances. Inherited property represented a contribution by one of the parties and was a factor to be taken into account.

This case was of some significance since it post-dated *Lambert v Lambert* and clearly reflects the thinking as to 'special contributions' in that case.[104] A similar conclusion was reached by Nicholas Mostyn QC in *GW v RW (Financial Provision: Departure from Equality)*.[105] Nevertheless, the fact that there might be room for more than one point of view on this issue was demonstrated by the decision of Munby J in *P v P (Inherited Property)*.[106] This was a case involving a family farm which had been in the husband's family for several generations. His Lordship held that fairness might demand a different approach if the inheritance were a pecuniary legacy which accrued during the marriage than if it were a landed estate which had been in one spouse's family for generations and had been brought into the marriage with an expectation that it would be retained in specie for future generations. In the instant case, the proper approach was to make an award based on the wife's reasonable needs for accommodation and income; to do more would be to tip the balance unfairly in her favour and unfairly against the husband.

1.40 The potential differences in judicial opinion at the highest level were revealed in the speeches of Lord Nicholls and Baroness Hale in *Miller/McFarlane*. *White v White* had already established that the contributions of the breadwinner are not to be favoured over those of the homemaker and childcarer. Both Lord Nicholls and Baroness Hale sought to deal with the vexed issue of the evaluation of special or exceptional contributions, such as, for example, those of an exceptionally gifted sportsman, musician or entrepreneur (these are the author's examples, not those of the court).

Lord Nicholls deprecated any lengthy and costly inquiry into such matters. The question was whether earnings of this character could be regarded as a 'special contribution', and thus as a good reason for departing from equality of division. The answer was that exceptional earnings were to be regarded as a factor pointing away from equality of division when, but only when, it would be inequitable to proceed otherwise. The wholly exceptional nature of the earnings must be, to borrow a phrase more familiar in a different context, obvious and gross.

---

[103] [2002] EWHC 2996 (Fam), [2003] 1 FLR 1142.
[104] [2002] EWCA Civ 1685, [2003] 1 FLR 139, CA. Cases such as *M v M (Financial Provision: Valuation of Assets)* [2002] Fam Law 509 and *H v H (Financial Contributions: Special Contribution)* [2002] 2 FLR 1021 which arrive at the opposite conclusion may be distinguished and doubted for that reason.
[105] [2003] EWHC 611 (Fam), [2003] 2 FLR 108.
[106] [2004] EWHC 1364 (Fam), [2005] 1 FLR 576.

Baroness Hale agreed, also equating contributions with conduct. The words she added are important and worth repeating.

> 'Section 25(2)(f) of the 1973 Act does not refer to the contributions which each has made to the parties' accumulated wealth, but to the contributions they have made (and will continue to make) to the welfare of the family. Each should be seen as doing their best in their own sphere. Only if there is such a disparity in their respective contributions to the welfare of the family that it would be inequitable to disregard it should this be taken into account in determining their shares.'

1.41 The difference between Lord Nicholls and Baroness Hale related to the relevance of 'non-matrimonial property'. Lord Nicholls' approach was that non-matrimonial property should be viewed as all property which the parties bring with them into the marriage or acquire by inheritance or gift during the marriage (plus perhaps the income or fruits of that property), while matrimonial property should be viewed as all other property. The yardstick of equality should apply generally to matrimonial property (although the shorter the marriage, the smaller the matrimonial property is in the nature of things likely to be). But the yardstick is not so readily applicable to non-matrimonial property, especially after a short marriage, but in some circumstances even after a long marriage.

Baroness Hale's approach took a more limited concept of matrimonial property, as embracing 'family assets' (cf *Wachtel v Wachtel*[107]) and family businesses or joint ventures in which both parties work (cf *Foster v Foster*[108]). In relation to such property she agreed that the yardstick of equality may readily be applied. However, she identified other 'non-business-partnership, non-family assets', to which that yardstick may not apply with the same force particularly in the case of short marriages; these included not merely (a) property which the parties bring with them into the marriage or acquire by inheritance or gift during the marriage (plus perhaps its income or fruits), but also (b) business or investment assets generated solely or mainly by the efforts of one party during the marriage.

Baroness Hale's view was that the source of assets may be taken into account but that this would become less important with the passage of time; she points out that the court is directed to take account of the length of the marriage. She continued:

> 'If the assets are not "family assets", or not generated by the joint efforts of the parties, then the duration of the marriage may justify a departure from the yardstick of equality of division. As we are talking here of a departure from that yardstick, I would prefer to put this in terms of a reduction to reflect the period of time over which the domestic contribution has or will continue rather than in terms of accrual over time.'

---

[107] [1973] Fam 72 at 90, per Lord Denning MR.
[108] [2003] EWCA Civ 565; [2003] 2 FLR 299, 305, para 19, per Hale LJ.

Baroness Hale concluded, on this issue:

> 'This is simply to recognise that in a matrimonial property regime which still starts with the premise of separate property, there is still some scope for one party to acquire and retain separate property which is not automatically to be shared equally between them. The nature and the source of the property and the way the couple have run their lives may be taken into account in deciding how it should be shared.'

Lord Mance approved this approach.

Given this approval, and the fact that Lord Hoffman expressly identified himself with Baroness Hale's speech and not with that of Lord Nicholls (Lord Hope favouring both equally), it could perhaps fairly be said that the true ratio of this case on this issue is that expressed by Baroness Hale and not that of Lord Nicholls. However, that was not an end of the debate as to 'exceptional' or 'special' contributions. When he gave his judgment in *Charman v Charman* at first instance[109] Coleridge J observed that:

> 'For the past nearly five years, since *White*, courts at every level have been wrestling with the question of whether or not in departing from equality and striving for fairness it is proper to take into account and give weight to exceptional wealth creation by one spouse. In reading and re-reading all the now familiar authorities, attempting to expose and explain the underlying principles, one is reminded of a frenzied butterfly hunter in a tropical jungle trying to entrap a rare and elusive butterfly using a net full of holes. As soon as it appears to have been caught it escapes again and the pursuit continues.'

The matter was considered in some detail when *Charman* reached the Court of Appeal for obvious reasons; this was a case involving very considerable assets (£138m) which it was common ground had almost entirely been generated by the exceptional and in every way 'special' efforts and ingenuity of the husband.[110] Giving the judgment of the court, Sir Mark Potter P said:

> 'It was inevitable, so it seems to us, that the notion of a special contribution should have "survived" the decision in *Miller* [as to which, see below]. The statutory requirement in every case to consider the contributions which each party has made to the welfare of the family, as well as those which each is likely to make to it, would be inconsistent with a blanket rule that their past contributions to its welfare must be afforded equal weight. Nevertheless the difficulty attendant upon a comparison of their different contributions and the danger of its infection by discrimination against the home-maker led the House in *Miller* heavily to circumscribe the situations in which it would be appropriate to find that one party had made a special contribution, in the sense of a contribution by one unmatched by the other, which, for the purpose of the sharing principle, should lead to departure from equality. In this regard the House was unanimous.'

---

[109] [2006] EWHC 1879 (Fam).
[110] For a similar case with a similar result see *Sorrell v Sorrell* [2005] EWHC 1717, [2006] 1 FLR 497.

The court declined the invitation to identify a figure as a 'threshold' beyond which a special contribution would be appropriate, considering it dangerous to do so. Nevertheless, it was prepared to give guidance (at para [90]) as to 'the appropriate range of percentage adjustment to be made in cases in which the court is satisfied that the principle requires departure from equality'. Even there, however, it was said that 'it is necessary however to bear in mind that fair despatch of some cases may require departure even from the range which we propose'.

The guidance offered was as follows:

(1) The adjustment should be significant as opposed to token. The court found it hard to conceive that where such a special contribution was established the percentages should be nearer equality than 55%–45%.

(2) Equally, it should not be too great. The court approved Coleridge J's comment that 'I think you need to be careful, after a very long marriage, to give a wife half of what you give the husband'. The judgment of the Court of Appeal continued:

> 'Arbitrary though it is, our instinct is the same, namely that, even in an extreme case and in the absence of some further dramatic feature unrelated to it, fair allowance for special contribution within the sharing principle would be most unlikely to give rise to percentages of division of matrimonial property further from equality than 66.6%–33.3%.'

1.42 A separate (though often overlapping) issue from 'special contributions' is that of 'non-marital property', that is property that has been acquired or brought in by one party before the marriage or eg by a lottery win. How the court should treat such assets has been the cause of considerable litigation and it cannot be said that there is one clear answer at present. Clearly the views of Lord Nicholls and Baroness Hale in *Miller/McFarlane* (see **1.41** above) provide the starting point for discussion but since that date the law has been refined in various ways.

1.43 The two leading authorities are the decisions of the Court of Appeal in *Robson v Robson*[111] and *Jones v Jones*.[112] In *Robson* Ward LJ set out guidance for dealing with big money cases involving inherited wealth, and stated the following principles:

• The words of the statute are the first source of authority, and judicial glosses should be avoided.

• Inherited wealth forms part of the property and resources of the parties and so must be taken into account under s 25(2)(a). It must not be quarantined.

---

[111] [2010] EWCA Civ 1171.
[112] [2011] EWCA Civ 41.

- Inherited wealth that has not been earned can be treated differently from wealth accrued by joint efforts. The nature of the inheritance may be relevant.

- Relevant s 25 factors to be taken into account are the duration of the marriage, the time during which the wealth has been enjoyed by the parties, the standard of living and the extent to which that has been afforded by drawing on the wealth.

- The more and longer the wealth has been enjoyed by the marriage the less fair it is that it should be ring-fenced and excluded from distribution.

In *Jones v Jones* Wilson LJ adopted a slightly different approach involving two stages. First, the scale of the matrimonial property to be excluded should be identified and then the resulting matrimonial property should be divided in accordance with the equal sharing principle.

Wilson LJ considered the issue further in *K v L (Non-Matrimonial Property: Special Contribution)*[113] where the Court of Appeal had to consider the significance of the wife's inherited wealth, which had grown enormously in value during the marriage and which had been ring-fenced and allowed to grow. He held that the importance of the source of the assets may, rather than will, diminish over time and preferred the dictum of Lord Nicholls in *Miller/McFarlane* to that of Baroness Hale. (The appeal against the order of Bodey J (reported as *K v L (Ancillary Relief:Inherited Wealth)*[114]) which had made an award in favour of the husband based on need was dismissed.)

1.44 There have been a number of decisions at first instance that have sought to apply the guidance given from above. In *N v F (Financial Orders: Pre-Acquired Wealth)*[115] Mostyn J set out the principles to be followed in such cases, adding that these cases are fact-specific and very discretionary. The longer a marriage went on, the easier it was to say that by virtue of the mingling of the pre-acquired wealth with the fruits of the marriage, the supplier had in effect agreed to share it. Where the court considered that the existence of pre-acquired wealth should be reflected in an order, a two-stage approach (as set out in *Jones v Jones*) should follow. The court should:

- Determine whether the existence of the marital property should be reflected in the order at all. That depended on questions of duration and mingling.

- If it was fair to do so, it should decide how much of the pre-marital assets should be excluded.

- The remaining property should then be divided equally.

---

[113] [2011] EWCA Civ 550.
[114] [2010] EWHC 1234 (Fam).
[115] [2011] EWHC 586 (Fam).

- The fairness of the approach should then be tested by the overall percentage technique.

- Finally, the question of need must be considered.

1.45 However, this approach has not been universally followed. Given that, as Mostyn LJ reminds us, many of these cases are fact-specific, it is unnecessary to analyse all reported cases on this topic. Some of the most significant are as follows:

- In *J v J (Financial Orders: Wife's Long-Term Needs)*[116] the husband argued that his share in the proceeds of a business should be excluded from consideration because it was acquired before the marriage and he owed his father business expenses. Moylan J said the correct approach was to start with the principle of need and then to consider the sharing principle. Where the result suggested by the needs principle was greater than that suggested by the sharing principle, the former should prevail.

- In *AR v AR (Treatment of Inherited Wealth)*[117] the total wealth of parties was between £21m and £24m. All but £1m was in the husband's name. The source of his wealth was a business developed by his father and brother. Moylan J held that the sharing principle can apply to non-matrimonial property if justified by the circumstances of the case. Nothing had happened to the non-matrimonial property to change it into matrimonial property. The principle best guiding the court was need; this could encompass the length of the marriage, the wife's contributions and the standard of living. The court's objective is fairness, not certainty.

- In *S v AG (Financial Orders: Lottery Prize)*[118] Mostyn J had to consider the best approach to money derived from a share of £500,000 in a lottery prize that the wife had won in 2000. She had invested the money in a home in which she and her new husband lived and that was now worth £495,000 subject to a mortgage of £305,000. In an apparent effort to defeat the husband's claims, the wife had transferred £250,000 to a third party. Both parties were otherwise of modest means. The husband sought, and was granted, a lump sum of £85,000 to assist him in his retirement. Mostyn J said that it would be a rare case where the sharing principle would lead to a distribution to a claimant of non-matrimonial property. However, an award to meet needs was commonplace. The husband was not entitled to anything like an equal share but 15–20% would be fair.

- In *GS v L (Financial Remedies: Pre-Acquired Assets; Needs)*[119] Eleanor King J found that the husband had come into the marriage with substantial assets. However, those assets (except the husband's pension)

---

[116] [2011] EWHC 1010 (Fam).
[117] [2011] EWHC 2717 (Fam).
[118] [2011] EWHC 2637 (Fam).
[119] [2011] EWHC 1759 (Fam).

were required to satisfy the immediate and long-term needs of the wife and children. With minor adjustments, the assets were divided equally.

- In *Y v Y (Financial Orders: Inherited Wealth)*[120] Baron J had to consider a case where the husband was beneficially entitled to a very substantial estate that had been originally acquired by his grandparents. The wife sought a substantial lump sum. Baron J said that the wife's needs were to be interpreted fairly, on application of the statute, in the context of the factor that the wealth was inherited. The wealth was derived from the husband's family, which made it prima facie non-matrimonial property and placed it in a special category. As such, the court should be slow to invade it without good reason, but the fact that property is inherited will carry little if any weight where the claimant's financial needs cannot be met without recourse to it. The wife was awarded a lump sum of £8,738,000 (32.5% of the total assets). The award was needs based and did involve sharing assets that would be invaded to cover the award. In this case needs, and the right to sharing, were the same thing.

1.46 Some more recent cases demonstrate that the courts are concerned to prevent excessive litigation over what is and what is not matrimonial property; the reader is referred to the cases discussed at **1.14**.

In *S v S (Ancillary Relief: Importance of FDR)*[121] the judge at first instance had 'ring-fenced' certain assets of the wife because they had emanated from her family in 1996 and always treated by her as her separate property. That decision was overturned on appeal and the properties brought into the general 'pot'; this was a needs case and the money was needed to fund homes and lifestyle.

Non-financial contributions

1.47 If the only contributions which the court could consider were financial, a wife and mother who had stayed at home to look after children would be at a distinct disadvantage. Thus it is that the court is directed to have regard to the value to the family of a non-working party. It may be that before the decision of the House of Lords in *White v White*[122] the guidance which was given as to how, if at all, such contributions should be weighed in the balance against financial contributions was not entirely clear. For example, it was held that it was wrong to make a distinction between cases where a wife makes actual financial contributions to the assets of the family and those in which her contribution is indirect.[123] However, in another, admittedly unusual, case,[124] it was held that, where there were ample assets and the wife had made a full

---

[120] [2012] EWHC 2063 (Fam).
[121] [2008] 1 FLR 944, Baron J.
[122] [2001] 1 AC 596, [2000] 2 FLR 981.
[123] *Vicary v Vicary* [1992] 2 FLR 271, CA, cited with approval in *Conran v Conran* [1997] 2 FLR 615 by Wilson J.
[124] *W v W (Judicial Separation: Ancillary Relief)* [1995] 2 FLR 259 (husband was 87, wife 78; wife's reasonable needs were limited).

contribution to the welfare of the family but had not contributed directly to the build-up of the family assets, the remarks in *Wachtel v Wachtel*,[125] to the effect that there should be a starting point of equality, should be confined to division of the family home and not to division of the family assets as a whole.

In *White v White*,[126] it was held that it is a principle 'of universal application' that there can be no discrimination between husband and wife in their respective roles. Different roles are assumed for many different reasons. Whatever the division of labour, fairness dictates that this should not prejudice either party when considering the statutory factors. There should be no bias in favour of the money-earner and against the homemaker and childcarer.

This principle was developed in *Lambert v Lambert*.[127] Here, judges were given clear guidance as to how to deal with issues of contributions. Any bias in favour of a breadwinner is an example of gender discrimination and therefore to be disapproved:[128]

> 'The danger of gender discrimination resulting from a finding of special financial contribution is plain.'

The statutory requirement to consider all the s 25 factors does not require a detailed critical appraisal of the performance of each of the parties during the marriage:[129]

> 'Couples who cannot agree division are entitled to seek a judicial decision without exposing themselves to intrusion, indignity, and possible embarrassment of such an appraisal.'

Special financial contributions are dealt with above. However, it should not be forgotten that not all special contributions are financial. In *Charman v Charman*, above, it was pointed out at para [80] that:

> 'The notion of a special contribution to the welfare of the family will not successfully have been purged of inherent gender discrimination unless it is accepted that such a contribution can, in principle, take a number of forms; that it can be non-financial as well as financial; and that it can thus be made by a party whose role has been exclusively that of a home-maker.'

1.48 It is, perhaps, necessary to say again that no one factor is to be regarded as intrinsically more important than the others; the court must take an overall view.

---

[125] [1973] Fam 72.
[126] See **1.10**.
[127] [2002] EWCA Civ 1685, [2003] 1 FLR 139.
[128] Ibid, per Thorpe LJ at para 45.
[129] Ibid, para 38.

In another unusual case,[130] it was said that the proper approach is to survey the wife's reasonable requirements and then place her contributions and all other factors in the balance, taking into account the nexus between the contributions and the creation of the resources.

Future contributions

1.49   The court must take account of the future as much as of the past. This will normally be relevant when one party is to care for the children of the family, and the longer the dependency the greater the significance of this factor. If one party is unable, for financial reasons, to make any significant contribution to the future welfare of the family, so that the burden will inevitably fall on the other party, this might well be a significant factor.

Since the advent of CSA 1991, and the virtual impossibility of contracting out of child support in most cases, the considerable sums which many 'non-resident parents' will have to pay is a future contribution which cannot be ignored.

CONDUCT

1.50   The court is directed to have regard to:[131]

'... the conduct of each of the parties, if that conduct is such that it would in the opinion of the court be inequitable to disregard it.'

As has been emphasised before, no one factor is normally the sole determining factor in any application, and there are few examples of cases where conduct has been a major determining matter.[132] Such examples as there are may be summarised as follows.

Financial conduct

1.51   Cases where it can be demonstrated that the behaviour of one party has had a clear (and, impliedly, detrimental) effect on the fortunes of the parties are the most usual examples of conduct having a real significance. In one case, the husband had dissipated the family capital, and the court held that he could not be allowed to fritter away assets and then claim as much of what was left as if he had behaved reasonably.[133] In another case, the husband, a farmer, had brought about financial disaster and his own bankruptcy; in the words of the judge he had 'obstinately, unrealistically and selfishly trailed on to eventual disaster, dissipating in the process not only his own money but his family's

---

[130]   *Conran v Conran* [1997] 2 FLR 615; unusual because of the size of the parties' wealth if for no other reason.

[131]   MCA 1973, s 25(2)(g).

[132]   In *McCartney v Mills McCartney* [2008] 1 FLR 1508, Bennett J declined to hear evidence or argument about conduct on the ground that it would make little or no difference to the final result.

[133]   *Martin v Martin* [1976] Fam 335.

money, his friends' money, the money of commercial creditors unsecured and eventually his wife's money'.[134] Even so, he was not deprived of all entitlement but was restricted to the minimum sum needed to rehouse himself.

These decisions may perhaps be contrasted with another,[135] in which a wife had inherited her mother's estate and then sold part to her daughter at an undervalue, thereby depleting her own assets. The argument that this was 'financial conduct' was rejected, but the actions of the wife were held to be clearly relevant as one of the circumstances.

In another case, it was held that although the husband's conduct in relation to certain financial transfers was such that it would be inequitable to ignore it, the approach should be not to fix a sum as a penalty, but rather an evaluation based on all the relevant factors taken in the round.[136]

An unusual situation arose in *W v W*.[137] Both parties had agreed not to pursue allegations of conduct but the husband then sought to argue that, because of the wife's drinking, her contributions were 'negative'. Wilson J said that 'negative contributions' was an unhelpful oxymoron. Where a nil contribution or conduct were alleged, the allegations should be put in those terms.

More comment on dissipated assets will be found at **1.22**

Non-financial conduct

1.52 In previous editions of this book, a summary of what were believed to be the leading cases where conduct was found to be relevant were included. This task was made easier and more authoritative by the judgment of Stanley Burton J in *S v S*.[138] His Lordship had to consider whether or not the alleged conduct in that case should be taken into account. He was at pains to point out that he did not normally sit in the Family Division and so relied on the two expert counsel[139] appearing before him. He dealt with the position as follows:

'I have been told by Counsel that there are only rare cases in the reports where this has occurred. I have been taken to what I believe must be all of them. The examples given include:

(i)   *Armstrong v Armstrong* [1974] SJ 579: wife shoots husband with his shotgun with intent to endanger life.
(ii) *Jones v Jones* [1976] Fam 8: husband attacks wife with a razor and inflicts serious injuries: there are financial consequences (wife rendered incapable of working).

---

[134] *Beach v Beach* [1995] 2 FLR 160, per Thorpe J. See also *Le Foe v Le Foe and Woolwich plc* [2001] 2 FLR 970.
[135] *Primavera v Primavera* [1992] 1 FLR 16, CA.
[136] *H v H (Financial Relief: Conduct)* [1998] 1 FLR 971.
[137] [2001] Fam Law 656, Wilson J.
[138] [2006] EWHC 2793.
[139] Mr Nicholas Mostyn QC and Mr Philip Moor QC.

(iii) *Bateman v Bateman* [1979] 2 WLR 377: wife twice inflicts stab wounds on her husband with a knife.

(iv) *S v S* [1982] Fam Law 183: husband commits incest with children of the family.

(v) *Hall v Hall* [1984] FLR 631: wife stabs husband in the abdomen with a knife.

(vi) *Kyte v Kyte* [1987] 3 AER 1041: wife facilitates the husband's attempted suicide.

(vii) *Evans v Evans* [1989] 1 FLR 351: wife incites others to murder the husband.

(viii) *K v K* [1990] 2 FLR 225: husband's serious drink problem and "disagreeable" behaviour led to the forced sale of the matrimonial home and serious financial consequences to the wife.

(ix) *H v H* [1994] 2 FLR 801: serious assault and an attempted rape of wife by husband: and financial consequences because the consequent imprisonment of husband destroyed his ability to support her.

(x) *A v A* [1995] 1 FLR 345: husband assaults the wife with a knife.

(xi) *C v C* (Bennett J 12 December 2001 unreported): wife deliberately drugged husband to make him very sleepy and then while he was in a somnolent state placed a bag over his head, which she held in such a way that the husband could not breathe. Although it was found that the wife did not have an intent to kill, Bennett J concluded that the husband did believe that she was trying to kill him, and that her aim was to make him so believe.

(xii) *Al-Khatib v Masry* [2002] 1 FLR 1053: husband guilty of "very grave" misconduct in abducting the children of the marriage in contempt of court.

(xiii) *H v H* [2006] 1 FLR 990: very serious assault by husband on wife with knife, leading to 12 years' imprisonment for attempted murder and with financial consequences, namely destroying her Police career.'

His Lordship's comments on these cases were as follows:

'As will be seen, it is not suggested that there were any financial consequences from the conduct of which the Applicant complains in this case, which factor may have exacerbated, in the judgment of Scott Baker J, the facts in *K v K* referred to at (viii) above. However, that case apart, all of the conduct found in those cases appears of manifest seriousness. Apart from the statutory provision, and the words of Ormrod J in *Wachtel* quoted by Baroness Hale above, there is a certain amount of recurrent phraseology: "If the courts were in these circumstances not to discharge the order, the public might think that we had taken leave of our senses" (per Balcombe LJ at 355 in *Evans* at (vii) above): Sir Roger Ormrod in *Hall* at (v) above describes (at 632) the conduct as "gross and obvious" which has "nothing to do with the ordinary run of fighting and quarrelling in an unhappy marriage" and which the judge's "sense of justice required to be taken into account": Bennett J in *C* at (xi) above, asks whether "it would be repugnant to any sense of justice for the wife to receive any award at all". Mr Mostyn QC pointed to the words of Sir George Baker P in *W v W* [1976] Fam 107 at 110D when he referred to the sort of conduct which would cause the ordinary mortal to throw up his hands and say "… surely that woman is not going to get a full award": and, in the course of submissions, he suggested a test of applying what he called the "gasp factor".'

One case which was, perhaps surprisingly omitted from this pantheon of wrongdoing was *Clark v Clark*[140] which was described by Thorpe LJ as 'one of the most extraordinary marital histories that I have ever encountered' and 'as baleful as any to be found in the family law reports'. The wife was 36 years younger than the husband. At the date of the marriage, he was rich while her liabilities exceeded her assets. The marriage was never consummated. Over the 5-year marriage, she persuaded him to purchase a number of properties, most of which were vested in her sole name. In addition, she acquired shares, a racehorse, a Bentley and a boat. The husband was coerced into transferring a large house into the wife's name, and he was then forced to live as a virtual prisoner in part of the house while she occupied the larger part with her lover. He attempted suicide, and when he returned home he was again confined as a virtual prisoner, the wife removing his telephone and gate buzzer. He was eventually rescued by relatives.

The judge found that the wife had exercised undue influence over the husband, that this was a short marriage, that the husband's contributions had been enormous while hers were negligible and that her marital and litigation conduct must be condemned in the strongest terms. Nevertheless, he awarded her a lump sum of £552,500. Both parties appealed.

The wife's appeal was dismissed and the husband's appeal allowed. The judge had fallen into manifest error in allowing the wife £552,500. He had failed to reflect his findings on the wife's misconduct in his award; it would be hard to conceive of a case of graver marital misconduct. This was a rare case in which litigation misconduct should be reflected in the substantive award. However, to leave the wife with nothing was impracticable since that would have required her to make substantial repayments to the husband, and the lump sum was reduced to £125,000.

For a case where the conduct of both parties was equally reprehensible and so cancelled each other out and had no effect on the award see the judgment of Mostyn J in *FZ v SZ (Ancillary Relief: Conduct: Valuations)*.[141]

Conduct in the course of the proceedings

1.53 The conduct of the parties during and in relation to the proceedings may be a relevant factor. In *B v B (Real Property: Assessment of Interests)*,[142] it was held that a wife whose conduct in relation to discovery and dishonest statements had amounted to contempt as well as conduct which it was inequitable to disregard should have the award which she would otherwise have received reduced to take account of the conduct. However, this may be a decision which will rarely be followed. In another case,[143] where a wife had knowingly misrepresented her true financial position and failed in her duty to

---

[140] [1999] 2 FLR 498, CA.
[141] [2010] EWHC 1630 (Fam), [2011] 1 FLR 64.
[142] [1988] 2 FLR 490.
[143] *P v P (Financial Relief: Non-disclosure)* [1994] 2 FLR 381.

give full disclosure, Thorpe J held that, while accepting that such behaviour was conduct which it would be inequitable to disregard, this should be reflected in an order for costs rather than a reduction of the share of the assets.[144]

In *Al Khatib v Masry*[145] the husband had been highly obstructive and unco-operative in the wife's application for ancillary relief and the court observed that it would be difficult to imagine a worse case of litigation misconduct. The husband had also abducted the children to Saudi Arabia. It was thought that the husband's assets were at least £50m. The wife was awarded a lump sum of £10m, a *Duxbury* award of £5.5m and a 'fighting fund' for legal costs of £2.5m to assist her to recover the children.

In *M v M (Ancillary Relief: Conduct)* it was held that the husband's conduct both in respect of gambling and his disregard of court orders should not be disregarded. Such conduct should be taken into account in a broad way and not with mathematical precision and affected the order and not just the costs.

Finally, mention should be made of *Hall v Hall*.[146] Here, a wife had steadfastly refused to take part in the husband's application for ancillary relief and, clearly in desperation, the district judge had transferred all the assets to the husband. The Court of Appeal held that this was the wrong approach; the husband's counsel should have dissuaded the judge from making an order which went beyond the husband's own case, and the denial of the wife's entitlement to equality was a wholly disproportionate response to her 'tardy engagement' in the proceedings.

For discussion of the position where the court has preferred to penalise litigation misconduct by an order for costs and has deprecated the practice of reflecting its displeasure in an increased financial award see **17.11**.

LOST BENEFITS

1.54   The court is directed to have regard to:[147]

> '... in the case of proceedings for divorce or nullity of marriage, the value to each of the parties to the marriage of any benefit which, by reason of the dissolution or annulment of the marriage, that party will lose the chance of acquiring.'

This is the factor most frequently relied on when loss of pension benefits is an issue, and its significance is clear.

---

[144] A similar result occurred in *T v T (Interception of Documents)* [1994] 2 FLR 1083 where a wife had obtained documents belonging to the husband by reprehensible means. See also *Tavoulareas v Tavoulareas* [1998] 2 FLR 418, CA.

[145] [2002] EWHC 108 (Fam), [2002] 1 FLR 1053.

[146] [2008] EWCA Civ 350, [2008] 2 FLR 575.

[147] MCA 1973, s 25(2)(h).

1.55 The Pensions Act 1995 amended the MCA 1973 to introduce a new s 25B which is concerned entirely with pensions. The original reference to pensions in s 25(2)(h) has been deleted, and the court is now directed to have regard to the value to each of the parties of any benefit which, by reason of the dissolution or annulment of the marriage, that party will lose the chance of acquiring.

Since pensions are now adequately covered elsewhere, it would seem that this is now to be a 'catch-all' provision, and it is difficult to think of circumstances which would be applicable to this subsection only and which would not be covered by some other provision.

As was seen above, pensions have been removed from the s 25(2) factors and given their own place in s 25B. Pensions is a very important subject which is considered in some detail in Chapter 10.

Here, it is only necessary to consider the requirement on the court to consider the subject; s 25B(1) in effect adds further s 25(2) factors to be considered in every case.

It is provided that the matters to which the court is to have regard under s 25(2) include:

(a) in the case of paragraph (a) (ie when considering the income, means, etc of the parties) any benefits under a pension scheme which a party to a marriage has or is likely to have; and

(b) in the case of paragraph (h) (ie loss of benefits) any benefits under a pension scheme which, by reason of the dissolution or annulment of the marriage, a party to the marriage will lose the chance of acquiring.

It is also provided that, in relation to benefits under a pension scheme, the words 'in the foreseeable future' should be regarded as being deleted from s 25(2)(a).

The result of this is that, in every case, it is necessary to consider the benefits which either party may receive from a pension scheme, no matter how remote that event may seem. In the same way, the effect on the other party of the loss of any such pension benefits must be calculated.

Section 25B(2) goes on to direct the court as to how it should consider dealing with loss of pension benefits. This is best considered in Chapter 10 on pensions.

AGREEMENTS

1.56 There is no specific mention of agreements in s 25 but they are generally agreed at least to be one of the 'circumstances' which the court must take into account. The traditional attitude of the courts to agreements was the somewhat paternalistic statement in *Hyman v Hyman*[148] that 'the wife cannot by her own covenant preclude herself from invoking the jurisdiction of the court or preclude the court from the exercise of that jurisdiction'. Previous editions of this book have contained detailed examinations of the way in which the courts have sought to qualify that doctrine and bring it into line with the wishes of divorcing couples and their advisers. Most of this is now of historical interest only due to the decision of the Supreme Court in *Radmacher (formerly Granatino) v Granatino*.[149]

1.57 The issue in *Radmacher v Granatino* was how far the terms of a pre-nuptial contract should dictate the result of a husband's application for ancillary relief; the wife, who was extremely wealthy, sought to rely on the agreement to limit the husband's claim. However, the decision of the Court goes far beyond that issue and gives guidance as to the manner in which the court should deal with all agreements, whether made pre- or post-marriage.

The most common kinds of agreement which need to be considered are:

- post-nuptial agreements made (normally) on separation to compromise claims;

- pre-nuptial agreements; and

- agreements to settle litigation.

The first two will be considered together, since the same principles now apply. First, however, a short account of the reasoning of the Supreme Court in arriving at its decision may be helpful.

Radmacher v Granatino

1.58 The most recent previous occasion on which the issue of pre-nuptial contracts had been determined at the highest level was the decision of the Privy Council (on appeal from the courts of the Isle of Man) in *MacLeod v MacLeod*.[150] In that case, it was said that:

> 'Post-nuptial agreements ... are very different from pre-nuptial agreements. The couple are now married. They have undertaken towards one another the obligations and responsibilities of the married state. A pre-nuptial agreement is no longer the price which one party may extract for his or her willingness to marry.' (para 36)

In *Radmacher v Granatino* the Supreme Court disapproved this statement:

---

[148]   [1929] AC 602.
[149]   [2010] UKSC 42, [2010] 2 FLR 1900.
[150]   [2008] UKPC 64.

'60. ... we do not see why different principles must apply to an agreement concluded in anticipation of the married state and one concluded after entry into the married state.

61. This is not to say that there are no circumstances where it is right to distinguish between an ante-nuptial and a post-nuptial agreement. The circumstances surrounding the agreement may be very different dependent on the stage of the couple's life together at which it is concluded, but it is not right to proceed on the premise that there will always be a significant difference between an ante- and a post-nuptial agreement. Some couples do not get married until they have lived together and had children.'

At para 63, the judgment continues:

'In summary, we consider that the Board in *MacLeod* was wrong to hold that post-nuptial agreements were contracts but that ante-nuptial agreements were not. That question did not arise for decision in that case any more than in this and does not matter anyway. It is a red herring. Regardless of whether one or both are contracts, the ancillary relief court should apply the same principles when considering ante-nuptial agreements as it applies to post-nuptial agreements.'

It seems therefore conclusively to be the case that, when considering whether or not an agreement should be adhered to or departed from, the same principles will be applied irrespective of whether the agreement is pre-nuptial or post-nuptial.

1.59 The Supreme Court also dealt with the question of whether the usual rules as to validity of a contract applied. At para 62 the question was asked:

'Is it important whether or not post-nuptial or ante-nuptial agreements have contractual status? The value of a contract is that the court will enforce it. But in ancillary relief proceedings the court is not bound to give effect to nuptial agreements, and is bound to have regard to them, whether or not they are contracts. Should they be given greater weight because in some other context they would be enforceable? Or is the question of whether or not they are contracts an irrelevance?'

In *MacLeod*, the Board had been concerned with whether the agreement in that case was a contract properly so-called. The view of the Supreme Court was that this was not important but that there were clearly factors which would justify the court in departing from the terms of a contract. These will be considered below.

The general approach to agreements

1.60 At the end of para [75] of the majority judgment, the Supreme Court advanced the following general proposition to govern the correct approach to pre- or post-nuptial agreements:

'The court should give effect to a nuptial agreement that is freely entered into by each party with a full appreciation of its implications unless in the circumstances prevailing it would not be fair to hold the parties to their agreement.'

This is now, therefore, the general rule to be applied in all cases. Two areas of discussion are therefore suggested and must be considered. They are, first, the factors which might lead a court to consider that the agreement was not freely entered into (for the sake of convenience these are here described as 'vitiating factors'), and secondly, the circumstances in which a court might consider it was not fair to hold the parties to the agreement. These two sets of issues might overlap in some cases but they are in fact distinct.

Vitiating factors

1.61   The Supreme Court considers these factors in detail in paras [71] to [73]. Here, they may be summarised as follows:

(1)   Material lack of disclosure or information, and lack of sound legal advice. However, this is subject to the qualification that:

> '... if it is clear that a party is fully aware of the implications of an ante-nuptial agreement and indifferent to detailed particulars of the other party's assets, there is no need to accord the agreement reduced weight because he or she is unaware of those particulars. What is important is that each party should have all the information that is material to his or her decision, and that each party should intend that the agreement should govern the financial consequences of the marriage coming to an end.'

(2)   The parties must have intended that the agreement should be effective. This cannot always be inferred from the mere existence of the agreement.

(3)   Any of the standard vitiating factors in contract such as duress, fraud, illegality or misrepresentation.

(4)   Unconscionable conduct such as undue pressure (falling short of duress) would be likely to reduce the weight to be placed on an agreement.

(5)   Unworthy behaviour such as exploitation of a dominant position to secure an advantage would reduce or eliminate the value of an agreement.

The Court added the following important observations.

> 'The circumstances of the parties at the time of the agreement will be relevant. Those will include such matters as their age and maturity, whether either or both had been married or been in long-term relationships before. For such couples their experience of previous relationships may explain the terms of the agreement, and may also show what they foresaw when they entered into the agreement. What may not be easily foreseeable for less mature couples may well be in contemplation of

more mature couples. Another important factor may be whether the marriage would have gone ahead without an agreement, or without the terms which had been agreed. This may cut either way.'

The foreign element

1.62 The Supreme Court then considered the factors which might enhance the weight to be placed on an agreement, the most important of which is a foreign element. This was dealt with succinctly as follows:

> 'When dealing with agreements concluded in the past, and the agreement in this case was concluded in 1998, foreign elements such as those in this case may bear on the important question of whether or not the parties intended their agreement to be effective. In the case of agreements made in recent times and, a fortiori, any agreement made after this judgment, the question of whether the parties intended their agreement to take effect is unlikely to be in issue, so foreign law will not need to be considered in relation to that question.'

Fairness

1.63 Having, as it were, cleared the decks by dealing with such of the above factors as may be relevant, the court must then deal with what the Supreme Court described as the difficult question of the circumstances in which it might not be fair to hold the parties to an agreement. It began with the observation that the reason why the court should give weight to a nuptial agreement is that there should be respect for individual autonomy. The court should accord respect to the decision of a married couple as to the manner in which their financial affairs should be regulated. It would be paternalistic and patronising to override their agreement simply on the basis that the court knows best. This is particularly true where the parties' agreement addresses existing circumstances and not merely the contingencies of an uncertain future.

1.64 The factors which might lead to argument over whether an agreement was unfair were summarised as follows:

(1) **Children of the family**. A nuptial agreement cannot be allowed to prejudice the reasonable requirements of any children of the family.

(2) **Non-matrimonial property**. Where one or both parties own property at the date of the marriage or anticipate receiving such property, and wish to make provision for that property in the event of the dissolution of the marriage, there is nothing inherently unfair in such an arrangement and there may be a good objective reason for it such as obligations to other family members.

(3) **Future circumstances**. Where a pre-nuptial agreement attempts to address the contingencies, unknown and often unforeseen, of the couple's future relationship there is more scope for future events to make it unfair to hold them to their agreement. The circumstances of parties often change over

time in ways or to an extent which either cannot be or was not envisaged. The longer the marriage has lasted, the more likely it is that this will be the case.

The Supreme Court considered the hypothetical case of a pre-nuptial agreement providing for no recovery by each spouse from the other in the event of divorce, where the marriage had seen the formation of a fortune which each spouse had played an equal role in their different ways in creating, but the fortune was in the hands for the most part of one spouse rather than the other. It asked whether it would be right to give the same weight to their early agreement as in another perhaps very different example. It concluded that the answer was likely to be 'no'. Of the three strands identified in *White v White* and *Miller/McFarlane*, it was the first two, needs and compensation, which could most readily render it unfair to hold the parties to a pre-nuptial agreement. The parties were unlikely to have intended that their agreement should result, in the event of the marriage breaking up, in one partner being left in a predicament of real need, while the other enjoyed a sufficiency or more, and such a result was likely to render it unfair to hold the parties to their agreement. If the devotion of one partner to looking after the family and the home had left the other free to accumulate wealth, it was likely to be unfair to hold the parties to an agreement that entitled the latter to retain all that he or she had earned.

However, where these considerations did not apply and each party was in a position to meet his or her needs, fairness might well not require a departure from their agreement as to the regulation of their financial affairs in the circumstances that had come to pass. It was in relation to the third strand, sharing, that the court would be most likely to make an order in the terms of the nuptial agreement in place of the order that it would otherwise have made.

Case law since Radmacher

1.65 As is always the case, this decision of the Supreme Court was not the last word on the subject and there have been a number of cases where the proper approach to an agreement has been in issue. The first reported case following was *Z v Z (Financial Remedies: Marriage Contract)*.[151] The parties, who were French, had made a marriage contract in France in 1994. The marriage broke down in 2008 by which time the parties were living in London. In his judgment Moor J said that, had it not been for the agreement, this would have been a case for equal division of assets. However, the burden on someone arguing that a marital agreement had been varied was a heavy one, and there had to be clearest evidence before a court would contemplate using this as a reason for not enforcing the agreement. Further, even where the parties have made an agreement as to capital, there can still be a substantial liability for to provide ongoing support for a spouse and children.

---

[151] [2011] EWHC 2878 (Fam).

In *V v V (Prenuptial Agreement)*[152] an award at first instance was set aside on the ground that the judge had failed to give proper weight to a 'marriage settlement'. This settlement provided a good and powerful reason for departing from an equal division of assets and was capable of founding an award that differed from the one that would have been made had it not been entered into.

These decisions therefore reflect the changed emphasis on the weight to be placed on an agreement. However, other decisions demonstrate the need for an agreement to be freely agreed and fair in all respects.

In *Kremen v Agrest (Financial Remedy: Non-Disclosure: Post-Nuptial Agreement)*[153] Mostyn J said that it only be in would be an unusual case that, absent legal advice and full disclosure, a party could be taken to have freely entered into a marital agreement with full appreciation of its implications.

In *GS v L (Financial Remedies; Pre-acquired Assets: Need)*[154] the parties had signed a post-marriage agreement in Spain. The judge held that neither party had a full appreciation of what it meant and there was no common understanding. It was therefore ignored.

1.66 The agreement also has to be intended as an agreement that might bind the parties in the event of separation. In *F v F (Financial Remedies: Pre-marital Wealth)*[155] the parties during the marriage had made a shareholders agreement reclassifying and assigning shares in a family company between the parties and providing for salaries etc. In the financial proceedings following divorce the issue of whether this agreement was a maintenance agreement under s 34 MCA 1973 arose. It was held that it was not; the definition of financial agreements covered only agreements made with the expressed or clearly implied purpose of governing the parties' financial affairs including in the event of separation.

Agreements to compromise litigation

1.67 Whether or not an agreement to compromise litigation has been made and, if so, in what terms, may be in dispute. In *Xydhias v Xydhias*,[156] there were prolonged negotiations shortly before trial, which led to the wife asking for the trial to be vacated and for a short directions appointment. The wife applied successfully for an order in the terms of an agreement made between the parties, the husband failing in his purported withdrawal of all previous offers. The husband appealed, unsuccessfully, to the circuit judge and thence to the Court of Appeal. His appeal was dismissed.

It was held that it was a fundamental principle that an agreement for the compromise of an ancillary relief application did not give rise to an agreement

---

[152] [2011] EWHC 3230 (Fam).
[153] [2012] EWHC 45 (Fam).
[154] [2011] EWHC 1759 (Fam).
[155] [2012] EWHC 438 (Fam).
[156] [1999] 1 FLR 683, CA.

enforceable in law; ordinary contractual principles did not apply. The award of ancillary relief was always fixed by the court. The court had a discretion in determining whether an accord had been reached, but if the court decided that agreement had been reached it might have to consider whether the terms of the agreement were vitiated by, for example, non-disclosure or one of the *Edgar v Edgar*[157] factors.

In every case, the court must carry out its independent discretionary review under s 25. In this case, it was held that an agreement had been reached.

This development was extended in *Rose v Rose*[158] where, at the end of a financial dispute resolution (FDR) appointment, the judge was told that the parties had come to terms and it was left to counsel to draw up an agreed order. This draft order was agreed but the husband then sought to resile from it. On reference back to the judge, the judge refused to convert the agreement to an order. On appeal, an order was made in the terms of the agreement; it mattered not that the hearing had been an FDR appointment.

However, in *Soulsbury v Soulsbury*[159] the view was expressed, per curiam, that the conclusion expressed by Thorpe LJ in *Xydhias* that an agreement to compromise a claim was not enforceable until converted into a court order was too wide. If there were negotiations leading to agreement there was a duty to seek the court's approval. However, even an agreement subject to the approval of the court was binding on the parties to the extent that neither could resile from it.[160] The position is therefore that two differently composed Courts of Appeal have expressed different views on this topic, both per curiam. It remains to be seen what will come of this.

Clearly, however, in the light of these decisions, when parties are negotiating at court and an agreement is reached, it is wise for the advocates to agree between themselves and record when a *Xydhias* agreement has been made.

Law Commission

1.68   The interested reader is directed to the powerful dissenting judgment of Baroness Hale (the only family lawyer and the only woman on the court). The Law Commission is currently holding a consultation exercise, which is discussed in more detail in Chapter 22.

---

[157]   [1980] 1 WLR 1410.
[158]   [2002] EWCA Civ 208, [2002] 1 FLR 978.
[159]   [2008] 1 FLR 90, CA.
[160]   The court relied on *Goodinson v Goodinson* [1954] 2 QB 118; *Gould v Gould* [1970] 1 QB 275 and *Smallman v Smallman* [1972] Fam 25.

SELF-SUFFICIENCY

1.69 So far, we have considered the factors which the court is directed to have in its mind when deciding whether, and if so, in what manner, to make an order for ancillary relief. No one factor is more important than any other; the court must weigh them all in its mind, and make a balanced judgment.

However, there is a further factor to which the court is directed to have regard, and that is the possibility of the parties achieving self-sufficiency. It has already been seen that, when considering the financial means of the parties, the court must consider what increase in the earning capacity of the parties it would be reasonable to expect them to acquire. This is reinforced by s 25A, which directs the court, when making a periodical payments order or secured periodical payments order, to consider whether the financial obligations of the parties to each other should be terminated as soon as the court considers it just and reasonable. In such circumstances, the court must also consider whether it should direct that no further application may be made.

1.70 There is therefore a positive obligation on the court to consider imposing a clean break in every case. Whether or not this will be the result depends on the circumstances of the case, and the position is, perhaps, not as clear as it might be. This is considered further in Chapter 2.

GUIDELINES IN CHILDREN ORDERS CASES

1.71 So far, the factors for the consideration of the court have been exclusively confined to orders between the parties to the marriage. When the court makes an order for a child, different criteria apply, and these are contained in s 25(3). These are considered further in Chapter 11.

WHEN MAY ORDERS BE MADE?

1.72 An order for maintenance pending suit may be made at any time after the filing of the petition. Other orders, such as orders for periodical payments, a lump sum or property adjustment, may only be made on or after the grant of a decree.[161]

Interim capital provision is discussed further in Chapter 4.

Mr Nicholas Mostyn QC, sitting as a deputy High Court judge in *Rossi v Rossi*, expressed certain views as to whether there is a time-limit on applications for ancillary relief. These statements have authority in the sense that they are from the High Court, but there may be room for doubt about whether they are universally shared.

---

[161] MCA 1973, ss 22–24.

Jurisdiction

1.73 Jurisdiction to make orders for ancillary relief (except for those after a foreign decree – see Chapter 14) depends on the grant of a decree of divorce, nullity or judicial separation. Whether or not the court may make an order for ancillary relief is therefore the same question as whether it has jurisdiction to entertain the proceedings leading to the decree.

This is now governed by the EU Council Regulation on Jurisdiction and the Recognition and Enforcement of Judgments in Matrimonial Matters and in Matters of Parental Responsibility for Joint Children (known as 'Brussels IIA'). This is binding on all EU Member States except Denmark and applies to all proceedings filed after 1 March 2001.

The Regulation deals with the jurisdiction of the court in matrimonial cases and in 'civil proceedings relating to parental responsibility for the children of both spouses'. As to matrimonial cases (eg divorce), Art 3 sets out a multiple choice of jurisdictional factors which do not have a hierarchy; ie no one factor is more important than any other. The factors are:

- both spouses' habitual residence;

- the last habitual residence of both spouses, one spouse still being habitually resident there;

- the respondent spouse's habitual residence;

- in cases of a joint application, either spouse's habitual residence;

- the applicant's habitual residence based on 12 months' residence immediately before the application;

- the applicant's habitual residence based on 6 months' residence immediately before the application coupled with nationality or (in the case of the UK or Ireland) domicile; and

- the nationality of both the spouses or (in the case of the UK and Ireland) their domicile.

Where no Member State has jurisdiction under the above factors, jurisdiction is determined according to the laws of each State.

Where courts have concurrent jurisdiction, a court must defer to the court first seised of the case unless it needs to take protective measures in urgent cases. A court is seised of a case when the documents instituting the proceedings 'or other equivalent document' is lodged with the court, provided that steps are taken to serve it or, when it has to be served before issue, when it is received by the authority responsible for service.

1.74 Schedule 1 to the Domicile and Matrimonial Proceedings Act 1973 makes provision for a stay of proceedings where there are proceedings affecting the marriage in another jurisdiction. Such a stay may be obligatory (Sch 1, para 8) or discretionary (Sch 1, para 11).

Questions of jurisdiction can assume some importance in cases of ample means where it is thought that the approach of the courts of England and Wales may be more, or less, generous than that to be found elsewhere.[162]

---

[162] See eg *de Dampierre v de Dampierre* [1987] 2 FLR 300, HL; *W v W (Financial Relief: Appropriate Forum)* [1997] 1 FLR 257; *S v S (Divorce: Staying Proceedings)* [1997] 2 FLR 100; *Butler v Butler (Nos 1 and 2)* [1997] 2 FLR 311, CA; *C v C (Divorce: Stay of English Proceedings)* [2001] 1 FLR 624.

Chapter 2

PERIODICAL PAYMENTS

INTRODUCTION

2.1   Periodical payments can be distinguished from other forms of financial orders by the fact that they constitute a continuing obligation, normally an obligation to pay a weekly or monthly sum, as opposed to a once and for all payment such as a lump sum or a transfer of property. A further distinction is that they can be varied, whereas, with certain exceptions, the general principle is that there can be only one order for payment of a lump sum or transfer of property. This type of relief is what was once called, and which the layperson may still call, 'maintenance'.

Periodical payments ordered to be paid before decree absolute of divorce or decree of judicial separation are called maintenance pending suit.

DEFINITIONS

2.2   Periodical payments are not defined by FPR 2010. This is because they are a type of financial order, which is defined as any of the orders mentioned in s 21(1) of MCA 1973. It is therefore to the statute that reference must be made.

2.3   One of the types of financial provision order contained in s 21(1)(a) is an order that a party must make, in favour of another person, such periodical payments, for such term, as may be specified (a 'periodical payments order').[1] This is the statutory authority for this type of order.

WHO MAY APPLY?

2.4   Only a party to the marriage or a child of the family may apply for periodical payments.[2] A party who has remarried cannot apply for periodical payments, even if the application is made before remarriage.[3] Orders for children are dealt with in Chapter 11.

---

[1]   MCA 1973, s 21(1)(a).
[2]   Heading to Part II of MCA 1973.
[3]   MCA 1973, s 28(3).

PROCEDURE

2.5 The procedure for applying for periodical payments is the same as for any other form of ancillary relief. Reference should therefore be made to Chapter 16.

GENERAL PRINCIPLES

2.6 As with any other form of financial order, orders for periodical payments are rarely made in isolation; they are usually part of a combination of the various forms of remedies, including lump sum, property adjustment and provision for children (whether made by the Child Support Agency or the court). When the court comes to decide whether or not an order for periodical payments should be made and, if so, in what sum, it must have regard to the needs of the parties and the ability of the paying party to meet the needs of the other party by these means. Such an exercise will normally be carried out after the court, at least notionally, has allocated the available capital. In particular, the court must have regard to the factors set out in s 25 of MCA 1973; these are considered in general terms in Chapter 1. Case-law is perhaps of even more uncertain value in this field than when considering other forms of ancillary relief.[4]

However, one important principle has been established by the case of *McFarlane v McFarlane;*[5] for a detailed discussion see **2.16** et seq. The principle established was that periodical payments are not limited to maintenance, but can include provision for compensation and to reflect any capital imbalance between the parties.

HOW DOES THE COURT MAKE ITS ORDERS?

2.7 Orders are made after consideration of the evidence and in the light of the factors in s 25. However, it would be logical to divide the reasoning process as follows:

- whether an order for periodical payments should be made at all;

- consideration of the amount of the order;

- whether any order should be limited in time.

These will be considered in turn.

---

[4] See e g *Sharpe v Sharpe* (1981) Fam Law 121, (1981) *The Times*, 7 February.
[5] [2006] 1 FLR 1186, HL.

Should there be an order at all?

2.8 Provided the party applying for periodical payments has not remarried, there is no absolute bar to an order being made. If the means of the parties are such that either the applicant does not need support or the respondent is unable to provide any support, an order would not normally be made. It may also be that, on consideration of all the factors, the court will decide that in the case before it the obligations of the parties to each other should be terminated and that there should be a clean break.[6]

However, provided both need and ability to pay can be demonstrated, the following matters may be relevant in making an initial decision as to whether an order should be made.

Earning capacity/potential

2.9 The court is required to have regard to the financial means of the parties at the time or in the foreseeable future[7] '... including in the case of earning capacity any increase in that capacity which it would in the opinion of the court be reasonable to expect a party to the marriage to take steps to acquire.' The court may not, therefore, consider only the means of the parties at the time of the hearing. It is required to inquire into whether or not a party, particularly the applicant, could take reasonable steps to improve her position and even render herself self-sufficient.

Cohabitation

2.10 A party who is cohabiting is not thereby precluded from applying for periodical payments. His or her financial position will clearly have to be considered in the light of the cohabitation, which will be one of the circumstances which the court is directed to consider. In some circumstances, cohabitation may be a source of considerable financial advantage; in others, quite the contrary. The principles have been lucidly set out as follows:[8]

> 'First, cohabitation is not to be equated with marriage. In performing its functions under the Matrimonial Causes Act 1973 (as amended) ... cohabitation is not to be given decisive weight. Secondly, cohabitation is, however, a relevant factor in that it bears upon the financial circumstances, particularly upon the assessment of the wife's financial needs. But to me it seems above all that the court should strive to discern the realities in determining what weight to give to the factor of cohabitation, particularly since the subjective presentation of the parties often seeks to disguise or distort the realities.'

---

[6] For a detailed consideration of the clean break, see **2.29** et seq.
[7] MCA 1973, s 25(2)(a).
[8] *Atkinson v Atkinson* [1995] 2 FLR 356 per Thorpe J. See also *Hepburn v Hepburn* [1989] 1 FLR 373; *MH v MH* (1982) 3 FLR 429; *Suter v Suter and Jones* [1987] Fam 111, and *Atkinson v Atkinson* [1988] 2 FLR 353 at 356 per Waterhouse J.

As to what constitutes cohabitation, it has been held[9] that, whilst it is impossible to produce a comprehensive list of criteria to determine the existence of cohabitation, relevant factors were living together in the same household; a sharing of daily life; stability and a degree of permanence; finances; a sexual relationship; children; intention and motivation; and the opinion of the reasonable person with normal perceptions.

The traditional statement of the law as set out above has been the subject of some judicial attack and it may be doubtful how long the present law will remain undisturbed. In *K v K (Periodical Payments: Cohabitation)*[10] Coleridge J referred to the 'social revolution' which has occurred and said that this should be recognised by the law. In the instant case he found that the cohabitation of the wife could not be ignored as a circumstance of the case and that the husband should be expected to support the wife for a shorter period than that envisaged by a previous consent order. However, he felt constrained by Court of Appeal authority from going further.

In *Fleming v Fleming*[11] it was held that *Atkinson* did not require revisiting. The principle that cohabitation was not to be equated with remarriage was as sound as ever.

> '... we do not consider that the right approach to a case of this kind is to seek to apply the so-called one-third rule. The right approach is rather to consider the disposable income of each party apart from any order and then to see what order will produce a redistribution of the disposable incomes which is fair and just in all circumstances.'

In *H v H (Financial Provision)*[12] Singer J made no findings as to the wife's cohabitation, even though she was pregnant and admitted she was in a permanent relationship. The appeal is reported as *Grey v Grey*.[13] The appeal was allowed and the issue of spousal maintenance remitted to the judge. It was held that post-separation cohabitation is a relevant factor for the court to take into account when considering the appropriate level of spousal maintenance. The judge should have attached significant weight to the wife's new relationship and investigated and assessed its financial consequences. The approach set out in *Fleming* was sound and sufficiently flexible to enable courts to do justice.

Conduct

2.11 Conduct of the parties is dealt with in more detail in Chapter 1. Here it may suffice to say that, although it is unusual for conduct to play a major part

---

9   In *Kimber v Kimber* [2000] 1 FLR 383. See also *Crake v Supplementary Benefits Commission* [1982] 1 All ER 498; *Re J (Income Support: Cohabitation)* [1995] 1 FLR 660.
10   [2005] EWHC 2886 (Fam), [2006] 2 FLR 468.
11   [2003] EWCA Civ 1841, [2004] 1 FLR 667.
12   [2009] EWHC 494 (Fam), [2009] 2 FLR 795.
13   [2009] EWCA Civ 1424, [2010] 1 FLR 1764.

in the award of financial remedies, there may be rare cases in which the conduct of one party has been such as to disentitle him or her from any relief.

Length of marriage

2.12 Special considerations arising from short marriages are considered in Chapter 1.

What should be the amount of the order?

2.13 It would be misleading to think that there is a conventional starting point for the quantification of a periodical payments order. Some older cases contain references to, for example, the 'one-third starting point'.[14] However, this is not now regarded as a proper approach.[15]

The only proper starting point is s 25. The particular factor which is normally important as an initial figure is the 'financial needs, obligations and responsibilities'[16] of the applicant party; these must be reduced to a figure which the court considers necessary to enable the applicant to live at a standard which is appropriate in the light of the other s 25 factors such as the standard of living during the marriage, the contributions of the parties and the length of the marriage. From this figure must be deducted the actual or potential income of that party; this will include non-means related State benefits such as retirement pension or child benefit, but not lone parent benefit. However, the ability of one party to increase her income by the proper use of State benefits cannot be overlooked. For example, working tax credit and child tax credit are clearly appropriate benefits for many working mothers on low incomes and should be applied for. They are available for families, including lone parents, who have one or more children, work more than 16 hours per week, and have savings of £8,000 or less. Applications are made to HM Revenue and Customs, who assess the sums payable.

2.14 Having ascertained the needs of the applicant party, the court must then assess the ability of the other party to meet those needs. This will involve consideration of that party's needs, obligations and responsibilities and all the other s 25 factors. It will also involve assessment of that party's financial means.

Clearly, one party cannot be ordered to pay money which he does not have. Nor should he normally be required to pay such sums as will reduce him to below subsistence level.[17] However, this is not inflexible, particularly where the court considers that the paying party has assumed obligations recklessly and

---

[14] For a comparatively recent example, see *Sibley v Sibley* (1981) 2 FLR 121, in which the principle did not seem to be challenged. See also, however, *Ward v Ward and Greene* (1980) 1 FLR 368: 'the one-third rule is only a starting point'.

[15] See e g *Saunders v Saunders* (1980) 1 FLR 121, per Brandon LJ.

[16] MCA 1973, s 25(2)(b).

[17] *Stockford v Stockford* (1982) 3 FLR 58, CA.

without proper regard to his liability to the applicant and/or the children of the family, or even where they have been assumed voluntarily.[18] In one case,[19] where the parties were comparatively affluent, Thorpe LJ observed that a 'conventional adjudication' would be to say that half the husband's net available income should be earmarked for the support of the wife and (two) children. This resulted in a figure of £20,000 from which it was necessary to deduct a Child Support Agency assessment of £7,500, the final sum being rounded down to £12,000 pa. However, this should not be taken as a 'rule' and perhaps is more akin to a maximum amount or even a starting point.

When calculating the incomes of the parties, the net figures (after income tax and national insurance contributions) are taken. Periodical payments are not taxable income in the hands of the recipient, nor is tax relief available on periodical payments orders.[20]

2.15 It is at this final stage that the court may wish to consider the proportion of the paying party's income which it is proposing to pay to the applicant and to consider the justice of the case in the round. Because of the essentially practical nature of this exercise, there are few reported cases on the appropriate proportion. It has been observed[21] that 'it has never been the custom in ancillary relief litigation to look with scrupulous care at the budget items of the prospective payer. Of course it is incumbent on the judge to cross-check to ensure that the adjudication that meets the applicant's needs is an adjudication which the respondent can afford'. It is difficult to improve on the reported words of Ormrod LJ in what is now a comparatively old case:[22]

> '... the court, in all cases, must apply the provisions of s 25 of the Matrimonial Causes Act 1973 ... without superimposed judicial glosses ... it becomes necessary to assess the actual impact of any order for periodical payments on the parties' respective financial means ... The court must, therefore, look broadly at the overall position rather than enter upon a detailed investigation of household budgets ... In essence, it involves, working out ... on the basis of [a] hypothetical order [the position of the parties] ... The two figures [payer's and payee's positions as a result of the hypothetical order] can then be compared and related to the respective needs, and the hypothetical order adjusted accordingly. This is the "net effect" method ...'

In all but the simplest cases, therefore, it is essential to prepare a 'net effect schedule' to demonstrate what will be the result of the order which is being proposed for each of the parties. This would involve starting with the net incomes from all sources for each party, making allowance for any tax changes which may occur as a result of the proposed order (though these are unlikely to be many), and deducting (or adding, as the case may be) the amount of the

---

[18]   See *Campbell v Campbell* [1998] 1 FLR 828, CA.
[19]   *Scheeres v Scheeres* [1999] 1 FLR 241, CA.
[20]   See **2.28**.
[21]   By Thorpe LJ in *Campbell v Campbell* (above).
[22]   *Stockford v Stockford* (above).

proposed order. This will show the total income of each party if the order is made, and this figure can then be compared with each party's reasonable needs or requirements.

Once again, it should be noted that periodical payments are not limited to the maintenance of the receiving party though one has to say that the practical effect of this will only be felt in cases where the means of the parties are considerable.

Periodical payments after Miller/McFarlane

2.16 The question of whether, and if so to what extent, equality should apply to periodical payments as opposed to capital has been debated since *White* and was the subject of the combined appeals of *McFarlane v McFarlane* and *Parlour v Parlour*.[23] The general principles enunciated by the House of Lords in *Miller/McFarlane* are discussed in detail in Chapter 1. Here, the discussion is limited to equality and periodical payments, where the general thrust of the Court of Appeal's judgment was not disturbed, save in the important respect that the 5-year term imposed on Mrs McFarlane's order was removed.

Thorpe LJ put it like this:

'If the decision in *White v White* introduces the yardstick of equality for measuring a fair division of capital why should the same yardstick not be applied as the measure for the division of income?'

2.17 In the *Parlour* case, before Bennett J, the judge at first instance, the wife argued that she should receive the same proportion of the husband's income as that which had been agreed in respect of his capital, namely 37%. This would give her £444,000 pa for herself and the three children. The husband contended for a global figure of £120,000 pa.

The wife's argument, in a nutshell, was that an earning capacity developed during marriage was a resource or thing of value which should be equitably shared, and that an award of periodical payments should not be confined to the wife's maintenance needs. The husband argued for restriction to reasonable needs.

Bennett J said that to confine periodical payments to needs or reasonable requirements would be a faulty exercise of discretion. That would apply only one matter in s 25(2) and ignore the rest. To award only 10% of the husband's income 'is thoroughly mean and would be unfair'. However, to award her £444,000 would be 'an unprincipled and unfair award'. The court 'must seek a way that does justice to the parties and which does not, so far as is possible, impose a glass ceiling on the one hand but which does not hand out capital on the other'.

---

[23]   [2004] EWCA Civ 872.

2.18 In the *McFarlane* case, the first hearing was before District Judge Redgrave who found that the parties' contributions to this long marriage had been different but of equal value. The wife's contributions had enabled the husband to create a working environment which had produced greater rewards, in respect of which she should have her fair share. It was unreasonable to expect the wife to take steps to improve her earning capacity in the foreseeable future.

The order made was for £250,000 pa, ie 33.18% of the husband's net income, to be index-linked. In the Court of Appeal Thorpe LJ commented at para [23] that 'implicit within the district judge's reasoning is first the conclusion that the wife should have the same opportunity as the husband to make provision for the years of retirement and second the conclusion that she should have the means with which to insure herself and the children against the risk of premature cessation of the husband's high professional earnings'.

The husband appealed on several grounds and the first appeal was heard by Bennett J who said:

> '... it is my judgment, with all due respect to the district judge, that, having given the wife an award from which she is likely to be able to save large sums of money and thereby accumulate capital, it is no answer to say, as she did, that it is a matter for the wife whether she chooses to make provision for pension and other matters.'

He therefore chose to exercise his discretion afresh. He asked the question 'what figure should then be substituted for £250,000?' and answered:

> '... the quantification of periodical payments is more an art than a science. The parameters of s 25 are so wide that it might be said that it is almost impossible to be "scientific". In my judgment, I would be doing justice to both parties if I award the wife £180,000 per annum by way of periodical payments.'

2.19 In the Court of Appeal, Thorpe LJ observed that:

> '... the skeleton arguments prepared for the appeals ... address the very general question: what should be the principles governing an award of periodical payments during joint lives or until remarriage in any case where the net income of the payer significantly exceeds what both parties need in order to meet their outgoings at the standard of living which the court has found to be appropriate.'

As far as *McFarlane* was concerned, the court decided that Bennett J had erred in interfering with the district judge's order which was therefore restored (applying *Cordle v Cordle*) subject only to the imposition of a 5-year term (subsequently removed by the House of Lords) and removal of the index-linking provision. In *Parlour*, Thorpe LJ observed that Mr Parlour, a professional footballer, might be nearing the end of his playing career and continued:

'These considerations only underline the obvious need for a substantial proportion of the income in the present fat years to be stored up against the future famine. Again I conclude that it would be wrong in principle to leave the responsibility and opportunity to the husband alone. The wife's and the children's needs were put at £150,000 by the judge. To award her the global figure of £444,000 per annum sought by Mr Mostyn allows her and obliges her to lay-up £294,000 per annum as a reserve against the discharge of her periodical payments order. I would in this case order a four-year extendable term. Hopefully a clean break will be achievable then on an assessment of the husband's earning capacity at thirty-five years of age and the wife's independent fortune derived from the original capital settlement augmented by the substantial annual surplus built into her periodical payments order in the interim.'

2.20 The Court of Appeal was at pains to emphasise that the two cases before it were exceptional and outside the normal run of ancillary relief applications which come before the court. The exceptional factors were the very large incomes of the parties coupled with the fact that there was insufficient capital to provide a clean break now. One might also add the fact that the wives in both cases had no immediate prospect of improving their earning capacity and had to care for young children. The predominating factor therefore became how best to prepare for a clean break in years to come.

However, even if the effect of the judgment were limited to that class of case, it might still have a significant effect. As Thorpe LJ pointed out, there must be many high-earning professional couples who will find themselves in a similar financial situation.

2.21 One important lesson from the Court of Appeal's judgment is that periodical payments cannot be limited to the needs of the receiving party. To do so would be to concentrate on one s 25(2) factor to the exclusion of the others. This was upheld by the House of Lords decision. In his speech at para [31] Lord Nicholls said:

'There is nothing in the statutory ancillary relief provisions to suggest Parliament intended periodical payments orders to be limited to payments needed for maintenance. Section 23(1)(a) empowers the court, in quite general language, to order one party to the marriage to make to the other "such periodical payments, for such term, as may be specified in the order". In deciding whether, and how, to exercise this power the statute requires the court to have regard to all the circumstances of the case: s 25(1). The court is required to have particular regard to the familiar wide-ranging checklist set out in s 25(2). These provisions, far from suggesting an intention to restrict periodical payments to the one particular purpose of maintenance, suggest that the financial provision orders in s 23 were intended to be flexible in their application.

[32] In particular, I consider a periodical payments order may be made for the purpose of affording compensation to the other party as well as meeting financial needs. It would be extraordinary if this were not so. If one party's earning capacity has been advantaged at the expense of the other party during the marriage it would be extraordinary if, where necessary, the court could not order the advantaged party to pay compensation to the other out of his enhanced earnings

when he receives them. It would be most unfair if absence of capital assets were regarded as cancelling his obligation to pay compensation in respect of a continuing economic advantage he has obtained from the marriage.'

2.22 It has to be said that the judgments do not assist in deciding what proportion of the payer's income should be taken. In *Parlour's* case, the wife's submission was that the division of income should be in the same proportions as the division of capital and that submission succeeded. The wife had conceded that a departure from equality of capital was appropriate. One has to ask whether, if that concession had not been made and if the court had divided capital equally, the division of income would also have been equal.

Little help is derived from the *McFarlane* case because the Court of Appeal merely restored the district judge's order, on *Cordle* principles, and the district judge had not stated any particular principle in arriving at her figure of £250,000 pa. Needs had been put at £128,000 and the eventual award was about one-third of the husband's net income. Bennett J was similarly imprecise when he reduced the figure to £180,000 merely saying that he thought this would do justice to both parties. The imposition of a term is of course important.

In the Court of Appeal, Wall LJ was clearly unsure as to what, if any principle, should replace the emphasis on needs. He felt it necessary to fall back on the words of Ormrod LJ in *Martin v Martin* 26 years ago:

'... the court should preserve, so far as it can, the utmost elasticity to deal with each case on its own facts. Therefore it is a matter of trial and error and imagination on the part of those advising clients.'

This of course, was echoed by Thorpe LJ in *White v White* and *Parra v Parra*. Practitioners may therefore find it difficult to draw any more general lessons from this case than others in the past.

Some useful guidance may be derived from the treatment of the *McFarlane* case on the subsequent variation application made by the wife. This is considered in detail in Chapter 13.

2.23 Words of caution have been expressed by Charles J in *H v H*.[24] His Lordship said that the fact that both parties are free to terminate a marital relationship means that by reference to the rationale of compensation the lower earner is not entitled to long-term economic parity. The aim is self-sufficiency. Nevertheless , in this case, fairness required that the wife receive an extra award to reflect her contribution over the years of partnership which had led to the husband's increased earning capacity.

---

[24]   [2007] 2 FLR 548.

Should the order be limited in duration?

2.24 Section 25A of the MCA 1973 contains the statutory authority for the 'clean break'. This is considered as a topic in its own right at **2.29**. Here, it should merely be noted that, in addition to s 25A(1) which requires the court to consider whether the financial obligations of the parties to each other should be terminated, s 25A(2) requires the court in every case where it makes a periodical payments order to consider whether it would be appropriate to require those payments to be made only for such term as would in the opinion of the court be sufficient to enable the party in whose favour the order is made to adjust without undue hardship to the termination of his or her financial dependence on the other party.

Further detail is contained at **2.29** et seq.

MAINTENANCE PENDING SUIT

2.25 The jurisdiction to make an order for periodical payments depends on the grant of a decree. Any order for periodic maintenance before that time is called maintenance pending suit. Once a petition has been filed:[25]

> '... the court may make an order for maintenance pending suit, that is to say, an order requiring either party to the marriage to make to the other such periodical payments for his or her maintenance and for such term, being a term beginning not earlier than the date of the presentation of the petition and ending with the date of the determination of the suit, as the court thinks reasonable.'

There is no special law relating to this form of relief and such applications invariably turn on their own facts. The court must use the usual s 25 factors, the only difference being that the application will be normally to deal with a short-term position rather than the permanent situation.

M v M (Maintenance Pending Suit)[26] was a case where the parties were very rich. The judge awarded the wife maintenance pending suit of £330,000 p a, holding that in the instant case the court must have regard to the standards of the very rich and not to middle-class standards. He also held that a decision as to maintenance pending suit should not be taken as a pointer to the future.

In *TL v ML*[27] it was held that the sole criterion for determining an application for maintenance pending suit is 'reasonableness', ie fairness. It was emphasised that there should always be before the court a specific budget for the application for maintenance pending suit.

---

[25] MCA 1973, s 22.

[26] [2002] EWHC 317 (Fam), [2002] 2 FLR 123.

[27] [2005] EWHC 2680 (Fam), [2006] 1 FLR 1263.

Further guidance was given by Coleridge J in *S v M (Maintenance Pending Suit)*.[28] It was emphasised that frequently these are not straightforward cases that can be dealt with in 30 minutes. Care should therefore be taken to ensure that adequate time is allowed for the application.

2.26 One of the problems of parties to matrimonial proceedings, particularly wives, is that they may be (and now, of course, invariably are) ineligible for public funding because of some modest accumulation of capital but have insufficient resources to pursue their rights against their spouse. This is made more acute when the spouse is wealthy, litigious or obstructive.[29] To some extent, this difficulty was overcome by the decision of Holman J in *A v A (Maintenance Pending Suit: Provision for Legal Fees)*.[30] Holman J ordered maintenance pending suit to include £4,000 per month towards legal costs, backdated to the discharge of the wife's certificate of public funding. He said that the costs of the matrimonial proceedings were not in a different category from other expenses; in fact, they were the wife's most urgent and pressing need. There was no authority excluding such an element as a matter of law. Holman J emphasised that the court should be cautious in including such a costs element in an order, and it may be noted that in this case the husband was of great wealth and the combined costs exceeded £350,000.

In *G v G (Maintenance Pending Suit: Costs)*[31] it was held that *A v A* was correctly decided and that maintenance pending suit could include an element for costs. The principle was further reinforced in *Minwalla v Minwalla.*[32]

In *Moses-Taiga v Moses-Taiga*[33] it was held that a costs element would only be included in an order for maintenance pending suit in an exceptional case. However, a more positive approach was given by the Court of Appeal in *Currey v Currey*.[34] Here, it was held that the principles applicable to determining whether support to meet legal costs should be given are no different whether under s 22 or under s 31 (variation applications). The initial overarching enquiry is into whether the applicant for a costs allowance can demonstrate that she cannot reasonably procure legal advice and representation by any other means. Thus, to the extent that she has assets, the applicant must demonstrate that they cannot reasonably be deployed whether directly or as means of raising a loan. She also has to demonstrate that she cannot reasonably procure legal services by offering a charge on ultimate capital recovery.

For the form of order, see below. For the general principles of costs see Chapter 17.

---

[28] [2013] Fam Law 271.
[29] See *Sears Tooth v Payne Hicks Beach and Others* [1997] 2 FLR 116 at 118H–119A per Wilson J.
[30] [2001] 1 FLR 377.
[31] [2003] Fam Law 393.
[32] [2004] EWHC 2823 (Fam), [2005] 1 FLR 771.
[33] [2005] EWCA Civ 1013, [2006] 1 FLR 1074.
[34] [2006] EWCA Civ 1338, [2007] 1 FLR 946.

FORM OF ORDER

2.27 Precedents for orders for periodical payments will be found at Appendix A. Any order for periodical payments is for the joint lives of the parties, and is therefore discharged on the death of either.

The form of an order for maintenance pending suit including a costs element was considered in *TL v ML and Others*[35] where it was held that the order should be expressed as including a legal expenses component of, eg £50,000 payable at the rate of, eg £2,000 per month, upon the applicant undertaking to pay such legal expenses to her solicitors to be credited against any costs order which she may ultimately recover against the respondent.

TAX CONSIDERATIONS

2.28 Before the budget of 1988, tax relief was available on orders for periodical payments, and the computation of the fiscal benefits to be derived from various orders occupied much of the time of family lawyers. That fiscal regime was abolished by the Finance Act 1988, and the position until April 2000 was that recipients of periodical payments were no longer taxed on their receipts, and paying parties were allowed a flat rate annual sum by way of tax relief, or the actual sum paid, whichever was the lesser. From 6 April 2000, the position is different again. Tax relief on maintenance is largely abolished as from this date. Relief is retained only where one or both of the parties was aged 65 or over as at 5 April 2000. Relief under 'old orders' (ie those made before 30 June 1988) has also ended.

THE CLEAN BREAK

Introduction

2.29 When periodical payments were considered at **2.1**, it was noted that the difference between that form of ancillary relief and the others is that periodical payments are a continuing form of relief whereas relief of a capital nature can normally be given only once. The standard form of order for periodical payments provides for payments during the joint lives of the parties and until the payee shall remarry. Periodical payments may therefore continue during the lifetime of the payer and may be varied at any time. Until the passage into law of MFPA 1984, it was possible to terminate the right of one party to apply for periodical payments only by consent.[36] However, as a result of that statute, the provisions of which are now contained in s 25(2)(a) and s 25A of MCA 1973, it is now possible for the court to terminate the right to periodical payments without consent; this provision is generally known as the 'clean break'.

---

[35] [2005] EWHC 2680 (Fam), [2006] 1 FLR 1263.
[36] See eg *Dipper v Dipper* [1981] Fam 31.

2.30 The meaning of the term 'clean break' is clear: once the break has occurred, neither party has any continuing financial claim on the other. When this change in the law occurred in 1984, it was generally considered to be an enlightened measure, and the desirability of a clean break in most cases has come to be regarded as axiomatic. During the period since then, judicial dicta have varied but it has seemed that the legal profession and the public generally have accepted, perhaps uncritically, the need for a clean break wherever possible. However, as will be seen, it may be that this has come about because of a failure to consider carefully the provisions of the statute.

Statutory provisions

2.31 The clean break provisions in MCA 1973 fall under four categories. The first of the changes effected in 1984 was that s 25(2)(a) was amended. This contains the statutory factors to which the court must have regard in respect of the means, including income, of the parties. The 1984 change was to add, after the reference to the income, etc of the parties, the words:[37]

'... including in the case of earning capacity any increase in that capacity which it would in the opinion of the court be reasonable to expect a party to the marriage to take steps to acquire.'

This may be taken, therefore, to represent the presumption of the desirability of self-sufficiency.[38]

2.32 Section 25A is more detailed. The second clean break provision is s 25A(1) which provides that whenever the court exercises any of its powers under ss 22A–24A, (except when making an interim order):

'... it shall be the duty of the court to consider whether it would be appropriate so to exercise those powers that the financial obligations of each party towards the other will be terminated as soon after the grant of the decree as the court considers just and reasonable.'

2.33 Thirdly, s 25A(2) provides that where the court decides to make an order for periodical payments or secured periodical payments in 'favour' of a party to the marriage:

'... the court shall, in particular, consider whether it would be appropriate to require those payments to be made or secured only for such term as would in the opinion of the court be sufficient to enable the party in whose favour the order is made to adjust without undue hardship to the termination of his or her financial dependence on the other party.'

The fourth provision is s 25A(3), which contains the power to dismiss and prevent further applications. When the court exercises its powers under MCA

---

[37] MCA 1973, s 25(2)(a).
[38] Supported by some judicial dicta, e g Ward J in *B v B (Financial Provision)* [1990] 1 FLR 20.

1973 to make an order for ancillary relief in favour of a party and considers that no continuing obligation should be imposed on either party to make or secure periodical payments in favour of the other, it may '... dismiss the application with a direction that the applicant shall not be entitled to make any future application in relation to that marriage for an order under section 23(1)(a) or (b) above.'

Summary of statutory provisions

2.34 The position may therefore be summarised as follows:

(1)　When considering the earning capacity of either party, the court must consider whether it would be reasonable to expect that party to take steps to increase such capacity.[39]

(2)　When making any order for ancillary relief (except an interim order), the court must consider whether the obligations of the parties to each other should be terminated.[40] If the court does come to that conclusion, the next paragraph is unnecessary.

(3)　When it does decide to make an order for periodical payments or secured periodical payments the court must consider whether such order should be for a limited term only, such term being that which is sufficient to enable the receiving party to adjust without undue hardship to termination.[41]

(4)　The above provisions are positive duties for the court. These matters must be considered in every case.

(5)　This duty of the court must be exercised after consideration of all the factors contained in s 25. It is only after proper consideration of all those factors, that the court can come to an informed decision.

(6)　When the court decides that there should be termination, it must effect this by the orders set out in s 25A(3).[42]

(7)　These provisions apply only to divorce and nullity cases. They do not apply to judicial separation.

Judicial guidance as to when a clean break is appropriate

2.35 As might have been expected, there have been many decided cases in which the court has given guidance on when a clean break is appropriate.[43]

---

[39]　MCA 1973, s 25(2)(a).
[40]　MCA 1973, s 25A(1).
[41]　MCA 1973, s 25A(2).
[42]　MCA 1973, s 25A(3).
[43]　See, e g *Waterman v Waterman* [1989] 1 FLR 380 (term order for 5 years when child would be

However, as will have been seen above, the decision which the court must make is not always one single issue. In many cases, the court will have to make two decisions:

(1)　whether the obligations of the parties towards each other should be terminated (the immediate clean break); and, if not,

(2)　whether they should be terminated at some future time (the delayed clean break).

These two possibilities are the subject of different, though sometimes overlapping, case-law.

When a delayed clean break is adopted, the separate question arises of whether a direction under s 28(1A) should be given and, if not, whether the term for periodical payments may be extended. These possibilities must be considered separately.

Should there be an immediate clean break?

2.36　Dicta from two cases will be considered shortly. Like all fields of law, this is an evolving and constantly changing area and these cases contain the guidance which is most likely to predict accurately the approach of the higher courts. Accordingly, it may be that some of the earlier examples of the way in which the court has exercised its discretion will be of less importance than might previously have been the case, and those cases will, therefore, be summarised rather than set out in detail.

2.37　It is striking that s 25A(1) gives no guidance to the court as to how its discretion should be exercised. This is in contrast to s 25A(2) which seems to suggest that periodical payments should only be for a fixed term if, at the end of that term, the payee has adjusted without undue hardship to the loss of dependency. It might be thought that that test is also appropriate to s 25A(1), but that is not what the statute says.

Cases in which the principle of an immediate clean break has been approved by the court may be categorised as 'big money cases' and 'no money cases', 'intermediate cases' providing more of a problem.

Examples of the former are *Gojkovic v Gojkovic*,[44] and *F v F (Duxbury Calculation: Rate of Return)*.[45] These cases will be considered in more detail in

---

10, wife working as secretary, short marriage); *Suter v Suter and Jones* [1987] 2 FLR 232, CA (nominal order where wife with young children and uncertainties as to her future); *M v M (Financial Provision)* [1987] 2 FLR 1 (47-year-old wife, no prospect of self-sufficiency, no clean break); *Whiting v Whiting* [1988] 2 FLR 189 (wife self-sufficient, husband unemployed, no clean break; this is generally accepted to be an untypical decision).
[44]　[1990] 1 FLR 140, CA.
[45]　[1996] 1 FLR 833.

Chapter 4 (big money cases) but it will be seen that the important factor was that it was possible to provide sufficient funds from ample capital resources to secure a fund from which the wife's income needs could be met for her lifetime. Accordingly, the rationale for the dismissal of all continuing claims in such cases seems to have been that true self-sufficiency could be achieved by an order for redistribution of capital.

This trend has continued in two recent reported cases. In *Vaughan v Vaughan*[46] inequality of division of capital in favour of a wife was justified by the need for a clean break, though on appeal[47] it was held that the judge had erred in his appraisal of the husband's income and effectively given priority to the hypothetical claims of a second wife. In *CR v CR*[48] the court ordered a lump sum to be paid by instalments, as the husband was unable to pay it in one sum, to avoid the need for a continuing periodical payments order and to ensure a lump sum.

2.38 In the 'no money' cases, such as *Ashley v Blackman*,[49] the rationale for the immediate clean break has been that there never was and never would be any prospect of the husband paying periodical payments and so, for the achievement of certainty and the avoidance of further unnecessary litigation, an immediate clean break was the only sensible answer.

F v F (Clean Break: Balance of Fairness)[50] was a case involving assets of £3.48m which included shares in a family company worth £2.8m. The husband argued that the illiquidity of his company justified a departure from equality. After making orders to secure the wife's housing, Singer J ordered the husband to pay periodical payments of £75,000 p a. Here a clean break was neither feasible nor just. Where assets exceeded needs good reason must be found for departing from equality. The order for periodical payments would enable both parties to share in the results of the company's performance until a clean break was feasible.

It is, perhaps, in the intermediate cases that the courts have been placed in the most difficult position. In many such cases, it is clear that the income of the paying party (normally the husband) is such that a periodical payments order would cause hardship, while, at the same time, the income of the other party is not such as to entitle the court to find her to be self-supporting. There may have been a tendency, at least until the advent of CSA 1991, to make clean break orders where a matrimonial home was transferred to a mother so that children continued to live in the family home.[51] Nevertheless, there is clear authority that a direction under s 28(1A) prohibiting further applications

---

[46]   [2008] 1 FLR 1108, CA.
[47]   [2010] EWCA Civ 349.
[48]   [2008] 1 FLR 323.
[49]   [1988] 2 FLR 278.
[50]   [2003] 1 FLR 847.
[51]   See e g *Clutton v Clutton* [1991] 1 FLR 242 at 245 per Lloyd LJ.

should not be made where there are young children.[52] In *SRJ v DWJ (Financial Provision)*,[53] it was held that there is no presumption in favour of a clean break; in this case, there was a young child, and it was observed that it is difficult to achieve a financial clean break when there cannot be a personal clean break between the parties.

In another case,[54] where the husband had been ordered to pay periodical payments but had obstinately failed to do so, it was held that these developments demonstrated that the order made was not appropriate or practical, and that a clean break should be imposed to put an end to the expensive process of enforcement. It should, however, be noted that there were sufficient capital assets to enable the court to award a lump sum of the wife's capitalised maintenance requirements.

2.39 If the 'no money cases' are put to one side, it seems that the courts look to the test contained in s 25A(2) in order to make a decision under s 25A(1), an approach which is wholly reasonable even though it might seem not to be dictated by the words of the statute. This is not an insignificant point, since the two cases about to be considered were concerned with s 25A(2) and not s 25A(1). Nevertheless, the principles set out in the judgments of Ward LJ in these cases seem to establish authoritative guidelines for both subsections.

2.40 In *Flavell v Flavell*,[55] the court was concerned with a wife aged 54 who had a very limited earning capacity and no pension. The judge at first instance observed that it was not usually appropriate to provide for the termination of periodical payments in the case of a woman in her mid-50s, an opinion which Ward LJ endorsed with his approval. Ward LJ continued:

> 'The words of [s 25A(2)] do not impose more than an aspiration that the parties should achieve self-sufficiency. The power of the court to terminate dependency can, however, be exercised only in the event that adjustment can be made without undue hardship. There is, in my judgment, often a tendency for these orders to be made more in hope than in serious expectation. Especially in judging the case of ladies in their middle years the judicial looking into a crystal ball very rarely finds enough of substance to justify a finding that adjustment can be made without undue hardship. All too often, these orders are made without evidence to support them.'

---

[52] See *N v N (Consent Order: Variation)* [1993] 2 FLR 868 at 883 per Roch LJ for a clear statement of this principle. See also *Mawson v Mawson* [1994] 2 FLR 985 for a more mixed message (wife with young child, Thorpe J ordered term of 9 months but no s 28(1A) direction as this would not be appropriate where young child involved, complication because previous agreement to which the parties should be held). See also *B v B (Mesher Order)* [2002] EWHC 3106 (Fam), [2003] 2 FLR 285 (no presumption of term order in short marriage).

[53] [1999] 2 FLR 176, CA.

[54] *Fournier v Fournier* [1998] 2 FLR 990, CA.

[55] [1997] 1 FLR 353, CA.

2.41 Ward LJ gave further guidance in *C v C (Financial Relief: Short Marriage)*.[56] The facts of this case are unimportant save that it may be noted that, as its name suggests, it was concerned with a short marriage where the husband was comparatively wealthy. The judge at first instance had awarded the wife a lump sum and periodical payments of a level which, on appeal, was described as being 'at the top of the bracket' but which was nevertheless upheld. Ward LJ summarised the proper approach of the court as follows:

'(1) The first task is to consider a clean break which pursuant to s 25A(1) requires the court to consider whether it would be appropriate to exercise its powers so that the financial obligations of each party towards the other will be terminated as soon after the grant of the decree as the court considers just and reasonable.'

(It may be noted that no guidance is given as to how this exercise is to be carried out.)

'(2) If there is to be no clean break, and a periodical payments order is to be made, then the court must decide pursuant to s 25 what amount is to be ordered. The duration of the marriage is a factor relevant to the determination of quantum.

(3) If a periodical payments order is made, whether for 5p per annum or whatever, the question is whether it would be appropriate to impose a term because in the absence of such a direction the order will endure for joint lives or until the remarriage of the payee: see s 28(1)(a).

(4) The statutory test is this: is it appropriate to order periodical payments only for such a term as in the opinion of the court would be sufficient to enable the payee to adjust without undue hardship to the termination of financial dependence on the paying party?

(5) What is appropriate must of necessity depend on all the circumstances of the case including the welfare of any minor child and the s 25 checklist factors, one of which is the duration of the marriage. It is, however, not appropriate simply to say, "this is a short marriage therefore a term must be imposed".

(6) Financial dependence being evident from the very making of an order for periodical payments, the question is whether, in the light of all the circumstances of the case, the payee can adjust – and adjust without undue hardship – to the termination of financial dependence and if so when. The question is, can she adjust, not should she adjust. In answering that question, the court will pay attention not only to the duration of the marriage but to the effect the marriage and its breakdown and the need to care for any minor children has had and will continue to have on the earning capacity of the payee and the extent to which she is no longer in the position she would have been in but for the marriage, its consequences and its breakdown. It is highly material to consider any difficulties the payee may have in entering or re-entering the labour market, resuming a fractured career and making up any lost ground.

---

[56]   [1997] 2 FLR 26, CA.

(7)   The court cannot form its opinion that a term is appropriate without evidence to support its conclusion. Facts supported by evidence must, therefore, justify a reasonable expectation that the payee can and will become self-sufficient. Gazing into the crystal ball does not give rise to such a reasonable expectation. Hope, with or without pious exhortations to end dependency, is not enough.

(8)   It is necessary for the court to form an opinion not only that the payee will adjust, but also that the payee will have adjusted within the time that is fixed. The court may be in a position of such certainty that it can impose a deferred clean break by prohibiting an extension of the term pursuant to s 28(1A). If, however, there is any doubt about when self-sufficiency will be attained, it is wrong to require the payee to apply to extend the term. If there is uncertainty about the appropriate length of the term, the proper course is to impose no term but to leave the payer to seek the variation and if necessary go through the same exercise, this time pursuant to s 31(7)(a).'

In *L v L (Financial Remedies: Deferred Clean Break)*[57] a district judge had made a periodical payments order in favour of the wife for joint lives. On appeal, Eleanor King J substituted a term order for two years five months with a bar on further applications. There was evidence that the wife could soon become self-sufficient, and the husband had undertaken responsibility for school fees, which the district judge had failed to consider. The proper approach was summarised by Ward LJ in *C v C (Financial Relief: Short Marriage)*.[58]

Summary

2.42   These words have been quoted in full since they are likely to be studied by practitioners and courts for some time to come. Nevertheless, a short summary may assist. The proper approach is as follows:

(a)   to consider whether an immediate clean break is appropriate. No guidance is given as to the principles to guide the court in this, but, by inference from the decided cases and by analogy with s 25(2), it would seem that the court should be satisfied that the payee is, or may become by order of the court, self-sufficient (the court would also be entitled to take this view if there was no future possibility of any financial contribution by one party to the other);

(b)   if the court decides that an immediate clean break is not appropriate and that a periodical payments order (of whatever amount) should be made, the court must consider whether this should be for a finite term. The court may limit such an order only if satisfied that the payee will at the end of the term have adjusted to the termination of support without undue hardship. Such a conclusion may be reached only by evidence;

---

[57]   [2011] EWHC 2207 (Fam).
[58]   [1997] 2 FLR 26, CA.

(c) there seems to be no justification for an order for a fixed term without a direction that no further applications should be made. The requirements for both are identical;

(d) where the court is in any doubt about the position, a deferred clean break order should not be made.

An important gloss has now been added by the dicta of the House of Lords in *Miller/McFarlane* (see **2.16** et seq). As previously discussed, the House held that periodical payments are not to be limited to maintenance but may include an element of compensation. Lord Nicholls put it in this way (paras [37]–[39]):

'[37] This statutory statement of principle raises a question of a similar nature to that affecting the whole of s 25. By s 25A(1) and (2) duties are imposed on the court but the court is left with a discretion. The court is required to "consider" whether it would be "appropriate" to exercise its powers in a particular way. But the section gives no express guidance on the type of circumstance which would render it inappropriate for the court to bring about a clean break.

[38] In one respect the object of s 25A(1) is abundantly clear. The subsection is expressed in general terms. It is apt to refer as much to a periodical payments order made to provide compensation as it is to an order made to meet financial needs. But, expressly, s 25A(1) is not intended to bring about an unfair result. Under s 25A(1) the goal the court is required to have in mind is that the parties' mutual financial obligations should end as soon as the court considers just and reasonable.

[39] Section 25A(2) is focused more specifically. It is concerned with the termination of one party's "financial dependence" on the other "without undue hardship". These references to financial dependence and hardship are apt when applied to a periodical payments order making provision for the payee's financial needs. They are hardly apt when applied to a periodical payments order whose object is to furnish compensation in respect of future economic disparity arising from the division of functions adopted by the parties during their marriage. If the claimant is owed compensation, and capital assets are not available, it is difficult to see why the social desirability of a clean break should be sufficient reason for depriving the claimant of that compensation.'

The clean break on variation

2.43 It should be noted that the duty of the court to consider terminating financial dependency applies as much on a variation application as on an application for periodical payments.[59]

---

[59] *Fleming v Fleming* [2003] EWCA Civ 1841, [2004] 1 FLR 667. For variation generally see Chapter 13.

Direction under the Inheritance (Provision for Family and Dependants) Act 1975

2.44   Since a clean break order, whether immediate or deferred, is designed to terminate all continuing financial obligations between the parties, it would be illogical if this were to change on the death of one of the parties. Nevertheless, this could be the case in the absence of provision to the contrary, since a former spouse is among the class of persons on whom s 1(1)(b) of the Inheritance (Provision for Family and Dependants) Act 1975 confers the right to apply for financial relief from the estate of a deceased person.

Thus it is that s 15(1) of the 1975 Act provides that, on the grant of an order for divorce or separation or of a decree of nullity, or at any time thereafter, the court may, if it considers it just to do so and on the application of either party to the marriage, order that the other party shall not be entitled on the death of the applicant to apply for an order under the 1975 Act.

This is now a standard order which is made whenever a clean break order is made, and, normally, it would be justified. Nevertheless, it clearly requires separate consideration by the court and a separate decision that the order is just must be made. There might be circumstances, such as the no money cases, in which an immediate clean break could be justified for pragmatic reasons but it would not necessarily follow that the right to apply under the 1975 Act should be prohibited. Further, such an order could be made only if one of the parties asked the court to do so.

Extension of terms

2.45   Where a direction is given under s 28(1A) of MCA 1973 that no further applications may be made, that is final and the court may not entertain an application for the term of a periodical payments order to be extended. This is not the case when a fixed-term order is made without such a direction. Arguably this should never happen, but it is possible for such orders to be made and the court has had to adjudicate on the position. The position is, in fact, quite simple. Provided the application to vary is made before the expiration of the term, the court has jurisdiction to entertain it.[60] However, if the term has expired, or the event on which the periodical payments were to cease has passed, the right to apply to vary is lost.[61]

Form of order

2.46   Precedents for the various clean break orders will be found at Appendix A.

---

[60]   *Richardson v Richardson* [1994] 1 FLR 286.

[61]   Once the application is made, the hearing, and the order, can take place after the term has expired. See *Jones v Jones* [2000] 2 FLR 307, CA, disapproving *G v G (Periodical Payments: Jurisdiction)* [1997] 1 FLR 368, CA.

Chapter 3

SECURED PERIODICAL PAYMENTS

INTRODUCTION

3.1 Secured periodical payments are in some ways a curious hybrid, and are probably comparatively rare. The order incorporates an assessment of the amount of periodical payments which should be paid, with an order that they be secured, ie that security be provided for them, by some capital deposit.

The general principles on which orders for ancillary relief are made have already been considered, as have the detailed principles for assessment of the quantum of periodical payments. It is unnecessary to consider either here. Instead, it is proposed to consider the special circumstances which might give rise to an order for secured periodical payments and the practical consequences of such an order.

STATUTORY PROVISIONS

3.2 It is provided that:[1]

> 'On granting a decree of divorce, a decree of nullity of marriage or a decree of judicial separation, or at any time thereafter (whether, in the case of a decree of divorce or nullity of marriage, before or after the decree is made absolute), the court may make ...
>
> (b) an order that either party to the marriage shall secure to the other to the satisfaction of the court, such periodical payments, for such term, as may be so specified.'

It will be noted that this is one of the types of orders which can be made only after decree.

3.3 There are other statutory provisions concerning the procedure for making an order which will be considered below.

NATURE OF THE ORDER

3.4 A precedent for the order will be found at Appendix A, precedent 9. It will be seen that the order requires the paying party to secure to the payee for a

---

[1] MCA 1973, s 23(1)(b).

specified term the annual sum of periodical payments upon such security as may satisfy the court. The various elements of such an order are therefore as follows.

Secure

3.5   The order does not require the payer to make payments to the payee; it merely requires him to provide the fund out of which the payments may be made. In a leading case it was said that the order was 'an order to secure and nothing else. Under it the only obligation of the husband is to provide the security; having done that, he is under no liability. He enters into no covenant to pay and never becomes a debtor in respect of the payments'.[2]

The term

3.6   The court must specify the term, which may be for any term the court thinks fit, subject to certain statutory restrictions. It is provided that:[3]

> '... in the case of a secured periodical payments order, the term shall begin not earlier than the date of the making of an application for the order, and shall be so defined as not to extend beyond the death or, where the order is made on or after the grant of such a decree [ie a decree of divorce or nullity], the remarriage of the party in whose favour the order is made.'

The term must therefore be expressed to end on the death or remarriage of the payee. However, it may survive the death of the paying party.

If the court considers a limited term order with a 'clean break' direction appropriate, this can be incorporated into the order.

The amount to be secured

3.7   The quantum of the periodical payments will be assessed in the usual way.

The security

3.8   The fund to be provided is in the discretion of the court. The order will either specify the asset or order 'security to be agreed or referred to the district judge in default of agreement'. The asset provided will either be an income-producing asset such as a portfolio of securities or a non-income-producing asset. In the latter case, and sometimes in the former also, it is necessary to provide for sale to provide income.

---

2   *Barker v Barker* [1952] P 184.
3   MCA 1973, s 28(1)(b).

An order imposing a general charge on all the husband's assets has been expressly disapproved by the Court of Appeal as 'sweeping and indiscriminate'.[4] It must be specific.

Although it has been said[5] that where there is ample free capital the whole of the order should be secured, it is necessary to have regard to all the circumstances of the case, including, in particular, the s 25 factors, and the order must be reasonable.

3.9 It is almost invariably necessary to require a deed to be lodged by the paying party as well as the asset itself, to give effect to the order. This would be necessary to ensure that the asset, which would remain vested in the name of the paying party, provides the payments to the payee. Where problems arise, the court may refer the matter to one of the conveyancing counsel of the court for settlement of a proper instrument to be executed by all parties.[6] Further, where the paying party refuses or neglects to execute the document, an order may be made for the district judge or some other person to sign on his behalf.[7]

The court also has power to order one party to lodge documents which are necessary for the preparation of the deed.[8]

WHEN WILL SUCH AN ORDER BE MADE?

3.10 The circumstances in which it might be appropriate to make an order for secured periodical payments can best be seen by considering the advantages to the payee of such an order. The principal advantage is that the payments are secure; the fund is there to make them safe and the payments will survive the death of the paying party or his bankruptcy or disappearance.

In order to be persuaded that this order is appropriate therefore, the court would normally have to come to the conclusion that there were dangers against which the payee needed protection and also, of course, that a capital fund was available for this purpose.

3.11 The nature of the problem was well illustrated by *Aggett v Aggett*.[9] The judge pointed out that the court was always reluctant to burden with security something which was the sole or main asset of the respondent, but on the other hand the court was loath to leave a wife in circumstances in which it seemed clear that the husband might well leave her penniless. One had to consider

---

4   *Barker v Barker* (above).
5   In *Shearn v Shearn* [1931] P 1.
6   MCA 1973, s 30.
7   Ibid.
8   Senior Courts Act 1981, s 39 and County Courts Act 1984, s 38.
9   [1962] 1 All ER 190, CA.

whether the fears expressed on the wife's behalf were sufficiently cogent to justify making an order for security which would not be made if there was no reality in those fears.[10]

VARIATION AND AMENDMENT

3.12　The security may be varied or changed at any time; where this cannot be agreed the court may order a variation. Likewise, an order for secured provision may be varied by increasing or reducing the amount payable or by discharging it.[11] The order survives the death of the paying party, but can be varied after death in the light of the circumstances at the time. The fact that a wife has the benefit of a secured order does not prevent her from applying for provision from her former husband's estate.

---

[10]　See also *Shearn v Shearn* [1931] P 1; *Naish v Naish* (1916) 32 TLR 487.
[11]　See MCA 1973, s 31, and Chapter 13.

Chapter 4

LUMP SUM ORDERS

INTRODUCTION

4.1   A lump sum order is an order that one party pay to the other a sum of money. It is therefore to be contrasted with a property adjustment order, which requires the transfer of some specified real or personal property, and a periodical payments order which requires the payment of regular periodic (weekly, monthly or annual) sums by way of maintenance. An order for a lump sum is normally, therefore, a means of adjusting the capital resources of the parties on the dissolution of the marriage. The reasons for such an order might be various, but of course could only be based on the normal s 25(2) factors. Although in this chapter it is not intended to deal with housing needs and the matrimonial home,[1] it should be noted that in many cases the housing needs of one or both of the parties are the principal needs which the order is intended to meet. Where a wife's capital claims have been fully resolved by a property adjustment order, the application for a lump sum should be dismissed so that both parties know that capital claims are not thereafter live between them.[2]

Unlike a periodical payments order, a lump sum order is intended to be a final order and, with certain limited exceptions, may be made only once.

4.2   As with most classes of relief, it would be unusual for only a lump sum order to be made. Most orders for ancillary relief contain a variety of types of order such as lump sum, periodical payments, property adjustment and so on. The exception to this might be where there are ample funds, and the purpose of the order is to fund continuing periodical payments for life; this would be known as a *Duxbury* order and this is considered below at **4.14**.

Because of this factor, it has been thought appropriate to include in this chapter a section on so-called 'big money' cases. As will be seen, some of the principles to be observed in such cases are not confined to big money but have significance across the board.

By a process of logical extension, there will then follow a section of the special features which arise when one of the assets of the parties is a business.

---

[1]   See Chapter 5.
[2]   *Scheeres v Scheeres* [1999] 1 FLR 241.

STATUTORY PROVISION

4.3   A lump sum order is a financial provision order.[3] On granting a decree of divorce, nullity or judicial separation or at any time thereafter the court may make an order 'that either party to the marriage shall pay to the other such lump sum as may be so specified'.[4] The powers of the court in this respect are exercisable only after the grant of a decree. They are therefore classed as final orders.

NUMBER OF LUMP SUMS

4.4   The statute refers to 'lump sum or sums'. This does not mean that more than one lump sum order may be made, but rather that only one order may be made, which order may provide for the payment of one or more lump sums.[5] The order may also provide for payment by instalments, or for payment to be deferred, and, in that event, for the payment of interest.[6]

In *CR v CR*,[7] where there was inadequate capital at the time of the order to meet all the wife's needs, a lump sum by instalments was ordered to avoid the need for a continuing periodical payments order and to ensure a clean break.

An order for the payment of lump sums over time is not necessarily an order for payment by instalments, but may be merely an order for the payment of several lump sums on different dates. This difference may be of practical importance since an order for a series of lump sums cannot be varied save as to timing whereas an order for payment by instalments can be varied as to quantum and not merely as to timing.[8]

A lump sum payable by instalments can be varied; for further details see Chapter 13.

4.5   With the limited exception mentioned below, there is at present no provision for interim lump sums. After the decision of Waite J in *Barry v Barry*,[9] it was thought that the court had the power to appropriate capital of the parties to one or other of them on an interim basis, on the understanding that the asset thereby acquired would be brought into account on the eventual distribution of assets at the final hearing. This supposed power was developed

---

[3]   MCA 1973, s 21(1)(c).

[4]   MCA 1973, s 23(1)(c).

[5]   *Coleman v Coleman* [1973] Fam 10.

[6]   MCA 1973, s 23(6). For an interesting example of an order to pay a lump sum by instalments see *R v R (Lump Sum Repayments)* [2003] EWHC 3197 (Fam), [2004] 1 FLR 928 where Wilson J ordered a husband to pay lump sums equivalent to the wife's obligations under a 20-year repayment mortgage, ie £30,000 forthwith and then 240 payments to cover the instalments.

[7]   [2008] 1 FLR 323.

[8]   *Hamilton v Hamilton* [2013] EWCA Civ 13.

[9]   [1992] Fam 140.

in other cases on the basis of the inherent jurisdiction of the court[10] and also the court's powers to order sale under the Rules of the Supreme Court 1965 (RSC), Ord 31, r 1, as applied by FPR 1991, r 2.64,[11] which then applied.

This line of cases was comprehensively demolished by the Court of Appeal; in *Wicks v Wicks*,[12] each of the supposed bases of jurisdiction was considered and, with regret, found wanting, and the law is therefore as it was before *Barry v Barry* was decided. There is no way in which the court may order an interim lump sum.

For the limited circumstances in which the court might order a sale of a property under TLATA before determining any application for a financial remedy see **7.10**.

4.6   The court does, however, have limited powers to provide for payments of sums of money on an interim basis for immediate needs. It is provided that:[13]

> '... an order under this section [s 23] that a party to a marriage shall pay a lump sum to the other party may be made for the purpose of enabling that other party to meet any liabilities or expenses reasonably incurred by him or her in maintaining himself or herself or any child of the family before making an application for an order under this section in his or her favour.'

This is a little used provision, but its utility is clear. It could be used where for some reason a periodic order was inappropriate, but the applicant had some pressing need, for example some school fees, a council tax bill, or a major car repair which could not be met out of income. It would seem that the purpose for which the lump sum would be required must be limited to the maintenance of the applicant or a child, and so the subsection could not be used for major housing requirements; perhaps, however, it could be used to require the payment of a deposit on rented accommodation.

For an example (not an authority) of an order made under this subsection, see *Askew-Page v Page*.[14]

HOW ARE LUMP SUM ORDERS CALCULATED?

4.7   As always, it must be said that the only starting point for the court is the s 25 factors. There is no justification for taking any proportion of the assets as any kind of 'rule of thumb' baseline.[15] The power to award a lump sum was, in fact, only introduced in 1970 and then incorporated into the MCA 1973. It may fairly be regarded as one of the most important developments in modern family

---

[10]   *F v F (Ancillary Relief: Substantial Assets)* [1995] 2 FLR 45.
[11]   *Green v Green* [1993] 1 FLR 326.
[12]   [1998] 1 FLR 470, per Ward LJ.
[13]   MCA 1973, s 23(3)(a).
[14]   [2001] Fam Law 794, Bath County Court, HHJ Meston QC.
[15]   See e g *Potter v Potter* (1983) 4 FLR 331, CA.

law. In one of the early cases, it was emphasised that a lump sum was not simply another way of quantifying maintenance; the court might take into account all the factors laid down in the Act. It was essential that the court should retain complete flexibility of approach in the light of the circumstances of the case, present, past, and insofar as one could make a reliable estimate, future.[16] This, of course, has been overtaken by the comprehensive rationales contained in the speeches in *White v White* and *Miller/McFarlane* (as to which see **1.8** et seq).

4.8   In another case,[17] Thorpe J held that the discretionary power of the court to adjust capital shares between the parties should not be exercised unless there is a manifest need for intervention upon the application of the s 25 criteria. In particular, the idea that an applicant was entitled to a 'nest egg' against a 'rainy day' was expressly disapproved; any specific award of capital must have an evidential justification.[18]

The conventional wisdom set out above is now subject to several qualifications arising out of the decisions of the House of Lords in *White v White*[19] and *Miller/McFarlane*.[20] Both these cases, and the legal position arising from them, are considered in detail at **1.8** et seq and reference should be made to that section of this book. However, some further comments can be added in the context of lump sums and will now be set out.

First, it is necessary to bear in mind the fundamental distinction between those cases where assets do not exceed needs and those where they do. For the sake of clarity, the latter can be referred to as 'big money cases'.

Cases where assets do not exceed needs

4.9   In this class of case, the function of the court, with the help of the practitioner, is to manage scarce funds so that the most pressing needs of the parties are met. By definition, there is not enough money to go round and so the court has to apply a 'hierarchy of needs'. Where there is a child, the first consideration will normally be to try to provide a home for the parent with care and the child. Where there are sufficient funds, the court will then try to make such order as enables the non-resident parent to rehouse himself or herself.

This will normally take up most of the parties' funds, but if any money is left over the court will then consider any item for which a need is proved.

---

[16]   *Trippas v Trippas* [1973] Fam 134, CA. See also *Hobhouse v Hobhouse* [1999] 1 FLR 961, CA.
[17]   *H v H (Financial Provision: Capital Allowance)* [1993] 2 FLR 335.
[18]   Disapproving *Re Besterman dec'd* [1984] Ch 458. But see *A v A (Financial Provision)* [1998] 2 FLR 180, where Singer J 'rounded up' the appropriate provision.
[19]   [2000] 2 FLR 981.
[20]   [2006] 1 FLR 1186, HL.

BIG MONEY CASES

4.10   Cases involving assets surplus to needs are fundamentally different from the cases considered above. It is still necessary to be guided by the s 25 factors but with the addition of the 'yardstick of equality'. By definition, there are sufficient funds to meet the needs of the parties. The role of the court is therefore now to achieve a just result in the light of s 25 and reference should be made to the section on the post-*White* and *Miller/McFarlane* position in Chapter 1.

As to what constitutes a 'big money' case, it is interesting (and, perhaps surprising) that in *D v D (Lump Sum: Adjournment of Application)*[21] Connell J considered that a case where the total assets were £700,000 and the husband earned £230,000 pa net was such a case on the ground that the available assets clearly exceeded the parties' needs for housing and income.

4.11   There will now be considered two particular aspects of this class of case, namely the 'millionaire's defence' and *Duxbury* funds.

The millionaire's defence

4.12   The fact that an approach based on a mathematical proportion is even less appropriate in big money cases than is normally the case is underlined by a number of decisions establishing what was known as 'the millionaire's defence'. This so-called defence, or argument, was to the effect that since the means of the paying party are such as to enable the payer to meet any award which the court could conceivably make based on the payee's reasonable requirements, it is unnecessary to give detailed and possibly costly disclosure of the full extent of the payer's means. This was also known as the '*Thyssen* defence', after the parties in the leading case on the point.[22] There, the husband deposed in his affidavit to very substantial and complicated assets worth over £400m, and concluded by saying, 'I would meet any order the court decides to make in relation to the financial dispute between the petitioner and myself'. The wife applied for detailed discovery, designed to support her assertion that the husband's wealth was, in reality, in excess of £1,000m. It was held that, since there was more than ample wealth to make a very substantial financial order to support the wife in luxury for the rest of her life, and the largest award which could be made would not be significantly increased by proof of a larger fortune, the limited discovery which had been offered was all that was reasonably necessary.

4.13   This decision was followed in another case in which the assets of the husband were 'only' £8m.[23] However, it is not to be taken as carte blanche for a less than careful or conscientious approach. In another case[24] in which the

---

[21]   [2001] 1 FLR 633.
[22]   *Thyssen-Bornemisza v Thyssen-Bornemisza (No 2)* [1985] FLR 1069.
[23]   *B v B (Discovery: Financial Provision)* [1990] 2 FLR 180.
[24]   *F v F (Ancillary Relief: Substantial Assets)* [1995] 2 FLR 45.

assets of the husband were between £150m and £200m, it was held that, while a restrictive approach to the wife's questionnaire was justified, this did not entitle the husband to refuse reasonably framed questions designed to establish the broad realities of the case and to illuminate issues as to past dealings. The death blow to the millionaires' defence might seem to have been delivered by the dicta of Thorpe LJ in *Parlour v Parlour* and *Mcfarlane v Mcfarlane* (as to which see **2.16** et seq); his Lordship said:

'We were told by the Bar that a practice has grown up for substantial earners to decline any statement of their needs on the grounds that they can afford any order that the court is likely to make. These appeals must put an end to that practice.'

The *Duxbury* fund

4.14 As was mentioned above, one of the characteristics of big money cases is that there is normally sufficient liquid capital to provide a fund of money from which one party's income for life can be derived. A well-settled practice was established by which, once a payee's reasonable income needs have been established, a calculation could be made to quantify the capital sum required to fund that income for life on an inflation-proof basis. This was based on a computer program into which it was necessary to feed such information as the age of the recipient, and certain assumptions as to tax bands, inflation and so on were made.

Until very recently the best guidance as to the weight to be placed on such calculations was to be found not in the case from which the calculation derives its name[25] but in the words of Ward J in *B v B (Financial Provision)*.[26] Here it was pointed out that, as a result of the observations made in *Preston v Preston*,[27] accountants had devised a computer program which could calculate the lump sum which, if invested on the assumptions as to life expectancy, rates of inflation, return on investment, growth of capital, incidence of income tax, will produce enough to meet the recipient's needs for her life. Ward J concluded that, if their calculation were accepted as no more than a tool for the judge's use, it was a very valuable help to him in many cases.[28]

4.15 In other cases[29] it has been emphasised that a *Duxbury* calculation cannot by itself provide the answer as to the sum to which a wife is entitled, and that there is a danger that it might be regarded as having achieved a status far beyond that which it had in the original case. There are also obvious uncertainties in trying to calculate the rate of return for any investment over a long period.

---

[25] *Duxbury v Duxbury* [1987] 1 FLR 7.
[26] [1990] 1 FLR 20.
[27] [1982] Fam 17, [1981] 3 WLR 619, CA.
[28] For background information on the origins of the computer program, see also the article by its originator Mr Timothy Lawrence at [1990] Fam Law 12.
[29] See *F v F (Duxbury Calculation: Rate of Return)* [1996] 1 FLR 833; *Gojkovic v Gojkovic* [1992] Fam 40 at 48E; *Vicary v Vicary* [1992] 2 FLR 271 at 278B.

It has been said that '*Duxbury* is a tool and not a rule', and that 'the utility of the *Duxbury* methodology depends in part upon the skill of the user. It must be applied with flexibility, with a due recognition of its limitations and with intelligent perception of special features which are capable of being incorporated within the computer program.'[30]

It was held in one case[31] that a *Duxbury* calculation was not appropriate because the wife had a life expectancy in excess of 40 years.

It would therefore always have been wrong to treat the result of a *Duxbury* calculation as being anything other than the probable best guess as to the sum which needs to be provided. There was room for argument over the method used and whether the whole basis of the *Duxbury* calculation should be changed.[32] However, the court was greatly assisted by such calculations and they should be regarded as indispensable in appropriate cases.[33]

As readers will know all too well, we live in troubled economic times and what has been said about *Duxbury* calculations may seem to some a relic of the past in mid-2011. Quite how a sensible prediction of interest and growth rates can be made when interest rates are 0.5% and growth may well fall in the current year is difficult to see. It may be that the status quo ante will be resumed at some stage in the future but, for the moment, one can only say that there are severe difficulties in the way of making any reliable calculation.

For some time the courts were troubled by the so-called '*Duxbury* paradox', arising from the fact that, when a *Duxbury* calculation was appropriate, the older (and possibly more deserving) spouse recovered a lower amount than a younger spouse, because the calculation is based, in part, on life expectancy. This paradox was to some extent made easier by the comments of Lord Nicholls in *White v White*,[34] where it was said that the proper application of the 'yardstick of equality' would resolve the problem in any event.

BUSINESS CASES

4.16   Many cases involving lump sums and, a fortiori, substantial amounts of money, are cases where one of the assets is a business owned by one or both of the parties. Where the business is a 'private' business, ie one in which the parties themselves have a controlling interest and which provides the source of the family's prosperity, particular considerations arise. The court has two essential

---

[30]   Per Thorpe LJ in *White v White* [1998] 2 FLR 310. See also *A v A (Elderly Applicant: Lump Sum)* [1999] 2 FLR 969 and *G v G (Financial Provision: Separation Agreement)* [2000] 2 FLR 18, Connell J.

[31]   *Fournier v Fournier* [1998] 2 FLR 990, CA.

[32]   See 'Is Duxbury misleading? Yes, it is' at [2001] Fam Law 747.

[33]   While expert advice may be needed in complicated cases, an indispensable source of information, giving helpful tables, etc is the publication *At a Glance*, published and annually updated by the Family Law Bar Association.

[34]   [2000] 2 FLR 981, HL. See also **4.10**.

functions in such cases. The first is to establish a value for the parties' interests in the business, as part of its duty under s 25(2)(a). The second is to decide how that value should be reflected in the final distribution.

4.17 As to the issue of valuation, it should be remembered that, until very recently, the conventional wisdom was that the court will avoid making any final order the effect of which would be that the business would have to be sold against the will of the party wishing to continue in the business; in most cases, the business would be regarded as the provider of income, now and in the future, and not as a source of liquid capital. It follows that any valuation should not be in the same detail as would be employed by someone wishing to buy the company but rather to establish a reasonably accurate figure for the income which the business could generate, and its eventual value as, for example, the source of a pension annuity.

4.18 There was a wealth of authority to establish this point. In *Potter v Potter*[35] there had been extensive and costly accountancy evidence to establish a precise value of a small business; the judge then awarded the wife one-third of the value of the assets. On appeal it was pointed out that the valuation of a business in these circumstances was a 'necessarily hypothetical exercise because the only way that it can be done is for those valuing it to assume that the business would be sold and that, of course, is the one thing which is not going to happen and very rarely does happen'. Such a valuation was 'an almost wholly irrelevant consideration', and the proper approach was to take the wife's reasonable needs and balance them against the husband's ability to pay.

In another case,[36] where there was a family company with a value of £1.2m to £1.5m, it was said that all that was required was 'the broadest evaluation of the company's worth to enable the court to decide the wife's reasonable requirements'. If there was liquidity in the company which could be realised to meet her requirements then the final order would take that liquidity into account; if there was none, in the sense that the company (the source of the breadwinner's income) would be damaged, then the court should look elsewhere.

This decision was cited in *Evans v Evans*[37] in support of one of the propositions laid down for the guidance of the profession in these cases. It was emphasised that, while it may be necessary to obtain a broad assessment of the value of a shareholding in a private company, it is inappropriate to undertake an expensive and meaningless exercise to achieve a precise valuation of a private company which will not be sold.

It must be said that it is now necessary to approach these cases with a degree of caution. *White v White* has introduced a new set of principles, particularly in cases of substantial assets, and in *N v N (Financial Provision: Sale of*

---

[35]   (1983) 4 FLR 331, CA.
[36]   *P v P (Financial Provision)* [1989] 2 FLR 241.
[37]   [1990] 1 FLR 319.

Company),[38] it was said that the older authorities disapproving the sale of the golden goose might no longer apply. The same judge (Coleridge J) held, in *R v R (Financial Relief: Company Valuation)*[39] that the valuation of companies was more of an art than a science.[40]

In *D v D and B Ltd*[41] it was held that in cases involving private companies a commercial/company law solution might be preferable to a clean break based on valuations. Practitioners should not confine their approach to valuations and liquidity but should consider commercially realistic alternatives and periodical payments. If they do not have such expertise they should consult others.

4.19 These warnings must, however, still be borne in mind, as must the point that the value of one of the assets is only one (even if the most important) factor which the court will take into account in the s 25 exercise. Nevertheless, the court does still have the duty to place some value on a business, and the following comments are designed to offer some guidance as to how that might be approached.

Businesses can of course take a variety of forms. What is to follow is not concerned with shares in publicly quoted companies, since their value is a matter of public record and should cause no difficulty. Here, we are concerned with sole traders, partnerships and limited companies.

The only exceptions to the principle that a detailed and precise valuation is inappropriate would be where one party was likely in the near future to convert his or her interest in the business into a liquid form, for example by sale, retirement or takeover, or where the wife had acquired a quantifiable interest in the business, for example by a direct financial contribution or by working in the business.[42] Perhaps the best test as to the latter point would be to ask whether the wife would be able to prove some beneficial interest in the business if she were a stranger and not involved in matrimonial proceedings; if this were the case, she would be entitled to an interest in the business in her own right, and not only as part of the s 25 exercise, and a more detailed examination might be appropriate.[43]

4.20 If any valuation of the business is to be carried out with a view to relying on it in court proceedings or advice to a client, it will at some stage become necessary to instruct an accountant. A lawyer who relied on his or her own expertise for such a purpose would be in grave danger of an action for negligence. Nevertheless, there are several reasons why the family lawyer should

---

[38] [2001] 2 FLR 69, Coleridge J.
[39] [2005] 2 FLR 365.
[40] For an interesting example of valuation of a minority interest in a company, see the decision of Charles J in *A v A* [2004] EWHC 2818 (Fam), [2006] 2 FLR 115.
[41] [2007] 2 FLR 653, Charles J.
[42] See e g *Gojkovic v Gojkovic* [1990] 1 FLR 140, CA.
[43] See *White v White* [1998] 2 FLR 310, CA.

be familiar with methods of valuation. First and foremost, such knowledge enables the lawyer to scrutinise the evidence of experts, to understand the terms which are used, and, if necessary, to challenge it. It is the court which makes the final decision as to such issues, and lawyers must be able to make intelligent and informed submissions to the court, based on an understanding of what the experts have been saying. Secondly, when a case is at an early stage, the lawyer should be able to make a provisional estimate of what a business is likely to be worth, with a view to advising the client and deciding how to conduct the application.

4.21 The value of any business is normally what a willing purchaser would pay for it on an arm's length basis. There are three bases of valuation which an interested purchaser would normally use; these are the asset basis, the dividend yield basis, and the earnings basis. Frequently, a calculation is done on each of these bases and then the results compared to obtain a cross-checked final result.

The asset basis produces the figure which would be obtained if the assets were sold and the business closed down. The problem for the family lawyer with this basis is that the book value of the assets as shown in the balance sheet is almost invariably wrong and of no assistance in calculating the market value of the assets. Expert valuation of the assets is therefore essential, but it would also be necessary to take account of the legal and other costs involved in closing down a business. For the reasons given above, businesses are rarely closed down to provide a lump sum, so, in addition to being the most difficult, this basis of valuation is unlikely to be the one finally relied on by the court.

4.22 The dividend yield basis is equally unlikely to provide a final answer. It gives the value to a potential purchaser who is principally interested in the dividend income from the company. It involves dividing the gross dividend by the required rate of return to give a value per share. It is therefore necessary to select the rate of return required. This method is usually employed as a cross-check on the result of a calculation on the earnings basis.

The earnings basis of valuation is therefore likely to be the most useful starting point. It involves first establishing the maintainable earnings of the business. This figure will be derived from one or more sources; one would be the most recent year's gross profits. Another would be the average of the last 3 years' gross profits. These could then be compared to obtain the final figure. This figure must then be adjusted to take account of such matters as inappropriate payments of various kinds (eg adding back excessive remuneration or pension contributions) and tax at the current rate must then be deducted.

The figure for maintainable earnings must then be multiplied by the P/E (profits: earnings) ratio appropriate for that type of business. This ratio can be obtained from the FT Actuaries Share Index, published daily, which should be rounded down to the nearest whole number. The resulting figure may then have to be discounted to take account of the size of the business.

4.23 To be able to carry out the calculations as above, or to instruct an expert, certain documents are necessary, and should be obtained at an early date. At the very least the last 3 years' accounts must be obtained; these will enable a preliminary valuation to be done. If an expert is to be instructed he will say what he wants, but this will include the Memorandum and Articles of Association of a company, shareholders' agreements and internal documents relating to business plans and forecasts, board minutes and cash flow projections.

Once again, it should be emphasised that the family lawyer should not try to be his or her own expert witness nor to rely on what has been said above as anything other than a guide to help find a way through the thickets of a complicated field. Nevertheless, if it succeeds in giving that limited amount of help, it should prove useful.

Where one spouse is involved in a company, the other frequently thinks that he or she must have some interest not immediately apparent on the face of the accounts and, of course, that may be true; identifying such benefits is one of the tasks of the expert. However, it is important to retain a sense of reality. The judgment in *Ben Hashem v Al Shayif*[44] contains a comprehensive analysis of the principle to be applied; in order to pierce the corporate veil it is necessary to demonstrate not only control of a company but also impropriety linked to the company structure, ie (mis)use of the company as a device to conceal a wrongdoing entirely outside the company. The question is whether the company is being used as a facade.

4.24 As was said at **4.16**, after ascertaining the value of the parties' interests in a business, the court must then decide what to do with those figures. The facts of *White v White*[45] and its general relevance have already been considered in Chapter 1. In the Court of Appeal, Thorpe LJ said that the dominant feature of the case was that from first to last the parties traded as equal partners. Had the partnership been dissolved by the death of either party, the extent of the estate of the deceased partner would have been established according to the law of partnership. Equally, the wife was entitled to her share on dissolution by mutual agreement. Later in the judgment, he said that where the parties had during marriage elected for a financial regime which made each financially independent, one gain might be said to be that they may thereby have obviated the need to embark upon ancillary relief litigation in the event of divorce.

In the light of these principles, Thorpe LJ said that the first fundamental issue was what was the financial worth of the parties on the immediate dissolution of the partnership; the second was whether the court should exercise its powers under s 23 or s 24 to increase the wife's share; the third was, if no, whether the court should exercise its powers to reduce the wife's share. He concluded by saying that 'it offends my sense of fairness that a wife who has worked for over

---

[44]   [2008] EWHC 3380, Munby J.
[45]   [1998] 2 FLR 310, CA.

30 years equally and not nominally in partnership should exit with anything less than her legal entitlement in the absence of extraordinary features'.

Butler-Sloss LJ agreed, adding that there would of course be partnership cases where the starting point for the spouses would have to be adjusted upwards or downwards in the circumstances of the individual case, particularly where there were children. Where the spouses were shown to be genuine partners, the dissolution of their partnership both in marriage and in business ought not to require the intervention of the courts.

4.25 As is now well known, the decision of the Court of Appeal was not upset by the House of Lords, but the dicta of Lord Nicholls suggest that in certain respects the reasoning of the lower court was not to be accepted.[46] As to this specific issue, the House of Lords did not disagree with Thorpe LJ in principle, but expressed the hope that, in the light of the yardstick of equality, it would not be necessary to have a prolonged investigation of the parties' interests in most cases. See also the section on 'fairness' at **1.7** et seq.

TAX CONSIDERATIONS

4.26 Since this is not a textbook on revenue law, only the briefest mention is to be made of this subject; however, it is important that family lawyers be aware of the tax implications of any proposed order. This will normally involve taking expert advice.

The simplest explanation of this topic is that the sale or transfer of any asset, other than the sole or principal residence of a person, may attract capital gains tax. The tax is on the gain between acquisition and disposal, subject to 'indexation'. When spouses are separated, and assets are sold by one of them to provide a lump sum, tax is, in principle, payable on the gain achieved by the sale. When a matrimonial home, in which both parties have continued to live, is transferred to one of them, the private residence exemption should apply. This also applies even where the transferor has left the home, provided the transferee has continued to live in it.

Before the court can decide whether to order a lump sum payment which is to be funded by the sale of assets, therefore, the tax implications of any sale must be ascertained, and the net effect of these incorporated in the calculations leading to the order.

---

[46]   See **1.8**.

Chapter 5

TRANSFER OF PROPERTY ORDERS AND HOUSING NEEDS

INTRODUCTION

5.1 Transfer of property orders and housing needs are both topics which, clearly, have to be considered. It has been thought appropriate to combine them in one chapter because of the obvious overlapping nature of the subjects. Nevertheless, it should be remembered that the meeting of housing needs is not the sole purpose of a transfer of property order.

A transfer of property order is an order that one party transfer to the other some property. In most cases this will be real property, such as land or a dwelling-house. However, personal property such as shares, chattels, or even the matrimonial dog may also be the subject of a transfer of property order. The essential nature of the order is that an identifiable and specific item of property is ordered to be transferred; it therefore differs from a lump sum order, which provides for the payment of a sum of money.

5.2 The housing needs of the parties are, almost invariably, a high priority in any ancillary relief application. In many cases, particularly in the lower financial range, the matrimonial home is the sole or principal asset, and the whole case revolves around the housing needs of the parties and their children. The significance of this will be explored in more detail at **5.6** et seq.

The subject of transfers of tenancy will be considered at **5.21** et seq. A tenancy may be the subject of a transfer of property order, but there may also be an application pursuant to Part IV of the Family Law Act 1996 (FLA 1996).

The wording of transfer of property orders may be particularly important, and is considered in some detail at **5.10** et seq.

STATUTORY PROVISION

5.3 A transfer of property order is a type of property adjustment order,[1] the other two types being settlement of property orders and variation of settlement; the latter two are dealt with elsewhere. This is the most common form of property adjustment order.

---

[1] MCA 1973, s 21(2)(a).

It is provided that:[2]

> '... on granting a decree of divorce, a decree of nullity of marriage or a decree of judicial separation or at any time thereafter (whether, in the case of a decree of divorce or of nullity of marriage, before or after the decree is made absolute) the court may make ...
>
> (a)   an order that a party to the marriage shall transfer to the other party, to any child of the family or to such person as may be specified in the order for the benefit of such a child such property as may be so specified, being property to which the first-mentioned party is entitled, either in possession or reversion.'

It will be noted that the order may be made only on or after the grant of a decree; there is no provision for interim orders. It will also be seen that the court may make 'an order'; the court may not make more than one order, although it may, of course, provide for the transfer of more than one item of property in the same order.

Clearly, the person ordered to transfer may only transfer property which he is entitled to transfer, ie that which he owns. However, this may include property in which he has a joint interest (eg with the applicant) or a reversionary interest.

The provisions as to children are considered in more detail in Chapter 11.

RULES

5.4   There are certain requirements in the Family Procedure Rules 2010 (FPR 2010) which are specific to transfer of property orders; these are considered in more detail in Chapter 16.

THE BASIS ON WHICH ORDERS ARE MADE

5.5   As always, it must be said that the only basis on which the court makes any financial order is the consideration and balancing of the factors in MCA 1973, s 25, and the position is no different in relation to transfer of property orders. The proper approach to ancillary relief is dealt with in more detail in Chapter 1 and need not be considered in such detail here. Nevertheless, the question of housing needs is usually important, and it is therefore appropriate to consider that as a preliminary matter.

5.6   In one leading case,[3] Thorpe LJ said that it was one of the paramount considerations in applying the s 25 criteria to endeavour to stretch what was available to cover the need of each party for a home, particularly where there

---

[2]   MCA 1973, s 24(1)(a).
[3]   *M v B (Ancillary Proceedings: Lump Sum)* [1998] 1 FLR 53, CA.

were young children involved. Obviously the primary carer needed whatever was available to make a main home for the children, but it was of importance, albeit of lesser importance, that the other party should have a home of his own where the children could enjoy their contact time with him. In any case, where there was, by stretch and a degree of risk-taking, the possibility of a division to enable both parties to rehouse themselves, that was an exceptionally important consideration and one which would almost invariably have a decisive impact on the outcome. In the instant case, the resources were available to make a division which would, just about, enable each to rehouse and the judge's order, which had awarded the husband a lump sum of an insufficient size, was set aside and a larger sum awarded.

5.7 This is an important restatement of, and compelling authority for, a general principle which the courts have normally striven to observe. That the need for a roof over one's head is one of the most basic human needs is a principle which hardly needs restating, and housing must, therefore, be one of the most important financial needs to be met pursuant to s 25(2)(b). However, it has also been emphasised[4] that the statement of the desirability of the non-caring parent having his or her accommodation should not be elevated into a rigid rule of law; there was no rule of law that each party must be able to purchase a property, and each case depends on its own facts.

Sometimes, when assets are severely limited, the needs of one party have to give way to the needs of the family as a whole and the requirement to treat the welfare of the children as the first consideration pursuant to s 25(1). A home for the minor children is normally the principal requirement. However, that does not always mean that they should continue to occupy the former matrimonial home; that may be a desirable objective in many cases, but where they could be satisfactorily rehoused in cheaper accommodation, thereby releasing capital for the rehousing of the non-carer, that is an option which should be adopted.

Each case will, of course, turn on its own facts. Ability to borrow is an important feature of such cases, and is regarded as a resource under s 25(2)(a).

5.8 The fact that one party (and the children) have to occupy a particular property does not always mean that that party is entitled to the sole ownership of that property. In the following section the various options for the court are considered, and clearly an outright transfer is not always appropriate. Where a property could be sold after the children had ceased to need it as their residence and some capital released for the non-carer, this is an option which the court should consider. This might be attractive where the non-carer was going to be under a continuing obligation to pay periodic payments as well as sacrificing all his capital. However, the factors which might persuade a court to the contrary view are:

---

4   In *Piglowska v Piglowski* [1999] 2 FLR 763, HL.

- the desire of most parties for finality;

- the undesirability in some cases of maintaining a link between the non-carer and the carer;

- uncertainty as to the future ability of the carer to rehouse himself or herself once the children had gone;

- the value of the property in question;

- the length of time which was likely to elapse before the property could be sold; and

- the fact that ownership of a property, particularly one of modest value, is not always a markedly superior position to that of someone entitled to reasonably secure rented accommodation.

5.9   When assessing housing needs, the court must take account of the effect of its proposed order on those directly affected by its decision; in one case,[5] that was described as 'the court's primary if not exclusive concern'. In that case the judge had held that he should not make an order which might be regarded as usurping the role of the local housing authority, but on appeal this was held to be an incorrect approach. Phillips LJ said that he did not see how the court could perform its duty without taking into account what would happen to those deprived of the right to live in the matrimonial home. However, he went on to say that this necessarily involved having regard to the effect of the local authority housing policy, and he did not think it correct to describe the effect of such an approach as being to manipulate housing lists or to usurp the function of the council.

The fact that one party may be eligible for local authority housing is therefore a valid consideration, although, once again, each case will turn on its own facts.

TYPES OF TRANSFER OF PROPERTY ORDERS

5.10   Once the court has decided the overall scheme of its disposition this must be incorporated into an order, and in many cases the order might take a variety of forms. In this section it is intended to set out the various types of order which may be made. Some of these orders, while being property adjustment orders, would properly fall under the heading of settlement of property or variation of settlement orders; however, for convenience, they are all set out here. Forms of order will be found at Appendix A.

5.11   Although it may seem simplistic to make this point, it is extremely important for the practitioners to have seen the deeds or land certificate to the

---

[5]   *Jones v Jones* [1997] 1 FLR 27, CA.

property well before the application is heard. The information which lay clients give about ownership of property is not always accurate and it is important to be aware of the exact nature of the title and any incumbrances.

As a final preliminary point, it should be noted that there are many references in the text and elsewhere to trusts for sale of land. As a result of the Trusts of Land and Appointment of Trustees Act 1996 (TLATA 1996), trusts for sale have been replaced by trusts of land. The wording of any orders now made will therefore have to reflect that change.

Outright transfer

5.12 The simplest form of order which can be made is for one party to transfer to the other his or her estate or interest (whether sole or joint) in a property.[6] When the property to be transferred is mortgaged, the order would have to provide either for the simultaneous redemption of the mortgage (eg by a separate order for payment of a lump sum for this purpose), or for the transfer to be subject to the existing charge (this would be the case even if the order did not provide for it). A mortgagee cannot prevent a transfer, but if the property were merely transferred subject to the charge, the property would be at risk if the terms of the mortgage were not observed and the transferor would continue to be liable under the mortgage covenants.

This frequently has to be the position. However, an order in these circumstances should normally also contain an undertaking by the transferee to perform the obligations of the mortgage and to indemnify the transferor against liability under the mortgage.

In *Fisher-Aziz v Aziz*[7] it was said that, as a matter of general principle, if a wife in occupation of a former matrimonial home (having primary regard to the needs of any children) sought the transfer of the property in preference to the proceeds of sale of the property, she should normally succeed, provided she can secure the release of the co-owner from the mortgage. It should perhaps be noted that in this case there was no available equity so the issue of any payment to the husband did not arise.

5.13 A possible variation of this type of outright transfer order would be to transfer in return for some consideration. This consideration could take the form of a cash payment, or the discharge of the transferor's obligation to pay periodical payments by a clean break order.[8] The latter order might be appropriate where the value of the property transferred was roughly equivalent to the value of the lost benefits. It might also be appropriate where it was clear that the transferor would be unable to make any significant contribution to the

---

[6] As was done in *Hanlon v Hanlon* [1978] 1 WLR 592, CA. If the house were to be sold, neither party could rehouse themselves on 50% of the proceeds. The husband was earning significantly more and it was better that the parties knew where they stood.

[7] [2010] EWCA Civ 673.

[8] As in *Mortimer v Mortimer-Griffin* [1986] 2 FLR 315, CA.

support of the transferee, and it was important for the transferee (and any children) to have settled accommodation. In *Lawrence v Bertram (Judgment on Preliminary Issue)*[9] it was held that the court had jurisdiction to order a transfer of property on condition that the transferee pay the transferor a fixed sum.

In the absence of other factors, it would not be appropriate where the value of the interest transferred was significantly less than the lost benefits. The desire of the transferee for certainty should not obscure the need for her advisers to have regard to the circumstances in which a clean break order is inappropriate.[10]

Similarly, a potential transferor should be aware that, even if the transferee's right to periodical payments can be extinguished, the same does not apply to the children, and even if a mother undertook not to claim for the children this would not be binding on the Child Support Agency.

Transfer subject to charge

5.14   An order may provide for the transfer to one party of a property, subject to a charge in favour of the transferor for payment of a sum of money. Such a payment would be required either on a fixed date[11] or on the occurrence of a certain event or the first of certain events, such as the death or remarriage of the transferee, the children attaining their majority or ceasing full-time education or some other event.[12] The payment to be made could be expressed as a fixed monetary amount, but it is more common, and normally preferable, for it to be a percentage of the gross or net proceeds of sale.[13]

Orders frequently provide for the enforcement of the charge on the remarriage or cohabitation of the transferee. Where there are dependent children, this should be subject to the proviso that any enforcement on this ground should be subject to the leave of the court. In any event, the provision as to cohabitation is liable to raise problems, since cohabitation may be difficult to define and, even if proved, may not endure. Perhaps a better form of words would be: 'if any adult person other than the [transferee] and the children of the family occupies the property as his or her home for a period, whether continuous or cumulative, in excess of six months save with the written consent of the [transferor]'.

An order that the property 'stand charged' with payment of a certain sum on terms is valid and will be recognised by the Land Registry. However, this may be a less desirable form of order than the alternative which is to order the transfer in return for the delivery to the transferor of a charge duly executed by

---

9   Croydon County Court [2004] Fam Law 323. This is a decision of a circuit judge in a county court and is therefore only a persuasive authority but there seems no reason to doubt it.
10   See generally **2.29** et seq.
11   *Knibb v Knibb* [1987] 2 FLR 396.
12   As in *Hector v Hector* [1973] 1 WLR 1122, CA.
13   See *McDonnell v McDonnell* (1976) 120 SJ 87, CA.

the transferee, such charge to be in a form agreed between the solicitors for the parties and, in default of agreement, to be settled by the district judge. The parties and, in default, the court, then retain some control over the terms on which the transferee occupies the property.

5.15 A brief but not exhaustive list of the possible problems which should be eliminated by a properly drawn charge is as follows.

(a) The right to redeem. In the absence of this, a mortgagee entitled to eg 30% of the net proceeds of sale could insist on a sale of the property.

(b) Provision for determination of the value of the property in the event of dispute, eg by a chartered surveyor.

(c) A bare charge for moneys on demand entitles the chargee to possession of the property without proof of breach of any term. Even where this does not apply, a chargee is entitled to take possession on breach, eg if the charge is not redeemed on the fixed date. The charge should be so drawn as to prevent either of these possibilities.

(d) Where there is no prior mortgage, or that mortgage is redeemed, the chargee is entitled to hold the deeds. This might not be desirable in many post-matrimonial situations.

(e) Unless there is express power to tack, the chargor cannot raise any further money on the security of the property. The power to lease should also be restricted.

(f) The right to move house and transfer the charge to another property, eg during the minority of the children should be considered.

Mesher orders

5.16 A *Mesher* order, so called after the eponymous case,[14] is essentially a postponement of the exercise of a trust for sale until a named event occurs; this is normally connected with the children of the family. In the case itself, the order was for the matrimonial home to be held on trust for sale for the parties in equal shares, and that the house be not sold for so long as the child of the family was under the age of 17 or until further order.[15] The wife was to live there rent-free but had to pay the outgoings, and capital repayments of the mortgage were to be shared equally. Strictly speaking, it is a settlement order rather than a transfer of property order.

---

[14] *Mesher v Mesher and Hall* [1980] 1 All ER 126, CA.

[15] 'Until further order' entitles the court to make an order for earlier sale, if appropriate, but not to postpone the sale; see *Carson v Carson* [1983] 1 WLR 285, CA, and *Norman v Norman* (1983) 4 FLR 446.

Such an order may be amended to take account of the circumstances of a particular case. For example, the 'trigger event' for sale of the house could be expressed as the first of various occurrences including the death or remarriage of the carer spouse, the children continuing in full-time education, or further order; the division of the proceeds of sale could be other than equal; and the occupying party could be required to pay an occupation rent.[16]

5.17 Some of the comments on orders for transfer subject to chargeback set out at **5.14** apply equally to *Mesher* orders. The orders can also be refined to provide for the exclusive occupation of the home by the occupying party.[17] However, there are more fundamental objections to *Mesher* orders which cannot always be met by different wordings, and whether the court's objectives could be met by other means should always be considered.

One reason why a *Mesher* order might be unsuitable would be the undesirability in a particular case of the parties remaining joined together in property ownership. However, the principal objection to these orders is the state of uncertainty in which the parties might be left. When these orders were more fashionable, there were many cases in which 'the chickens came home to roost' a number of years later, and it was found that one or even both parties were unable to rehouse themselves from the available funds.[18]

In *B v B (Mesher Order)*[19] it was held that a *Mesher* order was inappropriate where there was a young child, and the commitment of the mother to child rearing would mean that her ability to generate capital would be much less than that of her husband. The result would be inequality of outcome which was discriminatory and unacceptable. This is an interesting gloss on the meaning of equality in the post-*White* and *Lambert* world.

With that in mind, and in the light of the requirement for the court to strive to make such order as will enable both parties to rehouse themselves, it can be said that it would now be unusual for the court to make a *Mesher* order unless it were satisfied, by credible evidence, either that the eventual net proceeds of sale would be sufficient to provide for both parties, or that, for some reason, this was not necessary or desirable.

For a recent example of a *Mesher* order see *Mansfield v Mansfield*.[20] The husband had received damages for personal injuries of £500,000, which he invested in a property in which he and the wife lived before the breakdown of the marriage. The wife left with the children and the district judge awarded her £285,000 for the purchase of a property. The circuit judge rejected the husband's appeal, which was, however, allowed by the Court of Appeal, which

---

[16]   As in *Harvey v Harvey* [1982] Fam 83, CA.

[17]   See *Allen v Allen* [1986] 2 FLR 265, CA.

[18]   See *Mortimer v Mortimer-Griffin* [1986] 2 FLR 315, CA; *Carson v Carson* (above); *Norman v Norman* (above); *Thompson v Thompson* [1985] FLR 863, CA.

[19]   [2002] EWHC 3106 (Fam), [2003] 2 FLR 285.

[20]   [2011] EWCA Civ 1056.

substituted a *Mesher* order, under which the husband would recover one-third of the value of the property on the children's majority. This would recognise the origin of the family capital and the special purpose for which it had been provided.

5.18 In summary, therefore, there may well be cases in which a *Mesher* order would be suitable, but in most cases an alternative form of order will probably be preferable.

Martin orders

5.19 A *Martin* order[21] is, in effect, a refinement of a *Mesher* order. It provides for the postponement of the trust for sale and for the division of the net proceeds when sold, but also provides for the property to be settled on the occupying party for life or until remarriage or voluntary removal. Such orders have been further refined to provide for the occupying party to pay an occupation rent,[22] or for the right of occupation to terminate on the wife's cohabitation. A more sophisticated form of order was that in *Chamberlain v Chamberlain*[23] where it was ordered that the property should not be sold until every child of the family had ceased to receive full-time education or thereafter without leave of the court or with the consent of the parties.

Martin orders are clearly appropriate where the justice of the case demands that one party be entitled to occupy a property for as long as he or she wishes, but it is not intended to deprive the other party of his or her capital entitlement for ever and even in the event of the other party's death.

Other orders

5.20 The orders set out above are the principal types of orders made for transfer of property and/or settlement of property. It should not be forgotten that the court may also order the immediate sale of a property and the division of the net proceeds of sale in whatever proportions appear appropriate in suitable cases.

An interesting case involving transfer of shares in a company is *C v C (Company Shares)*[24] where Coleridge J held that, where a wife had played a part, and wished to continue to play a part in the future of a company, there had to be a compelling reason why she should not be entitled to do so. Where the wife had made out a sensible case for holding shares, the court should, in fairness, accede to it.

---

[21] Named after *Martin v Martin* [1978] Fam 12, CA. See also *Bateman v Bateman* [1979] Fam 25; *Clutton v Clutton* [1991] 1 FLR 242, CA.

[22] *Harvey v Harvey* (above).

[23] [1973] 1 WLR 1557, CA.

[24] [2003] 2 FLR 493.

TRANSFER OF TENANCY

5.21 When the interest or estate which the parties to an ancillary relief application have in a property is a tenancy and not ownership of the property, different considerations arise from those already considered. In principle, the court must deal with the application in the same way as any other, namely by application of the s 25 factors. However, there are additional matters to be borne in mind.

Perhaps, at the outset, it should be made clear that most of the tenancies which will be the subject of an application will be local authority or social housing tenancies. This is because most tenancies in the private sector are now shorthold tenancies which are likely to contain a covenant against assignment (as to which, see **5.22**) or to be of so short a period as not to be worth transferring.

5.22 It has been held[25] that a tenancy is 'property' for the purposes of s 24(1)(a) and is therefore capable of being transferred pursuant to an order. There are two ways in which such an order may be obtained, and the choice will depend on the terms of the tenancy.

While the court has jurisdiction to make an order for transfer of a tenancy under s 24(1)(a), it should not exercise its discretion to do so when its order would be rendered ineffective by a covenant against assignment or where it would interfere with the statutory duties and discretion of a local housing authority.[26] If, therefore, there is a covenant against assignment, so that the tenant has contractually agreed not to assign, it has been said that it is doubtful that the court would transfer the tenancy.[27]

However, this statement may be subject to doubt, at least as far as council tenants are concerned, since in another decision of the Court of Appeal[28] it was described as out of date on the ground that, since the Housing Act 1980, council tenants had security of tenure and even the right to buy.

In any event, the position would be different where the local housing authority had expressly declined to become involved on behalf of either party but made it clear that it had no objection to transfer.

5.23 In a case where s 24 could not be invoked, an application for transfer of tenancy may be made under FLA 1996, Sch 7. This empowers the court to order the transfer of a protected or statutory tenancy, a statutory tenancy within the meaning of the Rent (Agriculture) Act 1976, a secure tenancy within the meaning of the Housing Act 1985, s 79, or an assured tenancy or assured

---

[25] *Thompson v Thompson* [1976] Fam 25, CA.
[26] See *Regan v Regan* [1977] 1 WLR 84; *Hale v Hale* [1975] 1 WLR 931. See also *Newlon Housing Trust v Alsulaimen* [1997] 1 FLR 914, CA.
[27] Most recently in *Newlon Housing Trust v Alsulaimen* (above).
[28] *Jones v Jones* [1997] 1 FLR 27, CA.

agricultural tenancy within the meaning of Part I of the Housing Act 1988. In the case of spouses, past or present, the court has jurisdiction to make an order whenever it has power to make a property adjustment order.

It will be noted that shorthold tenancies are not included in the list of tenancies which may be transferred. However, secure tenancies are included, and the Act provides a procedure for allowing landlords to be heard and provides a checklist for the guidance of the court. It is for this reason that it can be said that even where there is a covenant against assignment, the court has jurisdiction to consider an application under this statute.

5.24   The procedure for applying for a transfer of tenancy under FLA 1996, Sch 7 is set out in FPR 2010, Part 8, Chapter 7.

Chapter 6

SETTLEMENT OF PROPERTY ORDERS AND VARIATION OF SETTLEMENTS

INTRODUCTION

6.1   As was seen in Chapter 5, when dealing with transfer of property orders, settlement of property orders and transfer of property orders are both types of property adjustment order and, to a large extent, overlap. For example, a *Mesher* order,[1] often regarded as a typical transfer of property order, is in reality a settlement of property order. The distinction is, for most purposes, immaterial, and in Chapter 5 the general principles governing the making of all such orders involving property were considered. In this chapter, therefore, it is proposed to consider only the special characteristics of settlement orders and also the subject of variation of settlement.

STATUTORY PROVISION

6.2   The power to order settlement of property or variation of settlement is contained in s 24 of MCA 1973 which provides that on granting a decree of divorce, a decree of nullity of marriage, or a decree of judicial separation or at any time thereafter (whether, in the case of a decree of divorce or of nullity of marriage, before or after the decree is made absolute) the court may make one or more of the following orders, that is to say:[2]

'(b)   an order that a settlement of such property as may be so specified, being property to which a party to the marriage is so entitled, be made to the satisfaction of the court for the benefit of the other party to the marriage and of the children of the family or either or any of them;

(c)   an order varying for the benefit of the parties to the marriage and of the children of the family or either or any of them any ante-nuptial or post-nuptial settlement (including such a settlement made by will or codicil) made on the parties to the marriage, other than one in the form of a pension arrangement (within the meaning of section 25D ...);

(d)   an order extinguishing or reducing the interest of either of the parties to the marriage under any settlement, other than one in the form of a pension arrangement (within the meaning of section 25D ...).'

---

[1]   *Mesher v Mesher and Hall* [1980] 1 All ER 126, CA.
[2]   MCA 1973, s 24(1).

6.3   These orders are, therefore, only capable of being made after decree. There is no provision for any interim relief of this nature.

WHAT IS A SETTLEMENT?

6.4   This is considered in more detail at **6.9**.

6.5   With the exception of *Mesher* and *Martin*[3] type orders, settlement orders are quite rare today. The reason for this is the comparatively sophisticated range of orders of other kinds available under the statute, and the fact that settlements of land are unusual in any circumstances in contemporary conditions. It is therefore not proposed to spend much time considering the requirements for settlement orders.

6.6   It should be noted that the power to settle is not limited in any way. When, therefore, the court considers that a settlement order is appropriate, it may do so in a wide variety of ways.[4] Since, with the exception of *Mesher* or *Martin* orders, this will be quite unusual, it is not proposed to consider the matter further here.

VARIATION OF SETTLEMENT

6.7   As has been seen, the statute confers on the court wide jurisdiction to vary or discharge settlements. This was once an important part of the court's jurisdiction on marriage breakdown, but has become comparatively rare. When marriage settlements were common and the court had restricted powers, the power to vary the settlement was clearly significant. Now that such settlements are less common and, in any event, the court enjoys wide discretionary powers, it is unusual for the court to have to exercise this branch of its jurisdiction. A modern example of a case in which the court would have had no means of providing for a party (in terms of pension provision) except by way of variation of settlement is *Brooks v Brooks*, considered at **6.10**.

6.8   Having said that, it must also be said that the approach of the court when dealing with such applications must be exactly the same as in any other ancillary relief application. The s 25 factors must be observed, and the interest of either party under a settlement is one of the assets to be brought into the calculations under s 25(2)(a). It will be for the court to consider the settlement in the light of the overall picture, and to decide how, if at all, it should be varied.

6.9   The first matter to be proved is, of course, that there is an ante-nuptial or post-nuptial settlement. The court interprets the term 'settlement' in a liberal manner and is not constrained by conveyancing concepts. The form is not the

---

3   *Martin v Martin* [1976] Fam 335.
4   For an example, see *Tavoulareas v Tavoulareas* [1998] 2 FLR 418, CA.

most important element; settlements can range from the strict settlement which would be easily recognised by a chancery lawyer to a mere covenant to pay periodic amounts. The settlement may be contained in a separation agreement, a will or codicil, or any document.

What is important is that the settlement provide for the financial benefit of one of the spouses and with reference to their married state.[5] A mere gift between spouses, or by a third party to a spouse, does not of itself create a settlement. An agreement to pay sums of money to a spouse after the marriage came to an end has been held to lack the required nuptial element.[6]

6.10 In *Brooks v Brooks*,[7] the parties had married in 1977 and in 1980 the husband's company set up a non-contributory pension scheme for him. It included the right for him to elect on retirement to give up a portion of his pension to provide on his death a deferred pension to his spouse or other person financially dependent on him. It was held that this was a post-nuptial settlement which the court could vary. The significance of *Brooks v Brooks* in terms of pensions has now diminished due to the effect of the Welfare Reform and Pensions Act 1999 (WRPA 1999) (see **10.17**).

In his speech, Lord Nicholls conceded the wide interpretation given to 'settlement' and said that the disposition must be one which makes some form of continuing provision for both or either of the parties to the marriage, with or without provision for their children. A disposition which conferred an immediate, absolute interest in an item of property would not constitute a settlement; in such a case, the appropriate remedy (if remedy were needed) would be a property transfer order or property settlement order. The authorities had consistently given a wide meaning to settlement in this context and had spelled out no precise limitation. A disposition which created interests in succession in specified property would cause no difficulty, nor where such interests were concurrent but discretionary. Concurrent joint interests, such as where parties to a marriage hold the matrimonial home as joint tenants or tenants in common, were 'near the borderline' but there was (rightly) authority[8] for holding this to be within the scope of the section. Income provision from settled property would readily qualify, and it was 'only a short step' to include income provision which took the form of an obligation by one party to the marriage to make periodical payments to the other.

6.11 In *Charamalous v Charamalous*[9] it was held that, provided it existed at the date of the order, the court has jurisdiction under s 24(1)(c) to vary a settlement that, at the date it was made, was ante- or post-nuptial, notwithstanding that, prior to the date of the order, the features that made it nuptial had been removed. In this case the court accorded primacy to the

---

[5] *Prescott (formerly Fellowes) v Fellowes* [1958] P 260, CA.
[6] *Young v Young* [1962] P 27, CA.
[7] [1996] 1 AC 375, [1995] 2 FLR 13, HL.
[8] In *Brown v Brown* [1959] P 86.
[9] [2004] 2 FLR 1093, CA.

ancillary relief regime over the trust regime and emphasised the incapacity of individuals to elect out of it. The nuptial character or otherwise of a settlement was held to be a question of fact.

For a recent example of a case where the court found that there was not a post-nuptial settlement see *K v K*.[10]

6.12 The powers of the court to vary the settlement are wide:

- the capital or income can be given to either party or to the children;[11]

- the interest of a party under the settlement can be extinguished;

- the settlement may be terminated; the property contained in the settlement may be resettled.[12]

When the property contained in the settlement is the matrimonial home, the various options adopted in transfer of property orders may be employed. The court has the power to require separate representation of children where there may be a conflict of interest,[13] and other third parties must be given the right to be heard.[14] It has been held that, on an application under this section the court has power to remove a trustee.[15]

In the older cases it was held that the court would not interfere with the terms of a settlement more than was necessary to do justice between the parties.[16] Clearly, today the court has wide powers of redistribution, and is more prepared to intervene in the parties' affairs than was once the case. Nevertheless, in a 1989 case[17] dealing with a post-nuptial settlement, Ewbank J said that his first consideration was the welfare of the children and the second consideration was that he should not interfere with the settlement more than was necessary for the purposes of the s 25 factors. In another more recent case[18] involving a lump sum (and not variation of settlement), Thorpe J said that the discretionary powers of the court to adjust capital shares between the parties should not be exercised unless there was a manifest need for intervention upon the application of the s 25 criteria; it might be said that this statement of principle echoes the older cases on this subject and is equally valid

---

[10]   [2007] EWHC 3485 (Fam).
[11]   See eg *E v E* [1990] 2 FLR 233; *Jump v Jump* [1883] 8 PD 159.
[12]   *Bacon v Bacon* [1947] P 151.
[13]   FPR 2010, r 9.11.
[14]   FPR 2010, r 9.13.
[15]   *E v E (Financial Provision)* [1990] 2 FLR 233, per Ewbank J; for a different, albeit older, view, see *Compton v Compton and Hussey* [1960] P 201.
[16]   See eg *Smith v Smith and Graves* (1887) 12 PD 102; *Ulrich v Ulrich and Felton* [1968] 1 All ER 67; *Egerton v Egerton* [1949] 2 All ER 238, CA.
[17]   *E v E* [1990] 2 FLR 233.
[18]   *H v H (Financial Provision: Capital Allowance)* [1993] 2 FLR 335 at 348.

in this context. As always, these older cases must be re-read in the light of *White v White*[19] and *Miller/McFarlane*[20] and, indeed, now *Radmacher v Granatino*.[21]

The law on variation of post-nuptial settlements is extensively reviewed in *Ben Hashem v Al Sharif*.[22] Here, it was held that, while the jurisdiction to vary such a settlement under s 24(1)(c) of MCA 1973 is unfettered and, in theory, unlimited, a settlement should not be interfered with more than is necessary to do justice between the parties.

[19] [2001] 1 AC 596.
[20] [2006] 1 FLR 1186.
[21] [2010] UKSC 42.
[22] [2008] EWHC 2380.

Chapter 7

ORDERS FOR SALE

INTRODUCTION

7.1 The effect of an order for ancillary relief is frequently that property must be sold. This may happen as a direct result of the order, for example if the former matrimonial home is to be sold, or perhaps when some asset has to be sold to provide a lump sum for one of the parties. This chapter will consider briefly the types of order for sale which may be made and the law and practice involved.

ORDER FOR SALE UNDER SECTION 24A OF MCA 1973

7.2 Statutory power of sale is provided by s 24A which provides that:[1]

'Where the court makes under section 23 or 24 of this Act a secured periodical payments order, an order for the payment of a lump sum or a property adjustment order, then, on making that order or at any time thereafter, the court may make a further order for the sale of such property as may be specified in the order, being property in which or in the proceeds of sale of which either or both of the parties to the marriage has or have a beneficial interest, either in possession or reversion.'

7.3 This power of sale is, therefore, ancillary to the principal capital order which has been made, and is only exercisable if such an order has been made.[2] An order for a lump sum, property adjustment or secured provision takes effect only on decree absolute, so no order could be made under this section to take effect before that time.[3] Subject to that proviso, the order may be made either at the same time as making the principal order or at any time thereafter; however, it must be the case that the court could not make such an order if the principal order had been complied with.

The order may contain a provision that it shall not take effect until the occurrence of an event specified by the order or the expiration of a period so specified. The court has, therefore, considerable discretion as to the terms which it imposes.

7.4 Section 24A also contains further provisions ancillary to the power to order sale. It is provided that any order for sale may contain such consequential

---

[1]   MCA 1973, s 24A(1).
[2]   *Thompson v Thompson* [1986] Fam 38.
[3]   MCA 1973, s 24A(3).

or supplementary provisions as the court thinks fit and, without prejudice to the generality of those provisions, may include:[4]

'(a) provision requiring the making of a payment out of the proceeds of sale of the property to which the order relates, and

(b) provision requiring any such property to be offered for sale to a person or class of persons specified in the order.'

The order could, therefore, for example, require the sale of a property owned by the respondent, and the payment of a lump sum from the proceeds of sale with the balance to be paid to the respondent; or the sale of a jointly owned former matrimonial home, with a requirement that one of the parties to the marriage and his or her cohabitant be entitled to bid. It is not uncommon for such orders to provide that the property be sold for the best offer received in excess of a certain figure.

What the order cannot do is require payments to third parties such as creditors who have no connection with the property or the sale thereof;[5] it would be proper to include an order for payment of estate agents' charges but not for payment of debts owed by the parties.

7.5 When the property in respect of which sale is sought is owned jointly by one of the parties and a third party, it is provided that:[6]

'... before deciding whether to make an order under this section in relation to that property, it shall be the duty of the court to give that other person an opportunity to make representations with respect to the order; and any representations made by that other person shall be included among the circumstances to which the court is required to have regard under section 25(1) ...'

It follows from this that the court must direct service of all relevant proceedings on the third party; procedure for this is considered in more detail at **16.9**. In *Ram v Ram (No 2)*[7] it was held that the court's power under s 24A is limited to property in which either or both of the parties has or have a beneficial interest in possession or reversion. Thus, where a bankruptcy order has been made and the property therefore vested in the trustee, the bankrupt has no beneficial interest even after his discharge.

HOW IS JURISDICTION EXERCISED?

7.6 There is no separate set of guidelines applicable to orders under s 24A. An order under this section is an order to which s 25 applies, and the exercise of

---

[4] MCA 1973, s 24A(2).
[5] *Burton v Burton* [1986] 2 FLR 419.
[6] MCA 1973, s 24A(6).
[7] [2004] EWCA Civ 1684, [2005] 2 FLR 75.

the court's discretion will be governed by the usual s 25 factors. An order under s 24A may be made if the court considers it necessary to do so to achieve its purpose pursuant to s 25.

INTERIM ORDERS

7.7   There is no power to make an interim order for sale under s 24A or, indeed, under any other provision. This is considered in more detail at **4.5**.

FPR 2010, RULE 9.24

7.8   FPR 2010, r 9.24(1) provides that, where the court has made an order under MCA 1973, s 24A, the Matrimonial and Family Proceedings Act 1984, s 17(2), or the Civil Partnership Act 2004, Sch 5, Part 3 or Sch 7, para 9(4), it may order any party to deliver up to the purchaser or any other person possession of the land, including any interest in, or right over, land, receipt of rents or profits relating to it, or both.

7.9   It has been held that RSC Ord 31, r 1 does not permit the court to order an interim sale of a property pending the final resolution of an application for ancillary relief.[8]

THE TRUSTS OF LAND AND APPOINTMENT OF TRUSTEES ACT 1996

7.10   Under s 30 of the Law of Property Act 1925 (LPA 1925), when property was held on trust for sale (which was always the case when jointly owned) either trustee could apply to the court for an order for sale, which would be granted unless, for example, it could be found that the purposes for which the trust was established (such as the provision of a family home) had not been fulfilled. Section 30 has now been repealed by the Trusts of Land and Appointment of Trustees Act 1996 (TLATA 1996) and, for the purposes of this chapter, the important part of this statute is s 14 which permits the court to order sale.

The difference between s 14 and LPA 1925, s 30 is that there is now no presumption as to an order for sale. Instead, the court is directed by s 15 to have regard to various matters such as the intentions of the persons who created the trust, the purposes for which the property is held, the welfare of any minor occupying the property, and the interests of any secured creditor.

7.11   It is unlikely that it will be necessary to make an application under s 14 in the course of an application for financial relief. Nevertheless, the statutory powers exist, and it may be necessary to have them in mind as a fall-back position in some situations.

---

[8]   *Wicks v Wicks* [1998] 1 FLR 470, CA.

This was in fact the case in *Miller-Smith v Miller-Smith*.[9] Here it was held that where the court is confronted by an application under TLATA 1996 between separated spouses it should ask itself whether the issues raised by the application can reasonably be left to be resolved within an application for financial relief following divorce. In the circumstances of this case, where the house was larger than required to meet the wife's needs and it was unlikely that the financial relief proceedings would be determined within another year, the Court of Appeal upheld a decision that the house should be sold.

For further discussion in the context of insolvency, see Chapter 12.

---

9   [2009] EWCA Civ 1297, [2010] 1 FLR 1402.

Chapter 8

AVOIDANCE OF DISPOSITION AND OTHER INJUNCTIONS

INTRODUCTION

8.1   The course of an application for a financial remedy does not always run smoothly. Sometimes, orders are not obeyed, parties are less than frank, and, in extreme cases, there may be a concerted effort to defeat the just entitlement of one of the parties by the other party. The court therefore has to have powers to overcome such stratagems.

These powers may be summarised as follows:

(a)   the power to prevent or set aside a disposition under s 37 of the MCA 1973;

(b)   a similar power under the inherent jurisdiction of the court;

(c)   the power to grant a freezing injunction;

(d)   the power to grant a search order.

8.2   These powers and remedies will be considered in turn. The first is by far the most common.

APPLICATIONS UNDER SECTION 37 OF MCA 1973 FOR AN AVOIDANCE OF DISPOSITION ORDER

8.3   It is provided that:[1]

'Where proceedings for financial relief are brought by one person against another, the court may, on the application of the first-mentioned person –

(a)   if it is satisfied that the other party to the proceedings is, with the intention of defeating the claim for financial relief, about to make any disposition or to transfer out of the jurisdiction or otherwise deal with any property, make such order as it thinks fit for restraining the other party from so doing or otherwise for protecting the claim;

---

[1]   MCA 1973, s 37(2).

(b)   if it is satisfied that the other party has, with that intention, made a reviewable disposition and that if the disposition were set aside financial relief or different financial relief would be granted to the applicant, make an order setting aside the disposition;

(c)   if it is satisfied, in a case where an order has been obtained under any of the provisions mentioned in subsection (1) above by the applicant against the other party, that the other party has, with that intention, made a reviewable disposition, make an order setting aside the disposition;

and an application for the purposes of paragraph (b) above shall be made in the proceedings for the financial relief in question.'

8.4   Section 37(2) refers to s 37(1) which is a definition section. There, it is provided that, for the purposes of s 37:[2]

'... "financial relief" means relief under any of the provisions of sections 22, 23, 24, 24B, 27, 31 (except subsection (6)) and 35 above, and any reference in this section to defeating a person's claim for financial relief is a reference to preventing financial relief from being granted to that person, or to that person for the benefit of a child of the family, or reducing the amount of any financial relief which might be so granted, or frustrating or impeding the enforcement of any order which might be or has been made at his instance under any of those provisions.'

By FPR 2010, r 2.3 an order for avoidance of disposition is a financial order. By r 9.3 an avoidance of disposition order means, in addition to orders under MCA 1973, s 37, orders under similar provisions in the statutes relating to financial relief after overseas divorce and dissolution of civil partnerships. Orders after overseas divorce are considered in Chapter 15, and this book is not concerned with civil partnerships.

Issues arising out of the remedy under s 37 will now be considered in turn.

Two types of remedy

8.5   Section 37 gives the right to apply for two distinct remedies. The first, which is pre-emptive, is the power of the court to prevent a disposition before it has been made. Thus, for example, a spouse who threatened to transfer assets to another person, or to squander some asset, could be ordered not to do so; banks or other financial institutions can be served with copies of any order made which would normally have the result of freezing transactions.

The second is the power to undo or set aside any disposition which has been made. Where a spouse transfers assets to another with the intention of putting them out of reach of the court, the person to whom the assets were transferred can be ordered to transfer them back so that they may form part of the funds available for distribution between the parties. This provision itself falls into two

---

[2]   MCA 1973, s 37(1).

categories, namely the power to set aside in anticipation of the hearing of an application for a financial remedy, and the power to set aside at or after the hearing.

Separate factors obviously govern these two remedies, but there are a number of common factors which will be considered.

The requirement for an application for a financial remedy

8.6 Section 37 is a remedy ancillary to an application for a financial remedy; there cannot be a free-standing s 37 application. Subsection (2) begins by requiring that financial proceedings are brought by one person against another, and there can be no application under s 37 unless this has happened. Where the applicant is a petitioner, or a respondent who has filed an answer, the application for a financial remedy contained in the petition or answer will be deemed sufficient for this purpose, although it would normally be considered right to require a Form A to have been issued; s 37 is a discretionary remedy, and the court would not normally think it right to make an order unless satisfied that the application for financial relief was to proceed.

The application for financial relief may be filed at court at the same time as the s 37 application. In cases of urgency, the court will accept an undertaking to file the application by a fixed date.

8.7 'Financial relief' is defined by s 37(1) as, in effect, an application for either a financial provision order, a property adjustment order, an order for maintenance pending suit, an order on the ground of neglect to maintain, or a variation order.

Only the applicant can apply

8.8 After reciting the need for an application for financial relief by one person against another, s 37(2) sets out the remedies which may be granted 'on the application of the first mentioned person', ie the applicant for financial relief. A respondent to such an application who had made no prayer for financial relief in an answer would have no right to apply under s 37. This is perhaps a formal hurdle only because all the respondent would have to do would be to file a notice of application, but the point should be noted.

What is a 'disposition'?

8.9 The section provides that 'disposition' does not include provision made by will or codicil, but that it does include any conveyance, assurance or gift of property of any description, whether made by an instrument or otherwise.[3] Apart from this, no attempt is made to define the term, but clearly it includes any act, deed or transaction which has the effect of transferring ownership or

---

[3] MCA 1973, s 37(6).

possession from one person to another. It has been held to include a legal charge on real property.[4] It has also been held that failure to deal with property, as opposed to a positive dealing, is not a disposition.[5] A notice to quit a periodic tenancy is not a disposition and cannot be set aside under s 37.[6]

'With the intention of defeating the claim for financial relief'

8.10   The court must be satisfied that, in the case of a pre-emptive application, the disposition or transfer is to be made, or, in the case of a post-disposition or transfer application, has been made, with the intention of defeating the applicant's claim for financial relief. The onus of proof is on the applicant, and if this burden is not discharged the order cannot be made. However, it has been held that the question which the judge must ask himself is whether he is 'satisfied', and that it is inappropriate to add tests such as 'beyond reasonable doubt' or 'on the balance of probabilities'.[7]

To some extent, the task of the applicant is made easier by s 37(1) which goes some way to defining 'defeating the claim'. Here, it is said that this means any of the following:[8]

(a)   preventing (any) financial relief from being granted to the applicant, either for herself or for a child;

(b)   reducing the amount of any financial relief which might otherwise be granted;

(c)   frustrating or impeding the enforcement of any order for financial relief which might be made or which has been made.

The court will therefore have to find that one of these results is more likely than not to happen if an order is not made.

8.11   This leaves the question of proving 'intention'. Where it is found that one of the outcomes set out above is likely to occur, the court would have no difficulty in deducing that the respondent to the application intended that to happen. A person is deemed to intend the normal consequences of his actions, and where, for example, the inevitable result of a transfer of a property to someone else would be that the funds available for distribution between the spouses would be diminished, it would almost inevitably have to be found that the transferor had intended that consequence.

Different factors might arise where there could be more than one reason for the disposition or transfer, particularly where it could also be said that the funds

---

[4]   *Whittingham v Whittingham* [1979] Fam 9, CA.
[5]   *Crittenden v Crittenden* [1990] 2 FLR 361, CA.
[6]   *Newlon Housing Trust v Alsulaimen* [1998] 2 FLR 690, HL.
[7]   *K v K (Avoidance of Reviewable Disposition)* (1983) 4 FLR 31, CA.
[8]   MCA 1973, s 37(1).

available for distribution would not be diminished. For example, a person whose livelihood depended on the sale and purchase of assets should not be prevented from trading for no other reason than a pending ancillary relief application, and a person involved in any business should not be subjected to unusual and unreasonable restrictions. In the context of marriage breakdown, it is not unusual for the parties to be both deeply suspicious of each other and resentful of any interference with their normal activities. The court has to distinguish these cases from those where there is evidence that some deliberate attempt to defeat the claim is being or has been made.[9]

In *Mubarak v Mubarik*[10] it was held that s 37 requires an actual intention to defeat a claim to be in existence at the time of the disposition; here, the court could not be satisfied that the husband had made the disposition with the intention of defeating the claim for ancillary relief (as opposed to tax evasion).

Special considerations in applications to set aside dispositions

8.12 As has already been mentioned, the power to set aside a disposition is distinct from the power to prevent a disposition. Clearly, once a disposition or transfer has been made, it may be that third parties have acquired rights in the property concerned, and different considerations arise from those when it is sought to prevent a disposition from taking place. The various relevant factors will now be considered.

Reviewable dispositions

8.13 For a disposition or transfer to be set aside, it has to be 'reviewable'. This term is defined by the section. First, it is provided that:[11]

'... any disposition made by the other party to the proceedings for financial relief in question (whether before or after the commencement of those proceedings) is a reviewable disposition for the purposes of subsection (2)(b) and (c) above unless it was made for valuable consideration (other than marriage) to a person who, at the time of the disposition, acted in relation to it in good faith and without notice of any intention on the part of the other party to defeat the applicant's claim for financial relief.'

8.14 The significance of this is that it will be presumed that any disposition is reviewable unless the respondent to the application (and the transferee) can establish all the matters mentioned, namely:

(a) valuable consideration (for this purpose, marriage does not count);

---

[9] See *Smith v Smith* (1973) Fam Law 80; the court must be satisfied that a disposition is in fact about to take place, and also that its intention is to defeat the applicant's claim. There is no general power to freeze a party's assets pending the hearing of an application for financial relief.

[10] [2007] 2 FLR 364, Holman J.

[11] MCA 1973, s 37(4).

(b)   transferee acting in good faith;[12]

(c)   transferee without any notice of transferor's intention to defeat applicant's claim.

The onus will therefore be on the respondent or transferee to satisfy the court of these matters. This applies to any transfer or disposition which the respondent has made.[13]

The limitations of s 37 were demonstrated by the decision in *Ansari v Ansari*.[14] Here, the husband and a third party had conspired to defeat the wife's claim; a house which was owned by the husband was transferred to the third party who then charged it to a bank for a large sum. The bank had notice of the wife's family home rights. The wife's application to set aside the charge failed, on the ground that the husband was not a party to the bank's charge which was therefore not a reviewable disposition made by 'the other party'. It was also held, per curiam, that even if the charge had been a reviewable disposition, the bank would have been able to rely on s 37(4). The fact that the bank had notice of the wife's rights did not mean that it had notice of the husband's intention to defeat the wife's claims.

Presumption of intention to defeat claim in some cases

8.15   The section goes further. It is provided that:[15]

> 'Where an application is made under this section with respect to a disposition which took place less than three years before the date of the application or with respect to a disposition or other dealing with property which is about to take place and the court is satisfied –
>
> (a)   in a case falling within subsection (2)(a) or (b) above, that the disposition or other dealing would (apart from this section) have the consequence, or
> (b)   in a case falling within subsection (2)(c) above, that the disposition has had the consequence,
>
> of defeating the applicant's claim for financial relief, it shall be presumed, unless the contrary is shown, that the person who disposed of or is about to dispose of or

---

[12]   See *Whittingham v Whittingham* [1979] Fam 9, CA; at the very least lack of good faith involves lack of honesty, and may require something akin to fraud.

[13]   There is no general rule that anyone acquiring an interest in property from someone he knows to be divorced thereby has notice of an application for financial relief. However, the facts may indicate constructive notice. A bank may be under an obligation to make inquiries, and a lender who knows that an aspirant borrower has been involved in divorce proceedings is obliged to ask him whether his spouse has any potential interest in a property sought to be charged; however, it is under no obligation to verify information given by the borrower unless the spouse is in occupation of the property. See *Whittingham v Whittingham* (above); *B v B (P Ltd Intervening) (No 2)* [1995] 1 FLR 374, CA.

[14]   [2008] EWCA Civ 1456.

[15]   MCA 1973, s 37(5).

deal with the property did so, or, as the case may be, is about to do so, with the intention of defeating the applicant's claim for financial relief.'

8.16 This subsection therefore erects a further hurdle which the respondent or transferee must cross. Where the disposition was either less than 3 years before the application, or, in the case of an application to prevent a disposition, has not yet been made, and it is established to the satisfaction of the court that its effect will be to defeat the applicant's claim for financial relief (as defined in s 37(1): see **8.7**) it will be presumed that the intention was or is to defeat the claim for financial relief unless the respondent is able to prove the contrary.

Consequential directions

8.17 When an order is made setting aside a disposition, the court must give consequential directions as it thinks fit for giving effect to the order, including directions requiring the making of any payments or the disposal of any property.

How will the court exercise its discretion?

8.18 Even if the court finds in favour of the applicant on the issues of intention to defeat the claim, etc the position remains that the court 'may' make an order under s 37; the final disposal is subject to the discretion of the court. Clearly, each case will turn on its own facts, and, as always, the factors set out in s 25 apply.

In deciding whether or not to grant an order under s 37(2)(a) (a pre-emptive order), and assuming that the intention on the part of the respondent had been proved, the court would normally feel obliged to make an order unless it could be demonstrated that the disposition or transfer need not affect the final result because there would be more than enough capital left to provide for any order which the court could conceivably make.

In deciding whether or not to set aside a disposition, the same consideration will apply, but the court will also have to weigh up the hardship which would be caused to the transferee if the disposition were set aside against that which would be caused to the applicant if it were not set aside.

Foreign property

8.19 It has been held that an order under s 37 can be granted even though the property in question is outside England and Wales.[16] The court might, in the exercise of its discretion, decline to make any order which would be unenforceable, but that would not per se prevent an application being made and an order granted in appropriate cases.

---

[16]   *Hamlin v Hamlin* [1986] 1 FLR 61, CA.

Procedure

8.20 By FPR 2010, r 9.6(1) the Part 18 procedure applies to applications for an avoidance of a disposition order. By r 9.6(2) the application may be made without notice to the respondent.

In *ND v KP (ex parte application)*[17] Mostyn J re-affirmed the principle that an ex parte order is an exceptional remedy and should only be sought where there is good cause and clear evidence. An application for an ex parte order should only be made where there is positive evidence that to give notice would lead to irretrievable prejudice to the applicant.

This was in fact a case involving a freezing order, but it is submitted that his Lordship's comments apply to all forms of without notice application.

Rule 18.2 confirms that an applicant may use the Part 18 procedure where the application is made within existing proceedings. The procedure is set out in rr 18.4–18.12. Briefly, an application must be filed which must set out what order the applicant is seeking and why the order is sought. A draft of the order sought must be attached to the application. Part 17 requires the application notice to be verified by a statement of truth if the applicant intends to rely on the notice as evidence. The applicant seems, therefore, to have the choice of either putting all the supporting evidence in the notice of application and verifying it by a statement of truth or of filing a separate statement which would also need to be so verified.

When an order is made without notice, or where the applicant is proceeding on notice, at least 7 days notice of the hearing or return date as the case may be, must be given.

Rule 2.62 of the now repealed FPR 1991 provided that where practicable an application for an avoidance of disposition order should be heard at the same time as any related application for ancillary relief. There seems to be no corresponding provision in the 2010 rules, though the commonsense of the previous provision is clear.

Forms

8.21 Suggested draft orders will be found at Appendix A.

APPLICATIONS FOR AVOIDANCE OF DISPOSITION UNDER THE INHERENT JURISDICTION OF THE COURT

8.22 As has been seen, s 37 contains a series of requirements which the court must find to have been fulfilled before an order under that section may be made. However, there may be occasions when, although the evidence might not

---

[17]   [2011] EWHC 457 (Fam).

support a positive finding under s 37, the justice of the case demands that some injunctive relief be granted. In such circumstances, it has been held that the court is not powerless, since it may invoke its inherent jurisdiction. Whether or not a county court enjoys any inherent jurisdiction may be a matter for debate. The practice in the Principal Registry is that applications invoking the inherent jurisdiction are transferred to the High Court and heard by a judge.

In *Shipman v Shipman*[18] it was held that, although the requirements of s 37 (including in particular the intention to defeat the wife's claim) could not be met, the court had an inherent jurisdiction to freeze assets which might be put beyond the reach of the applicant; in deciding whether or not to exercise its discretion in favour of the applicant, the court was not bound by the many restrictions and safeguards which must be observed when granting a worldwide freezing injunction (as to which see **8.25** et seq).

8.23   Another example of the court's ability to grant an injunction to preserve the status quo is provided by the decision of Thorpe J in *Poon v Poon*.[19] In that case, the parties were directors and shareholders of a family company. Proceedings for ancillary relief were pending, and the wife proposed to remove the husband from his position in the company and replace him with her current boyfriend; she was in a position to do this since other members of her family were also shareholders. Thorpe J said that, pending a final hearing, every effort was made to preserve the status quo. Although the company was a separate entity, it was not an entity in which any other individual or non-family member had any interest; it was unthinkable that the wife should be allowed to proceed to emasculate the husband's interest. Accordingly, an injunction was granted restraining the wife from placing her proposals before the general meeting.

8.24   However, a word of caution may be in order. The inherent jurisdiction of the court was considered by the Court of Appeal in *Wicks v Wicks*,[20] a case which dealt with a different issue, namely the power of the court to order an interim sale of property, and it was held that, for that purpose at least, the court did not have inherent jurisdiction. Ward LJ pointed out that the inherent jurisdiction related to the procedural and not the substantive law. In the instant case:

> 'Under the cloak of ensuring fair play, the judge was in fact making orders affecting the parties' substantive rights, and that must be governed by the general law and rules, not by resort to a wide judicial discretion derived from the court's inherent jurisdiction ... The reality [in *Wicks*] is that the wife is seeking the enforcement of rights which the Matrimonial Causes Act 1973 does not grant her. She wants an order for sale before s 24A allows the court to order it.'

---

[18]   [1991] 1 FLR 250, Anthony Lincoln J; see also *Roche v Roche* (1981) Fam Law 243, CA, and *Walker v Walker* (1983) 4 FLR 455.

[19]   [1994] 2 FLR 857.

[20]   [1998] 1 FLR 470, CA; discussed in more detail at **4.5**.

It remains to be seen whether these comments as to the inherent jurisdiction will ever be used to overturn the line of authorities referred to in this section, or, indeed, whether it would be held that these injunctions affected the substantive rather than the procedural rights of the parties. For the time being the decisions remain good law, and at least one of them is a decision of the Court of Appeal. However, the possibility of development should not be ignored.

FREEZING INJUNCTIONS

8.25   Freezing injunctions were originally called *Mareva* injunctions after the name of the vessel in the leading case on the subject.[21] Although this was a mercantile case, the principles laid down are applicable to family cases.

The essence of such an injunction is that the respondent to the application is forbidden to remove from the jurisdiction of the court (ie from England and Wales) funds or property until the trial of the action or matter. The onus is on the applicant to show that it is likely that she will recover a capital sum or property at the final hearing and that there is a danger that the court's order may be emasculated by the respondent removing funds out of the court's reach.

8.26   The statutory basis is s 37 of the Senior Courts Act 1981 (SCA 1981). This is applied to county courts by the County Courts Act 1984 (CCA 1984), s 38. The county court, therefore, has jurisdiction in a family matter,[22] but under normal circumstances a freezing injunction, particularly where the issues are contested, should be transferred to the High Court.[23] A freezing injunction may be worldwide (ie applying to assets outside the jurisdiction) or limited to assets within the jurisdiction.

8.27   The law and practice relating to freezing injunctions is clearly both complicated and of a specialist nature, and it is not proposed to say more in detail about it in this book. The rules relating to such applications are contained in Part 20 and essential material is contained in Practice Direction 20A in the FPR 2010. This practice direction is set out in full in Appendix B and contains detailed and practical guidance which is obviously required reading for anyone contemplating such an application.

SEARCH ORDERS

8.28   Similar comments to those contained in the previous paragraph apply to search orders. These orders were originally called *Anton Piller* orders after the

---

[21]   *Mareva Cia Naviera SA v International Bulkcarriers SA, The Mareva* [1980] 1 All ER 213n, CA.
[22]   See MFPA 1984, s 32.
[23]   *Practice Direction (Family Business: Distribution of Business)* [1992] 3 All ER 151.

eponymous case[24] in which they were first made, were of mercantile or commercial origin, and have been adapted for use in family proceedings.[25] Such orders now have a statutory basis in s 7 of the Civil Procedure Act 1997. The Practice Direction referred to in the previous paragraph also governs practice and procedure in these cases. A suggested form for a search order will be found at Appendix A, Precedent 3.

8.29 A search order may be granted where it appears that the respondent to the application has in his possession documents or other material relevant to the application for financial relief, that he has not disclosed them, and that there is a real possibility that he may destroy them before an application can be made inter partes. The order is therefore always made ex parte, and its effect is that the applicant or her agent is empowered to enter the respondent's premises and to seize and remove documents or material of the classes specified in the order. By s 7 of the 1997 Act, an order may be made against 'any person'.

The order is, therefore, extremely drastic and has been described as being 'at the extremity of the court's powers'.[26] Such orders are therefore rarely made, and where it eventually appears that the search was fruitless, severe penalties in costs will be inflicted on the applicant.[27] It remains to be seen whether the decision of Moylan J in *Imerman v Imerman*[28] results in an increase of search applications in respect of allegedly improperly retained documents..

8.30 An application for a search order made in county court proceedings must be transferred to the High Court.

---

[24] *Anton Piller KG v Manufacturing Processes Ltd* [1976] Ch 55, [1976] 1 All ER 779, CA.
[25] See *Emanuel v Emanuel* [1982] 2 All ER 342; *Kepa v Kepa* (1983) 4 FLR 515.
[26] *Anton Piller KG v Manufacturing Processes Ltd* (above), per Ormrod LJ.
[27] As in *Burgess v Burgess* [1996] 2 FLR 34.
[28] [2009] EWHC 3486 (Fam), [2010] 2 FLR 752.

Chapter 9

CONSENT ORDERS

INTRODUCTION

9.1   Not all applications for a financial order result in a final contested hearing. Some applications are agreed from the outset; some become agreed in the course of the proceedings but before the final hearing; and yet more are settled at the doors of the court. The principles applicable to these different classes of case are the same, but there are differences in procedure.

A consent order is defined by MCA 1973 as 'an order in the terms applied for to which the respondent agrees';[1] in effect, it is an order which both parties to the application for financial relief ask the court to make without hearing evidence or argument. Before considering the procedural steps necessary for a consent order and the requirements to be observed when drafting such an order, it will be necessary to consider the duty of the court on such occasions, and the general principles applicable to applications for consent orders.

The circumstances in which a consent order may be set aside are considered in detail in Chapter 18.

THE DUTY OF THE COURT

9.2   It is a fundamental principle of family law in England and Wales that the rights of the parties are not finally declared until the court has made an order endorsing their agreement; any attempt to oust the jurisdiction of the court is likely to fail, and the parties cannot know that their agreement is final until the court has made an order incorporating its terms.[2]

It is a further fundamental principle that the court has a duty to scrutinise and approve whatever agreement is put before it. The position was authoritatively established in *Livesey (formerly Jenkins) v Jenkins*,[3] where the position as to consent orders was summarised as follows:

- the jurisdiction of the court to make orders for financial relief is derived entirely from statute, namely MCA 1973;

---

[1]   MCA 1973, s 33A(3).
[2]   *Pounds v Pounds* [1994] 1 FLR 775, CA. See also **1.54** as to agreements generally.
[3]   [1985] AC 424, HL.

- the function of the court when making such orders is exactly the same when the application is by consent as when the hearing is contested;

- s 25 of MCA 1973 prescribes a list of matters to which the court is required to have regard;

- it follows that the court must consider the merits of any consent application in the light of the s 25 factors, and only make the order if it appears to be just and reasonable.

The position was well set out in a later case,[4] where it was said that in consent applications for ancillary relief:

'... the court does not act, it has been said, as a rubber stamp. The judge will be concerned, whether the order be made by consent or imposed after argument, to be satisfied that the criteria of ss 25 and 25A of the Matrimonial Causes Act 1973 have been duly applied.'

Having said that, it should also be said that the function of the court is not to scrutinise the agreed terms and evidence in the same way as it would on a defended hearing.[5] It is submitted that the court's role is limited to satisfying itself that the proposed order is within the band of reasonable discretion and that it does not, on the face of it, offend any obvious principle. For a case where there was a dispute as to whether an agreement had been made at all, see *Xydhias v Xydhias*[6] discussed at **1.67**.

9.3   It follows from what has been said that the court cannot perform its statutory functions unless it has the information and material on which to base its assessment. When the question of setting aside consent orders is considered in Chapter 18, the importance of full and frank disclosure will become apparent; this was one of the major issues in *Livesey v Jenkins*. Another important result of that case was that it became necessary to establish procedures to give the court the required information when it was considering a consent application, and this will now be considered.

INFORMATION REQUIRED BY THE COURT

9.4   After some uncertainty following *Livesey v Jenkins* as to what would be required by the court in order to carry out its investigations, statutory authority was provided by s 33A of MCA 1973. This provides that:[7]

'... on an application for a consent order for financial relief the court may, unless it has reason to think that there are other circumstances into which it ought to

---

4   *Pounds v Pounds* [1994] 1 FLR 775, CA.
5   Ibid.
6   [1999] 1 FLR 683, CA.
7   MCA 1973, s 33A(1).

inquire, make an order in the terms agreed on the basis only of the prescribed information furnished with the application.'

'Prescribed' means prescribed by rules of court, and these are to be found in FPR 2010, r 9.26.

This provides that the applicant must file two copies of a draft of the order in the terms sought, one of which must be endorsed with a statement signed by the respondent to the application signifying agreement. Further, each party must file with the court and serve on the other party, a statement of information in the form referred to in Practice Direction 5A. Where each party's statement of information is contained in one form, it must be signed by both the applicant and respondent to certify that they have read the contents of the other party's statement. Where each party's statement of information is in a separate form, the form of each party must be signed by the other party to certify that they have read the contents of the statement contained in that form.

Practice Direction 5A requires the statements of information to contain the following:

'(a) the duration of the marriage, the age of each party and of any minor or dependent child of the family;

(b) an estimate in summary form of the approximate amount of value of the capital resources and net income of each party and of any minor child of the family;

(c) what arrangements are intended for the accommodation of each of the parties and any minor child of the family;

(d) whether either party has remarried or has any present intention to marry or to cohabit with another person;

(dd) where the order includes provision to be made under s 24B, 25B or 25C of the Act of 1973, a statement confirming that the person responsible for the pension arrangement in question has been served with the documents required by rule 2.70(11) and that no objection to such an order has been made by that person within 14 days from such service;

(e) where the terms of the order provide for a transfer of property, a statement confirming that any mortgagee of the property has been served with notice of the application and that no objection to such a transfer has been made by the mortgagee within 14 days from such service; and

(f) any other especially significant matters.'

Unless the court directs otherwise, the applicant and the respondent need not attend the hearing of an application for a consent order. Normally, the district judge would only require parties to attend where, on the face of it, the order seemed unfair or something needed to be explained.

EXCEPTIONS TO THE GENERAL RULE

9.5   Sometimes a consent order is requested at a hearing where the parties have come to an agreement. In such circumstances, by r 9.26(5) the court may dispense with the filing of the statements of information and give directions for the information which would otherwise be required to be given in such a statement in such a manner as it thinks fit. Normally, where the parties had filed Forms E and counsel or solicitors had filed a case outline, no further documentation should be required.

It is important to make the point that there are no other circumstances in which the statements may be dispensed with; it certainly is not acceptable for parties or their advisers to send the court a consent order with an invitation to read the Forms E or other evidence on the court file, however recent that evidence may be.

9.6   A diversion from the established practice was approved by Coleridge J in *S v P*.[8] His Lordship directed that draft consent orders approved by the collaborative law process could be approved in the Urgent Ex Parte Applications List without it being necessary to go through the normal procedure. This procedure could only be used where every aspect of the documentation was agreed, the hearing was not more than 10 minutes, and the documentation was lodged with the judge the night before. It was emphasised that this procedure would be kept under review and the implication is that it must not be allowed to get out of hand.

NOTES ON DRAFTING CONSENT ORDERS

9.7   It is clearly important that all orders should be correctly drafted. This is more than usually important in the case of consent orders. In the first place, the drafting of the order is in the hands of the parties' advisers, who therefore assume responsibility for the order and any defects in it. In the second place, in most cases of a consent order, the application is considered by the court in the absence of the parties, and any matter which requires amendment or further inquiry by the court results in delay and, probably, additional cost for the lay client.[9]

The following paragraphs include common causes of query by the court.

The distinction between matters which may be ordered and those which may not

9.8   In *Livesey v Jenkins* it was pointed out that the powers of the court in respect of financial relief are entirely statutory; if the power to make a certain order cannot be identified in MCA 1973, that order cannot be made:[10]

---

[8]   [2008] 2 FLR 2040.
[9]   For an example of the problems which can be caused by lack of care in a drafting order, see *McGladdery v McGladdery* [1999] 2 FLR 1102.
[10]   *Livesey v Jenkins* [1984] AC 424, HL, per Lord Brandon.

'When a consent order is drafted it is essential that all its terms should come clearly within the court's powers conferred on it by sections 23 and 24 of the Act of 1973.'

Having said that, frequently there are matters of fact which the parties wish to have recorded, or agreements which are essential to the proper performance of the overall arrangement which the parties have made which cannot be brought within the terms of the statute but which, nevertheless, should appear in the order. One of the most common reasons for rejection of a consent order is a failure on the part of the draftsman to recognise the difference between the various parts of the order.

The distinction which must be made is between recitals of fact, recitals of agreement, undertakings, and orders. These will be considered in turn.

Recitals of fact

9.9   Most of the important factual matters, such as the declared means of the parties, will have been set out in the Form filed with the court, so it should not normally be necessary to recite detailed facts in the preamble to the order itself. Nevertheless, there are certain matters which it may be thought helpful for the court to have on the face of the order (eg that the former matrimonial home has been sold and the proceeds divided in certain proportions). There may also be important matters which have been in dispute, and which the party agreeing to compromise wishes to have placed on record unambiguously, so that if it later appeared that any such recited matter was not true it would be easier for that party to establish that he or she was misled.

Recitals of agreement

9.10   An agreement should be recited in the preamble to the order if it is an integral part of the overall settlement between the parties, but is not a matter which could properly be worded as an undertaking (as to which, see below). This might be the case, for example, where one party agreed that the other should be given the conduct of a sale, or be allowed to occupy premises until sale. It would also be the case where one party agreed to indemnify the other in respect of liability under a contract. In the event of a breach of any such agreement, the remedy of the aggrieved party would be to institute separate proceedings for breach of contract rather than trying to enforce the order in the preamble to which the agreement was recited.

Another useful recital of agreement (or of the existence of an agreement) would arise when the parties had made a written agreement for the support of a child pursuant to s 8(5) of CSA 1991.[11]

---

[11]   See also the Child Maintenance (Written Agreements) Order 1993, SI 1993/620; but note **11.12**.

Undertakings

9.11 The difference between an agreement and an undertaking is that in the case of an undertaking the person giving the undertaking is making a promise to the court and not to the other party.[12] The expectation is therefore that the court would be able to punish any breach of undertaking, for example by committal to prison.

In *Livesey v Jenkins*, Lord Brandon drew the distinction between obligations which could be the subject of an order of the court and those which could not, pointed out that the latter should be drawn as undertakings, and observed that 'such undertakings are, needless to say, enforceable as effectively as direct orders'.[13] This statement clearly has the unanimous authority of the highest court and must be taken to be correct. Nevertheless, the position is not entirely free from doubt, and it may be that not all undertakings are as easily enforceable as has been suggested.

9.12 Until the decision of the Court of Appeal in *Mubarak v Mubarak*,[14] there was no doubt that an undertaking by one party to pay money to the other party is capable of being enforced by judgment summons.[15]

In an effort to resolve the debates which have raged as to the enforcement of undertakings, Practice Direction 33A now contains detailed guidance. It is provided that any undertaking for the payment of money that has effect as if it was an order made under MCA 1973, Part 2 may be enforced as if it was an order and Part 33 applies accordingly.

The form of any such undertaking must be endorsed with a notice setting out the consequences of disobedience, as follows:

> 'If you fail to pay any sum of money which you have promised the court that you would pay, a person entitled to enforce the undertaking may apply to the court for an order. If it is proved that you have had the means to pay the sum but you have refused or neglected to pay that sum, you may be sent to prison.'

The person giving the undertaking must make a signed statement to the effect that he or she understands the terms of the undertaking being given and the consequences of failure to comply with it, as follows:

> 'I understand the undertaking that I have given, and that if I break my promise to the court to pay any sum of money, I may be sent to prison.'

---

[12]   Though, for the sake of completeness, it may be wise for the undertaking to be expressed as being to the court *and* to the other party.

[13]   [1984] AC 424, HL.

[14]   [2001] 1 FLR 698.

[15]   *Symmons v Symmons* [1993] 1 FLR 317.

The statement need not be given before the court in person (this would obviously be impracticable in the case of consent orders). It may be endorsed on the court copy of the undertaking or may be filed in a separate document such as a letter.

Dismissal of claims and clean break orders

9.13 This is mentioned only for the purpose of underlining what was said on the subject of the clean break in Chapter 2. The justification for a clean break is one of the most common reasons for inquiry and delay in the making of consent orders. The court must ask itself in every case whether, if the case were being considered on a contested basis, the claims of the parties would be dismissed. In Chapter 2 at **2.29** et seq, it is suggested that it may be that the Court of Appeal, by its dicta in recent decisions, has reminded courts that a clean break should certainly not be imposed as a matter of course, and only after careful consideration to ensure that the statutory criteria are met.

Some common faults

9.14 Most of the possible pitfalls have been suggested above. However, care should also be taken to ensure that all dates for the commencement of certain actions, and all matters of detail such as mortgage accounts or insurance policies are inserted; if there are blank spaces left in a form of order this will cause delay.

It is important that the prescribed Statement of Information should be completed in full.

While not, strictly speaking, a fault, one matter which is frequently not provided for is interest on any overdue sum ordered to be paid. It would avoid doubt if this were always included.

FORMS

9.15 Some standard precedents for use as preambles to consent orders will be found at Appendix A, Precedent 31.

Chapter 10

PENSIONS

INTRODUCTION

10.1 After the matrimonial home, a pension fund is, for many people, the most substantial financial investment they will ever make. It is also a resource which is most likely to be lost to one party, usually the wife, on divorce if no action is taken; in most cases a wife will lose the ability to enjoy with her husband not only the benefits of the lump sum and regular payments which he will receive on retirement but also the protection of the benefits which the pension scheme will confer on his death. It is clear that, as a matter of government policy, the value of the state retirement pension will diminish in relative terms in the future and that people will continue to be required to make their own pension provision to supplement the state scheme.

Pensions are therefore of the highest importance when dealing with financial relief. However, it was not until the 1990s that the courts were given any specific powers to make orders dealing with pensions. The present law on the subject remains complicated and can only be understood if explained in terms of its evolution. First, however, the various types of pension should be outlined.

There are effectively four[1] basic types of pension which the reader may meet. They are:

- Occupational salary related pensions – ie schemes set up by employers for the benefit of their employees where the beneficiary receives a pension on retirement calculated upon a formula based upon the salary earned by the employee and number of years of service. Most schemes had been based upon the final salary at retirement but increasingly schemes have adopted an average salary over years of employment. These schemes are also known as 'defined benefit' schemes and are common in the public sector and in many substantial companies. They are, however, very expensive for the employer and as a result many companies have moved to a different structure of pension scheme.

- Occupational money purchase schemes – again these are schemes set up by employers for the benefit of employees with contributions paid regularly by the employee and the employer which are invested. On retirement the employee is provided with a fund with which to purchase

---

[1] Before July 1988 it was possible also to invest in a Retirement Annuity Contract, but this has been replaced by the present form of personal pension scheme.

an annuity. Effectively this is therefore a long term savings plan with the added tax advantages which apply for pensions. Unlike defined benefit schemes the employee will not know exactly how much he or she will receive on retirement as it will depend upon the success of the investment and the cost of purchasing an annuity at the time of retirement. These schemes are also known as 'defined contribution' schemes and have become increasingly popular with employers as they provide a much cheaper way of providing pensions for employees.

- Personal pension schemes – these bear many similarities with occupational money purchase schemes as the contributions are paid to a pension provider for investment. On retirement the beneficiary may choose to purchase an annuity or draw down the fund over the years permitted under the legislation and may also be able to take 25% of the fund on retirement in cash. Personal pension schemes are therefore based upon the contributions made by an individual rather than those of an employer. Stakeholder schemes are very similar to personal pension schemes and there are other forms of personal pension which the reader may have contact with such as Self Invested Personal Pension Schemes (SIPPS) which again are a form of long term investment with tax benefits.

- State pensions – the basic state pension is based upon National Insurance Contributions paid during working life. It is paid from state pension age and it is governmental policy to increase the state pension age over time. In addition to the basic state pension there are also 'additional state pensions' provided under the state earnings related pension scheme (SERPS) and the state second pension (S2P). The additional state pensions were intended to supplement the basic state pension provision for those who did not have an employer's scheme to join. However in the 2012 budget the Government announced plans to move to a single tier pension scheme (replacing the existing three tier system of a basic pension, additional state pension and graduated pensions) for people retiring from 2017. The new flat rate scheme will not be eligible for pension sharing.

It is important to establish what type of pension is being considered and also to consider what form of benefits will be provided under the scheme upon retirement. As has been seen, salary-based schemes are particularly valuable as the benefits to be received on retirement are defined based upon years of service and the salary earned. In contrast money purchase type schemes (whether occupational or under personal schemes) are dependent upon other factors such as the success of the investment policies employed and the cost of providing an annuity on retirement. Some schemes, for example those which apply for the uniformed services, may provide for retirement at an age substantially lower than that which applies under the state scheme or most other occupational type schemes. Schemes may also provide for lump sums payable on death in service and for a lump sum to be taken on retirement in commutation of pension benefits.

The various ways in which a pension may now be dealt with by the court may be summarised as follows:

(1) as a general resource available for offsetting under MCA 1973, s 25B and s 25C;

(2) attachment under MCA 1973, ss 25B–25D;

(3) pension sharing.

Not all of these possibilities may be available in every case and it is particularly important when considering a variation of an order to check when the petition for divorce was initially filed as the court's powers to make orders for attachment or pension sharing were only introduced in 1996 and 2000 respectively. The various types of remedy will be compared in later sections of this chapter.

There is one further possibility which must also be examined, namely loss of pension as an example of hardship enabling a party to defend certain divorce proceedings under MCA 1973, s 10. This is considered in more detail later in this chapter.

Procedural aspects relating to pensions are considered in more detail in Chapter 16.

EVOLUTION OF THE COURTS' POWERS RELATING TO PENSIONS

10.2 Until 1996 the courts had no specific powers to deal with pension provision held by one party to the marriage. The pension benefits which one party had accrued were a resource to which the court would have regard under MCA 1973, s 25. If the pension was already in payment then it could be used to fund periodical payments to the other party and if a lump sum had been paid to the pension scheme member it could be used to finance a lump sum to the other party. However, the courts had no power to make orders which would share pension benefits which had accrued but which were not in payment or to attach part of those benefits in favour of the other party. The party with pension rights would therefore retain those rights on divorce and the other party would be deprived of any benefit arising from them including the benefit of sharing in the pension paid to the pension scheme member (including the lump sum) and any entitlement to a widow's pension payable on the death of that member. The court's only option was to take into account the fact that the pension scheme member would retain these pension benefits on divorce and 'offset' that by providing the other party with a larger share of the other resources.

A number of the relevant cases decided at this time focused upon the way in which the courts should take into account the benefits that had accrued under a pension scheme where the date at which the pension scheme member could claim the benefits was still many years away. For example, in *Hedges v Hedges*[2] where the pension was not payable for 20 years, Mustill LJ said:

> 'I note the existence of this sum but it seems to me that the time when it would fall to hand is so remote that is has little relevance except as a piece of background.'

In *Milne v Milne*,[3] however, after a 33-year marriage where the husband was a member of a pension scheme and had up to 10 years still to serve, the wife was awarded a lump sum equivalent to one half of the amount to which the husband or his estate should become entitled under the scheme, provided she was still surviving at that time. In *H v H (Financial Provision: Capital Allowance)*,[4] the pension had been earned over 13 years of service. Only 7 of those years were years of cohabitation. Thorpe J said that it was more important to look to '… the value of what has been earned during cohabitation than to look to the prospective value of what may be earned over the course of 25 or 30 years between separation and retirement age'

Although the courts therefore had the power to make lump sum orders as demonstrated by *Milne v Milne*, which could in some way share the benefits that had accrued through the pension scheme, the fact that in many cases pension benefits were not due to the member for many years and the lack of bespoke powers to deal with pensions therefore significantly limited the court's powers to deal fairly with pension assets on divorce. In cases where, as in *Hedges*, it was determined that the time for benefits was too remote, the pension scheme member would be left with the entire benefit with no 'compensatory' provision for the other party.

1996 reforms

10.3 The first set of reforms dealing specifically with pensions were inserted into MCA 1973 as ss 25B–25D and have been in force since 1 August 1996. The reforms apply to petitions filed after 1 July 1996. If a petition was filed before that date but an answer or cross petition was filed afterwards then the reforms do not apply.

These provisions had two main consequences. First of all, they prescribe the matters to which the court is to have regard in respect of pensions and secondly, they confer new powers on the courts to make orders directed to the trustees of pension schemes, including powers to order a lump sum to be paid from a pension scheme and to provide for what was then known as 'earmarking' of pension benefits (now known as 'attachment').

---

2   [1991] 1 FLR 196, [1991] Fam Law 267, CA.
3   (1981) 2 FLR 286, CA.
4   [1993] 2 FLR 335, [1993] Fam Law 520, FD.

The court's powers to make pension attachment orders will be considered in detail later in this chapter.

Matters to which the court must have regard

10.4 It is provided that the matters to which the court is to have regard under s 25(2) include:[5]

> '(a) in the case of paragraph (a) [ie the financial resources of the parties] any benefits under a pension arrangement which a party to the marriage has or is likely to have, and
> (b) in the case of paragraph (h) [ie the value to the parties of any benefit to be lost by reason of the divorce or annulment] any benefits under a pension arrangement which by reason of the dissolution or annulment of the marriage, a party to the marriage will lose the chance of acquiring,
>
> and, accordingly, in relation to benefits under a pension arrangement, section 25(2)(a) above shall have effect as if "in the foreseeable future" were omitted.'

Section 25(2)(a) requires the court to have regard to the financial resources which a party has 'or is likely to have in the foreseeable future'. The specific disapplication of these words means that the court is required to have regard to any pension benefit which either party is likely to have at any time, however far in the future; however, as will be seen, the fact that the court takes such matters into account does not in itself prescribe any particular method of dealing with them. A pension fund is, thus, a resource like any other and must be included in any list of assets supplied to the court.[6]

Paragraph (h), referred to in s 25B(1)(b), refers to 'the value to each of the parties ... of any benefit which, by reason of the divorce or annulment of the marriage, that party will lose the chance of acquiring'. Section 25B(1)(b) therefore makes specific what was implied in s 25(2)(h), namely that the court must look at the value of lost benefits, and the most significant aspect of this will normally be lost widow's benefits. These will be considered at **10.12**.

2000 reforms

10.5 As will be seen later the utility of the court's powers to make attachment orders was of limited effect. There was increasing pressure for the courts to be able to make orders which enabled them to permanently divide pensions which had been built up by the parties during the marriage. As a result the Welfare Reforms and Pensions Act 1999, which came into force on 1 December 2000, provided the courts with the power to make pension sharing orders. It only applies to pensions where the petition for divorce or nullity of marriage (not

---

5   MCA 1973, s 25B(1).
6   See Form E, para 2.16.

judicial separation) was filed after 1 December 2000, and for the first time enabled the court to effectively create two separate pensions from the pension member's scheme.

Summary so far

10.6 It can therefore be seen that the court's armoury of powers to deal with pensions is as follows:

(1) Pension sharing (where the petition was filed after 1 December 2000).

(2) Pension attachment (where the petition was filed on or after 1 July 1996).

(3) Offsetting (having taken into account the factors set out in s 25B and s 25C of MCA 1973) regardless of the date of petition.

Having briefly considered the range of powers available to the court when dealing with pensions, consideration must now be given to the way in which the benefits are to be valued for the purpose of the s 25 calculation and the circumstances in which they will be sufficiently significant to have an effect on the order.

VALUATION

10.7 The 1973 Act[7] provides for regulations to be made for the value of any benefits under a pension scheme to be calculated and verified for the purpose of orders under s 23. These regulations are contained in the Divorce etc (Pensions) Regulations 2000 (referred to as the 'Pensions Regulations 2000'),[8] the Pensions on Divorce etc (Provision of Information) Regulations 2000 (referred to as the 'Information Regulations 2000'),[9] and the Occupational Pension Schemes (Transfer Values) (Amendment) Regulations 2008 ('the 2008 Regulations').[10] These may be summarised as follows:

(1) The value of pension benefits shall be valued on a date to be specified by the court between one year before the date of petition and the date of order.[11]
The significance of this is not only that any direction by the court should specify the date for valuation but also that, strictly speaking, the court should be invited to specify such a date in all cases.

---

7   MCA 1973, s 25D(2)(e).
8   SI 2000/1123.
9   SI 2000/1048.
10 SI 2008/1050. These of course apply only to occupational pensions and not to the other types outlined at **10.1**.
11 Pensions Regulations 2000, reg 3(1)(a).

(2) If the party is an active member of an occupational pension scheme the value shall be the cash equivalent to which he would have acquired a right under s 94(1)(a) of the Pension Schemes Act 1993 if his pensionable service had terminated at the specified date;[12] if he is a deferred member of such a scheme the value shall be the cash equivalent of his rights acquired at termination of his pensionable service.[13]

(3) If the party is a member of a personal pension scheme the value shall be the cash equivalent to which he would have acquired a right under s 94(1)(b) of the Pension Schemes Act 1993 if he had made an application under s 95(1) at the specified date.[14]

The significance of the references to the 1993 Act is that ss 93–101 of that Act provide for the right of persons in occupational and personal pension schemes to take a 'cash equivalent transfer value' (CETV), and for the method of calculating and taking such value. The Cash Equivalent (CE), is by far the most common form of valuation to be used in cases involving pensions, and includes the value of the member's payment on retirement, the lump sum payable on retirement, the lump sum payable on death after leaving active service but before retirement, the lump sum payable on death after retirement, and the spouse's pension payable on the member's death. It does not include death in service benefits, future expectations nor discretionary benefits.

Because of the 2008 Regulations, different questions may now arise in respect of occupational pensions. Regulation 3 of the Pensions Regulations 2000 has been amended to refer merely to 'cash equivalents' (CE) and a new category of valuations has been established.[15]

(4) Managers of pension schemes must provide a CE to a party on request or when ordered within the period of 3 months beginning with the date of the request.[16]

(5) When asked, the managers must specify what proportion of the CE is attributable to any pension or other periodical payments to which a spouse of the member would or might become entitled in the event of the member's death.[17]

10.8 Although the CE is the conventional method of valuation, it is not the only one, and this method is not without its critics. It is sometimes argued that in defined contribution or money purchase schemes the CE is likely to be less than the actual value of the fund accrued for the member due to certain costs being deducted. In contrast in final salary and defined benefit schemes, the CE

---

[12] Information Regulations 2000, reg 3(3).
[13] Information Regulations 2000, reg 3(4).
[14] Information Regulations 2000, reg 3(5).
[15] For more detail on this complicated topic see David Salter 'Pension Transfer Values: The New Regime' [2008] Fam Law 1205.
[16] Information Regulations 2000, reg 2.
[17] Information Regulations 2000, reg 5.

may be considerably less than the true value of the lost benefits as the scheme actuary may adopt conservative assumptions to protect the remaining scheme members. Changes in the way CEs are calculated may also have a considerable impact. For example in 2011 the Government announced that price indexation of the benefits in public sector schemes would be calculated by using the Consumer Prices Index (CPI) rather than the Retail Prices Index (RPI). The RPI is usually a higher figure and as a result the CE of many public sector schemes reduced significantly.

It is therefore important to consider carefully what information has been provided by the pension member about the value of the benefits he has accrued within the pension scheme and whether any additional information is required to establish whether the figures provided represent a 'fair value'.

Obtaining basic information has been easier since the introduction of 'Form P' in 2005 which enables relevant information to be provided by the pension provider with authority given voluntarily by the scheme member or as directed in a court order.

In certain cases it is still important to consider whether an independent assessment of the true value of the pension benefits should be obtained from a pension actuary. This may be particularly important in defined benefits schemes and especially in those which provide for earlier than usual retirement dates such as in the uniformed services. It has also been necessary to calculate the percentage of the CE which will be required to provide each party with an equal income from the pension benefits accrued at retirement as the longer life expectancy for women meant that the cost of acquiring pension benefits for them was greater than for men. However a decision of the European Court of Justice in March 2011 that pricing insurance premiums based on life expectancy in this way was gender discrimination and would not be permitted from December 2012 also impacts on both the CE and the way in which the benefits need to be divided to ensure equality of income.

The court cannot, in principle, depart from the CE method of valuation, but it may be persuaded to take other matters into account, provided they were supported by expert evidence. In particular, evidence of matters not included in the CE, such as death in service benefits or discretionary benefits, might be admissible, as might evidence as to future expectations where it is deemed that the CE provided an inadequate indication as to its value.

10.9   Valuation of a pension in payment is a more open question. As was seen at **10.7**, the court has a complete discretion. One answer might be to do a *Duxbury* calculation.[18] It should also be noted that there is no prescribed method of valuation of either future pension rights or death in service benefits.

---

[18]   See **4.14**.

What weight is to be attached to the value of the benefits?

10.10 Having established the value of benefits, normally by a CE, what does the court do with it? What figure is to be brought into the calculation of assets? As has been seen, a pension is a unique type of asset. It has some similarities (particularly in the case of money purchase or personal pension schemes) with long term investment plans but the CE provides a capitalised value for an asset that has a restricted use in that it must be utilised to provide a long term income stream. How then should the courts compare the value of a pension with other assets such as the value of the matrimonial home, other investments or even the income that will be generated from one party's employment?. This is an issue which has concerned the courts in a number of cases when considering how to deal with pensions.

Although the pensions in the case were pensions in payment, the comments of Thorpe LJ in *Martin-Dye v Martin-Dye*[19] may be taken to be relevant to all pensions. His Lordship saw the matter as follows:

> 'Our focus is upon pensions in payment and cash equivalent benefits. They are to be characterised as "other financial resources" within the s 25(2)(a) classification. For they do not sit comfortably in the category of "property", since they are unrealisable and non-transferable. Nor do they sit comfortably in the category of "income" because, although purely an income stream, the income does not derive from future endeavour but from past employment or contribution which will generally have been effected during the years of marriage.
>
> This case provides a useful example of this analysis. The "property" consists of the houses and the investments. The "income" is the receipts anticipated from the parties continuing endeavours, the wife in her livery business and the husband in his fitted kitchen business. The "other financial resources" are their respective pensions in payment.'

Both Thorpe LJ and Dyson LJ agreed that it was artificial to regard pensions as being the same as other assets. In the words of Dyson LJ:

> 'It seems to me that in a case such as this the better course is to take the pensions out of the assets altogether and to make a pension-sharing order. This reflects the reality that the pensions are in truth non-transferable income streams and are quite different in kind from the other assets owned by the parties. In my judgment, it is artificial to say that the pensions are capital assets valued at £940,000 (husband) and £100,000 (wife). The reality is that the sole value of their pensions to the parties is that they produce gross incomes of £37,840 and £5,818 respectively. In my judgment, the judge below, in effect, mischaracterised the pensions as being, or being equivalent to, capital assets.'

In *Maskell v Maskell*[20] Thorpe LJ observed that the judge had made the seemingly somewhat elementary mistake of confusing present capital with a

---

[19] [2006] EWCA Civ 681, [2006] 2 FLR 901.
[20] [2001] EWCA Civ 858, [2003] 1 FLR 1138, CA.

right to financial benefits on retirement, only 25% of which maximum could be taken in capital terms, the other 75% being taken as an annuity stream. He simply failed to compare like with like.

However that is not to say there are never cases in which the court should aggregate the value of pensions with other assets. In his judgment in *Martin-Dye*, Dyson LJ said:

> 'But I do not read Thorpe LJ as saying that, as a matter of law, it is never open to the court to aggregate the value of pensions with that of other assets and distribute the resultant total value between the parties. Examples of where such an approach might be appropriate could be where the parties have pensions in payment which are of approximately equal value and/or where the value of the pensions is small in comparison with that of the other assets. It will all depend in the particular circumstances of the case.'

An example of case in which this was done is *Norris v Norris*.[21]

. As with so many aspects of s 25, there is no universal way of dealing with the weight to be attached to the value of pension benefits when apportioning assets on divorce. Each case must be viewed on its own facts but there are a number of points which can be validly made:

(1)   How valuable are the pensions? If they are of low value either as assets in their own right or as a proportion of the overall assets available in the case then it is more likely that the court will approach matters on the basis that the pension provision will be retained by the party who has the benefit without a substantial impact upon the overall division of the other assets.

(2)   How old are the parties and when will they expect the pension benefits to come into payment? Generally speaking the younger the parties are, the less significance the pension benefits will have on the overall division unless they reflect a substantial proportion of the overall assets. For older parties, however, the pensions may be a resource from which they may need to draw income in the relatively near future and active consideration must be given to using the pension benefits in a way which can provide for the needs of both parties in this way.

(3)   How long was the marriage and when were the pension benefits accrued? It is not uncommon for the pension benefits held by one party to have been built up over a substantial number of years before the marriage. In these cases reliance is frequently put upon the decision of Thorpe J in *H v H (Financial Provision: Capital Allowance)*[22] where the pension had been earned over 13 years of service but only 7 of those years were years when the parties were cohabiting during their marriage. Thorpe J said that it was more important to look to 'the value of what has been earned during

---

[21]   [2003] EWCA Civ 1084, [2003] 2 FLR 1124.
[22]   [1993] 2 FLR 335, [1993] Fam Law 520, FD.

cohabitation than to look to the prospective value of what may be earned over the course of the 25 or 30 years between separation and retirement age'. His approach in this case is often used to support a contention that the CE should be divided by the number of years' service so far and then multiplied by the length of the marriage (including pre-marital cohabitation where the parties proceeded seamlessly into marriage). It is noteworthy, however, that this decision was made before any of the pension reforms had been implemented and before the sea change in the courts' approach to division of capital which followed the decision of the House of Lords in *White v White*.[23] It is submitted that it may now be more appropriate to treat a pension which had been built up significantly during the period prior to a marriage as a contribution which one party has brought into the marriage. The court can then give appropriate weight to the value of the contribution when dividing up the assets rather than applying a formulaic approach which contrasts with the Court's general approach to dividing assets. However this must still be subject to the court's overriding duty to deal with a case in a way which provides a fair outcome and in particular to the importance of considering both parties' needs.

Summary

10.11 It is therefore recommended that when preparing a schedule of assets the value of the parties' pension provision should be set out in the overall capital summary but as a discrete item. In this way the overall position will be clear but attention will also be focused upon whether to make a 'bespoke order' in relation to the pension provision (probably by a pension sharing order) or to deal with any disparity in provision by offsetting.

LOSS OF WIDOW'S PENSION RIGHTS

10.12 On divorce or annulment of marriage, the party who is not a pension scheme member (normally the wife) is liable to lose two classes of benefits. The first, namely loss of the chance of sharing in the benefits payable under the scheme on retirement, has already been considered. The second is just as important for many wives; this is loss of the benefits of a widow's pension in the event of a husband's death. As has been seen, the court is specifically directed to have regard to the benefits under a pension scheme which a party to the marriage will lose the chance of acquiring.[24]

10.13 The value of the lost benefits should be comparatively simple to ascertain, since an obligation is imposed on managers or trustees of a pension scheme to specify what proportion of the CE is attributable to any pension or other periodical payments to which a spouse of the member would be or might

---

[23] [2000] 2 FLR 981.
[24] MCA 1973, s 25(2)(h).

become entitled in the event of the member's death.[25] However, once again, the CE method may be criticised on the ground that the proportion specified will represent only the estimated cost of providing a pension to an average widow of the member and presupposes termination of service as at the date of valuation. By contrast, s 25(2)(h) clearly requires consideration of the potential loss in the event that service is completed to normal retirement date. There may therefore be scope for expert evidence to supplement the CE information in appropriate cases.

10.14 Having established a figure for the value of the lost benefits, the next calculation is that of the sum which might be paid to compensate the wife for the loss of the chance of acquiring the widow's pension. This figure will be the sum which she would need to buy an annuity which would come into payment on her husband's death.[26] Both these figures should therefore be available for the use of the court.

However, it should not be supposed that a lump sum of this nature will be awarded as a matter of right in all cases. Where the value of the lost benefits is taken into account it will normally be as part of a greater lump sum which takes account of other matters, and any award will only be made after consideration of all the s 25 factors.

10.15 There is another area in which loss of widow's benefits is highly relevant, namely a divorce suit which is defended on the ground of grave financial hardship.[27] All that has been said so far is equally applicable to that class of case.

In such cases, if a respondent wife establishes a prima facie case of grave financial hardship, it is for the husband to make proposals to mitigate the hardship; if he does not do so, the petition must be dismissed. However, it would be wrong to suppose that a wife is entitled to be compensated pound for pound for what she will lose in consequence of the divorce; she has to show not that she will lose something by being divorced but that she will suffer grave financial hardship, which is a very different thing.[28]

It has been held that the proper approach for the court is first to determine whether it has been established that grave financial hardship will result from the divorce and secondly to decide whether in all the circumstances the marriage should be dissolved.[29] In many cases, the issue may be whether the husband is, in fact, in a position to do anything to remedy the hardship; the availability of State benefits will also be relevant.[30]

---

[25]   Information Regulations 2000, reg 2.
[26]   Tables for calculating the value of the lost benefits and of the cost of a replacement annuity will be found at table 16 of *At a Glance*. These should be used as a guide.
[27]   Under MCA 1973, s 5.
[28]   *Le Marchant v Le Marchant* [1977] 1 WLR 559, CA.
[29]   *Jackson v Jackson* [1993] 2 FLR 848, CA.
[30]   Ibid.

In another case[31] where the husband was a serving police officer, after a long marriage it was held that the husband's proposals came nowhere near mitigating the hardship; the hearing was adjourned generally to enable the parties to negotiate further.

WHAT ORDERS MAY BE MADE?

10.16 There follows separate sections on the type of orders the court can make namely pension sharing orders, pension attachment orders and offsetting orders. For the sake of completeness, it should be stated that the court may also make a lump sum order if, for example, the pension has recently come into payment and a lump sum has been paid to the pension member or make a periodical payments order against the pension scheme member using the income from his pension to fund the payments.

PENSION SHARING ORDERS

10.17 Pension sharing orders were introduced following the enactment of the Welfare Reform and Pensions Act 1999. They are therefore the most recent weapon in the court's armoury and are only available in cases where a petition for divorce or nullity was presented after 1 December 2000. Although they are the most recent addition to the court's powers, pension sharing orders have now become relatively routine and appear to be the most common method of dealing with pensions within ancillary relief proceedings. They are therefore worthy of the first consideration in this section.

10.18 A pension sharing order is defined under MCA 1973, s 21A as an order which:

(a) provides that one party's:

    (i) shareable rights under a specified pension arrangement; or
    (ii) shareable state scheme rights
    be subject to pension sharing for the benefit of the other party; and

(b) specifies the percentage value to be transferred.

Shareable rights under a specified pension arrangement refers to rights under a 'private' pension scheme (whether an occupational or personal scheme). Shareable state scheme rights refer to the rights under the state pension scheme. It is important to emphasise that only the additional state pension can be the subject of a pension sharing order. A pension sharing order cannot be made in respect of a basic state pension.

---

[31] *K v K (Financial Relief: Widow's Pension)* [1997] 1 FLR 35, FD.

10.19   Once implementation takes place, a pension sharing order results in the legal transfer of a specified proportion of the scheme member's pension rights to the other party. A 'pension debit' is applied to the transferor's fund reducing the value of his fund or benefits and a 'pension credit' is created for the transferee. The parties will then have separate pension rights in their own name completely independent of each other.

10.20   It is important to emphasise that it is the value of the cash equivalent of the transferor's relevant benefits on the valuation day which are subject to pension sharing. The percentage specified in the order will then be applied to that figure. The valuation on the implementation date will be likely to be different to the CE figure upon which the negotiations and court hearing have taken place. The figure may be more or less than the one used for that purpose.

The impact of this was illustrated in *H v H (Financial Relief: Pensions)*.[32] Baron J held that a pension sharing order can only be expressed as a straight percentage of the fund value. In that case the judge had originally awarded a pension sharing order of 48.49% which was equivalent to £900,000. There had, however, been a substantial delay during which period the husband's pension had increased in value by 10% as a result of in changes in the stock market. He had kept the wife's £900,000 in cash which had not therefore increased in the same manner. Baron J confirmed that the wife was to have 48.49% of the current value of the pension irrespective of the substantial increase in value since the date of the order, rather than the figure which the husband had retained in cash.

The person responsible for the pension arrangement has a period of time in which to effect the pension sharing and transfer the pension credit to the transferee. The implementation period is 4 months beginning with the day on which the order takes effect or the day on which the person responsible for the pension arrangement receives the order and prescribed information, whichever is the later. The prescribed information is contained in reg 5 of the Information Regulations 2000 and includes such matters as dates of birth, national insurance numbers and addresses. The information is now set out in the prescribed pension sharing annex form.

10.21   In some cases the party benefiting from the pension sharing order will remain within the original pension scheme (an internal transfer) and in other cases may transfer the pension credit into another scheme (an external transfer). In the case of most pension schemes an external transfer must be offered as an option. This is consistent with the general rules that apply to pensions enabling a scheme member to transfer his pension scheme into another scheme prior to the benefits becoming payable. However, in unfunded non-contributory public sector schemes such as those that apply for teachers, the NHS and uniformed services only an internal transfer will be permitted so that the beneficiary of the pension sharing order will become a member of that

---

[32]   [2009] EWHC 3739 (Fam), [2010] 2 FLR 173.

pension scheme. Some private sector schemes will offer the beneficiary of the pension sharing order the option of an internal transfer as well as an external transfer. It is, however, important to emphasise that even where an internal transfer takes place the pension credit remains entirely separate from and independent of the original member's pension rights. When considering the relative merits of an internal or external transfer if both options are available it is important to obtain expert advice.

Restrictions on making pension sharing orders

10.22 A pension sharing order may be made on divorce against one or more pensions. However, MCA 1973, s 24B provides that a pension sharing order may not be made in relation to a pension arrangement which is already the subject of a pension sharing order in relation to the marriage or has been the subject of pension sharing between the parties. On a variation a second pension sharing order cannot be made against the same pension. Furthermore a pension sharing order may not be made in relation to shareable state scheme rights if a pension sharing order has already been made in relation to those rights between the parties to the marriage. A pension sharing order may also not be made in relation to the rights of a person under a pension arrangement if there is in force a pension attachment order under s 25B or s 25C.

In summary, therefore, if there has already been a pension sharing order in relation to the same marriage then no pension sharing order (nor indeed an attachment order) is possible in relation to the same pension arrangement.

If there has been a prior pension sharing order made in relation to a previous marriage then pension sharing or an attachment order may be made in relation to the same pension arrangement. However, if there is a prior attachment order in force in relation to any marriage then no pension sharing order is possible in relation to the same pension arrangement.

PENSION ATTACHMENT (FORMERLY KNOWN AS EARMARKING)

10.23 Pension attachment orders (then known as earmarking) were one of the principal innovations of the changes introduced by the Pensions Act 1995 and now found in MCA 1973, ss 25B–25D. These orders are available for petitions filed after 1 July 1996 and are available upon a decree of divorce, nullity or judicial separation.

It is important to emphasise that attachment orders are not a separate form of financial provision order. They are orders for payment of periodical payments and lump sum orders pursuant to MCA 1973, s 23 against benefits held by the pension scheme member and providing for a proportion of the pension payments to be made direct to the former spouse by the pension provider at the time of payment. They are, therefore, effectively a form of enforcement of a periodical payments or lump sum order operating in a similar way to an attachment of earnings order against the member's pension provision.

10.24   The relevant statutory provisions, which apply whenever, having regard to any benefits under a pension scheme, the court determines to make an order under s 23, are as follows:[33]

'(4)   To the extent to which the order [ie the s 23 order] is made having regard to any benefits under a pension arrangement, the order may require the person responsible for the pension arrangement in question, if at any time any payment in respect of any benefits under the arrangement becomes due to the party with pension rights, to make a payment for the benefit of the other party.

(5)   The order must express the amount of any payment required to be made by virtue of subsection (4) as a percentage of the payment which becomes due to the party with pension rights.

(6)   Any such payment by the person responsible for the arrangement—
    (a)   shall discharge so much of his liability to the party with pension rights as corresponds to the amount of the payment, and
    (b)   shall be treated for all purposes as a payment made by the party with pension rights in or towards the discharge of his liability under the order.

(7)   Where the party with pension rights has a right of commutation under the arrangement, the order may require him to exercise it to any extent; and this section applies to any payment due in consequence of commutation in pursuance of the order as it applies to other payments in respect of benefits under the arrangement.'

10.25   The remaining statutory provisions are concerned exclusively with lump sums due under the pension scheme on death; they apply whenever the benefits which the party with pension rights has or is likely to have under a pension scheme include any lump sum payable in respect of his death. In such cases, the court may:[34]

'(a)   if the person responsible for the pension arrangement in question has power to determine the person to whom the sum, or any part of it, is to be paid, require him to pay the whole or part of that sum, when it becomes due, to the other party,

(b)   if the party with pension rights has power to nominate the person to whom the sum or any part of it is to be paid, require the party with pension rights to nominate the other party in respect of the whole or part of that sum,

(c)   in any other case, require the person responsible for the pension arrangement in question to pay the whole or part of that sum, when it becomes due, for the benefit of the other party instead of to the party to whom, apart from the order, it would be paid.'

The effect of all these provisions may now be considered.

---

[33]   MCA 1973, s 25B(4)–(7), as amended by WRPA 1999.
[34]   MCA 1973, s 25C(2), as amended by WRPA 1999.

Summary of attachment provisions

10.26 As mentioned above, these provisions came into force on 1 August 1996, and are only available for petitions filed on or after 1 July 1996 and in respect of applications made on or after 1 August 1996. The position may be summarised as follows.

(1) When the court makes an attachment order, whether by way of periodical payments or lump sum, it can order the trustees or managers (now known as 'the person responsible') to pay it on the husband's behalf.

(2) Payments of periodical payments are paid from the scheme members pension income on which he is taxed.

(3) A periodical payments attachment order is in reality no more than an attachment of earnings order against the pension fund.

(4) A periodical payments attachment order may apply immediately if the pension is in payment or be deferred, ie may be ordered to be paid at some future date and will then be, in effect, a deferred attachment order against the fund.

(5) A periodical payments attachment order will end on the death of either party, and is fully variable; this might mean that it could be varied before it had ever been paid.

(6) When the court is considering making a lump sum attachment order to be paid from pension benefits, it can require the pension fund member to exercise any commutation rights which he may enjoy. This can be for part or all of the benefits, and would be accompanied by an order requiring the trustees or managers to pay the commuted sum to the other party. However, a defect in the provisions is that the court cannot order the member to take his pension at any particular time.

(7) The court can order a lump sum attachment order from death benefits, and can force the member to nominate the other party to receive such death benefits.

(8) All lump sum attachment orders are variable.[35] In this, they are in stark contrast to other lump sum orders. It might be argued that the remarriage of a wife in whose favour such an order had been made would be ground for variation, particularly if her new husband was a man of means although this issue does not appear to have been the subject of any reported decisions.

---

[35] MCA 1973, s 31(2)(dd).

Restrictions on making pension attachment orders

10.27 MCA 1973, s 25B(7B) provides that a pension attachment order may not be made in relation to a pension arrangement which is the subject of a pension sharing order in relation to the same marriage. If, however, a pension sharing order has been made in relation to the pension arrangement in respect of a previous marriage then a pension attachment order may still be made. If, however, there is already in place a pension attachment order relating to any marriage in respect of a pension arrangement then a pension sharing order cannot be made for that pension arrangement. If, however, the pension attachment relates to an earlier divorce then a pension attachment order may still be made in respect of that pension on a subsequent divorce.

Judicial consideration of pension attachment

10.28 The first important case on the earmarking provisions (as they were then called) was the decision of Singer J in *T v T (Financial Relief: Pensions)*.[36] The wife had argued that the new provisions manifested an intention on the part of the legislature to require, and not just enable, a spouse in her position to be compensated for actual and not just potential loss of pension benefits. The judge, however, decided that the statute required the court 'in particular' to have regard to the pension benefits, etc and to consider how pension considerations 'should effect' the terms of the order it intended to make: that formulation in no way precluded the court from giving the answer 'not at all' to that question. He also rejected as unsustainable the wife's submission that the orders which could be made against pension providers were distinct from the other orders which could be made under s 23 and therefore rejected the contention that an attachment maintenance order would not terminate on the wife's remarriage. The wife had also argued for an order which required the trustees to pay her a proportion of the husband's pension on his retirement to reflect the duration of the marriage as a proportion of the time over which the pension benefits had accrued. In this case the pension benefits would not be payable for approximately 14 years after the court decision. A joint lives periodical payments order had been made and the judge saw no advantage in making an order for a deferred pension attachment order at that stage. The court would be in just as an effective a position to consider the quantum and form of the appropriate order at the time that the husband was due to take his pension. The wife had also argued for additional provision to compensate for the potential loss of her widow's pension if the husband predeceased her after commencing drawing his own pension. Again the judge declined to make an order to reflect the wife's potential pension loss and left it open to her to bring claims against the husband's estate. However, the judge did award the wife an order under s 25C(1) for a payment in respect of the lump sum due to the husband in the event of his death in service.

---

[36]   [1998] 1 FLR 1072.

A similar approach was taken in *Burrow v Burrow*[37] in which Cazalet J decided that the provisions of MCA 1973, ss 25B–25D did not create any entitlement as such for the wife to share in the pension provision. In deciding whether to make an attachment order and, if so, determining the quantum of the order, the court must simply exercise its discretion under the s 25 criteria.

10.29 These two cases highlight some of the major disadvantages with pension attachment orders. Perhaps the most important drawback with a periodical payment attachment order is that the order will cease upon the death of the pension scheme member. It only therefore provides limited financial security on retirement. The benefit of a pension attachment periodical payments order is also lost on upon the remarriage of the receiving party. The payments also only become payable once the scheme member draws his pension benefits. The legislation contains no provision for the court to order the benefits to be drawn at a particular date. Pension attachment also effectively prevents a clean break between the parties as the receiving spouse is continuing to receive periodical payments under the pension attachment order.

10.30 Pension attachment can therefore be considered as primarily a mechanism for ensuring that financial provision which is to be made from the proceeds of pension benefits is paid effectively. As such it is a 'means of payment' order rather than a distinct type of financial provision in its own right and provides the non scheme member with very little long term financial security. The court's powers to make orders in relation to death in service benefits can provide some useful 'insurance' for a wife who is dependent on maintenance provision for herself or her children and the power to order a husband to commute part of his benefits provides a useful way of ensuring that a lump sum may be available. However, the effect of these drawbacks and restrictions have led to pension attachment orders rarely being made particularly since pension sharing was implemented.

OFFSETTING

10.31 As has been emphasised offsetting is not a form of pension order. It is simply a way in which the court takes into account the fact that one party will retain certain pension benefits when dividing up the other available assets between the parties. One party therefore receives a larger share of the other assets to 'compensate' for the fact that the other party will retain the pension. The courts can obviously achieve this by using other financial provision powers including lump sum and periodical payments or property adjustment orders.

However, the difficulties referred to above in valuing and deciding what weight to give to pension benefits apply particularly when considering offsetting. How is the court to compare the value of the other available assets with that of the pension?

---

[37] [1999] 1 FLR 508.

What consideration should be given to, for example, the limited utility of the pension as a result of its restricted use or the impact of taxation. The reader is referred to the comments of the Court of Appeal in the *Maskell* and *Martin-Dye* cases referred to above to illustrate the difficulties which the courts have had in weighing up these issues.

In some cases additional evidence, often from an actuary, is provided to support considerations about the value to be taken into account when offsetting.

However, in practice it appears that the main drivers in determining what type of order will be made are the value of the pension provision, the availability of other resources and the parties' own priorities. If a pension sharing order is the preference then provided that the pension is not so small that the costs of implementation will be disproportionate then it will be made.

However, if offsetting is the preference then the amount will usually be determined by the size of the other resources that are available and the parties other needs for the use of those resources.

THE PENSION PROTECTION FUND

10.32 During periods of economic instability many defined benefit pension schemes established by employers have foundered when the company itself had had financial difficulties leaving the pension scheme unable to pay the benefits promised to its members.

In order to alleviate the hardship this caused to pension scheme members the Pension Protection Fund (PPF) was set up with effect from 6 April 2005 by the Pensions Act 2004. The PPF is effectively a form of insurance that can provide compensation to members of certain schemes where the employer is insolvent and has insufficient funds to pay the members' benefits.

After the qualifying insolvency event the pension scheme will enter a period of assessment of at least 12 months. If after the assessment period the scheme cannot meet its obligations the PPF assumes responsibility for it. As at February 2013 the PPF had taken responsibility for 595 schemes containing 153,101 members.

Benefits paid by the Pension Protection Fund

10.33 The members of schemes accepted into the PPF receive the following compensation:

- where the member had already reached retirement age – 100% of their benefits

- for a member who had not reached normal retirement age – 90% of benefits once they reach 65

In both cases the benefits payable are subject to the PPF cap of £34,867.04 at age 65 (as at April 2013). However the PPF does not provide any compensation for death in service benefits.

Court's powers to make orders where the Pension Protection Fund is involved

10.34 The PPF was not a pension arrangement against which a pension sharing order could be made. However the Pension Act 2008 introduced a number of additional provisions to the Matrimonial Causes Act 1973 enabling the courts to make specific orders in cases in which a party is receiving compensation under the PPF scheme and the relevant procedures are set out in FPR 2010 and the Pension Protection Fund (Pension Compensation Sharing and attachment on divorce etc) Regulations 2011[38] both of which came into effect on 6 April 2011.

The new provisions mean that a court can make a pension compensation sharing order (s 21B Matrimonial Causes Act 1973) and also enables the court to make pension compensation attachment orders (s 25A Matrimonial Causes Act 1973), which require the PPF to make the payment directly to and for the benefit of the other party.

Even if a petition/application for financial remedy had been issued prior to 6 April 2011 it can be amended to enable the party to apply for a pension compensation sharing or attachment order. Details of the procedure are set out in Chapter 16.

Orders made prior to the Pension Protection Fund assuming responsibility

10.35 Some orders may have been made but not implemented before the PPF took responsibility for the pension scheme. A pension sharing or attachment order may still be made using the usual procedure and CE valuation during the assessment period. However if the PPF assumes responsibility for the scheme at the end of the assessment period any outstanding pension sharing or attachment orders are implemented by the PPF.

Once the PPF assumes responsibility pension sharing and attachment orders are no longer available and the party must instead seek a pension compensation sharing order or pension compensation attachment order against the PPF using the new provisions.

---

[38] SI 2011/731.

Valuation of PPF benefits

10.36　Where an application is being made for a pension compensation sharing order or pension compensation attachment order a valuation should be requested. The valuation is the CE of providing the PPF benefit to the member on the date that the request is received.

HOW SHOULD THE COURT APPROACH THE USE OF ITS POWERS IN RELATION TO PENSIONS?

10.37　Before considering the question of how the court's armoury of powers should be deployed, the more fundamental question of what the court is trying to do in any particular case will have to be considered. The value of any benefits or potential benefits under the pension arrangement must first be ascertained; this has to be by way of the CE, but evidence may be admissible to show that the CE figure states the true value. In the current economic climate, when many occupational schemes are underfunded, new problems have arisen and the situation has not been helped by the 2008 Regulations which provide for new ways of valuing occupational pensions. Public service pensions are normally immune from market turmoil and therefore care must be taken not to carry out an exact 'like-for-like' comparison of such a pension with a pension which is not public service.

These are complicated issues and the advice of a pensions consultant is normally a wise investment.

Once the value is known, that figure is considered together with the values of the other assets and liabilities. What does the court do next?[39]

10.38　Pensions are part of the overall exercise to be performed under s 25. It used to be said that there was no intrinsic reason why the property rights of parties should be disturbed and that redistribution in itself was not the purpose of the litigation. Such a confident statement is no longer possible, and the reader is referred to the section on equality and fairness at **1.8** et seq. It is suggested that the court will now be concerned with equality of outcome where pensions are concerned and that overall fairness is likely to be an increasing preoccupation.

10.39　Assuming that the husband in most cases is the pension scheme member and that the wife has little or no pension provision, most cases will be approached on the basis of first considering whether or not the wife's reasonable needs include a need for pension provision. It is submitted that this is normally by no means the most pressing need, and the need for housing for

---

[39]　In what follows, the present author, by a different route, has come to roughly the same conclusions as those contained in an article entitled 'Pensions on divorce – Compensation or needs?' by Catherine Hallam and David Salter in [1997] Fam Law 608. A careful reading of that article is recommended.

the wife (and any dependent children) and her need for income would have been considered as the first priorities. However, assuming those needs to have been met, either from the wife's own resources or from redistribution of the assets, the pension position must be considered.

10.40 It is assumed that, in the kind of case in which pensions are relevant, the husband has some pension rights. It must further be assumed that his own needs for housing, income, etc have been met; in most cases it would clearly be wrong, for example, to provide the funds for the wife to re-house herself, to leave the husband with no adequate provision for housing and then to seek to attack his pension which might be the only asset or security he had left.

Given those assumptions, the pension needs of the wife would have to be considered. In considering these, the following questions would be relevant.

(1) How old is the wife? It seems to be generally accepted that the younger the parties (particularly the wife), and the longer the time before retirement, the less relevant is the pension issue. Quite how long this period has to be to make it irrelevant is debatable.[40] Clearly, a wife aged under 30, perhaps even under 35, would find it difficult to mount a successful attack on a husband's pension. Equally clearly, a wife aged over 50 would have little problem. Between those ages exists an area of uncertainty and potential for litigation.

(2) How old is the husband and how soon will the pension become payable? This question may be particularly relevant when there is a significant discrepancy in the parties' ages.

(3) In the light of all the circumstances of the case, what are the wife's reasonable needs? In the context of pensions, these needs might be subdivided into need for income after the retirement of the husband or after his death, and need for capital after his retirement or death. Where there is an order for periodical payments without limit, clearly there will be a need for a continuing source of income; this might be met by means of periodical payments or by a one-off capital payment. The position of the wife if the husband dies must be considered.

10.41 Having decided what the needs of the wife are, what is available must be considered; it is, of course, necessary to remember that the husband is entitled to a pension as well, so that his needs must be considered unless it seems that he will be able to provide adequately for himself from other assets. The needs of the wife might be met by one of the orders now to be considered.

In *Maskell v Maskell*[41] it was held that comparing present capital with a right to future benefits on retirement was not a like-for-like comparison. The judge

---

[40] See e g *H v H (Financial Provision: Capital Allowance)* [1993] 2 FLR 335 and *Hedges v Hedges* [1991] 1 FLR 196.
[41] [2001] EWCA Civ 858, [2003] 1 FLR 1138.

had confused present capital with a right to future financial benefits: only 25% could be taken as capital and the remainder as an annuity stream. This was an elementary mistake.

Points to consider when considering the use of the courts' powers to deal with pensions

Pension sharing orders

10.42 These powers are particularly useful for ensuring that incomes can be provided in retirement for both parties in a case in which one party has the majority of the pension assets. A pension sharing order provides security for the non-pension member spouse who will have ownership of her own scheme which is not in any way dependent upon the former spouse. It will enable the parties to proceed with a clean break.

However, there remain some significant disadvantages. The costs of pension sharing can be significant particularly where the pension benefits are relatively small. Problems may also arise where there is a significant age gap between the parties and the pension member will be entitled to draw his pension soon, although there is a significant delay before the non pension member can draw on his scheme. This may cause particular problems where there is a need for income in the short term. Care needs also to be taken about the impact of the loss in value arising through pension sharing.

Pension attachment orders

10.43 Attachment for income purposes under s 25B(4) may be useful in 'income gap' cases where a pension is already in payment to the scheme member but the other party would not be able to draw the pension for many years and needs income now. The same effect could of course be made by a periodical payments order but pension attachment provides a method of enforcement if it is anticipated that the pension scheme member may be unreliable. However, it still leads to a lack of security as payments depend upon the pension scheme member surviving and would end upon his death or upon the remarriage of the other party. The order would also be liable to variation.

Attachment for a capital sum under s 25B(4) would be useful if the wife was to receive a deferred lump sum from the husband's pension entitlement, perhaps where there was insufficient capital when the lump sum order was made and the only way in which to secure the money was from the pension fund. However, there would continue to be disadvantages as with the income order, particularly in view of the fact that the order can be varied.

An order requiring payment of capital from a commuted lump sum under s 25B(7) would be useful where a party is seeking a deferred lump sum which could be achieved by forcing the pension scheme member to commute part of his pension benefits in return for capital.

Attachment of death in service benefits (s 25C(2)(a)) was perhaps the most widely used part of the court's pension attachment powers as it provided the non pension scheme member with some form of security where she was financially dependent upon the other party either for her own periodical payments or for payments in respect of the children. On the death of the husband before retirement an order made under this provision would provide that any lump sum payable on his death (or part thereof) would be paid to the wife and an order could be made requiring the husband to nominate the wife as the person entitled to receive all or part of his benefits. However, this type of order is also liable to be varied.

Offsetting

10.44 This will have to be used in cases where pension sharing orders or attachment are unavailable (although this is now a relatively small proportion of cases) it may also be useful in cases where the parties have other priorities, for example where one party is keen to retain the matrimonial home but is unable to use other assets to acquire the other party's share without offsetting against the pension. It may also be more appropriate and attractive where the parties are young enough to build up alternative provision. It is more likely to be useful in cases where the pension provision is relatively small and therefore the costs of pension sharing may be disproportionate.

SUMMARY

10.45 This chapter is intended to give a brief overview of the type of pensions a practitioner may come across, the range of powers available to the court to deal with the pensions and the circumstances in which each type of power may be particularly important. It must, however, be emphasised when dealing with pensions that the court continues to use its discretion under MCA 1973, s 25 and the objective is, as always, to achieve a fair outcome.

Chapter 11

CHILDREN

INTRODUCTION

11.1 Any attempt to describe the significance of children in financial relief cases is bound to result in a somewhat muddled account. The welfare of any minor children of the family is the first consideration of the court,[1] but this does not mean that their interests take precedence over those of the adults in the case; the meaning of the 'first consideration' is considered in more detail at **1.14**. It certainly does not mean that the court must make orders for the support of children before it may deal with their parents; indeed, as will be seen, in most cases the court is precluded by statute from doing so.

11.2 The complicating factor in cases involving children is the CSA 1991, which is intended to provide support for most children. It will, therefore, be necessary to consider the principles of this Act at the outset, after which the principles for dealing with those cases in which the court has jurisdiction will be examined.

THE CHILD SUPPORT ACT 1991

11.3 The present law, which has been considerably amended, may be summarised as follows:

(a) In cases involving 'natural' children (ie children of both parties, whether by birth or adoption) jurisdiction to make orders for financial support was removed from the courts and vested in the Child Support Agency[2] (now the Child Maintenance and Enforcement Commission). The Commission assumed responsibility for the enforcement and collection of any maintenance required to be paid.

(b) A person with the care of children is described as 'the person with care' and the other parent is the 'non-resident parent' (formerly the 'absent parent').[3] A child is only subject to the Act if he was a 'qualifying child', ie a child of the person with care and the non-resident parent who lives with the person with care, and where all three are habitually resident in the UK.

---

[1] MCA 1973, s 25(1).
[2] CSA 1991, s 8(3).
[3] CSA 1991, s 3.

(c) Child maintenance is calculated under the Act according to a formula prescribed by the Act. In the original version of the formula there was no room for discretion or variation; indeed, one of the purposes of the Act was to depart from what was described as the 'discredited discretionary system' adopted by the courts. When it was found that this resulted in hardship, attempts were made to make the formula more flexible, but the principle that all jurisdiction must be derived from the Act remains.

(d) For historical reasons it should be recorded that there were two types of applications for assessment (now called a 'maintenance calculation') under the 1991 Act. The most significant of these and, it may be argued, the type of case for which the whole system was designed, was where the person with care was in receipt of state benefits. Here, the Secretary of State could require her to make an application under s 6, and exact penalties if she did not co-operate. This type of application has now disappeared (see below). The other type of application was made under s 4 by the person with care herself when she was not in receipt of benefits.

11.4 This is not the place for a detailed examination of the principles of the 1991 Act.[4] Instead, the following matters will be considered:

(a) the basic principles of the formula; and

(b) exceptions to the Act.

As has already been emphasised, the formula has been changed twice, first in 2003 and again in 2008. The pre-2003 and pre-2008 formulae are of mainly historical interest; they were considered in previous editions of this book and will not be considered further here. Readers should be aware that the 'old system' will still apply in some cases and that the system to be explained hereafter may apply only to new cases from 10 December 2012.

The significance of the Act in relation to cases to which it does not apply and where the court has jurisdiction will be considered at **11.27**

Basic principles of the formula from November 2008[5]

11.5 The parents of a qualifying child are called the parent with care (PWC) and the non-resident parent (NRP). What used to be called a 'maintenance assessment' is now a 'maintenance calculation'. The income of the PWC is ignored and the calculation is based entirely on the income of the PWC, being a percentage of his gross income depending on the number of children.

---

[4]   For a comprehensive account, see Bird *Child Support – The New Law* (Family Law, 2002). For a practical guide to calculating child support assessments see Bird *Child Support Calculation Kit 2003/2004* (Family Law).

[5]   Subject to their being brought into force by statutory instrument: see footnote 11.

11.6 From the beginning of the child support system the formula for determining how much a NRP should pay has been contained in para 2 of Sch 1 to the CSA 1991. This has now been amended by para 3 of Sch 4 to CMOPA 2008, which was brought into effect by statutory instrument[6] on 10 December 2012. The general rule now is that the basic rate is a percentage of the gross weekly income of the NRP calculated as follows:

- 12% where the NRP has one qualifying child;

- 16% where the NRP has two qualifying children;

- 19% where the NRP has three or more qualifying children.

This is therefore on the face of it a simple calculation. If, for example, the NRP earns £400 per week gross and has one qualifying child the child support maintenance will be £48 per week. Where there are two children it would be £64 per week and where there are three or more children it would be £76 per week.

11.7 However, the calculation is not as simple as might appear at first sight since, in effect, CSA 1991 reintroduces a two-tier system of earnings of the NRP, so that higher earners do not pay the full basic rate. Where the gross weekly income of the non-resident parent exceeds £800 (or £41,600 per annum) the percentages mentioned above apply only to the first £800, but the slice of the income above £800 per week is subject to deduction of the following percentages:

- one qualifying child 9%;

- two qualifying children 12%;

- three or more qualifying children 15%.[7]

There is a cap, or limit, on the income of the NRP that is taken into account. After the changes of 2000 this figure was £2,000 per week net; it is now[8] £800 per week gross (equivalent to £153,846 per annum.) plus a percentage of the balance over that figure depending on whether he has one qualifying child (9%), two qualifying children (12%) or three or more qualifying children (15%). (For the position as to top-up orders, where income exceeds £3,000 per week, see **11.11** below.)

11.8 However, the calculation contains two other complications. The first of these relates to 'relevant other children' of the NRP. Relevant other children are defined as children other than qualifying children in respect of whom the NRP or his or her partner receives child benefit or such other children as may be

---

[6] Child Maintenance and Other Payments Act 2008 (Commencement No 10 and Transitional Provisions) Order 2012, SI 2012/3042.

[7] CMOPA 2008, Sch 4, para 3(2).

[8] From 10 December 2012: see CSA 1991, s 3 above.

prescribed;[9] as there has never been any other class of children it may be assumed that this is a complete definition.

In effect, therefore, other relevant children are children of the NRP or his or her partner who are living with the NRP. No account is taken of the income of the partner, whether as child maintenance or otherwise.

The allowance which is made is by way of a deduction from the gross income of the NRP before it falls to be considered for deduction of the basic rate. The percentages are:

- 12% for one relevant other child;

- 16% for two relevant children;

- 19% for three or more relevant children.[10]

11.9 Gross weekly income is determined in such manner as prescribed by regulations.[11] These regulations may in particular provide for the Child Maintenance and Enforcement Commission (the Commission) to estimate any income or make an assumption as to any fact where, in its view, the information at its disposal is unreliable, insufficient or relates to an untypical period in the life of the non-resident parent.[12]

11.10 The system contains a large number of exceptions, special cases etc which are detailed and need not be considered here. The following are the principal matters of which the reader should be aware. As always with child support, the calculation is more complex than might appear to be the case, and the stages through which the calculation must go are outlined below.

(1) No child maintenance is payable when the NRP has a net income of below £5 or his income is of a prescribed description (eg students and prisoners).

(2) When the NRP's net income is £100 per week or less, or he receives any benefit, pension or allowance prescribed for this purpose, or he or his partner receive any benefit prescribed for this purpose, and the nil rate does not apply, the flat rate of £5 per week applies.

(3) Where the NRP has a partner who is also an NRP, and the partner is a person with respect to whom a maintenance calculation is in force, and the NRP or his partner receive any benefit prescribed for this purpose, the nil rate applies.

---

9   CSA 1991, Sch 1, para 10C(2).
10   CMOPA 2008, Sch 4, para 3(3), amending CSA 1991, Sch 1, para 2.
11   CSA 1991, Sch 1, para 10(1).
12   CSA 1991, Sch 1, Part I, para 10(2).

(4) When neither the nil rate nor a flat rate applies, and the NRP's net income is between £100 and £200 per week, the reduced rate applies.[13]

(5) When none of the previous categories is applicable, the basic rate applies. This is a percentage of the net weekly income of the NRP and is 15% where there is one qualifying child, 20% for two children and 25% for three or more.

(6) Income of the NRP exceeding £2,000 per week is ignored. The maximum sum payable under a maintenance calculation is therefore £500 per week, but the provisions as to applications to the court for 'top-up' orders are maintained.

(7) Where the NRP has more than one qualifying child, living with different PWCs, the rate of maintenance liability is divided by the number of qualifying children and shared among the PWCs according to the number of qualifying children living with that PWC.

(8) The amount of the maintenance calculation may be reduced if the NRP has one or more qualifying children with him for more than a certain number of nights per annum. The amount of decrease in respect of each child is as follows:

Number of nights with NRP	Fraction to subtract
52 to 103	One-seventh
104 to 155	Two-sevenths
156 to 174	Three-sevenths
175 or more	One-half

If the PWC is providing for more than one qualifying child of the NRP, the applicable decrease is the sum of the appropriate fractions in the table divided by the number of qualifying children. If the applicable fraction is one-half in relation to any qualifying child in the care of the PWC, the total amount payable to the PWC is then to be further decreased by £7 for each such child. Finally, if the application of these provisions would reduce the weekly amount of child support payable by the NRP to the PWC to less than £5 per week, the NRP has to pay £5 per week.

Changes from 2008

11.11 Section 1 of the Child Maintenance and Other Payments Act 2008 (CMOPA 2008) has replaced the CSA with the Child Maintenance and Enforcement Commission ('the Commission') and the detail is contained in Sch 1. Section 2 sets out the objectives of the Commission, the main objective

---

[13] Reduced rate is defined in CSA 1991, Sch 1, para 3.

being 'to maximise the number of those children who live apart from one or both of their parents for whom effective maintenance arrangements are in place'.

This is to be supported by the following subsidiary objectives:[14]

(a) to encourage and support the making and keeping by parents of appropriate voluntary maintenance arrangements for their children; and

(b) to support the making of applications for child support maintenance under the 1991 Act and to secure compliance when appropriate with parental obligations under that Act.

The general functions of the Commission are then defined as being the functions relating to child support transferred to it from the Secretary of State by this Act, and such other functions as may be conferred by any other enactment.[15] In addition, the Secretary of State, by regulation, may provide for additional functions.[16]

The Commission is enjoined to exercise its functions effectively and efficiently,[17] and is directed to take steps for the promotion of child maintenance and for the provision of information to parents to help them to secure effective voluntary arrangements.[18]

Sections 7 and 8 contain authority for the Commission to make agency arrangements and for the contracting out of any of its services. Finally, the Secretary of State retains the power to give guidance to the Commission and, perhaps more significantly, general or specific directions as to the exercise of its functions.

11.12 The formula for calculating child maintenance remains in Sch 1, which has, however, been amended. The formula which existed as a result of the Child Support, Pensions and Social Security Act 2000 (CSPSSA 2000) was a completely different formula from that contained in the 1991 Act. That formula was based on a 'maintenance requirement' for the children of any family and the apportionment of that requirement between the parents on the basis of their respective incomes and allowable outgoings. The revised formula in the CSPSSA 2000 was based entirely on a percentage of the non-resident parent's income. The formula now contained in the CMOPA 2008 is based on this, but is calculated on the gross income of the non-resident parent rather than the net income as previously was the case. This calculation is not as simple as might have been hoped. Provision is made for variation of the formula in certain cases, and this is at the discretion of the Secretary of State. Subject to variation,

---

[14] CMOPA 2008, s 2(2).
[15] CMOPA 2008, s 3(1).
[16] CMOPA 2008, s 3(2).
[17] CMOPA 2008, s 3(3).
[18] CMOPA 2008, ss 4 and 5.

however, the intention of the 1991 Act remains: by reference to the formula a 'correct' decision should be arrived at in every case.

The belief that the proper application of the formula would give an unchallengeable answer was given as the reason why the role of the courts had been rendered unnecessary and explains the thinking behind the system of revision and appeal. The formula was originally applied to the facts of a particular case in the same way as if calculating a benefit such as income support. This has now changed only in the sense that the formula is, ostensibly, easier to calculate since it requires only a pocket calculator. In the original 1991 formula, no element of discretion was possible. When the Act was amended in 1995 an element of discretion was introduced in the shape of departure directions. That element of discretion has been carried into the new law under the name of variation.

The purity of the original doctrine has therefore been sullied and made more unpredictable by the introduction of a discretionary element. However, in most cases the basic principle remains and the proponents of the amended Act envisage that the formula will reign undisturbed.[19]

WHEN MAY APPLICATIONS BE MADE TO THE COURT?

11.13   As was explained above, one of the principal features of the 1991 Act is that it is intended that the jurisdiction of the court shall be excluded and replaced by that of the Secretary of State. In *R (Kehoe) v Secretary of State for Work and Pensions*[20] it was held that the intention of the 1991 Act was to replace – except as expressly retained by the Act itself – any pre-existing rights of either a child or parent to periodical payments for the maintenance of that child. The applicant mother had no right that she could exercise against the father and accordingly she could not assert that she had an arguable civil right that entitled her under Art 6(1) of HRA 1998 to a determination by the court. However, the Act itself contains various exceptions to this principle, and further exceptions have been provided for as a result of the Agency's inability to handle all the tasks originally intended for it. These may be summarised as follows.

(a) Cases where the Commission does not have jurisdiction

11.14   The Commission (previously the Secretary of State) has jurisdiction only where the child is under 18 years of age and is the natural or adopted child of a person with care and a non-resident parent, and all three are habitually resident in the UK. It follows that stepchildren, children aged over 18, and

---

[19]   For a detailed examination of the provisions of CMOPA 2008 see R Bird and D Burrows *Child Maintenance – the New Law* (Family Law, 2008).

[20]   [2004] EWCA Civ 225, [2004] 1 FLR 1132. Upheld on appeal at [2005] UKHL 48, [2005] 2 FLR 1249, HL. The PWC had no right she could enforce against the NRP apart from judicial review. The maintenance obligation was enforceable only by the Secretary of State.

cases where any one of the parties or child are not habitually resident are excluded from the jurisdiction of the Commission and fall within the jurisdiction of the court.

(b) Applications to the court permitted by the Act

11.15 The Act allows applications to the court to be made in addition to a calculation by the Commission (previously the Secretary of State) in certain cases:

(i) 'Topping up', ie when the maximum amount payable under the formula has been reached; in such cases the court may make an order for such additional amount as is appropriate.[21]

(ii) Additional educational expenses. An order may be made 'solely for the purposes of requiring the person making or securing the making of periodical payments fixed by the order to meet some or all of the expenses incurred in connection with the provision of ... instruction or training'.[22] The most obvious way in which this might be used is to obtain an order for the payment of school fees, but the provision is not limited to this.

(iii) Disabled or blind children. Where a disability living allowance is paid to or in respect of a child, or no such allowance is paid but the child is disabled, an order may be made solely for the purpose of requiring the person making the payments 'to meet some or all of any of the expenses attributable to the child's disability'.[23]

In the case of (i) above, it is a prerequisite that a maintenance calculation has been made. This is not necessary in the two other cases.

(c) Certain consent orders

11.16 A court may make an order where 'a written agreement (whether or not enforceable) provides for the making, or securing, by a non-resident parent of the child of periodical payments to or for the benefit of the child; and the maintenance order which the court makes is, in all material respects, in the same terms as that agreement'.[24] In order to be satisfied of its jurisdiction, therefore, the court may need to see a copy of the written agreement.

---

[21] CSA 1991, s 8(6).
[22] CSA 1991, s 8(7).
[23] CSA 1991, s 8(8). By s 8(9), a child is disabled if he is blind, deaf or dumb or is substantially and permanently handicapped by illness, injury, mental disorder or congenital deformity or such other disability as may be prescribed.
[24] CSA 1991, s 8(5).

It should also be noted that the CSA 1991 provides that 'nothing in this Act shall be taken to prevent any person from entering into a maintenance agreement'.[25]

(d) Capital orders

11.17   There is nothing in the CSA 1991 to prevent a lump sum order or a property adjustment order in favour of a child (but see **11.25**).

(e) Applications under 'transitional provisions'

11.18   It was always envisaged that the Agency would not be able to take on all cases immediately and that there would have to be a phased take up. What began as transitional provisions seem to have achieved a degree of permanence, but there seems little point in summarising the position further since, with the advent of the new formula, this will be a diminishing problem.

(f) Variation and duration of orders

11.19   As was noted above, the court has jurisdiction to make orders for child maintenance where there is no maintenance calculation in effect and the parties have agreed the terms of such order in writing. Such an order, once made, may be varied. Until the coming into force of the new provisions in 2003, this prevented any application for a maintenance calculation under s 4 of the 1991 Act. The position after implementation of the new provisions was different. By s 4(10) of the 1991 Act, as amended by CSPSSA 2000, the Secretary of State could make a maintenance calculation, provided that one year has elapsed from the date of the order. Advisers should therefore be aware that any agreement made and reflected in a consent order may last only for one year, and the message would seem to be that orders should, as far as possible, be in terms similar to those of a maintenance calculation.

APPLICATIONS TO THE COURT

11.20   For the purposes of this book, it will be assumed that any application to the court in respect of children will be made under the provisions of MCA 1973. For the sake of completeness, however, it should be noted that, where the court has jurisdiction, applications may be made under the provisions of Sch 1 to the Children Act 1989. The principles governing the exercise of the court's discretion under the 1989 Act are virtually identical to those under MCA 1973.

The rules governing the procedure for applications in respect of children are contained in Chapter 3 of Part 9 of the FPR 2010. It is provided that the following persons may apply for an order:

---

[25]   CSA 1991, s 9(2).

- any person in whose favour a residence order has been made with respect to a child of the family, and any applicant for such an order;

- any other person who is entitled to apply for a residence order with respect to a child;

- a local authority, where an order has been made under s 31(1)(a) of the 1989 Act placing a child in its care;

- the Official Solicitor, if appointed the children's guardian of a child of the family under r 16.24; and

- a child of the family who has been given permission to apply for a financial remedy.

Jurisdiction

11.21   The powers of the court to make financial provision orders and property adjustment orders have been set out in the chapters applicable to each of the various forms of relief (eg periodical payments, lump sum, etc). It will be noted that in each case the court has jurisdiction to make an order of the kind described for the benefit of a child of the family. 'Child of the family' is defined as, in relation to the parties to a marriage:[26]

'(a)   a child of both those parties; and
(b)   any other child, not being a child who is placed with those parties as foster parents by a local authority or voluntary organisation, who has been treated by both of those parties as a child of their family.'

Age limits

11.22   The basic principle is that 'no financial provision order and no order for a transfer of property under section 24(1)(a) … shall be made in favour of a child who has attained the age of eighteen'.[27] It is also provided that the term specified in any order for periodical payments or secured periodical payments in favour of a child:[28]

'(a)   shall not in the first instance extend beyond the date of the birthday of the child next following his attaining the upper limit of the compulsory school age … unless the court considers that in the circumstances of the case the welfare of the child requires that it should extend to a later date; and
(b)   shall not in any event, subject to subsection (3) below, extend beyond the date of the child's eighteenth birthday.'

---

[26]   MCA 1973, s 52(1).
[27]   MCA 1973, s 29(1).
[28]   MCA 1973, s 29(2).

11.23 Section 29(3) will be considered below. However, the principle is that no order may be made in respect of a child who is aged over 18, or which extends beyond the age of 18. Moreover, any periodic order for a child should not extend beyond the child's seventeenth birthday unless the court considers that the welfare of the child requires such an order.

However, there is an exception to this principle. It is provided that the limitations on orders for children aged over 18 or extending beyond that age shall not apply:[29]

'... if it appears to the court that –

(a) the child is, or will be, or if an order were made without complying with either or both of those provisions would be, receiving instruction at an educational establishment or undergoing training for a trade, profession or vocation, whether or not he is also, or will also be, in gainful employment; or

(b) there are special circumstances which justify the making of an order without complying with either or both of those provisions.'

The effect of this is that when a child is, or will be, in education or training, whether full-time or part-time, an order may be made for or to him. 'Special circumstances' are not defined, but would probably include cases where the 'child' was unable to be self-sufficient because of some mental or physical disability.

11.24 The usual wording of an order for a child under the age of 17 is that the payments continue 'until the said child shall attain the age of seventeen years or ceases full-time education if later or further order'.

Principles on which the court exercises its jurisdiction

11.25 When the court exercises its jurisdiction in respect of a child, it is directed to have regard in particular to the following matters:[30]

'(a) the financial needs of the child;

(b) the income, earning capacity (if any), property and other financial resources of the child;

(c) any physical or mental disability of the child;

(d) the manner in which he was being and in which the parties to the marriage expected him to be educated or trained;

(e) the considerations mentioned in relation to the parties to the marriage in paragraphs (a), (b), (c) and (e) of subsection (2).'

The matters referred to in (e) are the income, capital, etc of each of the parties, their needs, obligations and responsibilities, the standard of living enjoyed by the family and any mental or physical disability of either party.

---

29   MCA 1973, s 29(3).
30   MCA 1973, s 25(3).

11.26 In addition to the matters prescribed above, when the court is exercising its powers against a party to the marriage in favour of a child of the family who is not the child of that party, the court is directed to have regard:[31]

> '(a)   to whether that party assumed any responsibility for the child's maintenance, and, if so, to the extent to which, and the basis upon which, that party assumed such responsibility and to the length of time for which that party discharged such responsibility;
> (b)   to whether in assuming and discharging such responsibility that party did so knowing that the child was not his or her own;
> (c)   to the liability of any other person to maintain the child.'

Periodic orders for children

11.27 The quantification of an order for periodical payments for a child must be approached on the same basis as any other periodical payments order, ie by assessing the reasonable needs and requirements of the child in the light of the statutory factors set out above and then determining the ability of the parents to provide for such needs and requirements. Both parents have an obligation to provide for a child, and the court would normally expect this obligation to be regarded as a prior responsibility by both of them. However, this principle must be tempered by the recognition of the fact that the 'non-resident parent' has to maintain himself and discharge any proper responsibilities which he may have assumed; the latter may include a new family.[32] In one case it was said that:[33]

> 'The respondent husband is entitled to order his life in such a way as will hold in reasonable balance the responsibilities to his existing family which he carries into his new life, as well as his proper aspirations for that new future. In all life, for those who are divorced as well as for those who are not divorced, indulging one's whims or even one's reasonable desires must be held in check by the constraints imposed by limited resources and compelling obligations.'

11.28 Whatever view is eventually taken of the parents' ability to pay, it is normally necessary to make a provisional assessment of the child's needs. In many cases, the formula prescribed by the CSA 1991 will assist as a starting point, and a 'child support calculation' is always useful in such cases. Indeed, in *E v C (Child Maintenance)*,[34] where a family proceedings court had declined to vary an order for £5 per week against a father who was unemployed and in receipt of benefit, Douglas Brown J allowed the appeal and observed that the justices would have done well to consider what a child support assessment would have been (in the instant case it would have been a nil assessment). While that assessment would not have been binding on the court, it would have been strongly persuasive. It was the practice of professional judges to ask about a child support assessment, and it would be helpful for justices to do likewise.

---

[31]   MCA 1973, s 25(4).
[32]   See eg *R v R* [1988] 1 FLR 89, CA.
[33]   *Delaney v Delaney* [1990] 2 FLR 457, CA, at 461, per Ward J.
[34]   [1996] 1 FLR 472.

Support for this view is now to be found in *GW v RW (Financial Provision: Departure from Equality)*,[35] a case involving very substantial assets. It was held that, in fixing a child maintenance award in a case where the Agency lacked jurisdiction, the appropriate starting point was almost invariably the figure thrown up by the new child support rules.

This case is, therefore, authority for considering what a child support calculation would be in all cases involving a child. It could not be the last word, since the court is bound by s 25(3) and (4) and not by the CSA 1991 when dealing with children's cases, but it would at least be a useful starting point. It is suggested that these principles supersede the earlier practice of adopting income support figures (in lower income cases) or the National Foster Care Association recommendations (in cases of greater affluence) as a starting point.

Different considerations apply in very 'big money' cases. In *M v M (Financial Relief: Substantial Earning Capacity)*[36] the award was for £25,000 pa per child, increasing to £35,000 pa for a child with special needs. In the celebrated case of *McCartney v Mills McCartney*[37] the award was for £35,000 pa for one child aged 4, plus school fees and the cost of a nanny not to exceed £30,000 pa. All sums were index-linked.

Capital provision for children

11.29 As was observed when the exceptions to the CSA 1991 were being considered, there is nothing in the Act to prevent a lump sum order or property adjustment order in favour of a child, even when a child support calculation is in force. However, it must be said that such orders are rare, since it is difficult to show that a child, as distinct from the parent with whom he lives, has a need or reasonable requirement for capital. There is, in principle, no justification for the children to expect to share in their parents' capital assets on or after the dissolution of marriage,[38] although settlement orders may be made in exceptional cases.[39]

An example of a capital order for children in somewhat unusual circumstances is *V v V (Child Maintenance)*,[40] where the father, having invited the judge to determine the level of child maintenance, then refused to consent to the judge's proposed order. The judge awarded the children lump sums, saying that, in those circumstances, it was right to seek to reflect the balance of the provision in another form of order.

The cases brought under the Children Act 1989, Sch 1, in which property has been ordered to be transferred for the benefit of children, support this general

---

[35] [2003] EWHC 611 (Fam), [2003] 2 FLR 108, Nicholas Mostyn QC.
[36] [2004] 2 FLR 236.
[37] [2008] 1 FLR 1508.
[38] *Lilford (Lord) v Glyn* [1979] 1 All ER 441; *Kiely v Kiely* [1988] 1 FLR 248, CA.
[39] See eg *Tavoulareas v Tavoulareas* [1998] 2 FLR 418, CA.
[40] [2001] 2 FLR 799, Wilson J.

proposition. Such cases have been brought when the parents have not been married and so the parent with care (normally the mother) has been unable to apply for provision in her own right.[41] The orders for transfer of capital to provide a home have all provided for the property to be held on trust until the majority of the child and then to return to the transferor. In *Phillips v Peace*[42] it was held that in an application under Sch 1 only one settlement of property order could be made.

An interesting insight into financial provision for a child is provided by *K v K (Ancillary Relief: Pre-nuptial Agreement)*.[43] This case is considered in more detail at **1.52**, but the important point is that, after a short marriage where there had been a pre-nuptial agreement, the wife was held to her agreement as to capital. However, the judge also ordered the husband to provide a home and furnishings for the mother and child at a cost of £1.2m (to revert to him in due course) and £15,000 pa for the child.

Given this decision, the decision of the Court of Appeal in *Re P (Child: Financial Provision)*[44] is also of interest, although it was clearly a most unusual case. Here, the parties were not married and the child was aged 2 years. The father was described as 'fabulously rich'. The court decided that a home in central London was appropriate and ordered the father to provide £1m for this purpose, £100,000 for decoration and furnishing, and £70,000 pa periodical payments, on the basis that the father undertook to pay school fees. The Court of Appeal gave further guidance as to the quantum of financial support for children in *F v G (Child: Financial Provision)*.[45] It was held that, although standard of living is not a factor which appears in the Children Act 1989, Sch 1, para 4(1), it is clearly among the totality of circumstances which the court must hold in view. The extent to which the unit of primary carer and child have become accustomed to a particular level of lifestyle can impact legitimately on an evaluation of a child's needs. The remainder of the case is an interesting example of the way the court may exercise its discretion but, as each case is fact-specific, no further comment need be made here.

In *W v J (Child: Variation of Periodical Payments)*[46] it was held that there was no jurisdiction to make an order for increased periodical payments for a child to cover legal costs to be incurred in forthcoming litigation between the parties.

---

[41] See eg *A v A (Minor: Financial Provision)* [1994] 1 FLR 657; *T v S (Financial Provision for Children)* [1994] 2 FLR 883; *Phillips v Peace* [1996] 2 FLR 230; *J v C (Child: Financial Provision)* [1999] 1 FLR 152. For the position where the mother was a joint owner of the house see *Re B (Child: Property Transfer)* [1999] 2 FLR 418.

[42] [2004] EWHC 3180 (Fam), [2005] 2 FLR 1212.

[43] [2003] 1 FLR 120.

[44] [2003] EWCA Civ 837, [2003] 2 FLR 865.

[45] [2004] EWHC 1848 (Fam), [2005] 1 FLR 261.

[46] [2003] EWHC 2657 (Fam), [2004] 2 FLR 300.

School fees

11.30 As was seen above, provision for school fees or other educational expenses is an area where the court always retains jurisdiction, whether or not a child support calculation has been or might be made. Since the Finance Act 1988, there has been no tax advantage to be gained by any particular form of order. A form of order will be found at Appendix A, Precedent 12.

In *T v T (Financial Provision: Private Education)*[47] the husband applied to be relieved of his obligation under a consent order to pay school fees. The application was dismissed and the husband ordered to pay £254,680.71 lump sum for fees. Bennett J held that he could afford to do so even if he had to sell some assets. This would still leave him securely housed.

However, sub nom *Tracey v Tracey*,[48] the Court of Appeal allowed in part the husband's appeal. This was allowed on the facts, important information not having been before Bennett J, and the lump sum was reduced. However, the principle was not affected.

INTERIM APPLICATIONS

11.31 The situation may (indeed, frequently does) arise in which a parent with the care of a child, normally the mother, is left without any support for a child, and, whether or not she seeks to recover any periodical payments or maintenance payment suit for herself, wishes to obtain support for a child. In many such cases the provisions of the CSA 1991 prohibit her from applying to the court for an order for the child, but the Commission (previously the Child Support Agency) may well take many months to deal with any application under s 4.

11.32 In such cases, there is nothing to prevent the court from making an order for the mother which includes support for the child. Such an order has to be expressed as remaining in force 'until a child support calculation is made'. When the order is made up partly of the mother's maintenance and partly the child's, the court would add the words 'whereupon this order shall be reduced by the amount of any such calculation'. Such an order would not be possible where the mother had remarried. Indeed, any such order is only legitimate where there is a genuine and substantial amount of spousal support in the order; where the order in reality relates only to children, it is not legitimate.[49]

---

[47] [2005] EWHC 2119 (Fam), [2006] 1 FLR 903.
[48] [2006] EWCA Civ 734, [2007] 1 FLR 196.
[49] *Dorney-Kingdom v Dorney-Kingdom* [2000] 2 FLR 855, CA.

Chapter 12

INSOLVENCY AND RIGHTS OF CREDITORS

INTRODUCTION

12.1 In this chapter it is intended to consider the effect on the parties of the bankruptcy of one of them. It also seems convenient at this point to consider the position of one or both of the parties when a creditor has a charge, whether by virtue of a mortgage deed or a charging order, over the matrimonial home. The two situations are different, but the effect on the party who is not insolvent or the object of the judgment or charge may seem to be similar; a third party is perceived to wish to deprive that party of what she regards as hers.

THE INSOLVENCY ACT 1986 AND SALE OF THE MATRIMONIAL HOME

12.2 When a person becomes bankrupt, the whole of his estate vests in his trustee in bankruptcy,[1] who is then under an obligation to realise the bankrupt's assets for the benefit of the creditors. One of the assets will be any property in which the bankrupt has a legal or beneficial interest, and this will frequently include the matrimonial home. If a property is held by the bankrupt and another as joint tenants, the bankruptcy severs the joint tenancy;[2] the result of this is that the trustee and the other co-owner hold the property as tenants in common in equal shares. Where the property was held as tenants in common, the trustee holds the share which the bankrupt previously held.

12.3 The trustee is then in the position of any joint owner in the sense that he may apply to the court for an order for sale, previously under s 30 of the Law of Property Act 1925 (LPA 1925) and now under s 14 of the Trusts of Land and Appointment of Trustees Act 1996 (TLATA 1996).[3] However, the trustee is in a different position from other joint owners because the Insolvency Act 1986 (IA 1986) prescribes the duties of the court in such circumstances. It is provided[4] that, on application for an order for sale, the court shall make such order:

---

[1] IA 1986, s 306.
[2] *Re Gorman (A Bankrupt)* [1990] 2 FLR 284.
[3] As to when time begins to run for the purposes of the Limitation Act 1980, s 20(1), see *Gotham v Doodes* [2006] EWCA Civ 1080, [2007] 1 FLR 373; the right to receive the money could not predate an order for sale. Until the order for sale, the charge is merely a deferred charge.
[4] By IA 1986, s 336(4).

'... as it thinks just and reasonable having regard to –

(a)   the interests of the bankrupt's creditors,
(b)   the conduct of the spouse or former spouse, so far as contributing to the bankruptcy,
(c)   the needs and financial resources of the spouse or former spouse,
(d)   the needs of any children, and
(e)   all the circumstances of the case other than the needs of the bankrupt.'

It will be seen that the court is afforded a certain degree of discretion when considering such applications. However, this may be more apparent than real since it is further provided[5] that when the application is made more than one year after the bankruptcy the court 'shall assume, unless the circumstances of the case are exceptional, that the interests of the bankrupt's creditors outweigh all other considerations'.

12.4   The result of these provisions is that applications for orders for sale are rarely made before one year has elapsed, and, when they are eventually made, there is little or no dispute that an order must be made. It is clearly difficult to prove that the circumstances of a particular case are exceptional, and the courts have accepted the clear intention of the insolvency legislation which puts the interests of the creditors to the forefront. In one case,[6] the fact that the wife and children would be rendered homeless was described as 'not an exceptional circumstance. It is a normal circumstance and is the result, the all too obvious result, of a husband having conducted the financial affairs of the family in a way that has led to bankruptcy'. In another case, Hoffmann J decided that, since the half share which the bankrupt's wife would receive would not be sufficient to rehouse her and the children, the order for sale and possession should not be enforced until the youngest child was 16 years old. The Court of Appeal allowed the trustee's appeal and said that an order for immediate sale should have been made. The eviction of the wife, with all the consequent problems, was not exceptional but was 'one of the melancholy consequences of debt and improvidence with which every society has been familiar'.[7] A similar result was reached in *Barca v Mears*[8] but it should be noted that in that case the learned judge said that the *Re Citro* approach might be incompatible with Convention rights and might need re-examining in light of the European Convention.

12.5   However, it is not impossible to prove exceptional circumstances.[9] In *Re Holliday*,[10] the husband had presented his own petition in bankruptcy as a tactical move to defeat his wife's claims. No creditors were pressing and he was

5   By IA 1986, s 336(5).
6   *Re Lowrie (A Bankrupt)* [1981] 3 All ER 353.
7   *Re Citro (A Bankrupt)* [1991] Ch 142, CA.
8   [2004] EWHC 2170 (Ch).
9   For another example of the application of the relevant principles leading to an order for sale, see the judgment of Lawrence Collins J in *Dean v Stout* [2005] EWHC 3315 (Ch), [2006] 1 FLR 725.
10   [1981] 3 All ER 353.

in a position to discharge his debts out of income. The judge postponed sale for 5 years. In *Re Bailey*,[11] although an order for sale was made, it seems to have been accepted that if a house had been specially converted to meet the needs of a disabled child, the circumstances could properly be described as exceptional.

In *Judd v Brown*,[12] the fact that the wife was suffering from cancer and had to undergo a course of chemotherapy was held to be an exceptional circumstance and the trustee's application for an order for sale was refused. A slightly different result was reached in *Re Raval (A Bankrupt)*,[13] where the bankrupt's wife suffered from schizophrenia and it was thought that 'adverse life events' might cause a relapse. The former matrimonial home was the only asset but there was a substantial equity. Possession was suspended for one year.

In *Re Bremner*,[14] the bankrupt husband was aged 79, suffering from cancer, and unlikely to survive more than 6 months. It was held that the wife's need to care for him was distinct from the husband's needs and was exceptional; sale was deferred with marketing not to begin until 3 months after the husband's death.

An example to the contrary is *Donohoe v Ingram*[15] where the bankrupt's partner applied for sale to be postponed on the ground that the home was needed for the children and the creditors would be paid in full by 2017. It was held that the case was not sufficiently similar to *Holliday* to permit a deviation from the usual *Re Citro* approach.

In *Mekarska v Ruiz and Bowden (Trustee in Bankruptcy)*[16] a wife's application to annul the husband's bankruptcy was refused, partly because at the date of the bankruptcy order he was plainly unable to pay his debts and his motivation in petitioning had not been to defeat the wife's claims. *Per curiam*, the judge said that where a person affected by a bankruptcy order considers that the order should not have been made, they must act immediately to have it annulled or suspended.

12.6   The position of a spouse who has no legal or beneficial interest in the home is different from that of the spouse with such an interest, in that when the house is sold she will recover nothing. However, in terms of her right of occupation, her position is very similar. A spouse with no legal or beneficial interest has matrimonial home rights,[17] which include the right not to be evicted save by order of the court. A former spouse has similar rights provided

---

[11]   [1977] 1 WLR 278.
[12]   [1998] 2 FLR 360.
[13]   [1998] 2 FLR 718.
[14]   [1999] 1 FLR 912. See also *Claughton v Charalamabous* [1999] 1 FLR 740, CA (the court must make a value judgment and look at all the circumstances); the process leaves little scope for interference by an appellate court.
[15]   [2006] 2 FLR 1084.
[16]   [2011] EWHC 913 (Fam).
[17]   FLA 1996, s 30.

an order to that effect has been made before decree absolute.[18] A trustee in bankruptcy who wishes to obtain a possession order must apply to the court having jurisdiction in the bankruptcy.[19] The factors which the court must take into account are those already set out above where the spouse is a joint owner. In *Byford v Butler*[20] it was held that a wife who had continued to live in the former matrimonial home after the bankruptcy was entitled to credit for mortgage interest paid, subject to the trustee's right to set off occupation rent.

12.7 Finally, in this section, the position of a bankrupt spouse who has the care of children must be considered. A person who has a beneficial interest in a property, has been adjudged bankrupt, and who has living with him in the property any person under the age of 18 has the right not to be evicted without order of the court.[21] On an application for sale made by a trustee, the court must have regard to 'the interests of the creditors, to the bankrupt's financial resources, to the needs of the children, and to all the circumstances of the case other than the needs of the bankrupt'.[22] There is a similar provision in respect of applications made one year after the bankruptcy to that set out above.[23]

Effect of bankruptcy on order for financial relief

12.8 All that has been said so far in this chapter assumes that the bankruptcy has pre-dated any order for financial relief; once the bankruptcy occurs, there is normally little point in considering such applications, and the provisions of the IA 1986 apply. Where a party has presented his or her own petition for bankruptcy in order to defeat the claim of the other in principle the other party may apply to annul the bankruptcy on the ground that it should not have been made under s 282(1)(a). However, the onus of proof lies on the applicant and if, in fact, the bankrupt was unable to pay his debts on the date of the bankruptcy, his motives are irrelevant.[24]

What must now be considered is the position when a bankruptcy order is made after an order for financial relief has been made, and what, if any, effect the bankruptcy will have on the order and its implementation.

The answer to this will depend on the type of order which has been made, and each must be considered in turn. It should, however, be noted that the same regime and rationales apply when there has not been an order but a transfer pursuant to an agreement which has not led to an order.[25]

---

[18] FLA 1996, s 33(5).
[19] IA 1986, s 336(3).
[20] [2004] 1 FLR 56.
[21] IA 1986, s 337(2).
[22] IA 1986, s 337(5).
[23] IA 1986, s 337(6).
[24] *Whig v Whig* [2008] 1 FLR 453.
[25] *Segal v Pasram* [2008] 1 FLR 271.

Property adjustment orders

12.9 The court has no jurisdiction to make a property adjustment order against a bankrupt spouse.[26]

A common danger which may be encountered by a party in whose favour a property adjustment order has been made is that the transaction, ie the transfer of property pursuant to the order, may be set aside on an application by the trustee in bankruptcy. The trustee has the right to apply to the court[27] for an order to set aside any transaction 'at an undervalue' made within a specified period before the day of the presentation of the bankruptcy petition. The fact that the transfer has been made pursuant to an order of the court does not prevent it from being the object of such an application.[28]

However, in *Mountney v Treharne*,[29] where the court had ordered the transfer of a house to the wife but a bankruptcy order was made in respect of the husband before the transfer was signed, it was held that the order had the effect of conferring on the wife an equitable interest in the property at the moment it took effect, ie on decree absolute. The trustee in bankruptcy therefore took the property subject to the wife's equitable interest.[30] For the position in a similar case involving pension policies see **12.15**.

The specified period is 5 years unless it can be shown that the other party was not insolvent at the date of the transaction and that he did not become insolvent because of it, in which case it is 2 years.[31]

12.10 Whether or not a transaction was at an undervalue will depend on the facts of the case. For example, if it could be shown that a former husband and wife had agreed to transfer the property of one of them to the other in an attempt to defeat creditors, and had obtained an order of the court to that effect, it is virtually certain that the transaction would be set aside. On the other hand, it was thought that, if an order for transfer of property were made for the housing of a spouse and children in the normal way and after consideration of the s 25 factors, it might be difficult to establish that the transaction was at an undervalue and that this might also be the case where the property transferred was on a clean break basis, and in settlement of all a wife's claims including her right to periodical payments.

This may have been clarified by the decision of the Court of Appeal in *Hill v Haines*.[32] Here, in the proceedings for ancillary relief, the district judge had ordered, inter alia, that the husband transfer to the wife all his interest in the former matrimonial home. The husband was subsequently adjudged bankrupt.

---

[26] *McGladdery v McGladdery* [1999] 2 FLR 1102.
[27] Under IA 1986, s 339.
[28] MCA 1973, s 39.
[29] [2002] EWCA Civ 1174, [2002] 2 FLR 930, CA.
[30] This would not have been the case had decree absolute not been pronounced.
[31] See IA 1986, s 341.
[32] [2007] EWHC 1012 (Ch), [2007] All ER (D) 72 (May).

Following the bankruptcy, trustees of the bankrupt were appointed and they applied for an order to set aside the transfer of property pursuant to s 339 of the IA 1986. The application was refused and the trustees appealed against the refusal of their application. They submitted that the transfer was a transaction at an undervalue either under s 339(3)(a) or (c) of the Act in view of the fact that the property adjustment order had not involved the respondent giving consideration and certainly not such that could be measured in money or money's worth within the meaning of s 339(3)(c). The wife submitted that a transferee under a transfer made pursuant to a property transfer order was to be regarded as having given consideration equivalent to the value of the property being transferred, unless the case was an exceptional one where it could be demonstrated that the property transferred was obtained by fraud or some broadly similar exceptional circumstance. The appeal was allowed. The judge held that the district judge had been wrong to conclude that the transfer of the property pursuant to the order made in favour of the respondent by the matrimonial court was not a transaction at an undervalue. The transaction had been at an undervalue by application of s 339(3)(a) of the Act and in any event on an application of s 339(3)(c).

However, to the relief of most ancillary relief practitioners, this was not the last word. The wife's appeal was allowed by the Court of Appeal[33] which held that the judge had been wrong to find that that parties to an ancillary relief order do not give consideration. The ability of a spouse to apply for ancillary relief is a right conferred by law, and the court may make an order entitling one party to property at the expense of the other. That property is prima facie the value of the right. Release or compromise of a claim can therefore constitute valuable consideration.

A different result was obtained in *Avis v Turner and Avis*[34] where it was held that where there is an ancillary relief order postponing sale until certain events (eg a *Martin* or *Mesher* order) the bankrupt's share is not protected from an application by the trustee under s 339 until the occurrence of the events. Section 335A(3) gives priority to the interests of the creditors save in specified circumstances.

12.11 Any disposition of property made by a bankrupt between the date of the presentation of the petition and the date of the bankrupt's property vesting in the trustee is void unless made with the consent of the court or subsequently ratified by the court.[35]

---

[33] See [2008] 1 FLR 1192, CA.
[34] [2008] 1 FLR 482, CA. See also the same case reported at [2008] Fam Law 1185 where, on the facts, it was held that the circumstances of the case were not exceptional.
[35] IA 1986, s 284(1).

Lump sum orders

12.12 The point made at **12.11** should be noted; for these purposes, a lump sum payment would be a disposition of property. Subject to that point, the issues arising as to lump sums are:

(a) whether or not a lump sum could be set aside by the court on the trustee's application;

(b) whether it can be enforced against a bankrupt's estate;

(c) irrespective of (b), whether an order will be made against a bankrupt's estate.

12.13 As to the first point, it would seem that, for the lump sum to be successfully attacked by the trustee, it would have to constitute a preference.[36] When a bankrupt has given a preference within the time specified by the IA 1986, the court may make such order as is necessary to restore the position to what it would have been had the preference not been made.[37] The specified times are the same as those applicable to transfers at an undervalue (see **12.9**). The fact that the lump sum had been paid pursuant to an order of the court would not prevent it from being classed as a preference.[38]

There is no mention in the IA 1986 of a lump sum constituting a transfer at an undervalue, and no authority as to whether this might be possible.

12.14 The second point may arise when a lump sum order has been made and the paying party then becomes bankrupt (or, as may be the case, is already bankrupt). Any obligation arising under an order made in family or domestic proceedings is not provable in bankruptcy.[39] The effect of this is that, so long as the bankrupt remains bankrupt, the order cannot be enforced against his estate. However, it also follows that the order survives the bankruptcy and may be enforced after the bankrupt's discharge, or during the bankruptcy by other methods, for example a judgment summons. Prior to 2005 it was held that even though a lump sum order cannot be proved in a bankruptcy, there is no reason in principle why an unpaid lump sum should not found a bankruptcy petition.[40] However, by virtue of the Insolvency (Amendment) Rules 2005,[41]

---

[36] For example, see *Trowbridge v Trowbridge* [2003] 2 FLR 231.

[37] IA 1986, s 340(1) and (2).

[38] IA 1986, s 340(6).

[39] Insolvency Rules 1986, r 12.3(2)(a). See also *Woodley v Woodley (No 2)* [1993] 2 FLR 477, CA.

[40] *Russell v Russell* [1998] 1 FLR 936; *Wheatley v Wheatley* [1999] 2 FLR 205 (where the husband's repeated failures to pay and the presence of other creditors made the strategy justifiable). For the position in a voluntary arrangement, see *Re Bradley-Hole (A Bankrupt)* [1995] 2 FLR 838 and *Re A Debtor; JP v A Debtor* [1999] 1 FLR 926. For the position where bankruptcy is based on a foreign order, see *Cartwright v Cartwright (No 2)* [2002] EWCA Civ 931, [2002] 2 FLR 610, CA.

[41] SI 2005/527.

with effect from 1 April 2005 lump sum and costs orders made within family proceedings are provable in bankruptcy.

12.15   In *Re Nunn (Bankruptcy: Divorce: Pension Rights)*[42] the husband was ordered to pay one-half of the lump sums which he would receive under his pension policies. He was then made bankrupt. It was held that the wife had no rights as against the trustee in bankruptcy; the court lacked jurisdiction to make an order for payment in any form which created an equitable interest or security.

12.16   Finally, the jurisdiction of the court to make an order against an undischarged bankrupt must be considered. In view of what has been said above, there will be little point in such an application in most cases. However, there is no reason in principle why such an order should not be made; the only restriction is that the court must consider the bankrupt's ability to pay.[43] In one case,[44] it was shown that there would be a substantial surplus in the bankruptcy, and an order for a lump sum of £450,000 was upheld. The only caveat was that the judge must have a clear picture of the assets and liabilities of the bankrupt so that he can determine what assets the bankrupt will have in the foreseeable future.

12.17   The fact that a spouse seeks a bankruptcy order in order to defeat a claim for ancillary relief is not a matter which the court may take into account under s 37 of the MCA 1973. In such a case, the appropriate remedy is to apply to the bankruptcy court for an annulment of the bankruptcy.[45] In *Paulin v Paulin*[46] it was said that an individual who was made bankrupt on his own petition who was shown to have made a dishonest statement of his affairs and on the date of presentation of the petition to have had assets substantially exceeding liabilities would find it difficult to resist annulment of the bankruptcy.

Periodical payments orders

12.18   Orders for periodic maintenance for a spouse or child are probably the class of order for financial relief which is most vulnerable to attack after bankruptcy. After bankruptcy, the income of the bankrupt may be claimed by the trustee as part of the bankrupt's estate.[47] The court may make an income payments order, which requires the bankrupt to make payments from his

---

[42]   [2004] 1 FLR 1123.
[43]   *Woodley v Woodley (No 2)* (above).
[44]   *Hellyer v Hellyer* [1996] 2 FLR 579, CA.
[45]   *F v F (Divorce: Insolvency: Annulment of Bankruptcy Order)* [1994] 1 FLR 359. See also *Couvaras v Wolf* [2002] 2 FLR 107.
[46]   [2009] EWCA Civ 221, [2009] 2 FLR 354.
[47]   IA 1986, s 307(1).

income to the trustee for the benefit of the creditors;[48] this order may continue to have effect after discharge from bankruptcy.[49]

When assessing the amount of an income payments order, the court must leave the bankrupt with sufficient to meet the reasonable domestic needs of the bankrupt and his family, defined in this context as the persons who are living with the bankrupt and are dependent on him.[50] It is therefore not difficult to see that any order for periodical payments made before bankruptcy is at great risk of not being paid in full or even at all once the paying party is made bankrupt.

An order for periodical payments or maintenance pending suit is not provable in the bankruptcy.[51] Similarly, although an order for costs made in ancillary relief proceedings is a 'bankruptcy debt' within the meaning of s 382(1) of the IA 1986, it has been held that it would be difficult to envisage any circumstances in which the court could properly make a bankruptcy order based on such an unprovable debt.[52] On the other hand, an order in favour of a bankrupt may be claimed by the trustee by way of an application for an income payments order.[53]

THE RIGHTS OF THIRD-PARTY CREDITORS

12.19 In general, while the court must take account of the proper liabilities of either party when performing the s 25 exercise,[54] it does not have to put the interests of creditors before those of the parties to the marriage and the children. There is no jurisdiction to make an order for payment to any person other than the parties or a child.

The only exception to this general rule is the position of a creditor which has a secured interest over any property which is the object of an application by either party. When procedure is considered in Chapter 16, it will be seen that a mortgagee or chargee is one of the persons who must be served with notice of any application for a property adjustment order, and who have the right to be heard on the application. This is not normally a situation which causes difficulty, since the court would not order transfer of any property if the transferee was unable to maintain the mortgage payments from some source of funds, whether private or public.

12.20 However, some difficulties have arisen and may arise when either a mortgagee has a charge which is repayable on demand, or is a creditor which

---

[48] IA 1986, ss 310(1) and 385(1).
[49] IA 1986, ss 310(5) and 280(2)(c).
[50] IA 1986, ss 310(2) and 385(1).
[51] Insolvency Rules 1986, r 12.3(2)(a).
[52] *Levy v Legal Services Commission* [2001] 1 FLR 435, CA. See also *Wehmeyer v Wehmeyer* [2001] 2 FLR 84.
[53] IA 1986, ss 310(1) and 283(1)(b).
[54] MCA 1973, s 25(2)(b).

has obtained a charging order to secure a judgment debt. The position is most difficult when only one of the parties is liable in respect of the judgment debt and the charging order is over that party's interest in a jointly owned property and a dispute arises as to whether the interests of the non-liable party and the family or those of the creditor are to have precedence. Such a dispute will not normally arise on the application for the charging order itself, but more commonly arises on an application for an order for sale or on an application to vary the charging order.

In *Harman v Glencross*,[55] it was held first that, in such a case, the application for the charging order to be varied should be transferred to the Family Division (or to the Divorce County Court), so that the court might be fully apprised of all the circumstances of the case. The court should strike a balance between the creditor's normal expectation that an order enforcing a money judgment lawfully obtained would be made, and the hardship to the wife and children that such an order could entail. Where, as in this case, the wife's right of occupation would not be adequately protected under the LPA 1925, s 30, an order with *Mesher*-type terms would normally be appropriate.

It was also said in this case that where the application for the charging order to be made absolute is heard before the commencement of divorce proceedings, the court should normally make the order sought. Where the charging order nisi has been made after the filing of the petition, the court considering the application for the charging order absolute should bear in mind that the court is holding the balance not only between the wife and the husband but also between the wife and the judgment creditor, and should make only such order as is necessary to protect the wife's right to occupy the home.

12.21 In another case,[56] it was held that there was no automatic predominance for either claim. Every case depended on striking a fair balance between the normal expectations of the creditor and the hardship to the wife and children if an order were made. The use of the term 'hardship' necessarily implied that there would be instances in which a wife and/or children would be compelled, in the interests of justice to the judgment creditor, to accept a provision for their accommodation which fell below the level of adequacy. The court, having weighed all the circumstances, was required to make only such orders as might be necessary to protect the wife's right to occupy the home, albeit not on a permanent basis.

By virtue of the TLATA 1996, trusts are no longer trusts for sale and the court should therefore be able to take a more balanced view of competing interests.[57]

---

[55] [1984] FLR 652, FD.
[56] *Austin-Fell v Austin-Fell and Midland Bank* [1989] 2 FLR 497.
[57] See *Mortgage Corporation v Shaire* [2000] 1 FLR 973. For an example of the disadvantaged position of a spouse as against the creditors of a bankrupt, see *Ram v Ram, Ram and Russell* [2004] EWCA Civ 1452, [2005] 2 FLR 63.

This issue was argued on behalf of a wife in *Bank of Ireland Mortgages v Bell and Bell*[58] where a judge at first instance had refused to order the sale of a property on the application of the creditor on the grounds that it had been purchased as a family home, was occupied by the wife and son, and the wife was in poor health. On appeal, it was held that while s 15 of the TLATA 1996 had given scope for some change to the court's previous practice, a powerful consideration was whether a creditor was receiving proper recompense for being kept out of his money of which repayment was overdue. Here, the house had ceased to be the family home when the husband left, the son was nearly 18 and the wife's ill health might at best have justified only postponement of the sale. Sale was ordered.

---

[58]   [2001] 2 FLR 809, CA.

Chapter 13

VARIATION

INTRODUCTION

13.1 The orders which may be made under the MCA 1973 may be divided into those which can be reconsidered and, if appropriate, changed or varied, and those which are 'final orders' and which cannot normally be changed. With certain limited exceptions, only periodic orders can be varied. The general principle of the MCA 1973 is that a capital order cannot be varied, save as to detail.

The statutory powers to vary are contained in s 31 of the MCA 1973, which must be considered in detail. There is some case-law as to the way the courts should approach such cases, and this must also be considered.

STATUTORY PROVISIONS

What orders can be varied?

13.2 Section 31 begins by defining the types of order to which it applies. Since s 31 is intended to be a comprehensive code, it may be taken that unless an order appears in the list of orders in s 31(2), it cannot be varied.

It is provided that:[1]

'This section [ie s 31] applies to the following orders, that is to say –

(a) any order for maintenance pending suit and any interim order for maintenance;
(b) any periodical payments order;
(c) any secured periodical payments order;
(d) any order made by virtue of section 23(3)(c) or 27(7)(b) above (provision for payment of a lump sum by instalments);
(dd) any deferred order made by virtue of section 23(1)(c) (lump sums) which includes provision made by virtue of –
(i) section 25B(4), or
(ii) section 25C,
(provision in respect of pension rights);

---

[1] MCA 1973, s 31(2).

(e)   any order for a settlement of property under section 24(1)(b) or for a variation of settlement under section 24(1)(c) or (d) above, being an order made on or after the grant of a decree of judicial separation;

(f)   any order made under section 24A(1) above for the sale of property;

(g)   a pension sharing order under section 24B above which is made at a time before the decree has been made absolute.'

13.3 The powers of the court in respect of each of these types of order are set out in s 31(1). It is provided that:

'Where the court has made an order to which this section applies, then, subject to the provisions of this section and of section 28(1A) above, the court shall have power to vary or discharge the order or to suspend any provision thereof temporarily and to revive the operation of any provision so suspended.'

Section 28(1A) is the section of the Act which empowers the court to direct that no further applications may be made. The reference to s 28(1A) therefore reminds the court that, when such a direction has been given, the order may not be varied.

13.4 The principles observed by the court when considering an application will be set out at **13.11** et seq. First, however, some particular considerations applicable to certain types of orders must be considered.

Capital orders

13.5 As was seen above, lump sum orders and property adjustment orders cannot be varied and they are not included in the list of variable orders in s 31(2). Little more need be said, save that when any dispute arises as to the precise meaning of an order, the question which must be asked is whether the order was intended to be, and can reasonably be construed as being, a final resolution of all issues between the parties. Where that is the case, and the order is in effect a lump sum order, property adjustment order or settlement of property order, it must be a final order and cannot be varied.[2]

A lump sum order payable by instalments can by varied (see **4.4**). This power to vary extends to quantum as well as to timing, but this is not the case where the order is merely for a series of lump sums payable at different times.[3] In *Myerson v Myerson* the availability of the power to vary was given as one reason for declining to allow an appeal against a consent order.[4]

---

[2]   See *Dinch v Dinch* [1987] 2 FLR 162, HL; *Peacock v Peacock* [1991] 1 FLR 324; *Hill v Hill* [1998] 1 FLR 198, CA.

[3]   *Hamilton v Hamilton* [2013] EWCA Civ 13.

[4]   [2009] EWCA Civ 282, [2009] 2 FLR 147.

Maintenance pending suit and periodical payments

13.6 When an order of this type is varied the court has power to remit any arrears which have accrued.[5] It may also, of course, either increase or decrease the rate of payment or discharge the order.

Since November 1998, the court has also enjoyed the valuable power[6] to substitute a lump sum order or property adjustment order when it discharges a periodical payments order and also, where the petition was filed on or after 1 December 2000, to make a pension sharing order. This in effect allows the court to capitalise maintenance. When substituting a lump sum order on discharging a periodical payments order, the court is not limited to a mathematical calculation of the capital equivalent of the ongoing periodical payments but may consider what lump sum would be fair in all the circumstances.[7] The court may also order that no further applications may be made for periodical payments, secured periodical payments, or an extension of any term granted by the court.

In *Pearce v Pearce*[8] Thorpe LJ summarised his general conclusions on this issue as follows:

(1)   On dismissing an entitlement to future periodical payments, the court's function is not to reopen capital claims but to substitute for the periodical payments order such other order or orders as will both fairly compensate the payee and at the same time complete the clean break.

(2)   In surveying what substitute order or orders should be made, first consideration should be given to the option of carving out of the payor's pension funds a pension for the payee equivalent to the discharged periodical payments order.

When the court decides to vary or discharge a periodical payments order or secured periodical payments order it may direct that the variation or discharge shall not take effect until the expiration of such period as may be specified in the order.[9]

Secured periodical payments

13.7 The comments made above apply equally to secured periodical payments. There is also a provision[10] to deal with the position where a person liable to make secured payments has died. In principle, an order for secured

---

5   MCA 1973, s 31(2A).
6   MCA 1973, s 31(7A) and (7B), introduced by FLA 1996, Sch 8, para 7; the remedy established by *S v S* [1987] 1 FLR 71 is now therefore obsolete.
7   *Cornick v Cornick (No 3)* [2001] 2 FLR 1240, Charles J.
8   [2003] EWCA Civ 1054, [2003] 2 FLR 1144.
9   MCA 1973, s 31(10).
10   MCA 1973, s 31(6).

periodical payments survives the death of the paying party; his obligation was to provide the security for the payments, and these will continue after his death.[11] It is therefore provided that the person entitled to payments or the personal representatives of the deceased may apply for an order for the proceeds of sale of a property to be used for securing the payments, but, save with leave of the court, no such application may be made later than 6 months after the date on which representation in regard to the deceased's estate is taken out.

Lump sum payable by instalments

13.8 As has already been said, in principle, a lump sum order cannot be varied. The provision in s 31(2) is limited to the question of payment by instalments. It only applies when the court's original order provided for payment by instalments rather than by one single payment. The power of the court is, therefore, to reduce or increase the size of the instalments or to change the frequency of the payments. In practice, of course, the court could render a lump sum order ineffective by so reducing the instalments that it would never be paid, but this would be unusual.

Provision in respect of pension rights

13.9 Pensions are dealt with in detail in Chapter 10. The types of orders which are covered by s 31(2)(dd) are, first, orders under s 25B(4) which enable the court to 'attach' a pension lump sum, and secondly, orders under s 25C which contain a similar power including the power to compel the trustees or a party with pension rights to nominate the other party as the payee. The essential nature of these provisions is that a deferred order is made requiring the trustees of a pension scheme to make a payment or payments out of the scheme to the party who is not the scheme member at some future date.

The effect of this provision is that the court may vary any such order, whether it is of a periodic or capital nature at any time after the order is made. This might be before the order had come into effect.

It is provided that, in respect of these types of orders, s 31 shall cease to apply on the death of either of the parties to the marriage.[12]

Settlement of property or variation of settlement

13.10 The powers of the court under s 31 in relation to these types of orders are limited[13] to orders made in judicial separation proceedings and also to applications:

---

[11] See **3.12**.
[12] MCA 1973, s 31(2B).
[13] MCA 1973, s 31(4).

'... made in proceedings –

(a) for the rescission of the decree of judicial separation by reference to which the order was made, or
(b) for the dissolution of the marriage in question.'

This provision therefore recognises that a decree of judicial separation leaves the parties still married to each other. If the decree itself is rescinded, any justification for the order must fall away, and if the marriage is dissolved, the court has wider powers as to a clean break, and the position may need to be reconsidered.

THE PRINCIPLES ON WHICH THE COURT EXERCISES ITS DISCRETION

13.11 The principles which govern the exercise of the court's discretion are contained in s 31(7) and fall into three parts. First, it is provided that:[14]

'... the court shall have regard to all the circumstances of the case, first consideration being given to the welfare while a minor of any child of the family who has not attained the age of eighteen ...'

This provision requires little comment. The meaning of 'the first consideration' has already been considered at **1.14**.

Secondly, it is provided that:[15]

'... the circumstances of the case shall include any change in any of the matters to which the court was required to have regard when making the order to which the application relates.'

Thirdly, it is provided that:[16]

'... in the case of a periodical or secured periodical payments order made on or after the grant of a decree of divorce or nullity of marriage, the court shall consider whether in all the circumstances and after having regard to any such change it would be appropriate to vary the order so that payments under the order are required to be made or secured only for such further period as will in the opinion of the court be sufficient ... to enable the party in whose favour the order was made to adjust without undue hardship to the termination of those payments.'

Then, in a provision which applies only to secured periodical payments, it is also provided that:[17]

---

[14] MCA 1973, s 31(7).
[15] MCA 1973, s 31(7).
[16] MCA 1973, s 31(7)(a).
[17] MCA 1973, s 31(7)(b).

'... in a case where the party against whom the order was made has died, the circumstances of the case shall also include the changed circumstances resulting from his or her death.'

The clean break on variation applications

13.12 The significance of the reference to termination of payments is clear. On a variation application, the court must perform the same task of inquiry into whether or not there should be a clean break as would be performed on an original application. The principles of the clean break are considered in detail at **2.29** et seq and need not be considered further here, save to say that the courts have adopted a variety of approaches to the termination of payments on a variation application, depending on the circumstances of the case.[18] (See also **13.6**.)

In *Fleming v Fleming*[19] it was held that on an application for variation the court was under a duty to consider terminating financial dependence provided such outcome could be achieved without undue hardship and that this principle was much enhanced where there was a previous term order.

Changes in circumstances

13.13 The court must consider all the circumstances including any change there may have been in any of the matters to which it was originally directed to have regard under s 25. The requirement to have regard to all the circumstances therefore dictates a complete review of all relevant matters; the changes since the order was made are merely one of the aspects to be considered. It is not correct merely to look at what has changed since the order was made.[20]

Having said that, it is inevitable that the court will require some change in the circumstances before it varies an order; otherwise, a dissatisfied litigant could apply repeatedly for variation as a method of appeal or challenge. The starting point must be that the order was correctly made. In a case[21] involving variation of a consent order, it was said that 'the court should not adopt an approach which differs radically from the approach taken by the parties themselves in assessing quantum of maintenance when the original order was made'; the same could be said of the approach adopted by the court in a contested case.

13.14 Some comparatively recent cases demonstrate, in different ways, the tendency of the courts to try not to depart radically from the spirit of the original order. In *VB v JP*[22] the original order had allocated 34% of the

---

[18] See e g *Morris v Morris* [1985] FLR 1176; *Sandford v Sandford* [1986] 1 FLR 412; *Richardson v Richardson (No 2)* [1994] 2 FLR 1051; *Ashley v Blackman* [1988] Fam 85; *Jones v Jones* [2000] 2 FLR 307.

[19] [2004] 1 FLR 667.

[20] *Lewis v Lewis* [1977] 3 All ER 992, CA.

[21] *Boylan v Boylan* [1988] 1 FLR 282 per Booth J.

[22] [2008] 1 FLR 742, Sir Mark Potter P.

husband's net income to the wife and children when he was earning £340,000 pa net. At the time of the variation application, his earnings had increased to £450,000 pa net. At the request of the husband, the wife had given up her career to fulfil a domestic role. The order was increased from £34,000 pa to £65,000 pa which continued to give the wife about 33% of the husband's income, the President holding that *Miller/McFarlane* principles did not apply to variation applications.

A similar result was obtained in *Lauder v Lauder.*[23]

In *Hvorostovsky v Horostovsky*[24] it was said that there was much to be said for trial judges directing themselves by reference to Charles J's rule of fairness in *Cornick v Cornick (No 3)*[25] (see **13.6**) namely that, as an income fall justifies an application for downwards variation so an income rise justifies an upward variation.[26]

In *North v North*[27] it was held that a paying party is not an insurer against all financial hazards, nor is he responsible for needs created by the other's financial mismanagement.

13.15 In *Primavera v Primavera,*[28] the husband was ordered to pay the wife periodical payments of £10,000 pa less tax, and a lump sum of £72,000. The wife was a beneficiary of her mother's estate, part of which was a house. The wife agreed to sell her share of the house to one of her daughters for the district valuer's valuation, which was considerably less than the true value, with the result that she received much less than she would otherwise have done. She applied to vary her periodical payments, and Booth J increased the order to £28,000 pa. The husband was a wealthy man. On appeal, Booth J's conclusion that there was no reason why the wife should not have regarded the inheritance as hers to do with as she wished was upheld. However, it was emphasised that an important factor was that the husband was wealthy and well able to pay the increased order; the position might be very different where the parties were of more modest means and the inheritance would have made a material difference to the total means of both parties.

It was also held that, although financial mismanagement by a party was not a relevant factor in this case, it could well be a relevant circumstance in an appropriate case.

---

[23] [2007] 2 FLR 802, Baron J.
[24] [2009] EWCA Civ 791.
[25] [2001] 2 FLR 1240.
[26] One might think that practitioners did not need Charles J or even the Court of Appeal to explain this simple truth.
[27] [2008] 1 FLR 158.
[28] [1992] 1 FLR 16, CA.

Useful guidance has been given by Charles J in *McFarlane v McFarlane*.[29] Readers will be familiar with this case (see **1.9** et seq) from when it was before the House of Lords; this was the wife's application for a variation of the periodical payments order made then. Since the previous hearings the husband's income had increased. The approach adopted by the court and agreed by the parties was to use the concept of the husband's surplus income after deducting payments for children and essential living expenses and then to give consideration to what an application of the surplus (plus the wife's own capital and other income) would be likely to produce for the wife for the rest of her life. The husband planned to retire in 2014. The wife was awarded 40% of the husband's income up to £750,000, 20% of the balance up to £1m, and 10% of any income above that figure. Charles J emphasised that it would be wrong to isolate the principle of compensation and treat it as if it were a damages claim.

PROCEDURE

13.16 An application to vary is contained within the definition of 'financial remedy'.[30] There are therefore no separate rules applicable to such an application, and it should be conducted according to the normal rules applicable to ancillary relief.[31]

FORMS OF ORDER

13.17 Forms of order for variation applications will be found at Appendix A, Precedent 32.

VARIATION SUBJECT TO CONDITIONS

13.18 In *Mubarak v Mubarik*[32] the husband applied to vary. He was in default of earlier orders and had been found to be dishonest. It was held that *Hadkinson v Hadkinson*[33] was still good law and was an important discretionary power of last resort – see also *Corbett v Corbett*.[34] The court could impose conditions on the husband proceeding with his application. It must consider:

(a)   whether the husband was in contempt;

(b)   whether he caused an impediment to the course of justice;

---

[29]   [2009] EWHC 891 (Fam), [2009] 2 FLR 1322.
[30]   FPR 2010, r 2.3.
[31]   See Chapter 16.
[32]   [2004] EWCA 1158 (Fam), [2004] 2 FLR 932.
[33]   [1952] P 285.
[34]   [2003] EWCA Civ 559, [2003] 2 FLR 385.

(c) whether there was any other effective way of securing justice;

(d) whether the contempt was wilful;

(e) whether it was appropriate to impose conditions and if so what would be appropriate.

A similar result may be found in *Laing v Laing*.[35] Here, the district judge had made it a condition of the continuation of the husband's variation application that he pay arrears of periodical payments and also reduced periodical payments to the wife. The husband appealed. The President held that the jurisdiction to make such an order was not dependent on the amount of the arrears but on the situation of the parties, the circumstances of the non-payment, and the effect of the non-payment on the course of justice in the particular case. Key questions were whether justice was being impeded and whether there was no other effective method of securing compliance with the order. It was not limited to breaches of a capital sum order.

---

[35] [2007] EWHC 3152 (Fam), Sir Mark Potter P.

Chapter 14

MISCELLANEOUS APPLICATIONS

INTRODUCTION

14.1 In this chapter, it is intended to deal with certain types of application which, although they must be mentioned, do not merit a chapter to themselves. They are:

(a) applications under MCA 1973, s 27;

(b) applications under MCA 1973, s 10(2);

(c) alteration of agreements.

APPLICATIONS UNDER MCA 1973, SECTION 27

14.2 The marginal note to s 27 of the MCA 1973 reads 'Financial provision in cases of neglect to maintain', and the section is intended to provide a remedy for financial relief exercisable by courts exercising family jurisdiction. The essential difference from the other types of relief described in this book is that the exercise of the jurisdiction conferred by s 27 does not depend on the grant of a decree of divorce, nullity or judicial separation nor even the filing of a petition. It is a 'free-standing' remedy, and the application is by way of an originating application.

14.3 Before 1970, applications for neglect to maintain were quite common, but for some time, s 27 has been little used. It was thought that it might assume a more prominent role when FLA 1996 came into force but that is now, at most, an academic possibility.

14.4 It is provided that either party to a marriage may apply to the court for an order on the ground that the other party:[1]

'(a) has failed to provide reasonable maintenance for the applicant, or
(b) has failed to provide, or to make a proper contribution towards, reasonable maintenance for any child of the family.'

Jurisdiction to make the order is the same as in other matrimonial causes.[2]

---

[1] MCA 1973, s 27(1).
[2] MCA 1973, s 27(2). See **1.69**.

The orders which the court may make in favour of the applicant are orders for periodical payments, secured periodical payments, and a lump sum.[3] There is jurisdiction to make similar orders for a child, but the effect of CSA 1991, s 8 reduces the value of those provisions. The court may also make a lump sum order for the purpose of enabling any liabilities or expenses to be met;[4] this is a similar provision to that contained in s 23(3).[5] The court also has jurisdiction to make interim orders.[6]

14.5 In deciding whether or not the respondent has failed to provide reasonable maintenance for the applicant, and, if so, what order to make, the court is directed to:[7]

> '... have regard to all the circumstances of the case including the matters mentioned in section 25(2) above and where an application is also made under this section in respect of a child of the family who has not attained the age of eighteen, first consideration shall be given to the welfare of the child while a minor.'

The court has therefore to take account of the usual s 25 factors.[8] Since the marriage has not yet been dissolved, the termination of the parties' financial dependence on each other does not arise.

14.6 There are few authorities under the modern law to indicate how the courts exercise their discretion; this may be because s 27 has been little used, and also, perhaps, because when used the orders are often only of temporary duration. The duty of both parties to a marriage to maintain each other is an established part of English law;[9] what is reasonable will depend on the circumstances of the case.

The wording of the statute was changed in 1978,[10] the old formula of 'wilful neglect to maintain' being replaced by the present 'failure to maintain'. It had been held that the common law rule that a husband has no duty to maintain a wife who has committed adultery which he has not connived at, nor by his conduct conduced to, applied to the duty to provide reasonable maintenance under s 27.[11] However, it is thought that the change in the wording of the statute, which omits the word 'wilful' and introduces some general guidelines, means that the law is no longer simply a procedure for enforcing the common law duty to maintain, and therefore that the rule that adultery is a bar no longer applies.[12]

---

3   MCA 1973, s 27(6).
4   MCA 1973, s 27(7).
5   See **4.6**.
6   MCA 1973, s 27(5).
7   MCA 1973, s 27(3).
8   See Chapter 1.
9   *Northrop v Northrop* [1968] P 74, CA.
10   By Domestic Proceedings and Magistrates' Courts Act 1978, s 63(1); see also MFPA 1984, s 4.
11   *Gray v Gray* [1976] Fam 324; *Newmarch v Newmarch* [1978] Fam 79.
12   This certainly was the intention of the Law Commission; see Law Com No 77, paras 2.15, 9.11, and 9.24(c).

14.7 There is no separate procedure for making applications under s 27 (this is a change from the previous position). An application under s 27 is defined by FPR 2010, r 2.3 as a financial remedy; r 9.1 states that Part 9 applies to applications for a financial remedy, and r 9.5(2) specifically refers to s 27 applications and requires them to be issued in a divorce county court. The procedure is therefore the same as for any other financial relief application.

APPLICATIONS UNDER MCA 1973, SECTION 10(2)

14.8 In 1969, for the first time, the law of divorce was changed to allow 'no fault' divorce.[13] For the first time, a divorce could be granted on the ground that the parties had lived apart for 2 years and the respondent consented to the grant of a decree, or that they had lived apart for 5 years even though the respondent did not consent to the grant of a decree; in the latter case, an 'innocent party' could be divorced against her will. These provisions are now s 1(2)(d) and (e) of the 1973 Act.

Because of these then novel provisions, it was thought right to include in the legislation special protection for respondents in such cases, and this protection survives unchanged in the modern law as s 10(2). The only significant advantage which can be obtained by an application under s 10(2) as opposed to a conventional application for a financial remedy is that the filing of the notice of application prevents the grant of decree absolute,[14] which can, in appropriate cases, be postponed until proper provision has been made.

When an application under s 10(2) is made, it is common to apply for other financial remedies in the usual way at the same time.

14.9 The section therefore applies where the court has granted a decree nisi under s 1(2)(d) or (e) and the respondent applies for her financial position to be considered; when the decree was also on the basis of one of the other facts in s 1 the section does not apply.[15] The application must clearly be made before decree absolute or it will lose its purpose.

It is provided that the court hearing the application:[16]

> '... shall consider all the circumstances, including the age, health, conduct, earning capacity, financial resources and financial obligations of each of the parties, and the financial position of the respondent as, having regard to the divorce, it is likely to be after the death of the petitioner should the petitioner die first ...'

The statute imposes two duties on the court: first, to consider the age, health and general financial position of the parties and any issue of conduct which

---

[13] Divorce Reform Act 1969, s 2.
[14] MCA 1973, s 10(3).
[15] MCA 1973, s 10(2).
[16] MCA 1973, s 10(3).

may be relevant, and, secondly, to consider what the position of the respondent would be if the petitioner died first. Section 10(3) then continues:

> '... and, subject to subsection (4) below, the court shall not make the decree absolute unless it is satisfied –
>
> (a)   that the petitioner should not be required to make any financial provision for the respondent, or
> (b)   that the financial provision made by the petitioner for the respondent is reasonable and fair or the best that can be made in the circumstances.'

14.10   The court must, therefore, satisfy itself either that no financial provision need be made, or that the provision made is fair and reasonable, or the best in the circumstances. The latter case (best in the circumstances) would apply where the provision made was inadequate but there were insufficient funds to do better.

As indicated, there is provision for exception made in s 10(4) which provides that the court may, if it thinks fit, make the decree absolute notwithstanding the requirements of s 10(3), if:[17]

> '(a)   it appears that there are circumstances making it desirable that the decree should be obtained without delay, and
> (b)   the court has obtained a satisfactory undertaking from the petitioner that he will make such financial provision for the respondent as the court may approve.'

Both parts of this requirement must be met before the court could act under s 10(4).

14.11   As was said in the introduction to this part, the only separate usefulness of s 10(2) is to hold up decree absolute until all financial matters have been concluded. When the person in need of protection is the petitioner, an application under s 10(2) is unnecessary as well as impossible. In *Wickler v Wickler*,[18] where the respondent applied for decree absolute under s 9(2) of MCA 1973, the petitioner having failed to apply, it was held that the court had power to refuse the application unless and until he complied with orders as to ancillary relief. There always will be a residue of cases where a respondent feels that the only way to ensure proper relief is to make an application under s 10(2); these will nearly always be cases where she will lose all rights under the husband's pension scheme on the grant of decree absolute.[19]

14.12   By FPR 2010, r 2.3 an application under s 10(2) is defined as a financial remedy. The Part 9 procedure therefore applies. Further details are given in chapter 16.

---

[17]   MCA 1973, s 10(4).
[18]   [1998] 2 FLR 326, Bracewell J.
[19]   For examples, see *Cumbers v Cumbers* [1975] 1 All ER 1, CA; *Grigson v Grigson* [1974] 1 All ER 748, CA; *Garcia v Garcia* [1991] 3 All ER 451, CA.

ORDERS FOR ALTERATION OF AGREEMENTS DURING LIFETIMES OF PARTIES

14.13 Section 35 of the MCA 1973 applies where there is a maintenance agreement subsisting, and each of the parties is, for the time being, either domiciled in or resident in England and Wales.[20] In those circumstances, either party may apply to the court for an order making such alterations in the agreement:[21]

'(i) by varying or revoking any financial arrangements contained in it, or

(ii) by inserting in it financial arrangements for the benefit of one of the parties to the agreement or a child of the family,

as may appear to that court to be just having regard to all the circumstances, including, if relevant, the matters mentioned in section 25(4) above; and the agreement shall have effect thereafter as if any alteration made by the order had been made by agreement between the parties and for valuable consideration.'

Section 25(4) refers to the liability of a step-parent. This is the only specific s 25 factor to be mentioned. Otherwise, the court must consider all the circumstances.

14.14 Before it can make such an order, the court must be satisfied either:[22]

'(a) that by reason of a change in the circumstances in the light of which any financial arrangements contained in the agreement were made or, as the case may be, financial arrangements were omitted from it (including a change foreseen by the parties when making the agreement), the agreement should be altered so as to make different, or, as the case may be, so as to contain, financial arrangements, or

(b) that the agreement does not contain proper financial arrangements with respect to any child of the family.'

The second provision may now be of little effect due to CSA 1991.

14.15 There are other matters of detail in the section. It should be noted that application may be made to a magistrates' court under s 35, provided the parties are resident in England and Wales and at least one of the parties resides in the area of that court.[23] The powers of the magistrates are limited to issues of periodical payments.[24]

14.16 By FPR 2010, r 2.3 an application under s 35 is defined as a financial remedy. The procedure under Part 9 therefore applies.

---

[20] MCA 1973, s 35(1).
[21] MCA 1973, s 35(2).
[22] MCA 1973, s 35(2).
[23] MCA 1973, s 35(3).
[24] MCA 1973, s 35(3).

Chapter 15

FINANCIAL RELIEF AFTER OVERSEAS DIVORCE

INTRODUCTION

15.1 The various forms of financial relief described in this book, with the exception of applications under s 27 of the MCA 1973, all depend on the grant of a decree of divorce, nullity or judicial separation (or at least the filing of a petition for such relief). Without a petition and, in the case of a final order, a decree, the court can do nothing. The type of relief about to be described in this chapter is different, in that the basis for jurisdiction is an overseas divorce or other order. There are two stages in such applications. First, the court must grant permission to apply. Secondly, the court will adjudicate on the application; in this case, the relief it may grant is practically identical to that which would be granted after a decree of the English and Welsh courts.

JURISDICTION

15.2 It is provided that an application for financial relief may be made where:[1]

'(a) a marriage has been dissolved or annulled, or the parties to a marriage have been legally separated, by means of judicial or other proceedings in an overseas country, and
(b) the divorce, annulment or legal separation is entitled to be recognised as valid in England and Wales.'

Remarriage of the applicant is a bar to an application in relation to that marriage.[2]

15.3 The classes of divorce etc which would be recognised as valid are those set out in the Recognition of Divorces and Legal Separations Act 1971, ss 2–6.

15.4 Jurisdiction therefore depends on the existence of a divorce etc which would be recognised and on the requirements of MFPA 1984, s 15, which provides that the court shall have jurisdiction if any of the following three jurisdictional requirements are satisfied:

---

[1] MFPA 1984, s 12(1).
[2] MFPA 1984, s 12(2).

(1) domicile of either party at the date of application for leave or as at the divorce etc;

(2) the habitual residence of either party for one year ending with either the application for leave or the divorce etc;

(3) either party having, at the date of the application for leave, a beneficial interest in possession in a dwelling-house in England and Wales which was at some time in the marriage a matrimonial home of the parties to the marriage.

15.5 If the proposed respondent is domiciled in a contracting State within the meaning of the Civil Jurisdiction and Judgments Act 1982,[3] a further complication may arise. The general theme of the 1982 Act is that a respondent who is in a contracting State must be sued there. However, the Act does not apply to rights in property arising out of a matrimonial relationship, nor to maintenance.

APPLICATIONS FOR PERMISSION

15.6 The first step the applicant must take is to apply for permission, and it is provided that the court shall not grant permission unless it considers that there is substantial ground for the making of an application for such an order.[4] Clearly, the court would first have to be satisfied that it had jurisdiction, as explained above. However, that would not be an end of the matter, since s 16 provides that:[5]

> '... the court shall consider whether in all the circumstances of the case it would be appropriate for such an order to be made by a court in England and Wales, and if the court is not satisfied that it would be appropriate the court shall dismiss the application.'

There follows a list of the matters to which the court must have particular regard. These include:[6]

- the connection which the parties have with England and Wales, the country where the divorce etc was granted, or any other country;

- the financial benefit which the applicant or a child has or is likely to have received in the foreign proceedings;

- the financial relief awarded by any foreign court and the likelihood of any such order being complied with;

---

3   Most countries in western Europe are contracting States.
4   MFPA 1984, s 13.
5   MFPA 1984, s 16(2).
6   MFPA 1984, s 16(2)(a)–(i).

- the right to apply in any other jurisdiction;

- availability of property in this country;

- length of time since divorce etc.

15.7 The procedure for an application is contained in FPR 2010, Part 6. The application must be made in the Principal Registry except where r 9.26 applies (this relates to consent orders and provides that the application may be made to the court where the consent application is proceeding). The application must be heard by a judge but not a district judge. However, when permission is granted, the court may direct that the substantive application may be heard by a district judge of the principal registry.

The applicant may apply for an order that the application be made without notice, but some reason for this must be given; where the application is without notice, the respondent has the right to apply to set the order aside. The procedure to be followed is that set out in Part 18.

The application for permission is a crucial step. The court has to be satisfied as to the 'substantial ground for the making of an application', and if, on the application for permission, it is clear that if permission were granted the substantive application would fail, permission should not be granted.[7] The burden is on the person bringing the application, and it was held, in a case where there had been a connection with England before the marriage but the connection with the foreign jurisdiction was now stronger, that permission should not be granted.[8]

It has been held that the mischief which the Act was designed to redress is a narrow one, and does not include the case of a foreign court of competent jurisdiction making an order which has neither been appealed nor impugned.[9] While there is no absolute rule of law that permission will not be granted where the sole motive is to enforce a foreign order, in practice permission will only rarely be granted in such circumstances.[10] Permission was refused in one case where the wife, wisely or unwisely, had allowed the breakdown of her marriage to be referred to the courts in France; she was not to be allowed to relitigate here an issue which had been taken to its conclusion there.[11] In another case, it was held that it was essential to demonstrate that the applicant was suffering some injustice before the court could find that there was a substantial ground[12] but in a later decision of the Court of Appeal it was said that the judge had gone too far and his decision should not be followed.[13]

---

[7]   *Holmes v Holmes* [1989] Fam 47, CA.
[8]   *Z v Z (Financial Provision: Overseas Divorce)* [1992] 2 FLR 291.
[9]   *Hewitson v Hewitson* [1995] Fam 100, CA.
[10]   *Jordan v Jordan* [1999] 2 FLR 1069, CA.
[11]   *M v M (Financial Provision after Foreign Divorce)* [1994] 1 FLR 399.
[12]   *N v N (Foreign Divorce: Financial Relief)* [1997] 1 FLR 900, per Cazalet J.
[13]   *Jordan v Jordan* (above).

The relationship between the grant of permission and the substantive application was considered in detail in *Agbaje v Agbaje* which is examined at **15.9**.

ORDERS WHICH MAY BE MADE

15.8 Once the vital step of obtaining permission has been taken (and assuming that the order is not set aside), the applicant may proceed with the application for financial relief. The powers of the court are contained in ss 14, and 17 to 26 of MFPA 1984. Broadly speaking, the court has power to make all the types of order it could make if the divorce etc had been granted in England and Wales, including avoidance of disposition. The matters to which the court must have regard are contained in s 18, and are similar to those in s 25.

Examples of cases where substantive orders have been made after the grant of permission are found in two recent cases. In *A v S (Financial Relief After Overseas US Divorce and Financial Proceedings)*[14] the parties had been divorced in Texas, and the Texan court had made an order in financial proceedings awarding the wife almost nothing, based on the Texan doctrine of community of property. Before the marriage, the wife lived in a house in England which the husband had purchased for her occupation; after the marriage she had moved to live with him in Texas. The Texan court ordered her to leave the house in England to which she had returned, and she applied for relief in the English court. Bodey J held that extreme caution had to be exercised when a mature foreign jurisdiction had already adjudicated and there was also a problem because the wife had repeatedly lied in the Texan proceedings. Nevertheless, there was an injustice which could be remedied by the application of the discretionary approach, and the wife had a real need for financial help. It was only appropriate to intervene to the minimum extent necessary so as to remedy the injustice perceived. The wife was awarded £60,000.

In *M v L (Financial Relief After Overseas Divorce)*[15] there had been a 30-year delay between divorce and the application. The fact that the divorce had been in South Africa was anomalous, since the case should always have been an English one. The wife had remained dependent on the husband through voluntary payments. Coleridge J declined to divide the husband's capital on modern principles, but made an award of periodical payments based on what it would be reasonable for her to have in all the circumstances.

15.9 The decision of the Supreme Court in *Agbaje v Agbaje*[16] is the first important guidance to be issued on a review of a substantive order under Part III and also contains guidance as to the relationship between the grant of permission and the approach of the court on making a substantive order. The

---

[14]   [2003] 1 FLR 431.
[15]   [2003] 2 FLR 425.
[16]   [2010] UKSC 13, [2010] 1 FLR 1813.

facts of the case need not be set out in detail. Essentially, Coleridge J made an order granting a Nigerian wife £275,000; this was set aside by the Court of Appeal. It was said that the judge had failed to address the issue of comity and had not identified why this was an exceptional case; the parties' connection with Nigeria was more significant than with England and the Nigerian court, which had made an award to the wife, had not done her a serious injustice.

The decision of the Court of Appeal was set aside by the Supreme Court and the decision of Coleridge J restored. The following guidance was given:

(1) The principal object of the filter mechanism is to prevent wholly unmeritorious claims being pursued to oppress or blackmail a former spouse. The threshold is not high; 'substantial' means 'solid'.

(2) Once a judge has given reasons for deciding that the threshold has been crossed, the approach to setting aside should be (as under the CPR) exercised only where there is a compelling reason to do so.

(3) Section 16 does not require the court to consider whether it is appropriate for an order to be made but only whether it is appropriate for an order to be made by the court of England and Wales. It does not determine the criteria by which the question of whether financial provision should be made is determined.

(4) Part III contains no reference to hardship, injustice or exceptionality. Hardship and injustice are not pre-conditions.

(5) Mere disparity between the award made by the foreign court and what would be awarded on an English divorce is insufficient to trigger the application of Part III. Nor is hardship or injustice a condition, but if either factor is present it may make it appropriate for an order to be made.

(6) The following general principles should be applied. First, primary consideration should be given to the welfare of any children of the marriage. Secondly, it will never be appropriate to make an order which gives the claimant more than he or she would have been awarded had all the proceedings taken place within this jurisdiction. Thirdly, where possible, the order should have the result that provision is made for the reasonable needs of both spouses. Subject to this, the court has a broad discretion.

The decision in *Agbaje* was followed in *Traversa v Freddi*[17] where it was said that it is inevitable in practice that the court will look comparatively at the parties' respective degrees of closeness with the two jurisdictions involved. In this case, it was held that the foreign jurisdiction had not produced an overall unjust result.

---

[17] [2009] EWHC 2101 (Fam), [2010] 1 FLR 324, Charles J.

15.10 In *Z v A (Financial Remedy after Overseas Divorce)*[18] Coleridge J after observing that the proper interpretation of ss 16-18 was set out in *Agjabe v Agjabe* (supra), particularly at paras [70] and [73] per Lord Collins, added that there was a scale of award dependent on the parties' connections (or lack of connections) with this jurisdiction. He said that where the English connections were very strong there was no reason why the application should not proceed as if it were made in purely English proceedings under MCA 1973. This emphasis appears to be a new element in the guidance and it will be interesting to see if it is repeated by higher courts.

---

[18]   [2012] EWHC 1434 (Fam).

Chapter 16

PROCEDURE

INTRODUCTION

16.1 The Family Procedure Rules 2010 (FPR 2010) Part 9 and the accompanying practice directions, which came into force on 6 April 2011, set out the rule dealing with applications for a financial remedy. FPR 2010, r 3.3 defines this term to include a wide range of family proceedings within which courts can make financial orders including for example applications under Sch 7 of the Children Act 1989 and certain applications under the Matrimonial and Family Proceedings Act 1984. The court's powers to make orders which were formerly known as ancillary relief orders are now collectively defined as 'financial orders' and that terminology is used in this chapter.

Although the FPR 2010 make substantial amendments to the rules and practice dealing with many aspects of family proceedings, the provisions relating to applications for financial orders have not changed significantly from the ancillary relief procedural rules which had applied under the old regime. The new provisions are set out in Part 9 of the FPR 2010 but will be familiar to practitioners who have worked under the ancillary relief procedure which has been in operation since 2000. The new rules follow a style similar to the Civil Procedure Rules 1998 (CPR) and at their heart have the overriding objective which is set out in Part 1 of the rules. In addition to considering the specific provisions for financial orders set out in Part 9 of the rules, the practitioner will also need to be familiar with other aspects of the new rules which apply to all family proceedings (including those for financial orders) such as the provisions relating to experts (which were changed significantly in January 2013), costs, evidence (including the provisions relating to statements of truth) and the courts general case management powers.

ISSUE OF PROCEEDINGS

16.2 Applicants for a financial order may be classified into:

(a) those who have included a prayer for a financial order in a petition or answer;

(b) petitioners who have not included such a prayer in their petition;

(c) respondents.

Those in class (a) may apply for a financial order in the manner described in **16.5** et seq.[1] Those in class (b) must apply for permission to make the application. The Family Procedings Rules 1991 which have been replaced by the FPR 2010 made specific provision for making an application of this kind. There appears to be no equivalent provision in the FPR 2010 and so it would appear that an application should be made in accordance with the procedure set out in FPR 2010, Part 18. If the decree nisi has not yet been pronounced, the appropriate method to apply for permission is to apply to the district judge for leave to amend the petition by including such a prayer. The amended petition must then be re-served on the respondent unless he has already consented to the application. When the application to the court is for a consent order leave is not required.

If the application is made after decree nisi, it must be made on notice to the respondent by filing Form A, supported by a statement explaining why the petition contained no such prayer. The application may be made at the trial of the application, but, for obvious reasons, it is preferable to make the application well in advance.

The reasons for the omission may be many and various. It may have been a simple mistake; the respondent may have promised to support the petitioner and then failed to do so; circumstances may have changed since the filing of the petition. Permission is not to be granted as of right; some reason must be given.[2]

16.3   The principle behind the rule requiring the prayer in the petition is that a respondent is entitled to know from the outset what claims are being made against him. It follows that the most likely reason why permission would be refused would be that the respondent had been led to believe that there would be no such claim, that such a belief was reasonable in the circumstances, and that he had acted to his detriment on the strength of this belief.[3] In such circumstances, the longer the delay on the part of the applicant the greater the chance of a refusal of permission.

However, refusal of permission is uncommon. The applicant has a statutory right to apply, and should not be deprived of this by some technical defect. It has been held[4] that the court ought not to refuse permission in any case where it seems that the applicant has a seriously arguable case for financial order; accordingly, any statement in support of the application should, in addition to dealing with the reason for the omission, deal with the applicant's means, the respondent's means insofar as the applicant is aware of them, and the general merits of the case.

---

[1]   FPR 2010, r 9.4.
[2]   *Marsden v Marsden* [1973] 2 All ER 851.
[3]   As in *Marsden v Marsden* (above).
[4]   *Chatterjee v Chatterjee* [1976] Fam 199, CA.

16.4 A respondent who has not filed an answer or even an acknowledgement of service has an unfettered right to be heard on any question relating to an application for a financial order. This would include making an application.

16.5 Subject to what has been said above, either the petitioner or the respondent may apply for a financial order. A party who has remarried may not apply for a financial order.[5] However, the application can be made in the petition or answer and so Form A does not have to precede any remarriage. Where a claim for financial order was made in the petition, and no claim was made by the respondent until the petitioner subsequently made her application, it was held[6] that the remarriage of the respondent did not bar him from applying for an order in the course of the petitioner's application; the petitioner had applied and she could seek an order against herself (even though she had not done so here!). Therefore the court had jurisdiction. The position would have been different had the petitioner made no application.

The persons who may apply for financial orders for a child are set out in r 9.10, and include parents and others who might normally be regarded as being in loco parentis and also any child of the family who has been given leave to intervene in the cause for the purpose of applying for financial orders.[7] Where the application is for a variation of settlement, the court must, unless it is satisfied that the proposed variation does not adversely affect the rights of the child or children concerned, direct that the children be separately represented on the application.[8]

THE OVERRIDING OBJECTIVE

16.6 FPR 2010 Part 1 sets out 'The Overriding Objective' of the rules. This is a concept familiar to practitioners as it had been contained in those provisions of the Family Proceedings Rules 1991 which applied to ancillary relief. Following the introduction of the FPR 2010, however, the overriding objective now applies when the court exercises any powers set out under the Family Procedure Rules or interprets any rule. It is emphasised that the overriding objective is to enable the court to deal with cases justly, having regard to any welfare issues involved. This includes ensuring that a case is dealt with expeditiously and fairly, in ways which are proportionate to the nature, importance and complexity of the issues, ensuring that the parties are on an equal footing, saving expense and allotting to it an appropriate share of the court's resources taking into account the need to allot resources to other cases. These provisions follow closely the overriding objective which is a central feature of the CPR.

---

[5]   MCA 1973, s 28(3).
[6]   *Whitehouse-Piper v Stokes* [2008] EWCA Civ 1049.
[7]   FPR 2010, r 9.10(1)(f).
[8]   FPR 2010, r 9.11(1).

ISSUE OF APPLICATION

16.7 An application for a financial order falls within the definition of relevant family proceedings set out in the pre-application protocol for mediation information and assessment which is part of PD 3A of the Family Procedure Rules 2010. As a result, before an applicant makes an application to the court for a financial order, he or she should first contact a family mediator to arrange to attend an information meeting about family mediation and other forms of alternative dispute resolution. There are certain exceptions to this requirement, including where the applicant or another party in a dispute concerning financial issues is bankrupt, where the parties are in agreement and there is no dispute to mediate or where the whereabouts of the other party are unknown. There are also exceptions where any party has, to the applicant's knowledge, made an allegation of domestic violence against the other party resulting in a police investigation or the issuing of civil proceedings within the last 12 months, and where the prospective application is to be made without notice to the other party.

When issuing an application for a financial order, the form FM1 completed by the applicant or his solicitor must accompany the application. Where a party has attended a mediation information and assessment meeting, the form must also be completed by the mediator.

The implementation of the pre-action protocol, with effect from 6 April 2011, reflects government policy to continue to encourage the use of mediation rather than court proceedings in family disputes. However, attendance at mediation or even at a mediation information and assessment meeting is not compulsory. The FM1 form includes a section in which an applicant who has not attended the mediation information and assessment meeting and does not fall within any of the exceptions to the requirement to do so can explain why he has not attended. The practice direction states that if court proceedings are taken, the court will wish to know at the first hearing whether mediation has been considered by the parties. In considering the conduct of any relevant family proceedings (including an application for a financial order) the court will take into account any failure to comply with the protocol and may refer the parties to a meeting with a mediator before the proceedings continue further. It is anticipated that this would be a step which the court would be expected to consider at the first appointment. This is a new procedural requirement and it will take some time to establish the extent to which the courts will seek to emphasise the importance of its provisions by, for example, requiring parties to attend mediation before taking any other procedural steps after the first appointment. It is anticipated that practice will differ between courts, even between individual district judges.

Notice of application is made by filing Form A. The application should be made in the county court or district registry of the High Court where the proceedings seeking a 'matrimonial order' for a divorce, judicial separation or dissolution of a civil partnership are taking place. An application under MCA

1973, s 10(2) is made in Form B.[9] It will be noted that, except in s 10(2) applications, the parties are referred to as 'the applicant' and 'the respondent'; a respondent to the main suit may be the applicant in the ancillary relief application.

At this stage, no statement or other evidence is filed. The parties receive a notice in Form C which informs them of the date of the first appointment (FA) and the requirements as to the filing of evidence. The court allocates a date for hearing of the FA not less than 12 weeks and not more than 16 weeks after the date of issue.[10] The documents must then be served on the respondent to the application by the court within 4 days.[11] If the applicant wishes to serve the respondent he must notify the court and then do so within 4 days of receiving the notice of hearing from the court and file a certificate of service at or before the first appointment.

SERVICE AND PARTIES

16.8 Once the Form A has been issued, the court serves it on the respondent within 4 days of the date of issue.[12] The documents are sent either to the solicitors who are on the record as acting for the other party[13] or to the party in person where no solicitor is acting for him.[14] In certain circumstances, service may also be effected by DX or fax.[15] When the application is for a variation of settlement, a copy of the application must be served by the applicant on the trustees of the settlement and the settlor if living.[16] In the case of an application for avoidance of disposition, the same documents must be sent by the applicant to the person in whose favour the disposition is alleged to have been made.[17] If the application contains an application for pension sharing or pension attachment it must be served on the person responsible for the pension arrangement or on the Pension Protection Fund Board if the PPF has taken responsibility for the scheme and a pension compensation sharing order or pension compensation attachment order is sought.

When the application is for a property adjustment order, a copy of the application must be served by the applicant on any mortgagee or other person of whom particulars are given in the form. It is not necessary to serve a copy of the evidence in support, but any person so served may make a request in writing to the court, within 14 days after service, for a copy of the applicant's Form E.[18]

---

[9]   FPR 2010, PD5A.
[10]   FPR 2010, r 9.12(1)(a).
[11]   FPR 2010, r 9.12(1)(b).
[12]   FPR 2010, r 9.12(1).
[13]   FPR 2010, r 9.25.
[14]   FPR 2010, r 9.12(1)(a).
[15]   FPR 2010, r 9.12(1)(b).
[16]   FPR 2010, r 9.12(1)(b)(i).
[17]   FPR 2010, r 6.11.
[18]   FPR 2010, r 6.12.

Sometimes it is necessary to join other parties, for example persons with whom the respondent jointly owns property. RSC Ord 15, r 6(2)(b) allowed the joinder of 'any person between whom and any party ... there may exist a question or issue arising out of ... any relief or remedy claimed'; under the FPR 1991 these rules applied in family proceedings in the High Court and county court as there was no other provision contained in the rules. This issue was confirmed by the Court of Appeal in *Goldstone v Goldstone*[19] in which a contention that CPR applied when the court considered the gender of parties was rejected and the court confirmed that the proceedings were properly regarded as family proceedings rather than chancery.

> 'In its essence the claim remains a claim by the wife against her husband. Ultimately it is a claim for discretionary relief. In this, as in many cases, there must be a preliminary issue trial to establish the extent of the assets over which the discretion is ultimately exercised. Here, as in many cases, the preliminary issue trial determines the claims and the rights of third parties. The preliminary issue trial is pendent on the originating application. It has no independent existence.'

The Court of Appeal then confirmed the approach which had been taken by Nicholas Mostyn QC then sitting as a deputy high court judge in *TL v ML (Ancillary Relief: Claim against Assets of Extended Family)*[20] in which he stated that in every case where a dispute arises about the ownership of property in ancillary relief proceedings between a spouse and a third party the following steps should ordinarily happen:

(1)   the third party should be joined to the proceedings at the earliest opportunity;

(2)   direction should be given for the issue to be fully pleaded by points of claim and points of defence;

(3)   separate witness statements should be directed in relation to the dispute;

(4)   the dispute should be directed to be heard separately as a preliminary issue before the financial dispute resolution appointment.

The position in relation to the application of the RSC has changed following the implementation of the FPR 2010 which remove the 'default application' of the RSC to family proceedings. This issue was considered by Hughes LJ in the *Goldstone* case. His opinion, albeit obiter, was that following implementation of the FPR 2010, joinder of third parties to family proceedings would be governed by the court's wide case management powers, contained in FPR 2010, r 4.1, the application of the overriding objective in FPR 2010, r 1.1 and the court's duty to manage cases in FPR 2010, r 1.4(1), which contains a specific provision that the court's duty to actively manage cases included identifying at an early stage the issues and who should be a party to the proceedings. Any remaining doubt

[19]   [2011] EWCA Civ 39.
[20]   [2005] EWHC 2860 (Fam), [2006] 1 FLR 1263.

about the appropriate procedure to be followed has been resolved by the amendments of the FPR now contained in FPR 9.26B which enables the court to add a party if it is desirable so that the court can resolve all matters in dispute in the proceedings or to remove a party if it is not desirable for him or her to continue to be a party to the proceedings on the court's own initiative or on an application made in accordance with the Part 18 procedure. Any such application must be supported by evidence setting out the proposed new party's interest in, or connection with, the proceedings (unless the court directs otherwise).

16.9 The Family Proceedings Rules 1991 provided that where an affidavit or document contained an allegation of adultery or of an improper association with a named person, then, if the court so directed, it must be endorsed with a notice in Form M14, and a copy of the affidavit or of such part thereof as the court may direct, endorsed as aforesaid, should be served on that person by the person who files the affidavit, and the person against whom the allegation is made should be entitled to intervene in the proceedings by applying for directions within 7 days of the service of the affidavit on him.

The court has a discretion as to whether to make an order for service on a named person, and one of the problems about this rule is that it is frequently overlooked until the trial of the application, by which time, in most cases, it would not be cost-effective to do anything about it. The intention of the rule, clearly, is that anyone whose name is mentioned in an affidavit is entitled to know about it and to have the opportunity to deny what is said. Difficulties could be avoided if the following procedure were adopted.

(1) The person drafting the document should be satisfied that it really is necessary to name the person concerned. This might be necessary where it was alleged that the other party was cohabiting and that this had some relevance to the issues but, even then, unless the cohabitation was in dispute it would not be necessary to name the other party.

(2) Where a person is named, a copy of the statement, or of the relevant part, should be sent to him or her or to any solicitors acting, with a letter asking if the named person wishes to be formally served or to make any representations.

(3) After the time specified in the letter has elapsed, a letter should be sent to the district judge pointing out the relevant passage in the statement, informing the court of any reply from the named person, and asking for a direction. There appears to be no corresponding rule in FPR 2010 setting out the specific procedure to be followed in cases of this kind but it is suggested that the guidance set out above should still be followed to prevent difficulties arising.

SPECIAL RULES RELATING TO PENSIONS

16.10   Specific rules relating to the action required by a person with pension rights are set out in FPR 2010, r 9.30. This provides that when the court fixes the first appointment date a party with pension rights must request the person responsible for the pension arrangement under which he is likely to have benefits to provide the information referred to in reg 2(2) of the Pensions on Divorce etc (Provision of Information) Regulations 2000.[21] This relates to the valuation of pension rights or benefits. The person with pension rights must make this request within 7 days of the date upon which he receives notification of the date of the first appointment and must then supply the information to the other party (together with the name and address of the person responsible for the pension arrangements) within 7 days of receipt of that information. It is specifically provided that a request for this information need not be made where the party with pension rights is already in possession of or has requested a relevant valuation of the pension rights or benefits under the pension arrangement. Information relating to each party's pension rights must be set out in the Form E Financial Statement. Rule 9.15(7)(c) provides that at the first appointment the court may in a case where a pension sharing order or pension attachment order is requested direct any party with pension rights to file and serve a pension enquiry form (Form P) completed in full or in part as the court may direct. Form P was introduced in 2005 with the intention of providing a cheaper and more cost effective procedure for providing detailed information about a party's pension rights than the procedure which had previously been followed.

Similar provisions are applied by FPR 2010, rr 9.38–9.45 where the application is made for a pension compensation sharing order (PCSO) or pension compensation attachment order (PCAO) in respect of a pension scheme that has been transferred to the Pension Protection Fund (PPF). The 'party with compensation rights' must request the PPF Board to provide information about the valuation of entitlement to the PPF compensation within seven days of notification of the date of the Form A and pass on that information to the other party within seven days of receipt.

If an application for a PCSO or PCAO is made in the Form A (or subsequently added to an existing application) it must be served on the PPF Board. The rules also contain provisions which apply where the PPF becomes involved in a pension scheme during the course of an application for a financial order which includes an application for a pension sharing order or pension attachment order in respect of the other party's pension rights in respect of that scheme.

Where the party receives notification that the scheme is undergoing an assessment period and/or where the PPF has assumed responsibility for the scheme he must send to the other party within seven days of receipt a copy of the notification valuation summary and any other information which the PPF

---

[21]   SI 2000/1048.

Board is required to supply. He must also request in writing a forecast of the member's compensation entitlement and send a copy to the other party within seven days of receipt.

Confirmation from the party with pension rights that a scheme is in an assessment period will enable the court and the other party to consider the options available for dealing with the rights under that scheme. In the event that the PPF assumes responsibility for a scheme an application can be made, where appropriate, to amend the application for the financial order to include an application for a PCSO or PCAO. As at February 2013 the PPF had taken responsibility for 595 schemes and a further 200 had been subject to a period of assessment.

FILING OF EVIDENCE

16.11 Evidence is given by each party completing Form E. These forms must be filed at court and simultaneously exchanged not less than 35 days before the date of the FA.[22] Form E is a comprehensive document which requires the parties to set out full details of the marriage, their children, their property and income and financial needs and obligations, and enables them to provide information about any specific MCA 1973, s 25 matter (such as contributions) on which they rely.[23] Form E is a statement verified by a statement of truth. It is intended that the information contained in Form E will be all the information which the court will need in the majority of cases.

Form E must have attached to it any documents required by the form itself and any other documents necessary to clarify or explain any of the information contained in the form. It must also attach certain specified documents in relation to the party's pension arrangement or, where relevant, the pension protection fund. It may not annex or exhibit any other documents.[24] At this stage, no further disclosure or inspection of document may be requested or given except as specifically provided for in the FPR 2010.[25]

16.12 The intention is that in relatively simple cases it should be possible to use the first appointment as a financial dispute resolution (FDR) appointment (see **16.27**) but this cannot happen where one side is waiting for important documents from the other. As the rules provide that no voluntary disclosure may be given before the first appointment it is important to ensure that all documents that would be relevant in a standard case are annexed to Form E in order to improve the prospect of a settlement taking place at (or even before) the first appointment.

---

[22] FPR 2010, r 9.13(2).
[23] FPR 2010, r 9.13(4).
[24] FPR 2010, r 9.14(2).
[25] FPR 2010, r 9.14(4).

16.13   Form E therefore requires the annexation of the following documents:

- any property valuation obtained within the last 6 months (paras 2.1 and 2.2);

- bank or building society statements for the past 12 months for any account held (para 2.3);

- surrender value quotations in respect of any life insurance policies (para 2.5);

- the last 2 years' accounts and any other document used as a basis for valuation of business assets (para 2.11) and for income from business (para 2.16);

- any valuation of pension rights and information about Pension Protection Fund Compensation actually available (para 2.13); and

- the last three payslips and most recent P60 (para 2.15).

This list is a useful summary of requirements to hand to clients in a financial remedy case at an early stage. It has been held that:[26]

> '... solicitors advising the makers of Forms E have, as officers of the court, an important responsibility to ensure that true and realistic figures are inserted in a Form E. And deponents have a greater responsibility to ensure that their Forms E are truthful and honest. The rubric at the beginning of the Form ... is not mere window dressing.'

16.14   The fairly strict limits imposed by the rule can clearly cause difficulties when one party fails to co-operate; disclosure of the Forms E must be simultaneous, and if the date of the FA is drawing near there may seem to be insufficient time to prepare the case. The date of the FA may be vacated only with permission of the court,[27] and the courts are generally slow to permit any variation in the timetable.

In these circumstances, the applicant's solicitor should immediately apply without notice to the district judge for an order that the respondent file and exchange his Form E within, say, 7 days of the service of the order upon him. If this does not produce the desired result, it may be that there will be no alternative to seeking an adjournment of the FA at the FA itself; in such circumstances, there is no reason why the court should not assess the wasted costs and order the respondent to pay them within 14 days.

16.15   Where a party is unavoidably prevented from sending any document required by Form E, he must at the earliest opportunity serve copies of that

---

[26]   FPR 2010, r 9.14(1).
[27]   For a complete list, see Form E itself in FPR 2010, PD5A, set out as Appendix B of this book.

document on the other party and file a copy with the court together with a written explanation of the failure to send it with Form E.[28]

OTHER DOCUMENTS TO BE SERVED

16.16 At least 14 days before the hearing of the FA, each party must file at court and serve on the other an important series of documents, designed to clarify the case and narrow the issues.[29] These are as follows:

- a concise statement of the issues between the parties (see **16.17**);

- a chronology;

- either a questionnaire setting out by reference to the statement of issues any further information or documents requested or a statement that no such information is requested; and

- notice in Form G (see **16.23**).

The importance of these documents will be seen when they are considered in turn.

THE STATEMENT OF APPARENT ISSUES

16.17 One of the documents which both parties must file at court and serve on each other before the hearing of the FA is the statement of apparent issues. This is an important document, and, in a well-prepared case, should be the central document for the district judge at the FA, since the principal purpose of that hearing is to define the issues in the case. It is essential, therefore, that the parties and their advisers should have contemplated the issues and committed their thoughts to writing before the FA. The Forms E of both parties will have concluded by stating the terms of the order which each party seeks, and it should therefore be possible to identify the issues in the case.

16.18 It is unnecessary to set out a laborious list of each and every issue on which the parties do not agree. For example, it would be unnecessary to record that 'the wife asserts that the cost of her gas and electricity is £800 per annum whereas the husband says it should be only £550 per annum', or that 'the wife says that the husband has an improper relationship with Mrs X, but the husband denies this'.

Proper issues might read, for example:

---

[28]   FPR 2010, r 9.14(3).
[29]   FPR 2010, r 9.14(5).

- 'The wife asserts that the matrimonial home should be transferred to her, to provide a home for her and the children; the husband says that the wife's housing needs can be met by a lump sum payment of £x which should be paid to her from the proceeds of sale of the home.'

- 'The husband states that there should be a clean break on payment to the wife of £x and says that the wife could acquire an earning capacity of £y per annum and make herself self-sufficient within 12 months. The wife says that her earning capacity is uncertain and unpredictable, and that, in any event, as long as the children are of school age, there should be no dismissal of her claims.'

- 'The wife asserts that her separate capital amounts to £z, acquired in the following manner [brief details] and that this is the minimum sum which should be paid to her before consideration of the s 25 factors. The husband denies this claim, and says that the majority of the wife's notional capital came from him or his family.'

16.19 It is unnecessary to continue at great length. The importance of the statement of apparent issues, and the requirement on the parties to formulate these in a manner which will enable the court to use the statement as the foundation of its deliberations, is obvious.

QUESTIONNAIRES AND REQUESTS FOR DOCUMENTS

16.20 It is of the essence of the current procedure that no disclosure of documents may be sought or given after the issue of the application and before the FA, except as provided for under the rule.[30] The intention of the rule is that the 35 days between the exchange of the Forms E and the FA shall be taken up with deciding what further information and documents are needed, and formulating the questionnaire and request for documents. The importance of these provisions and, in particular, the court's control over the disclosure and inspection process was emphasised by the Court of Appeal in its decision in *Imerman v Imerman*,[31] when considering an appeal brought by a husband (following a first instance decision by Moylan J) concerning the wife's ability to use documents obtained by her brothers from the hard drive of a computer that they had shared with the husband. At first instance these documents had been admitted as evidence in accordance with the long standing approach taken by the family courts following the decision in *Hildebrand v Hildebrand*[32] which had allowed the use in evidence of confidential private documents contained by one spouse concerning the financial affairs of the other, provided that no force was used in obtaining the documents and that copies of the documents found were produced and the original documents returned to the other party. As part of its reasoning for overturning Moylan J's decision and disapproving the way in

---

[30] FPR 2010, r 9.14(4).
[31] [2010] EWCA Civ 908, [2010] 2 FLR 814.
[32] [1992] 1 FLR 244.

which the 'Hildebrand' approach had been used in family cases, the Court of Appeal in *Imerman* emphasised that it was only at the point at which a party is required to file and serve Form E that the duty arises to provide disclosure of assets. In the *Imerman* case when the documents from the husband's computer had been downloaded prior to exchange of Forms E the husband had been under no duty of financial disclosure.

The Court of Appeal also emphasised that the Family Proceedings Rules 1991 closely regulated the discovery of documents and how such documents should be tendered by way of evidence and at what time. These provisions are also contained in FPR 2010. It stressed that it was a matter for the court to determine what evidence is admissible and whether it should be admitted after carrying out a balancing exercise of the rights contained in the ECHR, namely one spouse's right to a fair trial and freedom of expression against the other's right to privacy.

The questionnaire and request for documents must be filed at court and served on the other party not later than 14 days before the hearing of the FA.[33] At the same time, it is necessary to file and serve a statement of the apparent issues between the parties and confirmation that all relevant persons have been served.[34]

It is important to note that care should be taken with the questionnaire and request for documents, since it is provided that, between the FA and the financial dispute resolution appointment, no party shall be entitled to the production of further documents save with permission of the court.[35] It is therefore intended that the district judge at the FA shall deal comprehensively and finally with all issues of disclosure and questionnaires, and those orders will be based on the requests before him. The questionnaire should also focus on the issues in dispute between the parties which will need to be resolved in order to enable the court to achieve the objective of a fair outcome. Questions about issues that are of little or no significance to the outcome of the case will simply increase costs that the parties incur and should be dealt with robustly by the district judge.

THE FIRST APPOINTMENT

16.21 The FA is conducted by the district judge. The parties to the case must attend every hearing in addition to the lawyers unless the court otherwise directs.[36] By now, the Forms E, questionnaires, requests for documents, and statements of apparent issues should be on the court file, and the district judge should have read them in advance.

---

[33] FPR 2010, r 9.14(5).
[34] FPR 2010, r 9.14(6).
[35] FPR 2010, r 9.16(1).
[36] FPR 2010, r 9.15(8).

The other vital document which each party must produce at the FA is the 'written estimate of the solicitor and client costs hitherto incurred on his behalf'.[37] This document (as updated) must be produced at every hearing, and this is the first of these occasions. It should have been agreed with the client in advance, and is an open statement, the contents of which the district judge should state publicly in the presence of the parties.

In order to improve the prospects of settlement at a first appointment it is helpful for the court to have a schedule of assets showing concisely the resources and assets available to the parties. This enables the court and the parties to focus upon those issues which are relevant to resolving the dispute between them. Many practitioners routinely produce a document of this kind at a first appointment, although the previous rules which applied to ancillary relief did not require this. One of the relatively few changes under the FPR 2010 (and one which is to be welcomed) is set out in PD 9A, Part 4.1 which provides that the parties should, if possible, exchange and file a summary of the case agreed between them, a schedule of assets agreed between them and details of any directions that they seek including, where appropriate, the name of any expert they wish to be appointed.

16.22 The objective of the district judge at the FA is defined in r 9.15(1) as 'defining the issues and saving costs'. Definition of the issues has already been discussed above. The district judge's specific duties are set out in r 9.15(2) and (3). He must decide to what extent questionnaires should be answered and documents produced, direct valuations and expert evidence, and decide whether any further evidence is required from the parties (for example, on issues as to contributions). In all this, he will be guided by his definition of what the issues in the case are to be and by the overriding objective. The district judge will be able to exercise the wide ranging case management powers set out in FPR 2010, Part 4.

16.23 Having declared what the issues are to be, and directed the filing of the further evidence necessary to bring the issues on for hearing, including any directions of valuation of assets and obtaining and exchanging expert evidence if required, the district judge must then consider the future progress of the case. This will involve a decision as to whether the FA is to be treated as the FDR appointment.[38] Both parties should have filed and served Form G indicating whether or not they will be in a position to proceed to FDR there and then, but, even where they have not done so, the district judge may inquire as to whether this is possible. When the FA is to be so treated, he will conduct the FDR hearing (as to which see **16.26**) and then, if necessary, direct the final hearing. If FDR is not dealt with there and then, he will direct an FDR appointment and a final hearing shortly thereafter, unless he thinks the case suitable for mediation or out-of-court private negotiation.[39] In directing the

---

[37] FPR 2010, r 9.27(1).
[38] FPR 2010, r 9.15(7).
[39] FPR 2010, r 9.15(5).

final hearing, the district judge must determine the judicial level at which the case will be heard, ie either by district judge, High Court judge or (more rarely) circuit judge.

16.24 There are a very few cases where the normal procedure can be bypassed and where the court decides to adjudicate on one discrete issue which will have an overwhelming determinative effect. The authority for such an approach is derived from the decision of Coleridge J in *Crossley v Crossley*.[40] Here, the parties, both of mature age and independently wealthy, had married late in life after making a pre-nuptial agreement to the effect that, in the event of divorce, neither would make any claim on the other. When, after divorce, the wife applied for ancillary relief, the husband issued notice to show cause why her application should not be resolved in accordance with the agreement. Coleridge J agreed with this approach, ordered Forms E with no documentation, and adjourned the FA to resolve the issue. The wife's appeal was dismissed; it was held that, while the agreement was only one aspect of the case and did not relieve the court of its duty to consider all the s 25 factors, in this case it was of magnetic importance. The ancillary relief rules were not a straitjacket and the overriding objective governed all. The judge had a duty to identify issues at an early stage and deal with the case in a manner proportionate to the means of the parties.

This approach was also adopted in *S v S (Ancillary Relief)*.[41] Clearly, this method of dealing with a case cannot be limited to cases involving agreements, though it is difficult to think of another issue which might qualify. In any event, such an application is anything but routine and will only be appropriate in a limited number of situations. A party wishing to avail himself of this procedure should issue a notice to show cause returnable at the FA, supported by a witness statement exhibiting the agreement and any correspondence leading up to it.

EXPERT EVIDENCE

16.25 The rules relating to expert evidence in all family proceedings were changed significantly in January 2013.

The amended FPR 2010, r 25 reiterates that in family proceedings a party cannot put expert evidence before the court without permission of the court (FPR 2010, r 25.3(1)). However in place of the previous provision limiting expert evidence to that which was reasonably required to resolve the proceedings FPR 2010, r 25.3(1) now states that expert evidence is restricted to that which 'in the opinion of the Court is necessary to the Court to resolve the proceedings'. Commenting on the new wording before its introduction Munby P said that the new test is intended to be significantly more stringent that the

---

40   [2007] EWCA Civ 1491, [2008] 1 FLR 1467.
41   [2008] EWHC 2038 (Fam), [2009] 1 FLR 254.

old and that the test of what is 'necessary' sets a hurdle which is on any view significantly higher than the old test of what is 'reasonably required'.

The new rules and Practice Direction 25B dealing with the duties of an expert reiterate that it is the duty of experts to help the Court on matters within their expertise and that their overriding duty is to the court rather than to the person by whom they were instructed or paid.

The factors that the court is to have regard when deciding whether to give permission in financial remedy proceedings are set out in FPR 2010, r 25.2(2) and include the issues to which the evidence would relate, the questions that the court would require the expert to answer, the impact on the timetable, duration and conduct of the case, any failure to comply with the rules dealing with the way in which the application is to be made and the cost of the expert evidence.

The application for permission to put expert evidence before the court should be made as soon as possible and in any event no later than the first appointment. It should be made in an application in accordance with FPR 2010, Part 18 with details of the name, field of expertise and issues that the expert is to address and a draft order. The parties and the court are required to consider whether a single joint expert (SJE) should be appointed and for the court if necessary to decide the identity of the SJE and even to determine the consents of the letter of instruction.

If permission is given the expert evidence should be given in a written report and the FPR 2010, r 25.10 sets out a 'default provision' for proportionate questions that are intended to seek clarification of the report to be put back to the expert within 10 days of receipt and to be answered within the timetable specified by the court. Failure by the expert to answer the questions may lead to the party who instructed the expert being unable to rely on the expert report and/or being unable to recover the expert's fees from the other party even if a costs order is made.

The court will only direct an expert to attend to give evidence if it is necessary in the interests of justice to do so.

It must be emphasised that in financial remedy proceedings (in contrast to proceedings relating to children) a party can obtain an expert's report without seeking permission from the court, although PD 25D encourages parties to agree to use a single joint expert. However it cannot put it before the court (in any form) without the court's permission. The rules also make provision for discussions between experts and for an expert to seek directions from the court. The expert is to be provided with copies of the relevant orders within two days of receipt. Interestingly, after the final hearing the expert is also to be informed in writing by the instructing party about the court's determination and the use made of the expert's evidence.

In addition to PD 25B which sets out further provisions about the duties of the report and the arrangements for an expert to attend Court and is of general application to all experts instructed in family proceedings, PD 25D sets out specific provisions for financial remedy proceedings including the use of single joint experts.

PD 25D 3.3 emphasises the importance of preliminary inquiries of the proposed expert to ensure that they are able to meet the court's timetable and to ensure that the work requested is within their expertise. It is also emphasised that if there is insufficient time to make a formal application pursuant to FPR 2010, Part 18 a letter should be sent to the other party and the court before the hearing is to take place. The information required by FPR 2010, r 25(2)(a) together with information about the likely cost of the report and the expert's availability should be provided when the application is made.

The letter of instruction should be sent to the expert within five business days of permission being granted.

16.26 Guidance as to the practice to be followed when instructing an expert was given by the President's Ancillary Relief Advisory Group in the *Best Practice Guide for Instructing a Single Joint Expert* (the '*Best Practice Guide*') in December 2002.[42]

What follows is a summary of the *Best Practice Guide*.

(1) Where expert evidence is sought to be relied on, parties should if possible agree on a single joint expert (SJE) whom they can jointly instruct.

(2) Before instructions are given, the parties should establish the SJE's availability, fees, and expertise. They should also agree between themselves the proportions in which the SJE's fees are to be shared.

(3) When the court directs a report from an SJE, the order should:

    (a) identify the SJE;
    (b) specify the task to be performed;
    (c) provide for instructions in a joint letter;
    (d) specify the time for sending the joint letter, the date for the report and the dates for written questions to be sent and answered; and
    (e) make any provision as to fees which are appropriate.

(4) Supplementary instructions to the SJE should not be given unless both parties agree or the court sanctions them.

(5) Communications by the SJE must be addressed to both parties.

---

42 [2003] 1 FLR 573.

(6)   Any meeting with the SJE must be proportionate and should be with both parties and/or their advisers.

This guidance remains very helpful but specific reference should now be made to FPR 2010, Part 25 and to the practice direction attached.

THE FINANCIAL DISPUTE RESOLUTION HEARING

16.27   The FDR appointment was one of the innovations of the new procedure for ancillary relief introduced in 2000 after the earlier operation of the pilot scheme. Its purpose is to give the parties an opportunity to put their fundamental positions to the district judge and to each other, and for the district judge to make such comments as he or she may consider to be helpful, and it is hoped that this process may facilitate a settlement. It is normally helpful for solicitors and/or counsel and their clients to arrive at court some time before the appointed time to enable them to negotiate. This is frequently a process which continues over the course of a day.

The FDR appointment is a privileged occasion; it must be treated as a meeting held for the purposes of discussion and negotiation[43] and the fact that without prejudice offers must be filed at court does not make them admissible in evidence if they would not otherwise be admissible.[44] The district judge who conducts the FDR appointment must have no further involvement with the matter other than to conduct any further FDR appointment.[45]

There is no reason why, in a case which is likely to be tried by a High Court or circuit judge, a judge of that rank should not conduct the FDR appointment. A judge who has conducted an FDR may only do one of three things, viz to make a consent order, give directions for trial, or adjourn for a further FDR.[46] However, in an earlier case it was held that a judge who has dealt with an FDR which has led to a consent order is not thereafter precluded from dealing with an application to vary that order;[47] whether that is still good law remains to be seen.

16.28   Not later than 7 days before the FDR appointment, the applicant must file at court details of all offers, proposals and responses thereto; at the end of the appointment, all such documents must be returned.[48] At the appointment, the parties must, of course, file their up-to-date written costs estimates.

---

[43]   FPR 2010, r 9.17(1).
[44]   FPR 2010, r 9.17(3).
[45]   FPR 2010 r 9.17(2).
[46]   *Myerson v Myerson* [2008] EWCA Civ 1376.
[47]   *G v G* [2006] EWHC 1993, [2007] 1 FLR 237.
[48]   FPR 2010, r 9.17(5).

It is provided by the rule that 'parties attending the appointment must use their best endeavours to reach agreement on the matters in issue between them'.[49] The role of the district judge is, essentially, to ensure that the parties have a full opportunity to exchange offers and counteroffers and to encourage them to reach a settlement. It is not part of a district judge's duties to mediate between the parties, if for no other reason than that he or she may lack mediation skills. However, this is not to say that the district judge does not have a creative role to play. It is now generally accepted that the district judge should indicate to the parties how he or she sees the case, and what he or she thinks are the principal issues. The district judge may choose not to predict the likely outcome (although many district judges will assume this burden) but is likely to indicate how he or she would approach the case and try to eliminate what he or she sees as any unrealistic expectations. In essence, the FDR appointment is designed for settlement seeking. It has been recognised that the approach judges and practitioners take when dealing with FDRs differ widely between courts. As a result the Family Justice Council produced Best Practice Guidance on the conduct of FDRs in December 2012. This document is required reading for solicitors preparing for the FDR, advocates and the judges themselves.

In *Rose v Rose*[50] the parties had reached agreement at an FDR appointment and gone away to prepare a draft order, which was subsequently agreed. The husband then sought to resile from the agreement. On appeal, it was held that the fact that the agreement was made at an FDR appointment made no difference and the order should be made.

16.29 At the conclusion of the FDR appointment, if an agreement is reached, the district judge may make a consent order.[51] The appointment may be adjourned for a further FDR appointment if that seems likely to assist the parties, or the district judge may give directions to lead to the final hearing. This may include the filing of evidence, which should only be necessary in a limited number of cases; all the financial information should have been contained in the Forms E and replies to questionnaires, and where there is a particular issue, the court may have directed the filing of witness statements limited to those issues. It might seem, therefore, that a further narrative statement of the evidence-in-chief which a party intends to give would, in the run-of-the-mill case, be contrary to the spirit of the new rules and constitute a return to the old narrative affidavit, and that it should only be necessary in a case which is likely to be lengthy and complex. In *W v W (Ancillary Relief: Practice)*,[52] Wilson J said that it would be desirable in cases of greater wealth for the evidence to be broadened by narrative affidavits but, it is submitted, this decision does not detract from the generality of what has been said above and in the event that the parties are directed to file a statement it should be limited to those aspects of the s 25 factors that are at the heart of the issues in dispute between the parties and require determination by the court.

---

49 FPR 2010, r 9.17(6).
50 [2002] 1 FLR 978, CA.
51 FPR 2010, r 9.17(8).
52 [2000] Fam Law 473.

16.30 One of the principal reasons why cases involving substantial assets reach a final hearing and cannot be resolved before is that there is a genuine dispute as to the amount of the assets, coupled with allegations of lack of good faith and failure to disclose. In *OS v DS (Oral Disclosure: Preliminary Hearing)*[53] Coleridge J devised a novel procedure for resolving issues at an early stage. At a directions appointment he ordered a three-day preliminary/oral discovery hearing, to take oral evidence and resolve questions of joinder. This enabled the judge to make findings and resolved the issues with great savings of costs and court time. It is unlikely that this procedure will be used in more than a small proportion of cases but it remains a useful tool to bear in mind in appropriate cases. It may be anticipated that the introduction of wider case management powers in FPR 2010, Part 4 and the central importance of the overriding objective when exercising its powers will encourage more creative approaches of this kind.

THE FINAL HEARING

16.31 The Family Proceedings Rules 1991, r 2.62 contained provisions which made it clear that the role of the District Judge at the final hearing was quasi inquisatorial. There appears to be no corresponding provision in FPR 2010. However, there is no reason to believe that the long standing approach will change and indeed the prominence now given to the overriding objective as well as the extensive case management powers contained in FPR 2010, Part 4 emphasise the importance of the District Judge taking a pro-active role.

The procedure at the final hearing will therefore follow the approach in place from the 1991 rules. In particular, the former practice as to bundles, skeleton arguments, etc applies (see *Practice Direction of 10 March 2000 (Family Proceedings: Court Bundles)*[54] in Appendix B). Three particular provisions that were first applied by the 2000 procedural reforms and remain in the FPR 2010 should be emphasised. First, as has already been seen, the district judge who conducted the FDR appointment may not hear the application. Secondly, not less than 14 days before the hearing, the applicant must file with the court and serve on the other party a concise statement setting out the nature and amount of the orders which he or she proposes to invite the court to make, and the respondent must reply within 7 days thereafter. No privilege attaches to these documents, so they are open offers.[55] These documents are then before the court and should focus the scope of the hearing. Thirdly, the 2010 Rules contain more elaborate provisions as to costs. Full details of these provisions will be found in Chapter 17.

---

[53]　[2004] EWHC 2376 (Fam), [2005] 1 FLR 675.
[54]　[2000] 1 FLR 536.
[55]　FPR 2010, r 9.28.

INSPECTION APPOINTMENTS

16.32 A problem which frequently arises is that one of the parties to the case, or a third party, fails to produce for inspection some document which is potentially important for the preparation of the application. To solve this problem, the Family Proceedings Rules 1991 introduced a new provision which provided that any party may apply to the court for an order that any person attends an appointment (an 'inspection appointment') before the court and produces any documents to be specified or described in the order, the production of which appears to the court to be necessary for disposing fairly of the application for ancillary relief or for saving costs. This provision, which was previously called a 'production appointment' has been described as 'an extraordinarily useful addition to the range of powers available to the court', with the caveat that 'the very breadth of the power does, however, present opportunity for abuse'.[56] The provision enables the court to exercise a wide discretion, and should be directed to saving costs or achieving a just result. Perhaps surprisingly FPR 2010 does not appear to contain specific provision for an appointment of this kind. In view of the breadth of the case management powers in Part 4 of the new rules it would be surprising if the courts did not interpret its provisions in a way which enables the useful procedure to still be employed and it is suggested that the guidance below will continue to be applied.

The procedure is principally invoked against third parties, since, as was seen above, a party to the application may be ordered to produce documents and this can, if necessary, be enforced by penal sanctions. The rule is, therefore, principally useful when trying to obtain documents from a third party against whom, normally, an order may not be made in the proceedings. The most common classes of persons against whom orders are sought are the cohabitant of one of the parties, and some person or body (such as a bank, or business partner) with whom the other party has a financial relationship.

16.33 The first stage in obtaining an inspection order is to apply to the district judge, using the FPR 2010, Part 18 procedure, on notice to the other party but not the person against whom the order is sought. The notice of application should specify the order sought, with details of the documents to be disclosed, and should be supported by a statement of truth sworn by the applicant or his or her solicitor setting out all factual matters relied upon. It will normally be the case that the other party has refused or failed to produce the evidence which is sought, and the statement should give particulars of this refusal or failure.

The court will bear in mind that, when the documents sought are the personal documents of the third party, he or she is entitled to privacy and should not normally be required to disclose them to others. The court must, therefore, be satisfied that there is prima facie evidence that the documents relate to a relevant issue in the proceedings and that the evidence which they will provide cannot be obtained in any other way. For example, it is frequently the case that

---

[56]   *B v B (Production Appointment: Procedure)* [1995] 1 FLR 913, per Thorpe J.

the means of a cohabitant are irrelevant, and in such a case it would be necessary to show that the financial positions of the cohabitant and the other party were so interlinked as to make it necessary to see the cohabitant's documents.

16.34 The Family Proceedings Rules 1991 specifically provided that no person shall be compelled by an order to produce any document at an inspection appointment which he could not be compelled to produce at the hearing of the application for ancillary relief. In *Frary v Frary*,[57] the husband cohabited with a wealthy woman with whom he said he had no financial relationship and who did not support him. On appeal, a production order was set aside. It was observed that the rule did not change the law but merely brought forward the time at which a witness might be compelled to attend court. In this case, the applicant had no intention of calling the third party, neither she nor the respondent had made any secret of their relationship and there was no particular relevance in the precise limits of the third party's means. There was nothing to make it a proper exercise of the court's discretion to order the appellant, a stranger to the proceedings, to attend and be examined at the trial or to produce documents.

On the other hand, in *D v D (Production Appointment)*,[58] the husband's attempts to obtain proper disclosure of the wife's considerable means had been obstructed and frustrated. Thorpe J made a production order requiring the wife's accountant to attend and produce his files, such disclosure being on a broad basis in view of the earlier obstructions and having the effect of overriding any professional privilege.

In *M v M (Ancillary Relief: Conduct: Disclosure)*[59] it was held that the existing case law on disclosure against a third party had been strengthened rather than weakened by Art 8 of the ECHR.

16.35 When an inspection order is made, the person concerned is directed to attend court and to produce any documents named in the order. Such a person is entitled to be legally represented at the appointment.

INTERIM ORDERS

16.36 A problem which may arise is that an applicant for ancillary relief is in urgent need of interim support and cannot wait for up to 16 weeks for the FA. It is therefore provided that a party may apply at any stage of the proceedings for an order for maintenance pending suit, interim periodical payments or an interim variation order.[60] It is implicit that such an application can be made only where a full application for ancillary relief is pending, so one or other

---

[57] [1993] 2 FLR 696.
[58] [1995] 2 FLR 497.
[59] [2006] Fam Law 923.
[60] FPR 2010, r 9.7(1).

party must have issued Form A. The application for an interim order is made in accordance with FPR 2010, Part 18 application, and the day fixed for the hearing must be not less than 14 days after the issue of the application, notice of which must be served forthwith on the other party.[61]

When, as will normally be the case, the application is made before the filing of Forms E, the applicant must file with the court and serve on the other party written evidence explaining why the order is necessary and giving the necessary information about his or her financial circumstances.[62] Not less than 7 days before the hearing, the other party must file and serve a short statement about his or her means unless he or she has already filed Form E.[63]

VARIATION APPLICATION

16.37 A variation application pursuant to MCA 1973, s 31 is an application for a financial order and therefore falls to be dealt with in exactly the same way as any other application, by the filing of Form A and Forms E and the fixing of an FA and FDR. This will be the procedure to be adopted in the majority of variation cases since, clearly, the court will need to know the whole financial position of a party even where only periodical payments are in dispute.

However, there may be a limited number of cases where there genuinely can be no point in requiring lengthy disclosure of means, for example where an increase in the amount payable under an old order for a child is the only issue. In these circumstances, FPR 2010, r 9.8 provides that an application can be made for an interim variation order following the procedure set out in **16.38**. Once a determination has been made at the interim hearing, the court can be invited to make the order a final order to dispose of the application and to vacate the FA. In this way, time and costs could be saved.

It is emphasised, however, that this procedure would only be appropriate in the simplest cases.

THE PROTOCOLS

16.38 One of the innovations of the CPR, which govern civil proceedings other than family proceedings, was the introduction of protocols which govern how practitioners deal with the preparation of cases up to the issue of proceedings. These protocols have the force of law in the sense that the court may refer to them once proceedings have been issued when deciding whether or not various orders should be made and when deciding issues of costs.

---

[61] FPR 2010, Pt 18.
[62] FPR 2010, r 9.7(3).
[63] FPR 2010, r 9.7(4).

The Family Procedure Rules 2010 contain two protocols relevant to proceedings for seeking a financial order. The first is the pre-application protocol for mediation information and assessment which was considered at **16.7**. The other is the protocol attached to PD 9A. It follows to a large extent the structure and content of the protocol devised by the Lord Chancellor's Advisory Group on ancillary relief which was introduced by a Practice Direction on 25 May 2000. It is required reading for all practitioners and in particular the following points should be noted:

- Where there is pre-action disclosure and inspection it must be dealt with cost-effectively and in line with the overriding objective.

- While there is sometimes an advantage in preparing disclosure before proceedings are commenced, solicitors must bear in mind the objective of controlling costs and in particular the costs of disclosure of documents.

- Solicitors should consider at an early stage and keep under review whether mediation would be appropriate.

- Proportionality must be borne in mind at all times.

- Parties should seek to clarify their claims and identify the issues as soon as possible.

- Wherever possible, valuations should be by a joint valuer.

Chapter 17

COSTS

INTRODUCTION

17.1   In all forms of litigation, the incidence of costs is one of the primary considerations and causes of concern for the lay client. When lawyers are instructed, they have to be paid, and in the absence of any order to the contrary, the client has to pay. A client who is successful in most forms of civil litigation expects to recover his or her costs from the unsuccessful party; when he or she does so, the unsuccessful party has a double burden to pay, but the successful party rarely recovers all costs and normally still has something to pay. In short, while costs may be an area of the law which the intelligent client can understand, it will rarely bring much satisfaction.

17.2   If what has been said applies to all litigation, the problems caused thereby are magnified in family cases and, in particular, in financial relief. The average litigant, pursuing, for example, an action for damages or a boundary dispute, normally has a choice as to whether to proceed with the action or abandon it, and this decision can be taken on rational grounds. The person caught up in a dispute as to the occupation of the family home, or the financial support of the other party usually has no such choice. Family disputes go to the heart of most people's lives, in both a financial and an emotional sense, and when, as is the case in most run-of-the-mill disputes, something as intimate as a person's home is involved, it is difficult, if not impossible, for the litigants to adopt a detached approach.

17.3   If these general comments are applied to the particular problems in applications for a financial remedy, the most common difficulty faced by the parties and by the court is that the money which is paid to lawyers is money which the parties can normally ill afford to lose, since it is needed for meeting the needs and reasonable requirements of the parties and their children. The court frequently has to face the difficulty of being asked to make an order for costs which will upset a finely balanced distribution of property which it has taken care to work out; if the order for costs is not made, the party who has behaved unrealistically may benefit, but if it is made the whole basis of the order may disappear. Two overriding considerations emerge from this. The first is that the parties must be made and kept aware of the economic facts of their case, and the second is that the lawyers involved must ensure that the case is conducted in the most cost-effective manner consistent with the interests of the client. The problems inherent in family litigation have led to the sweeping changes in the general principles of costs which are described in **17.4** et seq.

This chapter is not going to deal in detail with the rules as to assessment of costs (previously known as 'taxation'). The minutiae of such matters are best left to more specialist publications. Instead, the matters to be considered are those which have most direct relevance to the subject of ancillary relief. They are:

(a)   some general principles of costs;

(b)   the effect of the FPR 1991 and the FPR 2010, including the effect on *Calderbank* offers.

SOME GENERAL PRINCIPLES OF COSTS

17.4   Previous editions of this book have contained a detailed account of the elaborate system of rules and case-law which governed costs in ancillary relief cases. This body of law is now obsolete, save in respect of applications made before 3 April 2006.[1] With effect from 3 April 2006 the Family Proceedings (Amendment) (No 6) Rules 2005[2] took effect, and the 1991 rules were amended accordingly. (The detail of which applications are governed by these changes is complicated – see **17.6**.) These amended rules have been incorporated more or less unchanged in the FPR 2010.

The general rule

17.5   FPR 2010, r 28.3(2) makes it clear that this rule contains discrete and self-contained provisions as to costs in ancillary relief proceedings by providing that CPR, r 44.3(1)–(5) (ie those rules which govern costs in other civil proceedings and provide, inter alia, that costs are in the discretion of the court and normally follow the event) shall not apply to financial remedy proceedings.[3] CPR, r 44.3(6)–(9) continues to apply to financial remedy proceedings but that rule relates to the mechanics of assessment of costs and not the principles governing the award of costs.

17.6   Rule 28.3(5) begins by providing that 'the general rule in ancillary relief proceedings is that the court will not make an order requiring one party to pay the costs of another party'.

As will be seen, the rule will make an exception to that general principle but it is worth pausing at this point to reinforce the general effect of the rule. The general principle with which all lawyers are familiar and which governs other civil proceedings, namely that the 'loser' pays the costs of the 'winner' no longer applies to financial remedy proceedings. There are many reasons for this change of legislative position, which cannot all be considered here. However, the principal reasons for the change were first, the difficulty in many cases of

---

[1]   Interested readers should refer to the 5th edition.
[2]   SI 2005/352.
[3]   See **1.3** for definition of 'ancillary relief'.

establishing which party was the winner and which the loser; secondly, the fact that breakdown of marriage and the need to re-order family assets should be regarded as a misfortune falling on both parties rather than the fault of either of them; thirdly, the award of costs subsequent to the main substantive order in any particular case frequently distorted the intentions of the order itself. It might also be said that previous attempts to improve the rules relating to costs, as detailed in the 5th edition of this book, had led to an extremely complicated and self-contradictory set of rules.

The general rule, therefore, is that each party will bear his or her costs, whether incurred at the final hearing or in an interim application. The way the court will treat such costs is dealt with at **17.14**.

Exceptions to the general rule

17.7   Rule 28.3(6) contains the exception to the general rule and provides:

> '... the court may make an order requiring one party to pay the costs of another party at any stage of the proceedings where it considers it appropriate to do so because of the conduct of a party in relation to the proceedings (whether before or during them).'

The matters to which the court must have regard in deciding whether or not to make such an order are then set out, but at this stage the following points should be noted. First, the only matter which may trigger an order for costs is 'the conduct of a party'. Secondly, it is only conduct 'in relation to the proceedings' which will be taken into account. 'Conduct' in the general sense, as considered at **1.50** et seq, is not to be taken into account. This conduct may therefore be described as 'litigation misconduct'.

Thirdly, the court may order costs 'at any stage of the proceedings'. Applications for costs orders may therefore be made at any stage where it seems appropriate.

In *Malialis v Malialis*[4] the width of discretion of a trial judge to make a costs order even where the general rule is that there should be no order as to costs was emphasised.

17.8   Rule 28.3(7) then sets out the matters which should guide the court, as follows:

> '(7)   In deciding what order (if any) to make under paragraph (6), the court must have regard to –
>   (a)   any failure by a party to comply with these Rules, any order of the court or any practice direction which the court considers relevant;
>   (b)   any open offer to settle made by a party;

---

4   [2012] EWCA Civ 1748.

(c)   whether it was reasonable for a party to raise, pursue or contest a particular allegation or issue;

(d)   the manner in which a party has pursued or responded to the application or a particular allegation or issue;

(e)   any other aspect of a party's conduct in relation to the proceedings which the court considers relevant; and

(f)   the financial effect on the parties of any costs order.'

Examples of the operation of these rules might be as follows.

Failure to comply with rules, orders, etc

17.9 Obvious examples of this would be failure to file Form E on time, or failure to comply with an order as to information, which led to a further application to the court.

Open offers

17.10 This rule must be read with the rule as to offers to settle contained in r 28.3(8); 'no offer to settle which is not an open offer to settle shall be admissible at any stage of the proceedings ...'. (There is an exception to this which relates to FDR appointments only and is not relevant here.)

The only offers which may be considered are therefore open offers, ie the open position of a party revealed to the court in the course of the proceedings. The previous jurisprudence as to '*Calderbank* letters' is now firmly abolished and out of date. The requirement to make offers is contained in and limited to r 9.28(1) which provides that:

'(1) Not less than 14 days before the date fixed for the final hearing of an application for a financial remedy, the applicant must (unless the court directs otherwise) file with the court and serve on the respondent an open statement which sets out concise details, including the amounts involved, of the orders which the applicant proposes to ask the court to make.

(2) Not more than 7 days after service of a statement under paragraph (1), the respondent must file with the court and serve on the applicant an open statement which sets out concise details, including the amounts involved, of the orders which the respondent proposes to ask the court to make.'

It must be emphasised that these rules as to costs and offers are not intended to bring in the old 'winner gets his costs' provision by the back door; the purpose of open offers is to enable the court and the parties to know what the issues are rather than retrospectively to apportion blame for protracted litigation. There remains some uncertainty as to when a court might think it appropriate to make an order for costs in reliance on this part of the rule. The following tentative suggestions are made with the intention of helping to clarify the position but it must be emphasised that these are suggestions only and that only judicial decisions will give accurate guidance.

(a) There is clearly every incentive to parties to make their positions clear by means of open offers to settle. Such offers to settle could be revised or amended in the light of changing developments.

(b) Such offers should not normally be made until disclosure is complete. A party against whom a costs order is sought could reasonably argue that he or she was not in a position to decide whether or not to accept an offer until all relevant information was available and that, if any order was to be made, it should only be in respect of work done after that date.

(c) It is not intended that any party who fails to beat an open offer made by the other will automatically be liable to costs. The general rule remains that there will be no order as to costs. Presumably the court will take account of whether or not the 'unsuccessful' party made any open offer and, if so, the gap between the open positions of the parties and the stage at which any offer was made. Although the rule avoids the use of the term 'unreasonable', one cannot avoid the conclusion that reasonableness may be a factor. It may well be that, where one party has throughout made a reasonable offer, or a series of reasonable offers to settle which the other has ignored, and the final result accords with the offers made, the court will feel entitled to condemn the unsuccessful party in costs.

(d) Slightly different principles apply to a party who has not made any open proposals before trial; where one party adopts an unreasonable position and fails to make sensible open proposals for trial, this may amount to unreasonable conduct and attract a costs penalty.[5]

This does not mean that 'without prejudice' offers cannot continue to be made. No doubt this will be the case and such offers will remain a useful part of the procedure. It does mean, however, that such offers will not be admissible in any arguments as to costs.

Whether reasonable to raise or pursue allegations or issues and the manner in which allegations or issues were pursued or responded to

17.11 The significance of these two provisions is fairly clear. A party who raises an issue of, e g conduct, or alleged concealed assets, and pursues the issue in the face of all the evidence, is going to be liable to pay the other party's additional costs incurred in dealing with such issues. In the same way, a party who causes the other party unnecessary work by failing to provide the necessary information or to concede an obvious issue is also exposing himself to a liability for costs.

---

[5] *H v H* [2008] EWHC 935 (Fam); *McCartney v Mills McCartney* [2008] 1 FLR 1508 at para [230].

In *M v M*,[6] Eleanor King J ordered a wife to pay costs after she had shifted ground of a certain issue twice. In *B v B (Ancillary Relief)*,[7] Moylan J ordered a husband who had fought doggedly and lost on a trust issue to pay the costs of that issue; the husband had been entirely responsible for the manner in which the case had been litigated.

Any other aspect of conduct in relation to the proceedings which the court considers relevant

17.12 This is a 'catch-all' provision, and means that the other matters mentioned in r 28.3(7) are not exclusive. One can only say that for such conduct to be 'caught' by this provision, it would presumably be necessary for it to have increased the costs which the other party had to pay.

For an example of a case where a father was ordered to pay the mother a lump sum to fund her costs in a protracted contact application see *R v F (Child Maintenance:Costs of Contact Proceedings)*.[8]

The financial effect on the parties of a costs order

17.13 The significance of this is that, even if the court decided it was appropriate to make a costs order, it must still take account of what the financial consequences of such an order would be. For example, where the court decided that a parent should have a property or sum of money to provide a home for children, and that to make a costs order, however, richly deserved, would have the effect of making it impossible for that parent to provide the home, it might well decide that it should not make the costs order.

How will costs be treated?

17.14 Given that the general rule is that each party bears his or her own costs, and that costs are a necessary part of life, the question of how the court will deal with the costs is of great importance. Costs still due should presumably be regarded as a debt due from the client, and, in order to be fair, it is arguable that costs already paid should be added back (as was done in *Leadbeater v Leadbeater*).[9]

Useful guidance has been given by Wilson LJ in *Currey v Currey*,[10] where he said that the proper treatment of liabilities for costs will generally be to regard them as debts to be considered when the judge is making his substantive award,

---

6 [2009] EWHC 1941 (Fam), [2010] 1 FLR 256. It should be noted that an appeal against this decision, reported as *Marano v Marano* [2010] EWCA Civ 119, [2010] 1 FLR 1903 was dismissed.

7 [2009] EWHC 3422 (Fam), [2010] 2 FLR 887.

8 [2011] 2 FLR 991.

9 [1985] FLR 789.

10 [2006] EWCA Civ 1338, [2007] 1 FLR 946.

with an allowance for costs (eg a lump sum on account of costs – see **17.22**) being fully consonant with the thrust of the new rules to cater for costs at an earlier stage than hitherto.

Generally, when preparing schedules of assets for a final or interim hearing, it will be proper to include the total amount of costs paid by and still due from a party as a liability of that party. A judge retains the ability to distinguish between costs reasonably incurred and those unreasonably incurred and only to allow the former.[11]

The practice of increasing a financial award to take account of the litigation or other misconduct of a party has been deprecated in several cases.

In *R v R (Financial Remedies: Needs and Practicalities)*[12] Coleridge J said that as a matter of principle the pursuit of the add-back principle or approach to costs should be discouraged. It flies in the face of the no order starting point and leads to debates about costs by the back door.

In *GS v L (Financial Remedies: Costs)*[13] the judge declined to adopt an add-back approach to costs. She later decided this was an appropriate case for an issue-based costs order.

In *Ezair v Ezair*[14] the judge sought to reflect the husband's litigation misconduct by increasing a lump sum to the wife from £322,000 to £500,000. On appeal, it was held that, while the judge was entitled to recognise the husband's misconduct, it was unorthodox simply to inflate the lump sum and that the safe and orthodox approach was to make a distinct costs order.

Procedure

17.15 Procedural requirements as to the new costs rules are contained in r 9.27 which provides as follows:

'(1) Subject to paragraph (2), at every hearing or appointment each party must produce to the court an estimate of the costs incurred by him up to the date of that hearing or appointment.

(2) Not less than 14 days before the date fixed for the final hearing of an application for ancillary relief, each party must (unless the court directs otherwise) file with the court and serve on each other party a statement giving full particulars of all costs in respect of the proceedings which he has incurred or expects to incur, to enable the court to take account of the parties' liabilities for costs when deciding what order (if any) to make for a financial remedy '

---

[11] *RH v RH* [2008] EWHC 347 (Fam), Singer J. Although this case was governed by the old costs regime, there is no reason to think that it will not be followed under the new regime.
[12] [2011] EWHC 3093 (Fam).
[13] [2011] EWHC 2116 (Fam).
[14] [2010] EWCA Civ 893.

Estimates and statements of costs must be in Forms H1 and H2 to PD 5A which will be found at Appendix B. The purpose of these forms, which require much more detail than their predecessors, is to enable parties to justify what they tell the court about their liability for costs and to enable the court to examine such submissions. They are therefore very important and should be taken far more seriously than were the previous costs estimates.

17.16 Provisions are made relating to the first appointment (FA) and to the FDR appointment (generally, see Chapter 16). Rule 9.15 sets out the responsibilities of the district judge at the FDA, which includes r 9.15(6) as follows:

> '[the district judge]

> (e)   in considering whether to make a costs order under rule 2.71(4), must have particular regard to the extent to which each party has complied with the requirement to send documents with the financial statement;'

It should also be noted that the rule as to the admissibility of without prejudice offers does not apply at the FDR appointment. Therefore, when parties comply with the rule which requires them to file details of offers and counteroffers 7 days before the FDR, this includes without prejudice offers and counteroffers.

17.17 When a party intends to apply for an order for costs against the other party, he or she must follow paragraph 4 of the President's Practice Direction which reads as follows:

> 'Parties who intend to seek a costs order against another party in proceedings to which rule 2.71 of the Family Proceedings Rules 1991 applies should ordinarily make this plain in open correspondence or in skeleton arguments before the date of the hearing. In any case where summary assessment of costs awarded under rule 2.71 of the Family Proceedings Rules 1991 would be appropriate parties are under an obligation to file a statement of costs in CPR Form N260 (see CPR Practice Direction supplementing Parts 43 to 48 (Costs), Section 13 and paragraph 6 below).'

This is self-explanatory.

The basis of assessment

17.18 Although the detail of this subject is not to be considered, practitioners must know which of the various (and potentially confusing) regimes of assessment applies to ancillary relief cases.

17.19 CPR, Part 44 contains certain provisions as to principle which must be considered.

There are two bases of assessment, namely the standard basis and the indemnity basis.[15] Unless otherwise specified, assessment is on the standard basis.[16] In funded cases, assessment is always on the standard basis. When the order for costs is on the inter partes basis with no funded element involved, the court may order costs on the indemnity basis, but this is unusual. The difference between the two bases is that on the standard basis the taxing officer must resolve any doubt in favour of the paying party, whereas on the indemnity basis the taxing officer must award all costs save where they are found to be unreasonable in amount or where they were unreasonably incurred.[17]

Generally speaking, indemnity costs are more generous and are more likely to reflect the actual cost to the client, and are frequently awarded when the court wishes to demonstrate its disapproval of some action by the paying party which has led to the order for costs. However, it has been emphasised that to make a full indemnity order against a party 'is a Draconian thing to do',[18] and it would be rare for the whole costs of an application to be on that basis.

What use should the court make of costs estimates?

17.20 In *Leadbeater v Leadbeater*,[19] Balcombe J was given the information as to the parties' costs and posed the following question: 'the question of principle which arises here is how should I treat these costs in estimating the assets of the parties and in particular those of the wife in finding out what she has available for her needs?' His Lordship adopted the following formula: there should be added back into a party's assets what had already been paid by that party on account of costs, less only such part of those costs as would never be recoverable inter partes (ie solicitor and own client costs) and any costs which might be recovered on taxation as inter partes costs. Any future liability for costs should be omitted from that party's liabilities except such part as might properly never be recoverable. The justification for this approach was that if, in estimating the wife's present capital position and, in particular, what money she had available to buy a house, the money which she had already spent on costs was not included in her assets and her future liability for costs was included, the court would be anticipating the order as to costs which it might make.

This decision was followed in an appeal from a district judge's order where the district judge had awarded the husband a lump sum to meet his housing needs and declined to make an order for costs in favour of the wife, even though her *Calderbank* offer equalled if not exceeded the award, on the ground that it would defeat a settlement which would meet the husband's needs. Singer J

---

[15] CPR, r 44.4(1).
[16] CPR, r 44.4(4).
[17] CPR, r 44.4(2) and (3).
[18] *H v H (Clean Break: Non-disclosure: Costs)* [1994] 2 FLR 309, a case where the husband had been criticised for lack of disclosure, but the judge thought that justice could be done by making a standard basis order.
[19] [1985] FLR 789.

allowed the appeal as to costs. The district judge had not conducted the exercise recommended and authorised by Balcombe J in *Leadbeater v Leadbeater*, and had therefore fallen into error.[20]

However, in *Wells v Wells*,[21] the Court of Appeal observed, per curiam, that the *Leadbeater* practice had been introduced on the premise that the assessment of an applicant's needs without both adding back payments made and disregarding liability for unpaid costs incurred and to be incurred would effectively anticipate the costs order that would eventually be made. However, in the modern world, few, if any, litigate on credit and solicitors require to be in funds at all stages. Judges must not lose sight of this reality. The *Leadbeater* mechanism should never be automatic and was probably most useful in cases where one party had paid money out and the other had obtained security, or where the court suspects some element of contrivance or artificiality in the arrangements set up by one party.

17.21 Before the introduction of the new costs rules it was often thought that the relevance of *Leadbeater* was limited, and, as has been seen, it was frequently not followed. However, it is now suggested that the new costs rules have given the decision a new lease of life. Since the costs incurred and yet to be incurred by a party are regarded as a debt or obligation of that party or, where paid, have reduced the capital available to that party, it is necessary to take them into account in some way, and the mechanism suggested in *Leadbeater* has the virtue of a logical approach and may assist the court to arrive at a fair result.

LUMP SUM ORDERS AS TO COSTS

17.22 When one party is ordered to pay the costs of the other party, the normal order is for those costs to be assessed if not agreed. In *Leary v Leary*,[22] the judge found that the long duration and complexity of the application for ancillary relief had been due to the husband's failure to disclose his financial situation and concluded that the wife should be indemnified against the costs incurred as a result of the husband's action. In order to prevent further delay and litigation arising out of taxation, she ordered the husband to pay to the wife a lump sum of £31,000 under the provisions of RSC Ord 62, r 9, that sum being based on an itemised schedule of costs prepared by the wife's solicitors in accordance with the Practice Direction. The Court of Appeal dismissed the husband's appeal. RSC Ord 62, r 9(4) conferred on the court unlimited discretion to award a gross sum to avoid protracted taxation proceedings. It was necessary to warn the parties of the court's intention to act in this way. There was no justification for the suggestion that the court should only use Ord 62, r 9 in simple cases or cases involving small amounts, provided the court exercised its discretion in a judicial manner according to the facts of each

---

20   *A v A (Costs Appeal)* [1996] 1 FLR 14.
21   [2002] 2 FLR 97, CA.
22   [1987] 1 FLR 384.

individual case. While this decision pre-dated the provisions for summary assessment and other provisions now found in the CPR, there is no reason to think that the principle established by this case has changed.

It should be noted that where the court has ordered one party to pay costs, it may order an amount to be paid before the costs are assessed (CPR, r 44.3(7)).

LEGAL AID

17.23 Previous editions of this book have contained details of public funding, or legal aid, for financial remedy cases. It now seems that public funding is to be withdrawn for all, or all but the narrowest band of entitlement, and there seems little point therefore in repeating this information.

ORDERS FOR PAYMENTS ON ACCOUNT OF COSTS

17.24 See **2.25** for orders for maintenance pending suit which may include provision for costs. See also **17.22**as to payments on account.

In addition, since 1 April 2013 the court has the power[23] to make a Legal Services Order that compels one spouse to pay to the other an amount for the purpose of enabling the receiving party to obtain legal services for the purposes of the proceedings. This may be a one-off payment, a payment by installments or a deferred payment. Such an order can be made more than once during proceedings. Section 22ZB sets out the matters that the court must take into account, which include such matters as the relative means of the parties, the subject matter of the proceedings, the conduct of the applicant, and the likely effect of the order on the paying party. The court may not make such an order unless satisfied that the applicant would not otherwise reasonably be able to obtain appropriate legal advice for the purposes of the proceedings. In particular the court must be satisfied that the applicant could not obtain a loan or obtain legal services by offering a charge over property.

WASTED COSTS ORDERS

17.25 Provision for wasted costs orders is made in the SCA 1981, s 51(6) and (7) whereby costs incurred as result of any improper, unreasonable or negligent act or omission on the part of any legal or other representative may be visited on that individual or firm. The procedure is contained in CPR, r 48.7 and the Practice Direction to Part 48. Generally, a court will deal with a wasted costs application in two stages; first, a determination as to whether there is material before it which might lead to a wasted costs order, and then a second stage after notice to show cause has been given to the legal representative.

---

[23]   Under ss 22ZA and 22ZB MCA 1973.

In *B v B (Wasted Costs: Abuse of Process)*,[24] Wall J held that there were circumstances in family proceedings which may render it appropriate to hear applications for wasted costs orders in the course of the proceedings and to dispense with the two-stage process.

For further discussion of the principles governing the making of a wasted costs order against solicitors see the judgment of Mostyn J in *Fisher Meredith v JH and PH (Financial Remedy: Appeal: Wasted Costs)*[25][26]

PRECEDENTS FOR ORDERS FOR COSTS

17.26   See Appendix A, Precedent 45 for precedents for orders for costs.

SECURITY FOR COSTS

17.27   There is no general jurisdiction to order security for costs in family cases. FPR 2010, Part 20 provides for security for costs in cases brought under that part, that is to say applications for freezing injunctions and related remedies, but this part does not apply to general applications for a financial remedy.

---

[24]   [2001] 1 FLR 843. In this case, Wall J ordered the wasted costs of an unmeritorious appeal to be apportioned as to 75% to counsel and 25% to the solicitors.

[25]   [2012] EWHC 408 (Fam).

[26]   *Bradley v Bradley* [2008] 2 FLR 1433, CA. Nor may the court stay a lump sum order in order to protect a party from costs orders.

Chapter 18

APPEALS AND SETTING ASIDE

INTRODUCTION

18.1 The appeals to be considered in this chapter are appeals in financial remedy cases. These are therefore appeals, in the county court, from district judge to circuit judge, and in the High Court from district judge to High Court Judge, and thereafter, in both courts, to the Court of Appeal. Not all challenges to district judge's orders are appeals, however, and in this chapter we also consider applications to set aside district judges' consent orders.

18.2 The rules governing the procedure for appeals in the county court and the High Court are now identical[1] and are contained in Part 30 of the FPR 2010 and in Practice Direction PD 30A. The various elements of these will now be considered in turn. It should be noted that the same rules, eg as to time limits, apply whether the appeal is from the district judge or the circuit or High Court judge.

PERMISSION REQUIRED

18.3 Rule 30.3 deals with permission to appeal. An appellant or respondent requires permission to appeal against a decision in proceedings where the decision appealed against was made by a district judge or a costs judge, unless para (2) applies (which is not the case here), or as provided by the Practice Direction. An application for permission to appeal may be made to the lower court at the hearing at which the decision to be appealed was made; or to the appeal court in an appeal notice.

Permission to appeal an order of a district judge is a new provision and dissatisfied practitioners should therefore be sure to make the application at the conclusion of the hearing.

Where the lower court refuses an application for permission to appeal, a further application for permission to appeal may be made to the appeal court. An application refused by the district judge may therefore be made to the circuit or High Court judge.

Such applications are normally considered without a hearing, but where, in such a case, the application is refused, the person seeking permission may

---

[1] FPR 2010, r 30.1.

request the decision to be reconsidered at a hearing.[2] A request for a hearing in such a case must be made within 7 days of service of the notice of refusal.[3]

18.4 Rule 30.7 provides that permission to appeal may be given only where the court considers that the appeal would have a real prospect of success, or there is some other compelling reason why the appeal should be heard.

An order giving permission may limit the issues to be heard, and be made subject to conditions.[4] As an example of conditions, in *C v C (Appeal: Hadkinson Order)*[5] it was held that there is power to require a sum of money to be deposited as a condition of appealing an order of a district judge. In *Radmacher v Granatino*[6] the Court of Appeal held that the appellant wife's gross and subsisting breaches of an order made this an extreme case and that the husband should be protected in the event that the appeal failed. Permission was granted subject to the wife paying a sum of money into the joint names of the solicitors and giving security for costs.

18.5 Under certain circumstances an appeal in a case which has been heard by a district judge in a county court may be transferred to the High Court for hearing by a High Court judge where it appears to the district judge, whether on the application of a party or otherwise, that the appeal raises a difficult or important question, whether of law or otherwise.

TIME LIMITS

18.6 An appellant must file the appellant's notice at the appeal court within such period as may be directed by the lower court (which may be longer or shorter than 21 days). However, where the court makes no such direction, the time limit is 21 days after the date of the decision of the lower court against which the appellant wishes to appeal.[7] The appellant's notice must be served on the respondent to the appeal as soon as practicable and in any event within 7 days.[8]

18.7 A respondent to an appeal who either is seeking permission to appeal from the appeal court, or wishes to ask the appeal court to uphold the order of the lower court for reasons different from or additional to those given by the lower court, must file a respondent's notice. The time for filing such notice depends on a number of factors; it must be filed within:

(a) such period as may be directed by the lower court; or

---

[2]   FPR 2010, rr 30.4 and 30.5.
[3]   FPR 2010, r 30.3(6).
[4]   FPR 2010, r 30.8.
[5]   [2010] EWHC 1656 (Fam), [2011] 1 FLR 434, Eleanor King J.
[6]   [2008] EWCA Civ 1304.
[7]   FPR 2010, r 30.4(2).
[8]   FPR 2010, r 30.4(4).

(b) where the court makes no such direction, 14 days beginning with whichever of the following dates is appropriate:

- the date on which the respondent is served with the appellant's notice where permission to appeal was given by the lower court; or permission to appeal is not required;
- the date on which the respondent is served with notification that the appeal court has given the appellant permission to appeal; or
- the date on which the respondent is served with notification that the application for permission to appeal and the appeal itself are to be heard together.[9]

18.8 Any application to vary the time required for appeal must be made to the appeal court. The parties to an appeal may not agree to vary the times.[10]

ROUTES OF APPEAL

18.9 The question of to whom or to what level of judge an appeal lies is dealt with in PD30A, para 2.1. Appeal from a district judge of a county court lies to a circuit judge (normally one who is 'ticketed' to deal with such appeals). Appeals from a district judge in a district registry of the High Court or from a district judge of the Principal Registry or a costs judge go to a High Court Judge. Appeals from circuit judges, recorders and High Court Judges go to the Court of Appeal.

CONTENTS OF NOTICE

18.10 Unsurprisingly, it is provided that the appeal notice must state the grounds of appeal.[11] Once served, the appeal notice may not be amended except with permission of the appeal court.[12] The appeal court may strike out the whole or part of an appeal notice, set aside permission to appeal in whole or in part, or impose or vary conditions upon which an appeal may be brought.[13] However, it is provided that the court will only exercise these powers where there is a compelling reason for doing so.[14]

POWERS OF APPELLATE COURT

18.11 Rule 30.11 provides that the appellate court has all the powers of the lower court. It may:

---

[9]   FPR 2010, r 30.5(4) and (5).
[10] FPR 2010, r 30.7(1) and (2).
[11] FPR 2010, r 30.6.
[12] FPR 2010, r 30.9.
[13] FPR 2010, r 3.10(1).
[14] FPR 2010, r 30.10(2).

(a)   affirm, set aside or vary any order or judgment made or given by the lower court;

(b)   refer any application or issue for determination by the lower court;

(c)   order a new hearing;

(d)   make orders for the payment of interest;

(e)   make a costs order.[15]

The appeal court may exercise its powers in relation to the whole or part of an order of the lower court.[16]

18.12   As to the principles applicable to the exercise of the appellate court's discretion, it is worth noting that these are the same whether the appellate court consists of a circuit or High Court judge on appeal from a district judge or the Court of Appeal on appeal from the circuit or High Court judge. The new rules in fact more or less repeat the amended FPR 1991, r 8.1(3) which was inserted in 2003. Rule 30.12 in its entirety reads as follows:

> '(1) Every appeal will be limited to a review of the decision of the lower court unless –
>
> (a)   an enactment or practice direction makes different provision for a particular category of appeal; or
> (b)   the court considers that in the circumstances of an individual appeal it would be in the interests of justice to hold a re-hearing.
>
> (2) Unless it orders otherwise, the appeal court will not receive –
>
> (a)   oral evidence; or
> (b)   evidence which was not before the lower court.
>
> (3) The appeal court will allow an appeal where the decision of the lower court was –
>
> (a)   wrong; or
> (b)   unjust because of a serious procedural or other irregularity in the proceedings in the lower court.
>
> (4) The appeal court may draw any inference of fact which it considers justified on the evidence.
>
> (5) At the hearing of the appeal a party may not rely on a matter not contained in that party's appeal notice unless the appeal court gives permission.'

---

[15]   FPR 2010, r 30.11(2).
[16]   FPR 2010, r 30.11(3).

Permission to appeal may be made subject to conditions.[17] In *Radmacher v Granatino*[18] the Court of Appeal held that the appellant wife's gross and subsisting breaches of an order made this an extreme case and that the husband should be protected in the event that the appeal failed. Permission was granted subject to the wife paying a sum of money into the joint names of the solicitors and giving security for costs.

18.13 The following are some examples of how the Court of Appeal has exercised its discretion as to whether or not to allow appeals. These were cases using almost identical rules and guidelines to the new rules.

In *Brisset v Brisset*[19] it was found that the circuit judge had been procedurally improper on an appeal from the district judge. His order was set aside and the court conducted its own appeal from the district judge.

In *Fallon v Fallon*[20] a High Court Judge declined to allow an appeal even though the district judge had clearly made a mistake of fact in his calculations and deliberations. The appeal was allowed.

In *Lyons v Lyons*[21] an appeal was allowed where the trial judge had made an obvious error. It was said that it was unfortunate that the errors had not been taken up when the judgment was delivered.

In *Kaur v Matharu*[22] a circuit judge on hearing an appeal allowed fresh (oral) evidence. On appeal it was held that the judge was clearly wrong. Although the court was not strictly bound by *Ladd v Marshall*[23] its discretion to admit fresh evidence should only be exercised in exceptional circumstances and when it was in the interests of justice so to do.

In *N v N (Financial Order: Appellate Role)*[24] a circuit judge had failed to direct himself correctly on the appellate function, based his decision to allow an appeal on a view of the evidence fundamentally at variance with the district judge's findings and erroneously exercised an independent discretion. The Court of Appeal held that these were compelling circumstances which justified giving permission for a second appeal and for allowing the appeal.

---

[17] CPR, r 52.3(7).
[18] [2008] EWCA Civ 1304.
[19] [2009] EWCA Civ 679, [2009] 2 FLR 1451.
[20] [2008] EWCA Civ 1653.
[21] [2010] EWCA Civ 177.
[22] [2010] EWCA Civ 930.
[23] [1954] 1 WLR 1489.
[24] [2011] EWCA Civ 940.

For a case where an appeal was allowed on grounds of error of law (which can include a failure to give proper reasons, a failure to apply the statutory test under s 25 MCA, and a failure to take account of relevant factors) see *V v V (Prenuptial Agreement)*.[25]

MATERIAL OMISSIONS

18.14   PD30A, paras 4.6–4.9 deal with the procedure where a party's advocate considers that there is a material omission from the judgment of the lower court. Before the drawing of the order the advocate should notify the lower court of the omission so that the court can consider this, rather than using the omission as an immediate ground of appeal. Where an application for permission to appeal on the ground of an omission is made to the lower court that court must consider the issue and, if it agrees that there was an omission, correct the omission. It may adjourn if necessary to consider the issue.

Where such an application is made to the appeal court, that court may, if it considers that there was an omission, adjourn the application and ask the lower court to correct the omission.

PROCEDURE

18.15   The procedure for appeals, including detail as to bundles of documents, skeleton arguments etc will be found in PD30A, para 5 et seq.

APPLICATIONS TO SET ASIDE CONSENT ORDERS

18.16   Since an order made by consent is made with the express agreement of the parties, there are clearly only limited grounds on which it might be set aside; an appeal cannot lie on the merits of the order, in the usual way. Any challenge to a consent order has, therefore, to attack the fundamental basis of the order, and there are four recognised ways of doing this. They are by alleging:

(a)   non-disclosure of some essential matter;

(b)   fraud or misrepresentation;

(c)   supervening events which invalidate the whole basis of the order; and

(d)   undue influence.[26]

---

[25]   [2011] EWHC 3230 (Fam).
[26]   *Tomney v Tomney* [1983] Fam 15. See also *L v L* below; pressure falling short of undue influence will not suffice.

These possibilities will be considered in turn, with (a) and (b) being considered together since, as will be seen, they are essentially variations on the same basic allegation, namely that the respondent to the application has in some way misled the applicant.[27]

The two means of attacking a consent order are applications for leave to appeal out of time and applications to set aside the order; the first is made by the normal appellate route from the court which made the order, while the second is made to the court which made the order.[28] It would seem that the former is more appropriate in the case of events occurring after the date of the order while the latter would be appropriate in the case of non-disclosure or fraud.

Non-disclosure, fraud and misrepresentation

18.17 The duty of full and frank disclosure has already been mentioned above, and was one of the principal issues in *Livesey (formerly Jenkins) v Jenkins*.[29] In that case the parties had settled their litigation by means of a consent order, but the wife had omitted to tell her former husband, or even her own solicitors, that she was intending to remarry; that remarriage was a significant matter and something which she should have disclosed. In his speech, Lord Brandon emphasised that the parties were under the same obligation as to complete disclosure in cases of consent orders as in contested proceedings, and said that in order to do justice to the husband it was necessary to set the order aside.

This decision confirmed a number of earlier decisions, notably *Robinson v Robinson (Disclosure)*,[30] where it was held that there was a duty on litigants in matrimonial proceedings to make full and frank disclosure of their property and financial resources; the power to set aside orders was not limited to cases of fraud and mistake but extended to material non-disclosure.

It was emphasised in *Livesey v Jenkins* that not every example of non-disclosure would result in the order being set aside. Orders will not be set aside if the disclosure would not have made any substantial difference to the order which the court would have made:[31]

'It will only be in cases where the absence of full and frank disclosure has led to the court making, either in contested proceedings or by consent, an order that is

---

[27] For a lengthy and comprehensive analysis of the various grounds on which an ancillary relief order may be challenged, see the judgment of Munby J in *L v L* [2006] EWHC 956 (Fam). Inter alia, his Lordship said that an order can never be set aside on the ground of bad legal advice.

[28] For a flow chart of the means by which an application to set aside an order may be made, see *B-T v B-T (Divorce Procedure)* [1990] 2 FLR 1 per Ward J, set out in Appendix A, Precedent 33.

[29] See **9.3**.

[30] (1983) 4 FLR 102, CA.

[31] *Livesey v Jenkins* [1984] AC 424, HL, per Lord Brandon.

substantially different from the order which would have been made if such disclosure had taken place that a case for setting aside can possibly be made good.'

18.18 In *Vicary v Vicary*,[32] a consent order was made on the basis that the husband's assets, including his shares in a private company, were £430,000. He did not disclose the fact that negotiations were taking place for the sale of the company, and, shortly thereafter, he sold his shares for £2.8m. The order was set aside.[33]

In *Rose v Rose*[34] a consent order was made in August 2001. At an FDR hearing the wife had claimed that her relationship with a boyfriend had cooled. However, the husband subsequently adduced evidence to show that they had planned to buy a house in Italy and spend part of each year there. He applied to set aside the consent order, but the wife successfully applied for a summary order striking out his application. It was held that the operative date for non-disclosure was the date of the order. On that date the husband had been aware of the relationship and had chosen not to cross-examine her on it. Even if the husband were able to prove non-disclosure, it was utterly unlikely that the wife's interest would be confined to a life interest in property as he now suggested. It was emphasised that a delay of one year in making an application of this kind is 'wholly unreasonable'.[35]

In *I v I (Ancillary Relief: Disclosure)*[36] a consent order had been made after an FDR at which the husband had failed to disclose that he was negotiating a new employment contract. The wife subsequently applied to set aside the order on the ground of non-disclosure. It was held that, if it had been disclosed, it would probably have made little difference to the final order and the appeal was dismissed.

Parties who applied on trivial grounds would be penalised in costs. In another case, the fact that there is no jurisdiction to vary a lump sum order nor to award a second lump sum was advanced to support the point that consent orders should not lightly be set aside.[37]

18.19 In *Boker-Ingram v Boker-Ingram*[38] after a consent order was made it was found that the husband had failed to disclose the advanced state of negotiations for his new contract. Charles J declined to set aside the order. On appeal, it was said that 'the judge's erudition may have blinded him to the simplicity of the case and its proper outcome'. The appeal was allowed.

---

[32] [1992] 2 FLR 271, CA.
[33] See also *Thompson v Thompson* [1991] 2 FLR 530, CA.
[34] [2003] EWHC 505 (Fam), [2003] 2 FLR 197.
[35] A point repeated in *Shaw v Shaw* [2002] EWCA Civ 1298, [2002] 2 FLR 1204, CA.
[36] [2008] EWCA 1167 (Fam).
[37] *Redmond v Redmond* [1986] 2 FLR 173.
[38] [2009] EWCA Civ 412.

In *Kingdon v Kingdon*[39] the husband failed to disclose that he had purchased shares in a new company which led to his being required to sell other shares resulting in a net gain for him of £1.2m. He continued to present a misleading picture and the wife applied to set aside the consent order. The trial judge found that there had been a material non-disclosure, but delclined to set aside the whole order, instead ordering the husband to pay an additional lump sum. The Court of Appeal dismissed the wife's appeal against this decision; there was no need to dismantle the consent order but merely to add to it. The court relied on the judgment of Thorpe LJ in *Williams v Lindley* (see **18.25**). In this case, however, re-consideration of all the s 25 factors was not necessary.

18.20 In *Robinson v Robinson*,[40] Ormrod LJ expressed the view that, while applications to set aside could be made by means of either a new action or an appeal to a higher court, there was much convenience in an application to the judge who made the original order who could determine the application and then go on, as the Court of Appeal could not, to make a new order in appropriate cases.

New or supervening circumstances

18.21 As has already been said, there is no jurisdiction to vary a lump sum order or property adjustment order on the ground of new circumstances or otherwise. Nevertheless, some procedure has to exist to deal with the kind of case where the whole factual basis on which the order was made has disappeared.

In *Barder v Caluori*,[41] a consent order was made by which the husband was ordered to transfer his interest in the former matrimonial home to the wife. One of the principal reasons for this order was that the wife had the care of the children. Shortly thereafter, the wife killed the children and herself. On appeal to the House of Lords, the principal issue was whether leave to appeal out of time should have been granted, but the reasons given in the speech of Lord Brandon may be applied to an application to the judge at first instance. Lord Brandon said that the court might properly exercise its discretion to grant leave to appeal out of time from an order for financial provision or property transfer on the ground of new events provided four conditions were met. These conditions were:

(1) that new events have occurred since the making of the order which invalidate the basis or fundamental assumption upon which the order was made, so that, if leave to appeal out of time were given, the appeal would be certain, or very likely, to succeed;

---

[39] [2010] EWCA Civ 1251.

[40] (1983) 4 FLR 102, CA. For a similar statement, see *Fournier v Fournier* [1998] 2 FLR 990, CA, per Lord Woolf MR.

[41] [1988] AC 20, sub nom *Barder v Barder (Caluori Intervening)* [1987] 2 FLR 480, HL.

(2)　that the new events should have occurred within a relatively short time of the order having been made. While that time could not be precisely defined, Lord Brandon thought it extremely unlikely that it could be as long as a year, and that in most cases it would be no more than a few months;

(3)　that the application should be made reasonably promptly in the circumstances of the case; and

(4)　that the grant of leave should not prejudice third parties who have acquired in good faith and for valuable consideration interests in property which is the subject matter of the order.

18.22 Inevitably, circumstances change after orders are made, and it must be emphasised that the courts will not set aside an order merely on the ground that things are now different from how they appeared at the time of the order.[42] In *Walkden v Walkden*[43] the husband had stated the value of his shares as £216,000 in his Form E. After a consent order was made he sold them for £1.8m. The Court of Appeal held that a court should first consider whether the consent order was vitiated by misrepresentation, fraud, undue influence or non-disclosure. If not, it should then consider whether there was a '*Barder* event'. Here there was no vititating factor and no *Barder* event because the sale was not unforeseen or unforeseeable and there had been no dramatic change in the company's performance.

In *Judge v Judge*[44] it was held that an application to set aside an order is not an application for ancillary relief and so the general rule that costs do not follow the event did not apply.

In *Richardson v Richardson*[45] Thorpe LJ emphasised that '*Barder* jurisprudence' is to be kept within very strict limits ; clearly such applications are not encouraged.

It seems that there are several common grounds for such applications which may conveniently be summarised as follows.

(1) Disputes as to the value of an asset

18.23 The position was summarised in *Cornick v Cornick*.[46] Where an asset which was correctly valued at the time of the order changes value within a relatively short period because of the natural processes of price fluctuation, leave to appeal should not be granted (and the order should not be set aside).

---

[42]　See e g *McGladdery v McGladdery* [1999] 2 FLR 1102.
[43]　[2009] EWCA Civ 627, [2010] 1 FLR 174.
[44]　[2009] EWCA Civ 1458, [2009] 1 FLR 1287.
[45]　[2011] EWCA Civ 79.
[46]　[1994] 2 FLR 530.

Where a wrong value was placed on an asset at the time of the order and, had this been known, a different order would have been made, provided that this was not the fault of the person alleging the mistake, leave to appeal may be granted (and the order set aside).

Where something unforeseen and unforeseeable has occurred since the date of the order which has altered the value of the assets so dramatically as to bring about a substantial change in the balance of the assets brought about by the order, then, provided the other three *Barder* conditions are met, the *Barder* principles may apply. The circumstances in which these conditions might apply are rare.[47]

18.24 At a time of rapid fluctuation of property prices, it is natural that there should be second thoughts about the wisdom of some consent orders. However, it will always be necessary to show that the facts fall within the principles set out above. For example, in one case[48] the Court of Appeal granted leave to appeal out of time on the ground that the actual value of a house was so much lower than the agreed valuation that the applicant could not be rehoused on the division of the proceeds of sale originally agreed. In another,[49] the division of the proceeds of sale would have been enough to rehouse the parties had the husband not 'disgracefully' delayed the sale by more than 3 years, and leave to appeal was granted on the basis that the fundamental assumption underlying the order, namely that the wife would be able to rehouse herself, had been falsified. However, in another case,[50] where the value of a house at the time of the order was £340,000 and at the time of the hearing of the application for leave to appeal 3 years later £250,000, leave to appeal was refused.

In *Kean v Kean*[51] a consent order was made in 2000 on the basis that the property was worth £500,000 to £550,000. No formal valuation was obtained. In the summer of 2001 the property was sold for £765,000 and the wife sought leave to appeal out of time. This application was refused on the ground that the estimate of the value was not a basis of, nor a fundamental assumption underlying the agreement. It was not certain that the court would have made a different order if the true value had been known. Moreover, the wife had to take some responsibility since she had been advised to take separate advice and had refused.

In *B v B (Ancillary Relief: Consent Order: Appeal out of Time)*[52] a wife sought leave to appeal on the ground, inter alia, of an error in valuation at trial. It was held that there was no evidence of an incorrect valuation at the date of the hearing and that none of the *Barder* conditions applied.

---

[47] See e g *Middleton v Middleton* [1998] 2 FLR 821, CA.
[48] *Heard v Heard* [1995] 1 FLR 970, CA.
[49] *Hope-Smith v Hope-Smith* [1989] 2 FLR 56, CA.
[50] *B v B (Financial Provision: Leave to Appeal)* [1994] 1 FLR 219. See also, for a contrary decision, *Heard v Heard* [1995] 1 FLR 970, CA.
[51] [2002] 2 FLR 28.
[52] [2007] EWHC 2472 (Fam), [2008] 1 FLR 1279.

(2) Remarriage or cohabitation

18.25 It has been seen above that in *Livesey v Jenkins* the fact that the wife failed to disclose to the husband her intention to remarry undermined the basis on which the order was made and was sufficient to enable the court to set it aside. This will, of course, not always be the case.[53] In another case,[54] where the wife had remarried since the order, it was held that the fact of her remarriage did not affect her entitlement to capital and this would have been the case even if she had been remarried at the time of the order. It is therefore necessary to demonstrate that the basis on which the order was made has been falsified before the application will stand any chance of success.

In *Williams v Lindley*[55] a consent order of 70/30 in favour of a wife had been made after the wife had denied any relationship with a certain man. Soon thereafter she married the man in question. A circuit judge refused the husband's application for a re-hearing but this was allowed by the Court of Appeal. It was held that the main foundation of the wife's case had been undermined, and Thorpe LJ added that, when approaching the 'supervening event', greater flexibility was needed; the court should move away from rigid prescription and reconsideration of all the s 25 factors was necessary.

In *Dixon v Marchant*[56] a husband claimed that he had been led to make a consent order capitalising the wife's periodical payments by her assertion that she was not cohabiting and did not intend to do so. Seven months later she remarried. His appeal was dismissed. The court held that he had to show on an objective test that there was a common assumption made by the parties and shared by the court that for an indefinite period to be measured in years rather than weeks or months the wife would not remarry.

(3) Death

18.26 The same principles apply in the case of the death of a party. It might be thought that where the basis of an order was the provision of a home for one party, the death of that party would invalidate the whole order, but that would be an over-simplistic view of the law. Death was, clearly, the background to *Barder v Caluori*, considered at **18.21**, and the principles set out there need not be repeated.

In *Amey v Amey*,[57] there had been an agreement between the parties which they intended to have approved by means of a consent order. However, before they could do so, the wife died. The husband sought to set aside the agreement. It was held that the mere fact of the wife's death was not sufficient; the agreement had been a fair distribution of assets on the basis of the wife's entitlement, and

---

[53] See e g *Cook v Cook* [1988] 1 FLR 521, CA.
[54] *B v B (Financial Provision: Leave to Appeal)* (above).
[55] [2005] EWCA Civ 103, [2005] 2 FLR 710.
[56] [2008] 1 FLR 655, CA.
[57] [1992] 2 FLR 89.

the only ground for setting it aside would be if the death had undermined the fundamental assumptions on which the order was made.

In *Barber v Barber*,[58] an order was made for the wife to have more than half the proceeds of sale of the former matrimonial home on the assumption that, though she was ill, she had at least 5 years to live. She died 3 months after the order was made. The order was set aside in part, on the ground that its fundamental basis had been invalidated. It was held that the proper approach was to start again and make an order on the basis of what the court would have done had it known at the date of the order what it now knew. This followed the decision of the court in *Smith v Smith (Smith and Others Intervening)*,[59] which established similar principles.

In *Reid v Reid*[60] the facts were that a consent order had awarded the wife £99,000 on a clean break basis. She had disclosed the fact that she suffered from ill health. Fifteen days after decree absolute she died. The husband sought leave to appeal out of time. The court held that her death 2 months after the order was a new event and attracted *Barder* principles. It was not reasonably foreseeable; the husband's needs had not been fully met by the order and the wife's death had invalidated the parties' perceptions of her needs. The husband would receive a lump sum of £37,000; the executor's arguments based on entitlement and contributions were not appropriate where assets were very limited.

(4) Other matters

18.27 For the sake of completeness, reference should be made to *Crozier v Crozier*,[61] where an application was made to set aside a clean break order with nominal maintenance for a child on the ground that the Child Support Agency, which had come into being since the making of the order, seemed likely to require the husband to pay a substantial amount by way of child maintenance. The application was refused, partly on the ground that parties could never agree to contract out of liability for a child.

In *S v S (Ancillary Relief: Consent Order)*[62] a consent order was made for a payment of £800,000 to the wife on a clean break basis one month before the House of Lords decision in *White v White*. The wife applied to set aside the order on the ground of a supervening event. The application was dismissed. It was held that, while a change in the law could be a supervening event, it must be unforeseeable. At the time of the order, the House was considering its judgment, and a change in the law was foreseeable.

---

[58]   [1993] 1 FLR 476, CA.
[59]   [1991] 2 FLR 432, CA.
[60]   [2004] 1 FLR 736, Wilson J.
[61]   [1994] 1 FLR 126.
[62]   [2002] 1 FLR 992.

18.28 In the present 'credit crunch' many orders have been made at a time when values, whether of shares or properties, were considerably greater than they are today, and it was widely anticipated that this would give rise to applications to set aside consent (and, indeed, other) orders. The decision of the Court of Appeal in *Myerson v Myerson*[63] was therefore awaited with keen interest.

In this case, the consent order had divided the assets, valued at the time at £25m, at 57% to the husband and 43% to the wife. The husband's retained assets were largely made up of his shareholding in his company. At the time of the order the shares were worth £15m (each share was valued at £2.99). By the time of the appeal the shares were trading at 27.5p. The husband had paid the first instalment (£7m) of a lump sum totalling £9.5m in April 2008. He had submitted that the original judge's jurisdiction should be extended to fundamentally rewrite the order at a future hearing as the order was no longer fair and the husband could not perform his remaining obligations (ie the lump sum instalments).

Thorpe LJ rejected the appeal even though it had 'dramatic features'. He relied on *Cornick*, and agreed with Hale J's reasoning in that case that the 'natural processes of price fluctuation' should not constitute a *Barder* event. He also added four other factors in this case that prevent the appeal succeeding:

(i) the husband, with all his knowledge and experience, had agreed the compromise;

(ii) the husband, in attempting to vary and offer the wife shares instead, was seeking to relieve himself of the consequences of his speculation;

(iii) he still has the opportunities as 'unusual opportunities are created for the most astute in a bear market'; and

(iv) the husband has already invoked the statutory power of variation concerning the instalments.

He went on as follows:

'There may be many who are contemplating an attempt to reopen an existing ancillary relief order on the grounds of subsequently encountered financial eclipse. All in that situation should ponder Hale J's analytical characterisation and ask themselves whether the events upon which they intend to rely can be bought within either the second or the third category. Even then they would be well advised to heed the warning that very few successful applications have been reported. I echo the words of Hale J that the natural processes of price fluctuation, whether in houses, shares, or any other property, and however dramatic, do not satisfy the *Barder* test.'

---

[63] [2009] EWCA Civ 282.

APPEAL OR SETTING ASIDE?

18.29 Where non-disclosure is alleged it would seem that the applicant to set aside has the choice of proceeding by way of appeal or by way of application to the first instance judge. In *Harris v Manahan*[64] it was clear that Thorpe and Ward LJJ held different opinions as to which was the most appropriate course. In the recent case of *Musa v Karim*[65] Thorpe LJ repeated that it was open to the applicant to choose the most suitable route and added that this difference of opinion needed to be resolved.

[64] [1997] 1 FLR 205 CA.
[65] [2012] EWCA Civ 1332, [2013] Fam Law 16.

Chapter 19

ENFORCEMENT

INTRODUCTION

19.1 In this chapter it is intended to give an outline of the types of enforcement available in respect of orders for financial remedies and the practical details of how to proceed in the most common types of enforcement. It should be noted that, although FPR 2010, Part 33 sets out the various forms of enforcement, the methods of enforcement themselves are contained in Parts 70 and 71 of the Civil Procedure Rules (CPR), and so a certain amount of cross-referencing is necessary. (More confusingly, in places the CPR refer back to the mainly superseded Rules of the Supreme Court (RSC) and County Court Rules (CCR) but it is hoped that it will not be necessary to go into too much detail about this.)

The preliminary step

19.2 Rule 33.3(1) provides that, except where a rule or practice direction otherwise requires, an application for an order to enforce an order for the payment of money must be made in a notice of application accompanied by a statement which must state the amount due under the order, showing how that amount is arrived at, and be verified by a statement of truth. This therefore is the initial requirement. A precedent for such a statement is contained within Form D50K referred to below. However, the next step is to decide how best the order can be enforced.

19.3 The litigant who has secured an order for a financial remedy, such as a periodical payments order or a lump sum order has to decide which remedy is most appropriate. In some cases the choice is clear and the position in such a case will be considered below from **19.6** onwards.

However, what should the litigant do when the choice is not clear? In the past, this has meant that fees and costs have sometimes been wasted when, for example, after an application for a third party debt order, it has transpired that there is no asset over which the order can take effect. For this reason, FPR 2010 have introduced a new form of procedure, contained in r 33.3(2) which provides as follows:

> 'The notice of application may either –
>
> (a)   apply for an order specifying the method of enforcement; or

(b)   apply for an order for such method of enforcement as the court may consider appropriate.' (This is Form D50K.)

In other words, where the applicant is unsure how to proceed, he or she may issue the application and leave it to the court to decide what form of enforcement is most appropriate.

19.4   When this second course is adopted, r 33.3(3) applies. This provides that where such an application is made, an order to attend court will be issued and r 71.2 (6) and (7) of the CPR will apply as if the application had been made under that rule. These rules are those designed to obtain information from judgment debtors and provide as follows:

'(6) A person served with an order issued under this rule must –

(a)   attend court at the time and place specified in the order;
(b)   when he does so, produce at court documents in his control which are described in the order; and
(c)   answer on oath such questions as the court may require.

(7) An order under this rule will contain a notice in the following terms –

"You must obey this order. If you do not, you may be sent to prison for contempt of court."'

At the hearing, therefore, the debtor must produce all evidence about his means and assets including any specifically requested in the notice of application. When the applicant has gathered all information necessary for her decision, she will presumably ask the judge to make an appropriate order. The intention of the rule changes is that the judge will be able to make such orders without the need for a separate application, and the respondent will have been given ample warning of the possibilities by the wording of Form D50K which will have been served on him. This reads as follows:

'At the hearing of this application the court may make an order by any of the following methods as it considers appropriate –

- An attachment of earnings order
- A third party debt order
- A charging order, stop order or stop notice
- A writ or warrant of execution (seizure and sale of personal property)
- The appointment of a receiver'

19.5   It may be, however, that the applicant is well acquainted with the assets of the debtor and is able to choose which remedy is most appropriate. Para 1.1 of Practice Direction 70 to the CPR provides as follows:

'1.1 A judgment creditor may enforce a judgment or order for the payment of money by any of the following methods:

(1)   a writ of fieri facias or warrant of execution (see RSC Orders 46 and 47 and CCR Order 26);

(2)   a third party debt order (see Part 72);

(3)   a charging order, stop order or stop notice (see Part 73);

(4)   in a county court, an attachment of earnings order (see CCR Order 27);

(5)   the appointment of a receiver (see Part 69).

1.2 In addition the court may make the following orders against a judgment debtor –

(1)   an order of committal, but only if permitted by –
     (a)   a rule; and
     (b)   the Debtors Acts 1869 and 1878
     (See RSC Order 45 rule 5 and CCR Order 28. Practice Direction RSC 52 and CCR 29 applies to an application for committal of a judgment debtor); and

(2)   in the High Court, a writ of sequestration, but only if permitted by RSC Order 45 rule 5.'

This succinctly summarises the options available, which will be briefly considered in turn.

EXECUTION

19.6   Execution is the seizure and sale of the debtor's goods, and takes the form of a writ of fiere facias in the High Court and a warrant of execution in the county court. The appropriate provisions are RSC Ord 47 and CCR Ord 26.

For the purposes of a warrant of execution, the Principal Registry is, in effect, treated as a county court.[1]

CHARGING ORDERS

19.7   This process is governed by the Charging Orders Act 1979, and CPR Part 73. Process may be issued in the High Court in respect of maintenance orders of the High Court or other orders of the High Court where the sum to be enforced is over £5,000; otherwise, the county court has exclusive jurisdiction.

The procedure is that an interim charging order is obtained by filing the statement in support, and then a date is fixed for the hearing of the on notice application for a final charging order. A charging order is most commonly granted over real property, but can be granted over shares, funds in court or other forms of property.

---

[1]   FPR 2010, r 33.6.

An interim charging order must be served on any joint owner and on any known creditor, who is then entitled to be heard at the on notice hearing. Once a charging order has been made, it is a security for the debt and the person in whose favour the order was made is in the position of a mortgagee. Any further enforcement has to be by way of an application for an order for sale.[2]

The court has no power to make a charging order on a debtor's entitlements under a pension scheme, as the debtor would have no beneficial interest under the trusts of the scheme.[3]

THIRD PARTY DEBT ORDER

19.8   The rules are contained in CPR Part 72. A third party debt order directs someone who owes money to the debtor (such as a bank, where the account is in credit, or a trade debtor) to make the payment to the creditor. As with a charging order, the procedure is that an interim order is granted upon the filing of the statement in support and a hearing is then fixed for the application for the final order.

ATTACHMENT OF EARNINGS

19.9   The primary authority for attachment of earnings orders is the Attachment of Earnings Act 1971, and the rules are contained in CCR Ord 27. CCR Ord 27, r 17 has particular relevance to maintenance orders. Although attachment of earnings is normally used to enforce orders for periodical payments, it can be used, for example, to recover an unpaid lump sum over a period of time. The essential features of an attachment of earnings order are that the court fixes a normal deduction rate (the weekly or monthly sum to be deducted from the debtor's earnings by his employer), and a protected earnings rate (the sum which the debtor must be allowed to keep). An attachment of earnings order is normally made in respect of earnings, but it can be used to deduct payments from a pension.

When the order to be enforced was made by a divorce county court, application for an attachment of earnings order must be made to that court.[4]

19.10   Attachment of earnings is unique among forms of enforcement in that a court which makes an order for periodical payments may make an attachment of earnings order at the same time, even if, as must be the case, no arrears have arisen.[5]

---

[2]   See TLATA 1996, s 14, and CCR Ord 31, r 4.
[3]   *Field v Field* [2003] 1 FLR 376.
[4]   CCR Ord 27, r 17(2).
[5]   Maintenance Enforcement Act 1991, s 1, and CCR Ord 27, r 17(4).

JUDGMENT SUMMONS

19.11 The power of the court to make an order on a judgment summons derives from the Debtors Act 1869, s 5.[6]

Procedure is governed by FPR 2010, r 33.10 which provides as follows:

'(1) An application for the issue of a judgment summons may be made –

(a) in the case of an order of the High Court –
   (i) where the order was made in matrimonial proceedings, to the principal registry, a district registry or a divorce county court, whichever in the opinion of the judgment creditor is most convenient;
   (ii) [not applicable] and
   (iii) in any other case, to the principal registry, a district registry or a designated county court, whichever in the opinion of the judgment creditor is most convenient;
(b) in the case of an order of a divorce county court, to whichever divorce county court is in the opinion of the judgment creditor most convenient; and
(c) [not applicable]

having regard (in any case) to the place where the debtor resides or carries on business and irrespective of the court or registry in which the order was made.

(2) An application must be accompanied by a statement which –

(a) complies with rule 33.3(1);
(b) contains all the evidence on which the judgment creditor intends to rely; and
(c) has exhibited to it a copy of the order.'

19.12 Rule 33.11 provides that if the debtor is in default under an order of committal made on a previous judgment summons in respect of the same order, a judgment summons must not be issued without the court's permission. A judgment summons and the statement referred to in r 33.10(2) must be served on the debtor personally not less than 14 days before the hearing and the debtor must be paid or offered a sum reasonably sufficient to cover the expenses of travelling to and from the court at which he is summoned to appear. Personal service of an application to commit is essential.

19.13 As to the hearing, r 33.14(1) sets out the rules to be observed.

'No person may be committed on an application for a judgment summons unless –

(a) where the proceedings are in the High Court, the debtor has failed to attend both the hearing that the debtor was summonsed to attend and the adjourned hearing;
(b) where the proceedings are in a county court, an order is made under section 110(2) of the County Courts Act 1984; or
(c) the judgment creditor proves that the debtor –

---

[6] Subject to Administration of Justice Act 1970, s 11.

> (i)   has, or has had, since the date of the order the means to pay the sum in respect of which the debtor has made default; and
>
> (ii)   has refused or neglected, or refuses or neglects, to pay that sum.'

It is further provided that the debtor may not be compelled to give evidence.

Rule 33.16 then sets out the various options open to the court on the hearing of a judgment summons. Where the order is for lump sum provision or costs; or where the order is an order for maintenance pending suit, an order for maintenance pending outcome of proceedings or an order for other periodical payments and it appears to the court that the order would have been varied or suspended if the debtor had made an application for that purpose, the court may make a new order for payment of the amount due under the original order, together with the costs of the judgment summons, either at a specified time or by instalments.

If the court makes an order of committal, it may direct its execution to be suspended on terms that the debtor pays to the judgment creditor the amount due; the costs of the judgment summons; and any sums accruing due under the original order, either at a specified time or by instalments.

All payments under a new order or an order of committal must be made to the judgment creditor unless the court directs otherwise.

19.14   Where an order of committal is suspended on such terms as are mentioned above, all payments made under the suspended order will be deemed to be made first, in or towards the discharge of any sums from time to time accruing due under the original order; and secondly, in or towards the discharge of a debt in respect of which the judgment summons was issued and the costs of the summons. The suspended order must not be executed until the judgment creditor has filed a statement of default on the part of the debtor.

19.15   For a case where an appeal was allowed after committal proceedings which were 'peppered with errors' see *Zuk v Zuk*.[7]

For a comprehensive review of the principles and approach which must be followed in these applications see the judgment of Mostyn J in *Bhura v Bhura*.[8]

APPOINTMENT OF A RECEIVER

19.16   A receiver may be appointed by the court by way of equitable execution whenever this is 'just and convenient'.[9] Procedure is governed by CPR Part 69. Application may be made at trial or at any time.

---

[7]   [2012] EWCA Civ 1871.

[8]   [2012] EWHC 3633 (Fam).

[9]   SCA 1981, s 37(1) and CCA 1984, s 38 but see *Field v Field* [2003] 1 FLR 376.

When an order is made, or application for an order has been made, an injunction may be granted in support of the order or application.

REGISTRATION OF ORDER IN A MAGISTRATES' COURT

19.17 An order for periodical payments made in a divorce county court may be registered for purposes of enforcement in a magistrates' court.[10] Once registration has been effected, any application to vary the amount of the order (as opposed to, for example, its duration) must be made in a magistrates' court.[11]

Procedure is governed by FPR 2010, r 32.15. Application is made by sending to the court officer at the court which made the order a certified copy of the maintenance order and two copies of the application.

An order for registration of an interim order or nominal order will not normally be made.

THE MAINTENANCE ENFORCEMENT ACT 1991

19.18 The Maintenance Enforcement Act 1991 has already been mentioned in connection with attachment of earnings. It should also be noted that, whenever the court makes a periodical payments order[12] or at any time thereafter,[13] it may direct that payment of the order be made in a specified manner such as by standing order or by direct debit.[14] This power may be exercised on application of either party or of the court's own motion.[15]

To enforce payment by this method, the court may order the paying party to open a bank account.[16]

EXECUTION OF DOCUMENTS BY NOMINATED PERSON

19.19 Sometimes, when an order is made for the transfer of property, the person ordered to transfer fails to do so. In those circumstances, the court may order that some other person execute the document on his behalf.[17] The proposed nominee is frequently the district judge but this need not be so; a

---

[10] Maintenance Orders Act 1958, s 2(1).
[11] Maintenance Orders Act 1958, s 4(5).
[12] Maintenance Enforcement Act 1991, s 1(1).
[13] Maintenance Enforcement Act 1991, s 1(3).
[14] Maintenance Enforcement Act 1991, s 1(4), (5).
[15] Maintenance Enforcement Act 1991, s 1(3).
[16] Maintenance Enforcement Act 1991, s 1(6).
[17] SCA 1981, s 39; CCA 1984, s 38.

partner in the applicant's firm of solicitors would be a more convenient person. Application for such an order may be made when the order for transfer is made, but, if it is not, it must be made on notice to the other party, supported by a statement as to the facts of the case. This remedy should always be used rather than an application to commit.[18]

SEQUESTRATION

19.20 Sequestration is a drastic method of enforcing an order to do an act (such as a payment of money, or transfer of property) within a specified time. The effect of the issue of a writ of sequestration is that the property of the defaulting party is bound by the sequestration until the money is paid or the act otherwise performed. Sequestration is in fact a means of punishing a contempt.

Procedure is governed by RSC Ord 46, r 5, and CCA 1984, s 38 (there are no separate county court rules relating to sequestration). Application must be made to a judge; in the High Court, application is made in the Family Division, and it is suggested that county court applications should be made to a divorce county court.

There are several reported examples of the use of sequestration in family cases.[19]

RECIPROCAL ENFORCEMENT

19.21 Maintenance and other orders may sometimes be registered in other jurisdictions for enforcement. The law is complicated and a variety of different statutes, depending on where it is sought to register and which Conventions apply, govern what may be done. For the detail the reader is referred to *The Family Court Practice*.[20] Procedure is governed by FPR 2010, Part 32.

---

[18] *Danchevsky v Danchevsky* [1975] Fam 17.
[19] *Sansom v Sansom* (1879) 4 PD 69; *Birch v Birch* (1883) 8 PD 163; *Hyde v Hyde* (1888) 13 PD 166; *Romilly v Romilly* [1964] P 22.
[20] *The Family Court Practice 2013*, Jordan Publishing, 2013.

Chapter 20

THE IMPACT OF THE HUMAN RIGHTS ACT 1998

INTRODUCTION

20.1 The enactment of the Human Rights Act 1998 (HRA 1998) means that all areas of the law of England and Wales are now subject to the overriding duty to comply with the provisions of the European Convention for the Protection of Human Rights and Fundamental Freedoms ('the Convention') which has applied to most of the rest of Europe since 1950. Family law, and ancillary relief in particular, is not exempt from this general requirement. The purpose of this chapter is not to provide a detailed examination of all the implications of the HRA 1998[1] but rather to draw attention to some of the major points which may impinge on the law and practice of ancillary relief.

20.2 The structure of this chapter will therefore be to examine the following matters:

(a)   the principal provisions of the HRA 1998;

(b)   the parts of the Convention which may affect ancillary relief;

(c)   the likely effect in practice of these provisions.

THE PRINCIPAL PROVISIONS OF THE HRA 1998

20.3 In this section it is proposed to consider the following:

*   duties of the court in respect of Convention rights;

*   declarations of incompatibility;

*   acts of 'public authorities';

*   remedies available.

---

[1]   For such a detailed examination, see Swindells et al *Family Law and the Human Rights Act 1998* (Jordans, 1999).

Before doing so, however, two key terms must be defined. 'Convention rights' means:[2]

> 'the rights and fundamental freedoms set out in –
>
> (a)　Articles 2 to 12 and 14 of the Convention,
> (b)　Articles 1 to 3 of the First Protocol, and
> (c)　Articles 1 and 2 of the Sixth Protocol,
>
> as read with Articles 16 to 18 of the Convention.'

'Protocol' means:[3]

> 'a protocol to the Convention –
>
> (a)　which the United Kingdom has ratified; or
> (b)　which the United Kingdom has signed with a view to ratification.'

Application and interpretation of Convention rights

20.4　HRA 1998, s 3 provides that, so far as possible, primary legislation and subordinate legislation must be read and given effect in a way which is compatible with the Convention rights. The overall effect is clear: domestic legislation must be read and interpreted in such a way as to give effect to and not to go against the letter or the spirit of Convention rights. The courts are directed as to their duties in this respect. A court or tribunal determining any question which has arisen in connection with a Convention right must take into account any:

(a)　judgment, decision, declaration or advisory opinion of the European Court of Human Rights (ECHR);

(b)　opinion of the Commission (ie the European Commission of Human Rights, now incorporated in the new ECHR) given in a report adopted under Art 31 of the Convention;

(c)　decision of the Commission in connection with Art 26 or Art 27(2) of the Convention; or

(d)　decision of the Committee of Ministers taken under Art 46 of the Convention,

whenever made or given, so far as, in the opinion of the court or tribunal, it is relevant to the proceedings in which that question has arisen.[4]

---

[2]　HRA 1998, s 1(1).
[3]　HRA 1998, s 1(5).
[4]　HRA 1998, s 2(1).

20.5 The duty of the court is therefore clear. Convention rights govern and have an overriding effect on the way the courts exercise their jurisdiction and, in deciding what Convention rights mean or imply, the court is given a menu of possible sources of law.

Declaration of incompatibility

20.6 Circumstances may arise in which a court finds it impossible to give effect to Convention rights because of the clear meaning of domestic law. In those circumstances, normally domestic law will prevail; the court may not strike down primary legislation, but may strike down delegated legislation provided the terms of the parent statute do not make that impossible.[5] However, that need not be an end of the matter. Whenever a court (as defined below) decides that a provision of the law of England and Wales is incompatible with a Convention right, it may make a declaration of that incompatibility.[6] This will not affect the validity, continuing operation or enforcement of the provision and is not binding on the parties to the proceedings in which it is given,[7] so that nothing will change in the instant case. However, it is thought that such a declaration would lead Parliament to change, or to consider changing, the offending provision.

Because of the potential importance of a declaration of incompatibility, this power is reserved to the High Court and above.[8]

Acts of public authorities

20.7 The HRA 1998 provides that it is unlawful for a public authority to act in a way which is incompatible with a Convention right.[9] This is of more significance than might first appear because 'public authority' includes a court or tribunal as well as 'any person certain of whose functions are functions of a public nature'.[10] It is therefore unlawful for a court to disregard, breach, or act otherwise than in accordance with, Convention rights. Acting unlawfully in this context would, therefore, include, in the case of a court, failing to have regard to s 3 (the obligation to read and give effect to domestic legislation in a way which is compatible with Convention rights) and failing to interpret Convention rights in accordance with s 2 (see **20.4**).

The individual who claims that a court or other body has acted unlawfully has, therefore, a right of action.

---

5 'Rights Brought Home: The Human Rights Bill' (Cm 3782) ('White Paper'), paras 2.13 and 2.15.
6 HRA 1998, s 4(2).
7 HRA 1998, s 4(6).
8 HRA 1998, s 4(5).
9 HRA 1998, s 6(1).
10 HRA 1998, s 6(3).

Remedies available

20.8   A person who claims that a public authority has acted or proposes to act in a way which is unlawful by virtue of these provisions must either bring proceedings against the authority in the 'appropriate court or tribunal' or rely on the Convention rights in 'any legal proceedings'.[11] 'Appropriate court or tribunal' means such court as may be determined by rules of court;[12] in the case of the public authority being a court, it is most likely that such proceedings will have to be by way of judicial review.

As to reliance on the Convention in 'any legal proceedings', it would seem that this means that the Convention rights may be relied on in argument in the proceedings in which the court has acted, or threatens to act, unlawfully. It is also specifically provided[13] that 'legal proceedings' includes an appeal against a decision of a court or tribunal; an unlawful act by a court could therefore constitute a ground of appeal.

If proceedings are brought by way of judicial review, an applicant will be taken to have a sufficient interest in relation to the unlawful act only if he or she is, or would be, a victim of the unlawful act.[14]

PARTS OF THE CONVENTION WHICH MAY AFFECT ANCILLARY RELIEF

20.9   In the section above, we have considered, in brief outline only, the way in which the HRA 1998 incorporates the Convention into the law of England and Wales. In this section, those Convention rights which may affect ancillary relief will be set out and briefly described. It must be borne in mind that the Convention covers all aspects of law and, by its nature, includes such matters as the right to life and liberty which do not normally impinge on ancillary relief applications. Nevertheless, as will be seen, there are several Convention rights which may have a profound effect on this area of law.

20.10   The rights guaranteed by the Convention which may concern family law in general, and ancillary relief in particular, are as follows:

- the right to a fair trial (Art 6);

- the right to respect for private and family life, home and correspondence (Art 8);

- the right to marry and found a family (Art 12);

---

[11]   HRA 1998, s 7(1).
[12]   HRA 1998, s 7(2).
[13]   By HRA 1998, s 7(6).
[14]   HRA 1998, s 7(4).

- freedom from discrimination in the field of Convention rights (Art 14); and

- the right to property (Art 1 of the First Protocol).

These will be considered in turn. It should be noted that Art 5 of the Seventh Protocol, which provides for equality of rights of spouses, has been omitted from HRA 1998. However, this may only be a temporary omission, and in view of its potential importance for ancillary relief, this Convention right will also be discussed.

The right to a fair trial

20.11 Article 6 of the Convention provides that 'everyone is entitled to a fair and public hearing within a reasonable time by an independent and impartial tribunal established by law'. This is one of the most important Convention rights for obvious reasons; the rule of law, which underpins the whole Convention, would be impossible without it.

The following points emerge from this:

- The individual must have right of access to a court.

- The proceedings must be fair.

- Any hearing must be within a reasonable time.

- The tribunal must be independent and impartial.

- The hearing, and pronouncement of any decision, must be in public.

20.12 Although it is impossible to deal with this topic in more than outline, it may be helpful to consider briefly how the guarantee of a 'fair hearing' has been interpreted. The following principles have been developed:

- The concept of 'equality of arms' has emerged. Each party must be afforded a reasonable opportunity to present his case, including his evidence, under conditions which do not place him at a substantial disadvantage vis-à-vis his opponent.[15]

- Both parties must have access to all evidence.[16]

- No one may be required to incriminate himself.[17]

---

[15] *Dombo Beheer BV v The Netherlands* (1994) 18 EHRR 213, para 33.
[16] See *Bönisch v Austria* (1985) 9 EHRR 191, where it was held that there was inequality between a court appointed expert and an expert for one of the parties.
[17] See e g *Saunders v UK* (1996) 23 EHRR 313, para 71.

- Reasons for any judgment must be given.

This Article has already had an effect. In *Mubarak v Mubarak (No 1)*,[18] the applicant had issued a judgment summons against her former husband for the non-payment of a lump sum order. An order was made against the husband by the judge at first instance. The husband appealed and in his judgment Brooke LJ observed that the HRA 1998, which had then been in force for 2 months:

> '... is doing work of considerable value in shining light into some of the dustier corners of our law. The experience of this case shows, at any rate to my satisfaction, that corners do not get much dustier than those inhabited by section 5 of the Debtors Act 1869 and the prescribed procedures under that Act.'

His Lordship referred to the new CPR Practice Direction – Committal Applications, which provided that the burden of proof was that the allegation be proved beyond reasonable doubt. It was not clear that that applied to judgment summonses, but Brooke LJ (and the court) emphasised that in order to comply with Art 6, it would have to do so. The husband's appeal was allowed and the President has now issued a Practice Direction to govern the judgment summons procedure in future (see **19.11**).[19]

Respect for private and family life

20.13   Article 8 provides that everyone has the right to respect for his private and family life, his home and his correspondence. The essential object of Art 8 is 'to protect the individual against arbitrary action by the public authorities';[20] it will be remembered that a court is a 'public authority'. It has also been held that 'respect for private life must also comprise to a certain degree the right to establish and develop relationships with other human beings'.[21]

The right to a home has been held to be a right to occupy a home and not to be expelled or evicted.[22] Telephone tapping has been held to be a violation of Art 8.[23]

The right to marry and found a family

20.14   Article 12 states that 'men and women of marriageable age have the right to marry and to found a family, according to the national laws governing the exercise of this right'. This is an absolute right in that the State has no right

---

18   [2001] 1 FLR 698, CA.
19   *President's Direction of 16 March 2001 (Committal Applications and Proceedings in which a Committal Order may be made)* [2001] 1 FLR 949.
20   *Kroon v The Netherlands* (1994) 19 EHRR 263.
21   *Niemitz v Germany* (1993) 16 EHRR 97.
22   *Wiggins v UK Application No 7456/76*, (1978) 13 DR 40.
23   *Klass v Germany* (1979–80) 2 EHRR 214.

to interfere with it.[24] However, the exercise of the right to marry is subject to the national laws of the contracting States.[25]

The right to freedom from discrimination

20.15 Article 14 provides that 'the enjoyment of the rights and freedoms set forth in this Convention shall be secured without discrimination on any ground such as sex, race, colour, language, religion, political or other opinion, national or social origin, association with a national minority, property, birth or other status'.

The right to property

20.16 Article 1 of the First Protocol provides that 'every natural person or legal person is entitled to the peaceful enjoyment of his possessions. No one shall be deprived of his possessions except in the public interest and subject to the conditions provided for by law and by the general principles of international law'.

The right to property is therefore guaranteed by the Protocol.

Equality of rights of spouses

20.17 Article 5 of the Seventh Protocol provides that 'spouses shall enjoy equality of rights and responsibilities of a private law character between them, and in their relations with their children, as to marriage, during marriage, and in the event of its dissolution. This Article shall not prevent States from taking such measures as are necessary in the interests of children'.

As was mentioned above, this Article has not been included in the HRA 1998, although it may well be included in the future. Its implications are discussed below.

THE EFFECT OF HRA 1998 IN PRACTICE

20.18 Perhaps the most interesting result of the HRA 1998 in relation to ancillary relief will be when Art 5 of the Seventh Protocol (Equality of Rights of Spouses) is introduced into domestic law; this has not yet happened but it may only be a matter of time. It is thought that the principal reason for its omission was the potential difficulties which the Government foresaw while the law of ancillary relief remained in its present state.[26] As shown in Chapter 21, during 1996 ministers expressed an interest in amending MCA 1973, s 25 to provide for some statement of equality as a starting point. In 1998, this issue

---

[24]   *X v UK* Application No 6564/74, (1975) 2 DR 105.
[25]   *F v Switzerland* (1987) 10 EHRR 411.
[26]   'Rights Brought Home: The Human Rights Bill' (Cm 3782), para 4.15.

was referred to the Lord Chancellor's Advisory Group, whose unanimous advice was that the existing law should not be changed.

Whatever the future shape of domestic legislation, it is clearly possible that Art 5, if incorporated into domestic law, could provide a fruitful source of litigation and argument. It is difficult to speculate as to what the result of such litigation would be, or as to the degree to which the ECHR would arrive at different conclusions from the courts of England and Wales. One possible difference of approach might arise from argument as to whether 'equality' means 'equality of outcome' although this argument was firmly rejected as a possibility in *Cowan v Cowan*.[27]

20.19   Turning to provisions which have been included in HRA 1998, the right to property under Art 1 of the First Protocol might give rise to some argument. The right to peaceful enjoyment of property may be interfered with when, for example, a property adjustment order is made. However, it is also provided that contracting States may control the use of property in accordance with the general interest by enforcing such laws as they deem necessary for the purpose, and there seem to be no reported cases which give any guidance as to how Art 1 might affect ancillary relief.

20.20   The right to a fair trial (Art 6) will clearly have an effect on ancillary relief. Some of the general implications have already been discussed at **20.12**. One issue which will have to be faced is the requirement for a public hearing and the public pronouncement of judgment; were this adopted, procedure would have to change. It might be that cases will continue to be heard in chambers with only the judgment being given in public, and, even then, it seems that it might be permissible for the parties to be referred to merely by their initials. Only time will tell.

It might also be argued that the obligation on parties to give full and frank disclosure could, in some cases, constitute a breach of the freedom from self-incrimination; again, we must await developments.

20.21   Finally, there are many examples in this book of cases where the court has had to consider the application of the ECHR to ancillary relief cases. The reader will find these at the appropriate places, but examples are *Mubarak v Mubarik*,[28] *Nicholls v Lan*,[29] *R (Kehoe) v Secretary of State for Work and Pensions*,[30] and *Barca v Mears*.[31]

---

[27]   [2001] EWCA Civ 679, [2001] 2 FLR 192, CA (as to which, see **1.52**).
[28]   [2006] EWHC 1260 (Fam), [2007] 1 FLR 722.
[29]   [2006] EWHC 1255 (Ch), [2007] 1 FLR 744.
[30]   [2005] UKHL 48, [2005] 2 FLR 1249, HL.
[31]   [2004] EWHC 2170 (Ch), [2005] 2 FLR 1.

Chapter 21

THE PROCEEDS OF CRIME ACT 2002

INTRODUCTION

21.1   Family lawyers have always had a potential difficulty in deciding what to do when it appeared that their client was involved in some illegal activity. Conflicting duties to the client, the court, their profession and the administration of justice have meant that difficult decisions have had to be made.

These dilemmas have been made more urgent by the coming into force of the Proceeds of Crime Act 2002 (POCA 2002). In one sense, POCA 2002 removes some of the dilemmas in that the lawyer's duties are now more clearly defined. However, these duties impose burdens on the family lawyer which are new, and it is the purpose of this chapter to alert the reader to the potential difficulties.

It must be emphasised that this chapter is not an exhaustive analysis of the whole of POCA 2002. It is merely intended to alert the family lawyer to the most obvious consequences of the Act in the hope that the traps may be recognised in practice.

THE PURPOSE OF POCA 2002

21.2   POCA 2002 is designed to help to fight organised crime. The philosophy behind the Act is that if the Crown can intercept and recover the proceeds of crime, thereby depriving the wrongdoer of the benefits of criminal activities, the incentive to crime will be diminished. Until now, it has been possible for the Crown Court to make confiscation orders, but that has been dependent on a criminal conviction. The court may exercise its powers under POCA 2002 without a criminal conviction and according to the civil standard of proof – the balance of probabilities. In this way, it is hoped, the process will be made more efficient and quick and criminals will no longer be able to enjoy the fruit of their labours.

POCA 2002 is also to some extent a codifying Act, which incorporates the former Drugs Trafficking Offences Act 1986.

As will be seen below, POCA 2002 is drafted in wide terms and the problem for the family lawyer (or any other kind of lawyer) is that provisions intended to defeat large-scale crime may have the unintended effect of 'catching' much smaller and possibly less heinous transactions; there is no de minimis level and every transaction, however small, which might come within the ambit of the Act can give rise to offences being committed.

MONEY LAUNDERING

21.3 Money laundering is dealt with in Part 7 of POCA 2002. It is one of the key concepts of the Act and the part which is most likely to impinge on the family lawyer. As its name implies, laundering occurs where the proceeds of crime are cleaned up and made apparently legitimate. This may be done, for example, by placing tainted money into the economy; cash may be paid to a solicitor for a purpose which fails, such as the purchase of a house, and is then repaid to the original payor by a solicitor's cheque. The first appearance of the money in the payor's accounts is the solicitor's cheque, which would not attract attention.

Money may also be layered, which means that it would be a part of a series of transactions designed to obscure the origin of the money. Finally, the money may be integrated legitimately into the economy, for example by being used to purchase a legitimate business.

Tax evasion is a criminal offence and is the crime which is most likely to taint money which is used in the family law context. Where the fortunes of parties to ancillary relief have been augmented by historic tax evasion, and those fortunes are to be divided between the parties at the conclusion of the proceedings, the lawyers may well find that they are caught by the Act.

The detail about money laundering is contained in the Money Laundering Regulations 2003 ('the Regulations').[1]

OFFENCES UNDER POCA 2002

21.4 A person commits an offence if he:

(1) conceals, disguises, converts, transfers or removes criminal property from England and Wales (s 327);

(2) enters into an arrangement which he knows, or suspects, will assist someone to acquire, retain, use or control criminal property by or for another person (s 328);

(3) acquires, uses or has possession of criminal property (s 329);

(4) fails to disclose a known or suspected money laundering offence; this includes the position where the defendant merely has reasonable grounds to suspect; this applies in the 'regulated sector' (s 330);

---

[1] SI 2003/3075.

(5) fails to disclose a money laundering offence; this applies to a nominated officer in the regulated sector (s 331);

(6) fails to disclose a money laundering offence as soon as practicable after the information comes to him; this applies to other nominated officers;

(7) 'tips off' after a s 337 or s 338 disclosure has been made so as to prejudice an investigation (s 333).

Defences and/or exceptions to the various offences are contained in ss 330(6) and (7) and 338.

21.5 Criminal property is the benefit from criminal conduct or something which represents the benefit (in whole or in part and whether directly or indirectly), and the person concerned knows or suspects that it constitutes or represents such a benefit.

Criminal conduct is conduct which is an offence in any part of the UK or would be an offence if it happened in the UK; this is the case even if it is legal in the jurisdiction in which it is done. This definition therefore covers all crimes, including crimes committed abroad, irrespective of by whom they were committed or the date on which they were committed. As an example of a potential difficulty, the United States of America can choose to apply its domestic legislation with extra-territorial effect, with the result that a case with a US connection may give rise to offences in respect of acts done in the UK which are not criminal in the UK.

21.6 Reporting must be made to the National Criminal Intelligence Service (NCIS). Once the report is made the solicitor or barrister cannot continue to act unless NCIS give the appropriate consent. NCIS has 7 working days in which to give this consent, but if consent is refused there is a further period of 31 days during which a restraint order may be applied for.

21.7 The duty to report is set out above. However, equally important is the duty not to tell the client that the report has been made. If a person makes an internal or external report and tells the client or anyone else that he has made a report or that there is an investigation he commits an offence. Note, however, that no offence of tipping off can be committed if no report has been made. Merely asking questions of the client to find out more information is not tipping off.

If a lawyer receives the information (leading him to suspect an offence) in privileged circumstances, he does not have to report. Privilege attaches to confidential communications made between a solicitor and his client in connection with the giving of legal advice or in connection with or in contemplation of legal proceedings and for the purpose of such proceedings. Privilege provides a defence to failure to report or tipping off. However, it would then be impossible for the lawyer to continue to act.

21.8   Solicitors are part of the regulated sector if they provide legal services which involve participation in a financial or real property transaction, whether by assisting in the planning or execution of transactions or otherwise by acting for or on behalf of a client.

JUDICIAL GUIDANCE AS TO THE OPERATION OF POCA 2002

21.9   The uncertainties about the effect on the legal profession of POCA 2002 led to a prompt application to the High Court in *P v P (Ancillary Relief: Proceeds of Crime)*[2] and the President handed down her judgment on 8 October 2003. This judgment was intended to give constructive guidance to the profession and its contents will be summarised below. However, as will be seen, this judgment has been to some extent overtaken by the judgment of the Court of Appeal in *Bowman v Fels* which is also summarised below.

(a) Whether and in what circumstances it is permitted to act in relation to an arrangement

21.10   There are a variety of ways in which a legal professional might become 'concerned in' an arrangement. It could not be the case that the offence under s 328 can only be committed at the point of execution of the arrangement. The act of negotiating an arrangement would equally amount to being 'concerned in' the arrangement.

The President said that the duties under s 328 of a barrister or solicitor engaged in family litigation are straightforward. There is nothing in that section to prevent a solicitor or barrister from taking instructions from a client. However, if having taken instructions the solicitor or barrister knows or suspects that he or she or his or her client will become involved in an arrangement that might involve the acquisition, retention, use or control of criminal property, then an authorised disclosure should be made and the appropriate consent sought under s 335. Therefore, if it seems to the solicitor or barrister that there are grounds for suspicion that any arrangement being sought from the court or negotiated between the parties is contrary to the requirements of s 328(1), then authorisation should be sought. It would seem that the position as set out above would apply equally to ss 327 and 329.

The President's view was that issues of legal professional privilege did not seem to arise under ss 327, 328 or 329 and there was no professional privilege exemption in these sections.

21.11   The effect of s 335 was that a person may make a disclosure, generally but not necessarily, to NCIS seeking consent to continue taking steps in

---

[2]   [2003] EWHC 2260 (Fam), [2004] 1 FLR 193.

relation to an arrangement. The person must not take any further steps in relation to the arrangement, until the person either:

(1) receives from NCIS notice of consent within 7 working days from the next working day after the disclosure is made ('the notice period' – s 335(5)), in which case the person may resume acting in relation to the arrangement (by virtue of s 335(3)); or

(2) hears nothing from NCIS within the notice period, in which case the person is treated as having deemed consent to resume acting in relation to the arrangement (by virtue of s 335(3)); or

(3) receives from NCIS notice of refusal of consent within the notice period, in which case the person must not act in relation to the arrangement for the duration of the moratorium period of 31 days starting with the day on which the person receives the refusal notice (by virtue of s 335(4)). Once the moratorium period has expired the person may resume acting in relation to the arrangement.

In practice, the longest possible time for which a person could be prevented from taking steps in relation to an arrangement, after sending a notice to the NCIS, would be 31 days plus 7 working days.

21.12 The President said that the consent procedures in ss 335 and 338 apply to those persons who make the authorised disclosure. So, for example, if a solicitor makes an authorised joint disclosure on behalf of himself, counsel and his client, then all three will be protected from prosecution. Indeed, where the solicitor acts for the innocent party, it would be sensible as a matter of practice for solicitors to make an authorised disclosure. If a solicitor is disclosing suspicions about his own client, it may, of course, be a different matter.

21.13 It was important for the legal profession to take into account that the Act makes no distinction between degrees of criminal property. An illegally obtained sum of £10 is no less susceptible to the definition of 'criminal property' than a sum of £1m. Parliament clearly intended this to be the case. The President said that whatever may be the resource implications, the legal profession would appear to be bound by the provisions of the Act in all cases, however big or small. If this approach is scrupulously followed by the legal advisers, the result is likely to have a considerable and potentially adverse impact upon the NCIS and would create serious consequential delays in listing and hearing family cases, including child cases.

(b) Whether and in what circumstances a legal adviser, having made an authorised disclosure, is permitted to tell others of this fact

21.14 Section 93D of the Criminal Justice Act 1988 (now repealed) contained a prohibition against tipping off in relation to criminal investigations of money laundering. In *Governor and Company of the Bank of Scotland v A Ltd*[3] the Court of Appeal considered the meaning of the legal professional exemption contained in s 93D(4) of the Criminal Justice Act 1988, a provision dealing with 'tipping off' in almost identical terms to s 333. In that case, the bank suspected that the moneys held in a client's account had been obtained by fraud. Lord Woolf CJ at para [7] of the judgment of the court said:

> 'During argument there was discussion as to the extent of the defence provided by s 93D(4). Mr Crow helpfully drew our attention to the similarity between the language of s 93D(4) and the scope of legal professional privilege. Based on this assistance, we conclude that the subsection broadly protects a legal adviser when that adviser is engaged in activities which attract legal professional privilege.'

The President said that passage would appear to support the protection given to members of the legal profession in carrying out their duties to their clients.

21.15 The President said that ss 333 and 342 specifically recognise a legal adviser's duty in ordinary circumstances to make the relevant disclosures, even where the result would be to tip off their client, where to do so would fall within the ambit of being in connection with the giving of legal advice or with legal proceedings actual or contemplated. A central element of advising and representing a client must be the duty to keep one's client informed and not to withhold information from him or her. Since the function of the Act is to regulate the proceeds of criminal behaviour, it is clear that in every circumstance where a solicitor believes an authorised disclosure to the NCIS is necessary there will be at least a suspicion of criminal purpose. If, as the NCIS suggests, ss 333(4) and 342(5) bite every time a party who is suspected of holding a criminal purpose is given notice that a disclosure has been or will be made to the NCIS (ie is 'tipped off'), then the legal professional exemptions in ss 333(3) and 342(4) would be rendered meaningless. Sections 333(4) and 342(5) must have some purpose and the interpretation suggested by the NCIS cannot be correct. The exemption is lost if a disclosure to a client is made 'with the intention of furthering a criminal purpose'. The natural meaning of those words would seem to be clear. The approach which the House of Lords took to the construction of the word 'held' in *R v Central Criminal Court ex parte Francis & Francis*[4] should not be transposed into this context in relation to the word 'made', nor would it be necessary or proper to attempt to do so. Whereas the purpose of holding documents can be tainted by the intention of any number of people (including client and third parties), the intention of a legal adviser in choosing to make a disclosure would seem to belong to the adviser alone. The context and purpose of this particular section of POCA 2002 is distinguishable from that in *Francis*, not least because the Act has specifically underlined the duty of disclosure by legal advisers.

---

3   [2001] EWCA Civ 52, [2001] 1 WLR 754.
4   [1989] 1 AC 346.

The President observed that even though the client's criminal intent disqualified him from claiming privilege, it did not disqualify him from his entitlement to be consulted by his lawyer without falling foul of the tipping off rules.

There might well be instances where a solicitor's disclosure to a client is in breach of s 333(4) or s 342(5), because the solicitor makes the disclosure with an improper purpose. In such a case the legal professional exemption would, of course, be lost. The President could not give a blanket guarantee to all family practitioners that they would never lose the protection of the exemption. But unless the requisite improper intention is there, the solicitor should be free to communicate such information to his or her client or opponent as is necessary and appropriate in connection with the giving of legal advice or acting in connection with actual or contemplated legal proceedings.

21.16 The President recognised that the conclusion she had reached might cause some difficulty to the investigating authorities. The time lines set out in ss 328, 335 and 338 are independent from the provisions of ss 333 and 342. Having complied with the obligations under s 328, there is nothing in the statute to require a solicitor to delay in informing his client. Either he is entitled to do so forthwith by virtue of the s 333(3) exemption, or if s 333(4) or s 342(5) bite, he is not entitled to do so at all. There is no middle ground.

Good practice

21.17 The President was, however, concerned that the purpose of the Act be respected, and that as a matter of good practice (as opposed to statutory obligation) the investigation authorities should be permitted time to do their job without frustration. In most cases, she could not see why a delay of, at most, 7 working days before informing a client would generally cause particular difficulty to the solicitor's obligations to his client or his opponent. Where appropriate consent is refused and a 31-day moratorium is imposed, best practice would suggest that the legal adviser and the NCIS (or other relevant investigating body) try to agree on the degree of information which can be disclosed during the moratorium period without harming the investigation. In the absence of agreement, or in other urgent circumstances where even a short delay in disclosure would be unacceptable (such as where a hearing or FDR is imminent, or orders for discovery require immediate compliance), the guidance of the court may be sought.

21.18 The Court of Appeal in *C v S and others*[5] set out a procedure to be followed where compliance with an order for disclosure of information in civil proceedings might reveal money laundering and cause the financial institution to be in breach of tipping off provisions under s 93D of the Criminal Justice Act 1988 (as amended). In *Governor and Company of the Bank of Scotland v*

---

[5]   [1999] 2 All ER 343.

A Ltd[6] the Court of Appeal suggested a similar procedure whereby the bank in that case could have made an application to the court naming the Serious Fraud Office as respondent. The application could be held in private and there would be no question of serving the customer since he would not be a party. The procedures suggested by the Court of Appeal in those two cases might usefully be adapted to the family financial proceedings where a disclosure has been made. Since the purpose of such an application is to protect the legal advisers and, in some cases, the client, the President could not see how one can impose an obligation on the NCIS to be the applicant (although the NCIS would however also be entitled to approach the court if it wished to do so). It would be appropriate for the legal advisers to make the application without notice to the other side, making the NCIS the respondent to the application. It would be an application, however, within the ambit of the existing court proceedings and there did not seem to be any difficulty at the moment in the court making any appropriate order, including, if in the High Court, declarations. In the present case the President granted declarations since the situation was entirely new and she did so to clarify the situation. It would not seem to be necessary for the court generally to grant declarations, but rather to deal with the practical consequences of the authorised disclosure to the NCIS. The application would be heard in private and the court should direct that any mechanical recording of the proceedings should not be disclosed or transcribed without the leave of the judge.

The President reminded legal advisers that it would not seem to be necessary to make repeated disclosures on the same facts, unless it is proposed to enter into a new arrangement or a variation of the same arrangement. Each time a further disclosure is made, time will start running again for 7 days or possibly 7 plus 31 days.

21.19 The President's judgment in *P v P* was not appealed. However, the same issues came to be considered by the Court of Appeal in *Bowman v Fels* and to some extent the guidance given by the President was modified.

Lord Justice Brooke, giving the judgment of the Court, said that on this appeal the Court was invited to determine whether s 328 meant that as soon as a lawyer acting for a client in legal proceedings discovered or suspected anything in the proceedings that might facilitate the acquisition, retention, use or control (usually by his own client or his client's opponent) of 'criminal property', he must immediately notify NCIS of his belief if he was to avoid being guilty of the criminal offence of being concerned in an arrangement which he knew or suspected facilitated such activity (by whatever means). This particular appeal focused on the applicability or otherwise of s 328 in a case where information comes to the attention of the lawyer for one of the parties in the course of legal proceedings and leads him to know or, more likely, suspect that the other party has engaged in money laundering

---

[6]   [2001] EWCA Civ 52, [2001] 1 WLR 754.

21.20 The central issue on this appeal was whether s 328 applied to the ordinary conduct of legal proceedings or any aspect of such conduct – including, in particular, any step taken to pursue proceedings and the obtaining of a judgment. A question not directly raised by the facts of the appeal, but which his Lordship thought it would not be sensible to ignore, was whether the section applied to any consensual steps taken or settlement reached during legal proceedings.

The fact that s 328 (unlike Art 7) applied to any person gave rise to the argument that s 328 applied to lawyers conducting legal proceedings. But there was a general problem about this argument which existed as much under the directives as under the more expanded domestic law.

21.21 After an exhaustive examination of the issues, his Lordship on behalf of the Court concluded that the proper interpretation of s 328 was that it was not intended to cover or affect the ordinary conduct of litigation by legal professionals. That included any step taken by them in litigation from the issue of proceedings and the securing of injunctive relief or a freezing order up to its final disposal by judgment. The Court did not consider that either the European or the UK legislator could have envisaged that any of these ordinary activities could fall within the concept of 'becoming concerned in an arrangement which ... facilitates the acquisition, retention, use or control of criminal property'.

Summarising the position, Brooke LJ said that legal proceedings were a State-provided mechanism for the resolution of issues according to law. Everyone had the right to a fair and public trial in the determination of his civil rights and duties which is secured by Art 6 of the Convention. Parliament could have intended that proceedings or steps taken by lawyers in order to determine or secure legal rights and remedies for their clients should involve them in 'becoming concerned in an arrangement which ... facilitates the acquisition, retention, use or control of criminal property', even if they suspected that the outcome of such proceedings might have such an effect.

21.22 Brooke LJ went on to consider what the position would be if the Court were wrong in its conclusion on the central issue. The question would remain whether on its true construction s 328 had the effect of overriding legal professional privilege and the terms on which lawyers were permitted to have access to documents disclosed in the litigation process. He therefore proceeded to apply to the interpretation of s 328 certain principles that were used to interpret English Acts of Parliament when there was not a European perspective. He observed that there was nothing in the language of s 328 to suggest that Parliament expressly intended to override legal professional privilege.

After further consideration, his Lordship said that the Court was of the firm opinion that it would require much clearer language than is contained in s 328 and its ancillary sections before a parliamentary intention could be gleaned to the effect that a party's solicitor is obliged, in breach of this implied duty to the court, and in breach of the duty of confidence he owes to his own client as his litigation solicitor, to disclose to NCIS a suspicion he may have that documents disclosed under compulsion by the other party evidence one of the matters referred to in s 328. It followed that on this narrower issue the Court was satisfied that even if, contrary to its primary view, s 328 was to be interpreted as including legal proceedings within its purview, it could not be interpreted as meaning either that legal professional privilege was to be overridden or that a lawyer was to breach his duty to the court by disclosing to a third party external to the litigation documents revealed to him through the disclosure processes.

DISTRIBUTION OF 'TAINTED' FUNDS

21.23 The issue of whether or not funds tainted by criminal activities of which the applicant spouse was aware and which are subject to possible confiscation may be distributed in ancillary relief proceedings was considered in *Customs and Excise Commissioners v A and another; A v A*,[7] and *CPS v Richards and Richards*.[8] The general rule was established that such assets should not ordinarily, as a matter of justice and public policy, be distributed in ancillary relief proceedings. That was not to say that the court is deprived of jurisdiction under the MCA 1973 nor that there are no circumstances in which such an order could be justified.

In *Stodgell v Stodgell*[9] a confiscation order was made after the husband had pleaded guilty to fraud and been sentenced to imprisonment. A judge held that the wife's application for ancillary relief should not proceed until the order had been discharged. The wife's appeal was dismissed. Non-complicity in the crime was a necessary but not sufficient condition for the wife to succeed where she was in competition with a confiscation order. She might also fail in other respects, such as the husband's assets being nil as a result of paying the confiscation order.

In *G v G*[10] it was held that in financial remedy proceedings involving co-existing confiscation proceedings neither of the two jurisdictions takes precedence. Both sets of legislation give rise to a discretion to be exercised on the facts of the particular case. The fact that a party has not been complicit in the fraud is no guarantee that she will succeed.

---

[7]   [2002] EWCA Civ 1039.
[8]   [2006] EWCA Civ 849.
[9]   [2009] EWCA Civ 243, [2009] 2 FLR 244.
[10]   [2010] Fam Law 572.

Chapter 22

FUTURE DEVELOPMENTS

INTRODUCTION

22.1 Family law is always subject to legislative change, and the purpose of this chapter is to alert the reader to the probable shape of things to come. As has been seen in this book, many of the most important developments over recent years have been judge-made and many would think that the law as it now stands needs a period of consolidation rather than reform. However, the will of Parliament is unpredictable and it is inevitable that there will be some changes, though probably not in ways one could predict.

REFORM OF MCA 1973, SECTION 25

22.2 As Lord Justice Thorpe points out in his foreword to this book, during the parliamentary passage of the FLA 1996, the then Lord Chancellor announced his intention of considering whether anything could be learned from the Scottish system of ancillary relief with a view to improving the system in England and Wales. This statement aroused little attention, but it became clear that these ideas were being pursued when the then parliamentary secretary in the Lord Chancellor's Department, Mr Geoffrey Hoon, announced, at the annual conference of the Solicitors Family Law Association in 1998 that the government was giving favourable consideration to adopting the Scottish concept of a presumption of equal sharing of matrimonial property (as defined in the Family Law (Scotland) Act 1985), and making pre-nuptial contracts enforceable, subject to various safeguards. This gave rise to some debate, although the only formal consultation which the government carried out was to invite the Lord Chancellor's Advisory Group on Ancillary Relief to comment. In the event, the Advisory Group advised against amendment of s 25 in this way, and no more came of the proposal. It is impossible to say that it will never be revisited.

The decisions of the House of Lords in *White v White* and *Miller/McFarlane* (as to which see Chapter 1) do not seem to have stopped the calls for a more predictable and formulaic approach. No doubt conscious of this continuing debate, in *Charman v Charman*[1] the Court of Appeal added a postscript entitled 'Changing the Law'. At the end of a lengthy review of the history, the Court identified the new problems which have arisen as follows:

---

[1]   [2007] EWCA Civ 503 at para [106] et seq.

'[116] However a social change that was not perhaps recognised in that decision was the extent to which the origins and the volume of big money cases were shifting. Most of the big money cases pre-*White* involved fortunes created by previous generations. The removal of exchange control restrictions in 1979, a policy that offered a favourable tax regime to very rich foreigners domiciled elsewhere, and a new financial era dominated by hedge-funds, private equity funds, derivative traders and sophisticated off-shore structures meant that very large fortunes were being made very quickly. These socio-economic developments coincided with a retreat from the preference of English judges for moderation. The present case well illustrates that shift. At trial Mr Pointer achieved for his client an award of £48 million. Before us he freely conceded that he could not have justified an award of more than £20 million on the application of the reasonable requirements principle. Thus, in very big money cases, the effect of the decision in *White* was to raise the aspirations of the claimant hugely. In big money cases the *White* factor has more than doubled the levels of award and it has been said by many that London has become the divorce capital of the world for aspiring wives. Whether this is a desirable result needs to be considered not only in the context of our society but also in the context of the European Union of which we are a singular Member State, in the sense that we are a common law jurisdiction amongst largely Civilian fellows and that in the determination of issues ancillary to divorce we apply the lex fori and decline to apply the law more applicable to the parties.

[117] In the case of *Cowan* the need for legislative review in the aftermath of the case of *White* was articulated: see paragraphs 32, 41 and 58. Undoubtedly the decision in *White* did not resolve the problems faced by practitioners in advising clients or by clients in deciding upon what terms to compromise.

[118] However this court adopted a cautious approach both in *Cowan* and in the later case of *Lambert*. In his submission Mr Singleton drew attention to an article by Joanna Miles in International Journal of Law, Policy and the Family 19 (2005) 242. He told us that he had incorporated the article in his argument for Mrs McFarlane in the House of Lords. The article criticises the earlier decision of this court in the conjoined appeals of *McFarlane* and *Parlour* [2005] Fam 171 for having declined the opportunity to identify principles underpinning the exercise of judicial discretion under the Act of 1973. The article is particularly interesting in that it demonstrates that the principles discussed in the article (needs, entitlement and compensation), were subsequently the principles identified by the House of Lords in deciding the conjoined appeals of *Miller* and *McFarlane*.'

Later, in relation to the European aspects, the Court had this to say:

'[124] Any harmonisation within the European region is particularly difficult, given that the Regulation Brussels I is restricted to claims for maintenance and the Regulation Brussels II Revised expressly excludes from its application the property consequence of divorce. In the European context this makes sense because in Civilian systems the property consequences of divorce are dealt with by marital property regimes. Almost uniquely our jurisdiction does not have a marital property regime and it is scarcely appropriate to classify our jurisdiction as having a marital regime of separation of property. More correctly we have no regime, simply accepting that each spouse owns his or her own separate property during the marriage but subject to the court's wide distributive powers in prospect upon a decree of judicial separation, nullity or divorce. The difficulty of harmonising our law concerning the property consequences of marriage and divorce and the law of the Civilian Member States is exacerbated by the fact that our law has so far given little status to pre-nuptial contracts. If, unlike the rest of Europe, the property consequences of divorce are to be regulated by the principles of needs, compensation and sharing, should not the parties to the marriage, or the projected marriage, have at the least the opportunity to order their own affairs otherwise by a nuptial contract? The White Paper, "Supporting Families", not only proposed specific reforms of section 25 but also to give statutory force to nuptial contracts. The government's subsequent abdication has not been accepted by specialist practitioners. In 2005 Resolution published a well argued report urging the government to give statutory force to nuptial contracts. The report was subsequently fully supported by the Money and Property Sub-Committee of the Family Justice Council.'

The Court of Appeal recommended research by the Law Commission, and particularly stressed the need to reform the law to include the enforceability of pre-nuptial contracts.[2] The calls to reform the law to make pre-nuptial contracts enforceable as such have become ever more strident and it seems highly likely that this will be a prime candidate for reform, particularly in a period when a higher than ever proportion of marriages are second and subsequent marriages.

So far, Parliament has shown no sign of wishing to embark on the time-consuming and unpredictable task of family law reform and there are many other issues demanding the attention of the present coalition government. However, the presence in the government of several socially liberal members (not all of one party) means that the future is more than usually unpredictable.

22.3 Following the close of the consultation on agreements in 2011 (as to which, see para 22.5 below) the Law Commission decided to consider two other significant aspects of the financial consequences of divorce and dissolution. (The Government announced that decision in February 2012 as part of its response to the Family Justice Review.)

These two aspects, which are the subject of a supplementary consultation, are:

(1)   the law relating to financial needs on divorce and dissolution; and

(2)   the legal status of 'non-matrimonial property'.

The Executive Summary of the consultation sets out its aims in the following terms:

---

2   Though it has to be said that this would not have achieved very much in *Charman*. When the parties married they had no money and would, no doubt, have agreed equal sharing at that stage.

'9. First, it seeks to recommend a fundamental and principled reform of the law relating to needs. What is lacking in the law is an objective, to tell the courts and the parties what is to be achieved by provision for needs. An objective would explain what is to be paid and why. The Supplementary Consultation Paper discusses what would be an appropriate objective for the meeting of needs. The options discussed in the paper are the following.

(1) Compensation for needs generated by the relationship. The spouse left less well-off by the divorce or dissolution would be entitled to support until he or she was able to attain the level of earnings and the living standard that he or she would have achieved but for (for example) choices made about childcare and career options in the interests of the couple together and their family.

(2) Support to enable a transition to independence. Marriage and civil partnership both typically involve a merging of lives and a giving up of independence; the ending of the partnership might well therefore include a financial adjustment that equalises, or evens out, the standards of living of the couple for a transitional period. Like compensation, this could generate very long-term support; the level of support would vary with the length of the marriage and also with the length of time expected to be spent caring for children, for example. In contrast to a compensatory basis for payment, this approach does not require the court or the parties to work out what position the claimant would have been in, but for the marriage or civil partnership.

(3) Support for a limited time so as to create incentives for independence. There is a concern that in allowing dependency, the law may be encouraging dependency; it may be that to impose artificial limits on the support available from a former spouse may have the useful effect of incentivising the quest for employment and independence. However, the Commission is not attracted to policies such as that in Scotland, where a three-year limit is placed upon support following divorce.

10. The Supplementary Consultation Paper goes on to ask whether financial support should continue to be determined by the court, at the judge's discretion, or whether it should be calculated by reference to a formula, so substituting greater predictability for individualised discretion. A number of other jurisdictions have taken this route, notably Canada, and the paper gives some examples of the sort of calculation that have been successful elsewhere.

11. However, the Law Commission stresses in the paper that other jurisdictions that have achieved fundamental reform of the law relating to needs have done so after years of research and piloting. This is an important area of social policy where it is important not to generate hardship, and vital that the interests of children are not sacrificed to the convenience of adults. Accordingly, the Commission's final Report (expected in the autumn of 2013) will make recommendations for principled reform but will also recommend further work before the law is changed.

12. [*Omitted*]

13. For most couples the only relevant area of the law on financial orders is the law relating to needs. Even if needs are met, there is nothing left over to share. However, for some wealthier families non-matrimonial property is important. The current law is that, once needs have been met, property received by either party by

gift or inheritance at any time, or property generated by either party before the marriage, is less likely than other property to be shared on divorce or dissolution.

14. The Supplementary Consultation Paper asks questions about:

(1)   the definition of non-matrimonial property;
(2)   whether there should be a rule that it is not shared;
(3)   whether that rule should be subject to the further rule that it must be shared if it is required to meet needs; and
(4)   whether non-matrimonial property can ever become matrimonial, either by the passage of time or because it has been sold and replaced or has appreciated in value as a result of investment or management by either party.'

There may also be a ECHR dimension to this issue which is discussed further in Chapter 20.

ENFORCEMENT

22.4   In 1997 the Advisory Group also made quite wide-ranging proposals for the reform of the procedure relating to enforcement of family financial orders, which were approved by public consultation. In previous editions of this book it was stated that it was thought that implementation of the recommendations was imminent. However, hopes were dashed and, for some time it seemed that this statement was hopelessly optimistic. Now, as will be seen from the chapter on enforcement, patience has been rewarded and the new FPR 2010 include the recommended changes.

HARMONISATION OF RULES OF COURT

22.5   As readers who have got this far will know, new harmonised rules are in force as from April 2011. The long wait is over.

AGREEMENTS

22.6   As was seen in Chapter 1, the Supreme Court in *Radmacher v Granatino*[3] has brought about considerable changes to the way in which the courts should approach agreements, including, of course, pre-nuptial agreements. Very soon after the decision of the Supreme Court, the Law Commission published a consultation paper on the subject, so the issue may, at some stage, be returned to Parliament (though it may be, of course, that Ministers will take the view that the law as it now exists needs no reform).

A key element in the thinking of the Law Commission may be the (sole) dissenting judgment of Baroness Hale in *Radmacher v Granatino*; the view may

---

[3]   [2010] UKSC 42; [2010] 2 FLR 1900.

be taken that, as the only family lawyer on the court, her position should have been accorded greater weight by her colleagues. At para 138 of the judgment, Baroness Hale summarised her disagreements with her colleagues as follows:

'I disagree with the view, mercifully obiter to the decision in this case, that ante-nuptial agreements are legally enforceable contracts. (2) I disagree with the view, also mercifully obiter to the decision in this case, that it is open to this court to hold that they are. (3) I disagree with the view that, in policy terms, there are no relevant differences between agreements made before and agreements made after a marriage. (4) I disagree with the way in which the majority have formulated the test to be applied by a court hearing an application for financial relief, which I believe to be an impermissible gloss upon the courts' statutory duties. However, I agree that the court must consider the agreement in the light of the circumstances as they now exist and that the way the matter was put by the Privy Council in *MacLeod v MacLeod* [2008] UKPC 64, [2010] 1 AC 298, was too rigid, and in some cases, too strong; and I broadly agree with the majority upon the relevant considerations which the court should take into account. (5) I disagree with the approach of the Court of Appeal to the actual outcome of this case, which the majority uphold. In my view it is inconsistent with the continued importance attached to the status of marriage in English law. This is independent of the weight to be attached to the agreement in this case. (6) I consider that the reform of the law on ante- and post-nuptial agreements should be considered comprehensively, not limited to agreements catering for future separation or divorce.'

22.7 It will be interesting to see how far, if at all, the final recommendations of the Law Commission, incorporate these views. In Part 5 of its paper, the Law Commission sets out the issues as follows:

'5.2 The assessment of fairness depends, potentially, upon a wide range of factors.[1] And although the decision in *Radmacher v Granatino* established that marital property agreements are no longer contractually void for public policy reasons, they will not be able to be enforced as contracts, because an attempt to enforce one as a contract could always be thwarted by an application for ancillary relief.[2]

5.3 For many people, therefore, the emerging acceptance of marital property agreements by the courts, which we charted in Part 3, culminating in the decision in *Radmacher v Granatino*, will not go far enough. The fact that the terms of a marital property agreement are always subject to the court's review means that it is never possible to be certain, in advance, that an agreement will determine the outcome of the ancillary relief process. We explored in Part 3 the reasons that might, according to the majority in the Supreme Court, make an agreement unfair. There is a long list. Many are highly subjective. Some are unusual factors; others, such as the presence of children, are part of the normal circumstances of marriage and civil partnership. Some of them are outside the control of the parties – for example, whether either of them has had a relationship before.

5.4 An agreement may be carefully drafted by lawyers familiar with the case law, in the hope that it will survive scrutiny. Separation agreements will normally do so, because they are formulated at the point when separation is about to happen rather than contemplating a possible future event. But couples can never be sure that their agreement will determine the financial consequences of divorce or dissolution; and legal advisers providing an expensive service in the negotiation of pre- or post-nuptial agreements cannot predict with any confidence the eventual success or otherwise of an agreement entered into on the advice they have given.

5.5 There have therefore been a number of calls for the reform of marital property agreements in the interests of autonomy and certainty. In order to achieve any significantly greater degree of certainty than is now available marital property agreements would have to be able to exclude the discretionary jurisdiction of the court. Whether there should be such reform is the major issue for this consultation …

[1]   The decision may make it more likely that parties who make a contract subsequently intend to be legally bound, at least if they have been properly advised: see *Radmacher v Granatino* [2010] UKSC 42 at [70].
[2]   [2010] UKSC 42 at [52].'

THE FAMILY JUSTICE REVIEW

22.8   The Family Justice Review, which was commenced in 2010, produced its interim report in 2011. Although most of the report is concerned with children's cases the possibility of reform and simplification of the law relating to financial remedies is mentioned, almost in passing. It remains to be seen what changes may be proposed in the final report. Any such changes would of course require primary legislation.

Chapter 23

A SUMMING UP

INTRODUCTION

23.1 Throughout this book, a number of recurring themes have appeared. One of the problems of writing any book of this kind is that the separate chapters on individual topics may appear to the reader to be self-contained, whereas the lessons to be learned from many of them apply across the board and should be borne in mind generally. Nevertheless, it would be irksome for the reader if the same messages were driven home in every chapter.

For these reasons, it has been thought appropriate to include in this final chapter the principal matters which anyone involved in an ancillary relief application should have in mind. First, the generally accepted principles on which the courts decide these matters will be outlined, with accompanying references as to where a longer exposition may be found. Then, some of the practical lessons for the conduct of an application will be considered.

THE PRIMACY OF THE STATUTE

23.2 Applications for ancillary relief are governed by s 25 of MCA 1973, which is a self-contained code which directs the court's attention to certain specified factors. Decided cases are of some assistance, but they can never replace the words of the statute.

23.3 Subject to the 'first consideration' of the welfare of the minor children, no single factor within s 25 is intrinsically more important than the others. All of them must be considered. In most cases, the facts of the case will mean that there is a 'gravitational pull' towards one or more factors which assume particular significance, but this does not mean that all the factors should not be considered. This paragraph should be borne in mind when reading all that now follows. Whatever the importance of cases such as *White v White* and *Miller/McFarlane*, and whatever stress is placed on 'sharing' and 'equality', time and again one is reminded that the speeches in the House were not some form of statutory amendment and that one must begin always with the statute.

THE IMPORTANCE OF FINDING THE FACTS

23.4 Notwithstanding what was said above, no case can proceed without accurate findings under s 25(2)(a). Until the income and capital of each of the parties is ascertained, the court cannot begin to consider whether the assets should be redistributed in accordance with any of the other factors. When determining the facts, the usual rules of evidence apply. The fact that a hearing is in chambers and may seem relatively informal should not deceive a practitioner or litigant into thinking that the court will make findings of fact on less than the normal civil standard of proof.

23.5   The court will be concerned, where this is relevant, to decide what is and is not 'matrimonial property', ie property acquired during the marriage (or any relevant period of pre-marital cohabitation) which is neither property inherited by either of the parties nor property which they owned well before the marriage or relevant period of cohabitation. However, it must be emphasised that this does not mean that such property is then excluded from the calculations. Generally speaking, the longer the marriage the less inclined a court will be to hive off any particular asset. Moreover, in cases where assets are not sufficient to meet the needs of both parties and one party has a greater need than the other, it is unlikely that this aspect of the matter will be decisive.

NO MATHEMATICAL STARTING POINT

23.6   There is no 'one-third rule' nor any other fractional starting point. When a judge has decided how the assets of the parties should be divided (if at all) in accordance with the s 25 factors, he may cross-check his proposals by considering the proportions of the joint assets which each party would have, but there is no absolute proportion with which either party must be left. The yardstick of equality (see below) is a useful cross-check at the end of the calculation to ensure fairness. However, having said that, it is a reasonable inference from the judgment of the Court of Appeal in *Charman v Charman*[1] that the concept of 'sharing' derived from *Miller v Miller* implies equal sharing and that this is now considerably more of a starting point than once it was.

REASONABLE NEEDS AND ABILITY TO PROVIDE

23.7   The reasonable needs as to capital and income of both parties must be considered. These will vary in every case, but will depend on the age and health of the parties in the light of the history of the marriage, and the responsibilities which they both have, particularly to children of the family. How far these needs can be met will depend on the means available.

THE IMPORTANCE OF HOUSING

23.8   The most important requirement for most people is to be housed, and the primary task of the court in average income and capital cases should be to

---

[1]   [2007] EWCA Civ 503, [2007] All ER (D) 425 (May) at [65]. See also the discussion at **1.11** et seq.

ensure that both are housed. Where there are dependent children, the housing of the parent with the care of the children must come first, even if this means that the other party is not rehoused as he would wish. However, rehousing of a parent with children does not mean that that parent must live in the former matrimonial home. The housing of the other parent is an important priority also, and where a parent and children can be adequately rehoused in cheaper accommodation with a proportion of the proceeds of sale, to enable the other parent to be rehoused, this should be done.

NO REDISTRIBUTION FOR ITS OWN SAKE

23.9   When either or both parties have capital, there is no presumption that it must be redistributed. Redistribution is only appropriate if required to do justice between the parties in the light of the s 25 factors. However, this must be balanced against what is said in the next paragraph.

THE YARDSTICK OF EQUALITY

23.10   When the court has performed its statutory functions of investigating all the s 25 factors, it must first arrive at a provisional and tentative view as to what is required before comparing that provisional view with what the result would be on the basis of equal division. If the provisional view does not approximate to equal division, the court must be able to articulate and express reasons, based on the s 25 criteria, as to why it should not do so. Where there are no such reasons, equality should prevail.

SELF-SUFFICIENCY

23.11   The court must have regard to the possibility of self-sufficiency and a clean break in every case. Nevertheless, a clean break should not be imposed where the evidence does not suggest that self-sufficiency will be achieved.

PENSIONS NOT A SEPARATE REGIME

23.12   The only reason for making the following point is the recent date of the legislative changes. Pensions are not a separate form of assets which must be re-allocated according to some discrete code. The extent to which the court will consider pensions relevant, and make orders in respect of them, will depend entirely on the application of the s 25 factors.

SOME PRACTICAL HINTS ON PREPARING A CASE

23.13 Practitioners acting for a party to ancillary relief proceedings should bear in mind all that has been said above. The following practical questions emerge and should be asked in every case:

(a)   What are the assets and incomes of both parties?

(b)   What are the needs of the parties? In particular:

    (i)   Where will the parent with care of a child (if any) live?
    (ii)   Where will the other party live?

(c)   What are the income needs of the parties, in particular your client? Be realistic; do not merely compile a wish list. What will it cost him or her to live?

(d)   How can these needs be met? Can your client support himself or herself? Are there other sources of funds?

(e)   What is the position as to pensions?

(f)   Can there be a clean break?

(g)   Having considered all the s 25 factors, is there some particular factor which is relevant to this case?

(h)   Finally, what would be the position if there were equal division? Is there some s 25 factor which makes equal division unjust?

Appendices

Appendix A

PRECEDENTS

1 Example of request for documents

[Heading]

Request for documents

1. Please provide accounts for the XYZ Co Ltd for the last three accounting years and any six-monthly draft accounts in respect of the period since the last prepared accounts.

2. Please supply copy bank statements in respect of every account in the Respondent's name or in respect of which the Respondent is a Signatory, whether solely or jointly with any other person, for the past 12 months and identify all credits and all debits over £250.

3. In respect of expenses on company business please supply copies of I.T. Form P 11D for the past two years.

4. The Respondent alleges in paragraph _____ of Form E that he owes *[name]* the sum of £_____. Please supply any memorandum of this debt and give full details of when it was incurred, for what purpose, whether any sums have been repaid and the Respondent's intentions as to repayment.

5. In connection with the Respondent's purchase of the property *[address]* please state the source of the deposit and legal fees and provide a copy of the application for a mortgage from the ABC Building Society.

6. Please disclose the Respondent's passport(s) since 2008.

7. Please state the cost of the Respondent's holiday in Bermuda in September 2009, state where the money came from and provide any documentation in existence with regard to it. Identify any payments in respect of that holiday in bank accounts or credit card accounts. In the absence of any such identifications state why none such exist.

8. In 2008 the Respondent's loan account with the XYZ Co Ltd stood at £10,741. Explain the source of this and account for any fluctuations since.

9. Please disclose all correspondence and any other relevant documentation with respect to the investigation by HMRC of the XYZ Co Ltd in 2005.

10. What connection has the Respondent with the DEF Finance Co with offices at *[address]*?

11. Please state the means of the Co-respondent *[or name of other person with whom Respondent is living]*, his/her income and capital and assets.

2 Order for inspection appointment

[*Heading*]

Upon hearing Counsel/the solicitor for the Applicant and Counsel/solicitor for the Respondent.

It is ordered that the Applicant/Respondent [*or* Miss G. H.] do attend the District Judge in chambers at [*address of court*] on [*day*], [*date*] at [*time*] and produce for inspection the documents specified or described in the schedule hereto.

And it is further ordered that the costs of this application be [as the court thinks fit].

THE SCHEDULE

[*set out the documents to be produced*]

3 Search order – discovery by order permitting entry of premises and search for documents

[*Heading*]

Upon hearing counsel for the Applicant on an *ex parte* application and upon reading the affidavit of _____ sworn the _____ day of [*month and year*].

And the Applicant by her counsel undertaking:

(1)   to serve this order together with a copy of the affidavit of [*the affidavit referred to above*] by a solicitor of the Supreme Court;

(2)   to abide by any order this court may make as to damages in case this court shall hereafter be of opinion that the Respondent shall have suffered any by reason of this order which the petitioner ought to pay;

(3)   to notify the Respondent or the person on whom this order is served by the solicitor of the Supreme Court who serves this order upon them that they may seek legal advice and to explain fairly and in everyday language the meaning or effect thereof;

(4)   [*any necessary undertaking to issue proceedings, e g to issue a summons to set aside an order allegedly obtained by deception or non-disclosure or the like*].

And the solicitors for the Applicant by counsel for the Applicant being their counsel for this purpose undertaking that all documents obtained as a result of this order will be retained in their safe custody until further order.

It is ordered that the Respondent or such person as shall appear to be in charge of the premises at [*address*] do forthwith permit the person who shall serve this order upon him, together with such persons not exceeding two as may be duly authorised by the Applicant, to enter the premises at [*address*] at any hour between 8 o'clock in the forenoon and 8 o'clock in the evening for the purpose of:

(a)   looking for and inspecting any of the following:

(i)   all documents relating to the Respondent's earnings, income and capital from [*date*] to date;

(ii)   all documents relating to the sale by the Respondent and the proceeds of sale of shares in any company and of any capital asset including [*description of asset*];

(iii)   all bank statements and building society passbooks and documents related thereto including pass books, cheque stubs, paid cheques and paying-in books;

(iv)   all documents relating to the purchase by the Respondent of [*description of asset allegedly purchased*] including documents relating to provision of the purchase price;

(b)   taking into the Applicant's solicitors' custody all and any of the above-mentioned documents and of making copies of the same and it is ordered that the Respondent and/or the person or person appearing for the time being to be in charge of the premises aforesaid do produce forthwith to the person serving this order all of the documents referred to in the above orders.

Liberty to apply.

4 Ex parte order permitting entry to premises and search for assets and documents

[*Heading*]

[*Undertakings by Applicant by counsel as in Precedent 3*]

And the solicitors for the Applicant by counsel for the Applicant being their counsel for this purpose undertaking that all property and documents inspected or obtained as a result of this order will be retained in their safe custody, save only that any precious metals, jewels or jewellery, watches [*add other specific items or classes of items that the search relates to*] may be released into the custody of [*name*] a jeweller for the purpose of valuing the same on the premises to which this order relates.

It is ordered that the Respondent do forthwith permit the person who shall serve this order upon him, together with such other persons not exceeding two in number as may be duly authorised by the Applicant, to enter the premises at [*address*] at any hour between 8 o'clock in the forenoon and 8 o'clock in the evening for the purpose of:

(a)   looking for and inspecting any of the following: (i) all jewels, semi-precious stones, amber, agate or similar, precious metals and alloys thereof, jewellery and similar valuable items, watches [*continue with specific items or classes of items to be searched for*]; (ii) all money; (iii) all documents relating to [*define according to circumstances*];

(b)   taking into the Applicant's solicitors' custody all and any of the above-mentioned documents and of making copies of the same and thereafter returning the originals to the Respondent's solicitors.

And it is further ordered that the Respondent do produce forthwith to the person serving this order all of the property and documents referred to herein and do open for inspection by the person serving this order any safe, cupboard, cabinet drawer and/or room at the said premises that is or appears to be locked.

Liberty to apply, costs reserved.

Dated the _____ day of [*month and year*].

GENERAL NOTE

Based on the order in *Kepa v Kepa* (1983) 4 FLR 515.

5   Maintenance pending suit order

[*Heading*]

It is ordered that the Respondent do pay or cause to be paid to the Applicant as from the _____ day of [*month and year*] maintenance pending suit at the rate of £250 per week payable weekly.

Dated the _____ day of [*month and year*].

GENERAL NOTE

Commencement date of order. This will usually be the date of the filing of the petition (it cannot be earlier). See MCA 1973, s 22.

Termination of order. The order will cease when the suit ceases to be pending, ie when a decree of judicial separation is made; when a decree nisi of divorce or nullity is made absolute or when the petition is dismissed.

Variation. The order is variable under MCA 1973, s 31; the words 'until further order' are customarily not inserted as it is most often the case that the order is intended to subsist for only a short time.

Order combined with periodical payments. Where, at the hearing of the application for maintenance pending suit, the court has jurisdiction to make an order for periodical payments, ie after decree nisi but before decree absolute, then, provided application has been duly made, the District Judge may make an order for maintenance pending suit and also for periodical payments (or interim periodical payments) to run from the date when the decree nisi is made absolute. The court can only consider periodical payments after a decree nisi has been pronounced and accordingly such a combined order can only be asked for where the hearing is after decree nisi and before decree absolute.

5A   Order for maintenance pending suit to include a costs element

It is ordered that the Respondent do pay or cause to be paid to the Applicant as from the _____ day of [*month and year*] maintenance pending suit at the rate of £3,000 per month payable monthly, such sum to include a legal expenses component of £50,000 payable at the rate of £2,000 per month, upon the Applicant undertaking to pay such legal expenses to her solicitors to be credited against any costs order which she may ultimately recover against the respondent.

6   Order for maintenance payments to be paid by standing order

And it is further ordered:

(1) That the said Maintenance pending suit/Periodical payments be paid by means of standing order to the Applicant's account at ABC Bank Plc, _____ Branch, account number 12345.

(2) That the Respondent forthwith give to his Bankers authority for payments of £ _____ per week/month to be made from his account to the Applicant's account no 12345 with ABC Bank Plc, _____ branch, on the _____ day of each month until further order of this court without the need for any further authority by the Respondent.

(3) That the application for an order pursuant to section 1(5) of the Maintenance Enforcement Act 1991 be adjourned for 21 days to enable the Respondent to open a bank account.

(4) The court being satisfied that the Respondent has failed without reasonable excuse to open an account out of which payments under this order may be made, that the Respondent do within 7 days from the date of this order [*or* from the order of service of this order] open such an account.

GENERAL NOTE

See **19.15**.

7 Periodical payments order for spouse

[*Heading*]

It is ordered that the above-named Respondent do make or cause to be made to the above-named Applicant as from the _____ day of [*month and year*] periodical payments for herself during their joint lives until [the _____ day of [*month and year*] or such earlier date as] he/she shall remarry or further order at the rate of £5,500 per annum payable monthly.

[And it is further ordered that the Applicant shall not be entitled to apply under section 31 of the Matrimonial Causes Act 1973 for an extension of the term specified above.]

Dated the _____ day of [*month and year*].

8 Order directing cessation of order made in magistrates' court

[*Heading*]

It is ordered, pursuant to section 28(1) of the Domestic Proceedings and Magistrates' Courts Act 1978, that the order of the _____ Magistrates dated the _____ day of [*month and year*] [insofar as the same relates to periodical payments for the Applicant *and/or* the child (*name in full*)] do cease to have effect from the _____ day of [*month and year*].

GENERAL NOTE

The county court and the High Court may order that a magistrates' court order made under Part 1 of the 1978 Act do cease to have effect (excluding an order for a lump sum under s 2 thereof). A county court or High Court order may implicitly supersede or revoke a magistrates' court order without specifically directing that it ceases to have effect.

9 Secured periodical payments order

[*Heading*]

It is ordered that the above-named Respondent do secure to the above-named Applicant for her life until [the _____ day of [*month and year*] or such earlier date as] she shall remarry or further order as from the _____ day of [*month and year*] the annual sum of £5,000 upon [*here state the nature of the securities or if they are not agreed or fixed at the time of making the order use the words* 'security to be agreed or referred to a District Judge in default of agreement'] and that in default of agreement as to the form of deed between the parties it be referred to conveyancing counsel of the High Court to settle the necessary deed or deeds.

[And it is further ordered that the Applicant shall not be entitled to apply under section 31 of the Matrimonial Causes Act 1973 for an extension of the term specified above.]

Dated the _____ day of [*month and year*].

10 Periodical payments order to child

[*Heading*]

It is ordered that the above-named Respondent do make to [*name of child in full*] as from the _____ day of [*month and year*] periodical payments until he/she shall attain the age of 17 years or further order at the rate of £25 per week payable weekly.

Dated the _____ day of [*month and year*].

GENERAL NOTE

Note the limitation on the power of the court, see **11.18**.

11 Order to parent or other person for child

[*Heading*]

It is ordered that the above-named Respondent do make to [*name of payee*] as from the _____ day of [*month and year*] periodical payments for the child [*name in full*] until he/she shall attain the age of 17 years or further order at the rate of £25 per week payable weekly.

Dated the _____ day of [*month and year*].

12 Order to include payment of school fees

[*Heading*]

It is ordered that the Respondent do pay or cause to be paid [to the child (*name in full*)] or [to the Applicant for the child (*name in full*)] as from the _____ day of [*month and year*] [until he/she shall attain the age of 17 years] *and/or* [he/she shall cease to receive full-time education] [whichever is the later/earlier] or until further order periodical payments [for himself/herself]:

(a)   of an amount equivalent to the school fees (but not the extras in the school bill) *or* (including (*specified extra*)) at the school the said child attends for each financial year (by way of three payments on _____ and _____ and _____) (payable monthly); together with

(b)   the sum of £ _____ per annum payable monthly in respect of the general maintenance of the said child.

And it is further ordered that payment of the school fees to the [Headmaster *or* Bursar *or* School Secretary] shall be a sufficient discharge of the Respondent's liability to pay to the Applicant for the said child the said school fees.

13   Lump sum orders

[*Heading*]

A. For Spouse or Former Spouse

It is ordered that the Respondent do, within 28 days from the date of this order, pay to the Applicant a lump sum of £25,000.

or

It is ordered that the Respondent do pay to the Applicant a lump sum of £25,000 by instalments as follows: £5,000 within 14 days from the date of this order; a further £10,000 on December 1, 2009 and the balance of £10,000 on March 1, 2010 and that the said instalments of £10,000 do carry interest at _____ per cent as from the date of this order until the dates when they are respectively due to be paid.

And it is further ordered that the said instalments of £10,000 be secured by a charge to be effected on the property [*address*].

or

It is ordered that the Respondent do pay to the Applicant within 12 months from today a lump sum of £50,000 and that the lump sum shall carry interest at the rate of _____ per cent as [from the date three months] from today until the date 12 months from today when the said sum is due to be paid.

or

(*Where the payee is a funded person and the Court has ordered that the lump sum is to be used for the purpose of purchasing a home for himself or his dependants.*)

It is ordered that the Respondent do, within 28 days from the date of this order, pay to the Applicant a lump sum of £75,000.

And it is certified for the purposes of regulation 21 of the Community Legal Service (Costs) Regulations 2000 that the lump sum of £75,000 has been ordered to be paid to enable the Applicant to provide a home for herself (and her dependants).

B. For or To Child

It is ordered that the Respondent do within 28 days from the date of this order [pay to the Applicant for the benefit of the child of the family (*name of child in full*) a lump sum of £5,000] *or* [pay to the child of the family (*name of child in full*) a lump sum of £5,000] [*insert details as to instalments, security and interest, if appropriate, as in A. above*].

C. For Spouse or Child under MCA 1973, s 23(3) – Urgent Application

It is ordered pursuant to section 23(3) of the Matrimonial Causes Act 1973 that the above-named Respondent do pay, within (*specified time*) from today, [to the Applicant] *or* [to the Applicant for the benefit of the child (*name in full*)] *or* [to the child (*name in full*)] the sum of £1,250 for the purpose of enabling [the Applicant]/[the said child] to meet liabilities (and/or expenses) reasonably incurred in maintaining [herself]/[the said child].

Dated the _____ day of [*month and year*].

GENERAL NOTE

An order under MCA 1973, s 23(3) may be made before applying for a lump sum order under s 23(1)(c) or (f). It is essentially a provision to enable a payment to be ordered to cover liabilities which cannot otherwise be met where such provision is urgently required. See **4.6**.

Lump sum for legally assisted person's home. The Community Legal Service (Costs) Regulations 2000, reg 21 provides for the deferment of the statutory charge, in respect of the assisted person's costs, over money recovered or over property recovered or preserved by order of the court or by agreement, if by the order or agreement the money recovered or the property is to be used to purchase a home for the assisted person or his dependants.

14   Order to transfer property to assisted person with direction that it be used as a home for funded person or his dependants

It is ordered that the Respondent do, within 28 days from today, transfer to the Applicant the property known as and situate at [*address*]; [*add any conditions such as* 'subject to the existing mortgage with the XYZ Building Society; the Applicant undertaking to indemnify the Respondent for any liability thereunder'].

And it is certified for the purposes of the Community Legal Service (Costs) Regulations 2000 that the property [*address*] has been preserved/recovered for the Applicant for use as a home for herself (and her dependants).

GENERAL NOTE

See General Note to Precedent 13.

15   *Mesher* order – house in joint names – party to be allowed to live there until child attains a certain age

[*Heading*]

It is ordered that the property [*address*] be held upon trust to hold the net proceeds of sale and rents and profits until sale in equal shares, provided that as long as the child [*name in full*] be under the age of 17 years or until further order the house be not sold; the Applicant to be at liberty to live there rent-free paying and discharging all rates, taxes and outgoings, including mortgage interest and indemnifying the Respondent thereof; and repayments of capital to be borne in equal shares.

Dated the _____ day of [*month and year*].

GENERAL NOTE

This precedent is based upon that in *Mesher v Mesher and Hall* [1980] 1 All ER 126, CA. The case was decided in 1973. The words 'or until further order' have been inserted as they or the words 'liberty to apply' or other words of more particular intent allow for a prior application for the sale of the property if circumstances so justify although not permitting an application to postpone sale after the term specified in the order. In such respect, the order is not variable.

The reference to 'trust for sale' has been omitted, see **5.11**.

16   A more elaborate form of *Mesher*-type order

[*Heading*]

It is ordered that the trust [for sale] upon which the Parties presently hold the property [*address*] be varied forthwith to provide that the Applicant and the Respondent do hold the said property [*or* It is ordered that the Respondent do transfer into the joint names of the Applicant and Respondent the property [*address*] to hold the same] upon trust as tenants in common in equal shares upon the statutory trusts for sale declared by the Law of Property Act 1925 and upon the following terms and conditions:

(a)   the property not to be sold without the prior written consent of both Parties or without the leave of the court until either (i) the child of the family [*name in full*] reaches the age of 18 years or completes her full-time education, whichever shall later occur; or (ii) the remarriage of the Applicant, whichever shall first occur;

(b)   the Applicant to be solely responsible for payment of all interest due under a subsisting mortgage upon the said property in favour of the ABC Building Society and to be responsible for half of the instalments of capital repayments due under the said mortgage;

(c)   the Respondent to be responsible for one half of the instalments of capital repayments due under the said mortgage;

(d)   the Parties to be equally liable and responsible for insuring the said property and for structural repairs upon the said property; in the event of any dispute in relation thereto, such dispute to be referred to arbitration by a surveyor/valuer appointed by agreement between the Parties' solicitors and in default of agreement as to the surveyor/valuer to be appointed by the President of the Royal Institution of Chartered Surveyors;

(e)   the Applicant to be responsible for all decorative repairs to the said property;

(f)   the Applicant to have exclusive possession of the said property until sale;

(g)   in the event of the Applicant wishing to move to another property prior to the aforesaid property being sold in pursuance of the foregoing terms and conditions, she be at liberty to sell and re-invest the proceeds of sale in another property, subject to clause (a) above (the consent of the Respondent not to be withheld unreasonably), which said property to be held upon the same trusts and the same terms and conditions and any surplus arising on the acquisition thereof to be divided equally between the parties;

(h)   the Applicant to have the right, at the end of the period in which she has exclusive possessions under the terms of this order, to purchase the Respondent's interest at a valuation to be agreed or, in default of agreement, to be determined by a valuer nominated by the President of the Royal Institution of Chartered Surveyors.

Liberty to apply as to implementation of this order.

Dated the _____ day of [*month and year*].

GENERAL NOTE

See also Precedent 22 where the post-nuptial settlement created by the purchase of the matrimonial home in joint names (both having contributed) is varied to provide that the trust continues subject to terms set out in the order.

See also Precedent 13 and General Note to Precedent 13 for appropriate wording where property transferred to a funded applicant, or preserved for him, is to be used to house him and his dependants with the property being charged in favour of the Legal Services Commission in respect of his costs.

17   *Mesher*-type order with provisions for extended right of occupation and for occupant to pay rent from a specified date

[*Heading*]

It is ordered:

(1)   that the property [*address*] be transferred by the Respondent into the joint names of the Applicant and Respondent on trust;

(2)   that upon sale the net proceeds of sale be divided in the proportion of two-thirds to the Applicant and one-third to the Respondent;

(3)   that such sale be postponed in any event until the youngest child of the family shall attain the age of 18 years or completes his full-time education whichever shall be the later;

(4)   that thereafter the said sale shall continue to be postponed during the lifetime of the Applicant or until she consents to such sale: provided that if she has remarried before the date referred to in clause (3) hereof, or remarries or cohabits with another man, thereafter the said property shall be sold forthwith and the proceeds of sale divided in accordance with the terms of clause (2) hereof;

(5)   that the Applicant be responsible, subject to the provisions of this clause, for all outgoings including mortgage repayments until the sale of the property from the date of this order, and to pay to the Respondent from the date referred to in clause (3) hereof, such sum by way of occupation rent of the premises as may be agreed, or in default, determined by the District Judge of the _____ County Court in

respect of his interest in the said property; the said occupation rent shall be one-third of such sum as represents a fair rent.

GENERAL NOTE

Based on the order in *Harvey v Harvey* [1982] 2 WLR 283, [1982] 1 All ER 693, CA. The terms of this order permit the Applicant to continue to live in the property for as long as it is reasonable for her to do so.

18 Order for transfer of property to applicant and charge imposed in favour of respondent in a fixed sum

[*Heading*]

It is ordered that the Respondent do transfer to the Applicant all his interest both legal and beneficial in the property [*address*] within [*specified time*] from today and that as from the date of transfer as aforesaid the said property do stand charged in favour of the Respondent for the sum of £ _____; such charge not to be enforced until (a) the death of the Applicant; (b) the sale of the property; or (c) the date when the youngest child of the family attains the age of _____ years whichever is the soonest.

Dated the _____ day of [*month and year*].

GENERAL NOTE

Based on the order in *Hector v Hector* [1973] 1 WLR 1122, [1973] 3 All ER 1070, CA. The order would be improved by the addition of a further qualification to the period of prohibition for enforcement of the charge to allow an earlier enforcement if circumstances warranted, e g 'such charge not to be enforced without leave of the court until (a) . . . (etc)'.

In *McDonnell v McDonnell* [1976] 1 WLR 34, the Court of Appeal held that an order giving a spouse a proportion of the value of the matrimonial home was to be preferred to a charge for a fixed amount. A charge for a fixed sum may be appropriate if the period for which it will be deferred is known to be short.

19 Alternative order for transfer of property to applicant and charge imposed in favour of respondent in a proportion

It is ordered that the Respondent do transfer to the Applicant all his interest both legal and beneficial in the property [*address*] within [eg 28 days] on condition that the Applicant deliver in return a charge over the said property executed by her for [eg 25%] of the gross/net proceeds of sale of the said property such charge to be in a form to be agreed between the solicitors for the Applicant and Respondent and in default to be settled by the District Judge and to be enforceable only on the first of the following events, namely:

[*adapt a* Mesher *or* Martin *order as the circumstances require*].

20   Suggested form of charge

HM Land Registry

Land Registration Acts 1925–1986

COUNTY AND DISTRICT

TITLE NUMBER

PROPERTY

DATE

In pursuance of an order of District Judge in the Divorce Registry/ _____
_____ County Court dated _____ in proceedings between the Mortgagor
and [*name of the husband*] bearing Number of Matter _____:

1. AB of [*address*] (hereinafter called 'the Mortgagor') hereby covenant with
BB of [*address*] (hereinafter called 'the husband') to pay to the husband on the
occurrence of the first of the events below mentioned [*or* on the _____ day of
month and year] (hereinafter called 'the specified dates')] the secured amount as
hereinafter defined:

(i)   The remarriage of the Mortgagor
(ii)   The death of the Mortgagor
(iii)   The sale of the property charged by this deed
(iv)   The child of the family [*name in full*] attaining the age of 17 years or
         ceasing full-time education or training whichever be the later
(v)   The further order of the Court

[*or, as the case may be. The specified dates will of course be the 'trigger events' as
set out in the Court order*].

2. The secured amount shall be [*as ordered by the Court, eg x per cent of the
gross or net proceeds of sale of the property, stating which sums are to be
deducted in calculating net proceeds of sale. The charge might profitably include
the right of the Mortgagor to redeem at a time other than one of the specified
dates without sale and for the value of the property to be determined by an
independent valuer in that event, should the parties not agree as to value*].

3. The husband will not before the first to happen of the specified dates call in
the husband's share or any part thereof provided always that notwithstanding
and without prejudice to the provisions hereof the power of sale applicable to
this charge shall for the protection of a purchaser be deemed to arise on the
date hereof.

4. The Mortgagor as beneficial owner hereby charges by way of legal mortgage
the land comprised in the title above referred to (hereinafter called 'the
property') with payment to the husband of the secured amount [*add, if
appropriate,* subject to the charge dated *etc*].

5. The Mortgagor further covenants with the husband that the Mortgagor:

(a)   will duly and punctually pay the instalments in respect of the said
         charge in favour of the XYZ Building Society

(b)   will at all times keep the property insured in accordance with the covenant contained in the first mortgage.

[*Add any further provisions thought appropriate, e g covenants to repair, the right to substitute the charge to a new property.*]

SIGNED AS A DEED by
AB in the presence of:

GENERAL NOTE

This form of charge is suggested as suitable in many cases, as merely to order a charge to be executed can cause further problems since the parties may not agree on the terms of the charge. Precedent 19 enables the court to specify in the order as many of the terms of the charge as seems necessary, e g the fact that it will or will not bear interest, who is to be responsible for insurance and repairs, and so on. This can make a form of order very unwieldy and it is suggested that if the form of charge is left to be agreed between the parties with liberty to apply to the District Judge to settle the form of charge or any of its terms, this may be the better solution; this should not be necessary where the order is by consent since all these matters should have been agreed beforehand.

In extreme cases, the District Judge may refer the settling of the charge to conveyancing counsel.

21   Order for sale and for possession

[And] it is [further] ordered that:

(1)   The property known as [*address*] be sold.
(2)   The Applicant's/Respondent's solicitors have conduct of the sale.
(3)   The net proceeds of sale after deduction of all sums due to mortgagees, estate agents, charges and the proper solicitor's costs of sale be divided as to _____ per cent to the _____ and per cent _____ to the _____ [*or* £ _____ to the _____ and the balance to the _____].
(4)   Liberty to apply for further directions as to the conduct of the sale.

And it is further ordered that the Applicant/Respondent do deliver possession of the said property to the Respondent/Applicant and vacate the same on the _____ day of [*month and year*].

GENERAL NOTE

Section 24A of MCA 1973 enables the court to make an order for sale on making a property adjustment order or at any time thereafter. Paragraph (3) of the order above would only be necessary when the proportions had not been stated earlier in the order.

22   Order varying settlement created by purchase in joint names (both having contributed) to the effect that the trust for sale continues on terms set out – *Mesher*-type provision with power to substitute property

[*Heading*]

It is ordered that the post-nuptial settlement comprised in the transfer dated _____ whereby the freehold property [*address*] registered at HM Land Registry under Title number _____ was transferred to the Applicant and the Respondent as tenants in common in equal shares be and the same is hereby varied so that the trust thereby created is and continues henceforth subject to the terms set out in the schedule to this order.

SCHEDULE

(a)   In this Schedule 'the trust period' shall mean the period beginning at the date of this order and continuing so long as the Applicant shall have the care and control of the children _____ and _____ or either of them or until the death of the Applicant or until the remarriage of the Applicant or until the last survivor of the said children attains the age of 17 (whichever shall first occur) or until such other date as the Applicant and the Respondent may jointly by deed appoint.

(b)   In this Schedule 'the property' shall mean the freehold property known as _____ registered at HM Land Registry under Title Number _____ and where the context admits any dwelling or flat purchased in substitution for the property pursuant to paragraph (h) hereof.

(c)   The Trustees shall be the Applicant and/or such other persons as may from time to time during the trust period be appointed by the Applicant and the Respondent jointly (or in default of agreement by the Court) in addition to or in substitution for either or both of them.

(d)   The Trustees shall not sell the property during the trust period so long as the Applicant resides and is entitled to reside therein without the Applicant's consent in writing.

(e)   During the trust period the net income of the property shall be held upon trust for the Applicant absolutely.

(f)   During the trust period the Applicant shall pay all rates and other outgoings payable in respect of the property and keep the same in good repair and condition and insured in the names of the Trustees against such risks and in such amount as the Trustees shall from time to time reasonably require.

(g)   During the trust period:

   (i)   the Applicant shall be entitled and the Trustees shall permit the Applicant to occupy the property or any part thereof as her residence rent-free;

   (ii)   so long as the Applicant occupies the property as aforesaid and herself remains a Trustee the Trustees shall at her request delegate to the Applicant (upon terms that the Applicant consents to use her best endeavours at her expense to obtain possession from any tenants prior to her ceasing to reside in the property) the powers of and incidental to leasing any parts of the property not occupied by her in respect of weekly or monthly lettings at rack rent she receiving all rents arising therefrom without being required to account for the same to the Trustees.

   But save as aforesaid the Trustees shall not delegate their powers and shall not without the consent of the Applicant and the Respondent in writing create any lease of or charge mortgage or otherwise encumber the property.

(h)   If during the trust period the Applicant shall at any time request the Trustees to sell the property or any other property purchased pursuant to this paragraph then provided the Applicant shall have used her best endeavours as aforesaid to ensure sale with vacant possession the Trustees shall sell the same as soon as reasonably practicable thereafter and shall at the like request of the Applicant apply all or any part of the net proceeds of sale in or towards the purchase of another freehold dwellinghouse or flat selected by the Applicant and any dwellinghouse or flat so purchased shall be assured to the Trustees upon trust for sale upon the same terms as the property as varied by this Order.

(i) Any proceeds of sale of the property not required for the purchase of another property pursuant to paragraph (g) hereof shall be invested by the Trustees during the trust period in or upon the acquisition or security of any property of whatsoever nature and wheresoever situate to the intent that the Trustees shall have the same full and unrestricted power of investing in all respects as if they were absolutely entitled thereto beneficially.

(j) In the event of the Respondent dying before the expiration of the trust period the rights and powers hereby reserved to him shall be exerciseable by his personal representatives.

Dated the _____ day of [*month and year*].

23   Order for variation of settlement (pensions)

[*Order as approved by Wilson J*]

1. The trusts of the pension scheme called 'The XYZ Pension Scheme' ('the Scheme') established by Interim Trust Deed dated [. . .] and presently governed by a Trust Deed dated [. . .] between H Limited (1) and the Respondent and others (2) be varied so as to provide as follows:

    (a) £107,000 of the funds of the Scheme forthwith be allocated to provide benefits for the Petitioner; being such sum as will with effect from _____ (being the date of the Petitioner's 60th birthday) and for her lifetime provide the Petitioner with an annuity per annum of an amount equal to £9,900 increased in line with increases in the Retail Prices Index from [*date of order*] on terms that the annuity will itself increase annually in course of payment during the Petitioner's lifetime in line with increases in the Retail Prices Index ('the Pension') and on further terms that:

        (i) The Petitioner will have the right to effect commutation to a lump sum of such part of the Pension as may be permitted by HMRC; and

        (ii) Subject to the consent of HMRC, the Petitioner will be entitled to take an immediate transfer of the whole of such proportion of the funds of the Scheme to a personal pension scheme or occupational pension scheme (as defined in section 1 of the Pension Schemes Act 1993) of her choice; and

        (iii) If HMRC do not give the consent sought in (ii) above, the Petitioner will have the right to effect a commutation to a lump sum of such part of the Pension as may be permitted by HMRC, such lump sum then being paid from the funds of the Scheme; and the trustees of the Scheme will secure the Pension and future increases on it with effect from [. . .] (after making reasonable allowances for any commutation) with an annuity contract or policy (effected with the UK office or branch of an insurance company nominated by the trustees and consented to by the Petitioner (such consent not to be unreasonably withheld, and the court to be the sole arbiter of any issue as to whether consent is or is not being unreasonably withheld) to which Part II of the Insurance Companies Act 1982 applies and which is authorised by or under section 3 or 4 of that Act to carry on ordinary long term insurance business as defined in that Act) which contains such limitation on benefits and dealing as may be required by HMRC.

(b)   the trustees of the scheme shall not exercise any powers of amendment vested in them so as to deprive the petitioner of the pension specified in (a) above.

GENERAL NOTE

Because of the effect of WRPA 1999, such orders will be of reduced interest. The term 'applicant' has therefore not been substituted for 'petitioner'.

24   *Martin*-type order – house in joint names – party to be allowed to live there for life

[*Heading*]

It is ordered that the property [*address*] be held by the Applicant and the Respondent upon trust for themselves as beneficial tenants in common and to divide the net proceeds of sale of the said property between themselves in equal shares such sale to be postponed until after the death or remarriage of the Applicant or until her voluntary removal therefrom whichever event first occurs and until such sale the Applicant shall have liberty to occupy the said property provided that the Applicant regularly and duly pays all instalments of capital and interest in respect of the mortgage on the said property to the ABC Building Society falling due after the [*specified date*] and the Respondent paying all instalments before that date.

Dated the _____ day of [*month and year*].

GENERAL NOTE

Based on the order in *Martin v Martin* [1978] Fam 12, [1977] 3 All ER 762, CA.

25   Order for transfer on payment and provision for sale in default

[*Heading*]

It is ordered:

(a)   that on or before [*date*] the Applicant do transfer to the Respondent all his interest, both legal and beneficial, in the property [*address*] and that the Respondent on such transfer do pay to the Applicant the sum of £ _____ .

(b)   that in the event that the said transfer shall not be completed by [the said date] the property be placed on the market for sale at the best price obtainable; the Applicant's solicitors to have the conduct of the sale and conveyancing and the net proceeds of sale, that is to say, the sum remaining after discharge of the mortgage to the ABC Building Society, estate agents costs of sale including VAT and the legal costs and disbursements including VAT, be divided equally between the Applicant and Respondent.

And it is recorded that, in the event of the said transfer being completed by [the said date] the Respondent undertakes to indemnify the Applicant against all liability under the mortgage to the ABC Building Society.

Dated the _____ day of [*month and year*].

26   Order dismissing claims to periodical payments, etc

[*Heading*]

It is ordered that the Applicant's application(s) for periodical payments [and a lump sum *and/or* a property adjustment order] do stand dismissed.

And it is directed that the Applicant shall not be entitled to make any further application in relation to the marriage of the Applicant and the Respondent for an order under section 23(1)(a) or (b) of the Matrimonial Causes Act 1973.

[And it is further ordered that neither party/the Applicant/the Respondent shall (not) on the death of the other party/the Respondent/the Applicant be entitled to apply for an order under section 2 of the Inheritance (Provision for Family and Dependants) Act 1975.]

Dated the _____ day of [*month and year*].

27   Order for execution of contract or conveyance on behalf of person refusing to do so or who cannot be found

[*Heading*]

It is ordered under and by virtue of section 39 of the Supreme Court Act 1981 [applied by virtue of section 38 of the County Courts Act 1984] that [*name and/or description of person nominated*] do sign the conveyance of [the contract for the sale of] the property [*address*] to [*name*] at the price of £ _____ on behalf of the Respondent.

Dated the _____ day of [*month and year*].

ENDORSEMENT ON TRANSFER OR CONTRACT

Signed, Sealed and Delivered by [*name and description*] on behalf of [*name*] pursuant to order made [*date*] under section 39 of the Supreme Court Act 1981 [applied by virtue of section 38 of the County Courts Act 1984] in the presence of:

[*Signature, description and address of witness*]

28 Injunction under MCA 1973, section 37 – interim injunction made ex parte (High Court)

[*Heading*]

Upon hearing counsel/solicitor for the Applicant and upon reading the affidavit of _____ sworn on [*date*] and the Applicant undertaking by her counsel to abide by any order the court may make as to damages in case the court shall hereafter be of opinion that the Respondent shall have sustained any by reason of this order which the Applicant ought to pay.

It is ordered and directed that the Respondent by himself, his agents or servants or otherwise be restrained, and an interim injunction until further order or until the hearing of the Applicant's summons (application) before District Judge [*name*] at [*address of court*] at 10.30 am on [*date*] is hereby granted restraining him from disposing of, transferring out of the jurisdiction or otherwise dealing with any monies received by him or receivable by him in respect of the estate of [*name*] deceased save the action of placing any such monies in either a bank deposit account or in a building society account in England. [*Or such other order as may be appropriate.*] Liberty to the Respondent to apply to discharge or vary this order on 48 hours' notice to the solicitor for the Applicant. Costs reserved.

Dated the _____ day of [*month and year*].

GENERAL NOTE

The action in respect of which the respondent to the application is enjoined and restrained from taking is, of course, merely an example and the precedent may be adapted to suit the purpose of the application. This is a form which may be used in the High Court. For the position in the county courts and divorce registry where the suit is not in the High Court, see Precedent 30.

29 Order setting aside disposition

[*Heading*]

It is ordered that the transfer by [*name*] the Respondent to [*name*] the Co-respondent of the property [*address*] [registered under title number _____ at HM Land Registry] on [*date*] be set aside and that the Co-respondent do within _____ days from the date hereof transfer the said property into the name of the Respondent.

GENERAL NOTE

If the transferee is not a party to the suit he or she will normally be added to the title of orders relating to avoidance of disposition proceedings as a respondent or defendant.

30   General form of injunction

Between
_____

□ Plaintiff
□ Applicant
□ Petitioner
(Tick whichever applies)

and
_____

□ Defendant
□ Respondent

In the

County Court

Case No.	Always quote this	
Plaintiff's Ref		
Defendant's Ref		

To[1]
of[2]

For completion by the Court

Issued on

Seal

If you do not obey this order you will be guilty of contempt of court and you may be sent to prison

(1) The name of the person the order is directed to

On the   of   20

the court considered an application for an injunction

The Court ordered that[1]

(2) The address of the person the order is directed to

is forbidden (whether by himself or by instructing or encouraging any other person)[3]

(3) The terms of the restraining order.
If the defendant is a limited company, delete the words in brackets and insert 'whether by its sevants, agents, officers or otherwise'

This order shall remain in force until (the   of
          20   at   o'clock unless before then it is
revoked by a) further order of the court

And it is ordered that[1]

shall[4]

(4) The terms of any orders requiring acts to be done

(5) Enter time (and place) as ordered	on or before[5]

(6) The terms of any other orders costs etc	It is further ordered that[6]

(7) Use when the order is temporary or ex parte otherwise delete

Notice of further hearing[7]

The court will re-consider the application and whether the order should continue at a further hearing

at

on   the   day   of

(8) Delete if order made on notice

20   at   o'clock

If you do not attend at the time shown the court may make an injunction order in your absence

You are entitled to apply to the court to re-consider the order before that day[8]

If you do not fully understand this application you should go to a Solicitor, Legal Advice Centre or a Citizen's Advice Bureau

---

The Court Office at
is open from 10 am to 4 pm Mon–Fri. When corresponding with the court, address all forms and letters to the Chief Clerk and quote the case number

---

GENERAL NOTE

This is the general form of injunction in Form N16 which must be used. The Marginal Notes act as a useful checklist.

For examples of the kind of orders which may be granted, see the precedents immediately preceding this.

31   Examples of agreements and undertakings to be recited in preambles to consent orders

(i) As to matrimonial home

(a)   The Applicant/Respondent undertaking to the court to continue to discharge the mortgage on the property [*address*] and the outgoings thereon, namely charges for rates, water rates, gas, electricity, insurance and telephone pending suit.

(b)   The Applicant/Respondent having agreed that the Respondent/ Applicant be at liberty to reside in the property [*address*] until its sale, as provided for in the order hereunder, and not to let or share or part with possession of the basement flat in the property otherwise than by a letting or parting with possession which does not give the tenant or occupier any security of tenure under the Rent Acts and, save as aforesaid, not to let or share or part with possession or occupation of the property except with the written permission of the [*other party*], such permission not to be withheld unreasonably.

(ii) As to insurances

(a) The Applicant/Respondent undertaking to the court to provide private medical insurance for the (other party and/or children) to provide benefits not less than those that exist under the policy funded by his employer (or alternatively to procure that the said children remain covered under his employer's said policy).

(b) The Applicant/Respondent undertaking to the court to undergo such medical examination as may be required by an insurance company to enable the Respondent/Applicant to insure his/her life.

(c) The Applicant/Respondent undertaking to the court to maintain the policy with the ABC Insurance Co PLC being number _____ maturing on [*date*] and to provide the Respondent/Applicant annually on January 1, in each year with proof of the maintenance of the said policy.

(iii) As to companies

(a) The Applicant/Respondent undertaking to the court that he/she will, for the consideration of £1 transfer to the Respondent/Applicant or to whomsoever he/she may direct or nominate his/her one share in the ABCD Co Ltd and resign his/her directorship therein and he/she hereby acknowledges that he/she has no claim against the said company.

(b) The Applicant/Respondent undertaking to the court to indemnify the _____ in respect of any capital gains tax liability consequent upon the transfer to him/her of the _____'s shareholding in the ABCD Co Ltd and in respect of any other tax liability that may be suffered by the _____ arising from the _____'s involvement in and work for the said Co.

(iv) As to children

(a) The Applicant/Respondent undertaking to the court to reimburse the _____ in respect of any expenditure on behalf of the children he/she incurs at the _____'s request.

(b) The Applicant/Respondent undertaking to the court to provide each year a return air ticket to enable the child of the family [*name in full*] to visit him in [*country*] for access on dates to be agreed each year by the parties.

(c) The Applicant/Respondent undertaking to the court to provide one-third of the increased cost of the school fees beyond the level of such fees at the date hereof in respect of the children.

(v) As to Jewish Gets

(a) The Applicant/Respondent hereby undertaking to the court

(i) to apply [within _____ weeks of this order *or* within _____ weeks from the date of the [decree nisi *or* decree absolute]] to the London Beth Din (Court of the Chief Rabbi) for a religious divorce (*Get*), and

(ii) thereafter to take all such steps as are directed by the Court of the Chief Rabbi to complete the *Get*, such completion to take place not later than [_____ weeks *or* _____ months] from the date of application to the Court of the Chief Rabbi; costs thereof to be [borne by the [Applicant]/[Respondent] *or* shared equally].

(b) The Applicant/Respondent hereby undertaking to the court, upon application by the Respondent/Applicant to the London Beth Din (Court of the Chief Rabbi) for a religious divorce (*Get*), to take all such steps as are directed by the Court of the Chief Rabbi to complete the *Get*, such completion to take place not later than _____ months from the date of application to the Court of the Chief Rabbi; costs thereof to be [borne by the [Applicant]/[Respondent] *or* shared equally].

GENERAL NOTE

There is considerable debate about whether and if so how, undertakings are enforceable. There is authority (see Chapter 9) that undertakings to pay money are enforceable by way of judgment summons or third party debt orders. Whatever the true position may be, it is submitted that the position can only be made more clear if the party giving the undertaking expressly states in the application for the order that he/she accepts his/her obligations by reason of the undertaking and signs such acknowledgment.

Such acknowledgment might read as follows:

'I [full name] understand that the undertakings which I have given to the court as set out above are enforceable against me in the same way as orders of the court, and that breach of an order to pay money is a contempt of court'

32 Variation of orders

[*Heading*]

1. It is ordered that the order herein dated the _____ day of [*month and year*] be varied and that, as from the _____ day of [*month and year*], the Respondent do pay [*continue as in such precedent as may be appropriate, setting out the terms of the new provision for maintenance pending suit or periodical payments*].

Part of prior order only to be varied
2. It is ordered that the order herein dated the _____ day of [*month and year*] insofar as it relates to periodical payments for the Applicant be varied and that as from [*continue as in above precedent*].

Dated the _____ day of [*month and year*].

Arrears remitted under s 31(2A) of MCA 1973
3. And it is ordered that the arrears outstanding at the date of this order under the said order dated _____ be and the same are hereby remitted [as to £ _____] *or* [as to arrears accrued due prior to [*date*]].

33   Setting aside orders for ancillary relief

Type of Order	Appeal	Fresh Action	Rehearing*
1. County Court District Judge by consent	Yes: without leave. Fresh evidence admissible without leave. Hearing *de novo*	Yes	Yes: apply to District Judge
2. High Court District Judge by consent	As above	As above	No
3. County Court Judge by consent	Yes: but only with leave of the Judge. Needs leave of CA to admit fresh evidence	As above	Yes: apply to the Judge
4. High Court Judge by consent	As above	As above	No
5. County Court District Judge after contested hearing	Yes: without leave. Fresh evidence admissible. Hearing *de novo*	As above	Maybe not
6. High Court District Judge after contested hearing	As above	As above	No
7. County Court Judge after contested hearing	Yes: but with leave of the Judge or the CA. Needs leave to admit fresh evidence	As above	Maybe not
8. High Court Judge	As above	As above	No

* So far as rehearings are concerned, see CCR Ord 37, r 1. The doubt expressed in categories 5 and 7 above stems from the possible interpretation of the words in CCR Ord 37, r 1 'when no error of the court at the hearing is alleged'.

GENERAL NOTE

Light has been shed on the appropriate procedure to be adopted when it is sought to set aside an order for ancillary relief by reason of alleged non-disclosure of material information by Ward J in *B-T v B-T* [1990] 2 FLR 1. The procedure depends upon whether the order was made in the High Court or in a county court and whether it was made by a district judge or by a judge. The applicability of three possible avenues to achieve setting aside is set out in the table adapted from Ward J's judgment.

34   Undertaking to request commencement of pension on stipulated date and with sufficient benefits to meet order

AND UPON the [Applicant/Respondent] undertaking to the court:

EITHER
[Occupational pension scheme]

to request the commencement of [his/her] pension under the _____ pension scheme [forthwith]/[upon [his/her] ceasing employment with any employer participating in the said scheme]/[on [*date*]]/[upon [his/her] attaining the age of _____ years] in such a form that there will be a sufficient [net annuity]/[sum available for commutation] payable under the terms of the said scheme to meet the requirements of paragraph _____ of this order

OR
[Personal/pension/retirement annuity contract]

to take any benefits under [his/her] pension policy with _____ [forthwith]/[no earlier than [his/her] _____ birthday]/[no later than [his/her] _____ birthday]/[on [*date*]] in such a form that there will be a sufficient [net annuity]/[sum available for commutation] payable under the terms of the said pension policy to meet the requirements of paragraph _____ of this order

35   Undertaking not to frustrate attachment order – personal pension/retirement annuity contract

AND UPON the [Applicant/Respondent] undertaking to the court not to draw any benefits from [his/her] [personal pension policy]/[retirement annuity contract] with [*company*] [by way of income withdrawal]/[in such form] so as to frustrate the provisions of paragraph _____ of this order without the written consent of the [Respondent/Applicant].

36   Undertaking as to death benefits (occupational pension scheme)

AND UPON the [Applicant/Respondent] undertaking to the court that [he/she] will within _____ days from the date of this order irrevocably nominate and keep nominated

EITHER

the [Respondent/Applicant] [provided that [he/she] shall not have remarried at the date of the [Applicant's/Respondent's] death]/[for so long as the periodical payments order contained in paragraph _____ below shall subsist]

OR

the child of the family [*name*] [for so long as the periodical payments order contained in paragraph _____ below shall subsist]

BOTH

to receive [£ _____]/[_____% of the lump sum payable] in the event of [his/her] death under the [Applicant's/Respondent's] pension scheme with _____ [or such scheme of which [he/she] may from time to time be a member] and to provide upon request by the [Respondent/Applicant] written evidence of receipt by the person responsible for such scheme or schemes of the said nomination.

37   Clean break recital: attachment order

AND UPON the Applicant and the Respondent agreeing that the nominal order for periodical payments in favour of the [Applicant/Respondent] contained in paragraph _____ of this order is intended solely to preserve the entitlement of the [Applicant/Respondent] to periodical payments upon the retirement of the [Respondent/Applicant] as provided for by paragraph [*attached periodical payments order*] of this order and that the [Applicant/Respondent] will not apply to the court to vary the said nominal order save that the [Applicant/Respondent] shall be at liberty to apply to vary the order for periodical payments contained in paragraph [*attached periodical payments order*] of this order during the subsistence of the said nominal order in the event of a reduction in benefits within the meaning of the Divorce etc (Pensions) Regulations 1996, reg 7 [*or* the Divorce etc (Pensions) Regulations 2000, reg 5] [*or as appropriate*].

38   Non-attached deferred lump sum order from pension

The [Applicant/Respondent] do pay or cause to be paid to the [Respondent/Applicant] a lump sum [of £ _____]/[equal to _____% of the [maximum] lump sum payable to the [Applicant/Respondent] upon [his/her] retirement under the terms of [the _____ pension scheme]/[[his/her] pension with _____]/[such scheme of which [he/she] may from time to time be a member]] within _____ days of receipt by the [Applicant/Respondent] of the said lump sum WITH THE PROVISO that the [Respondent/Applicant] shall be alive and shall not have remarried at the date of the [Applicant's/Respondent's] retirement.

39   Attached periodical payments order

(a)   As from [the date of this order]/[the [Respondent's/Applicant's] retirement under the terms of [his/her] pension with [*pension provider*]]/[the date the [Applicant/Respondent] first draws benefits under [his/her] personal pension with [*pension provider*]] the person responsible for the said pension do pay to the [Applicant/Respondent] on behalf of the [Respondent/Applicant] periodical payments at the rate of [£ _____]/[_____% of [his/her] net pension payable under the terms of the said pension] payable monthly [in advance] [to be increased annually on the anniversary of this order [in accordance with the Retail Prices Index subject to a maximum of _____% per annum]/[by the percentage of any increase in the amount of pension payable to the [Respondent/Applicant] under the terms of the said pension]/[in accordance with the following formula _____] during joint lives and during the period of payment of the [Respondent's/Applicant's] pension payable under the terms of the said pension until the [Applicant/ Respondent] shall remarry or further order].

(b)   Any such payment by the person responsible for the said pension shall be treated pursuant to the Matrimonial Causes Act 1973, s 25B(6) for all purposes as a payment by the [Respondent/Applicant] as the party with pension rights in or towards [his/her] liability under the terms of this order and such payment shall be appropriated from the pension to be paid to the [Respondent/Applicant] which shall be reduced accordingly.

40   Attached lump sum order

(a)   The person responsible for the [Applicant's/Respondent's] pension scheme with _____ do pay or cause to be paid to the [Respondent/Applicant] on behalf of the [Applicant/Respondent] a lump sum [of £ _____]/[equal to _____% of the maximum amount capable of commutation in accordance with the said pension scheme's approval by HMRC to the [Applicant/Respondent]] within _____ days of [his/her] [retirement]/[taking of benefits] under the terms of the said pension scheme WITH THE PROVISO THAT the [Respondent/ Applicant] shall be alive and shall not have remarried at the date of the [Applicant's/Respondent's] retirement or taking of benefits under the terms of the said pension scheme;

(b)   Any such payment by the person responsible for the said pension shall be treated pursuant to the Matrimonial Causes Act 1973, s 25B(6) for all purposes as a payment made by the [Applicant/Respondent] as the party with pension rights in or towards [his/her] liability under the terms of this order and shall be appropriated from the lump sum or pension to be paid to the [Applicant/Respondent] which shall be reduced accordingly.

GENERAL NOTE

A commutation order will also be required: see Precedent 41.

41   Commutation order

The [Applicant/Respondent] do upon commencement of payment of [his/her] pension scheme with _____ commute [the maximum amount capable of commutation in accordance with the said pension scheme's approval by HMRC]/[_____% of the maximum amount capable of commutation in accordance with the said pension schemes approval by HMRC]/[£ _____] to a lump sum under the terms of the said pension scheme.

42 Death benefits attachment order under MCA 1973, section 25C (occupational pension scheme)

(a) The person responsible for the _____ pension scheme do pay or cause to be paid to the [Applicant/Respondent] on behalf of the [Respondent/Applicant] [£ _____]/[[_____% of] the lump sum payable] in the event of [his/her] death under the terms of the said pension scheme [WITH THE PROVISO THAT the [Applicant/Respondent] shall be alive and not have remarried at the date when the said sum becomes payable].

(b) Any such payment by the person responsible for the said pension scheme shall be treated pursuant to the Matrimonial Causes Act 1973, s 25B(6) for all purposes as a payment made by the [Respondent/Applicant] as the party with pension rights in or towards [his/her] liability under the terms of this order.

43 Death benefits attachment order under MCA 1973, section 25C (personal pension/retirement annuity contract)

(a) The [Respondent/Applicant] do nominate within _____ from the date of this order in respect of any sum payable in the event of [his/her] death prior to drawing any benefits other than income withdrawals pursuant to the Finance Act 1995, s 58 and Sch 11 under [his/her] [personal pensions]/[retirement annuity contract] number _____ with [*pension provider*]

[*either*]

the [Respondent/Applicant] [provided that [he/she] shall be alive and not have remarried at the date of the [Applicant's/Respondent's] death]/[for so long as the periodical payments order contained in paragraph _____ below shall subsist]

[*or*]

the child of the family [name] [for so long as the periodical payments order contained in paragraph _____ below shall subsist]

[*both*]

to receive [£ _____/[_____%] of the said sum]

(b) Any such payment by the person responsible for the said pension scheme shall be treated pursuant to the Matrimonial Causes Act 1973, s 25B(6) for all purposes as a payment made by the [Respondent/Applicant] as the party with pension rights in or towards his liability under the terms of this order.

44   Pension sharing/attachment order

[*Heading as appropriate*]

[It is ordered that]

Provision is made in favour of the [Applicant/Respondent] by way of [pension sharing *and/or* pension attachment] in accordance with the [annex/annexes] to this order.

FORM: P3

PENSION INQUIRY FORM

Information needed when a Pension Sharing Order or Pension Attachment Order may be made

| (insert details of pension scheme here) |
| TO: |
| of |
| Reference Number: |

A. To be completed by Pension Scheme member or policy holder:	
Name of pension scheme member or policy holder:	
Address:	
Reference:	. ... Signature of Pension Scheme member or policy holder (The scheme member's signature is necessary to authorise the release of the requested information, unless a court order requiring the information is attached to this form.)

2. Solicitors details:
   Address:
   Reference:
   Tel:	

3. Address to which the form should be sent once completed if different from 2 above.	

B. To be completed by the Pension Arrangement.

This section deals with information required to be provided under the Pensions on Divorce etc (Provision of Information) Regulations 2000 SI1048/2000, Regulations 2 and 3 and Rule 2.70(2) of the Family Proceedings Rules 1991 as amended). If a request for a Cash Equivalent Transfer Value has been made, the pension arrangement has 3 months to provide the information or 6 weeks if notified that the information is needed in connection with matrimonial proceedings, or such shorter time as notified by the court. Otherwise, the information should be provided within one month or such shorter time as notified by the court.

If this information has already been prepared in a standard form please send this instead.

1. (a)	Please confirm that you have already provided a valuation of the member's pension rights to the scheme member or to the Court.	Yes	☐	No	☐
(b)	If the answer to (a) is no, details of the CETV quotation should be attached and the date on which it was calculated.				
2. Provide a statement summarising the way in which the valuation referred to above has been or will be calculated.					
3. State the pension benefits included in the valuation referred to in B1 above.					
4. (a)	Does the person responsible for the pension arrangement offer scheme membership to the person entitled to a pension credit?	Yes	☐	No	☐
(b)	If yes, does this depend on Employer and/or trustee approval?	Yes	☐	No	☐
5. If the answer to 4(a) is yes, what benefits are available to the person with the pension credit?					

6. *Charging Policy*					
Does the arrangement charge for providing information or implementing a pension sharing order?	Yes	☐	No	☐	
If so, please:					
– provide a list of charges; – indicate when these must be paid; and – whether they can be paid directly from benefits held in the scheme or policy, or the pension credit.					

C. To be completed by the pension arrangement.

This information is required to be provided by the pension arrangement under the Pension on Divorce (Provision of Information) Regulations 2000 S.I. 1048, Regulation 4 within 21 days of being notified that a pension sharing order may be made. If such notification has not already been given, please treat this document as notification that such an order may be made. Alternatively the Court may specify a date by which this information should be provided.

If this information has already been prepared in a standard form please send this instead.

1. The full name of the pension arrangement and address to which a pension sharing order should be sent.					
2. In the case of an occupational pension scheme only, is the scheme winding up? If so: – when did the winding up commence? and – give the name and address of the trustees who are dealing with the winding up	Yes	☐	No	☐	
3. In the case of an occupational pension scheme only, assuming that a calculation of the member's CETV was carried out on the day the pension scheme received notification that a pension sharing order may be made, would that CETV be reduced?	Yes	☐	No	☐	
4. As far as you are aware, are the member's rights under the pension scheme subject to any of the following:					
– a pension sharing order	Yes	☐	No	☐	
– a pension attachment order made under s 23 of the Matrimonial Causes Act 1973 (England and Wales), s 12 A(2) or (3) of the Family Law (Scotland) Act 1985 or under art 25 of the Matrimonial Causes (Northern Ireland) Order 1978	Yes	☐	No	☐	
– a forfeiture order	Yes	☐	No	☐	
– a bankruptcy order	Yes	☐	No	☐	
– an award of sequestration on a member's estate or the making of the appointment on his estate of a judicial factor under section 41 of the Solicitors (Scotland) Act 1980	Yes	☐	No	☐	
5. Do the member's rights include rights which are not shareable by virtue of regulation 2 of the Pension Sharing (Valuation) Regulations 2000? If so, please provide details.	Yes	☐	No	☐	
6. Does the pension arrangement propose to levy additional charges specified in Regulation 6 of the Pensions on Divorce (Charging) Regulations 2000? If so, please provide the scale of the additional charges likely to made.	Yes	☐	No	☐	
7. Is the scheme member a trustee of the pension scheme?	Yes	☐	No	☐	
8. If a pension sharing order is made, will the person responsible for the pension arrangement require information regarding the scheme member's state of health before implementing the pension sharing order?	Yes	☐	No	☐	
9. Does the person responsible for the pension sharing arrangement require any further information other than that contained in regulation 5 of the Pensions on Divorce etc (Provision of Information Regulations) 2000, before implementing any Pension Sharing Order? If so, specify what.	Yes	☐	No	☐	

D. To be completed by the pension arrangement.				
The following information should be provided if the scheme member requests it or the Court orders it pursuant to its powers under the Pensions on Divorce etc (Provision of Information) Regulations 2000, SI 1048/2000. Please note that pension arrangements may make an additional charge for providing this information.				
1. Disregarding any future service or premiums that might be paid and future inflation, what is the largest lump sum payment that the member would be entitled to take if s/he were to retire at a normal retirement age?				
2. What is the earliest date on which the member has the right to take benefits , excluding retirement on grounds of ill health?				
3. Are spouse's benefits payable?	Yes	☐	No	☐
4. What lump sum would be payable on death at the date of completion of this form?				
5. What proportion of the member's pension would be payable as of right to the spouse of the member if the member were to die (a) before retirement; and (b) after retirement, disregarding any future service or premiums that might be paid and future inflation.				
6. Is the pension in payment, drawdown or deferment? If so, which?				
7. Please provide a copy of the scheme booklet.				

DATE: . ...

FORM: P1

Pension Sharing Annex under	In the
Section 24B of the Matrimonial	
Causes Act 1973	*(County Court)
(Rule 2.70 (14) FPR 1991)	*(Principal Registry of the Family Division)
	Case No.
	Always quote this
	Transferor's Solicitor's Reference
	Transferee's Solicitor's Reference

The marriage of   and

Take Notice that:

On   the Court

made a pension sharing order under Part IV of the Welfare Reform and Pensions Act 1999.
[varied] [discharged] an order which included provision for pension sharing under Part IV of the
Welfare Reform and Pensions Act 1999 and dated

This annex to the order provides the person responsible for the pension arrangement with the
information required by virtue of the Family Proceedings Rules 1991 as amended.

A. *Transferor's Details*	
(i)　The full name by which the Transferor is known (ii)　All names by which the Transferor has been known (iii)　The Transferor's date of birth (iv)　The Transferor's address (v)　The Transferor's National Insurance Number	
B. *Transferee's Details*	
(i)　The full name by which the Transferee is known (ii)　All names by which the Transferee has been known (iii)　The Transferee's date of Birth (iv)　The Transferee's address (v)　The Transferee's National Insurance Number (vi)　If the Transferee is also a member of the pension scheme from which the credit is derived, or a beneficiary of the same scheme because of survivor's benefits, the membership number	
C. *Details of the Transferor's Pension Arrangement*	
(i)　Name of the arrangement (ii)　Name and address of the person responsible for the pension arrangement: (iii)　Policy Reference Number: (iv)　If appropriate, such other details to enable the pension arrangement to be identified: (v)　The specified percentage of the member's CETV to be transferred:	＿＿ . ＿＿＿%
D. *Pension Sharing Charges*	
It is directed that:	* The pension sharing charges be apportioned between the parties as follows: or * The pension sharing charges be paid in full by the Transferor. (*Delete as appropriate)

E. Where no Form M1 (Statement of Information for a Consent Order) is filed, the parties certify that they have received the information required by Regulation 4 of the Pensions on Divorce (Provision of Information) Regulations 2000 and that information is attached on Form P3 and that it appears from that information that there is power to make an order including provision under s.24B Matrimonial Causes Act 1973 (pension sharing).	
F. In cases where the transferee has a choice of an internal or external transfer, if the transferee has indicated a preference, indicate what this is.	☐ Internal Transfer ☐ External Transfer
G. *In the case of external transfer only (recommended but optional information)* (i) The name of the qualifying arrangement which has agreed to accept the pension credit. (ii) The address of the qualifying arrangement (iii) If known, the transferee's membership or policy number in the qualifying arrangement and reference number of the new provider (iv) The name, or title, business address, phone and fax numbers and email address of the person who may be contacted in respect of the discharge of liability for the pension credit on behalf of the Transferee. (This may be an Independent Financial Advisor, for example, if one is advising the Transferee or the new pension scheme itself.) (v) Please attach a copy of the letter from the qualifying arrangement indicating its willingness to accept the pension credit.	

Please complete boxes H to J where applicable		
H. Where the credit is derived from an occupational scheme which is being wound up, has the Transferee indicated whether he wishes to transfer his pension credit rights to a qualifying arrangement?	☐ Yes	☐ No
I. Where the pension arrangement has requested details of the Transferor's health, has that information been provided?	☐ Yes	☐ No
J. Where the pension arrangement has requested further information, has that information been provided?	☐ Yes	☐ No

Note: Until the information requested in A, B, (and as far as applicable G, H, I & J) is provided the Pension Sharing Order cannot be implemented although it may be made. Even if all the information requested has been provided, further information may be required before implementation can begin. If so, reasons why implementation cannot begin should be sent by the Pension arrangement to the transferor and transferee within 21 days of receipt of the Pension Sharing Order and this annex. THIS ORDER TAKES EFFECT FROM the date on which the Decree Absolute of Divorce or nullity is made or if later, either

a. 21 days from the date of this Order, unless an Appeal has been lodged, in which case
b. the effective date of the Order determining that appeal.

To the person responsible for the pension arrangement:
Take notice that you must discharge your liability within the period of 4 months beginning with the later of:

– the day on which this order takes effect; or
– the first day on which you are in receipt of –

    (a) the pension sharing order including this annex properly completed (and where appropriate any attachments);
    (b) the decree nisi and absolute of divorce or nullity of marriage;
    (c) the information contained in G, including any further information requested; and
    (d) payment of all outstanding charges requested by the pension scheme.

To the court

You must send the following documents to the person responsible for the pension arrangement (as set out in box C above), within 7 days of the making of decree absolute of divorce or nullity of marriage or the making of the order, whichever is the later.

–   A copy of the decree of divorce or nullity of marriage;
–   A copy of the certificate under the Family Proceedings Rules 1991, rule 2.51 that the decree has been made absolute; and
–   A copy of the order, or the order varying or discharging that order, including any annex to that order relating to that pension arrangement but no other annex to that order.

45   Orders for costs

[It is ordered that]

(1) The [Respondent/Applicant] pay to the [Applicant/Respondent] the costs of the application for ancillary relief [from *date*] [limited to the issue of, eg, the existence or extent of his interest in ABC Ltd] to be the subject of detailed assessment if not agreed [assessed in the sum of £ _____ to be paid by *date*].

(2) The [Respondent/Applicant] pay to the [Applicant/Respondent] the costs of the application for ancillary relief on the indemnity basis from [*date*] to be the subject of detailed assessment if not agreed and interest on those costs from [*date*] until payment at the rate of [*a rate not exceeding 10% above base rate*].

GENERAL NOTE

This is a general form of order for costs. The first words in brackets would apply where, for example, the receiving party had made an offer on a certain date which had 'beaten' the order made. The second set of words would apply where one party had succeeded on one important issue, or acted unreasonably in relation thereto.

Appendix B

LEGISLATION

MATRIMONIAL CAUSES ACT 1973

****

PART II
FINANCIAL RELIEF FOR PARTIES TO MARRIAGE AND CHILDREN OF FAMILY

Financial provision and property adjustment orders

21 Financial provision and property adjustment orders

(1) The financial provision orders for the purposes of this Act are the orders for periodical or lump sum provision available (subject to the provisions of this Act) under section 23 below for the purpose of adjusting the financial position of the parties to a marriage and any children of the family in connection with proceedings for divorce, nullity of marriage or judicial separation and under section 27(6) below on proof of neglect by one party to a marriage to provide, or to make a proper contribution towards, reasonable maintenance for the other or a child of the family, that is to say –

(a) any order for periodical payments in favour of a party to a marriage under section 23(1)(a) or 27(6)(a) or in favour of a child of the family under section 23(1)(d), (2) or (4) or 27(6)(d);

(b) any order for secured periodical payments in favour of a party to a marriage under section 23(1)(b) or 27(6)(b) or in favour of a child of the family under section 23(1)(e), (2) or (4) or 27(6)(e); and

(c) any order for lump sum provision in favour of a party to a marriage under section 23(1)(c) or 27(6)(c) or in favour of a child of the family under section 23(1)(f), (2) or (4) or 27(6)(f);

and references in this Act (except in paragraphs 17(1) and 23 of Schedule 1 below) to periodical payments orders, secured periodical payments orders, and orders for the payment of a lump sum are references to all or some of the financial provision orders requiring the sort of financial provision in question according as the context of each reference may require.

(2) The property adjustment orders for the purposes of this Act are the orders dealing with property rights available (subject to the provisions of this Act) under section 24 below for the purpose of adjusting the financial position of the parties to a marriage and any children of the family on or after the grant of a decree of divorce, nullity of marriage or judicial separation, that is to say –

(a) any order under subsection (1)(a) of that section for a transfer of property;

(b) any order under subsection (1)(b) of that section for a settlement of property; and

(c) any order under subsection (1)(c) or (d) of that section for a variation of settlement.

21A Pension sharing orders

(1) For the purposes of this Act, a pension sharing order is an order which –

(a) provides that one party's –
 (i) shareable rights under a specified pension arrangement, or
 (ii) shareable state scheme rights,
 be subject to pension sharing for the benefit of the other party, and

(b) specifies the percentage value to be transferred.

(2) In subsection (1) above –

(a) the reference to shareable rights under a pension arrangement is to rights in relation to which pension sharing is available under Chapter I of Part IV of the Welfare Reform and Pensions Act 1999, or under corresponding Northern Ireland legislation,

(b) the reference to shareable state scheme rights is to rights in relation to which pension sharing is available under Chapter II of Part IV of the Welfare Reform and Pensions Act 1999, or under corresponding Northern Ireland legislation, and

(c) 'party' means a party to a marriage.

Amendments—Inserted by WRPA 1999, Sch 3, para 2.

21B Pension compensation sharing orders

(1) For the purposes of this Act, a pension compensation sharing order is an order which –

(a) provides that one party's shareable rights to PPF compensation that derive from rights under a specified pension scheme are to be subject to pension compensation sharing for the benefit of the other party, and

(b) specifies the percentage value to be transferred.

(2) In subsection (1) –

(a) the reference to shareable rights to PPF compensation is to rights in relation to which pension compensation sharing is available under Chapter 1 of Part 3 of the Pensions Act 2008 or under corresponding Northern Ireland legislation;

(b) 'party' means a party to a marriage;

(c) 'specified' means specified in the order.

Amendments—Inserted by Pensions Act 2008, Sch 6, Pt 1.

21C Pension compensation: interpretation

In this Part –

'PPF compensation' means compensation payable under the pension compensation provisions;

'the pension compensation provisions' means –

(a) Chapter 3 of Part 2 of the Pensions Act 2004 (pension protection) and any regulations or order made under it,

(b) Chapter 1 of Part 3 of the Pensions Act 2008 (pension compensation on divorce etc) and any regulations or order made under it, and

(c) any provision corresponding to the provisions mentioned in paragraph (a) or (b) in force in Northern Ireland.

Amendments—Inserted by Pensions Act 2008, Sch 6, Pt 1.

Ancillary relief in connection with divorce proceedings etc

22 Maintenance pending suit

On a petition for divorce, nullity of marriage or judicial separation, the court may make an order for maintenance pending suit, that is to say, an order requiring either party to the marriage to make to the other such periodical payments for his or her maintenance and for such term, being a term beginning not earlier than the date of the presentation of the petition and ending with the date of the determination of the suit, as the court thinks reasonable.

23 Financial provision orders in connection with divorce proceedings etc

(1) On granting a decree of divorce, a decree of nullity of marriage or a decree of judicial separation or at any time thereafter (whether, in the case of a decree of divorce or of nullity of marriage, before or after the decree is made absolute), the court may make any one or more of the following orders, that is to say –

(a) an order that either party to the marriage shall make to the other such periodical payments, for such term, as may be specified in the order;

(b) an order that either party to the marriage shall secure to the other to the satisfaction of the court such periodical payments, for such term, as may be so specified;

(c) an order that either party to the marriage shall pay to the other such lump sum or sums as may be so specified;

(d) an order that a party to the marriage shall make to such person as may be specified in the order for the benefit of a child of the family, or to such a child, such periodical payments, for such term, as may be so specified;

(e) an order that a party to the marriage shall secure to such person as may be so specified for the benefit of such a child, or to such a child, to the satisfaction of the court, such periodical payments, for such term, as may be so specified;

(f)   an order that a party to the marriage shall pay to such person as may
        be so specified for the benefit of such a child, or to such a child, such
        lump sum as may be so specified;

subject, however, in the case of an order under paragraph (d), (e) or (f) above,
to the restrictions imposed by section 29(1) and (3) below on the making of
financial provision orders in favour of children who have attained the age of
eighteen.

(2) The court may also, subject to those restrictions, make any one or more of
the orders mentioned in subsection (1)(d), (e) and (f) above –

(a)   in any proceedings for divorce, nullity of marriage or judicial
        separation, before granting a decree; and
(b)   where any such proceedings are dismissed after the beginning of the
        trial, either forthwith or within a reasonable period after the dismissal.

(3) Without prejudice to the generality of subsection (1)(c) or (f) above –

(a)   an order under this section that a party to a marriage shall pay a lump
        sum to the other party may be made for the purpose of enabling that
        other party to meet any liabilities or expenses reasonably incurred by
        him or her in maintaining himself or herself or any child of the family
        before making an application for an order under this section in his or
        her favour;
(b)   an order under this section for the payment of a lump sum to or for the
        benefit of a child of the family may be made for the purpose of
        enabling any liabilities or expenses reasonably incurred by or for the
        benefit of that child before the making of an application for an order
        under this section in his favour to be met; and
(c)   an order under this section for the payment of a lump sum may
        provide for the payment of that sum by instalments of such amount as
        may be specified in the order and may require the payment of the
        instalments to be secured to the satisfaction of the court.

(4) The power of the court under subsection (1) or (2)(a) above to make an
order in favour of a child of the family shall be exercisable from time to time;
and where the court makes an order in favour of a child under subsection (2)(b)
above, it may from time to time, subject to the restrictions mentioned in
subsection (1) above, make a further order in his favour of any of the kinds
mentioned in subsection (1)(d), (e) or (f) above.

(5) Without prejudice to the power to give a direction under section 30 below
for the settlement of an instrument by conveyancing counsel, where an order is
made under subsection (1)(a), (b) or (c) above on or after granting a decree of
divorce or nullity of marriage, neither the order nor any settlement made in
pursuance of the order shall take effect unless the decree has been made
absolute.

(6) Where the court –

(a)   makes an order under this section for the payment of a lump sum; and
(b)   directs –

(i)   that payment of that sum or any part of it shall be deferred; or

(ii)   that the sum or any part of it shall be paid by instalments,

the court may order that the amount deferred or the instalments shall carry interest at such rate as may be specified by the order from such date, not earlier than the date of the order, as may be so specified, until the date when payment of it is due.

Amendments—AJA 1982, s 16.

24 Property adjustment orders in connection with divorce proceedings etc

(1) On granting a decree of divorce, a decree of nullity of marriage or a decree of judicial separation or at any time thereafter (whether, in the case of a decree of divorce or of nullity of marriage, before or after the decree is made absolute), the court may make any one or more of the following orders, that is to say –

(a)   an order that a party to the marriage shall transfer to the other party, to any child of the family or to such person as may be specified in the order for the benefit of such a child such property as may be so specified, being property to which the first-mentioned party is entitled, either in possession or reversion;

(b)   an order that a 'settlement' of such property as may be so specified, being property to which a party to the marriage is so entitled, be made to the satisfaction of the court for the benefit of the other party to the marriage and of the children of the family or either or any of them;

(c)   an order varying for the benefit of the parties to the marriage and of the children of the family or either or any of them any ante-nuptial or post-nuptial settlement (including such a settlement made by will or codicil) made on the parties to the marriage , other than one in the form of a pension arrangement (within the meaning of section 25D below);

(d)   an order extinguishing or reducing the interest of either of the parties to the marriage under any such settlement , other than one in the form of a pension arrangement (within the meaning of section 25D below);

subject, however, in the case of an order under paragraph (a) above, to the restrictions imposed by section 29(1) and (3) below on the making of orders for a transfer of property in favour of children who have attained the age of eighteen.

(2) The court may make an order under subsection (1)(c) above notwithstanding that there are no children of the family.

(3) Without prejudice to the power to give a direction under section 30 below for the settlement of an instrument by conveyancing counsel, where an order is made under this section on or after granting a decree of divorce or nullity of marriage, neither the order nor any settlement made in pursuance of the order shall take effect unless the decree has been made absolute.

Amendments—WRPA 1999, Sch 3, para 3.

24A Orders for sale of property

(1) Where the court makes under section 23 or 24 of this Act a secured periodical payments order, an order for the payment of a lump sum or a property adjustment order, then, on making that order or at any time thereafter, the court may make a further order for the sale of such property as may be specified in the order, being property in which or in the proceeds of sale of which either or both of the parties to the marriage has or have a beneficial interest, either in possession or reversion.

(2) Any order made under subsection (1) above may contain such consequential or supplementary provisions as the court thinks fit and, without prejudice to the generality of the foregoing provision, may include –

  (a)   provision requiring the making of a payment out of the proceeds of sale of the property to which the order relates, and
  (b)   provision requiring any such property to be offered for sale to a person, or class of persons, specified in the order.

(3) Where an order is made under subsection (1) above on or after the grant of a decree of divorce or nullity of marriage, the order shall not take effect unless the decree has been made absolute.

(4) Where an order is made under subsection (1) above, the court may direct that the order, or such provision thereof as the court may specify, shall not take effect until the occurrence of an event specified by the court or the expiration of a period so specified.

(5) Where an order under subsection (1) above contains a provision requiring the proceeds of sale of the property to which the order relates to be used to secure periodical payments to a party to the marriage, the order shall cease to have effect on the death or re-marriage of, or formation of a civil partnership by, that person.

(6) Where a party to a marriage has a beneficial interest in any property, or in the proceeds of sale thereof, and some other person who is not a party to the marriage also has a beneficial interest in that property or in the proceeds of sale thereof, then, before deciding whether to make an order under this section in relation to that property, it shall be the duty of the court to give that other person an opportunity to make representations with respect to the order; and any representations made by that other person shall be included among the circumstances to which the court is required to have regard under section 25(1) below.

Amendments—Inserted by Matrimonial Homes and Property Act 1981, s 7; amended by MFPA 1984, s 46(1), Sch 1, para 11; CPA 2004, s 261(1), Sch 27, para 42.

24B Pension sharing orders in connection with divorce proceedings etc

(1) On granting a decree of divorce or a decree of nullity of marriage or at any time thereafter (whether before or after the decree is made absolute), the court may, on an application made under this section, make one or more pension sharing orders in relation to the marriage.

(2) A pension sharing order under this section is not to take effect unless the decree on or after which it is made has been made absolute.

(3) A pension sharing order under this section may not be made in relation to a pension arrangement which –

(a) is the subject of a pension sharing order in relation to the marriage, or
(b) has been the subject of pension sharing between the parties to the marriage.

(4) A pension sharing order under this section may not be made in relation to shareable state scheme rights if –

(a) such rights are the subject of a pension sharing order in relation to the marriage, or
(b) such rights have been the subject of pension sharing between the parties to the marriage.

(5) A pension sharing order under this section may not be made in relation to the rights of a person under a pension arrangement if there is in force a requirement imposed by virtue of section 25B or 25C below which relates to benefits or future benefits to which he is entitled under the pension arrangement.

Amendments—Inserted by WRPA 1999, Sch 3, para 4.

24C Pension sharing orders: duty to stay

(1) No pension sharing order may be made so as to take effect before the end of such period after the making of the order as may be prescribed by regulations made by the Lord Chancellor.

(2) The power to make regulations under this section shall be exercisable by statutory instrument which shall be subject to annulment in pursuance of a resolution of either House of Parliament.

Amendments—Inserted by WRPA 1999, 19, Sch 3, para 4.

24D Pension sharing orders: apportionment of charges

If a pension sharing order relates to rights under a pension arrangement, the court may include in the order provision about the apportionment between the parties of any charge under section 41 of the Welfare Reform and Pensions Act 1999 (charges in respect of pension sharing costs), or under corresponding Northern Ireland legislation.

Amendments—Inserted by WRPA 1999, 19, Sch 3, para 4.

24E Pension compensation sharing orders in connection with divorce proceedings

(1) On granting a decree of divorce or a decree of nullity of marriage or at any time thereafter (whether before or after the decree is made absolute), the court

may, on an application made under this section, make a pension compensation sharing order in relation to the marriage.

(2) A pension compensation sharing order under this section is not to take effect unless the decree on or after which it is made has been made absolute.

(3) A pension compensation sharing order under this section may not be made in relation to rights to PPF compensation that –

(a)   are the subject of pension attachment,
(b)   derive from rights under a pension scheme that were the subject of pension sharing between the parties to the marriage,
(c)   are the subject of pension compensation attachment, or
(d)   are or have been the subject of pension compensation sharing between the parties to the marriage.

(4) For the purposes of subsection (3)(a), rights to PPF compensation 'are the subject of pension attachment' if any of the following three conditions is met.

(5) The first condition is that –

(a)   the rights derive from rights under a pension scheme in relation to which an order was made under section 23 imposing a requirement by virtue of section 25B(4), and
(b)   that order, as modified under section 25E(3), remains in force.

(6) The second condition is that –

(a)   the rights derive from rights under a pension scheme in relation to which an order was made under section 23 imposing a requirement by virtue of section 25B(7), and
(b)   that order –
       (i)   has been complied with, or
       (ii)   has not been complied with and, as modified under section 25E(5), remains in force.

(7) The third condition is that –

(a)   the rights derive from rights under a pension scheme in relation to which an order was made under section 23 imposing a requirement by virtue of section 25C, and
(b)   that order remains in force.

(8) For the purposes of subsection (3)(b), rights under a pension scheme 'were the subject of pension sharing between the parties to the marriage' if the rights were at any time the subject of a pension sharing order in relation to the marriage or a previous marriage between the same parties.

(9) For the purposes of subsection (3)(c), rights to PPF compensation 'are the subject of pension compensation attachment' if there is in force a requirement imposed by virtue of section 25F relating to them.

(10) For the purposes of subsection (3)(d), rights to PPF compensation 'are or have been the subject of pension compensation sharing between the parties to

the marriage' if they are or have ever been the subject of a pension compensation sharing order in relation to the marriage or a previous marriage between the same parties.

Amendments—Inserted by Pensions Act 2008, Sch 6, Pt 1.

24F Pension compensation sharing orders: duty to stay

(1) No pension compensation sharing order may be made so as to take effect before the end of such period after the making of the order as may be prescribed by regulations made by the Lord Chancellor.

(2) The power to make regulations under this section shall be exercisable by statutory instrument which shall be subject to annulment in pursuance of a resolution of either House of Parliament.

Amendments—Inserted by Pensions Act 2008, Sch 6, Pt 1.

24G Pension compensation sharing orders: apportionment of charges

The court may include in a pension compensation sharing order provision about the apportionment between the parties of any charge under section 117 of the Pensions Act 2008 (charges in respect of pension compensation sharing costs), or under corresponding Northern Ireland legislation.

Amendments—Inserted by Pensions Act 2008, Sch 6, Pt 1.

25 Matters to which court is to have regard in deciding how to exercise its powers under ss 23, 24 and , 24A, 24B and 24E

(1)   It shall be the duty of the court in deciding whether to exercise its powers under section 23, 24 , 24A, 24B or 24E above and, if so, in what manner, to have regard to all the circumstances of the case, first consideration being given to the welfare while a minor of any child of the family who has not attained the age of eighteen.

(2)   As regards the exercise of the powers of the court under section 23(1)(a), (b) or (c), 24 , 24A, 24B or 24E above in relation to a party to the marriage, the court shall in particular have regard to the following matters –

    (a)   the income, earning capacity, property and other financial resources which each of the parties to the marriage has or is likely to have in the foreseeable future, including in the case of earning capacity any increase in that capacity which it would in the opinion of the court be reasonable to expect a party to the marriage to take steps to acquire;

    (b)   the financial needs, obligations and responsibilities which each of the parties to the marriage has or is likely to have in the foreseeable future;

    (c)   the standard of living enjoyed by the family before the breakdown of the marriage;

    (d)   the age of each party to the marriage and the duration of the marriage;

    (e)   any physical or mental disability of either of the parties to the marriage;

(f)   the contributions which each of the parties has made or is likely in the foreseeable future to make to the welfare of the family, including any contribution by looking after the home or caring for the family;

(g)   the conduct of each of the parties, if that conduct is such that it would in the opinion of the court be inequitable to disregard it;

(h)   in the case of proceedings for divorce or nullity of marriage, the value to each of the parties to the marriage of any benefit ... which, by reason of the dissolution or annulment of the marriage, that party will lose the chance of acquiring.

(3)   As regards the exercise of the powers of the court under section 23(1)(d), (e) or (f), (2) or (4), 24 or 24A above in relation to a child of the family, the court shall in particular have regard to the following matters –

(a)   the financial needs of the child;

(b)   the income, earning capacity (if any), property and other financial resources of the child;

(c)   any physical or mental disability of the child;

(d)   the manner in which he was being and in which the parties to the marriage expected him to be educated or trained;

(e)   the considerations mentioned in relation to the parties to the marriage in paragraphs (a), (b), (c) and (e) of subsection (2) above.

(4)   As regards the exercise of the powers of the court under section 23(1)(d), (e) or (f), (2) or (4), 24 or 24A above against a party to a marriage in favour of a child of the family who is not the child of that party, the court shall also have regard –

(a)   to whether that party assumed any responsibility for the child's maintenance, and, if so, to the extent to which, and the basis upon which, that party assumed such responsibility and to the length of time for which that party discharged such responsibility;

(b)   to whether in assuming and discharging such responsibility that party did so knowing that the child was not his or her own;

(c)   to the liability of any other person to maintain the child.

Amendments—MFPA 1984, s 3; Pensions Act 1995, s 166; WRPA 1999, s 19, Sch 3, para 5; Pensions Act 2008, Sch 6, Pt 1.

25A   Exercise of court's powers in favour of party to marriage on decree of divorce or nullity of marriage

(1)   Where on or after the grant of a decree of divorce or nullity of marriage the court decides to exercise its powers under section 23(1)(a), (b) or (c), 24 , 24A, 24B or 24E above in favour of a party to the marriage, it shall be the duty of the court to consider whether it would be appropriate so to exercise those powers that the financial obligations of each party towards the other will be terminated as soon after the grant of the decree as the court considers just and reasonable.

(2)   Where the court decides in such a case to make a periodical payments or secured periodical payments order in favour of a party to the marriage, the

court shall in particular consider whether it would be appropriate to require those payments to be made or secured only for such term as would in the opinion of the court be sufficient to enable the party in whose favour the order is made to adjust without undue hardship to the termination of his or her financial dependence on the other party.

(3)   Where on or after the grant of a decree of divorce or nullity of marriage an application is made by a party to the marriage for a periodical payments or secured periodical payments order in his or her favour, then, if the court considers that no continuing obligation should be imposed on either party to make or secure periodical payments in favour of the other, the court may dismiss the application with a direction that the applicant shall not be entitled to make any future application in relation to that marriage for an order under section 23(1)(a) or (b) above.

Amendments—Inserted by MFPA 1984, s 3; amended by WRPA 1999, s 19, Sch 3, para 6; Pensions Act 2008, Sch 6, Pt 1.

25B   Pensions

(1)   The matters to which the court is to have regard under section 25(2) above include –

   (a)   in the case of paragraph (a), any benefits under a pension arrangement which a party to the marriage has or is likely to have, and
   (b)   in the case of paragraph (h), any benefits under a pension arrangement which, by reason of the dissolution or annulment of the marriage, a party to the marriage will lose the chance of acquiring,

and, accordingly, in relation to benefits under a pension arrangement, section 25(2)(a) above shall have effect as if 'in the foreseeable future' were omitted.

(2)   ...

(3)   The following provisions apply where, having regard to any benefits under a pension arrangement, the court determines to make an order under section 23 above.

(4)   To the extent to which the order is made having regard to any benefits under a pension arrangement, the order may require the person responsible for the pension arrangement in question, if at any time any payment in respect of any benefits under the arrangement becomes due to the party with pension rights, to make a payment for the benefit of the other party.

(5)   The order must express the amount of any payment required to be made by virtue of subsection (4) above as a percentage of the payment which becomes due to the party with pension rights.

(6)   Any such payment by the person responsible for the arrangement –

   (a)   shall discharge so much of his liability to the party with pension rights as corresponds to the amount of the payment, and

(b)   shall be treated for all purposes as a payment made by the party with pension rights in or towards the discharge of his liability under the order.

(7)   Where the party with pension rights has a right of commutation under the arrangement, the order may require him to exercise it to any extent; and this section applies to any payment due in consequence of commutation in pursuance of the order as it applies to other payments in respect of benefits under the arrangement.

(7A)   The power conferred by subsection (7) above may not be exercised for the purpose of commuting a benefit payable to the party with pension rights to a benefit payable to the other party.

(7B)   The power conferred by subsection (4) or (7) above may not be exercised in relation to a pension arrangement which –

(a)   is the subject of a pension sharing order in relation to the marriage, or
(b)   has been the subject of pension sharing between the parties to the marriage.

(7C)   In subsection (1) above, references to benefits under a pension arrangement include any benefits by way of pension, whether under a pension arrangement or not.

Amendments—Inserted by Pensions Act 1995, s 166; amended by WRPA 1999, ss 21, 88, Sch 4, para 1, Sch 13, Pt II.

25C   Pensions: lump sums

(1)   The power of the court under section 23 above to order a party to a marriage to pay a lump sum to the other party includes, where the benefits which the party with pension rights has or is likely to have under a pension arrangement include any lump sum payable in respect of his death, power to make any of the following provision by the order.

(2)   The court may –

(a)   if the person responsible for the pension arrangement in question has power to determine the person to whom the sum, or any part of it, is to be paid, require him to pay the whole or part of that sum, when it becomes due, to the other party,
(b)   if the party with pension rights has power to nominate the person to whom the sum, or any part of it, is to be paid, require the party with pension rights to nominate the other party in respect of the whole or part of that sum,
(c)   in any other case, require the person responsible for the pension arrangement in question to pay the whole or part of that sum, when it becomes due, for the benefit of the other party instead of to the person to whom, apart from the order, it would be paid.

(3) Any payment by the person responsible for the arrangement under an order made under section 23 above by virtue of this section shall discharge so much of his liability in respect of the party with pension rights as corresponds to the amount of the payment.

(4) The powers conferred by this section may not be exercised in relation to a pension arrangement which –

  (a) is the subject of a pension sharing order in relation to the marriage, or
  (b) has been the subject of pension sharing between the parties to the marriage.

Amendments—Inserted by Pensions Act 1995, s 166; amended by WRPA 1999, s 21, Sch 4, para 2.

25D Pensions: supplementary

(1) Where –

  (a) an order made under section 23 above by virtue of section 25B or 25C above imposes any requirement on the person responsible for a pension arrangement ('the first arrangement') and the party with pension rights acquires rights under another pension arrangement ('the new arrangement') which are derived (directly or indirectly) from the whole of his rights under the first arrangement, and
  (b) the person responsible for the new arrangement has been given notice in accordance with regulations made by the Lord Chancellor,

the order shall have effect as if it had been made instead in respect of the person responsible for the new arrangement.

(2) The Lord Chancellor may by regulations –

  (a) in relation to any provision of sections 25B or 25C above which authorises the court making an order under section 23 above to require the person responsible for a pension arrangement to make a payment for the benefit of the other party, make provision as to the person to whom, and the terms on which, the payment is to be made,
  (ab) make, in relation to payment under a mistaken belief as to the continuation in force of a provision included by virtue of section 25B or 25C above in an order under section 23 above, provision about the rights or liabilities of the payer, the payee or the person to whom the payment was due,
  (b) require notices to be given in respect of changes of circumstances relevant to such orders which include provision made by virtue of sections 25B and 25C above,
  (ba) make provision for the person responsible for a pension arrangement to be discharged in prescribed circumstances from a requirement imposed by virtue of section 25B or 25C above,
  (c), (d) (*repealed*)
  (e) make provision about calculation and verification in relation to the valuation of –
    (i) benefits under a pension arrangement, or

(ii)   shareable state scheme rights,

for the purposes of the court's functions in connection with the exercise of any of its powers under this Part of this Act.

(2A)   Regulations under subsection (2)(e) above may include –

(a)   provision for calculation or verification in accordance with guidance from time to time prepared by a prescribed person, and

(b)   provision by reference to regulations under section 30 or 49(4) of the Welfare Reform and Pensions Act 1999.

(2B)   Regulations under subsection (2) above may make different provision for different cases.

(2C)   Power to make regulations under this section shall be exercisable by statutory instrument which shall be subject to annulment in pursuance of a resolution of either House of Parliament.

(3)   In this section and sections 25B and 25C above –

'occupational pension scheme' has the same meaning as in the Pension Schemes Act 1993;

'the party with pension rights' means the party to the marriage who has or is likely to have benefits under a pension arrangement and 'the other party' means the other party to the marriage;

'pension arrangement' means –

(a)   an occupational pension scheme,

(b)   a personal pension scheme,

(c)   a retirement annuity contract,

(d)   an annuity or insurance policy purchased, or transferred, for the purpose of giving effect to rights under an occupational pension scheme or a personal pension scheme, and

(e)   an annuity purchased, or entered into, for the purpose of discharging liability in respect of a pension credit under section 29(1)(b) of the Welfare Reform and Pensions Act 1999 or under corresponding Northern Ireland legislation;

'personal pension scheme' has the same meaning as in the Pension Schemes Act 1993;

'prescribed' means prescribed by regulations;

'retirement annuity contract' means a contract or scheme approved under Chapter III of Part XIV of the Income and Corporation Taxes Act 1988;

'shareable state scheme rights' has the same meaning as in section 21A(1) above; and

'trustees or managers', in relation to an occupational pension scheme or a personal pension scheme, means –

(a)   in the case of a scheme established under a trust, the trustees of the scheme, and

(b)   in any other case, the managers of the scheme.

(4)   In this section and sections 25B and 25C above, references to the person responsible for a pension arrangement are –

(a) in the case of an occupational pension scheme or a personal pension scheme, to the trustees or managers of the scheme,

(b) in the case of a retirement annuity contract or an annuity falling within paragraph (d) or (e) of the definition of 'pension arrangement' above, the provider of the annuity, and

(c) in the case of an insurance policy falling within paragraph (d) of the definition of that expression, the insurer.

Amendments—Inserted by Pensions Act 1995, s 166; amended by WRPA 1999, ss 21, 88, Sch 4, para 3, Sch 13, Pt II.

25E The Pension Protection Fund

(1) The matters to which the court is to have regard under section 25(2) include –

(a) in the case of paragraph (a), any PPF compensation to which a party to the marriage is or is likely to be entitled, and

(b) in the case of paragraph (h), any PPF compensation which, by reason of the dissolution or annulment of the marriage, a party to the marriage will lose the chance of acquiring entitlement to,

and, accordingly, in relation to PPF compensation, section 25(2)(a) shall have effect as if 'in the foreseeable future' were omitted.

(2) Subsection (3) applies in relation to an order under section 23 so far as it includes provision made by virtue of section 25B(4) which –

(a) imposed requirements on the trustees or managers of an occupational pension scheme for which the Board has assumed responsibility in accordance with Chapter 3 of Part 2 of the Pensions Act 2004 (pension protection) or any provision in force in Northern Ireland corresponding to that Chapter, and

(b) was made before the trustees or managers of the scheme received the transfer notice in relation to the scheme.

(3) The order is to have effect from the time when the trustees or managers of the scheme receive the transfer notice –

(a) as if, except in prescribed descriptions of case –

(i) references in the order to the trustees or managers of the scheme were references to the Board, and

(ii) references in the order to any pension or lump sum to which the party with pension rights is or may become entitled under the scheme were references to any PPF compensation to which that person is or may become entitled in respect of the pension or lump sum, and

(b) subject to such other modifications as may be prescribed.

(4) Subsection (5) applies to an order under section 23 if –

(a) it includes provision made by virtue of section 25B(7) which requires the party with pension rights to exercise his right of commutation under an occupational pension scheme to any extent, and

(b) before the requirement is complied with the Board has assumed responsibility for the scheme as mentioned in subsection (2)(a).

(5) From the time the trustees or managers of the scheme receive the transfer notice, the order is to have effect with such modifications as may be prescribed.

(6) Regulations may modify section 25C as it applies in relation to an occupational pension scheme at any time when there is an assessment period in relation to the scheme.

(7) Where the court makes a pension sharing order in respect of a person's shareable rights under an occupational pension scheme, or an order which includes provision made by virtue of section 25B(4) or (7) in relation to such a scheme, the Board subsequently assuming responsibility for the scheme as mentioned in subsection (2)(a) does not affect –

(a) the powers of the court under section 31 to vary or discharge the order or to suspend or revive any provision of it, or

(b) on an appeal, the powers of the appeal court to affirm, reinstate, set aside or vary the order.

(8) Regulations may make such consequential modifications of any provision of, or made by virtue of, this Part as appear to the Lord Chancellor necessary or expedient to give effect to the provisions of this section.

(9) In this section –

'assessment period' means an assessment period within the meaning of Part 2 of the Pensions Act 2004 (pension protection) (see sections 132 and 159 of that Act) or an equivalent period under any provision in force in Northern Ireland corresponding to that Part;

'the Board' means the Board of the Pension Protection Fund;

'occupational pension scheme' has the same meaning as in the Pension Schemes Act 1993;

'prescribed' means prescribed by regulations;

'regulations' means regulations made by the Lord Chancellor;

'shareable rights' are rights in relation to which pension sharing is available under Chapter 1 of Part 4 of the Welfare Reform and Pensions Act 1999 or any provision in force in Northern Ireland corresponding to that Chapter;

'transfer notice' has the same meaning as in section 160 of the Pensions Act 2004 or any corresponding provision in force in Northern Ireland.

(10) Any power to make regulations under this section is exercisable by statutory instrument, which shall be subject to annulment in pursuance of a resolution of either House of Parliament.

Amendments—Inserted by Pensions Act 2004, Sch 12, para 3; amended by Pensions Act 2008, Sch 6, Pt 1.

25F Attachment of pension compensation

(1) This section applies where, having regard to any PPF compensation to which a party to the marriage is or is likely to be entitled, the court determines to make an order under section 23.

(2) To the extent to which the order is made having regard to such compensation, the order may require the Board of the Pension Protection Fund, if at any time any payment in respect of PPF compensation becomes due to the party with compensation rights, to make a payment for the benefit of the other party.

(3) The order must express the amount of any payment required to be made by virtue of subsection (2) as a percentage of the payment which becomes due to the party with compensation rights.

(4) Any such payment by the Board of the Pension Protection Fund –

(a) shall discharge so much of its liability to the party with compensation rights as corresponds to the amount of the payment, and

(b) shall be treated for all purposes as a payment made by the party with compensation rights in or towards the discharge of that party's liability under the order.

(5) Where the party with compensation rights has a right to commute any PPF compensation, the order may require that party to exercise it to any extent; and this section applies to any payment due in consequence of commutation in pursuance of the order as it applies to other payments in respect of PPF compensation.

(6) The power conferred by subsection (5) may not be exercised for the purpose of commuting compensation payable to the party with compensation rights to compensation payable to the other party.

(7) The power conferred by subsection (2) or (5) may not be exercised in relation to rights to PPF compensation that –

(a) derive from rights under a pension scheme that were at any time the subject of a pension sharing order in relation to the marriage, or a previous marriage between the same parties, or

(b) are or have ever been the subject of a pension compensation sharing order in relation to the marriage or a previous marriage between the same parties.

Amendments—Inserted by Pensions Act 2008, Sch 6, Pt 1.

25G Pension compensation: supplementary

(1) The Lord Chancellor may by regulations –

(a) make provision, in relation to any provision of section 25F which authorises the court making an order under section 23 to require the

Board of the Pension Protection Fund to make a payment for the benefit of the other party, as to the person to whom, and the terms on which, the payment is to be made;

(b) make provision, in relation to payment under a mistaken belief as to the continuation in force of a provision included by virtue of section 25F in an order under section 23, about the rights or liabilities of the payer, the payee or the person to whom the payment was due;

(c) require notices to be given in respect of changes of circumstances relevant to orders under section 23 which include provision made by virtue of section 25F;

(d) make provision for the Board of the Pension Protection Fund to be discharged in prescribed circumstances from a requirement imposed by virtue of section 25F;

(e) make provision about calculation and verification in relation to the valuation of PPF compensation for the purposes of the court's functions in connection with the exercise of any of its powers under this Part.

(2) Regulations under subsection (1)(e) may include –

(a) provision for calculation or verification in accordance with guidance from time to time prepared by a prescribed person;

(b) provision by reference to regulations under section 112 of the Pensions Act 2008.

(3) Regulations under subsection (1) may make different provision for different cases.

(4) The power to make regulations under subsection (1) is exercisable by statutory instrument which shall be subject to annulment in pursuance of a resolution of either House of Parliament.

(5) In this section and section 25F –

'the party with compensation rights' means the party to the marriage who is or is likely to be entitled to PPF compensation, and 'the other party' means the other party to the marriage;
'prescribed' means prescribed by regulations.

Amendments—Inserted by Pensions Act 2008, Sch 6, Pt 1.

26 Commencement of proceedings for ancillary relief etc

(1) Where a petition for divorce, nullity of marriage or judicial separation has been presented, then, subject to subsection (2) below, proceedings for maintenance pending suit under section 22 above, for a financial provision order under section 23 above, or for a property adjustment order may be begun, subject to and in accordance with rules of court, at any time after the presentation of the petition.

(2) Rules of court may provide, in such cases as may be prescribed by the rules –

(a) that applications for any such relief as is mentioned in subsection (1) above shall be made in the petition or answer; and

(b) that applications for any such relief which are not so made, or are not made until after the expiration of such period following the presentation of the petition or filing of the answer as may be so prescribed, shall be made only with the leave of the court.

Financial provision in case of neglect to maintain

27 Financial provision orders etc in case of neglect by party to marriage to maintain other party or child of the family

(1) Either party to a marriage may apply to the court for an order under this section on the ground that the other party to the marriage (in this section referred to as the respondent) –

(a) has failed to provide reasonable maintenance for the applicant, or

(b) has failed to provide, or to make a proper contribution towards, reasonable maintenance for any child of the family.

(2) The court shall not entertain an application under this section unless –

(a) the applicant or the respondent is domiciled in England and Wales on the date of the application; or

(b) the applicant has been habitually resident there throughout the period of one year ending with that date; or

(c) the respondent is resident there on that date.

(3) Where an application under this section is made on the ground mentioned in subsection (1)(a) above then, in deciding –

(a) whether the respondent has failed to provide reasonable maintenance for the applicant, and

(b) what order, if any, to make under this section in favour of the applicant,

the court shall have regard to all the circumstances of the case including the matters mentioned in section 25(2) above, and where an application is also made under this section in respect of a child of the family who has not attained the age of eighteen, first consideration shall be given to the welfare of the child while a minor.

(3A) Where an application under this section is made on the ground mentioned in subsection (1)(b) above then, in deciding –

(a) whether the respondent has failed to provide, or to make a proper contribution towards, reasonable maintenance for the child of the family to whom the application relates, and

(b) what order, if any, to make under this section in favour of the child,

the court shall have regard to all the circumstances of the case including the matters mentioned in section 25(3)(a) to (e) above, and where the child of the family to whom the application relates is not the child of the respondent, including also the matters mentioned in section 25(4) above.

(3B)   In relation to an application under this section on the ground mentioned in subsection (1)(a) above, section 25(2)(c) above shall have effect as if for the reference therein to the breakdown of the marriage there were substituted a reference to the failure to provide reasonable maintenance for the applicant, and in relation to an application under this section on the ground mentioned in subsection (1)(b) above, section 25(2)(c) above (as it applies by virtue of section 25(3)(e) above) shall have effect as if for the reference therein to the breakdown of the marriage there were substituted a reference to the failure to provide, or to make a proper contribution towards, reasonable maintenance for the child of the family to whom the application relates.

(4) (*repealed*)

(5)   Where on an application under this section it appears to the court that the applicant or any child of the family to whom the application relates is in immediate need of financial assistance, but it is not yet possible to determine what order, if any, should be made on the application, the court may make an interim order for maintenance, that is to say, an order requiring the respondent to make to the applicant until the determination of the application such periodical payments as the court thinks reasonable.

(6)   Where on an application under this section the applicant satisfies the court of any ground mentioned in subsection (1) above, the court may make any one or more of the following orders, that is to say –

   (a)   an order that the respondent shall make to the applicant such periodical payments, for such term, as may be specified in the order;
   (b)   an order that the respondent shall secure to the applicant, to the satisfaction of the court, such periodical payments, for such term, as may be so specified;
   (c)   an order that the respondent shall pay to the applicant such lump sum as may be so specified;
   (d)   an order that the respondent shall make to such person as may be specified in the order for the benefit of the child to whom the application relates, or to that child, such periodical payments, for such term, as may be so specified;
   (e)   an order that the respondent shall secure to such person as may be so specified for the benefit of that child, or to that child, to the satisfaction of the court, such periodical payments, for such term, as may be so specified;
   (f)   an order that the respondent shall pay to such person as may be so specified for the benefit of that child, or to that child, such lump sum as may be so specified;

subject, however, in the case of an order under paragraph (d), (e) or (f) above, to the restrictions imposed by section 29(1) and (3) below on the making of financial provision orders in favour of children who have attained the age of eighteen.

(6A) An application for the variation under section 31 of this Act of a periodical payments order or secured periodical payments order made under this section in favour of a child may, if the child has attained the age of sixteen, be made by the child himself.

(6B) Where a periodical payments order made in favour of a child under this section ceases to have effect on the date on which the child attains the age of sixteen or at any time after that date but before or on the date on which he attains the age of eighteen, then, if at any time before he attains the age of twenty-one an application is made by the child for an order under this subsection, the court shall have power by order to revive the first-mentioned order from such date as the court may specify, not being earlier than the date of the making of the application, and to exercise its powers under section 31 of this Act in relation to any order so revived.

(7) Without prejudice to the generality of subsection (6)(c) or (f) above, an order under this section for the payment of a lump sum–

(a) may be made for the purpose of enabling any liabilities or expenses reasonably incurred in maintaining the applicant or any child of the family to whom the application relates before the making of the application to be met;

(b) may provide for the payment of that sum by instalments of such amount as may be specified in the order and may require the payment of the instalments to be secured to the satisfaction of the court.

(8) *(repealed)*

Amendments—DMPA 1973, s 6(1); DPMCA 1978, ss 63, 89(2)(*b*), Sch 3; MFPA 1984, ss 4, 46(1), Sch 1, para 12; FLRA 1987, s 33(1), Sch 2, para 52.

Additional provisions with respect to financial provision and property adjustment orders

28 Duration of continuing financial provision orders in favour of party to marriage, and effect of remarriage or formation of civil partnership

(1) Subject in the case of an order made on or after the grant of a decree of a divorce or nullity of marriage to the provisions of sections 25A(2) above and 31(7) below, the term to be specified in a periodical payments or secured periodical payments order in favour of a party to a marriage shall be such term as the court thinks fit, except that the term shall not begin before or extend beyond the following limits, that is to say –

(a) in the case of a periodical payments order, the term shall begin not earlier than the date of the making of an application for the order, and shall be so defined as not to extend beyond the death of either of the parties to the marriage or, where the order is made on or after the grant of a decree of divorce or nullity of marriage, the remarriage of, or formation of a civil partnership by, the party in whose favour the order is made; and

(b)   in the case of a secured periodical payments order, the term shall begin not earlier than the date of the making of an application for the order, and shall be so defined as not to extend beyond the death or, where the order is made on or after the grant of such a decree, the remarriage of, or formation of a civil partnership by, the party in whose favour the order is made.

(1A)   Where a periodical payments or secured periodical payments order in favour of a party to a marriage is made on or after the grant of a decree of divorce or nullity of marriage, the court may direct that that party shall not be entitled to apply under section 31 below for the extension of the term specified in the order.

(2)   Where a periodical payments or secured periodical payments order in favour of a party to a marriage is made otherwise than on or after the grant of a decree of divorce or nullity of marriage, and the marriage in question is subsequently dissolved or annulled but the order continues in force, the order shall, notwithstanding anything in it, cease to have effect on the remarriage of, or formation of a civil partnership by, that party, except in relation to any arrears due under it on the date of the remarriage or formation of the civil partnership.

(3)   If after the grant of a decree dissolving or annulling a marriage either party to that marriage remarries whether at any time before or after the commencement of this Act or forms a civil partnership, that party shall not be entitled to apply, by reference to the grant of that decree, for a financial provision order in his or her favour, or for a property adjustment order, against the other party to that marriage.

Amendments—MFPA 1984, s 5; CPA 2004, s 261(1), Sch 27, para 43(1)–(5).

29 Duration of continuing financial provision orders in favour of children, and age limit on making certain orders in their favour

(1) Subject to subsection (3) below, no financial provision order and no order for a transfer of property under section 24(1)(*a*) above shall be made in favour of a child who has attained the age of eighteen.

(2) The term to be specified in a periodical payments or secured periodical payments order in favour of a child may begin with the date of the making of an application for the order in question or any later date or a date ascertained in accordance with subsection (5) or (6) below but –

(a)   shall not in the first instance extend beyond the date of the birthday of the child next following his attaining the upper limit of the compulsory school age (construed in accordance with section 8 of the Education Act 1996) unless the court considers that in the circumstances of the case the welfare of the child requires that it should extend to a later date; and

(b)   shall not in any event, subject to subsection (3) below, extend beyond the date of the child's eighteenth birthday.

(3) Subsection (1) above, and paragraph (*b*) of subsection (2), shall not apply in the case of a child, if it appears to the court that –

(a)   the child is, or will be, or if an order were made without complying with either or both of those provisions would be, receiving instruction at an educational establishment or undergoing training for a trade, profession or vocation, whether or not he is also, or will also be, in gainful employment; or

(b)   there are special circumstances which justify the making of an order without complying with either or both of those provisions.

(4) Any periodical payments order in favour of a child shall, notwithstanding anything in the order, cease to have effect on the death of the person liable to make payments under the order, except in relation to any arrears due under the order on the date of the death.

(5) Where –

(a)   a maintenance calculation ('the current calculation') is in force with respect to a child; and

(b)   an application is made under Part II of this Act for a periodical payments or secured periodical payments order in favour of that child –

(i)   in accordance with section 8 of the Child Support Act 1991, and

(ii)   before the end of the period of 6 months beginning with the making of the current calculation,

the term to be specified in any such order made on that application may be expressed to begin on, or at any time after, the earliest permitted date.

(6) For the purposes of subsection (5) above, 'the earliest permitted date' is whichever is the later of –

(a)   the date 6 months before the application is made; or

(b)   the date on which the current calculation took effect or, where successive maintenance calculations have been continuously in force with respect to a child, on which the first of those calculations took effect.

(7) Where –

(a)   a maintenance calculation ceases to have effect by or under any provision of the Child Support Act 1991; and

(b)   an application is made, before the end of the period of 6 months beginning with the relevant date, for a periodical payments or secured periodical payments order in favour of a child with respect to whom that maintenance calculation was in force immediately before it ceased to have effect,

the term to be specified in any such order made on that application may begin with the date on which that maintenance calculation ceased to have effect, or any later date.

(8) In subsection (7)(*b*) above, –

(a)   where the maintenance calculation ceased to have effect, the relevant date is the date on which it so ceased;

(b)   (*repealed*)

Amendments—MFPA 1984, s 5; SI 1993/623; Education Act 1996, s 582(1), Sch 37, para 136; CSPSSA 2000, ss 26, 85, Sch 3, para 3, Sch 9.

30   Direction for settlement of instrument for securing payments or effecting property adjustment

Where the court decides to make a financial provision order requiring any payments to be secured or a property adjustment order –

(a)   it may direct that the matter be referred to one of the conveyancing counsel of the court for him to settle a proper instrument to be executed by all necessary parties; and

(b)   where the order is to be made in proceedings for divorce, nullity of marriage or judicial separation it may, if it thinks fit, defer the grant of the decree in question until the instrument has been duly executed.

Variation, discharge and enforcement of certain orders etc

31 Variation, discharge etc of certain orders for financial relief

(1) Where the court has made an order to which this section applies, then, subject to the provisions of this section and of section 28(1A) above, the court shall have power to vary or discharge the order or to suspend any provision thereof temporarily and to revive the operation of any provision so suspended.

(2) This section applies to the following orders, that is to say –

(a)   any order for maintenance pending suit and any interim order for maintenance;

(b)   any periodical payments order;

(c)   any secured periodical payments order;

(d)   any order made by virtue of section 23(3)(*c*) or 27(7)(*b*) above (provision for payment of a lump sum by instalments);

(dd) any deferred order made by virtue of section 23(1)(*c*) (lump sums) which includes provision made by virtue of –
       (i)   section 25B(4),
       (ii) section 25C, or
       (iii) section 25F(2),
(provision in respect of pension rights or pension compensation rights);

(e)   any order for a settlement of property under section 24(1)(*b*) or for a variation of settlement under section 24(1)(*c*) or (*d*) above, being an order made on or after the grant of a decree of judicial separation;

(f)   any order made under section 24A(1) above for the sale of property.

(g)   a pension sharing order under section 24B above or a pension compensation sharing order under section 24E above which is made at a time before the decree has been made absolute.

(2A) Where the court has made an order referred to in subsection (2)(*a*), (*b*) or (*c*) above, then, subject to the provisions of this section, the court shall have power to remit the payment of any arrears due under the order or of any part thereof.

(2B) Where the court has made an order referred to in subsection (2)(*dd*)(ii) above, this section shall cease to apply to the order on the death of either of the parties to the marriage.

(3) The powers exercisable by the court under this section in relation to an order shall be exercisable also in relation to any instrument executed in pursuance of the order.

(4) The court shall not exercise the powers conferred by this section in relation to an order for a settlement under section 24(1)(*b*) or for a variation of settlement under section 24(1)(*c*) or (*d*) above except on an application made in proceedings –

(a)   for the rescission of the decree of judicial separation by reference to which the order was made, or
(b)   for the dissolution of the marriage in question.

(4A) In relation to an order which falls within paragraph (*g*) of subsection (2) above ('the subsection (2) order') –

(a)   the powers conferred by this section may be exercised –
    (i)   only on an application made before the subsection (2) order has or, but for paragraph (*b*) below, would have taken effect; and
    (ii)   only if, at the time when the application is made, the decree has not been made absolute; and
(b)   an application made in accordance with paragraph (*a*) above prevents the subsection (2) order from taking effect before the application has been dealt with.

(4B) No variation of a pension sharing order, or a pension compensation sharing order, shall be made so as to take effect before the decree is made absolute.

(4C) The variation of a pension sharing order, or a pension compensation sharing order, prevents the order taking effect before the end of such period after the making of the variation as may be prescribed by regulations made by the Lord Chancellor.

(5) Subject to subsections (7A) to (7G) below and without prejudice to any power exercisable by virtue of subsection (2)(*d*), (*dd*), (*e*) or (*g*) above or otherwise than by virtue of this section, no property adjustment order or pension sharing order, or pension compensation sharing order shall be made on an application for the variation of a periodical payments or secured periodical payments order made (whether in favour of a party to a marriage or in favour of a child of the family) under section 23 above, and no order for the payment of a lump sum shall be made on an application for the variation of a periodical payments or secured periodical payments order in favour of a party to a marriage (whether made under section 23 or under section 27 above).

(6) Where the person liable to make payments under a secured periodical payments order has died, an application under this section relating to that order (and to any order made under section 24A(1) above which requires the proceeds of sale of property to be used for securing those payments) may be made by the person entitled to payments under the periodical payments order or by the personal representatives of the deceased person, but no such application shall, except with the permission of the court, be made after the end of the period of six months from the date on which representation in regard to the estate of that person is first taken out.

(7) In exercising the powers conferred by this section the court shall have regard to all the circumstances of the case, first consideration being given to the welfare while a minor of any child of the family who has not attained the age of eighteen, and the circumstances of the case shall include any change in any of the matters to which the court was required to have regard when making the order to which the application relates, and –

   (a)   in the case of a periodical payments or secured periodical payments order made on or after the grant of a decree of divorce or nullity of marriage, the court shall consider whether in all the circumstances and after having regard to any such change it would be appropriate to vary the order so that payments under the order are required to be made or secured only for such further period as will in the opinion of the court be sufficient (in the light of any proposed exercise by the court, where the marriage has been dissolved, of its powers under subsection (7B) below) to enable the party in whose favour the order was made to adjust without undue hardship to the termination of those payments;

   (b)   in a case where the party against whom the order was made has died, the circumstances of the case shall also include the changed circumstances resulting from his or her death.

(7A) Subsection (7B) below applies where, after the dissolution of a marriage, the court –

   (a)   discharges a periodical payments order or secured periodical payments order made in favour of a party to the marriage; or

   (b)   varies such an order so that payments under the order are required to be made or secured only for such further period as is determined by the court.

(7B) The court has power, in addition to any power it has apart from this subsection, to make supplemental provision consisting of any of –

   (a)   an order for the payment of a lump sum in favour of a party to the marriage;

   (b)   one or more property adjustment orders in favour of a party to the marriage;

   (ba) one or more pension sharing orders;

   (bb) a pension compensation sharing order;

(c)   a direction that the party in whose favour the original order discharged or varied was made is not entitled to make any further application for –
(i)   a periodical payments or secured periodical payments order, or
(ii)   an extension of the period to which the original order is limited by any variation made by the court.

(7C) An order for the payment of a lump sum made under subsection (7B) above may –

(a)   provide for the payment of that sum by instalments of such amount as may be specified in the order; and
(b)   require the payment of the instalments to be secured to the satisfaction of the court.

(7D) Section 23(6) above applies where the court makes an order for the payment of a lump sum under subsection (7B) above as it applies where the court makes such an order under section 23 above.

(7E) If under subsection (7B) above the court makes more than one property adjustment order in favour of the same party to the marriage, each of those orders must fall within a different paragraph of section 21(2) above.

(7F) Sections 24A and 30 above apply where the court makes a property adjustment order under subsection (7B) above as they apply where it makes such an order under section 24 above.

(7G) Subsections (3) to (5) of section 24B above apply in relation to a pension sharing order under subsection (7B) above as they apply in relation to a pension sharing order under that section.

(7H) Subsections (3) to (10) of section 24E above apply in relation to a pension compensation sharing order under subsection (7B) above as they apply in relation to a pension compensation sharing order under that section.

(8) The personal representatives of a deceased person against whom a secured periodical payments order was made shall not be liable for having distributed any part of the estate of the deceased after the expiration of the period of six months referred to in subsection (6) above on the ground that they ought to have taken into account the possibility that the court might permit an application under this section to be made after that period by the person entitled to payments under the order; but this subsection shall not prejudice any power to recover any part of the estate so distributed arising by virtue of the making of an order in pursuance of this section.

(9) In considering for the purposes of subsection (6) above the question when representation was first taken out, a grant limited to settled land or to trust property shall be left out of account and a grant limited to real estate or to personal estate shall be left out of account unless a grant limited to the remainder of the estate has previously been made or is made at the same time.

(10) Where the court, in exercise of its powers under this section, decides to vary or discharge a periodical payments or secured periodical payments order,

then, subject to section 28(1) and (2) above, the court shall have power to direct that the variation or discharge shall not take effect until the expiration of such period as may be specified in the order.

(11) Where –

(a)   a periodical payments or secured periodical payments order in favour of more than one child ('the order') is in force;

(b)   the order requires payments specified in it to be made to or for the benefit of more than one child without apportioning those payments between them;

(c)   a maintenance calculation ('the calculation') is made with respect to one or more, but not all, of the children with respect to whom those payments are to be made; and

(d)   an application is made, before the end of the period of 6 months beginning with the date on which the assessment was made, for the variation or discharge of the order,

the court may, in exercise of its powers under this section to vary or discharge the order, direct that the variation or discharge shall take effect from the date on which the calculation took effect or any later date.

(12) Where –

(a)   an order ('the child order') of a kind prescribed for the purposes of section 10(1) of the Child Support Act 1991 is affected by a maintenance calculation;

(b)   on the date on which the child order became so affected there was in force a periodical payments or secured periodical payments order ('the spousal order') in favour of a party to a marriage having the care of the child in whose favour the child order was made; and

(c)   an application is made, before the end of the period of 6 months beginning with the date on which the maintenance calculation was made, for the spousal order to be varied or discharged,

the court may, in exercise of its powers under this section to vary or discharge the spousal order, direct that the variation or discharge shall take effect from the date on which the child order became so affected or any later date.

(13) For the purposes of subsection (12) above, an order is affected if it ceases to have effect or is modified by or under section 10 of the Child Support Act 1991.

(14) Subsections (11) and (12) above are without prejudice to any other power of the court to direct that the variation of discharge of an order under this section shall take effect from a date earlier than that on which the order for variation or discharge was made.

(15) The power to make regulations under subsection (4C) above shall be exercisable by statutory instrument which shall be subject to annulment in pursuance of a resolution of either House of Parliament.

Amendments—Matrimonial Homes and Property Act 1981, s 8(2); AJA 1982, s 51; MFPA 1984, s 6; SI 1993/623; Pensions Act 1995, s 166; FLA 1996, Sch 8, para 16(5)(*a*), (6)(*b*), (7) (as modified by SI 1998/2572); WRPA 1999, s 19, Sch 3, para 7; CSPSSA 2000, s 26, Sch 3, para 3; Pensions Act 2008, Sch 6, Pt 1.

32 Payment of certain arrears unenforceable without the leave of the court

(1) A person shall not be entitled to enforce through the High Court or any county court the payment of any arrears due under an order for maintenance pending suit, an interim order for maintenance or any financial provision order without the leave of that court if those arrears became due more than twelve months before proceedings to enforce the payment of them are begun.

(2) The court hearing an application for the grant of leave under this section may refuse leave, or may grant leave subject to such restrictions and conditions (including conditions as to the allowing of time for payment or the making of payment by instalments) as that court thinks proper, or may remit the payment of the arrears or of any part thereof.

(3) An application for the grant of leave under this section shall be made in such manner as may be prescribed by rules of court.

33 Orders for repayment in certain cases of sums paid under certain orders

(1) Where on an application made under this section in relation to an order to which this section applies it appears to the court that by reason of –

(a) a change in the circumstances of the person entitled to, or liable to make, payments under the order since the order was made, or

(b) the changed circumstances resulting from the death of the person so liable,

the amount received by the person entitled to payments under the order in respect of a period after those circumstances changed or after the death of the person liable to make payments under the order, as the case may be, exceeds the amount which the person so liable or his or her personal representatives should have been required to pay, the court may order the respondent to the application to pay to the applicant such sum, not exceeding the amount of the excess, as the court thinks just.

(2) This section applies to the following orders, that is to say –

(a) any order for maintenance pending suit and any interim order for maintenance;

(b) any periodical payments order; and

(c) any secured periodical payments order.

(3) An application under this section may be made by the person liable to make payments under an order to which this section applies or his or her personal representatives and may be made against the person entitled to payments under the order or her or his personal representatives.

(4) An application under this section may be made in proceedings in the High Court or a county court for –

(a) the variation or discharge of the order to which this section applies, or

(b) leave to enforce, or the enforcement of, the payment of arrears under that order;

but when not made in such proceedings shall be made to a county court, and accordingly references in this section to the court are references to the High Court or a county court, as the circumstances require.

(5) The jurisdiction conferred on a county court by this section shall be exercisable notwithstanding that by reason of the amount claimed in the application the jurisdiction would not but for this subsection be exercisable by a county court.

(6) An order under this section for the payment of any sum may provide for the payment of that sum by instalments of such amount as may be specified in the order.

Consent orders

33A Consent orders for financial provision on property adjustment

(1) Notwithstanding anything in the preceding provisions of this Part of this Act, on an application for a consent order for financial relief the court may, unless it has reason to think that there are other circumstances into which it ought to inquire, make an order in the terms agreed on the basis only of the prescribed information furnished with the application.

(2) Subsection (1) above applies to an application for a consent order varying or discharging an order for financial relief as it applies to an application for an order for financial relief.

(3) In this section –

'consent order', in relation to an application for an order, means an order in the terms applied for to which the respondent agrees;

'order for financial relief' means an order under any of sections 23, 24, 24A, 24B or 27 above; and

'prescribed' means prescribed by rules of court.

Maintenance agreements

34 Validity of maintenance agreements

(1) If a maintenance agreement includes a provision purporting to restrict any right to apply to a court for an order containing financial arrangements, then –

(a) that provision shall be void; but

(b) any other financial arrangements contained in the agreement shall not thereby be rendered void or unenforceable and shall, unless they are void or unenforceable for any other reason (and subject to sections 35 and 36 below), be binding on the parties to the agreement.

(2) In this section and in section 35 below –

'maintenance agreement' means any agreement in writing made, whether before or after the commencement of this Act, between the parties to a marriage, being –

    (a)   an agreement containing financial arrangements, whether made during the continuance or after the dissolution or annulment of the marriage; or

    (b)   a separation agreement which contains no financial arrangements in a case where no other agreement in writing between the same parties contains such arrangements;

'financial arrangements' means provisions governing the rights and liabilities towards one another when living separately of the parties to a marriage (including a marriage which has been dissolved or annulled) in respect of the making or securing of payments or the disposition or use of any property, including such rights and liabilities with respect to the maintenance or education of any child, whether or not a child of the family.

35   Alteration of agreements by court during lives of parties

(1)   Where a maintenance agreement is for the time being subsisting and each of the parties to the agreement is for the time being either domiciled or resident in England and Wales, then, subject to subsection (3) below, either party may apply to the court or to a magistrates' court for an order under this section.

(2)   If the court to which the application is made is satisfied either –

    (a)   that by reason of a change in the circumstances in the light of which any financial arrangements contained in the agreement were made or, as the case may be, financial arrangements were omitted from it (including a change foreseen by the parties when making the agreement), the agreement should be altered so as to make different, or, as the case may be, so as to contain, financial arrangements, or

    (b)   that the agreement does not contain proper financial arrangements with respect to any child of the family,

then subject to subsections (3), (4) and (5) below, that court may by order make such alterations in the agreement –

    (i)   by varying or revoking any financial arrangements contained in it, or

    (ii)   by inserting in it financial arrangements for the benefit of one of the parties to the agreement or of a child of the family,

as may appear to that court to be just having regard to all the circumstances, including, if relevant, the matters mentioned in section 25(4) above; and the agreement shall have effect thereafter as if any alteration made by the order had been made by agreement between the parties and for valuable consideration.

(3)   A magistrates' court shall not entertain an application under subsection (1) above unless both the parties to the agreement are resident in England and Wales the court acts in, or is authorised by the Lord Chancellor to act for, a

local justice area in which at least one of the parties is resident, and shall not have power to make any order on such an application except –

(a)   in a case where the agreement includes no provision for periodical payments by either of the parties, an order inserting provision for the making by one of the parties of periodical payments for the maintenance of the other party or for the maintenance of any child of the family;

(b)   in a case where the agreement includes provision for the making by one of the parties of periodical payments, an order increasing or reducing the rate of, or terminating, any of those payments.

(4)   Where a court decides to alter, by order under this section, an agreement by inserting provision for the making or securing by one of the parties to the agreement of periodical payments for the maintenance of the other party or by increasing the rate of the periodical payments which the agreement provides shall be made by one of the parties for the maintenance of the other, the term for which the payments or, as the case may be, the additional payments attributable to the increase are to be made under the agreement as altered by the order shall be such term as the court may specify, subject to the following limits, that is to say –

(a)   where the payments will not be secured, the term shall be so defined as not to extend beyond the death of either of the parties to the agreement or the remarriage of, or formation of a civil partnership by, the party to whom the payments are to be made;

(b)   where the payments will be secured, the term shall be so defined as not to extend beyond the death or remarriage of, or formation of a civil partnership by, that party.

(5)   Where a court decides to alter, by order under this section, an agreement by inserting provision for the making or securing by one of the parties to the agreement of periodical payments for the maintenance of a child of the family or by increasing the rate of the periodical payments which the agreement provides shall be made or secured by one of the parties for the maintenance of such a child, then, in deciding the term for which under the agreement as altered by the order the payments, or as the case may be, the additional payments attributable to the increase are to be made or secured for the benefit of the child, the court shall apply the provisions of section 29(2) and (3) above as to age limits as if the order in question were a periodical payments or secured periodical payments order in favour of the child.

(6)   For the avoidance of doubt it is hereby declared that nothing in this section or in section 34 above affects any power of a court before which any proceedings between the parties to a maintenance agreement are brought under any other enactment (including a provision of this Act) to make an order containing financial arrangements or any right of either party to apply for such an order in such proceedings.

Amendments—MFPA 1984, s 46(1), Sch 1, para 13; Justices of the Peace Act 1997, s 73(2), Sch 5, para 14; AJA 1999, s 106, Sch 15; CPA 2004, s 261(1), Sch 27, para 44; Courts Act 2003, Sch 8, para 169.

36 Alteration of agreements by court after death of one party

(1)   Where a maintenance agreement within the meaning of section 34 above provides for the continuation of payments under the agreement after the death of one of the parties and that party dies domiciled in England and Wales, the surviving party or the personal representatives of the deceased party may, subject to subsections (2) and (3) below, apply to the High Court or a county court for an order under section 35 above.

(2)   An application under this section shall not, except with the permission of the High Court or a county court, be made after the end of the period of six months from the date on which representation in regard to the estate of the deceased is first taken out.

(3)   A county court shall not entertain an application under this section, or an application for permission to make an application under this section, unless it would have jurisdiction by virtue of section 22 of the Inheritance (Provision for Family and Dependants) Act 1975 (which confers jurisdiction on county courts in proceedings under that Act if the value of the property mentioned in that section does not exceed £5,000 or such larger sum as may be fixed by order of the Lord Chancellor) to hear and determine proceedings for an order under section 2 of that Act in relation to the deceased's estate.

(4)   If a maintenance agreement is altered by a court on an application made in pursuance of subsection (1) above, the like consequences shall ensue as if the alteration had been made immediately before the death by agreement between the parties and for valuable consideration.

(5)   The provisions of this section shall not render the personal representatives of the deceased liable for having distributed any part of the estate of the deceased after the expiration of the period of six months referred to in subsection (2) above on the ground that they ought to have taken into account the possibility that a court might permit an application by virtue of this section to be made by the surviving party after that period; but this subsection shall not prejudice any power to recover any part of the estate so distributed arising by virtue of the making of an order in pursuance of this section.

(6)   Section 31(9) above shall apply for the purposes of subsection (2) above as it applies for the purposes of subsection (6) of section 31.

(7)   Subsection (3) of section 22 of the Inheritance (Provision for Family and Dependants) Act 1975 (which enables rules of court to provide for the transfer from a county court to the High Court or from the High Court to a county court of proceedings for an order under section 2 of that Act) and paragraphs (a) and (b) of subsection (4) of that section (provisions relating to proceedings commenced in county court before coming into force of order of the Lord Chancellor under that section) shall apply in relation to proceedings

consisting of any such application as is referred to in subsection (3) above as they apply in relation to proceedings for an order under section 2 of that Act.

Amendments—I(PFD)A 1975, s 26(1).

Miscellaneous and supplemental

37 Avoidance of transactions intended to prevent or reduce financial relief

(1)   For the purposes of this section 'financial relief' means relief under any of the provisions of sections 22, 23, 24, 24B, 27, 31 (except subsection (6)) and 35 above, and any reference in this section to defeating a person's claim for financial relief is a reference to preventing financial relief from being granted to that person, or to that person for the benefit of a child of the family, or reducing the amount of any financial relief which might be so granted, or frustrating or impeding the enforcement of any order which might be or has been made at his instance under any of those provisions.

(2)   Where proceedings for financial relief are brought by one person against another, the court may, on the application of the first-mentioned person –

(a)   if it is satisfied that the other party to the proceedings is, with the intention of defeating the claim for financial relief, about to make any disposition or to transfer out of the jurisdiction or otherwise deal with any property, make such order as it thinks fit for restraining the other party from so doing or otherwise for protecting the claim;

(b)   if it is satisfied that the other party has, with that intention, made a reviewable disposition and that if the disposition were set aside financial relief or different financial relief would be granted to the applicant, make an order setting aside the disposition;

(c)   if it is satisfied, in a case where an order has been obtained under any of the provisions mentioned in subsection (1) above by the applicant against the other party, that the other party has, with that intention, made a reviewable disposition, make an order setting aside the disposition;

and an application for the purposes of paragraph (b) above shall be made in the proceedings for the financial relief in question.

(3)   Where the court makes an order under subsection (2)(b) or (c) above setting aside a disposition it shall give such consequential directions as it thinks fit for giving effect to the order (including directions requiring the making of any payments or the disposal of any property).

(4)   Any disposition made by the other party to the proceedings for financial relief in question (whether before or after the commencement of those proceedings) is a reviewable disposition for the purposes of subsection (2)(b) and (c) above unless it was made for valuable consideration (other than marriage) to a person who, at the time of the disposition, acted in relation to it in good faith and without notice of any intention on the part of the other party to defeat the applicant's claim for financial relief.

(5)   Where an application is made under this section with respect to a disposition which took place less than three years before the date of the application or with respect to a disposition or other dealing with property which is about to take place and the court is satisfied –

(a)   in a case falling within subsection (2)(a) or (b) above, that the disposition or other dealing would (apart from this section) have the consequence, or

(b)   in a case falling within subsection (2)(c) above, that the disposition has had the consequence,

of defeating the applicant's claim for financial relief, it shall be presumed, unless the contrary is shown, that the person who disposed of or is about to dispose of or deal with the property did so or, as the case may be, is about to do so, with the intention of defeating the applicant's claim for financial relief.

(6)   In this section 'disposition' does not include any provision contained in a will or codicil but, with that exception, includes any conveyance, assurance or gift of property of any description, whether made by an instrument or otherwise.

(7)   This section does not apply to a disposition made before 1st January 1968.

Amendments—WRPA 1999, s 19, Sch 3, para 9.

38   Orders for repayment in certain cases of sums paid after cessation of order by reason of remarriage or formation of civil partnership

(1)   Where –

(a)   a periodical payments or secured periodical payments order in favour of a party to a marriage (hereafter in this section referred to as 'a payments order') has ceased to have effect by reason of the remarriage of, or formation of a civil partnership by, that party, and

(b)   the person liable to make payments under the order or his or her personal representatives made payments in accordance with it in respect of a period after the date of the remarriage or formation of the civil partnership in the mistaken belief that the order was still subsisting,

the person so liable or his or her personal representatives shall not be entitled to bring proceedings in respect of a cause of action arising out of the circumstances mentioned in paragraphs (a) and (b) above against the person entitled to payments under the order or her or his personal representatives, but may instead make an application against that person or her or his personal representatives under this section.

(2)   On an application under this section the court may order the respondent to pay to the applicant a sum equal to the amount of the payments made in respect of the period mentioned in subsection (1)(b) above or, if it appears to the court that it would be unjust to make that order, it may either order the respondent to pay to the applicant such lesser sum as it thinks fit or dismiss the application.

(3)   An application under this section may be made in proceedings in the High Court or a county court for leave to enforce, or the enforcement of, payment of arrears under the order in question, but when not made in such proceedings shall be made to a county court; and accordingly references in this section to the court are references to the High Court or a county court, as the circumstances require.

(4)   The jurisdiction conferred on a county court by this section shall be exercisable notwithstanding that by reason of the amount claimed in the application the jurisdiction would not but for this subsection be exercisable by a county court.

(5)   An order under this section for the payment of any sum may provide for the payment of that sum by instalments of such amount as may be specified in the order.

(6)   The designated officer for a magistrates' court to whom any payments under a payments order are required to be made, and the collecting officer under an attachment of earnings order made to secure payments under a payments order, shall not be liable –

(a)   in the case of the designated officer, for any act done by him in pursuance of the payments order after the date on which that order ceased to have effect by reason of the remarriage of, or formation of a civil partnership by, the person entitled to payments under it, and

(b)   in the case of the collecting officer, for any act done by him after that date in accordance with any enactment or rule of court specifying how payments made to him in compliance with the attachment of earnings order are to be dealt with,

if, but only if, the act was one which he would have been under a duty to do had the payments order not so ceased to have effect and the act was done before notice in writing of the fact that the person so entitled had remarried or formed a civil partnership was given to him by or on behalf of that person, the person liable to make payments under the payments order or the personal representatives of either of those persons.

(7)   In this section 'collecting officer', in relation to an attachment of earnings order, means the officer of the High Court, the district judge of a county court or the designated officer for a magistrates' court to whom a person makes payments in compliance with the order.

Amendments—AJA 1999, s 90, Sch 13, para 82; CPA 2004, s 261(1), Sch 27, para 43(1)–(4); Courts Act 2003, Sch 8, para 170.

39   Settlement etc made in compliance with a property adjustment order may be avoided on bankruptcy of settlor

The fact that a settlement or transfer of property had to be made in order to comply with a property adjustment order shall not prevent that settlement or transfer from being a transaction in respect of which an order may be made under section 339 or 340 of the Insolvency Act 1986 (transfers at an undervalue and preferences).

Amendments—Insolvency Act 1985, s 235(1), Sch 8, para 23; Insolvency Act 1986, s 439(2), Sch 14.

40 Payments etc under order made in favour of person suffering from mental disorder

(1) Where the court makes an order under this Part of this Act requiring payments (including a lump sum payment) to be made, or property to be transferred, to a party to a marriage and the court is satisfied that the person in whose favour the order is made ('P') lacks capacity (within the meaning of the Mental Capacity Act 2005) in relation to the provisions of the order then, subject to any order, direction or authority made or given in relation to P under that Act, the court may order the payments to be made, or as the case may be, the property to be transferred, to such person ('D') as it may direct.

(2) In carrying out any functions of his in relation to an order made under subsection (1), D must act in P's best interests (within the meaning of that Act).

Amendments—MCA 2005, s 67(1), Sch 6, para 19.

40A Appeals relating to pension sharing orders which have taken effect

(1) Subsections (2) and (3) below apply where an appeal against a pension sharing order is begun on or after the day on which the order takes effect.

(2) If the pension sharing order relates to a person's rights under a pension arrangement, the appeal court may not set aside or vary the order if the person responsible for the pension arrangement has acted to his detriment in reliance on the taking effect of the order.

(3) If the pension sharing order relates to a person's shareable state scheme rights, the appeal court may not set aside or vary the order if the Secretary of State has acted to his detriment in reliance on the taking effect of the order.

(4) In determining for the purposes of subsection (2) or (3) above whether a person has acted to his detriment in reliance on the taking effect of the order, the appeal court may disregard any detriment which in its opinion is insignificant.

(5) Where subsection (2) or (3) above applies, the appeal court may make such further orders (including one or more pension sharing orders) as it thinks fit for the purpose of putting the parties in the position it considers appropriate.

(6) Section 24C above only applies to a pension sharing order under this section if the decision of the appeal court can itself be the subject of an appeal.

(7) In subsection (2) above, the reference to the person responsible for the pension arrangement is to be read in accordance with section 25D(4) above.

Amendments—Inserted by WRPA 1999, s 19, Sch 3, para 10.

40B Appeals relating to pension compensation sharing orders which have taken effect

(1) This section applies where an appeal against a pension compensation sharing order is begun on or after the day on which the order takes effect.

(2) If the Board of the Pension Protection Fund has acted to its detriment in reliance on the taking effect of the order the appeal court –

    (a)   may not set aside or vary the order;

    (b)   may make such further orders (including a pension compensation sharing order) as it thinks fit for the purpose of putting the parties in the position it considers appropriate.

(3) In determining for the purposes of subsection (2) whether the Board has acted to its detriment the appeal court may disregard any detriment which in the court's opinion is insignificant.

(4) Section 24F (duty to stay) only applies to a pension compensation sharing order under this section if the decision of the appeal court can itself be the subject of an appeal.

Amendments—Inserted by Pensions Act 2008, Sch 6, Pt 1.

****

FAMILY PROCEDURE RULES 2010

SI 2010/2955

PART 1
OVERRIDING OBJECTIVE

1.1 The overriding objective

(1) These rules are a new procedural code with the overriding objective of enabling the court to deal with cases justly, having regard to any welfare issues involved.

(2) Dealing with a case justly includes, so far as is practicable –

    (a)   ensuring that it is dealt with expeditiously and fairly;

    (b)   dealing with the case in ways which are proportionate to the nature, importance and complexity of the issues;

    (c)   ensuring that the parties are on an equal footing;

    (d)   saving expense; and

    (e)   allotting to it an appropriate share of the court's resources, while taking into account the need to allot resources to other cases.

1.2 Application by the court of the overriding objective

The court must seek to give effect to the overriding objective when it –

(a)   exercises any power given to it by these rules; or

(b)   interprets any rule.

1.3 Duty of the parties

The parties are required to help the court to further the overriding objective.

1.4 Court's duty to manage cases

(1) The court must further the overriding objective by actively managing cases.

(2) Active case management includes –

(a)   encouraging the parties to co-operate with each other in the conduct of the proceedings;

(b)   identifying at an early stage –

    (i)   the issues; and

    (ii)   who should be a party to the proceedings;

(c)   deciding promptly –

    (i)   which issues need full investigation and hearing and which do not; and

    (ii)   the procedure to be followed in the case;

(d)   deciding the order in which issues are to be resolved;

(e)   encouraging the parties to use an alternative dispute resolution procedure if the court considers that appropriate and facilitating the use of such procedure;

(f)   helping the parties to settle the whole or part of the case;

(g)   fixing timetables or otherwise controlling the progress of the case;

(h)   considering whether the likely benefits of taking a particular step justify the cost of taking it;

(i)   dealing with as many aspects of the case as it can on the same occasion;

(j)   dealing with the case without the parties needing to attend at court;

(k)   making use of technology; and

(l)   giving directions to ensure that the case proceeds quickly and efficiently.

PART 2
APPLICATION AND INTERPRETATION OF THE RULES

2.1 Application of these Rules

(1) Unless the context otherwise requires, these Rules apply to family proceedings in –

(a)   the High Court;

(b)   a county court; and

(c)   a magistrates' court.

(2) Nothing in these rules is to be construed as –

(a)   purporting to apply to proceedings in a magistrates' court which are not family proceedings within the meaning of section 65 of the Magistrates' Courts Act 1980; or

(b)   conferring upon a magistrate a function which a magistrate is not permitted by statute to perform.

2.2 The glossary

(1) The glossary at the end of these rules is a guide to the meaning of certain legal expressions used in the rules, but is not to be taken as giving those expressions any meaning in the rules which they do not have in the law generally.

(2) Subject to paragraph (3), words in these rules which are included in the glossary are followed by 'GL'.

(3) The word 'service', which appears frequently in the rules, is included in the glossary but is not followed by 'GL'.

2.3 Interpretation

(1) In these rules –

'the 1958 Act' means the Maintenance Orders Act 1958;

'the 1973 Act' means the Matrimonial Causes Act 1973;

'the 1978 Act' means the Domestic Proceedings and Magistrates' Courts 1978;

'the 1980 Hague Convention' means the Convention on the Civil Aspects of International Child Abduction which was signed at The Hague on 25 October 1980;

'the 1984 Act' means the Matrimonial and Family Proceedings Act 1984;

'the 1986 Act' means the Family Law Act 1986;

'the 1989 Act' means the Children Act 1989;

'the 1990 Act' means the Human Fertilisation and Embryology Act 1990;

'the 1991 Act' means the Child Support Act 1991;

'the 1996 Act' means the Family Law Act 1996;

'the 1996 Hague Convention' means the Convention on Jurisdiction, Applicable Law, Recognition, Enforcement and Co-Operation in Respect of Parental Responsibility and Measures for the Protection of Children;

'the 2002 Act' means the Adoption and Children Act 2002;

'the 2004 Act' means the Civil Partnership Act 2004;

'the 2005 Act' means the Mental Capacity Act 2005;

'the 2008 Act' means the Human Fertilisation and Embryology Act 2008;

'adoption proceedings' means proceedings for an adoption order under the 2002 Act;

'Allocation Order' means any order made by the Lord Chancellor under Part 1 of Schedule 11 to the 1989 Act;

'alternative dispute resolution' means methods of resolving a dispute, including mediation, other than through the normal court process;

'application form' means a document in which the applicant states his intention to seek a court order other than in accordance with the Part 18 procedure;

'application notice' means a document in which the applicant states his intention to seek a court order in accordance with the Part 18 procedure;

'Assembly' means the National Assembly for Wales;

'bank holiday' means a bank holiday under the Banking and Financial Dealings Act 1971 –

    (a)   for the purpose of service of a document within the United Kingdom, in the part of the United Kingdom where service is to take place; and

    (b)   for all other purposes, in England and Wales.

'business day' means any day other than –

    (a)   a Saturday, Sunday, Christmas Day or Good Friday; or

    (b)   a bank holiday;

'care order' has the meaning assigned to it by section 31(11) of the 1989 Act;

'CCR' means the County Court Rules 1981, as they appear in Schedule 2 to the CPR;

'child' means a person under the age of 18 years who is the subject of the proceedings; except that –

    (a)   in adoption proceedings, it also includes a person who has attained the age of 18 years before the proceedings are concluded; and

    (b)   in proceedings brought under the Council Regulation, the 1980 Hague Convention or the European Convention, it means a person under the age of 16 years who is the subject of the proceedings;

'child of the family' has the meaning given to it by section 105(1) of the 1989 Act;

'children and family reporter' means an officer of the Service or a Welsh family proceedings officer who has been asked to prepare a welfare report under section 7(1)(a) of the 1989 Act or section 102(3)(b) of the 2002 Act;

'children's guardian' means –

    (a)   in relation to a child who is the subject of and a party to specified proceedings or proceedings to which Part 14 applies, the person appointed in accordance with rule 16.3(1); and

    (b)   in any other case, the person appointed in accordance with rule 16.4;

    'civil partnership order' means one of the orders mentioned in section 37 of the 2004 Act;

'civil partnership proceedings' means proceedings for a civil partnership order;

'civil partnership proceedings county court' means a county court so designated by the Lord Chancellor under section 36A of the 1984 Act;

'civil restraint order' means an order restraining a party –

(a) from making any further applications in current proceedings (a limited civil restraint order);

(b) from making certain applications in specified courts (an extended civil restraint order); or

(c) from making any application in specified courts (a general civil restraint order);

'Commission' means the Child Maintenance and Enforcement Commission;

'consent order' means an order in the terms applied for to which the respondent agrees;

'contact order' has the meaning assigned to it by section 8(1) of the 1989 Act;

'the Council Regulation' means Council Regulation (EC) No 2201/2003 of 27 November 2003 on jurisdiction and the recognition and enforcement of judgments in matrimonial matters and in matters of parental responsibility;

'court' means, subject to any rule or other enactment which provides otherwise, the High Court, a county court or a magistrates' court;

(rule 2.5 relates to the power to perform functions of the court.)

'court of trial' means –

(a) in proceedings under the 1973 Act, a divorce county court designated by the Lord Chancellor as a court of trial pursuant to section 33(1) of the 1984 Act; or

(b) in proceedings under the 2004 Act, a civil partnership proceedings county court designated by the Lord Chancellor as a court of trial pursuant to section 36A(1)(b) of the 1984 Act; and

(c) in proceedings under the 1973 Act pending in a divorce county court or proceedings under the 2004 Act pending in a civil partnership proceedings county court, the principal registry is treated as a court of trial having its place of sitting at the Royal Courts of Justice;

'court officer' means –

(a) in the High Court or in a county court, a member of court staff; and

(b) in a magistrates' court, the designated officer;

('designated officer' is defined in section 37(1) of the Courts Act 2003.)

'CPR' means the Civil Procedure Rules 1998;

'deputy' has the meaning given in section 16(2)(b) of the 2005 Act;

'designated county court' means a court designated as –

(a) a divorce county court;

(b) a civil partnership proceedings county court; or

(c) both a divorce county court and a civil partnership proceedings county court;

'detailed assessment proceedings' means the procedure by which the amount of costs is decided in accordance with Part 47 of the CPR;

'directions appointment' means a hearing for directions;

'district judge' –

(a)   in relation to proceedings in the High Court, includes a district judge of the principal registry and in relation to proceedings in a county court, includes a district judge of the principal registry when the principal registry is treated as if it were a county court;

(b)   in relation to proceedings in a district registry or a county court, means the district judge or one of the district judges of that registry or county court, as the case may be;

'district registry' means –

(a)   in proceedings under the 1973 Act, any district registry having a divorce county court within its district;

(b)   in proceedings under the 2004 Act, any district registry having a civil partnership proceedings county court within its district; and

(c)   in any other case, any district registry having a designated county court within its district;

'divorce county court' means a county court so designated by the Lord Chancellor pursuant to section 33(1) of the 1984 Act, including the principal registry when it is treated as a divorce county court;

'the European Convention' means the European Convention on Recognition and Enforcement of Decisions concerning Custody of Children and on the Restoration of Custody of Children which was signed in Luxembourg on 20 May 1980;

'filing', in relation to a document, means delivering it, by post or otherwise, to the court office;

'financial order' means –

(a)   an avoidance of disposition order;

(b)   an order for maintenance pending suit;

(c)   an order for maintenance pending outcome of proceedings;

(d)   an order for periodical payments or lump sum provision as mentioned in section 21(1) of the 1973 Act, except an order under section 27(6) of that Act;

(e)   an order for periodical payments or lump sum provision as mentioned in paragraph 2(1) of Schedule 5 to the 2004 Act, made under Part 1 of Schedule 5 to that Act;

(f)   a property adjustment order;

(g)   a variation order;

(h)   a pension sharing order; or

(i)   a pension compensation sharing order;

('variation order', 'pension compensation sharing order' and 'pension sharing order' are defined in rule 9.3)

'financial remedy' means –

(a)   a financial order;

(b)   an order under Schedule 1 to the 1989 Act;

(c)   an order under Part 3 of the 1984 Act;

(d)   an order under Schedule 7 to the 2004 Act;

(e)   an order under section 27 of the 1973 Act;

(f)   an order under Part 9 of Schedule 5 to the 2004 Act;

(g)   an order under section 35 of the 1973 Act;

> (h)   an order under paragraph 69 of Schedule 5 to the 2004 Act;
> (i)   an order under Part 1 of the 1978 Act;
> (j)   an order under Schedule 6 to the 2004 Act;
> (k)   an order under section 10(2) of the 1973 Act; or
> (l)   an order under section 48(2) of the 2004 Act;

'hearing' includes a directions appointment;

'hearsay' means a statement made, otherwise than by a person while giving oral evidence in proceedings, which is tendered as evidence of the matters stated, and references to hearsay include hearsay of whatever degree;

'inherent jurisdiction' means the High Court's power to make any order or determine any issue in respect of a child, including in wardship proceedings, where it would be just and equitable to do so unless restricted by legislation or case law;

(Practice Direction 12D (Inherent Jurisdiction (including Wardship Proceedings)) provides examples of inherent jurisdiction proceedings.)

'judge', in the High Court or a county court, means, unless the context requires otherwise, a judge, district judge or a person authorised to act as such;

'jurisdiction' means, unless the context requires otherwise, England and Wales and any part of the territorial waters of the United Kingdom adjoining England and Wales;

'justices' clerk' has the meaning assigned to it by section 27(1) of the Courts Act 2003;

'legal representative' means a –

> (a)   barrister;
> (b)   solicitor;
> (c)   solicitor's employee;
> (d)   manager of a body recognised under section 9 of the Administration of Justice Act 1985; or
> (e)   person who, for the purposes of the Legal Services Act 2007, is an authorised person in relation to an activity which constitutes the conduct of litigation (within the meaning of the Act),

who has been instructed to act for a party in relation to proceedings;

'litigation friend' has the meaning given –

> (a)   in relation to a protected party, by Part 15; and
> (b)   in relation to a child, by Part 16;

'the Maintenance Regulation' means Council Regulation (EC) No 4/2009 of 18th December 2008 on jurisdiction, applicable law, recognition and enforcement of decisions and co-operation in matters relating to maintenance obligations, including as applied in relation to Denmark by virtue of the Agreement made on 19 October 2005 between the European Community and the Kingdom of Denmark;

'matrimonial cause' means proceedings for a matrimonial order;

'matrimonial order' means –

> (a)   a decree of divorce made under section 1 of the 1973 Act;
> (b)   a decree of nullity made on one of the grounds set out in sections 11 or 12 of the 1973 Act;

(c) a decree of judicial separation made under section 17 of the 1973 Act;

'note' includes a record made by mechanical means;

'officer of the Service' has the meaning given by section 11(3) of the Criminal Justice and Court Services Act 2000;

'order' includes directions of the court;

'order for maintenance pending outcome of proceedings' means an order under paragraph 38 of Schedule 5 to the 2004 Act;

'order for maintenance pending suit' means an order under section 22 of the 1973 Act;

'parental order proceedings' has the meaning assigned to it by rule 13.1;

'parental responsibility' has the meaning assigned to it by section 3 of the 1989 Act;

'placement proceedings' means proceedings for the making, varying or revoking of a placement order under the 2002 Act;

'principal registry' means the principal registry of the Family Division of the High Court;

'proceedings' means, unless the context requires otherwise, family proceedings as defined in section 75(3) of the Courts Act 2003;

'professional acting in furtherance of the protection of children' includes –

(a) an officer of a local authority exercising child protection functions;

(b) a police officer who is –

(i)   exercising powers under section 46 of the Act of 1989; or

(ii) serving in a child protection unit or a paedophile unit of a police force,

(c) any professional person attending a child protection conference or review in relation to a child who is the subject of the proceedings to which the information regarding the proceedings held in private relates; or

(d) an officer of the National Society for the Prevention of Cruelty to Children;

'professional legal adviser' means a –

(a) barrister;

(b) solicitor;

(c) solicitor's employee;

(d) manager of a body recognised under section 9 of the Administration of Justice Act 1985; or

(e) person who, for the purposes of the Legal Services Act 2007, is an authorised person in relation to an activity which constitutes the conduct of litigation (within the meaning of that Act),

who is providing advice to a party but is not instructed to represent that party in the proceedings;

'property adjustment order' means –

(a) in proceedings under the 1973 Act, any of the orders mentioned in section 21(2) of that Act;

(b) in proceedings under the 1984 Act, an order under section 17(1)(a)(ii) of that Act;

(c) in proceedings under Schedule 5 to the 2004 Act, any of the orders mentioned in paragraph 7(1); or

(d) in proceedings under Schedule 7 to the 2004 Act, an order for property adjustment under paragraph 9(2) or (3);

'protected party' means a party, or an intended party, who lacks capacity (within the meaning of the 2005 Act) to conduct proceedings;

'reporting officer' means an officer of the Service or a Welsh family proceedings officer appointed to witness the documents which signify a parent's or guardian's consent to the placing of the child for adoption or to the making of an adoption order or a section 84 order;

'risk assessment' has the meaning assigned to it by section 16A(3) of the 1989 Act;

'Royal Courts of Justice', in relation to matrimonial proceedings pending in a divorce county court or civil partnership proceedings pending in a civil partnership proceedings county court, means such place as may be specified in directions given by the Lord Chancellor pursuant to section 42(2)(a) of the 1984 Act;

'RSC' means the Rules of the Supreme Court 1965 as they appear in Schedule 1 to the CPR;

'section 8 order' has the meaning assigned to it by section 8(2) of the 1989 Act;

'section 84 order' means an order made by the High Court under section 84 of the 2002 Act giving parental responsibility prior to adoption abroad;

'section 89 order' means an order made by the High Court under section 89 of the 2002 Act –

(a) annulling a Convention adoption or Convention adoption order;

(b) providing for an overseas adoption or determination under section 91 of the 2002 Act to cease to be valid; or

(c) deciding the extent, if any, to which a determination under section 91 of the 2002 Act has been affected by a subsequent determination under that section;

'Service' has the meaning given by section 11 of the Criminal Justice and Court Services Act 2000;

'the Service Regulation' means Regulation (EC) No. 1393/2007 of the European Parliament and of the Council of 13 November 2007 on the service in the Member States of judicial and extrajudicial documents in civil or commercial matters (service of documents), and repealing Council Regulation (EC) No. 1348/2000, as amended from time to time and as applied by the Agreement made on 19 October 2005 between the European Community and the Kingdom of Denmark on the service of judicial and extrajudicial documents in civil and commercial matters;

'specified proceedings' has the meaning assigned to it by section 41(6) of the 1989 Act and rule 12.27;

'welfare officer' means a person who has been asked to prepare a report under section 7(1)(b) of the 1989 Act;

'Welsh family proceedings officer' has the meaning given by section 35(4) of the Children Act 2004.

(2) In these rules a reference to –

   (a)   an application for a matrimonial order or a civil partnership order is to be read as a reference to a petition for –
      (i)   a matrimonial order;
      (ii)   a decree of presumption of death and dissolution of marriage made under section 19 of the 1973 Act; or
      (iii)   a civil partnership order,
      and includes a petition by a respondent asking for such an order;
   (b)   'financial order' in matrimonial proceedings is to be read as a reference to 'ancillary relief';
   (c)   'matrimonial proceedings' is to be read as a reference to a matrimonial cause or proceedings for an application for a decree of presumption of death and dissolution of marriage made under section 19 of the 1973 Act.

(3) Where these rules apply the CPR, they apply the CPR as amended from time to time.

Amendments—SI 2011/1328.

****

2.8 Court's discretion as to where it deals with cases

The court may deal with a case at any place that it considers appropriate.

2.9 Computation of time

(1) This rule shows how to calculate any period of time for doing any act which is specified –

   (a)   by these rules;
   (b)   by a practice direction; or
   (c)   by a direction or order of the court.

(2) A period of time expressed as a number of days must be computed as clear days.

(3) In this rule 'clear days' means that in computing the numbers of days –

   (a)   the day on which the period begins; and
   (b)   if the end of the period is defined by reference to an event, the day on which that event occurs,

are not included.

(4) Where the specified period is 7 days or less and includes a day which is not a business day, that day does not count.

(5) When the period specified –

   (a)   by these rules or a practice direction; or

(b)   by any direction or order of the court,

for doing any act at the court office ends on a day on which the office is closed, that act will be in time if done on the next day on which the court office is open.

2.10 Dates for compliance to be calendar dates and to include time of day

(1) Where the court makes an order or gives a direction which imposes a time limit for doing any act, the last date for compliance must, wherever practicable –

(a)   be expressed as a calendar date; and
(b)   include the time of day by which the act must be done.

(2) Where the date by which an act must be done is inserted in any document, the date must, wherever practicable, be expressed as a calendar date.

(3) Where 'month' occurs in any order, direction or other document, it means a calendar month.

****

PART 3
ALTERNATIVE DISPUTE RESOLUTION: THE COURT'S POWERS

3.1 Scope of this Part

(1) This Part contains the court's powers to encourage the parties to use alternative dispute resolution and to facilitate its use.

(2) The powers in this Part are subject to any powers given to the court by any other rule or practice direction or by any other enactment or any powers it may otherwise have.

3.2 Court's duty to consider alternative dispute resolution

The court must consider, at every stage in proceedings, whether alternative dispute resolution is appropriate.

3.3 When the court will adjourn proceedings or a hearing in proceedings

(1) If the court considers that alternative dispute resolution is appropriate, the court may direct that the proceedings, or a hearing in the proceedings, be adjourned for such specified period as it considers appropriate –

(a)   to enable the parties to obtain information and advice about alternative dispute resolution; and
(b)   where the parties agree, to enable alternative dispute resolution to take place.

(2) The court may give directions under this rule on an application or of its own initiative.

(3) Where the court directs an adjournment under this rule, it will give directions about the timing and method by which the parties must tell the court if any of the issues in the proceedings have been resolved.

(4) If the parties do not tell the court if any of the issues have been resolved as directed under paragraph (3), the court will give such directions as to the management of the case as it considers appropriate.

(5) The court or court officer will –

(a) record the making of an order under this rule; and
(b) arrange for a copy of the order to be served as soon as practicable on the parties.

(6) Where the court proposes to exercise its powers of its own initiative the procedure set out in rule 4.3(2) to (6) applies.

(By rule 4.1(7), any direction given under this rule may be varied or revoked.)

****

PART 9
APPLICATIONS FOR A FINANCIAL REMEDY

Chapter 1
Application and Interpretation

9.1 Application

The rules in this Part apply to an application for a financial remedy.

('Financial remedy' and 'financial order' are defined in rule 2.3)

9.2 Application of Magistrates' Courts Rules 1981

Unless the context otherwise requires, and subject to the rules in this Part, the following rules of the Magistrates' Courts Rules 1981 apply to proceedings in a magistrates' court which are family proceedings under section 65 of the Magistrates' Courts Act 1980 –

(a) rule 39(6) (method of making periodical payments);
(b) rule 41 (revocation etc. of orders for periodical payments);
(c) rule 43 (service of copy of order);
(d) rule 44 (remission of sums due under order);
(e) rule 45 (duty of designated officer to notify subsequent marriage or formation of civil partnership of person entitled to payments under a maintenance order);
(f) rule 48 (to whom payments are to be made);
(g) rule 49 (duty of designated officer to give receipt);
(h) rule 51 (application for further time);
(i) rule 62 (particulars relating to payment of lump sum under a magistrates' courts maintenance order etc. to be entered in register);
(j) rule 66 (register of convictions, etc.);
(k) rule 67 (proof of service, handwriting, etc);

(l)   rule 68 (proof of proceedings); and
(m)   rule 69 (proof that magistrates' court maintenance orders, etc, have not been revoked etc).

9.3 Interpretation

(1) In this Part –

'avoidance of disposition order' means –
  (a)   in proceedings under the 1973 Act, an order under section 37(2)(*b*) or (*c*) of that Act;
  (b)   in proceedings under the 1984 Act, an order under section 23(2)(*b*) or 23(3) of that Act;
  (c)   in proceedings under Schedule 5 to the 2004 Act, an order under paragraph 74(3) or (4); or
  (d)   in proceedings under Schedule 7 to the 2004 Act, an order under paragraph 15(3) or (4);

'the Board' means the Board of the Pension Protection Fund;
'FDR appointment' means a Financial Dispute Resolution appointment in accordance with rule 9.17;
'order preventing a disposition' means –
  (a)   in proceedings under the 1973 Act, an order under section 37(2)(*a*) of that Act;
  (b)   in proceedings under the 1984 Act, an order under section 23(2)(*a*) of that Act;
  (c)   in proceedings under Schedule 5 to the 2004 Act, an order under paragraph 74(2); or
  (d)   in proceedings under Schedule 7 to the 2004 Act, an order under paragraph 15(2);

'pension arrangement' means –
  (a)   an occupational pension scheme;
  (b)   a personal pension scheme;
  (c)   shareable state scheme rights;
  (d)   a retirement annuity contract;
  (e)   an annuity or insurance policy purchased, or transferred, for the purpose of giving effect to rights under an occupational pension scheme or a personal pension scheme; and
  (f)   an annuity purchased, or entered into, for the purpose of discharging liability in respect of a pension credit under section 29(1)(*b*) of the Welfare Reform and Pensions Act 1999 or under corresponding Northern Ireland legislation;

'pension attachment order' means –
  (a)   in proceedings under the 1973 Act, an order making provision under section 25B or 25C of that Act;
  (b)   in proceedings under the 1984 Act, an order under section 17(1)(*a*)(i) of that Act making provision equivalent to an order referred to in paragraph (*a*);

(c) in proceedings under Schedule 5 to the 2004 Act, an order making provision under paragraph 25 or paragraph 26; or

(d) in proceedings under Schedule 7 to the 2004 Act, an order under paragraph 9(2) or (3) making provision equivalent to an order referred to in paragraph (*c*);

'pension compensation attachment order' means –

(a) in proceedings under the 1973 Act, an order making provision under section 25F of that Act;

(b) in proceedings under the 1984 Act, an order under section 17(1)(a)(i) of that Act making provision equivalent to an order referred in to paragraph (*a*);

(c) in proceedings under Schedule 5 to the 2004 Act, an order under paragraph 34A; and

(d) in proceedings under Schedule 7 to the 2004 Act, an order under paragraph 9(2) or (3) making provision equivalent to an order referred to in paragraph (*c*);

'pension compensation sharing order' means –

(a) in proceedings under the 1973 Act, an order under section 24E of that Act;

(b) in proceedings under the 1984 Act, an order under section 17(1)(*c*) of that Act;

(c) in proceedings under Schedule 5 to the 2004 Act, an order under paragraph 19A; and

(d) in proceedings under Schedule 7 to the 2004 Act, an order under paragraph 9(2) or (3) making provision equivalent to an order referred to in paragraph (*c*);

'pension sharing order' means –

(a) in proceedings under the 1973 Act, an order making provision under section 24B of that Act;

(b) in proceedings under the 1984 Act, an order under section 17(1)(*b*) of that Act;

(c) in proceedings under Schedule 5 to the 2004 Act, an order under paragraph 15; or

(d) in proceedings under Schedule 7 to the 2004 Act, an order under paragraph 9(2) or (3) making provision equivalent to an order referred to in paragraph (*c*);

'pension scheme' means, unless the context otherwise requires, a scheme for which the Board has assumed responsibility in accordance with Chapter 3 of Part 2 of the Pensions Act 2004 (pension protection) or any provision in force in Northern Ireland corresponding to that Chapter;

'PPF compensation' has the meaning given to it –

(a) in proceedings under the 1973 Act, by section 21C of the 1973 Act;

(b) in proceedings under the 1984 Act, by section 18(7) of the 1984 Act; and

    (c)   in proceedings under the 2004 Act, by paragraph 19F of Schedule 5 to the 2004 Act;

'relevant valuation' means a valuation of pension rights or benefits as at a date not more than 12 months earlier than the date fixed for the first appointment which has been furnished or requested for the purposes of any of the following provisions –

    (a)   the Pensions on Divorce etc (Provision of Information) Regulations 2000;

    (b)   regulation 5 of and Schedule 2 to the Occupational Pension Schemes (Disclosure of Information) Regulations 1996 and regulation 11 of and Schedule 1 to the Occupational Pension Schemes (Transfer Value) Regulations 1996;

    (c)   section 93A or 94(1)(*a*) or (*aa*) of the Pension Schemes Act 1993;

    (d)   section 94(1)(*b*) of the Pension Schemes Act 1993 or paragraph 2(*a*) (or, where applicable, 2(*b*)) of Schedule 2 to the Personal Pension Schemes (Disclosure of Information) Regulations 1987;

    (e)   the Dissolution etc (Pensions) Regulations 2005;

'variation order' means –

    (a)   in proceedings under the 1973 Act, an order under section 31 of that Act; or

    (b)   in proceedings under the 2004 Act, an order under Part 11 of Schedule 5 to that Act.

(2) References in this Part to a county court are to be construed, in relation to proceedings for a financial order, as references to a divorce county court or a civil partnership proceedings county court, as the case may be.

(3)

    (a)   Where an application is made under Article 56 of, and using the form in Annex VII to, the Maintenance Regulation, references in this Part to 'financial statement' apply to the applicant as if for the words 'financial statement' were substituted 'the form in Annex VII to the Maintenance Regulation';

    (b)   Sub-paragraph (a) does not apply where the relief sought includes relief which is of a type to which the Maintenance Regulation does not apply.

Amendments—SI 2011/1328.

Chapter 2
Procedure for Applications

9.4 When an Application for a financial order may be made

An application for a financial order may be made –

    (a)   in an application for a matrimonial or civil partnership order; or

    (b)   at any time after an application for a matrimonial or civil partnership order has been made.

9.5 Where to start proceedings

(1) An application for a financial remedy must be filed –

(a) if there are proceedings for a matrimonial order or a civil partnership order which are proceeding in a designated county court, in that court; or

(b) if there are proceedings for a matrimonial order or a civil partnership order which are proceeding in the High Court, in the registry in which those proceedings are taking place.

(2) In any other case, in relation to the application set out in column 1 of the following table, column 2 sets out where the application must be filed.

Provision under which application is made	*Court where application must be filed*
Section 27 of the 1973 Act.	Divorce county court.
Part 9 of Schedule 5 to the 2004 Act.	Civil partnership proceedings county court.
Part 3 of the 1984 Act.	Principal Registry or, in relation to an application for a consent order, a divorce county court.
Schedule 7 to the 2004 Act.	Principal Registry or, in relation to an application for a consent order, a civil partnership proceedings county court.
Section 35 of the 1973 Act.	High Court, a divorce county court or a magistrates' court.
Paragraph 69 of Schedule 5 to the 2004 Act.	High Court, a civil partnership proceedings county court or a magistrates' court.
Schedule 1 to the 1989 Act.	High Court, designated county court or a magistrates' court.
Part 1 of the 1978 Act.	magistrates' court.
Schedule 6 to the 2004 Act.	magistrates' court.

(3) An application for a financial remedy under Part 3 of the 1984 Act or Schedule 7 to the 2004 Act which is proceeding in the High Court must be heard by a judge, but not a district judge, of that court unless a direction has been made that the application may be heard by a district judge of the principal registry.

(Rule 8.28 enables a judge to direct that an application for a financial remedy under Part 3 of the 1984 Act or Schedule 7 to the 2004 Act may be heard by a district judge of the principal registry.)

9.6 Application for an order preventing a disposition

(1) The Part 18 procedure applies to an application for an order preventing a disposition.

(2) An application for an order preventing a disposition may be made without notice to the respondent.

('Order preventing a disposition' is defined in rule 9.3.)

9.7 Application for interim orders

(1) A party may apply at any stage of the proceedings for –

  (a)   an order for maintenance pending suit;
  (b)   an order for maintenance pending outcome of proceedings;
  (c)   an order for interim periodical payments;
  (d)   an interim variation order; or
  (e)   any other form of interim order.

(2) The Part 18 procedure applies to an application for an interim order.

(3) Where a party makes an application before filing a financial statement, the written evidence in support must –

  (a)   explain why the order is necessary; and
  (b)   give up to date information about that party's financial circumstances.

(4) Unless the respondent has filed a financial statement, the respondent must, at least 7 days before the court is to deal with the application, file a statement of his means and serve a copy on the applicant.

(5) An application for an order mentioned in paragraph (1)(*e*) may be made without notice.

9.8 Application for periodical payments order at same rate as an order for maintenance pending suit

(1) This rule applies where there are matrimonial proceedings and –

  (a)   a decree nisi of divorce or nullity of marriage has been made;
  (b)   at or after the date of the decree nisi an order for maintenance pending suit is in force; and
  (c)   the spouse in whose favour the decree nisi was made has made an application for an order for periodical payments.

(2) The spouse in whose favour the decree nisi was made may apply, using the Part 18 procedure, for an order providing for payments at the same rate as those provided for by the order for maintenance pending suit.

9.9 Application for periodical payments order at same rate as an order for maintenance pending outcome of proceedings

(1) This rule applies where there are civil partnership proceedings and –

(a) a conditional order of dissolution or nullity of civil partnership has been made;

(b) at or after the date of the conditional order an order for maintenance pending outcome of proceedings is in force;

(c) the civil partner in whose favour the conditional order was made has made an application for an order for periodical payments.

(2) The civil partner in whose favour the conditional order was made may apply, using the Part 18 procedure, for an order providing for payments at the same rate as those provided for by, the order for maintenance pending the outcome of proceedings.

Chapter 3
Applications for Financial Remedies for Children

9.10 Application by parent, guardian etc for financial remedy in respect of children

(1) The following people may apply for a financial remedy in respect of a child –

(a) a parent, guardian or special guardian of any child of the family;

(b) any person in whose favour a residence order has been made with respect to a child of the family, and any applicant for such an order;

(c) any other person who is entitled to apply for a residence order with respect to a child;

(d) a local authority, where an order has been made under section 31(1)(*a*) of the 1989 Act placing a child in its care;

(e) the Official Solicitor, if appointed the children's guardian of a child of the family under rule 16.24; and

(f) a child of the family who has been given permission to apply for a financial remedy.

(2) In this rule 'residence order' has the meaning given to it by section 8(1) of the 1989 Act.

9.11 Children to be separately represented on certain applications

(1) Where an application for a financial remedy includes an application for an order for a variation of settlement, the court must, unless it is satisfied that the proposed variation does not adversely affect the rights or interests of any child concerned, direct that the child be separately represented on the application.

(2) On any other application for a financial remedy the court may direct that the child be separately represented on the application.

(3) Where a direction is made under paragraph (1) or (2), the court may if the person to be appointed so consents, appoint –

(a) a person other than the Official Solicitor; or

(b) the Official Solicitor,

to be a children's guardian and rule 16.24(5) and (6) and rules 16.25 to 16.28 apply as appropriate to such an appointment.

Chapter 4
Procedure in the High Court and County Court after Filing an Application

9.12 Duties of the court and the applicant upon issuing an application

(1) When an application under this Part is issued in the High Court or in a county court –

- (a) the court will fix a first appointment not less than 12 weeks and not more than 16 weeks after the date of the filing of the application; and
- (b) subject to paragraph (2), within 4 days beginning with the date on which the application was filed, a court officer will –
  - (i) serve a copy of the application on the respondent; and
  - (ii) give notice of the date of the first appointment to the applicant and the respondent.

(2) Where the applicant wishes to serve a copy of the application on the respondent and on filing the application so notifies the court –

- (a) paragraph (1)(*b*) does not apply;
- (b) a court officer will return to the applicant the copy of the application and the notice of the date of the first appointment; and
- (c) the applicant must, –
  - (i) within 4 days beginning with the date on which the copy of the application is received from the court, serve the copy of the application and notice of the date of the first appointment on the respondent; and
  - (ii) file a certificate of service at or before the first appointment.

(Rule 6.37 sets out what must be included in a certificate of service)

(3) The date fixed under paragraph (1), or for any subsequent appointment, must not be cancelled except with the court's permission and, if cancelled, the court must immediately fix a new date.

(4) In relation to an application to which the Maintenance Regulation applies, where the applicant does not already know the address of the respondent at the time the application is issued, paragraph (2) does not apply and the court will serve the application in accordance with paragraph (1).

Amendments—SI 2011/1328.

9.13 Service of application on mortgagees, trustees etc

(1) Where an application for a financial remedy includes an application for an order for a variation of settlement, the applicant must serve copies of the application on –

- (a) the trustees of the settlement;
- (b) the settlor if living; and
- (c) such other persons as the court directs.

(2) In the case of an application for an avoidance of disposition order, the applicant must serve copies of the application on the person in whose favour the disposition is alleged to have been made.

(3) Where an application for a financial remedy includes an application relating to land, the applicant must serve a copy of the application on any mortgagee of whom particulars are given in the application.

(4) Any person served under paragraphs (1), (2) or (3) may make a request to the court in writing, within 14 days beginning with the date of service of the application, for a copy of the applicant's financial statement or any relevant part of that statement.

(5) Any person who –

(a) is served with copies of the application in accordance with paragraphs (1), (2) or (3); or

(b) receives a copy of a financial statement, or a relevant part of that statement, following an application made under paragraph (4),

may within 14 days beginning with the date of service or receipt file a statement in answer.

(6) Where a copy of an application is served under paragraphs (1), (2) or (3), the applicant must file a certificate of service at or before the first appointment.

(7) A statement in answer filed under paragraph (5) must be verified by a statement of truth.

9.14 Procedure before the first appointment

(1) Not less than 35 days before the first appointment both parties must simultaneously exchange with each other and file with the court a financial statement in the form referred to in Practice Direction 5A.

(2) The financial statement must –

(a) be verified by an affidavit; and

(b) accompanied by the following documents only –

(i) any documents required by the financial statement;

(ii) any other documents necessary to explain or clarify any of the information contained in the financial statement; and

(iii) any documents provided to the party producing the financial statement by a person responsible for a pension arrangement, either following a request under rule 9.30 or as part of a relevant valuation; and

(iv) any notification or other document referred to in rule 9.37(2), (4) or (5) which has been received by the party producing the financial statement.

(2A) Where the application is made under Article 56 of, using the form in Annex VII to, the Maintenance Regulation, and the relief sought is limited to relief of a type to which that Regulation applies, the requirement of paragraph (2)(a) relating to verification by affidavit does not apply.

(3) Where a party was unavoidably prevented from sending any document required by the financial statement, that party must at the earliest opportunity –

  (a) serve a copy of that document on the other party; and
  (b) file a copy of that document with the court, together with a written explanation of the failure to send it with the financial statement.

(4) No disclosure or inspection of documents may be requested or given between the filing of the application for a financial remedy and the first appointment, except –

  (a) copies sent with the financial statement, or in accordance with paragraph (3); or
  (b) in accordance with paragraphs (5) and (6).

  (Rule 21.1 explains what is meant by disclosure and inspection.)

(5) Not less than 14 days before the hearing of the first appointment, each party must file with the court and serve on the other party –

  (a) a concise statement of the issues between the parties;
  (b) a chronology;
  (c) a questionnaire setting out by reference to the concise statement of issues any further information and documents requested from the other party or a statement that no information and documents are required; and
  (d) a notice stating whether that party will be in a position at the first appointment to proceed on that occasion to a FDR appointment.

(6) Not less than 14 days before the hearing of the first appointment, the applicant must file with the court and serve on the respondent confirmation –

  (a) of the names of all persons served in accordance with rule 9.13(1) to (3); and
  (b) that there are no other persons who must be served in accordance with those paragraphs.

Amendments—SI 2011/1328.

9.15 Duties of the court at the first appointment

(1) The first appointment must be conducted with the objective of defining the issues and saving costs.

(2) At the first appointment the court must determine –

  (a) the extent to which any questions seeking information under rule 9.14(5)(*c*) must be answered; and
  (b) what documents requested under rule 9.14(5)(*c*) must be produced,

and give directions for the production of such further documents as may be necessary.

(3) The court must give directions where appropriate about –

(a)   the valuation of assets (including the joint instruction of joint experts);

(b)   obtaining and exchanging expert evidence, if required;

(c)   the evidence to be adduced by each party; and

(d)   further chronologies or schedules to be filed by each party.

(4) If the court decides that a referral to a FDR appointment is appropriate it must direct that the case be referred to a FDR appointment.

(5) If the court decides that a referral to a FDR appointment is not appropriate it must direct one or more of the following –

(a)   that a further directions appointment be fixed;

(b)   that an appointment be fixed for the making of an interim order;

(c)   that the case be fixed for a final hearing and, where that direction is given, the court must determine the judicial level at which the case should be heard.

   (By rule 3.3 the court may also direct that the case be adjourned if it considers that alternative dispute resolution is appropriate.)

(6) In considering whether to make a costs order under rule 28.3(5), the court must have particular regard to the extent to which each party has complied with the requirement to send documents with the financial statement and the explanation given for any failure to comply.

(7) The court may –

(a)   where an application for an interim order has been listed for consideration at the first appointment, make an interim order;

(b)   having regard to the contents of the notice filed by the parties under rule 9.14(5)(*d*), treat the appointment (or part of it) as a FDR appointment to which rule 9.17 applies;

(c)   in a case where a pension sharing order or a pension attachment order is requested, direct any party with pension rights to file and serve a Pension Inquiry Form, completed in full or in part as the court may direct; and

(d)   in a case where a pension compensation sharing order or a pension compensation attachment order is requested, direct any party with PPF compensation rights to file and serve a Pension Protection Fund Inquiry Form, completed in full or in part as the court may direct.

(8) Both parties must personally attend the first appointment unless the court directs otherwise.

9.16 After the first appointment

(1) Between the first appointment and the FDR appointment, a party is not entitled to the production of any further documents except –

(a)   in accordance with directions given under rule 9.15(2); or

(b)   with the permission of the court.

(2) At any stage –

(a)   a party may apply for further directions or a FDR appointment;
(b)   the court may give further directions or direct that parties attend a FDR appointment.

9.17 The FDR appointment

(1) The FDR appointment must be treated as a meeting held for the purposes of discussion and negotiation.

(2) The judge hearing the FDR appointment must have no further involvement with the application, other than to conduct any further FDR appointment or to make a consent order or a further directions order.

(3) Not less than 7 days before the FDR appointment, the applicant must file with the court details of all offers and proposals, and responses to them.

(4) Paragraph (3) includes any offers, proposals or responses made wholly or partly without prejudice, but paragraph (3) does not make any material admissible as evidence if, but for that paragraph, it would not be admissible.

(5) At the conclusion of the FDR appointment, any documents filed under paragraph (3), and any filed documents referring to them, must, at the request of the party who filed them, be returned to that party and not retained on the court file.

(6) Parties attending the FDR appointment must use their best endeavours to reach agreement on matters in issue between them.

(7) The FDR appointment may be adjourned from time to time.

(8) At the conclusion of the FDR appointment, the court may make an appropriate consent order.

(9) If the court does not make an appropriate consent order as mentioned in paragraph (8), the court must give directions for the future course of the proceedings including, where appropriate –

(a)   the filing of evidence, including up to date information; and
(b)   fixing a final hearing date.

(10) Both parties must personally attend the FDR appointment unless the court directs otherwise.

****

Chapter 6
General Procedure

9.24 Power to order delivery up of possession etc.

(1) This rule applies where the court has made an order under –

(a)   section 24A of the 1973 Act;
(b)   section 17(2) of the 1984 Act;
(c)   Part 3 of Schedule 5 to the 2004 Act; or
(d)   paragraph 9(4) of Schedule 7 to the 2004 Act.

(2) When the court makes an order mentioned in paragraph (1), it may order any party to deliver up to the purchaser or any other person –

    (a)   possession of the land, including any interest in, or right over, land;

    (b)   receipt of rents or profits relating to it; or

    (c)   both.

9.25 Where proceedings may be heard

(1) Paragraph (2) applies to an application –

    (a)   for a financial order;

    (b)   under Part 3 of the 1984 Act; or

    (c)   under Schedule 7 to the 2004 Act.

(2) An application mentioned in paragraph (1) must be heard –

    (a)   where the case is proceeding in the county court, at any court of trial; and

    (b)   where the case is proceeding in the High Court –

        (i)   at the Royal Courts of Justice; or

        (ii)   in matrimonial or civil partnership proceedings, any court at which sittings of the High Court are authorised.

(3) An application for an order under –

    (a)   section 27 of the 1973 Act; or

    (b)   Part 9 of Schedule 5 to the 2004 Act,

must be heard in a court of trial or in the High Court.

(4) A court may transfer a case to another court exercising the same jurisdiction, either of its own initiative or on the application of one of the parties, if –

    (a)   the parties consent to the transfer;

    (b)   the court has held a hearing to determine whether a transfer should be ordered; or

    (c)   paragraph (5) applies.

(5) A court may transfer a case without a hearing if –

    (a)   the court has notified the parties in writing that it intends to order a transfer; and

    (b)   neither party has, within 14 days of the notification being sent, requested a hearing to determine whether a transfer should be ordered.

9.26 Applications for consent orders for financial remedy

(1) Subject to paragraph (5) and to rule 35.2 in relation to an application for a consent order –

    (a)   the applicant must file two copies of a draft of the order in the terms sought, one of which must be endorsed with a statement signed by the respondent to the application signifying agreement; and

(b)   each party must file with the court and serve on the other party, a statement of information in the form referred to in Practice Direction 5A.

(2) Where each party's statement of information is contained in one form, it must be signed by both the applicant and respondent to certify that they have read the contents of the other party's statement.

(3) Where each party's statement of information is in a separate form, the form of each party must be signed by the other party to certify that they have read the contents of the statement contained in that form.

(4) Unless the court directs otherwise, the applicant and the respondent need not attend the hearing of an application for a consent order.

(5) Where all or any of the parties attend the hearing of an application for a financial remedy the court may –

(a)   dispense with the filing of a statement of information; and
(b)   give directions for the information which would otherwise be required to be given in such a statement in such a manner as it thinks fit.

(6) In relation to an application for a consent order under Part 3 of the 1984 Act or Schedule 7 to the 2004 Act, the application for permission to make the application may be heard at the same time as the application for a financial remedy if evidence of the respondent's consent to the order is filed with the application.

> (The following rules contain provision in relation to applications for consent orders – rule 9.32 (pension sharing order), rule 9.34 (pension attachment order), rule 9.41 (pension compensation sharing orders) and rule 9.43 (pension compensation attachment orders).

9.26A Questions as to the court's jurisdiction or whether the proceedings should be stayed

(1) This rule applies to applications for maintenance where a question as to jurisdiction arises under –

(a)   the 1968 Convention;
(b)   the 1988 Convention;
(c)   the Lugano Convention; or
(d)   the Maintenance Regulation.

(2) If at any time after the issue of the application it appears to the court that it does not or may not have jurisdiction to hear an application, or that under the instruments referred to in paragraph (1) it is or may be required to stay the proceedings or to decline jurisdiction, the court must –

(a)   stay the proceedings, and
(b)   fix a date for a hearing to determine jurisdiction or whether there should be a stay or other order.

(3) The court officer will serve notice of the hearing referred to at paragraph (2)(b) on the parties to the proceedings.

(4) The court must, in writing –

    (a)   give reasons for its decision under paragraph (2), and

    (b)   where it makes a finding of fact, state such finding.

(5) The court may with the consent of all the parties deal with any question as to the jurisdiction of the court, or as to whether the proceedings should be stayed, without a hearing.

(6) In this rule –

    (a)   'the 1968 Convention' has the meaning given to it in the Civil Jurisdiction and Judgments Act 1982;

    (b)   'the 1988 Convention' and 'the Lugano Convention' have the meanings given to them in rule 34.1(2).

Amendments—SI 2011/1328.

Chapter 7
Estimates of Costs

9.27 Estimates of Costs

(1) Subject to paragraph (2), at every hearing or appointment each party must produce to the court an estimate of the costs incurred by that party up to the date of that hearing or appointment.

(2) Not less than 14 days before the date fixed for the final hearing of an application for a financial remedy, each party ('the filing party') must (unless the court directs otherwise) file with the court and serve on each other party a statement giving full particulars of all costs in respect of the proceedings which the filing party has incurred or expects to incur, to enable the court to take account of the parties' liabilities for costs when deciding what order (if any) to make for a financial remedy.

(3) This rule does not apply to magistrates' courts.

    (Rule 28.3 makes provision for orders for costs in financial remedy proceedings.)

9.28 Duty to make open proposals

(1) Not less than 14 days before the date fixed for the final hearing of an application for a financial remedy, the applicant must (unless the court directs otherwise) file with the court and serve on the respondent an open statement which sets out concise details, including the amounts involved, of the orders which the applicant proposes to ask the court to make.

(2) Not more than 7 days after service of a statement under paragraph (1), the respondent must file with the court and serve on the applicant an open statement which sets out concise details, including the amounts involved, of the orders which the respondent proposes to ask the court to make.

9.29 Application and interpretation of this Chapter

(1) This Chapter applies

(a)   where an application for a financial remedy has been made; and
(b)   the applicant or respondent is the party with pension rights.

(2) In this Chapter –

(a)   in proceedings under the 1973 Act and the 1984 Act, all words and phrases defined in sections 25D(3) and (4) of the 1973 Act have the meaning assigned by those subsections;
(b)   in proceedings under the 2004 Act –
all words and phrases defined in paragraphs 16(4) to (5) and 29 of Schedule 5 to that Act have the meanings assigned by those paragraphs; and
'the party with pension rights' has the meaning given to 'civil partner with pension rights' by paragraph 29 of Schedule 5 to the 2004 Act;
(c)   all words and phrases defined in section 46 of the Welfare Reform and Pensions Act 1999 have the meanings assigned by that section.

9.30 What the party with pension rights must do when the court fixes a first appointment

(1) Where the court fixes a first appointment as required by rule 9.12(1)(*a*) the party with pension rights must request the person responsible for each pension arrangement under which the party has or is likely to have benefits to provide the information referred to in regulation 2(2) of the Pensions on Divorce etc (Provision of Information) Regulations 2000.

> (The information referred to in regulation 2 of the Pensions on Divorce etc (Provision of Information) Regulations 2000 relates to the valuation of pension rights or benefits.)

(2) The party with pension rights must comply with paragraph (1) within 7 days beginning with the date on which that party receives notification of the date of the first appointment.

(3) Within 7 days beginning with the date on which the party with pension rights receives the information under paragraph (1) that party must send a copy of it to the other party, together with the name and address of the person responsible for each pension arrangement.

(4) A request under paragraph (1) need not be made where the party with pension rights is in possession of, or has requested, a relevant valuation of the pension rights or benefits accrued under the pension arrangement in question.

9.31 Applications for pension sharing orders

Where an application for a financial remedy includes an application for a pension sharing order, or where a request for such an order is added to an existing application for a financial remedy, the applicant must serve a copy of the application on the person responsible for the pension arrangement concerned.

9.32 Applications for consent orders for pension sharing

(1) This rule applies where –

 (a) the parties have agreed on the terms of an order and the agreement includes a pension sharing order;

 (b) service has not been effected under rule 9.31; and

 (c) the information referred to in paragraph (2) has not otherwise been provided.

(2) The party with pension rights must –

 (a) request the person responsible for the pension arrangement concerned to provide the information set out in Section C of the Pension Inquiry Form; and

 (b) on receipt, send a copy of the information referred to in sub-paragraph (*a*) to the other party.

9.33 Applications for pension attachment orders

(1) Where an application for a financial remedy includes an application for a pension attachment order, or where a request for such an order is added to an existing application for a financial remedy, the applicant must serve a copy of the application on the person responsible for the pension arrangement concerned and must at the same time send –

 (a) an address to which any notice which the person responsible is required to serve on the applicant is to be sent;

 (b) an address to which any payment which the person responsible is required to make to the applicant is to be sent; and

 (c) where the address in sub-paragraph (*b*) is that of a bank, a building society or the Department of National Savings, sufficient details to enable the payment to be made into the account of the applicant.

(2) A person responsible for a pension arrangement who receives a copy of the application under paragraph (1) may, within 21 days beginning with the date of service of the application, request the party with the pension rights to provide that person with the information disclosed in the financial statement relating to the party's pension rights or benefits under that arrangement.

(3) If the person responsible for a pension arrangement makes a request under paragraph (2), the party with the pension rights must provide that person with a copy of the section of that party's financial statement that relates to that party's pension rights or benefits under that arrangement.

(4) The party with the pension rights must comply with paragraph (3) –

 (a) within the time limited for filing the financial statement by rule 9.14(1); or

(b)   within 21 days beginning with the date on which the person responsible for the pension arrangement makes the request,

whichever is the later.

(5) A person responsible for a pension arrangement who receives a copy of the section of a financial statement as required pursuant to paragraph (4) may, within 21 days beginning with the date on which that person receives it, send to the court, the applicant and the respondent a statement in answer.

(6) A person responsible for a pension arrangement who files a statement in answer pursuant to paragraph (5) will be entitled to be represented at the first appointment, or such other hearing as the court may direct, and the court must within 4 days, beginning with the date on which that person files the statement in answer, give the person notice of the date of the first appointment or other hearing as the case may be.

9.34 Applications for consent orders for pension attachment

(1) This rule applies where service has not been effected under rule 9.33(1).

(2) Where the parties have agreed on the terms of an order and the agreement includes a pension attachment order, then they must serve on the person responsible for the pension arrangement concerned –

(a)   a copy of the application for a consent order;
(b)   a draft of the proposed order, complying with rule 9.35; and
(c)   the particulars set out in rule 9.33(1).

(3) No consent order that includes a pension attachment order must be made unless either –

(a)   the person responsible for the pension arrangement has not made any objection within 21 days beginning with the date on which the application for a consent order was served on that person; or
(b)   the court has considered any such objection, and for the purpose of considering any objection the court may make such direction as it sees fit for the person responsible to attend before it or to furnish written details of the objection.

9.35 Pension sharing orders or pension attachment orders

An order for a financial remedy, whether by consent or not, which includes a pension sharing order or a pension attachment order, must –

(a)   in the body of the order, state that there is to be provision by way of pension sharing or pension attachment in accordance with the annex or annexes to the order; and
(b)   be accompanied by a pension sharing annex or a pension attachment annex as the case may require, and if provision is made in relation to more than one pension arrangement there must be one annex for each pension arrangement.

9.36 Duty of the court upon making a pension sharing order or a pension attachment order

(1) A court which varies or discharges a pension sharing order or a pension attachment order, must send, or direct one of the parties to send –

    (a)   to the person responsible for the pension arrangement concerned; or

    (b)   where the Board has assumed responsibility for the pension scheme or part of it, the Board;

the documents referred to in paragraph (4).

(2) A court which makes a pension sharing order or pension attachment order, must send, or direct one of the parties to send to the person responsible for the pension arrangement concerned, the documents referred to in paragraph (4).

(3) Where the Board has assumed responsibility for the pension scheme or part of it after the making of a pension sharing order or attachment order but before the documents have been sent to the person responsible for the pension arrangement in accordance with paragraph (2), the court which makes the pension sharing order or the pension attachment order, must send, or direct one of the parties to send to the Board the documents referred to in paragraph (4).

(4) The documents to be sent in accordance with paragraph (1) to (3) are –

    (a)   in the case of –

        (i)   proceedings under the 1973 Act, a copy of the decree of judicial separation;

        (ii)   proceedings under Schedule 5 to the 2004 Act, a copy of the separation order;

        (iii)   proceedings under Part 3 of the 1984 Act, a copy of the document of divorce, annulment or legal separation;

        (iv)   proceedings under Schedule 7 to the 2004 Act, a copy of the document of dissolution, annulment or legal separation;

    (b)   in the case of divorce or nullity of marriage, a copy of the decree absolute under rule 7.31 or 7.32; or

    (c)   in the case of dissolution or nullity of civil partnership, a copy of the order making the conditional order final under rule 7.31 or 7.32; and

    (d)   a copy of the pension sharing order or the pension attachment order, or as the case may be of the order varying or discharging that order, including any annex to that order relating to that pension arrangement but no other annex to that order.

(5) The documents referred to in paragraph (1) must be sent –

    (a)   in proceedings under the 1973 Act and the 1984 Act, within 7 days beginning with the date on which –

        (i)   the relevant pension sharing or pension attachment order is made; or

        (ii)   the decree absolute of divorce or nullity or decree of judicial separation is made,

    whichever is the later; and

(b) in proceedings under the 2004 Act, within 7 days beginning with the
date on which –
  (i) the relevant pension sharing or pension attachment order is
  made; or
  (ii) the final order of dissolution or nullity or separation order is
  made,
whichever is the later.

9.37 Procedure where Pension Protection Fund becomes involved with the pension scheme

(1) This rule applies where –

(a) rules 9.30 to 9.34 or 9.36 apply; and
(a) the party with the pension rights ('the member') receives or has
received notification in compliance with the Pension Protection Fund
(Provision of Information) Regulations 2005 ('the 2005 Regulations') –
  (i) from the trustees or managers of a pension scheme, that there is
  an assessment period in relation to that scheme; or
  (ii) from the Board that it has assumed responsibility for the pension
  scheme or part of it.

(2) If the trustees or managers of the pension scheme notify or have notified
the member that there is an assessment period in relation to that scheme, the
member must send to the other party, all the information which the Board is
required from time to time to provide to the member under the 2005
Regulations including –

(a) a copy of the notification; and
(b) a copy of the valuation summary,

in accordance with paragraph (3).

(3) The member must send the information or any part of it referred to in
paragraph (2) –

(a) if available, when the member sends the information received under
rule 9.30(1); or
(b) otherwise, within 7 days of receipt.

(4) If the Board notifies the member that it has assumed responsibility for the
pension scheme, or part of it, the member must –

(a) send a copy of the notification to the other party within 7 days of
receipt; and
(b) comply with paragraph (5).

(5) Where paragraph (4) applies, the member must –

(a) within 7 days of receipt of the notification, request the Board in
writing to provide a forecast of the member's compensation
entitlement as described in the 2005 Regulations; and
(b) send a copy of the forecast of the member's compensation entitlement
to the other party within 7 days of receipt.

(6) In this rule –

'assessment period' means an assessment period within the meaning of
Part 2 of the Pensions Act 2004; and
'valuation summary' has the meaning assigned to it by the 2005 Regulations.

Chapter 9
Pension Protection Fund Compensation

9.38 Application and interpretation of this Chapter

(1) This Chapter applies –

(a) where an application for a financial remedy has been made; and
(b) the applicant or respondent is, the party with compensation rights.

(2) In this Chapter 'party with compensation rights' –

(a) in proceedings under the 1973 Act and the 1984 Act, has the meaning
given to it by section 25G(5) of the 1973 Act;
(b) in proceedings under the 2004 Act, has the meaning given to 'civil
partner with compensation rights' by paragraph 37(1) of Schedule 5 to
the 2004 Act.

**9.39 What the party with compensation rights must do when the court fixes a
first appointment**

(1) Where the court fixes a first appointment as required by rule 9.12(1)(*a*) the
party with compensation rights must request the Board to provide the
information about the valuation of entitlement to PPF compensation referred
to in regulations made by the Secretary of State under section 118 of the
Pensions Act 2008.

(2) The party with compensation rights must comply with paragraph (1) within
7 days beginning with the date on which that party receives notification of the
date of the first appointment.

(3) Within 7 days beginning with the date on which the party with
compensation rights receives the information under paragraph (1) that party
must send a copy of it to the other party, together with the name and address of
the trustees or managers responsible for each pension scheme.

(4) Where the rights to PPF Compensation are derived from rights under more
than one pension scheme, the party with compensation rights must comply
with this rule in relation to each entitlement.

9.40 Applications for pension compensation sharing orders

Where an application for a financial remedy includes an application for a
pension compensation sharing order or where a request for such an order is
added to an existing application for a financial remedy, the applicant must serve
a copy of the application on the Board.

9.41 Applications for consent orders for pension compensation sharing

(1) This rule applies where –

    (a)   the parties have agreed on the terms of an order and the agreement includes a pension compensation sharing order;

    (b)   service has not been effected under rule 9.40; and

    (c)   the information referred to in paragraph (2) has not otherwise been provided.

(2) The party with compensation rights must –

    (a)   request the Board to provide the information set out in Section C of the Pension Protection Fund Inquiry Form; and

    (b)   on receipt, send a copy of the information referred to in sub-paragraph (*a*) to the other party.

9.42 Applications for pension compensation attachment orders

Where an application for a financial remedy includes an application for a pension compensation attachment order or where a request for such an order is added to an existing application for a financial remedy, the applicant must serve a copy of the application on the Board and must at the same time send –

    (a)   an address to which any notice which the Board is required to serve on the applicant is to be sent;

    (b)   an address to which any payment which the Board is required to make to the applicant is to be sent; and

    (c)   where the address in sub-paragraph (*b*) is that of a bank, a building society or the Department of National Savings, sufficient details to enable the payment to be made into the account of the applicant.

9.43 Applications for consent orders for pension compensation attachment

(1) This rule applies where service has not been effected under rule 9.42.

(2) Where the parties have agreed on the terms of an order and the agreement includes a pension compensation attachment order, then they must serve on the Board –

    (a)   a copy of the application for a consent order;

    (b)   a draft of the proposed order, complying with rule 9.44; and

    (c)   the particulars set out in rule 9.42.

9.44 Pension compensation sharing orders or pension compensation attachment orders

An order for a financial remedy, whether by consent or not, which includes a pension compensation sharing order or a pension compensation attachment order, must –

    (a)   in the body of the order, state that there is to be provision by way of pension compensation sharing or pension compensation attachment in accordance with the annex or annexes to the order; and

(b) be accompanied by a pension compensation sharing annex or a pension compensation attachment annex as the case may require, and if provision is made in relation to entitlement to PPF compensation that derives from rights under more than one pension scheme there must be one annex for each such entitlement.

9.45 Duty of the court upon making a pension compensation sharing order or a pension compensation attachment order

(1) A court which makes, varies or discharges a pension compensation sharing order or a pension compensation attachment order, must send, or direct one of the parties to send, to the Board –

(a) in the case of –
  (i) proceedings under Part 3 of the 1984 Act, a copy of the document of divorce, annulment or legal separation;
  (ii) proceedings under Schedule 7 to the 2004 Act, a copy of the document of dissolution, annulment or legal separation;
(b) in the case of –
  (i) divorce or nullity of marriage, a copy of the decree absolute under rule 7.32 or 7.33;
  (ii) dissolution or nullity of civil partnership, a copy of the order making the conditional order final under rule 7.32 or 7.33;
(c) in the case of separation –
  (i) in the matrimonial proceedings, a copy of the decree of judicial separation;
  (ii) in civil partnership proceedings, a copy of the separation order; and
(d) a copy of the pension compensation sharing order or the pension compensation attachment order, or as the case may be of the order varying or discharging that order, including any annex to that order relating to that PPF compensation but no other annex to that order.

(2) The documents referred to in paragraph (1) must be sent –

(a) in proceedings under the 1973 Act and the 1984 Act, within 7 days beginning with the date on which –
  (i) the relevant pension compensation sharing or pension compensation attachment order is made; or
  (ii) the decree absolute of divorce or nullity or the decree of judicial separation is made, whichever is the later; and
(b) in proceedings under the 2004 Act, within 7 days beginning with the date on which –
  (i) the relevant pension compensation sharing or pension compensation attachment order is made; or
  (ii) the final order of dissolution or nullity or separation order is made, whichever is the later.

****

PART 19
ALTERNATIVE PROCEDURE FOR APPLICATIONS

19.1 Types of application for which Part 19 procedure may be followed

(1) The Part 19 procedure is the procedure set out in this Part.

(2) An applicant may use the Part 19 procedure where the Part 18 procedure does not apply and –

    (a)   there is no form prescribed by a rule or referred to in Practice Direction 5A in which to make the application;

    (b)   the applicant seeks the court's decision on a question which is unlikely to involve a substantial dispute of fact; or

    (c)   paragraph (5) applies.

(3) The court may at any stage direct that the application is to continue as if the applicant had not used the Part 19 procedure and, if it does so, the court may give any directions it considers appropriate.

(4) Paragraph (2) does not apply if a practice direction provides that the Part 19 procedure may not be used in relation to the type of application in question.

(5) A rule or practice direction may, in relation to a specified type of proceedings –

    (a)   require or permit the use of the Part 19 procedure; and

    (b)   disapply or modify any of the rules set out in this Part as they apply to those proceedings.

19.2 Applications for which the Part 19 procedure must be followed

(1) The Part 19 procedure must be used in an application made in accordance with –

    (a)   section 60(3) of the 2002 Act (order to prevent disclosure of information to an adopted person);

    (b)   section 79(4) of the 2002 Act (order for Registrar General to give any information referred to in section 79(3) of the 2002 Act); and

    (c)   rule 14.21 (directions of High Court regarding fathers without parental responsibility).

(2) The respondent to an application made in accordance with paragraph (1)(b) is the Registrar General.

19.3 Contents of the application

Where the applicant uses the Part 19 procedure, the application must state –

    (a)   that this Part applies;

    (b)   either –

        (i)   the question which the applicant wants the court to decide; or

(ii) the order which the applicant is seeking and the legal basis of the application for that order;

(c) if the application is being made under an enactment, what that enactment is;

(d) if the applicant is applying in a representative capacity, what that capacity is; and

(e) if the respondent appears or is to appear in a representative capacity, what that capacity is.

(Part 17 requires a statement of case to be verified by a statement of truth.)

19.4 Issue of application without naming respondents

(1) A practice direction may set out circumstances in which an application may be issued under this Part without naming a respondent.

(2) The practice direction may set out those cases in which an application for permission must be made by application notice before the application is issued.

(3) The application for permission –

(a) need not be served on any other person; and

(b) must be accompanied by a copy of the application which the applicant proposes to issue.

(4) Where the court gives permission, it will give directions about the future management of the application.

19.5 Acknowledgment of service

(1) Subject to paragraph (2), each respondent must –

(a) file an acknowledgment of service within 14 days beginning with the date on which the application is served; and

(b) serve the acknowledgment of service on the applicant and any other party.

(2) If the application is to be served out of the jurisdiction, the respondent must file and serve an acknowledgment of service within the period set out in Practice Direction 6B.

(3) The acknowledgment of service must –

(a) state whether the respondent contests the application;

(b) state, if the respondent seeks a different order from that set out in the application, what that order is; and

(c) be signed by the respondent or the respondent's legal representative.

19.6 Consequence of not filing an acknowledgment of service

(1) This rule applies where –

(a) the respondent has failed to file an acknowledgment of service; and

(b) the time period for doing so has expired.

(2) The respondent may attend the hearing of the application but may not take part in the hearing unless the court gives permission.

19.7 Filing and serving written evidence

(1) The applicant must, when filing the application, file the written evidence on which the applicant intends to rely.

(2) The applicant's evidence must be served on the respondent with the application.

(3) A respondent who wishes to rely on written evidence must file it when filing the acknowledgment of service.

(4) A respondent who files written evidence must also, at the same time, serve a copy of that evidence on the other parties.

(5) Within 14 days beginning with the date on which a respondent's evidence was served on the applicant, the applicant may file further written evidence in reply.

(6) An applicant who files further written evidence must also, within the same time limit, serve a copy of that evidence on the other parties.

19.8 Evidence – general

(1) No written evidence may be relied on at the hearing of the application unless –

(a)   it has been served in accordance with rule 19.7; or
(b)   the court gives permission.

(2) The court may require or permit a party to give oral evidence at the hearing.

(3) The court may give directions requiring the attendance for cross-examination[GL] of a witness who has given written evidence.

   (Rule 22.1 contains a general power for the court to control evidence.)

19.9 Procedure where respondent objects to use of the Part 19 procedure

(1) A respondent who contends that the Part 19 procedure should not be used because –

(a)   there is a substantial dispute of fact; and
(b)   the use of the Part 19 procedure is not required or permitted by a rule or practice direction,

must state the reasons for that contention when filing the acknowledgment of service.

(2) When the court receives the acknowledgment of service and any written evidence, it will give directions as to the future management of the case.

(Rule 19.7 requires a respondent who wishes to rely on written evidence to file it when filing the acknowledgment of service.)

(Rule 19.1(3) allows the court to make an order that the application continue as if the applicant had not used the Part 19 procedure.)

PART 20
INTERIM REMEDIES AND SECURITY FOR COSTS

Chapter 1
Interim Remedies

20.1 Scope of this Part

The rules in this Part do not apply to proceedings in a magistrates' court.

20.2 Orders for interim remedies

(1) The court may grant the following interim remedies –

    (a)   an interim injunction$^{(GL)}$;
    (b)   an interim declaration;
    (c)   an order –
        (i)   for the detention, custody or preservation of relevant property;
        (ii)   for the inspection of relevant property;
        (iii)   for the taking of a sample of relevant property;
        (iv)   for the carrying out of an experiment on or with relevant property;
        (v)   for the sale of relevant property which is of a perishable nature or which for any other good reason it is desirable to sell quickly; and
        (vi)   for the payment of income from relevant property until an application is decided;
    (d)   an order authorising a person to enter any land or building in the possession of a party to the proceedings for the purposes of carrying out an order under sub-paragraph (*c*);
    (e)   an order under section 4 of the Torts (Interference with Goods) Act 1977 to deliver up goods;
    (f)   an order (referred to as a 'freezing injunction$^{(GL)}$') –
restraining a party from removing from the jurisdiction assets located there; or
restraining a party from dealing with any assets whether located within the jurisdiction or not;
    (g)   an order directing a party to provide information about the location of relevant property or assets or to provide information about relevant property or assets which are or may be the subject of an application for a freezing injunction$^{(GL)}$;
    (h)   an order (referred to as a 'search order') under section 7 of the Civil Procedure Act 1997 (order requiring a party to admit another party to premises for the purpose of preserving evidence etc);

(i)   an order under section 34 of the Senior Courts Act 1981 or section 53 of the County Courts Act 1984 (order in certain proceedings for disclosure of documents or inspection of property against a non-party);

(j)   an order for a specified fund to be paid into court or otherwise secured, where there is a dispute over a party's right to the fund;

(k)   an order permitting a party seeking to recover personal property to pay money into court pending the outcome of the proceedings and directing that, if money is paid into court, the property must be given up to that party;

(l)   an order directing a party to prepare and file accounts relating to the dispute;

(m) an order directing any account to be taken or inquiry to be made by the court.

(2) In paragraph (1)(*c*) and (*g*), 'relevant property' means property (including land) which is the subject of an application or as to which any question may arise on an application.

(3) The fact that a particular kind of interim remedy is not listed in paragraph (1) does not affect any power that the court may have to grant that remedy.

20.3 Time when an order for an interim remedy may be made

(1) An order for an interim remedy may be made at any time, including –

(a)   before proceedings are started; and

(b)   after judgment has been given.

    (Rule 5.3 provides that proceedings are started when the court issues an application form.)

(2) However –

(a)   paragraph (1) is subject to any rule, practice direction or other enactment which provides otherwise; and

(b)   the court may grant an interim remedy before an application has been started only if –
    (i)   the matter is urgent; or
    (ii)   it is otherwise desirable to do so in the interests of justice.

(3) Where the court grants an interim remedy before an application has been started, it will give directions requiring an application to be started.

(4) The court need not direct that an application be started where the application is made under section 33 of the Senior Courts Act 1981 or section 52 of the County Courts Act 1984 (order for disclosure, inspection etc before starting an application).

20.4 How to apply for an interim remedy

(1) The court may grant an interim remedy on an application made without notice if it appears to the court that there are good reasons for not giving notice.

(2) An application for an interim remedy must be supported by evidence, unless the court orders otherwise.

(3) If the applicant makes an application without giving notice, the evidence in support of the application must state the reasons why notice has not been given.

(Part 4 lists general case-management powers of the court.)

(Part 18 contains general rules about making an application.)

20.5 Interim injunction to cease if application is stayed

If –

(a) the court has granted an interim injunction$^{(GL)}$ other than a freezing injunction; and

(b) the application is stayed$^{(GL)}$ other than by agreement between the parties,

the interim injunction$^{(GL)}$ will be set aside$^{(GL)}$ unless the court orders that it should continue to have effect even though the application is stayed.

Chapter 2
Security for Costs

20.6 Security for costs

(1) A respondent to any application may apply under this Chapter of this Part for security for costs of the proceedings.

(Part 4 provides for the court to order payment of sums into court in other circumstances.)

(2) An application for security for costs must be supported by written evidence.

(3) Where the court makes an order for security for costs, it will –

(a) determine the amount of security; and

(b) direct –

(i)   the manner in which; and

(ii) the time within which,

the security must be given.

20.7 Conditions to be satisfied

(1) The court may make an order for security for costs under rule 20.6 if –

(a) it is satisfied, having regard to all the circumstances of the case, that it is just to make such an order; and

(b) either –

  (i) one or more of the conditions in paragraph (2) applies; or
  (ii) an enactment permits the court to require security for costs.

(2) The conditions are –

  (a) the applicant is –

    (i) resident out of the jurisdiction; but
    (ii) not resident in a Brussels Contracting State, a Lugano Contracting State or a Regulation State, as defined in section 1(3) of the Civil Jurisdiction and Judgments Act 1982 the Maintenance Regulation or a Member State bound by the Council Regulation;

  (b) the applicant has changed address since the application was started with a view to evading the consequences of the litigation;

  (c) the applicant failed to give an address in the application form, or gave an incorrect address in that form;

  (d) the applicant has taken steps in relation to the applicant's assets that would make it difficult to enforce an order for costs against the applicant.

(3) The court may not make an order for security for costs under rule 20.6 in relation to the costs of proceedings under the 1980 Hague Convention.

(Rule 4.4 allows the court to strike out a statement of case.)

Amendments—SI 2011/1328.

20.8 Security for costs of an appeal

The court may order security for costs of an appeal against –

(a) an appellant;
(b) a respondent who also appeals,

on the same grounds as it may order security for costs against an applicant under this Part.

****

PART 30
APPEALS

30.1 Scope and interpretation

(1) The rules in this Part apply to appeals to –

(a) the High Court; and
(b) a county court.

(2) This Part does not apply to an appeal in detailed assessment proceedings against a decision of an authorised court officer.

(Rules 47.20 to 47.23 of the CPR deal with appeals against a decision of an authorised court officer in detailed assessment proceedings.)

(3) In this Part –

'appeal court' means the court to which an appeal is made;

'appeal notice' means an appellant's or respondent's notice;

'appellant' means a person who brings or seeks to bring an appeal;

'lower court' means the court from which, or the person from whom, the appeal lies; and

'respondent' means –

    (a) a person other than the appellant who was a party to the proceedings in the lower court and who is affected by the appeal; and

    (b) a person who is permitted by the appeal court to be a party to the appeal.

(4) This Part is subject to any rule, enactment or practice direction which sets out special provisions with regard to any particular category of appeal.

30.2 Parties to comply with the practice direction

All parties to an appeal must comply with Practice Direction 30A.

30.3 Permission

(1) An appellant or respondent requires permission to appeal –

    (a) against a decision in proceedings where the decision appealed against was made by a district judge or a costs judge, unless paragraph (2) applies; or

    (b) as provided by Practice Direction 30A.

(2) Permission to appeal is not required where the appeal is against –

    (a) a committal order; or

    (b) a secure accommodation order under section 25 of the 1989 Act.

(3) An application for permission to appeal may be made –

    (a) to the lower court at the hearing at which the decision to be appealed was made; or

    (b) to the appeal court in an appeal notice.

    (Rule 30.4 sets out the time limits for filing an appellant's notice at the appeal court. Rule 30.5 sets out the time limits for filing a respondent's notice at the appeal court. Any application for permission to appeal to the appeal court must be made in the appeal notice (see rules 30.4(1) and 30.5(3).)

(4) Where the lower court refuses an application for permission to appeal, a further application for permission to appeal may be made to the appeal court.

(5) Where the appeal court, without a hearing, refuses permission to appeal, the person seeking permission may request the decision to be reconsidered at a hearing.

(6) A request under paragraph (5) must be filed within 7 days beginning with the date on which the notice that permission has been refused was served.

(7) Permission to appeal may be given only where –

    (a)   the court considers that the appeal would have a real prospect of success; or

    (b)   there is some other compelling reason why the appeal should be heard.

(8) An order giving permission may –

    (a)   limit the issues to be heard; and

    (b)   be made subject to conditions.

(9) In this rule 'costs judge' means a taxing master of the Senior Courts.

30.4 Appellant's notice

(1) Where the appellant seeks permission from the appeal court it must be requested in the appellant's notice.

(2) Subject to paragraph (3), the appellant must file the appellant's notice at the appeal court within –

    (a)   such period as may be directed by the lower court (which may be longer or shorter than the period referred to in sub-paragraph (b)); or

    (b)   where the court makes no such direction, 21 days after the date of the decision of the lower court against which the appellant wishes to appeal.

(3) Where the appeal is against an order under section 38(1) of the 1989 Act, the appellant must file the appellant's notice within 7 days beginning with the date of the decision of the lower court.

(4) Unless the appeal court orders otherwise, an appellant's notice must be served on each respondent and the persons referred to in paragraph (5) –

    (a)   as soon as practicable; and

    (b)   in any event not later than 7 days,

after it is filed.

(5) The persons referred to in paragraph (4) are –

    (a)   any children's guardian, welfare officer, or children and family reporter;

    (b)   a local authority who has prepared a report under section 14A(8) or (9) of the 1989 Act;

    (c)   an adoption agency or local authority which has prepared a report on the suitability of the applicant to adopt a child;

    (d)   a local authority which has prepared a report on the placement of the child for adoption; and

    (e)   where the appeal is from a magistrates' court, the court officer.

30.5 Respondent's notice

(1) A respondent may file and serve a respondent's notice.

(2) A respondent who –

    (a)   is seeking permission to appeal from the appeal court; or

    (b)   wishes to ask the appeal court to uphold the order of the lower court for reasons different from or additional to those given by the lower court,

must file a respondent's notice.

(3) Where the respondent seeks permission from the appeal court it must be requested in the respondent's notice.

(4) A respondent's notice must be filed within –

    (a)   such period as may be directed by the lower court; or

    (b)   where the court makes no such direction, 14 days beginning with the date referred to in paragraph (5).

(5) The date referred to in paragraph (4) is –

    (a)   the date on which the respondent is served with the appellant's notice where –

        permission to appeal was given by the lower court; or

        permission to appeal is not required;

    (b)   the date on which the respondent is served with notification that the appeal court has given the appellant permission to appeal; or

    (c)   the date on which the respondent is served with notification that the application for permission to appeal and the appeal itself are to be heard together.

(6) Unless the appeal court orders otherwise, a respondent's notice must be served on the appellant, any other respondent and the persons referred to in rule 30.4(5) –

    (a)   as soon as practicable; and

    (b)   in any event not later than 7 days,

after it is filed.

(7) Where there is an appeal against an order under section 38(1) of the 1989 Act –

    (a)   a respondent may not, in that appeal, bring an appeal from the order or ask the appeal court to uphold the order of the lower court for reasons different from or additional to those given by the lower court; and

    (b)   paragraphs (2) and (3) do not apply.

30.6 Grounds of appeal

The appeal notice must state the grounds of appeal.

30.7 Variation of time

(1) An application to vary the time limit for filing an appeal notice must be made to the appeal court.

(2) The parties may not agree to extend any date or time limit set by –

(a)   these rules;
(b)   Practice Direction 30A; or
(c)   an order of the appeal court or the lower court.

(Rule 4.1(3)(a) provides that the court may extend or shorten the time for compliance with a rule, practice direction or court order (even if an application for extension is made after the time for compliance has expired).)

(Rule 4.1(3)(c) provides that the court may adjourn or bring forward a hearing.)

30.8 Stay

Unless the appeal court or the lower court orders otherwise, an appeal does not operate as a stay$^{(GL)}$ of any order or decision of the lower court.

30.9 Amendment of appeal notice

An appeal notice may not be amended without the permission of the appeal court.

30.10 Striking out appeal notices and setting aside or imposing conditions on permission to appeal

(1) The appeal court may –

(a)   strike out the whole or part of an appeal notice;
(b)   set aside permission to appeal in whole or in part;
(c)   impose or vary conditions upon which an appeal may be brought.

(2) The court will only exercise its powers under paragraph (1) where there is a compelling reason for doing so.

(3) Where a party was present at the hearing at which permission was given that party may not subsequently apply for an order that the court exercise its powers under paragraphs (1)(b) or (1)(c).

30.11 Appeal court's powers

(1) In relation to an appeal the appeal court has all the powers of the lower court.

(Rule 30.1(4) provides that this Part is subject to any enactment that sets out special provisions with regard to any particular category of appeal.)

(2) The appeal court has power to –

(a)   affirm, set aside or vary any order or judgment made or given by the lower court;
(b)   refer any application or issue for determination by the lower court;
(c)   order a new hearing;
(d)   make orders for the payment of interest;
(e)   make a costs order.

(3) The appeal court may exercise its powers in relation to the whole or part of an order of the lower court.

(Rule 4.1 contains general rules about the court's case management powers.)

(4) If the appeal court –

    (a)   refuses an application for permission to appeal;

    (b)   strikes out an appellant's notice; or

    (c)   dismisses an appeal,

and it considers that the application, the appellant's notice or the appeal is totally without merit, the provisions of paragraph (5) must be complied with.

(5) Where paragraph (4) applies –

    (a)   the court's order must record the fact that it considers the application, the appellant's notice or the appeal to be totally without merit; and

    (b)   the court must at the same time consider whether it is appropriate to make a civil restraint order.

30.12 Hearing of appeals

(1) Every appeal will be limited to a review of the decision of the lower court unless –

    (a)   an enactment or practice direction makes different provision for a particular category of appeal; or

    (b)   the court considers that in the circumstances of an individual appeal it would be in the interests of justice to hold a re-hearing.

(2) Unless it orders otherwise, the appeal court will not receive –

    (a)   oral evidence; or

    (b)   evidence which was not before the lower court.

(3) The appeal court will allow an appeal where the decision of the lower court was –

    (a)   wrong; or

    (b)   unjust because of a serious procedural or other irregularity in the proceedings in the lower court.

(4) The appeal court may draw any inference of fact which it considers justified on the evidence.

(5) At the hearing of the appeal a party may not rely on a matter not contained in that party's appeal notice unless the appeal court gives permission.

30.13 Assignment of appeals to the Court of Appeal

(1) Where the court from or to which an appeal is made or from which permission to appeal is sought ('the relevant court') considers that –

    (a)   an appeal which is to be heard by a county court or the High Court would raise an important point of principle or practice; or

(b) there is some other compelling reason for the Court of Appeal to hear it,

the relevant court may order the appeal to be transferred to the Court of Appeal.

(2) This rule does not apply to proceedings in a magistrates' court.

30.14 Reopening of final appeals

(1) The High Court will not reopen a final determination of any appeal unless –

(a) it is necessary to do so in order to avoid real injustice;
(b) the circumstances are exceptional and make it appropriate to reopen the appeal; and
(c) there is no alternative effective remedy.

(2) In paragraphs (1), (3), (4) and (6), 'appeal' includes an application for permission to appeal.

(3) This rule does not apply to appeals to a county court.

(4) Permission is needed to make an application under this rule to reopen a final determination of an appeal.

(5) There is no right to an oral hearing of an application for permission unless, exceptionally, the judge so directs.

(6) The judge will not grant permission without directing the application to be served on the other party to the original appeal and giving that party an opportunity to make representations.

(7) There is no right of appeal or review from the decision of the judge on the application for permission, which is final.

(8) The procedure for making an application for permission is set out in Practice Direction 30A.

****

32.1 Power of court to control evidence

(1) The court may control the evidence by giving directions as to –

(a) the issues on which it requires evidence;
(b) the nature of the evidence which it requires to decide those issues; and
(c) the way in which the evidence is to be placed before the court.

(2) In this Part, 'the 1950 Act' means the Maintenance Orders Act 1950.

(3) The court may limit cross-examination·

Amendments-SI 2011/1328.

32.2 Evidence of witnesses – general rule

(1) The general rule is that any fact which needs to be proved by the evidence of witnesses is to be proved –

    (a)   at trial, by their oral evidence given in public; and

    (b)   at any other hearing, by their evidence in writing.

(2) This is subject –

    (a)   to any provision to the contrary contained in these Rules or elsewhere; or

    (b)   to any order of the court.

32.3 Evidence by video link or other means

The court may allow a witness to give evidence through a video link or by other means.

32.4 Requirement to serve witness statements for use at trial

(1) A witness statement is a written statement signed by a person which contains the evidence which that person would be allowed to give orally.

(2) The court will order a party to serve on the other parties any witness statement of the oral evidence which the party serving the statement intends to rely on in relation to any issues of fact to be decided at the trial.

(3) The court may give directions as to –

    (a)   the order in which witness statements are to be served; and

    (b)   whether or not the witness statements are to be filed.

32.5 Cancellation of registration of a High Court order

(1) This rule applies where –

    (a)   the registration of a High Court order registered in the Court of Session or the Court of Judicature of Northern Ireland is cancelled under section 24(1) of the 1950 Act; and

    (b)   notice of the cancellation is given to a court officer in the court in which the order was made (who is the prescribed officer for the purposes of section 24(3)(*a*) of the 1950 Act).

(2) On receipt of a notice of cancellation of registration, the court officer will enter particulars of the notice in Part 1 of the register.

32.6 Application of this Chapter to a county court order

Rules 32.3 to 32.5 apply to an application to register a county court order as if –

    (a)   references to a High Court order were references to a county court order;

(b)   where the order is to be registered in Scotland, references to the Court of Session and the clerk of the Court of Session were references to the sheriff court and the sheriff-clerk of the sheriff court respectively; and

(c)   where the order is to be registered in Northern Ireland, references to the Court of Judicature of Northern Ireland and the registrar of Northern Ireland were references to the court of summary jurisdiction and the clerk of the court of summary jurisdiction respectively.

Section 3
Registration etc. of Scottish and Northern Irish orders

32.7 Registration of Scottish and Northern Irish orders

On receipt of a certified copy of a Scottish order or a Northern Irish order for registration, a court officer in the principal registry (who is the prescribed officer for the purposes of section 17(2) of the 1950 Act) will –

(a)   enter particulars of the order in Part 2 of the register;

(b)   notify the clerk of the Court of Session or the registrar in Northern Ireland, as the case may be, that the order has been registered; and

(c)   file the certified copy of the order and any statutory declaration, affidavit(GL) or statement as to the amount of any arrears due under the order.

32.8 Application to adduce evidence before High Court

The Part 18 procedure applies to an application by a person liable to make payments under a Scottish order registered in the High Court to adduce before that court any evidence on which that person would be entitled to rely in any proceedings brought before the court by which the order was made for the variation or discharge of the order.

32.9 Notice of variation etc. of Scottish and Northern Irish orders

(1) This rule applies where –

(a)   a Scottish order or a Northern Irish order, which is registered in the High Court, is discharged or varied; and

(b)   notice of the discharge or variation is given to a court officer in the High Court (who is the prescribed officer for the purposes of section 23(1)(*a*) of the 1950 Act).

(2) On receipt of a notice of discharge or variation, the court officer will enter particulars of the notice in Part 2 of the register.

32.10 Cancellation of registration of Scottish and Northern Irish orders

(1) The Part 18 procedure applies to an application for the cancellation of the registration of a Scottish order or a Northern Irish order in the High Court.

(2) The application must be made without notice to the person liable to make payments under the order.

(3) If the registration of the order is cancelled, the court officer will –

(a) note the cancellation in Part II of the register; and
(b) send written notice of the cancellation to –
  (i) the clerk of the Court of Session or the registrar in Northern Ireland, as the case may be; and
  (ii) the court officer in any magistrates' court in which the order has been registered in accordance with section 2(5) of the 1958 Act.

32.11 Enforcement

(1) The Part 18 procedure applies to an application for or with respect to the enforcement of a Scottish order or a Northern Irish order registered in the High Court.

(2) The application may be made without notice to the person liable to make payments under the order.

32.12 Inspection of register and copies of order

Any person –

(a) who is entitled to receive, or liable to make, payments under a maintenance order made by the High Court, the Court of Session or the Court of Judicature of Northern Ireland; or
(b) with the permission of the court,

may –

  (i) inspect the register; or
  (ii) request a copy of any order registered in the High Court under Part 2 of the 1950 Act and any statutory declaration, affidavit(GL) or statement filed with the order.

Chapter 3
Registration of Maintenance Orders under the 1958 Act

32.13 Interpretation

In this Chapter 'the register' means the register kept for the purposes of the 1958 Act.

32.14 Registration of orders – prescribed period

The prescribed period for the purpose of section 2(2) of the 1958 Act is 14 days.

> (Section 2(2) sets out the period during which an order, which is to be registered in a magistrates' court, may not be enforced)

32.15 Application for registration of a maintenance order in a magistrates' court

(1) An application under section 2(1) of the 1958 Act may be made by sending to the court officer at the court which made the order –

(a)   a certified copy of the maintenance order; and

(b)   two copies of the application.

(2) When, on the grant of an application, the court officer sends the certified copy of the maintenance order to the magistrates' court in accordance with section 2(2), the court officer must –

(a)   note on the order that the application for registration has been granted; and

(b)   send to the magistrates' court a copy of the application for registration of the order.

(3) On receiving notice that the magistrates' court has registered the order, the court officer must enter particulars of the registration in the court records.

32.16 Registration in a magistrates' court of an order registered in the High Court

(1) This rule applies where –

(a)   a maintenance order is registered in the High Court in accordance with section 17(4) of the 1950 Act; and

(b)   the court officer receives notice that the magistrates' court has registered the order in accordance with section 2(5) of the 1958 Act.

(2) The court officer must enter particulars of the registration in Part II of the register.

32.17 Registration in the High Court of a magistrates' court order

(1) This rule applies where a court officer receives a certified copy of a magistrates' court order for registration in accordance with section 2(4)(*c*) of the 1958 Act.

(2) The court officer must register the order in the High Court by –

(a)   filing the copy of the order; and

(b)   entering particulars in –

    (i)   the register; or

    (ii)   if the order is received in a district registry, the cause book or cause card.

(3) The court officer must notify the magistrates' court that the order has been registered.

32.18 Notice to admit facts

(1) A party may serve notice on another party requiring him to admit the facts, or the part of the case of the serving party, specified in the notice.

(2) A notice to admit facts must be served no later than 21 days before the trial.

(3) Where the other party makes any admission in response to the notice the admission may be used against him only –

    (a)   in the proceedings in which the notice to admit is served; and

    (b)   by the party who served the notice.

(4) The court may allow a party to amend or withdraw any admission made by him on such terms as it thinks just.

32.19 Notice to admit or produce documents

(1) A party shall be deemed to admit the authenticity of a document disclosed to him under Part 31 (disclosure and inspection of documents) unless he serves notice that he wishes the document to be proved at trial.

(2) A notice to prove a document must be served –

    (a)   by the latest date for serving witness statements; or

    (b)   within 7 days of disclosure of the document,

whichever is later.

32.20 Variation or discharge of an order registered in the High Court

(1) This rule applies where a maintenance order is registered in the High Court under Part 1 of the 1958 Act.

(2) If the court officer receives from the magistrates' court a certified copy of an order varying or discharging the maintenance order the court officer must –

    (a)   file the copy of the order;

    (b)   enter the particulars of the variation or discharge in –

        (i)   the register; or

        (ii)   if the order is received in a district registry, the cause book or cause card; and

    (c)   send notice of the variation or discharge to the court officer of a county court –

        (i)   who has notified the court officer of enforcement proceedings in that court relating to the maintenance order; or

        (ii)   to whom a payment is to be made under an attachment of earnings order made by the High Court for the enforcement of the registered order.

32.21 Cancellation of registration – orders registered in the High Court

(1) This rule applies where an order is registered in the High Court.

(2) A person giving notice under section 5(1) of the 1958 Act must give the notice to the court officer.

(3) The court officer must take the steps mentioned in paragraph (4) if –

    (a)   notice is given under section 5 of the 1958 Act; and

    (b)   the court officer is satisfied, by a witness statement by the person entitled to receive payments under the order that no enforcement proceedings in relation to the order, that were started before the giving of the notice, remain in force.

(4) The court officer must, if satisfied as mentioned in paragraph (3) –

    (a)   cancel the registration by entering particulars of the notice in the register or cause book (or cause card) as the case may be; and

    (b)   send notice of the cancellation to –

        (i)   the court which made the order; and

        (ii)   where applicable, to the magistrates' court in which the order was registered in accordance with section 17(4) of the 1950 Act.

(5) Where the cancellation results from a notice given under section 5(1) of the 1958 Act, the court officer must state that fact in the notice of cancellation sent in accordance with paragraph (4)(*b*).

(6) If notice is received from a magistrates' court that the registration in that court under the 1958 Act of an order registered in the High Court in accordance with section 17(4) of the 1950 Act has been cancelled, the court officer must note the cancellation in Part II of the register.

32.22 Cancellation of registration – orders registered in a magistrates' court

(1) Where the court gives notice under section 5(2) of the 1958 Act, the court officer must endorse the notice on the certified copy of the order of variation or discharge sent to the magistrates' court in accordance with rule 32.19(2).

(2) Where notice is received from a magistrates' court that registration of an order made by the High Court or a county court under Part 1 of the 1958 Act has been cancelled, the court officer must enter particulars of the cancellation in the place where the details required by rule 32.15(3) were entered.

Chapter 4
Registration and Enforcement of Custody Orders under the 1986 Act

32.23 Interpretation

In this Chapter –

    'appropriate court' means, in relation to –

        (a)   Scotland, the Court of Session;

        (b)   Northern Ireland, the High Court in Northern Ireland; and

        (c)   a specified dependent territory, the corresponding court in that territory;

    'appropriate officer' means, in relation to –

        (a)   the Court of Session, the Deputy Principal Clerk of Session;

        (b)   the High Court in Northern Ireland, the Ml;aster (Care and Protection) of that court; and

        (c)   the appropriate court in a specified dependent territory, the corresponding officer of that court;

    'Part 1 order' means an order under Part 1 of the 1986 Act;

    'the register' means the register kept for the purposes of Part 1 of the 1986 Act; and 'specified dependent territory' means a dependent territory specified in column 1 of Schedule 1 to the Family Law Act 1986 (Specified Dependent Territories) Order 1991.

32.24 Prescribed officer and functions of the court

(1) The prescribed officer for the purposes of sections 27(4) and 28(1) of the 1986 Act is the family proceedings department manager of the principal registry.

(2) The function of the court under sections 27(3) and 28(1) of the 1986 Act shall be performed by a court officer.

32.25 Application for the registration of an order made by the High Court or a county court

(1) An application under section 27 of the 1986 Act for the registration of an order made in the High Court or a county court may be made by sending to a court officer at the court which made the order –

   (a)   a certified copy of the order;
   (b)   a copy of any order which has varied the terms of the original order;
   (c)   a statement which –
      (i)   contains the name and address of the applicant and the applicant's interest under the order;
      (ii)   contains –
         (aa)   the name and date of birth of the child in respect of whom the order was made;
         (bb)   the whereabouts or suspected whereabouts of the child; and
         (cc)   the name of any person with whom the child is alleged to be;
      (iii)   contains the name and address of any other person who has an interest under the order and states whether the order has been served on that person;
      (iv)   states in which of the jurisdictions of Scotland, Northern Ireland or a specified dependent territory the order is to be registered;
      (v)   states that to the best of the applicant's information and belief, the order is in force;
      (vi)   states whether, and if so where, the order is already registered;
      (vii)   gives details of any order known to the applicant which affects the child and is in force in the jurisdiction in which the order is to be registered;
      (viii)   annexes any document relevant to the application; and
      (ix)   is verified by a statement of truth; and
   (d)   a copy of the statement referred to in paragraph (c).

(2) On receipt of the documents referred to in paragraph (1), the court officer will, subject to paragraph (4) –

(a)   keep the original statement and send the other documents to the appropriate officer;

(b)   record in the court records the fact that the documents have been sent to the appropriate officer; and

(c)   file a copy of the documents.

(3) On receipt of a notice that the document has been registered in the appropriate court the court officer will record that fact in the court records.

(4) The court officer will not send the documents to the appropriate officer if it appears to the court officer that –

(a)   the order is no longer in force; or

(b)   the child has reached the age of 16.

(5) Where paragraph (4) applies –

(a)   the court officer must, within 14 days of the decision, notify the applicant of the decision of the court officer in paragraph (4) and the reasons for it; and

(b)   the applicant may apply to a judge, but not a district judge, in private for an order that the documents be sent to the appropriate court.

32.26 Registration of orders made in Scotland, Northern Ireland or a specified dependent territory

(1) This rule applies where the prescribed officer receives, for registration, a certified copy of an order made in Scotland, Northern Ireland or a specified dependent territory.

(2) The prescribed officer will –

(a)   enter in the register –
   (i)   the name and address of the applicant and the applicant's interest under the order;
   (ii)   the name and date of birth of the child and the date the child will attain the age of 16;
   (iii) the whereabouts or suspected whereabouts of the child; and
   (iv)   the terms of the order, its date and the court which made it;

(b)   file the certified copy and accompanying documents; and

(c)   notify –
   (i)   the court which sent the order; and
   (ii)   the applicant,
   that the order has been registered.

32.27 Revocation and variation of an order made in the High Court or a county court

(1) Where a Part 1 order, registered in an appropriate court, is varied or revoked, the court officer of the court making the order of variation or revocation will –

(a)   send a certified copy of the order of variation or revocation to –

      (i)   the appropriate officer; and

      (ii)   if a different court, the court which made the Part 1 order;

  (b)   record in the court records the fact that a copy of the order has been sent; and

  (c)   file a copy of the order.

(2) On receipt of notice from the appropriate court that its register has been amended, this fact will be recorded by the court officer of –

  (a)   the court which made the order of variation or revocation; and

  (b)   if different, the court which made the Part 1 order.

32.28 Registration of varied, revoked or recalled orders made in Scotland, Northern Ireland or a specified dependent territory

(1) This rule applies where the prescribed officer receives a certified copy of an order made in Scotland, Northern Ireland or a specified dependent territory which varies, revokes or recalls a registered Part 1 order.

(2) The prescribed officer shall enter particulars of the variation, revocation or recall in the register and give notice of the entry to –

  (a)   the court which sent the certified copy;

  (b)   if different, the court which made the Part 1 order;

  (c)   the applicant for registration; and

  (d)   if different, the applicant for the variation, revocation of recall of the order.

(3) An application under section 28(2) of the 1986 Act must be made in accordance with the Part 19 procedure.

(4) The applicant for the Part 1 order, if not the applicant under section 28(2) of the 1986 Act, must be made a defendant to the application.

(5) Where the court cancels a registration under section 28(2) of the 1986 Act, the court officer will amend the register and give notice of the amendment to the court which made the Part 1 order.

32.29 Interim directions

The following persons will be made parties to an application for interim directions under section 29 of the 1986 Act –

  (a)   the parties to the proceedings for enforcement; and

  (b)   if not a party to those proceedings, the applicant for the Part 1 order.

32.30 Staying and dismissal of enforcement proceedings

(1) The following persons will be made parties to an application under section 30(1) or 31(1) of the 1986 Act –

  (a)   the parties to the proceedings for enforcement which are sought to be stayed(GL); and

  (b)   if not a party to those proceedings, the applicant for the Part 1 order.

(2) Where the court makes an order under section 30(2) or (3) or section 31(3) of the 1986 Act, the court officer will amend the register and give notice of the amendment to –

    (a)   the court which made the Part 1 order; and

    (b)   the applicants for –

        (i)   registration;

        (ii) enforcement; and

        (iii) stay or dismissal of the enforcement proceedings.

32.31 Particulars of other proceedings

A party to proceedings for or relating to a Part 1 order who knows of other proceedings which relate to the child concerned (including proceedings out of the jurisdiction and concluded proceedings) must file a witness statement which –

    (a)   states in which jurisdiction and court the other proceedings were begun;

    (b)   states the nature and current state of the proceedings and the relief claimed or granted;

    (c)   sets out the names of the parties to the proceedings and their relationship to the child;

    (d)   if applicable and if known, states the reasons why relief claimed in the proceedings for or relating to the Part 1 order was not claimed in the other proceedings; and

    (e)   is verified by a statement of truth.

32.32 Inspection of register

The following persons may inspect any entry in the register relating to a Part 1 order and may request copies of the order any document relating to it –

    (a)   the applicant for registration of the Part 1 order;

    (b)   a person who, to the satisfaction of a district judge, has an interest under the Part 1 order; and

    (c)   a person who obtains the permission of a district judge.

PART 33
ENFORCEMENT

Chapter 1
General Rules

33.1 Application

(1) The rules in this Part apply to an application made in the High Court and a county court to enforce an order made in family proceedings.

(2) Part 50 of, and Schedules 1 and 2 to, the CPR apply, as far as they are relevant and with necessary modification (including the modifications referred

to in rule 33.7), to an application made in the High Court and a county court to enforce an order made in family proceedings.

Section 1
Enforcement of orders for the payment of money

33.2 Application of the Civil Procedure Rules

Part 70 of the CPR applies to proceedings under this Section as if –

(a)   in rule 70.1, in paragraph (2)(*d*), 'but does not include a judgment or order for the payment of money into court' is omitted; and

(b)   rule 70.5 is omitted.

33.3 How to apply

(1) Except where a rule or practice direction otherwise requires, an application for an order to enforce an order for the payment of money must be made in a notice of application accompanied by a statement which must –

(a)   state the amount due under the order, showing how that amount is arrived at; and

(b)   be verified by a statement of truth.

(2) The notice of application may either –

(a)   apply for an order specifying the method of enforcement; or

(b)   apply for an order for such method of enforcement as the court may consider appropriate.

(3) If an application is made under paragraph (2)(*b*), an order to attend court will be issued and rule 71.2 (6) and (7) of the CPR will apply as if the application had been made under that rule.

33.4 Transfer of orders

(1) This rule applies to an application for the transfer –

(a)   to the High Court of an order made in a designated county court; and

(b)   to a designated county court of an order made in the High Court.

(2) The application must be –

(a)   made without notice; and

(b)   accompanied by a statement which complies with rule 33.3(1).

(3) The transfer will have effect upon the filing of the application.

(4) Where an order is transferred from a designated county court to the High Court –

(a)   it will have the same force and effect; and

(b)   the same proceedings may be taken on it,

as if it were an order of the High Court.

(5) This rule does not apply to the transfer of orders for periodical payments or for the recovery of arrears of periodical payments.

Section 2
Committal and injunction

33.5 General rule – committal hearings to be in public

(1) The general rule is that proceedings in the High Court for an order of committal will be heard in public.

(2) An order of committal may be heard in private where this is permitted by rule 6 of Order 52 of the RSC (cases in which a court may sit in private).

33.6 Proceedings in the principal registry treated as pending in a designated county court

(1) This rule applies where an order for the warrant of committal of any person to prison has been made or issued in proceedings which are –

    (a)   in the principal registry; and
    (b)   treated as pending in a designated county court or a county court.

(2) The person subject to the order will, wherever located, be treated for the purposes of section 122 of the County Courts Act 1984 as being out of the jurisdiction of the principal registry.

(3) Where –

    (a)   a committal is for failure to comply with the terms of an injunction(GL); or
    (b)   an order or warrant for the arrest or committal of any person is made or issued in proceedings under Part 4 of the 1996 Act in the principal registry which are treated as pending in a county court,

the order or warrant may, if the court so directs, be executed by the tipstaff within any county court.

33.7 Specific modifications of the CCR

(1) CCR Order 29, rule 1 (committal for breach of an order or undertaking) applies to –

    (a)   section 8 orders, except those referred to in paragraph (2)(*a*); and
    (b)   orders under the following sections of the 1989 Act –
        (i)   section 14A (special guardianship orders);
        (ii)   14B(2)(*b*) (granting of permission on making a special guardianship order to remove a child from the United Kingdom);
        (iii)   section 14C(3)(*b*) (granting of permission to remove from the United Kingdom a child who is subject to a special guardianship order); and
        (iv)   section 14D (variation or discharge of a special guardianship order),

as if paragraph (3) of that rule were substituted by the following paragraph –

'(3) In the case of a section 8 order (within the meaning of section 8(2) of the Children Act 1989) or an order under section 14A, 14B(2)(*b*), 14C(3)(*b*) or 14D of the Children Act 1989 enforceable by committal order under paragraph (1), the judge or the district judge may, on the application of the person entitled to enforce the order, direct that the proper officer issue a copy of the order, endorsed with or incorporating a notice as to the consequences of disobedience, for service in accordance with paragraph (2), and no copy of the order shall be issued with any such notice endorsed or incorporated save in accordance with such a direction.'.

(2) CCR Order 29, rule 1 applies to –

(a) contact orders to which a notice has been attached under section 11I of the 1989 Act or under section 8(2) of the Children and Adoption Act 2006;

(b) orders under section 11J of the 1989 Act (enforcement orders); and

(c) orders under paragraph 9 of Schedule A1 to the 1989 Act (orders following breach of enforcement orders),

as if paragraph (3) were omitted.

33.8 Section 118 County Courts Act 1984 and the tipstaff

For the purposes of section 118 of the County Courts Act 1984 in its application to the hearing of family proceedings at the Royal Courts of Justice or the principal registry, the tipstaff is deemed to be an officer of the court.

Chapter 2
Committal by way of Judgment Summons

33.9 Interpretation

In this Chapter, unless the context requires otherwise –

'order' means an order made in family proceedings for the payment of money;

'judgment creditor' means a person entitled to enforce an order under section 5 of the Debtors Act 1869;

'debtor' means a person liable under an order; and

'judgment summons' means a summons under section 5 of the Debtor's Act 1869 requiring a debtor to attend court.

33.10 Application

(1) An application for the issue of a judgment summons may be made –

(a) in the case of an order of the High Court –

(i) where the order was made in matrimonial proceedings, to the principal registry, a district registry or a divorce county court, whichever in the opinion of the judgment creditor is most convenient;

> > (ii) where the order was made in civil partnership proceedings, to the principal registry, a district registry or a civil partnership proceedings county court, whichever in the opinion of the judgment creditor is the most convenient; and
> > (iii) in any other case, to the principal registry, a district registry or a designated county court, whichever in the opinion of the judgment creditor is most convenient;
> (b) in the case of an order of a divorce county court, to whichever divorce county court is in the opinion of the judgment creditor most convenient; and
> (c) in the case of an order of a civil partnership proceedings county court, to whichever civil partnership proceedings county court is in the opinion of the judgment creditor most convenient,

having regard (in any case) to the place where the debtor resides or carries on business and irrespective of the court or registry in which the order was made.

(2) An application must be accompanied by a statement which –

> (a) complies with rule 33.3(1);
> (b) contains all the evidence on which the judgment creditor intends to rely; and
> (c) has exhibited to it a copy of the order.

33.11 Judgment summons

(1) If the debtor is in default under an order of committal made on a previous judgment summons in respect of the same order, a judgment summons must not be issued without the court's permission.

(2) A judgment summons must –

> (a) be accompanied by the statement referred to in rule 33.10(2); and
> (b) be served on the debtor personally not less than 14 days before the hearing.

(3) A debtor served with the judgment summons under paragraph (2)(*b*) must be paid or offered a sum reasonably sufficient to cover the expenses of travelling to and from the court at which the debtor is summoned to appear.

33.12 Successive judgment summonses

Subject to rule 33.11(1), successive judgment summonses may be issued even if the debtor has ceased to reside or carry on business at the address stated in the application for the issue of a judgment summons since the issue of the original judgment summons.

33.13 Requirement for personal service

In proceedings for committal by way of judgment summons, the following documents must be served personally on the debtor –

(a) where the court has summonsed the debtor to attend and the debtor has failed to do so, the notice of the date and time fixed for the adjourned hearing; and

(b) copies of the judgment summons and the documents mentioned in rule 33.10(2).

33.14 Committal on application for judgment summons

(1) No person may be committed on an application for a judgment summons unless –

(a) where the proceedings are in the High Court, the debtor has failed to attend both the hearing that the debtor was summonsed to attend and the adjourned hearing;

(b) where the proceedings are in a county court, an order is made under section 110(2) of the County Courts Act 1984; or

(c) the judgment creditor proves that the debtor –
 (i) has, or has had, since the date of the order the means to pay the sum in respect of which the debtor has made default; and
 (ii) has refused or neglected, or refuses or neglects, to pay that sum.

(2) The debtor may not be compelled to give evidence.

33.15 Orders for the benefit of different persons

Where an applicant has obtained one or more orders in the same application but for the benefit of different persons –

(a) where the judgment creditor is a child, the applicant may apply for the issue of a judgment summons in respect of those orders on behalf of the judgment creditor without seeking permission to act as the child's litigation friend; and

(b) only one judgment summons need be issued in respect of those orders.

33.16 Hearing of judgment summons

(1) On the hearing of the judgment summons the court may –

(a) where the order is for lump sum provision or costs; or

(b) where the order is an order for maintenance pending suit, an order for maintenance pending outcome of proceedings or an order for other periodical payments and it appears to the court that the order would have been varied or suspended if the debtor had made an application for that purpose,

make a new order for payment of the amount due under the original order, together with the costs of the judgment summons, either at a specified time or by instalments.

(2) If the court makes an order of committal, it may direct its execution to be suspended on terms that the debtor pays to the judgment creditor –

(a) the amount due;

(b)   the costs of the judgment summons; and

(c)   any sums accruing due under the original order,

either at a specified time or by instalments.

(3) All payments under a new order or an order of committal must be made to the judgment creditor unless the court directs otherwise.

(4) Where an order of committal is suspended on such terms as are mentioned in paragraph (2) –

(a)   all payments made under the suspended order will be deemed to be made –

(i)   first, in or towards the discharge of any sums from time to time accruing due under the original order; and

(ii)   secondly, in or towards the discharge of a debt in respect of which the judgment summons was issued and the costs of the summons; and

(b)   the suspended order must not be executed until the judgment creditor has filed a statement of default on the part of the debtor.

33.17 Special provisions as to judgment summonses in the High Court

(1) The court may summons witnesses to give evidence to prove the means of the debtor and may issue a witness summons for that purpose.

(2) Where the debtor appears at the hearing, the court may direct that the travelling expenses paid to the debtor be allowed as expenses of a witness.

(3) Where the debtor appears at the hearing and no order of committal is made, the court may allow the debtor's proper costs including compensation for any loss of earnings.

(4) When the court makes –

(a)   a new order; or

(b)   an order of committal,

a court officer must send notice of the order to the debtor and, if the original order was made in another court, to that court.

(5) An order of committal must be directed –

(a)   where the order is to be executed by the tipstaff, to the tipstaff; or

(b)   where the order is to be executed by a deputy tipstaff, to the county court within the district of which the debtor is to be found.

33.18 Special provisions as to judgment summonses in designated county courts

(1) Rules 1, 2, 3(2), 5, 7(3) and 9(2) of Order 28 of the CCR (which deal with the issue of a judgment summons in a county court and the subsequent procedure) do not apply to judgment summons issued in a designated county court.

(2) Rule 9(1) of Order 28 of the CCR (notification of order on judgment of High Court) applies to such a summons as if for the words 'the High Court' there were substituted the words –

(a) 'any other court' where they first appear; and
(b) 'that other court' where they next appear.

(3) Rule 7(1) and (2) of Order 28 of the CCR (suspension of a committal order) apply to such a summons subject to rule 33.16(2) and (3).

Chapter 3
Attachment of Earnings

33.19 Proceedings in the Principal Registry

The Attachment of Earnings Act 1971 and Order 27 of the CCR (attachment of earnings) apply to the enforcement of an order made in family proceedings in the principal registry which are treated as pending in a designated county court as if they were an order made by such a court.

Chapter 4
Warrant of Execution

33.20 Applications to vary existing orders

Where an application is pending for a variation of –

(a) a financial order;
(b) an order under section 27 of the 1973 Act; or
(c) an order under Part 9 of Schedule 5 to the 2004 Act,

no warrant of execution may be issued to enforce payment of any sum due under those orders, except with the permission of the district judge.

33.21 Section 103 County Courts Act 1984

Where a warrant of execution has been issued to enforce an order made in family proceedings pending in the principal registry which are treated as pending in a designated county court, the goods and chattels against which the warrant has been issued must, wherever they are located, be treated for the purposes of section 103 of the County Courts Act 1984 as being out of the jurisdiction of the principal registry.

Chapter 5
Court's Power to Appoint a Receiver

33.22 Application of the CPR

Part 69 of the CPR applies to proceedings under this Part.

Chapter 6
Orders to Obtain Information from Judgment Debtors

33.23 Application of the CPR

Part 71 of the CPR applies to proceedings under this Part.

Chapter 7
Third Party Debt Orders

33.24 Application of the CPR

(1) Part 72 of the CPR applies to proceedings under this Part with the following modifications.

(2) In rule 72.4 –

    (a)   in paragraph (1), for 'a judge' there is substituted 'the court'; and
    (b)   in paragraph (2), for 'judge' there is substituted 'court'.

(3) In rule 72.7, in paragraph (2)(*a*), after 'the Royal Courts of Justice' insert ', or the principal registry'.

(4) Rule 72.10 is omitted.

Chapter 8
Charging Order, Stop Order, Stop Notice

33.25 Application of the CPR

(1) Part 73 of the CPR applies to proceedings under this Part with the following modifications.

(2) In rule 73.1, paragraph (2), sub-paragraphs (*b*) and (*c*) are omitted.

(3) For rule 73.2, there is substituted 'This Section applies to an application by a judgment creditor for a charging order under section 1 of the 1979 Act.'.

(4) In rule 73.3, paragraph (2), sub-paragraphs (*b*) and (*c*) are omitted.

(5) In rule 73.4 –

    (a)   in paragraph (1), for 'a judge' there is substituted 'the court,'; and
    (b)   in paragraph (2), for 'judge' there is substituted 'court'.

(6) In rule 73.9, in the parenthesis after paragraph (1) –

    (a)   'and regulation 51.4 of the 1992 Regulations' is omitted;
    (b)   for 'provides' there is substituted 'provide', and
    (c)   ', or (where the 1992 Regulations apply) of the authority,' is omitted.

(7) In rule 73.10 –

    (a)   in paragraph (1), for 'a claim' there is substituted 'an application';
    (b)   in paragraph (2) and the parenthesis following it, for 'A claim' each time it appears there is substituted 'An application';
    (c)   in paragraph (3), for 'claimant' there is substituted 'applicant';
    (d)   in paragraph (4), for 'claim form' there is substituted 'application'; and

(e)   in paragraph (5), for 'claimant's' there is substituted 'applicant's'.

(8) In rule 73.11, 'funds in court or' is omitted.

(9) In rule 73.12 –

    (a)   paragraph (1)(*a*) is omitted;
    (b)   in paragraph (1)(*b*) 'other than securities held in court' is omitted;
    (c)   in paragraph (2), in sub-paragraph (*b*), for 'claim form' there is substituted 'application notice'; and
    (d)   in paragraph (3) –
        (i)   'or claim form' is omitted; and
        (ii)   for sub-paragraph (*b*) there is substituted 'the person specified in rule 73.5(1)(*d*)'.

(10) Rule 73.13 is omitted.

(11) In rule 73.14, in paragraph (1), 'other than securities held in court' is omitted.

(12) In rule 73.16 –

    (a)   in paragraph (*a*) for '; and' there is substituted '.'; and
    (b)   paragraph (*b*) is omitted.

PART 34
RECIPROCAL ENFORCEMENT OF MAINTENANCE ORDERS

34.1 Scope and interpretation of this Part

(1) This Part contains rules about the reciprocal enforcement of maintenance orders.

(2) In this Part –

    'the 1920 Act' means the Maintenance Orders (Facilities for Enforcement) Act 1920;
    'the 1972 Act' means the Maintenance Orders (Reciprocal Enforcement) Act 1972;
    'the 1982 Act' means the Civil Jurisdiction and Judgments Act 1982;
    'the 1988 Convention' means the Convention on jurisdiction and the enforcement of judgments in civil and commercial matters done at Lugano on 16 September 1988;
    'the Judgments Regulation' means Council Regulation (EC) No. 44/2001 of 22 December 2000 on jurisdiction and the recognition and enforcement of judgments in civil and commercial matters; and
    'the Lugano Convention' means the Convention on jurisdiction and the recognition and enforcement of judgments in civil and commercial matters, between the European Community and the Republic of Iceland, the Kingdom of Norway, the Swiss Confederation and the Kingdom of Denmark signed on behalf of the European Community on 30 October 2007.

(3) Chapter 1 of this Part relates to the enforcement of maintenance orders in accordance with the 1920 Act.

(4) Chapter 2 of this Part relates to the enforcement of maintenance orders in accordance with Part 1 of the 1972 Act.

(5) Chapter 3 of this Part relates to the enforcement of maintenance orders in accordance with –

    (a)   the 1982 Act;
    (b)   the Judgments Regulation;
    (c)   the Lugano Convention; and
    (d)   the Maintenance Regulation.

Amendments—SI 2011/1328.

34.2 Meaning of prescribed officer in a magistrates' court

(1) For the purposes of the 1920 Act, the prescribed officer in relation to a magistrates' court is the designated officer for that court.

(2) For the purposes of Part 1 of the 1972 Act and section 5(2) of the 1982 Act, the prescribed officer in relation to a magistrates' court is the justices' clerk for the local justice area in which the court is situated.

34.3 Registration of maintenance orders in magistrates' courts in England and Wales

Where a magistrates' court is required by any of the enactments referred to in rule 34.1(2) or by virtue of the Maintenance Regulation to register a foreign order the court officer must –

    (a)   enter and sign a memorandum of the order in the register kept in accordance with rules made under section 144 of the Magistrates' Courts Act 1980; and
    (b)   state on the memorandum the statutory provision under which the order is registered.

Amendments—SI 2011/1328.

Chapter 1
Enforcement of Maintenance Orders under the Maintenance Orders (Facilities for Enforcement) Act 1920

34.4 Interpretation

(1) In this Chapter –

'payer', in relation to a maintenance order, means the person liable to make the payments for which the order provides; and
'reciprocating country' means a country or territory to which the 1920 Act extends.

(2) In this Chapter, an expression defined in the 1920 Act has the meaning given to it in that Act.

34.5 Confirmation of provisional orders made in a reciprocating country

(1) This rule applies where, in accordance with section 4(1) of the 1920 Act, the court officer receives a provisional maintenance order.

(2) The court must fix the date, time and place for a hearing.

(3) The court officer must register the order in accordance with rule 34.3.

(4) The court officer must serve on the payer –

    (a)   certified copies of the provisional order and accompanying documents; and

    (b)   a notice –
        (i)   specifying the time and date fixed for the hearing; and
        (ii) stating that the payer may attend to show cause why the order should not be confirmed.

(5) The court officer must inform –

    (a)   the court which made the provisional order; and
    (b)   the Lord Chancellor,

whether the court confirms, with or without modification, or decides not to confirm, the order.

34.6 Payment of sums due under registered orders

Where an order made by a reciprocating country is registered in a magistrates' court, the court must order payments due to be made to the court officer.

    (Practice Direction 34A contains further provisions relating to the payment of sums due under registered orders.)

34.7 Enforcement of sums due under registered orders

(1) This rule applies to –

    (a)   an order made in a reciprocating country which is registered in a magistrates' court; and
    (b)   a provisional order made in a reciprocating country which has been confirmed by a magistrates' court.

(2) The court officer must –

    (a)   collect the monies due under the order in the same way as for a magistrates' court maintenance order; and
    (b)   send the monies collected to –
        (i)   the court in the reciprocating country which made the order; or
        (ii) such other person or authority as that court or the Lord Chancellor may from time to time direct.

(3) The court officer may take proceedings in that officer's own name for enforcing payment of monies due under the order.

34.8 Prescribed notice for the taking of further evidence

(1) This rule applies where a court in a reciprocating country has sent a provisional order to a magistrates' court for the purpose of taking further evidence.

(2) The court officer must send a notice to the person who applied for the provisional order specifying –

    (a)   the further evidence required; and
    (b)   the time and place fixed for taking the evidence.

34.9 Transmission of maintenance orders made in a reciprocating country to the High Court

A maintenance order to be sent by the Lord Chancellor to the High Court in accordance with section 1(1) of the 1920 Act will be –

    (a)   sent to the senior district judge who will register it in the register kept for the purpose of the 1920 Act; and
    (b)   filed in the principal registry.

34.10 Transmission of maintenance orders made in the High Court to a reciprocating country

(1) This rule applies to maintenance orders made in the High Court.

(2) An application for a maintenance order to be sent to a reciprocating country under section 2 of the 1920 Act must be made in accordance with this rule.

(3) The application must be made to a district judge in the principal registry unless paragraph (4) applies.

(4) If the order was made in the course of proceedings in a district registry, the application may be made to a district judge in that district registry.

(5) The application must be –

    (a)   accompanied by a certified copy of the order; and
    (b)   supported by a record of the sworn written evidence.

(6) The written evidence must give –

    (a)   the applicant's reason for believing that the payer resides in the reciprocating country;
    (b)   such information as the applicant has as to the whereabouts of the payer; and
    (c)   such other information as may be set out in Practice Direction 34A.

34.11 Inspection of the register in the High Court

(1) A person may inspect the register and request copies of a registered order and any document filed with it if the district judge is satisfied that that person is entitled to, or liable to make, payments under a maintenance order made in –

(a)   the High Court; or

(b)   a court in a reciprocating country.

(2) The right to inspect the register referred to in paragraph (1) may be exercised by –

(a)   a solicitor acting on behalf of the person entitled to, or liable to make, the payments referred to in that paragraph; or

(b)   with the permission of the district judge, any other person.

Chapter 2
Enforcement of Maintenance Orders under Part 1 of the 1972 Act

34.12 Interpretation

(1) In this Chapter –

(a)   'reciprocating country' means a country to which Part 1 of the 1972 Act extends; and

(b)   'relevant court in the reciprocating country' means, as the case may be –

   (i)   the court which made the order which has been sent to England and Wales for confirmation;

   (ii)   the court which made the order which has been registered in a court in England and Wales;

   (iii) the court to which an order made in England and Wales has been sent for registration; or

   (iv)   the court to which a provisional order made in England and Wales has been sent for confirmation.

(2) In this Chapter, an expression defined in the 1972 Act has the meaning given to it in that Act.

(3) In this Chapter, 'Hague Convention Countries' means the countries listed in Schedule 1 to the Reciprocal Enforcement of Maintenance Orders (Hague Convention Countries) Order 1993.

Amendments—SI 2011/1328.

34.13 Scope

(1) Section 1 of this Chapter contains rules relating to the reciprocal enforcement of maintenance orders under Part 1 of the 1972 Act.

(2) Section 2 of this Chapter modifies the rules contained in Section 1 of this Chapter in their application to –

(b)   the Hague Convention Countries; and

(c)   the United States of America.

(Practice Direction 34A sets out in full the rules for the Hague Convention Countries and the United States of America as modified by Section 2 of this Chapter.)

Amendments—SI 2011/1328.

Section 1
Reciprocal enforcement of maintenance orders under Part 1 of the 1972 Act

34.14 Application for transmission of maintenance order to reciprocating country

An application for a maintenance order to be sent to a reciprocating country under section 2 of the 1972 Act must be made in accordance with Practice Direction 34A.

34.15 Certification of evidence given on provisional orders

A document setting out or summarising evidence is authenticated by a court in England and Wales by a certificate signed, as the case may be, by –

(a)   one of the justices; or
(b)   the District Judge (Magistrates' Courts),

before whom that evidence was given.

> (Section 3(5)(*b*), 5(4) and 9(5) of the 1972 Act require a document to be authenticated by the court.)

34.16 Confirmation of a provisional order made in a reciprocating country

(1) This rule applies to proceedings for the confirmation of a provisional order made in a reciprocating country.

(2) Paragraph (3) applies on receipt by the court of –

(a)   a certified copy of the order; and
(b)   the documents required by the 1972 Act to accompany the order.

(3) On receipt of the documents referred to in paragraph (2) –

(a)   the court must fix the date, time and place for a hearing or a directions appointment; and
(b)   the court officer must send to the payer notice of the date, time and place fixed together with a copy of the order and accompanying documents.

(4) The date fixed for the hearing must be not less than 21 days beginning with the date on which the court officer sent the documents to the payer in accordance with paragraph (2).

(5) The court officer will send to the relevant court in the reciprocating country a certified copy of any order confirming or refusing to confirm the provisional order.

(6) This rule does not apply to the confirmation of a provisional order made in a reciprocating country varying a maintenance order to which sections 5(5) or 9(6) of the 1972 Act applies.

> (Section 5(5) and 7 of the 1972 Act provide for proceedings for the confirmation of a provisional order.)

(Provision in respect of confirmation of a provisional order varying a maintenance order under the 1972 Act is in rules made under section 144 of the Magistrates' Courts Act 1980).

(Rule 34.22 provides for the transmission of documents to a court in a reciprocating country.)

34.17 Consideration of revocation of a provisional order made by a magistrates' court

(1) This rule applies where –

(a) a magistrates' court has made a provisional order by virtue of section 3 of the 1972 Act;

(b) before the order is confirmed, evidence is taken by the court or received by it as set out in section 5(9) of the 1972 Act; and

(c) on consideration of the evidence the court considers that the order ought not to have been made.

(Section 5(9) of the 1972 Act provides that a magistrates' court may revoke a provisional order made by it, before the order has been confirmed in a reciprocating country, if it receives new evidence.)

(2) The court officer must serve on the person who applied for the provisional order ('the applicant') a notice which must –

(a) set out the evidence taken or received by the court;

(b) inform the applicant that the court considers that the order ought not to have been made; and

(c) inform the applicant that the applicant may –

    (i) make representations in relation to that evidence either orally or in writing; and

    (ii) adduce further evidence.

(3) If an applicant wishes to adduce further evidence –

(a) the applicant must notify the court officer at the court which made the order;

(b) the court will fix a date for the hearing of the evidence; and

(c) the court officer will notify the applicant in writing of the date fixed.

34.18 Notification of variation or revocation of a maintenance order by the High Court or a county court

(1) This rule applies where –

(a) a maintenance order has been sent to a reciprocating country in pursuance of section 2 of the 1972 Act; and

(b) the court makes an order, not being a provisional order, varying or revoking that order.

(2) The court officer must send a certified copy of the order of variation or revocation to the relevant court in the reciprocating country.

(Rule 34.22 provides for the transmission of documents to a court in a reciprocating country.)

34.19 Notification of confirmation or revocation of a maintenance order by a magistrates' court

(1) This rule applies where a magistrates' court makes an order –

(a) not being a provisional order, revoking a maintenance order to which section 5 of the 1972 Act applies;

(b) under section 9 of the 1972 Act, revoking a registered order; or

(c) under section 7(2) of the 1972 Act, confirming an order to which section 7 of that Act applies.

(2) The court officer must send written notice of the making, revocation or confirmation of the order, as appropriate, to the relevant court in the reciprocating country.

(3) This rule does not apply to a provisional order varying a maintenance order to which sections 5 or 9 of the 1972 Act apply.

(Section 5 of the 1972 Act applies to a provisional order made by a magistrates' court in accordance with section 3 of that Act which has been confirmed by a court in a reciprocating country.)

(Provision in respect of notification of variation of a maintenance order by a magistrates' court under the 1972 Act is made in rules made under section 144 of the Magistrates' Courts Act 1980.)

(Rule 34.22 provides for the transmission of documents to a court in a reciprocating country.)

34.20 Taking of evidence for court in reciprocating country

(1) This rule applies where a request is made by or on behalf of a court in a reciprocating country for the taking of evidence for the purpose of proceedings relating to a maintenance order to which Part 1 of the 1972 Act applies.

(Section 14 of the 1972 Act makes provision for the taking of evidence needed for the purpose of certain proceedings.)

(2) The High Court has power to take the evidence where –

(a) the request for evidence relates to a maintenance order made by a superior court in the United Kingdom; and

(b) the witness resides in England and Wales.

(3) The county court has power to take the evidence where –

(a) the request for evidence relates to a maintenance order made by a county court; and

(b) the maintenance order has not been registered in a magistrates' court under the 1958 Act.

(4) The following magistrates' courts have power to take the evidence, that is –

(a)   where the proceedings in the reciprocating country relate to a maintenance order made by a magistrates' court, the court which made the order;

(b)   where the proceedings relate to an order which is registered in a magistrates' court, the court in which the order is registered; and

(c)   a magistrates' court to which the Lord Chancellor sends the request to take evidence.

(5) A magistrates' court not mentioned in paragraph (4) has power to take the evidence if the magistrates' court which would otherwise have that power consents because the evidence could be taken more conveniently.

(6) The evidence is to be taken in accordance with Part 22.

Amendments—SI 2011/1328.

34.21 Request for the taking of evidence by a court in a reciprocating country

(1) This rule applies where a request is made by a magistrates' court for the taking of evidence in a reciprocating country in accordance with section 14(5) of the 1972 Act.

(2) The request must be made in writing to the court in the reciprocating country.

> (Rule 34.22 provides for the transmission of documents to a court in a reciprocating country.)

34.22 Transmission of documents

(1) This rule applies to any document, including a notice or request, which is required to be sent to a court in a reciprocating country by –

(a)   Part 1 of the 1972 Act; or

(b)   Section 1 of Chapter 2 of this Part of these rules.

(2) The document must be sent to the Lord Chancellor for transmission to the court in the reciprocating country.

34.23 Method of payment under registered orders

(1) Where an order is registered in a magistrates' court in accordance with section 6(3) of the 1972 Act, the court must order that the payment of sums due under the order be made –

(a)   to the court officer for the registering court; and

(b)   at such time and place as the court officer directs.

> (Section 6(3) of the 1972 Act makes provision for the registration of maintenance orders made in a reciprocating country.)

(2) Where the court orders payments to be made to the court officer, whether in accordance with paragraph (1) or otherwise, the court officer must send the payments –

(a) by post to either –
    (i) the court which made the order; or
    (ii) such other person or authority as that court, or the Lord Chancellor, directs; or
(b) if the court which made the order is a country or territory specified in the Practice Direction 34A –
    (i) to the Crown Agents for Overseas Governments and Administrations for transmission to the person to whom they are due; or
    (ii) as the Lord Chancellor directs.

(Practice Direction 34A contains further provisions relating to the payment of sums due under registered orders.)

34.24 Enforcement of payments under registered orders

(1) This rule applies where a court has ordered periodical payments under a registered maintenance order to be made to the court officer.

(2) The court officer must take reasonable steps to notify the payee of the means of enforcement available.

(3) Paragraph (4) applies where periodical payments due under a registered order are in arrears.

(4) The court officer, on that officer's own initiative –

(a) may; or
(b) if the sums due are more than 4 weeks in arrears, must,

proceed in that officer's own name for the recovery of the sums due unless of the view that it is unreasonable to do so.

34.25 Notification of registration and cancellation

(1) The court officer must send written notice to the Lord Chancellor of the due registration of orders registered in accordance with section 6(3), 7(5), or 10(4) of the 1972 Act.

(2) The court officer must, when registering an order in accordance with section 6(3), 7(5), 9(10), 10(4) or (5) or 23(3) of the 1972 Act, send written notice to the payer stating –

(a) that the order has been registered;
(b) that payments under the order should be made to the court officer; and
(c) the hours during which and the place at which the payments should be made.

(3) The court officer must, when cancelling the registration of an order in accordance with section 10(1) of the 1972 Act, send written notice of the cancellation to the payer.

Section 2
Modification of rules in Section 1 of this Chapter

Republic of Ireland

34.26 Application of Section 1 of this Chapter to the Republic of Ireland

(1) In relation to the Republic of Ireland, Section 1 of this Chapter has effect as modified by this rule.

(2) A reference in this rule and in any rule which has effect in relation to the Republic of Ireland by virtue of this rule to –

    (a)   the 1972 Act is a reference to the 1972 Act as modified by Schedule 2 to the Reciprocal Enforcement of Maintenance Orders (Republic of Ireland) Order 1993; and

    (b)   a section under the 1972 Act is a reference to the section so numbered in the 1972 Act as so modified.

(3) A reference to a reciprocating country in rule 34.12(1) and Section 1 of this Chapter is a reference to the Republic of Ireland.

(4) In the words in brackets at the end of rule 34.15 (certification of evidence given on provisional orders), for the sections mentioned substitute 'section 3(5)(*b*) or 5(3)'.

(5) Rules 34.16 (confirmation of provisional orders) and 34.21 (request for the taking of evidence by a court in a reciprocating country) do not apply.

(6) For rule 34.17 (consideration of revocation of a provisional order made by a magistrates' court) substitute –

'34.17 Consideration of confirmation of a provisional order made by a magistrates' court

    (1) This rule applies where –

        (a)   a magistrates' court has made a provisional order by virtue of section 3 of the 1972 Act;

        (b)   the payer has made representations or adduced evidence to the court; and

        (c)   the court has fixed a date for the hearing at which it will consider confirmation of the order.

    (2) The court officer must serve on the applicant for the provisional order –

        (a)   a copy of the representations or evidence; and

        (b)   written notice of the date fixed for the hearing.'

(7) For rules 34.18 and 34.19 (notification of variation or revocation) substitute –

'34.18 Notification of variation or revocation of a maintenance order by the High Court

Where the High Court makes an order varying or revoking an order to which section 5 of the 1972 Act applies the court officer must send –

(a)   a certified copy of the order of variation or revocation; and

(b)   a statement as to the service on the payer of the documents mentioned in section 5(3) of the 1972 Act,

to the court in the Republic of Ireland.

(Rule 34.22 provides for the transmission of documents to a court in a reciprocating country.)

34.19 Notification of revocation of a maintenance order by a magistrates' court

Where a magistrates' court makes an order revoking an order to which section 5 of the 1972 Act applies, the court officer must send written notice of the making of the order to the Lord Chancellor.

(Section 5 of the 1972 Act applies to a maintenance order sent to the Republic of Ireland in accordance with section 2 of that Act and a provisional order made by a magistrates' court in accordance with section 3 of that Act which has been confirmed by such a court.)

(Provision in respect of notification of variation of a maintenance order by magistrates' court under the 1972 Act is made in rules made under section 144 of the Magistrates' Courts Act 1980.)'

(8) For rule 34.23(2) (method of payment under registered orders), substitute –

'(2) Where the court orders payment to be made to the court officer, the court officer must send the payments by post –

(a)   to the payee under the order; or

(b)   where a public authority has been authorised by the payee to receive the payments, to that public authority.'.

(9) For rule 34.24 (enforcement of payments under registered orders), substitute –

'34.24 Enforcement of payments under registered orders

(1) This rule applies where periodical payments under a registered order are in arrears.

(2) The court officer must, on the written request of the payee, proceed in that officer's own name for the recovery of the sums due unless of the view that it is unreasonable to do so.

(3) If the sums due are more than 4 weeks in arrears the court officer must give the payee notice in writing of that fact stating the particulars of the arrears.'

(10) For rule 34.25 (notification of registration and cancellation) substitute –

'34.25 Notification of registration and cancellation

The court officer must send written notice to –

(a)   the Lord Chancellor, on the due registration of an order under section 6(3) or 10(4) of the 1972 Act; and

(b)   to the payer under the order, on –
   (i)   the registration of an order under section 10(4) of the 1972 Act; or
   (ii)   the cancellation of the registration of an order under section 10(1)

of that Act.'

(11) After rule 34.25 insert –

'34.25A Other notices under section 6 of the 1972 Act

(1) A notice required under section 6(6) or (10) of the 1972 Act must be in the form referred to in a practice direction.

(2) Where a magistrates' court sets aside the registration of an order following an appeal under section 6(7) of the 1972 Act, the court officer must send written notice of the court's decision to the payee.

> (Section 6(6) of the 1972 Act provides for notice of registration in a United Kingdom court of a maintenance order made in the Republic of Ireland, and section 6(10) of that Act for notice that a maintenance order made in the Republic of Ireland has not been registered in a United Kingdom court.)'

Sub-section 2
Hague Convention Countries

34.27 Application of Section 1 of this Chapter to the Hague Convention Countries

(1) In relation to the Hague Convention Countries, Section 1 of this Chapter has effect as modified by this rule.

(2) A reference in this rule, and in any rule which has effect in relation to the Hague Convention Countries by virtue of this rule to –

(a) the 1972 Act is a reference to the 1972 Act as modified by Schedule 2 to the Reciprocal Enforcement of Maintenance Orders (Hague Convention Countries) Order 1993; and

(b) a section under the 1972 Act is a reference to the section so numbered in the 1972 Act as so modified.

(3) A reference to a reciprocating country in rule 34.12(1) and Section 1 of this Chapter is a reference to a Hague Convention Country.

(4) Rules 34.15 (certification of evidence given on provisional orders), 34.16 (confirmation of provisional orders), 34.19 (notification of confirmation or revocation of a maintenance order by a magistrates' court) and 34.21 (request for the taking of evidence by a court in a reciprocating country) do not apply.

(5) For rule 34.17 (consideration of revocation of a provisional order made by a magistrates' court) substitute –

'34.17 Consideration of revocation of a maintenance order made by a magistrates' court

(1) This rule applies where –

(a) an application has been made to a magistrates' court by a payee for the revocation of an order to which section 5 of the 1972 Act applies; and

(b) the payer resides in a Hague Convention Country.

(2)   The court officer must serve on the payee, by post, a copy of any representations or evidence adduced by or on behalf of the payer.

(Provision relating to consideration of variation of a maintenance order made by a magistrates' court to which section 5 of the 1972 Act applies is made in rules made under section 144 of the Magistrates' Courts Act 1980.)'

(6) For rule 34.18 (notification of variation or revocation of a maintenance order by the High Court or county court) substitute –

'34.18 Notification of variation or revocation of a maintenance order by the High Court or a county court

(1) This rule applies if the High Court or a county court makes an order varying or revoking a maintenance order to which section 5 of the 1972 Act applies.

(2) f the time for appealing has expired without an appeal having been entered, the court officer will send to the Lord Chancellor –

    (a)   the documents required by section 5(8) of the 1972 Act; and
    (b)   a certificate signed by the district judge stating that the order of variation or revocation is enforceable and no longer subject to the ordinary forms of review.

(3) A party who enters an appeal against the order of variation or revocation must, at the same time, give written notice to the court officer.'

(7) For rule 34.23(2) (method of payment under registered orders) substitute –

'(2) Where the court orders payment to be made to the court officer, the court officer must send the payments by post to the payee under the order.'

(8) For rule 34.25 (notification of registration and cancellation) substitute –

'34.25 Notification of registration and cancellation

The court officer must send written notice to –

    (a)   the Lord Chancellor, on the due registration of an order under section 10(4) of the 1972 Act; and
    (b)   the payer under the order, on –
        (i)   the registration of an order under section 10(4) of the 1972 Act; or
        (ii)   the cancellation of the registration of an order under section 10(1) of the 1972 Act.'

(9) After rule 34.25 insert –

'34.25A General provisions as to notices

(1) A notice to a payer of the registration of an order in a magistrates' court in accordance with section 6(3) of the 1972 Act must be in the form referred to in a practice direction.

(Section 6(8) of the 1972 Act requires notice of registration to be given to the payer.)

(2) If the court sets aside the registration of a maintenance order following an appeal under section 6(9) of the 1972 Act, the court officer must send written notice of the decision to the Lord Chancellor.

(3) A notice to a payee that the court officer has refused to register an order must be in the form referred to in a practice direction.

> (Section 6(11) of the 1972 Act requires notice of refusal of registration to be given to the payee.)

(4) Where, under any provision of Part 1 of the 1972 Act, a court officer serves a notice on a payer who resides in a Hague Convention Country, the court officer must send to the Lord Chancellor a certificate of service.'

Sub-section 3
United States of America

34.28 Application of Section 1 of this Chapter to the United States of America

(1) In relation to the United States of America, Section 1 of this Chapter has effect as modified by this rule.

(2) A reference in this rule and in any rule which has effect in relation to the United States of America by virtue of this rule to –

(a) the 1972 Act is a reference to the 1972 Act as modified by Schedule 1 to the Reciprocal Enforcement of Maintenance Orders (United States of America) Order 2007; and
(b) a section under the 1972 Act is a reference to the section so numbered in the 1972 Act as so modified.

(3) A reference to a reciprocating country in rule 34.12(1) and Section 1 of this Chapter is a reference to the United States of America.

(4) Rules 34.15 (certification of evidence given on provisional orders), 34.16 (confirmation of provisional orders), 34.19 (notification of confirmation or revocation of a maintenance order made by a magistrates' court) and 34.21 (request for the taking of evidence in a reciprocating country) do not apply.

(5) For rule 34.17 (consideration of revocation of a provisional order made by a magistrates' court) substitute –

> **'34.17 Consideration of revocation of a maintenance order made by a magistrates' court**
>
> (1) This rule applies where –
>
> (a) an application has been made to a magistrates' court by a payee for the revocation of an order to which section 5 of the 1972 Act applies; and
> (b) the payer resides in the United States of America.
>
> (2) The court officer must serve on the payee by post a copy of any representations or evidence adduced by or on behalf of the payer.
>
> > (Provision relating to consideration of variation of a maintenance order made by a magistrates' court to which section 5 of the 1972 Act applies is made in rules made under section 144 of the Magistrates' Courts Act 1980.)'

(6) For rule 34.18 (notification of variation or revocation), substitute –

'34.18 Notification of variation or revocation

If the High Court or a county court makes an order varying or revoking a maintenance order to which section 5 of the 1972 Act applies, the court officer will send to the Lord Chancellor the documents required by section 5(7) of that Act.'.

(7) For rule 34.23(2) (method of payment under registered orders) substitute –

'(2) Where the court orders payment to be made to the court officer, the court officer must send the payments by post to the payee under the order.'

(8) For rule 34.25 (notification of registration and cancellation) substitute –

'34.25 Notification of registration and cancellation

The court officer must send written notice to –

    (a)   the Lord Chancellor, on the due registration of an order under section 10(4) of the 1972 Act; or

    (b)   the payer under the order, on –

        (i)   the registration of an order under section 10(4) of the 1972 Act; or

        (ii) the cancellation of the registration of an order under section 10(1) of that Act.'

Chapter 3
Enforcement of Maintenance Orders under the Civil Jurisdiction and Judgments Act 1982, the Judgments Regulation the Maintenance Regulation and the Lugano Convention

34.28A Application of this Chapter

(1) In this Chapter –

    (a)   references to a maintenance order include reference to a decision, a court settlement or an authentic instrument within the meaning of Article 2 of the Maintenance Regulation where that Regulation applies;

    (b)   references to the Hague Protocol are to the Protocol on the Law Applicable to Maintenance Obligations done at The Hague on 23 November 2007.

(2) In relation to the Maintenance Regulation –

    (a)   Section 1 applies to maintenance orders to which Sections 2 and 3 of Chapter IV of the Maintenance Regulation apply (decisions given in a Member State which does not apply the rules of the Hague Protocol, that is, Denmark, and decisions to which Sections 2 and 3 of Chapter IV of that Regulation apply by virtue of Article 75(2)(a) or (b));

    (b)   Section 2 applies to all maintenance orders made in a magistrates' court in England and Wales for which reciprocal enforcement is sought in any Member State of the European Union, including Denmark.

(Provision in respect of enforcement of maintenance orders to which Section 1 of the Maintenance Regulation applies (maintenance decisions given in Member States other than Denmark) is made in the Magistrates' Courts Rules 1981).

Amendments—SI 2011/1328.

Section 1
Registration and Enforcement in a Magistrates' Court of Maintenance Orders made in a Contracting State to the 1968 Convention, a Contracting State to the 1988 Convention, a Regulation State or a State bound by the Lugano Convention

34.29 Interpretation

In this Section –

(a) an expression defined in the 1982 Act has the meaning given to it in that Act subject to paragraph (b); and

(b) 'Regulation State' means a Member State of the European Union which does not apply the rules of the Hague Protocol, or, where registration is sought for a maintenance order to which Article 75(2)(a) or (b) of the Maintenance Regulation applies, the Member State of the European Union from which the order originated.

Amendments—SI 2011/1328.

34.29A Application under Article 30 of the Maintenance Regulation for a declaration of enforceability

An application under Article 30 of the Maintenance Regulation for a declaration of enforceability of a maintenance decision will be determined by the justices' clerk for the local justice area in which the court is situated.

Amendments—Inserted by SI 2011/1328

34.30 Registration of maintenance orders

(1) In this rule, 'assets to which the 1958 Act applies' means assets against which, after registration in the High Court, the maintenance order could be enforced under Part 1 of the 1958 Act.

(2) This rule applies where the court officer for a magistrates' court receives –

(a) an application under Article 31 of the 1968 Convention for the enforcement of a maintenance order made in a Contracting State other than the United Kingdom;

(b) an application under Article 31 of the 1988 Convention for the enforcement of a maintenance order made in a State bound by the 1988 Convention other than a Member State of the European Union;

(c) an application under Article 26 of the Maintenance Regulation for a declaration of enforceability of a maintenance order made in a Regulation State other than the United Kingdom; or

(d) an application under Article 38 of the Lugano Convention for the enforcement of a maintenance order made in a State bound by the Lugano Convention other than a Member State of the European Union.

(3) The court officer must –

(a) take such steps as appear appropriate for ascertaining whether the payer resides within the local justice area for which the court acts; and

(b) consider any available information as to the nature and location of the payer's assets.

(4) If the court officer is satisfied that the payer –

(a) does not reside within the local justice area for which the court acts; and

(b) does not have assets to which the 1958 Act applies,

the court officer must refuse the application and return the application to the Lord Chancellor stating the information the court officer has as to the whereabouts of the payer and the nature and location of the payer's assets.

(5) If the court officer is satisfied that the payer –

(a) does not reside within the local justice area for which the court acts; but

(b) has assets to which the 1958 Act applies,

then either –

(i) the court officer must register the order; or

(ii) if the court officer believes that the payer is residing within the local justice area in which another magistrates' court acts, the court officer may refuse the application and return the documents to the Lord Chancellor with the information referred to in paragraph (4) above.

(6) Except where paragraphs (4) or (5) apply, the court officer must register the order unless –

(a) in the case of an application under Article 31 of the 1968 Convention, Articles 27 or 28 of that Convention apply; and

(b) in the case of an application under Article 31 of the 1988 Convention, Articles 27 or 28 of that Convention apply.

(7) If the court officer refuses to register an order to which this rule relates the court officer must notify the applicant.

(8) If the court officer registers an order the court officer must send written notice of that fact to –

(a) the Lord Chancellor;

(b) the payer; and

(c) the applicant.

(9) If the court officer considers that it would be appropriate for all or part of a registered order to be enforced in the High Court the court officer must notify the applicant –

(a) that the court officer so considers it appropriate; and
(b) that the applicant may apply under the 1958 Act for the order to be registered in the High Court.

Amendments—SI 2011/1328.

34.31 Appeal from a decision relating to registration

(1) This rule applies to an appeal under –

(a) Article 36 or Article 40 of the 1968 Convention;
(b) Article 36 or Article 40 of the 1988 Convention;
(c) Article 32 of the Maintenance Regulation; or
(d) Article 43 of the Lugano Convention.

(2) The appeal must be to the magistrates' court –

(a) in which the order is registered; or
(b) in which the application for registration has been refused,

as the case may be.

Amendments—SI 2011/1328.

34.32 Payment of sums due under a registered order

(1) Where an order is registered in accordance with section 5(3) of the 1982 Act or Article 38 of the Judgments Regulation or Article 38 of the Lugano Convention, or declared enforceable under Article 26 of the Maintenance Regulation by virtue of registration the court must order that payment of sums due under the order be made –

(a) to the court officer for the registering court; and
(b) at such time and place as the court officer directs.

(2) Where the court orders payments to be made to the court officer, whether in accordance with paragraph (1) or otherwise, the court officer must send the payments by post either –

(a) to the court which made the order; or
(b) to such other person or authority as that court, or the Lord Chancellor, directs.

(Practice Direction 34A contains further provisions relating to the payment of sums due under registered orders.)

Amendments—SI 2011/1328.

34.33 Enforcement of payments under registered orders

(1) This rule applies where a court has ordered periodical payments under a registered maintenance order to be made to the court officer for a magistrates' court.

(2) The court officer must take reasonable steps to notify the payee of the means of enforcement available.

(3) Paragraph (4) applies where periodical payments due under a registered order are in arrears.

(4) The court officer, on that officer's own initiative –

    (a)   may; or
    (b)   if the sums due are more than 4 weeks in arrears, must,

proceed in that officer's own name for the recovery of the sums due unless of the view that it is unreasonable to do so.

34.34 Variation and revocation of registered orders

(1) This rule applies where the court officer for a registering court receives notice that a registered maintenance order has been varied or revoked by a competent court in a Contracting State to the 1968 Convention, a Contracting State to the 1988 Convention (other than a Member State of the European Union), a Regulation State or a State bound by the Lugano Convention, other than a Member State of the European Union.

(2) The court officer for the registering court must –

    (a)   register the order of variation or revocation; and
    (b)   send notice of the registration by post to the payer and payee under the order.

(3) Where the court officer for a registering court receives notice that a maintenance order registered in that court by virtue of the provisions of the Judgments Regulation has been varied or revoked by a competent court in another Member State of the European Union, the court officer must—

    (a)   note against the entry in the register that the original order so registered has been varied or revoked, as the case may be; and
    (b)   send notice of the noting of the variation or revocation, as the case may be, by post to the payer and payee under the order.'

Amendments—SI 2011/1328.

34.35 Transfer of registered order

(1) This rule applies where the court officer for the court where an order is registered considers that the payer is residing within the local justice area in England and Wales for which another magistrates' court acts.

(2) Subject to paragraph (4), the court officer must transfer the order to the other court by sending to that court –

(a) the information and documents relating to the registration;

(b) a certificate of arrears, if applicable, signed by the court officer;

(c) a statement giving such information as the court officer possesses as to the whereabouts of the payer and the nature and location of the payer's assets; and

(d) any other relevant documents which the court officer has relating to the case.

(3) The information and documents referred to in paragraph (2)(*a*) are those required, as appropriate, under –

(a) Articles 46 and 47 of the 1968 Convention;

(b) Articles 46 and 47 of the 1988 Convention;

(c) Article 53 of the Judgments Regulation;

(d) Article 53 of the Lugano Convention or;

(e) Article 28 or 29 of the Maintenance Regulation.

(4) If an application is pending in the registering court for the registration of the whole or part of the order in the High Court under Part 1 of the 1958 Act, the court officer must not transfer the order, or the part to which the application relates, under paragraph (2).

(5) The court officer must give notice of the transfer of an order to –

(a) the payee; and

(b) the Lord Chancellor.

(6) If an order is transferred, the court officer for the court to which it is transferred must register the order.

Amendments—SI 2011/1328.

34.36 Cancellation of registered orders

(1) Where the court officer for the registering court –

(a) has no reason to transfer a registered order under rule 34.35; and

(b) considers that the payer under the registered order is not residing within the local justice area for which the court acts and has no assets to which the 1958 Act applies,

the court officer must cancel the registration of the order.

(2) The court officer must –

(a) give notice of cancellation to the payee; and

(b) send the information and documents relating to the registration and the other documents referred to in rule 34.35(2) to the Lord Chancellor.

34.36A Directions as to stays, documents and translations

At any stage in proceedings for registration of a maintenance order under this Section of this Chapter, the court may give directions about the conduct of the proceedings, including –

(a) staying of proceedings in accordance with –
    (i) Article 30 or 38 of the 1968 Convention,
    (ii) Article 30 or 38 of the 1988 Convention,
    (iii) Article 37 or 46 of the Lugano Convention, or
    (iv) Article 25 or 35 of the Maintenance Regulation;
(b) the provision of documents in accordance with –
    (i) Article 48 of the 1968 Convention,
    (ii) Article 48 of the 1988 Convention,
    (iii) Article 55 of the Lugano Convention, or
    (iv) Article 29 of the Maintenance Regulation;
(c) the provision of translations in accordance with –
    (i) Article 48 of the 1968 Convention,
    (ii) Article 48 of the 1988 Convention,
    (iii) Article 55 of the Lugano Convention, or
    (iv) Article 28 of the Maintenance Regulation.

Amendments— SI 2011/1328.

Section 2
Reciprocal enforcement in a Contracting State or a Member State of the European Union of Orders of a court in England and Wales

34.37 (revoked)

Amendments—Revoked by SI 2011/1328.

34.38 Admissibility of Documents

(1) This rule applies to a document, referred to in paragraph (2) and authenticated in accordance with paragraph (3), which comprises, records or summarises evidence given in, or information relating to, proceedings in a court in another part of the UK, another Contracting State to the 1968 Convention or the 1988 Convention, Member State of the European Union or State bound by the Lugano Convention, and any reference in this rule to 'the court', without more, is a reference to that court.

(2) The documents referred to at paragraph (1) are documents which purport to –

(a) set out or summarise evidence given to the court;
(b) have been received in evidence to the court;
(c) set out or summarise evidence taken in the court for the purpose of proceedings in a court in England and Wales to which the 1982 Act the Judgments Regulation or the Maintenance Regulation applies; or
(d) record information relating to payments made under an order of the court.

(3) A document to which paragraph (1) applies shall, in any proceedings in a magistrates' court in England and Wales relating to a maintenance order to which the 1982 Act the Judgments Regulation or the Maintenance Regulation applies, be admissible as evidence of any fact stated in it to the same extent as oral evidence of that fact is admissible in those proceedings.

(4) A document to which paragraph (1) applies shall be deemed to be authenticated –

(a)   in relation to the documents listed at paragraph 2(*a*) or (*c*), if the document purports to be –
(i)   certified by the judge or official before whom the evidence was given or taken; or
(ii)   the original document recording or summarising the evidence, or a true copy of that document;
(b)   in relation to a document listed at paragraph (2)(*b*), if the document purports to be certified by a judge or official of the court to be, or to be a true copy of, the document received in evidence; and
(c)   in relation to the document listed at paragraph (2)(*d*), if the document purports to be certified by a judge or official of the court as a true record of the payments made under the order.

(5) It shall not be necessary in any proceedings in which evidence is to be received under this rule to prove the signature or official position of the person appearing to have given the certificate referred to in paragraph (4).

(6) Nothing in this rule shall prejudice the admission in evidence of any document which is admissible in evidence apart from this rule.

(7) Any request by a magistrates' court in England and Wales for the taking or providing of evidence by a court in another part of the United Kingdom or in another Contracting State to the 1968 Convention or the 1988 Convention or the Lugano Convention (other than a Member State of the European Union) for the purpose of proceedings to which the 1982 Act applies or by a court in Denmark for the purpose of proceedings to which the Maintenance Regulation applies,shall be communicated in writing to the court in question.

(Chapter 2 of Part 24 makes provision for taking of evidence by a court in another Member State of the European Union).

Amendments—SI 2011/1328.

34.39 Enforcement of orders of a magistrates' court

(1) This rule applies to applications to a magistrates' court under –

(a)   section 12 of the 1982 Act;
(b)   Article 40(2) of the Maintenance Regulation; or
(c)   article 54 of the Lugano Convention.

(2) A person who wishes to enforce in a Contracting State to the 1968 Convention, a Contracting State to the 1988 Convention (other than a Member State of the European Union), a Member State of the European Union or a State bound by the Lugano Convention (other than a Member State of the European Union) a maintenance order obtained in a magistrates' court must apply for a certified copy of the order.

(3) An application under this rule must be made in writing to the court officer and must specify –

(a)   the names of the parties to the proceedings;
(b)   the date, or approximate date, of the proceedings in which the maintenance order was made and the nature of those proceedings;
(c)   the Contracting State or Member State of the EuropeanUnion in which the application for recognition or enforcement has been made or is to be made; and
(d)   the postal address of the applicant.

(4) The court officer must, on receipt of the application, send a copy of the order to the applicant certified in accordance with a practice direction and where the Maintenance Regulation applies, a completed extract from the decision in the form of Annex II to that Regulation.

(5) Paragraph (6) applies where –

(a)   a maintenance order is registered in a magistrates' court in England and Wales; and
(b)   a person wishes to obtain a certificate giving details of any payments made or arrears accrued under the order while it has been registered, for the purposes of an application made or to be made in connection with that order in –
     (i)   another Contracting State to the 1968 Convention;
     (ii)   another Contracting State to the 1988 Convention (other than a Member State of the European Union);
     (iii) another Member State of the European Union;
     (iv)   another State bound by the Lugano Convention (other than a Member State of the European Union); or
     (v)   another part of the United Kingdom.

(6) The person wishing to obtain the certificate referred to in paragraph (5) may make a written application to the court officer for the registering court.

(7) On receipt of an application under paragraph (6) the court officer must send to the applicant a certificate giving the information requested.

> (Rule 74.12 (application for certified copy of a judgment) and 74.13 (evidence in support) of the CPR apply in relation to the application for a certified copy of a judgment obtained in the High Court or a county court.)

Amendments—SI 2011/1328.

34.40 Enforcement of orders of the High Court or a county court

Rules 74.12 (application for a certified copy of a judgment) and 74.13 (evidence in support) of the CPR(a) apply in relation to an application under Article 40(2) of the Maintenance Regulation for a certified copy of a judgment relating to maintenance obtained in the High Court or a county court (including the principal registry when treated as a divorce county court or a civil partnership proceedings county court), or for an extract relating to that judgment in the form of Annex II to that Regulation, as they do to applications under section 12 of the 1982 Act or article 54 of the Lugano Convention.

Amendments—Inserted by SI 2011/1328.

PART 35
MEDIATION DIRECTIVE

35.1 Scope and interpretation

(1) This Part applies to mediated cross-border disputes that are subject to Directive 2008/52/EC of the European Parliament and of the Council of 21 May 2008 on certain aspects of mediation in civil and commercial matters ('the Mediation Directive').

(2) In this Part –

'cross-border dispute' has the meaning given by article 2 of the Mediation Directive;
'mediation' has the meaning given by article 3(*a*) of the Mediation Directive;
'mediation administrator' means a person involved in the administration of the mediation process;
'mediation evidence' means evidence regarding information arising out of or in connection with a mediation process;
'mediator' has the meaning given by article 3(*b*) of the Mediation Directive; and
'relevant dispute' means a cross-border dispute that is subject to the Mediation Directive.

35.2 Relevant disputes: applications for consent orders in respect of financial remedies

(1) This rule applies in relation to proceedings for a financial remedy where the applicant, with the explicit consent of the respondent, wishes to make an application that the content of a written agreement resulting from mediation of a relevant dispute be made enforceable by being made the subject of a consent order.

(2) The court will not include in a consent order any matter which is contrary to the law of England and Wales or which is not enforceable under that law.

(3) The applicant must file two copies of a draft of the order in the terms sought.

(4) Subject to paragraph (5), the application must be supported by evidence of the explicit consent of the respondent.

(5) Where the respondent has written to the court consenting to the making of the order sought, the respondent is deemed to have given explicit consent to the order and paragraph (4) does not apply.

(6) Paragraphs (1)(*b*) and (2) to (6) of rule 9.26 apply to an application to which this rule applies.

35.3 Mediation evidence: disclosure and inspection

(1) Where a party to proceedings seeks disclosure or inspection of mediation evidence that is in the control of a mediator or mediation administrator, that

party must first obtain the court's permission to seek the disclosure or inspection, by an application made in accordance with Part 18.

(2) The mediator or mediation administrator who has control of the mediation evidence must be named as a respondent to the application and must be served with a copy of the application notice.

(3) Evidence in support of the application must include evidence that –

(a)   all parties to the mediation agree to the disclosure or inspection of the mediation evidence;

(b)   disclosure or inspection of the mediation evidence is necessary for overriding considerations of public policy, in accordance with article 7(1)(*a*) of the Mediation Directive; or

(c)   the disclosure of the content of an agreement resulting from mediation is necessary to implement or enforce that agreement.

(4) Where this rule applies, Parts 21 to 24 apply to the extent they are consistent with this rule.

35.4 Mediation evidence: witnesses and depositions

(1) This rule applies where a party wishes to obtain mediation evidence from a mediator or mediation administrator by –

(a)   a witness summons;

(b)   cross-examination with permission of the court under rule 22.8 or 23.4;

(c)   an order under rule 24.7 (evidence by deposition);

(d)   an order under rule 24.9 (enforcing attendance of witness);

(e)   an order under rule 24.10(4) (deponent's evidence to be given orally); or

(f)   an order under rule 24.12 (order for the issue of a letter of request).

(2) When applying for a witness summons, permission under rule 22.8 or 23.4 or order under rule 24.7, 24.9, 24.10(4) or 24.12, the party must provide the court with evidence that –

(a)   all parties to the mediation agree to the obtaining of the mediation evidence;

(b)   obtaining the mediation evidence is necessary for overriding considerations of public policy in accordance with article 7(1)(*a*) of the Mediation Directive; or

(c)   the disclosure of the content of an agreement resulting from mediation is necessary to implement or enforce that agreement.

(3) When considering a request for a witness summons, permission under rule 22.8 or 23.4 or order under rule 24.7, 24.9, 24.10(4) or 24.12, the court may invite any person, whether or not a party, to make representations.

(4) Where this rule applies, Parts 21 to 24 apply to the extent they are consistent with this rule.

****

PRACTICE DIRECTION 5A – FORMS

FPR PT 5, R 5.1

This Practice Direction supplements FPR Part 5, rule 5.1 (Forms)

Scope and interpretation

1.1 This Practice Direction lists the forms to be used in family proceedings on or after 6 April 2011. Table 1 lists the forms against the part of the FPR to which they are relevant, and Table 2 lists the forms individually with their description.

1.2 The forms may be –

(a) modified as the circumstances require, provided that all essential information, especially information or guidance which the form gives to the recipient, is included;

(b) expanded to include additional pages where that may be necessary, provided that any additional pages are also verified by a statement of truth.

1.3 Any reference in family proceedings forms to a Part, rule or Practice Direction is to be read as a reference to the equivalent Part, rule or Practice Direction in the FPR and any reference to a Practice Direction in any CPR form used in family proceedings is to be read as a reference to the equivalent Practice Direction in the FPR.

Forms for committal applications

2.1 Rule 33.1(2) applies Part 50 of, and Schedules 1 and 2 to the CPR, in so far as they are relevant and with necessary modification (including the modification referred to in rule 33.7), to an application made in the High Court and a county court to enforce an order made in family proceedings. The CPR Practice Direction 'RSC52 and CCR 29–Committal Applications' therefore applies with necessary modifications to the enforcement of such an order. The form to be used for a committal application is set out in that Practice Direction. Accordingly, where a committal application is made in existing proceedings, it must be commenced by filing an application notice under Part 18 in those proceedings (a form C2 where there are existing proceedings under the Children Act 1989, a form D11 where the existing proceedings are matrimonial or civil partnership proceedings, financial remedy proceedings and proceedings under Part 8 or otherwise a form FP2). Otherwise a committal application must be commenced by the issue of a Part 19 application notice (a form FP1).

Other Forms

3.1 Other forms may be authorised by practice directions.

Table 1

Index to forms

FPR Part	Forms
Part 3 Alternative Dispute Resolution (Family Mediation)	FM1
Part 6 Service	C9, D5, D89, FL415, FP6
Part 7 Matrimonial and Civil Partnership Proceedings	C60, D6, D8, D8 Notes, D8A, D8B, D8D, D8D Notes, D8N, D8N Notes, D11, D13B, D20, D36, D80A, D80B, D80C, D80D, D80E, D80F, D80G, D81, D84,
Part 8 Miscellaneous Applications	D50, D50A, D50B, D50C, D50D, D50E, D50F, D50G, D50H, D50J, D50K
Part 8 Chapter 5 Applications for declarations	C63, C64, C65, D70
Part 9 Applications for a Financial Remedy	Form A, Form A1, Form A2, Form B, Form E, Form E Notes, Form E1, Form E2, Form F, Form I, Form P, Form P1, Form P2, Form PPF, Form PPF1, Form PPF2
Part 10 Applications under Part 4 of the Family Law Act 1996	FL401, FL403, FL407, FL415
Part 11 Applications under Part 4A of the Family Law Act 1996	FL401A, FL403A, FL407A, FL430, FL431
Part 12 Applications in respect of children	C1, C1A, C2, C3, C4, C5, C8, C9, C11, C12, C13, C13A, C14, C15, C16, C17, C17A, C18, C19, C20, C61, C62, C66, C67, C68, C78, C79, C100, C110, C(PRA1), C(PRA2) C(PRA3), PLO1, PLO2, PLO3, PLO4, PLO5, PLO6, PLO8, PLO9, PLP10
Part 13 Applications under section 54 of Human Fertilisation and Embryology Act 2008	C51, C52, A64A, A101A

FPR Part	Forms
Part 14 Adoption	A4, A5, A50, A51, A52, A53, A54, A55, A56, A57 A58, A59, A60, A61, A62, A63, A50 Notes, A51 Notes, A52 Notes, A53 Notes, A54 Notes, A55 Notes, A56 Notes, A57 Notes, A58 Notes, A59 Notes, A60 Notes, A61 Notes, A 62 Notes, A63 Notes, A64, A65, A100, A101, A102, A103, A104, A105, A106, A107
Part 15 Representation of Protected Parties	FP9
Part 16 Representation of children	FP9
Part 18 Applications in proceedings	C2, D11, FP2
Part 19 Alternative Procedure for applications	FP1, FP1A, FP1B, FP3, FP5
Part 22 Evidence	N285
Part 24 Witnesses	FP25
Part 26 Notification of change of solicitor	FP8
Part 28 Costs	252, D254, D258, D258A, D258B, D258C, D259, Form H, Form H1, N260
Part 30 Appeals	N161, N161A, N161B, N162, N162A, N162, N164
Part 31 Registration of Orders under the Council Regulation, The Civil Partnership (Jurisdiction and Recognition of Judgements) Regulations 2005 and under the Hague Convention 1996	C60, C61, C62, C69, D180
Part 32 Registration and Enforcement of Orders	D151
Part 33 Enforcement	D62, N56, N323, N336, N337, N349, N379, N380
Part 34 Reciprocal Enforcement of Maintenance Orders	REMO 1, REMO 2

Table 2

List of Forms

Number	Name
A4	Application For Revocation Of An Order Freeing A Child For Adoption
A5	Application For Substitution Of One Adoption Agency For Another
A50	Application for a placement order Section 22 Adoption and Children Act 2002
A51	Application for variation of a placement order Section 23 Adoption and Children Act 2002
A52	Application for revocation of a placement order Section 24 Adoption and Children Act 2002
A53	Application for a contact order Section 26 Adoption and Children Act 2002
A54	Application for variation or revocation of a contact order Section 27(1)(*b*) Adoption and Children Act 2002
A55	Application for permission to change a child's surname Section 28 Adoption and Children Act 2002
A56	Application for permission to remove a child from the United Kingdom Section 28 Adoption and Children Act 2002
A57	Application for a recovery order Section 41 Adoption and Children Act 2002
A58	Application for an adoption order Section 46 Adoption and Children Act 2002
A59	Application for a Convention adoption order Section 46 Adoption and Children Act 2002
A60	Application for an adoption order (excluding a Convention adoption order) where the child is habitually resident outside the British Islands and is brought into the United Kingdom for the purposes of adoption Section 46 Adoption and Children Act 2002
A61	Application for an order for parental responsibility prior to adoption abroad Section 84 Adoption and Children Act 2002

Number	Name
A62	Application for a direction under section 88(1) of the Adoption and Children Act 2002
A63	Application for an order to annul a Convention adoption or Convention adoption order or for an overseas adoption or determination under section 91 to cease to be valid Section 89 Adoption and Children Act 2002
A50 Notes	Application for a placement order Section 22 Adoption and Children Act 2002 – Notes on completing the form
A51 Notes	Application for variation of a placement order Section 23 Adoption and Children Act 2002 – Notes on completing the form
A52 Notes	Application for revocation of a placement order Section 24 Adoption and Children Act 2002 – Notes on completing the form
A53 Notes	Application for a contact order Section 26 Adoption and Children Act 2002 – Notes on completing the form
A54 Notes	Application for variation or revocation of a contact order Section 27(1)(*b*) Adoption and Children Act 2002 – Notes on completing the form
A55 Notes	Application for permission to change a child's surname Section 28 Adoption and Children Act 2002 – Notes on completing the form
A56 Notes	Application for permission to remove a child from the United Kingdom Section 28 Adoption and Children Act 2002 – Notes on completing the form
A57 Notes	Application for a recovery order Section 41 Adoption and Children Act 2002 – Notes on completing the form
A58 Notes	Application for an adoption order Section 46 Adoption and Children Act 2002 – Notes on completing the form
A59 Notes	Application for a Convention adoption order Section 46 Adoption and Children Act 2002 – Notes on completing the form
A60 Notes	Application for an adoption order (excluding a Convention adoption order) where the child is habitually resident outside the British Islands and is brought into the United Kingdom for the purposes of adoption Section 46 Adoption and Children Act 2002 – Notes on completing the form

Number	Name
A61 Notes	Application for an order for parental responsibility prior to adoption abroad Section 84 Adoption and Children Act 2002 – Notes on completing the form
A62 Notes	Application for a direction under section 88(1) of the Adoption and Children Act 2002 – Notes on completing the form
A63 Notes	Application for an order to annul a Convention adoption or Convention adoption order or for an overseas adoption or determination under section 91 to cease to be valid Section 89 Adoption and Children Act 2002 – Notes on completing the form
A64	Application to receive information from court records Section 60(4) Adoption and Children Act 2002
A64A	Application to receive information from court records about a parental order Section 60(4) Adoption and Children Act 2002
A65	Confidential information
A100	Consent to the placement of my child for adoption with any prospective adopters chosen by the Adoption Agency Section 19 of the Adoption and Children Act 2002
A101	Consent to the placement of my child for adoption with identified prospective adopters Section 19 of the Adoption and Children Act 2002
A101A	Agreement to the making of a parental order in respect of my child Section 54 of the Human Fertilisation and Embryology Act 2008
A102	Consent to the placement of my child for adoption with identified prospective adopter(s) and, if the placement breaks down, with any prospective adopter(s) chosen by the adoption agency Section 19 of the Adoption and Children Act 2002
A103	Advance Consent to Adoption Section 20 of the Adoption and Children Act 2002
A104	Consent to Adoption The Adoption and Children Act 2002
A105	Consent to the making of an Order under Section 84 of the Adoption and Children Act 2002

Number	Name
A106	Withdrawal of Consent Sections 19 and 20 of the Adoption and Children Act 2002
A107	Consent by the child's parent to adoption by their partner The Adoption and Children Act 2002
C1	Application for an Order
C1A	Allegations of harm and domestic violence (Supplemental information form)
C2	Application For permission to start proceedings For an order or directions in existing proceedings To be joined as, or cease to be, a party in existing family proceedings under the Children Act 1989
C3	Application for an order authorising search for, taking charge of and delivery of child
C4	Application for an order for disclosure of a child's whereabouts
C5	Local Authority application concerning the registration of a child-minder or a provider of day care
C8	Confidential contact details
C9	Statement of service
C11	Supplement for an application for an Emergency Protection Order
C12	Supplement for an application for a warrant to assist a person authorised by an Emergency Protection Order
C13	Supplement for an application for a Care or Supervision Order
C13A	Supplement for an application for a Special Guardianship Order Section 14A Children Act 1989
C14	Supplement for an application for authority to refuse contact with a child in care
C15	Supplement for an application for contact with a child in care
C16	Supplement for an application for a Child Assessment Order
C17	Supplement for an application for Education Supervision Order

Number	Name
C17A	Supplement for an application for an extension of an Education Supervision Order
C18	Supplement for an application for a Recovery Order
C19	Application for a warrant of assistance
C20	Supplement for an application for an order to hold a child in Secure Accommodation
C51	Application for a Parental Order Section 54 Human Fertilisation and Embryology Act 2008
C52	Acknowledgement of an application for a Parental Order
C60	Certificate referred to in Article 39 of Council Regulation (EC) No. 2201/ 2003 of 27 November 2003 concerning judgments on parental responsibility
C61	Certificate referred to in Article 41(1) of Council Regulation (EC) No. 2201/2003 of 27 November 2003 concerning judgments on rights of access
C62	Certificate referred to in Article 42(1) of Council Regulation (EC) No. 2201/2003 of 27 November 2003 concerning the return of the child
C63	Application for declaration of parentage under section 55A of the Family Law Act 1986
C64	Application for declaration of legitimacy or legitimation under section 56(1)(*b*) and (2) of the Family Law Act 1986
C65	Application for declaration as to adoption effected overseas under section 57 of the Family Law Act 1986
C66	Application for inherent jurisdiction order in relation to children
C67	Application under the Child Abduction and Custody Act 1985 or Article 11 of Council Regulation (EC) 2201/2003
C68	Application for international transfer of jurisdiction to or from England and Wales
C69	Application for registration, recognition or non recognition of a judgment under Council Regulation (EC) 2201/2003
C78	Application for attachment of a warning notice to a contact order

Number	Name
C79	Application related to enforcement of a contact order
C100	Application under the Children Act 1989 for a residence, contact, prohibited steps, specific issue section 8 order or to vary or discharge a section 8 order
C110	Application under the Children Act 1989 for a care or supervision order
C(PRA1)	Parental Responsibility Agreement
C(PRA2)	Step Parent Parental Responsibility Agreement
C(PRA3)	Parental Responsibility Agreement Section 4ZA Children Act 1989 (Acquisition of parental responsibility by second female parent)
D5	Notice to be indorsed on documents served in accordance with rule 6.14
D6	Statement of Reconciliation
D8	Divorce/dissolution/(judicial) separation petition
D8 Notes	Supporting notes for guidance on completing a divorce/dissolution/(judicial) separation petition
D8A	Statement of arrangements for children
D8B	Answer to a divorce/dissolution/(judicial) separation or nullity petition
D8D	Petition for a presumption of death decree/order and the dissolution of a marriage/civil partnership
D8D Notes	Supporting notes for guidance on completing a petition for a presumption of death decree/order and the dissolution of a marriage/civil partnership
D8N	Nullity petition
D8N Notes	Supporting notes for guidance on completing a nullity petition
D11	Application Notice
D13B	Affidavit in support of a request to dispense with service of the divorce/dissolution/nullity (judicial) separation petition on the Respondent
D20	Medical Examination: statement of parties & inspector

Number	Name
D36	Notice of Application for Decree Nisi to be made Absolute or Conditional Order to be made final
D50	Notice of application on ground of failure to provide maintenance or for alteration of maintenance agreement during parties' lifetime
D50A	Notice of proceedings and acknowledgement of service – maintenance/property proceedings
D50B	Application under Section 17 of the Married Women's Property Act 1882/Section 67 of the Civil Partnership Act 2004/Application to transfer a tenancy under the Family Law Act 1996 Part IV
D50C	Application on ground of failure to provide maintenance
D50D	Application for alteration of maintenance agreement after the death of one of the parties
D50E	Application for permission to apply for financial relief after overseas divorce/dissolution etc under section 13 of the Matrimonial and Family Proceedings Act 1984/paragraph 4 of Schedule 7 to the Civil Partnership Act 2004
D50F	Application for financial relief after overseas divorce etc under section 12 of the Matrimonial and Family Proceedings Act 1984/paragraph 4 to Schedule 7 to the Civil Partnership Act 2004
D50G	Application to prevent transactions intended to defeat prospective applications for financial relief
D50H	Application for alteration of maintenance agreement during parties lifetime
D50J	Application for an order preventing avoidance under section 32L of the Child Support Act 1991
D50K	Notice of Application for Enforcement by such method of enforcement as the court may consider appropriate
D62	Request for issue of Judgment Summons
D70	Application for Declaration of Marital/Civil Partnership Status
D80A	Affidavit in Support of divorce/(judicial) separation – adultery

Number	Name
D80B	Affidavit in Support of divorce/dissolution (judicial) separation – unreasonable behaviour
D80C	Affidavit in Support of divorce/dissolution/(judicial) separation – desertion
D80D	Affidavit in Support of divorce/dissolution/(judicial) separation – 2 years consent
D80E	Affidavit in Support of divorce/dissolution/(judicial) separation – 5 years separation
D80F	Affidavit in Support of annulment – void marriage/civil partnership
D80G	Affidavit in support of annulment – voidable marriage/civil partnership
D81	Statement of information for a Consent Order in relation to a financial remedy
D84	Application for a decree nisi/conditional order or (judicial) separation decree/order
D89	Request for personal service by a court bailiff
D151	Application for registration of maintenance order in a magistrates' court
D180	Concerning judgements in matrimonial matters
D252	Notice of commencement of assessment of bill of costs.
D254	Request for a default costs certificate
D258	Request for a detailed assessment of hearing
D258A	Request for detailed assessment (legal aid only)
D258B	Request for detailed assessment (Costs payable out of a fund other than the Community Legal Service Fund)
D258C	Request for detailed assessment hearing pursuant to an order under Part III of the Solicitors Act 1974
D259	Notice of appeal against a detailed assessment (divorce)
FL401	Application for a non molestation order/an occupation order
FL401A	Application for a Forced Marriage Protection Order
FL403	Application to vary, extend or discharge

Number	Name
FL403A	Application to vary, extend or discharge Forced Marriage Protection Orders
FL407	Applications for warrant of Arrest
FL407A	Application for warrant of arrest for a Forced Marriage Protection Order
FL415	Statement of service
FL430	Application for leave to apply for a Forced Marriage Protection Order
FL431	Application to join/cease as a party to Forced Marriage Protection Proceedings
FM1	Family Mediation Information and Assessment Form FM1
Form A	Notice of intention to proceed with an application for a financial order (NOTE: This form should be used whether the applicant is proceeding with an application in the petition or making a free standing application)
Form A1	Notice of intention to proceed with an application for a financial remedy (other than a financial order) in the county or high court
Form A2	Notice of intention to proceed with an application for a financial remedy in the magistrates court
Form B	Notice of an application to consider the financial position of the Respondent after the divorce/dissolution
Form E	Financial Statement for a financial order or for financial relief after an over seas divorce or dissolution etc
Form E Notes	Form E (Financial Statement for a financial order or for financial relief after an overseas divorce or dissolution etc) Notes for guidance
Form E1	Financial Statement for a financial remedy (other than a financial order or financial relief after an overseas divorce/dissolution etc) in the county or high court
Form E2	Financial Statement for a financial remedy in the magistrates court
Form F	Notice of allegation in proceedings for financial remedy
Form H	Estimate of costs (financial remedy)
Form H1	Statement of Costs (financial remedy)

Number	Name
Form I	Notice of request for periodical payments order at the same rate as order for interim maintenance pending outcome of proceeding
Form P	Pension inquiry form
Form P1	Pension sharing annex
Form P2	Pension attachment annex
Form PPF	Pension Protection Fund Inquiry Form
Form PPF 1	Pension Protection Fund sharing annex
Form PPF 2	Pension Protection Fund attachment annex
FP1	Application under Part 19 of the Family Procedure Rules 2010
FP1A	Application under Part 19 of the Family Procedure Rules 2010 Notes for applicant on completing the application (Form FP1)
FP1B	Application under Part 19 of the Family Procedure Rules 2010 Notes for respondent
FP2	Application notice Part 18 of the Family Procedure Rules 2010
FP3	Application for injunction (General form)
FP5	Acknowledgment of service Application under Part 19 of the Family Procedure Rules 2010
FP6	Certificate of service
FP8	Notice of change of solicitor
FP9	Certificate of suitability of litigation friend
FP25	Witness Summons
N56	Form for replying to an attachment of earnings application (statement of means)
N161	Appellant's Notice
N161A	Guidance Notes on Completing the Appellant's Notice
N161B	Important Notes for Respondents
N162	Respondent's Notice
N162A	Guidance Notes for Completing the Respondent's Notice

Number	Name
N163	Skeleton Argument
N164	Appellant's Notice
N260	Statement of costs (summary assessment)
N285	General Affidavit
N323	Request for Warrant of Execution
N336	Request and result of search in the attachment of earnings index
N337	Request for attachment of earnings order
N349	Application for a third party debt order
N379	Application for a charging order on land or property
N380	Application for charging order on securities
PLO1	Application for a care order or supervision order: Supplementary form
PLO2	The local authority's case summary
PLO3	Draft case management order
PLO4	Allocation record and timetable for the child(ren)
PLO5	Directions and allocation on issue of proceedings
PLO6	Directions and allocation at first appointment
PLO8	Standard Directions on Issue
PLO9	Standard Directions at First Appointment
PLP10	Order Menu – Directions Revised Private Law Programme
REMO 1	Notice of Registration
REMO 2	Notice of Refusal of Registration.

****

PRACTICE DIRECTION 7C – POLYGAMOUS MARRIAGES

FPR PTS 7, 9 AND 18

This Practice Direction supplements FPR Part 7 (procedure for applications in matrimonial and civil partnership proceedings), Part 9 (applications for a financial remedy) and Part 18 (procedure for other applications in proceedings).

Scope of this Practice Direction

1.1 This practice direction applies where an application is made for –

(a)　a matrimonial order;

(b)　an order under section 27 of the 1973 Act;

(c)　an order under section 35 of the 1973 Act;

(d)　an order under the 1973 Act which is made in connection with, or with proceedings for any of the above orders; or

(e)　an order under Part 3 of the 1984 Act,

and either party to the marriage is, or has during the course of the marriage, been married to more than one person (a polygamous marriage).

Polygamous marriages

2.1 Where this practice direction applies the application must state –

(a)　that the marriage is polygamous;

(b)　whether, as far as the party to the marriage is aware, any other spouse (that is, a spouse other than the spouse to whom the application relates) of that party is still living (the 'additional spouse'); and

(c)　if there is such an additional spouse –

　　(i)　the additional spouse's name and address;

　　(ii)　the date and place of the marriage to the additional spouse.

2.2 A respondent who believes that the marriage is polygamous must include the details referred to in paragraph 2.1 above in the acknowledgment of service if they are not included in the application.

2.3 The applicant in any proceedings to which this practice direction applies must apply to the court for directions as soon as possible after the filing of the application or the receipt of an acknowledgment of service mentioning an additional spouse.

2.4 On such an application or of its own initiative the court may –

(a)　give the additional spouse notice of any of the proceedings to which this practice direction applies; and

(b)　make the additional spouse a party to such proceedings.

2.5 In any case where the application or acknowledgment of service states that the marriage is polygamous (whether or not there is an additional spouse) a court officer must clearly mark the file with the words 'Polygamous Marriage'. The court officer must also check whether an application under paragraph 2.4 has been made in the case and, where no application has been made, refer the file to the court for consideration.

References in decrees to section 47 of the 1973 Act

3.1 Every decree nisi and decree absolute which is made in respect of a polygamous marriage must refer to the fact that the order is made with reference to section 47 of the 1973 Act.

****

PRACTICE DIRECTION 9A – APPLICATION FOR A FINANCIAL REMEDY

FPR PT 9

This Practice Direction supplements FPR Part 9

Introduction

1.1 Part 9 of the Family Procedure Rules sets out the procedure applicable to the financial proceedings that are included in the definition of a 'financial remedy'.

1.2 The procedure is applicable to a limited extent to applications for financial remedies that are heard in magistrates' courts (namely, those under section 35 of the Matrimonial Causes Act 1973, paragraph 69 of Schedule 5 to the Civil Partnership Act 2004, Part I of the Domestic Proceedings and Magistrates' Courts Act 1978, Schedule 1 to the Children Act 1989 and Schedule 6 to the Civil Partnership Act 2004). However, unless the context otherwise requires, this Practice Direction does not apply to proceedings in a magistrates' court.

1.3 Where an application for a financial remedy includes an application relating to land, details of any mortgagee must be included in the application.

Pre-application protocol

2.1 The 'pre-application protocol' annexed to this Direction outlines the steps parties should take to seek and provide information from and to each other prior to the commencement of any application for a financial remedy. The court will expect the parties to comply with the terms of the protocol.

Costs

3.1 Rule 9.27 applies in the High Court and county court. The rule requires each party to produce to the court, at every hearing or appointment, an estimate of the costs incurred by the party up to the date of that hearing or appointment.

3.2 The purpose of this rule is to enable the court to take account of the impact of each party's costs liability on their financial situations. Parties should ensure that the information contained in the estimate is as full and accurate as possible and that any sums already paid in respect of a party's financial remedy costs are clearly set out. Where relevant, any liability arising from the costs of other proceedings between the parties should continue to be referred to in the appropriate section of a party's financial statement; any such costs should not be included in the estimates under rule 9.27.

3.3 Rule 28.3 provides that the general rule in financial remedy proceedings is that the court will not make an order requiring one party to pay the costs of another party. However the court may make such an order at any stage of the proceedings where it considers it appropriate to do so because of the conduct of a party in relation to the proceedings.

3.4 Any breach of this practice direction or the pre-application protocol annexed to it will be taken into account by the court when deciding whether to depart from the general rule as to costs.

Procedure before the first appointment

4.1 In addition to the matters listed at rule 9.14(5), the parties should, if possible, with a view to identifying and narrowing any issues between the parties, exchange and file with the court –

(a)   a summary of the case agreed between the parties;
(b)   a schedule of assets agreed between the parties; and
(c)   details of any directions that they seek, including, where appropriate, the name of any expert they wish to be appointed.

4.2 Where a party is prevented from sending the details referred to in (c) above, the party should make that information available at the first appointment.

Financial Statements and other documents

5.1 Practice Direction 22A (Written Evidence) applies to any financial statement filed in accordance with rules 9.14 or 9.19 and to any exhibits to a financial statement. In preparing a bundle of documents to be exhibited to or attached to a financial statement, regard must be had in particular to paragraphs 11.1 to 11.3 and 13.1 to 13.4 of that Direction. Where on account of their bulk, it is impracticable for the exhibits to a financial statement to be retained on the court file after the First Appointment, the court may give directions as to their custody pending further hearings.

5.2 Where the court directs a party to provide information or documents by way of reply to a questionnaire or request by another party, the reply must be verified by a statement of truth. Unless otherwise directed, a reply to a questionnaire or request for information and documents shall not be filed with the court.

(Part 17 and Practice Direction 17A make further provision about statements of truth)

Financial Dispute Resolution (FDR) Appointment

6.1 A key element in the procedure is the Financial Dispute Resolution (FDR) appointment. Rule 9.17 provides that the FDR appointment is to be treated as a meeting held for the purposes of discussion and negotiation. Such meetings have been developed as a means of reducing the tension which inevitably arises in family disputes and facilitating settlement of those disputes.

6.2 In order for the FDR to be effective, parties must approach the occasion openly and without reserve. Non-disclosure of the content of such meetings is vital and is an essential prerequisite for fruitful discussion directed to the settlement of the dispute between the parties. The FDR appointment is an important part of the settlement process. As a consequence of *Re D (Minors) (Conciliation: Disclosure of Information)* 1993 Fam 231, evidence of anything said or of any admission made in the course of an FDR appointment will not be admissible in evidence, except at the trial of a person for an offence committed at the appointment or in the very exceptional circumstances indicated in *Re D*.

6.3 Courts will therefore expect –

(a) parties to make offers and proposals;
(b) recipients of offers and proposals to give them proper consideration; and
(c) (subject to paragraph 6.4), that parties, whether separately or together, will not seek to exclude from consideration at the appointment any such offer or proposal.

6.4 Paragraph 6.3(*c*) does not apply to an offer or proposal made during alternative dispute resolution.

6.5 In order to make the most effective use of the first appointment and the FDR appointment, the legal representatives attending those appointments will be expected to have full knowledge of the case.

6.6 The rules do not provide for FDR appointments to take place during proceedings in magistrates' courts.

(Provision relating to experts in financial remedy proceedings is contained in the Practice Direction supplementing Part 25 of the FPR relating to Experts and Assessors in Family Proceedings)

Consent orders

7.1 Rule 9.26(1)(*a*) requires an application for a consent order to be accompanied by two copies of the draft order in the terms sought, one of which must be endorsed with a statement signed by the respondent to the application signifying the respondent's agreement. The rule is considered to have been properly complied with if the endorsed statement is signed by solicitors on record as acting for the respondent; but where the consent order applied for contains undertakings, it should be signed by the party giving the undertakings as well as by that party's solicitor.

> (Provision relating to the enforcement of undertakings is contained in the Practice Direction 33A supplementing Part 33 of the FPR)

7.2 Rule 9.26(1)(*b*) requires each party to file with the court and serve on the other party a statement of information. Where this is contained in one form, both parties must sign the statement to certify that each has read the contents of the other's statement.

7.3 Rule 35.2 deals with applications for a consent order in respect of a financial remedy where the parties wish to have the content of a written mediation agreement to which the Mediation Directive applies made the subject of a consent order.

Section 10(2) of the Matrimonial Causes Act 1973 and section 48(2) of the Civil Partnership Act 2004

8.1 Where a respondent who has applied under section 10(2) of the Matrimonial Causes Act 1973, or section 48(2) of the Civil Partnership Act 2004, for the court to consider his or her financial position after a divorce or dissolution elects not to proceed with the application, a notice of withdrawal of the application signed by the respondent or by the respondent's solicitor may be filed without leave of the court. In this event a formal order dismissing or striking out the application is unnecessary. Notice of withdrawal should also be given to the applicant's solicitor.

8.2 An application under section 10(2) or section 48(2) which has been withdrawn is not a bar to making in matrimonial proceedings, the decree absolute and in civil partnership proceedings, the final order.

Maintenance Orders – registration in magistrates' courts

9.1 Where periodical payments are required to be made to a child under an order registered in a magistrates' court, section 62 of the Magistrates' Courts Act 1980 permits the payments to be made instead to the person with whom the child has his home. That person may proceed in his own name for variation, revival or revocation of the order and may enforce payment either in his own name or by requesting the designated officer of the court to do so.

9.2 The registration in a magistrates' court of an order made direct to a child entails a considerable amount of work. Accordingly, when the court is considering the form of an order where there are children, care should be taken not to make orders for payment direct where such orders would be of no benefit to the parties.

Pensions

10.1 The phrase 'party with pension rights' is used in FPR Part 9, Chapter 8. For matrimonial proceedings, this phrase has the meaning given to it by section 25D(3) of the Matrimonial Causes Act 1973 and means 'the party to the marriage who has or is likely to have benefits under a pension arrangement'. There is a definition of 'civil partner with pension rights' in paragraph 29 of Schedule 5 to the Civil Partnership Act 2004 which mirrors the definition of 'party with pension rights' in section 25D(3) of the 1973 Act. The phrase 'is likely to have benefits' in these definitions refers to accrued rights to pension benefits which are not yet in payment.

PPF Compensation

11.1 The phrase 'party with compensation rights' is used in FPR Part 9, Chapter 9. For matrimonial proceedings, the phrase has the meaning given to it by section 25G(5) of the Matrimonial Causes Act 1973 and means the party to the marriage who is or is likely to be entitled to PPF compensation. There is a definition of 'civil partner with compensation rights' in paragraph 37(1) of Schedule 5 to the Civil Partnership Act 2004 which mirrors the definition of 'party with compensation rights' in section 25G(5). The phrase 'is likely to be entitled to PPF Compensation' in those definitions refers to statutory entitlement to PPF Compensation which is not yet in payment.

Annex – Pre-application protocol

Notes of guidance

Scope of the Protocol

1 This protocol is intended to apply to all applications for a financial remedy as defined by rule 2.3. It is designed to cover all classes of case, ranging from a simple application for periodical payments to an application for a substantial lump sum and property adjustment order. The protocol is designed to facilitate the operation of the procedure for financial remedy applications.

2 In considering the options of pre-application disclosure and negotiation, solicitors should bear in mind the advantage of having a court timetable and court managed process. There is sometimes an advantage in preparing disclosure before proceedings are commenced. However, solicitors should bear in mind the objective of controlling costs and in particular the costs of discovery and that the option of pre-application disclosure and negotiation has risks of excessive and uncontrolled expenditure and delay. This option should only be encouraged where both parties agree to follow this route and disclosure is not likely to be an issue or has been adequately dealt with in mediation or otherwise.

3 Solicitors should consider at an early stage and keep under review whether it would be appropriate to suggest mediation and/or collaborative law to the clients as an alternative to solicitor negotiation or court based litigation.

4 Making an application to the court should not be regarded as a hostile step or a last resort, rather as a way of starting the court timetable, controlling disclosure and endeavouring to avoid the costly final hearing and the preparation for it.

First letter

5 The circumstances of parties to an application for a financial remedy are so various that it would be difficult to prepare a specimen first letter. The request for information will be different in every case. However, the tone of the initial letter is important and the guidelines in paragraphs 14 and 15 should be followed. It should be approved in advance by the client. Solicitors writing to an unrepresented party should always recommend that he seeks independent legal advice and enclose a second copy of the letter to be passed to any solicitor instructed. A reasonable time limit for an answer may be 14 days.

Negotiation and settlement

6 In the event of pre-application disclosure and negotiation, as envisaged in paragraph 12 an application should not be issued when a settlement is a reasonable prospect.

Disclosure

7 The protocol underlines the obligation of parties to make full and frank disclosure of all material facts, documents and other information relevant to the issues. Solicitors owe their clients a duty to tell them in clear terms of this duty and of the possible consequences of breach of the duty, which may include criminal sanctions under the Fraud Act 2006. This duty of disclosure is an ongoing obligation and includes the duty to disclose any material changes after initial disclosure has been given. Solicitors are referred to the Good Practice Guide for Disclosure produced by Resolution (obtainable from the Administrative Director, 366A Crofton Road, Orpington, Kent BR2 8NN) and can also contact the Law Society's Practice Advice Service on 0870 606 2522.

The Protocol

General principles

8 All parties must always bear in mind the overriding objective set out at rules 1.1 to 1.4 and try to ensure that applications should be resolved and a just outcome achieved as speedily as possible without costs being unreasonably incurred. The needs of any children should be addressed and safeguarded. The procedures which it is appropriate to follow should be conducted with minimum distress to the parties and in a manner designed to promote as good a continuing relationship between the parties and any children affected as is possible in the circumstances.

9 The principle of proportionality must be borne in mind at all times. It is unacceptable for the costs of any case to be disproportionate to the financial value of the subject matter of the dispute.

10 Parties should be informed that where a court is considering whether to make an order requiring one party to pay the costs of another party, it will take into account pre-application offers to settle and conduct of disclosure.

Identifying the issues

11 Parties must seek to clarify their claims and identify the issues between them as soon as possible. So that this can be achieved, they must provide full, frank and clear disclosure of facts, information and documents, which are material and sufficiently accurate to enable proper negotiations to take place to settle their differences. Openness in all dealings is essential.

Disclosure

12 If parties carry out voluntary disclosure before the issue of proceedings the parties should exchange schedules of assets, income, liabilities and other material facts, using the financial statement as a guide to the format of the disclosure. Documents should only be disclosed to the extent that they are required by the financial statement. Excessive or disproportionate costs should not be incurred.

Correspondence

13 Any first letter and subsequent correspondence must focus on the clarification of claims and identification of issues and their resolution. Protracted and unnecessary correspondence and 'trial by correspondence' must be avoided.

14 The impact of any correspondence upon the reader and in particular the parties must always be considered. Any correspondence which raises irrelevant issues or which might cause the other party to adopt an entrenched, polarised or hostile position is to be discouraged.

Summary

15 The aim of all pre-application proceedings steps must be to assist the parties to resolve their differences speedily and fairly or at least narrow the issues and, should that not be possible, to assist the court to do so.

FORMS

FORM A

Notice of [intention to proceed with] an application for a financial order	To be completed by the Applicant	
	Name of court	**Case No.**
	Name of Applicant	
	Name of Respondent	

Respondent('s Solicitor(s)) name and address

Please note that this form should only be completed if you are applying for a financial order.

If you are applying for a financial remedy other than a financial order in the county court please complete Form A1.

If you are applying for a financial remedy in the magistrates court please complete Form A2.

(please tick the appropriate boxes)

The Applicant intends:

☐ **to apply** to the Court for:

☐ **to proceed** with the application in the [application][answer] for:

☐ **to apply to vary:**

☐ an order for maintenance pending suit/ outcome of proceedings

☐ a secured provision order

☐ a lump sum order

☐ a property adjustment order (please provide address)

☐ a periodical payments order

☐ a pension sharing order

☐ a pension attachment order

☐ a pension compensation sharing order

☐ a pension compensation attachment order

continued over the page ⇨

© Crown Copyright 2011

Please tick the appropriate box below if an application is made for any periodical payments or secured periodical payments for children:

- ☐ and there is a written agreement made before 5 April 1993 about maintenance for the benefit of children

- ☐ and there is a written agreement made on or after 5 April 1993 about maintenance for the benefit of children

- ☐ but there is no agreement, tick any of the boxes below to show if you are applying for payment:

    ☐ for a stepchild or stepchildren

    ☐ in addition to child support maintenance already paid under a Child Support Agency assessment

    ☐ to meet expenses arising from a child's disability

    ☐ to meet expenses incurred by a child in being educated or training for work

    ☐ when either the child **or** the person with care of the child **or** the absent parent of the child is not habitually resident in the United Kingdom

    ☐ Other (please state)

Have you attended a mediation information/assessment meeting as suggested in the pre-action protocol and/or attached Form FM1?   ☐ Yes   ☐ No

Signed   Dated D D / M M / Y Y Y Y

             (Applicant) (Applicant's solicitor)

2

FORM A1

Notice of [intention to proceed with] an application for a financial remedy (other than a financial order) in the county or High Court

To be completed by the Applicant	
Name of court	Case No.
Name of Applicant	
Name of Respondent	

Please note that this form should only be completed if you are applying for a financial remedy other than a financial order in the county court.

If you are applying for

- a financial order in the county court please complete Form A
- a financial remedy in the magistrates court please complete Form A2
- financial relief after overseas divorce etc under Part 3 of the Matrimonial and Family Proceedings Act 1984 please complete D50F
- financial provision under section 27 of the Matrimonial Causes Act 1973/Part 9 of Schedule 5 to the Civil Partnership Act 2004 please complete D50C
- alteration of a maintenance agreement under section 35 of the Matrimonial Causes Act 1973/ paragraph 69 of Schedule 5 to the Civil Partnership Act 2004 please complete D50H

1. The Applicant intends: **(please tick the appropriate boxes)**

    ☐ **to apply** to the Court for:

    ☐ **to apply to vary:**

    ☐ a periodical payment order
    ☐ a lump sum order
    ☐ a secured periodical payments order
    ☐ Other (please specify)

    ☐ a settlement of property for the benefit of the child(ren) (please provide address below)
    ☐ a transfer of property for the benefit of the child(ren) (please provide address below)

2. **If an application is made for** any periodical payments or secured periodical payments for children please complete this section:

    ☐ there is a written agreement made before 5 April 1993 about maintenance for the benefit of children;

    ☐ there is a written agreement made on or after 5 April 1993 about maintenance for the benefit of children; or

    ☐ there is no agreement, tick any of the boxes below to show if you are applying for payment:

    ☐ for a stepchild or stepchildren

    ☐ in addition to child support maintenance already paid under a Child Support Agency assessment

    ☐ to meet expenses arising from a child's disability

    ☐ to meet expenses incurred by a child in being educated or training for work

    ☐ when either the child **or** the person with care of the child **or** the absent parent of the child is not habitually resident in the United Kingdom

    If none of the above applies, the court may not have jurisdiction to hear the application for periodical payments.

3. Has the Child Support Agency made any calculation of maintenance in respect of the child(ren)

☐ Yes   ☐ No

If Yes, state briefly your reasons for making this application to the court including any reasons why the Child Support Agency is no longer dealing with your claim or any reasons why you need additional maintenance to top up payments made through the Child Support Agency:

4. Have you attended a mediation information/assessment meeting as provided in the pre-action protocol and/or attached Form FM1?

☐ Yes   ☐ No

5. **Applicant's details**

Name of Applicant

Applicant's address (including postcode)

Postcode ☐☐☐ ☐☐☐

Telephone no.

Ref.

Email address

6. **Respondent's details**

Name of Respondent

Respondent's address (including postcode)

Postcode ☐☐☐ ☐☐☐

Telephone no.

Ref.

Email address

7. Have there been any previous court orders or written agreements regarding financial arrangements?

☐ Yes   ☐ No

If Yes, please attach a copy of the order, or if the order is not available please state the date, the terms, the parties and the court below:

8. Are you applying for a financial remedy in relation to a child?

☐ Yes   ☐ No   (If No, please complete the statement of truth)

(If Yes, please complete the tables below for each child continuing on additional sheets if necessary, and then complete the statement of truth)

Name of child 1	
Date of birth	D D / M M / Y Y Y Y
Gender	☐ Male ☐ Female
Relationship to Applicant	
Relationship to Respondent	
Country of residence (if not England or Wales)	

Name of child 2	
Date of birth	D D / M M / Y Y Y Y
Gender	☐ Male ☐ Female
Relationship to Applicant	
Relationship to Respondent	
Country of residence (if not England or Wales)	

Statement of Truth   *delete as appropriate

*[I believe] [the Applicant believes] that the facts stated in this application are true

*I am duly authorised by the Applicant to sign this statement

Print full name	
Name of Applicant's solicitor's firm	

Signed _____   Dated D D / M M / Y Y Y Y

(Applicant) (Litigation friend) (Applicant's solicitor)

Position or office held

(if signing on behalf of firm or company)

Proceedings for contempt of court may be brought against a person who makes or causes to be made, a false statement in a document verified by a statement of truth.

3

FORM A2

<table>
<tr><td rowspan="3">

Notice of [intention to proceed with] an application for a financial remedy in the magistrates' court

</td><td colspan="2">To be completed by the Applicant</td></tr>
<tr><td>Name of court</td><td>Case No.</td></tr>
<tr><td colspan="2">Name of Applicant

Name of Respondent</td></tr>
</table>

Please note that this form should only be completed if you are applying for a financial remedy order in the magistrates' court.

If you are applying for

- a financial order in the county court please complete Form A.
- a financial remedy other than a financial order in the county court please complete Form A1 or other applicable form.
- alteration of a maintenance agreement under section 35 of the Matrimonial Causes Act 1973/ paragraph 69 of Schedule 5 to the Civil Partnership Act 2004 please complete D50H

(please tick the appropriate boxes)

1. The Applicant intends:

    ☐ **to apply** to the Court for:

    ☐ **to apply to vary**:

        ☐ a periodical payment order

        ☐ a lump sum order

2. **If an application is made for** any periodical payments or secured periodical payments for children please complete this section:

    ☐ there is a written agreement made before 5 April 1993 about maintenance for the benefit of children;

    ☐ there is a written agreement made on or after 5 April 1993 about maintenance for the benefit of children; or

    ☐ there is no agreement, tick any of the boxes below to show if you are applying for payment:

        ☐ for a stepchild or stepchildren

        ☐ in addition to child support maintenance already paid under a Child Support Agency assessment

        ☐ to meet expenses arising from a child's disability

        ☐ to meet expenses incurred by a child in being educated or training for work

        ☐ when either the child **or** the person with care of the child **or** the absent parent of the child is not habitually resident in the United Kingdom

If none of the above applies, the court may not have jurisdiction to hear the application for periodical payments.

Form A2 Notice of [intention to proceed with] an application for a financial remedy in the magistrates' court (04.11)

© Crown Copyright 2011

1

3. Have you attended a mediation information/assessment meeting as provided in the pre-action protocol and/or attached Form FM1?

☐ Yes ☐ No

4. **Applicant's details**

Name of Applicant

Applicant's address (including postcode)

Postcode

Telephone no.

Ref.

Email address

5. **Respondent's details**

Name of Respondent

Respondent's address (including postcode)

Postcode

Telephone no.

Ref.

Email address

6. Have there been any previous court orders or written agreements regarding financial arrangements?

☐ Yes ☐ No

If Yes, please attach a copy of the order, or if the order is not available please state the date, the terms, the parties and the court below:

continued over the page ⇨

2

Statement of Truth   *delete as appropriate

*[I believe] [the Applicant believes] that the facts stated in this application are true

*I am duly authorised by the Applicant to sign this statement

Print full name

Name of Applicant's
solicitor's firm

Signed   Dated [D D]/[M M]/[Y Y Y Y]

    (Applicant) (Litigation friend) (Applicant's solicitor)

    Position or office held
    (if signing on behalf of firm
    or company)

**Proceedings for contempt of court may be brought against a person who makes or
causes to be made, a false statement in a document verified by a statement of truth.**

FORM B

Notice of an application to consider the financial position of the Respondent after the divorce/dissolution

To be completed by the Respondent	
Name of court	Case No.
Name of Applicant	
Name of Respondent	

The Respondent intends to apply to the Court under

*[section 10(2) of the Matrimonial Causes Act 1973 for the Court to consider the financial position of the Respondent after the divorce]

*[section 48(2) of the Civil Partnership Act 2004 for the Court to consider the financial position of the Respondent after the dissolution of the civil partnership].

Signed [   ]   Dated [D D / M M / Y Y Y Y]

(Respondent) (Respondent's solicitor)

FORM C

Notice of a First Appointment	**In the**	
	Case No. *Always quote this number*	
	Applicant's Solicitor's reference	
	Respondent's Solicitor's reference	

Take Notice that

By [35 days before the hearing date] you must file with the Court a statement which gives full details of your property and income. You must sign and swear the statement. At the same time each party must exchange a copy of the statement with the [legal representative of the] other party. You will therefore need to contact the other party [or their legal representative] not later than the above date and agree when the exchange shall take place. The exchange may be carried out by post. You must use the standard form of statement (Form E) which you may obtain from the Court office.

By [14 days before the hearing date] you must file with the Court and the [legal representative of the] other party:

- a concise statement of the apparent issues between yourself and the other party;
- a chronology;
- a questionnaire setting out the further information and documents you require from the other party,
  or a statement that no information or documents are required;
- a Notice in Form G.

The First Appointment will be heard by
[name of judge/the District Judge] [in chambers] at [place of hearing]

on [date of hearing]

at [time of hearing]
The probable length of the hearing is [time estimate]

You and your legal representative, if you have one, must attend the appointment. At the appointment you must provide the Court with a written estimate (in Form H) of any legal costs which you have incurred.

Non-compliance may render you liable to costs penalties.

Dated: [Date]

FORM D

Notice of a Financial Dispute Resolution Appointment

In the	
Case No. *Always quote this number*	
Applicant's Solicitor's reference	
Respondent's Solicitor's reference	

Take Notice that

By [7 days before the hearing date] the Applicant must provide the court with details of all offers, proposals and responses concerning the Application.

An appointment for a Financial Dispute Resolution will take place at

[place of hearing]

on [date of hearing]

at [time of hearing]
The probable length of the hearing is [time estimate]

At the Appointment

- You and your legal representative, if you have one, must attend the appointment.

- The hearing will define, as far as possible, the issues in this matter and explore the possibility of settlement. If the matter proceeds to a full hearing, the date of the full hearing will be fixed.

- You must provide the court with a written estimate (in Form H) of any legal costs.

Dated: [Date]

FORM E

Financial statement for a financial order or for financial relief after an overseas divorce or dissolution etc	To be completed by the relevant party	
	Name of court	Case No.
of	Name of Applicant	
	Name of Respondent	

☐ Husband ☐ Wife ☐ Civil partner

(please tick appropriate boxes)

Dated ☐ ☐ / ☐ ☐ / ☐ ☐ ☐ ☐   **The parties are**

	and	

Who is the

☐ husband ☐ wife ☐ civil partner
☐ Petitioner ☐ Applicant ☐ Respondent in the
☐ divorce ☐ dissolution ☐ nullity
☐ (judicial) separation ☐ financial relief application

Applicant in this matter

Who is the

☐ husband ☐ wife ☐ civil partner
☐ Petitioner ☐ Applicant ☐ Respondent in the
☐ divorce ☐ dissolution ☐ nullity
☐ (judicial) separation ☐ financial relief application

Respondent in this matter

This form should only be completed in applications for a financial order or for financial relief after an overseas divorce/dissolution etc. If the application is for any other financial remedy in the county court please complete Form E1. If the application is for a financial remedy in the magistrates court please complete Form E2.

Please fill in this form fully and accurately. Where any box is not applicable, write 'N/A'.

You have a duty to the court to give a full, frank and clear disclosure of all your financial and other relevant circumstances.

A failure to give full and accurate disclosure may result in any order the court makes being set aside.

If you are found to have been deliberately untruthful, criminal proceedings may be brought against you for fraud under the Fraud Act 2006.

The information given in this form must be confirmed by an affidavit. Proceedings for perjury may be brought against a person who makes or causes to be made, a false statement in a document confirmed by an affidavit.

You must attach documents to the form where they are specifically sought and you may attach other documents where it is necessary to explain or clarify any of the information that you give.

Essential documents that must accompany this statement are detailed in the form.

If there is not enough room on the form for any particular piece of information, you may continue on an attached sheet of paper.

If you are in doubt about how to complete any part of this form you should seek legal advice.

This statement is filed by

Name and address of solicitor

1 General Information

1.1	Full name			

1.2	Date of birth	Date	Month	Year		1.3	Date of the marriage/ civil partnership	Date	Month	Year

1.4	Occupation	

1.5 Date of the separation

Date	Month	Year

Tick here if not applicable ☐

1.6 Date of the

	Petition for divorce/ dissolution/nullity/ (judicial) separation			Decree nisi/ conditional order/ (judicial) separation order			Decree absolute/ final order (if applicable)		
	Date	Month	Year	Date	Month	Year	Date	Month	Year

1.7 If you have subsequently married or formed a civil partnership, or will do so, state the date

Date	Month	Year

1.8 Are you living with a new partner?   Yes ☐   No ☐

1.9 Do you intend to live with a new partner within the next six months?   Yes ☐   No ☐

1.10 Details of any children of the family

Full names	Date of birth			With whom does the child live?
	Date	Month	Year	

1.11 Details of the state of health of yourself and the children if you think this should be taken into account

Yourself	Children

2

1.12 Details of the present and proposed future educational arrangements for the children.

Present arrangements	Future arrangements

1.13 Details of any child support maintenance calculation or any maintenance order or agreement made in respect of any children of the family. If no calculation, order or agreement has been made, give an estimate of the liability of the non-resident parent in respect of the children of the family under the Child Support Act 1991.

1.14 If this application is to vary an order, attach a copy of the order and give details of the part that is to be varied and the changes sought. You may need to continue on a separate sheet.

1.15 Details of any other court cases between you and your spouse/civil partner, whether in relation to money, property, children or anything else.

Case No	Court	Type of proceedings

1.16 Your present residence and the occupants of it and on what terms you occupy it (e.g. tenant, owner-occupier).

Address	Occupants	Terms of occupation

3

2 Financial Details

Part 1 Real Property (land and buildings) and Personal Assets

2.1 Complete this section in respect of the family home (the last family home occupied by you and your spouse/civil partner) if it remains unsold.

Documentation required for attachment to this section:

a) A copy of any valuation of the property obtained within the last six months. If you cannot provide this document, please give your own realistic estimate of the current market value

b) A recent mortgage statement confirming the sum outstanding on **each** mortgage

Property name and address	
Land Registry title number	
Mortgage company name(s) and address(es) and account number(s)	
Type of mortgage	
Details of who owns the property and the extent of your legal and beneficial interest in it (i.e. state if it is owned by you solely or jointly owned with your spouse/civil partner or with others)	
If you consider that the legal ownership as recorded at the Land Registry does not reflect the true position, state why	
Current market value of the property	
Balance outstanding on any mortgage(s)	
If a sale at this stage would result in penalties payable under the mortgage, state amount	
Estimate the costs of sale of the property	
Total equity in the property (i.e. market value less outstanding mortgage(s), penalties if any and the costs of sale)	

TOTAL value of your interest in the family home: Total A | £

4

2.2 Details of your interest in any other property, land or buildings. Complete one page for each
property you have an interest in.

Documentation required for attachment to this section:
a) A copy of any valuation of the property obtained within the last six months. If you cannot
provide this document, please give your own realistic estimate of the current market value
b) A recent mortgage statement confirming the sum outstanding on **each** mortgage

Property name and address	
Land Registry title number	
Mortgage company name(s) and address(es) and account number(s)	
Type of mortgage	
Details of who owns the property and the extent of your legal and beneficial interest in it (i.e. state if it is owned by you solely or jointly owned with your spouse/civil partner or with others)	
If you consider that the legal ownership as recorded at the Land Registry does not reflect the true position, state why	
Current market value of the property	
Balance outstanding on any mortgage(s)	
If a sale at this stage would result in penalties payable under the mortgage, state amount	
Estimate the costs of sale of the property	
Total equity in the property (i.e. market value less outstanding mortgage(s), penalties if any and the costs of sale)	
Total value of your interest in this property	

TOTAL value of your interest in ALL other property: Total B £

2.3 Details of all personal bank, building society and National Savings Accounts that you hold or have held at any time in the last twelve months and which are or were either in your own name or in which you have or have had any interest. This applies whether any such account is in credit or in debit. For joint accounts give your interest and the name of the other account holder. If the account is overdrawn, show a minus figure.

Documentation required for attachment to this section:
For each account listed, all statements covering the last 12 months.

Name of bank or building society, including branch name	Type of account (e.g. current)	Account number	Name of other account holder (if applicable)	Balance at the date of this statement	Total current value of your interest

TOTAL value of your interest in ALL accounts: (C1) £ 0.00

2.4 Details of all investments, including shares, PEPs, ISAs, TESSAs, National Savings Investments (other than already shown above), bonds, stocks, unit trusts, investment trusts, gilts and other quoted securities that you hold or have an interest in. (Do not include dividend income as this will be dealt with separately later on.)

Documentation required for attachment to this section:
Latest statement or dividend counterfoil relating to each investment.

Name	Type of Investment	Size of Holding	Current value	Name of any other account holder (if applicable)	Total current value of your interest

TOTAL value of your interest in ALL holdings: (C2) £ 0.00

6

2.5 Details of all life insurance policies including endowment policies that you hold or have an interest in. Include those that do not have a surrender value. Complete one page for each policy.

| Documentation required for attachment to this section: |
| A surrender valuation of each policy that has a surrender value. |

Name of company			
Policy type			
Policy number			
If policy is assigned, state in whose favour and amount of charge			
Name of any other owner and the extent of your interest in the policy			
Maturity date (if applicable)	Date	Month	Year
Current surrender value (if applicable)			
If policy includes life insurance, the amount of the insurance and the name of the person whose life is insured			
Total current surrender value of your interest in this policy			

TOTAL value of your interest in ALL policies: (C3) | £

2.6 Details of all monies that are OWED TO YOU. Do not include sums owed in director's or partnership accounts which should be included at section 2.11.

Brief description of money owed and by whom	Balance outstanding	Total current value of your interest

TOTAL value of your interest in ALL debts owed to you: (C4) | £ | 0.00

7

2.7 Details of all cash sums held in excess of £500. You must state where it is held and the currency it is held in.

Where held	Amount	Currency	Total current value of your interest

TOTAL value of your interest in ALL cash sums: (C5)	£ 0.00

2.8 Details of personal belongings individually worth more than £500.

INCLUDE:
- Cars (gross value)
- Collections, pictures and jewellery
- Furniture and house contents

Brief description of item	Total current value of your interest

TOTAL value of your interest in ALL personal belongings: (C6)	£ 0.00
Add together all the figures in boxes C1 to C6 to give the TOTAL current value of your interest in personal assets: TOTAL C	£ 0.00

8

2 Financial Details   Part 2 Capital: Liabilities and Capital Gains Tax

2.9 Details of any liabilities you have.

EXCLUDE liabilities already shown such as:
- Mortgages
- Any overdrawn bank, building society or National Savings accounts

INCLUDE:
- Money owed on credit cards and store cards
- Bank loans
- Hire purchase agreements

List all credit and store cards held including those with a nil or positive balance. Where the liability is not solely your own, give the name(s) of the other account holder(s) and the amount of your share of the liability.

Liability	Name(s) of other account holder(s) (if applicable)	Total liability	Total current value of your interest in the liability

TOTAL value of your interest in ALL liabilities: (D1) £   0.00

2.10 If any Capital Gains Tax would be payable on the disposal now of any of your real property or personal assets, give your estimate of the tax liability.

Asset	Total Capital Gains Tax liability

TOTAL value of ALL your potential Capital Gains Tax liabilities: (D2) £

Add together D1 and D2 to give the TOTAL value of your liabilities: TOTAL D £   0.00

2 Financial Details   Part 3 Capital: Business assets and directorships

2.11 Details of all your business interests. Complete one page for each business you have an interest in.

Documentation required for attachment to this section:
a) Copies of the business accounts for the last two financial years
b) Any documentation, if available at this stage, upon which you have based your estimate of the current value of your interest in this business, for example a letter from an accountant or a formal valuation.
    It is not essential to obtain a formal valuation at this stage

Name of the business	
Briefly describe the nature of the business	
Are you (please tick appropriate box)	☐ Sole trader ☐ Partner in a partnership with others ☐ Shareholder in a limited company
If you are a partner or a shareholder, state the extent of your interest in the business (i.e. partnership share or the extent of your shareholding compared to the overall shares issued)	
State when your next set of accounts will be available	
If any of the figures in the last accounts are not an accurate reflection of the current position, state why. For example, if there has been a material change since the last accounts, or if the valuations of the assets are not a true reflection of their value (e.g. because property or other assets have not been re-valued in recent years or because they are shown at a book value)	
Total amount of any sums owed to you by the business by way of a director's loan account, partnership capital or current accounts or the like. Identify where these appear in the business accounts	
Your estimate of the current value of your business interest. Explain briefly the basis upon which you have reached that figure	
Your estimate of any Capital Gains Tax that would be payable if you were to dispose of your business now	
Net value of your interest in this business after any Capital Gains Tax liability	

TOTAL value of ALL your interests in business assets: TOTAL E | £ |

10

2.12 List any directorships you hold or have held in the last 12 months (other than those already disclosed in Section 2.11).

11

2 Financial Details

Part 4 Capital: Pensions and Pension Protection Fund (PPF) Compensation

2.13 Give details of all your pension rights and all PPF compensation entitlements, including prospective entitlements. Complete a separate page for each pension or PPF compensation entitlement.

EXCLUDE:

- Basic State Pension

INCLUDE (complete a separate page for each one):

- Additional State Pension (SERPS and State Second Pension (S2P))
- Free Standing Additional Voluntary Contribution Schemes (FSAVC) separate from the scheme of your employer
- Membership of ALL pension plans or schemes
- PPF compensation entitlement for each scheme you were a member of which has transferred to PPF

Documentation required for attachment to this section:

a) A recent statement showing the cash equivalent (CE) provided by the trustees or managers of each pension arrangement; for the additional state pension, a valuation of these rights or for PPF a valuation of PPF compensation entitlement

b) If any valuation is not available, give the estimated date when it will be available and attach a copy of your letter to the pension company, administrators, or PPF Board from whom the information was sought and/or state the date on which an application for a valuation of an Additional State Pension was submitted to the Department of Work and Pensions

Name and address of pension arrangement or PPF Board	
Your National Insurance Number	
Number of pension arrangement or reference number or PPF compensation reference number	
Type of scheme e.g. occupational or personal, final salary, money purchase, additional state pension, PPF or other (if other, please give details)	
Date the CE, PPF compensation or additional state pension was calculated	Date Month Year
Is the pension in payment or drawdown? (please answer Yes or No)	☐ Yes ☐ No
State the CE quotation, the additional state pension valuation or PPF valuation of those rights	
If the arrangement is an occupational pension arrangement that is paying reduced CEs, please quote what the CE would have been if not reduced. If this is not possible, please indicate if the CE quoted is a reduced CE	
Is the PPF compensation capped? (please answer Yes or No)	☐ Yes ☐ No

TOTAL value of ALL your pension assets: TOTAL F | £

2 Financial Details   Part 5 Capital: Other assets

2.14 Give details of any other assets not listed in Parts 1 to 4 above.

INCLUDE (the following list is not exhaustive):
- Any personal or business assets not yet disclosed
- Unrealisable assets
- Share option schemes, stating the estimated net sale proceeds of the shares if the options were capable of exercise now, and whether Capital Gains Tax or income tax would be payable
- Business expansion schemes
- Futures
- Commodities
- Trust interests (including interests under a discretionary trust), stating your estimate of the value of the interest and when it is likely to become realisable. If you say it will never be realisable, or has no value, give your reasons
- Any asset that is likely to be received in the foreseeable future
- Any asset held on your behalf by a third party
- Any asset not disclosed elsewhere on this form even if held outside England and Wales

You are reminded of your obligation to disclose all your financial assets and interests of ANY nature.

Type of asset	Value	Total NET value of your interest

TOTAL value of ALL your other assets: TOTAL G | £

13

2 Financial Details   Part 6 Income: Earned income from employment

2.15 Details of earned income from employment. Complete one page for each employment.

Documentation required for attachment to this section:
a) P60 for the last financial year (you should have received this from your employer shortly after the last 5th April)
b) Your last three payslips
c) Your last Form P11D if you have been issued with one

Name and address of your employer	
Job title and brief details of the type of work you do	
Hours worked per week in this employment	
How long have you been with this employer?	
Explain the basis of your income i.e. state whether it is based on an annual salary or an hourly rate of pay and whether it includes commissions or bonuses	
Gross income for the last financial year as shown on your P60	
Net income for the last financial year i.e. gross income less income tax and national insurance	
Average net income for the last three months i.e. total income less income tax and national insurance divided by three	
Briefly explain any other entries on the attached payslips other than basic income, income tax and national insurance	
If the payslips attached for the last three months are not an accurate reflection of your normal income briefly explain why	
Details and value of any bonuses or other occasional payments that you receive from this employment not otherwise already shown, including the basis upon which they are paid	
Details and value of any benefits in kind, perks or other remuneration received from this employer in the last year (e.g. provision of a car, payment of travel, accommodation, meal expenses, etc.)	
Your estimate of your net income from this employment for the next 12 months. If this differs significantly from your current income explain why in box 4.1.2	

Estimated TOTAL of ALL net earned income from employment for the next 12 months: TOTAL H   £

14

2 Financial Details   Part 7 Income: Income from self-employment or partnership

2.16 You will have already given details of your business and provided the last two years accounts at section 2.11. Complete this section giving details of your income from your business. Complete one page for each business.

Documentation required for attachment to this section:

a) A copy of your last tax assessment or, if that is not available, a letter from your accountant confirming your tax liability

b) If net income from the last financial year and estimated net income for the next 12 months is significantly different, a copy of management accounts for the period since your last account

Name of the business	
Date to which your last accounts were completed	
Your share of gross business profit from the last completed accounts	
Income tax and national insurance payable on your share of gross business profit above	
Net income for that year (using the two figures directly above, gross business profit less income tax and national insurance payable)	
Details and value of any benefits in kind, perks or other remuneration received from this business in the last year e.g. provision of a car, payment of travel, accommodation, meal expenses, etc.	
Amount of any regular monthly or other drawings that you take from this business	
If the estimated figure directly below is different from the net income as at the end date of the last completed accounts, briefly explain the reason(s)	
Your estimate of your net annual income for the next 12 months	

Estimated TOTAL of ALL net income from self-employment or partnership for the next 12 months: TOTAL I   £

15

2 Financial Details

Part 8 Income: Income from investments
e.g. dividends, interest or rental income

2.17 Details of income received in the last financial year (the year ended last 5th April), and your estimate of your income for the current financial year. Indicate whether the income was paid gross or net of income tax. You are not required to calculate any tax payable that may arise.

Nature of income and the asset from which it derived	Paid gross or net	Income received in the last financial year	Estimated income for the next 12 months

Estimated TOTAL investment income for the next 12 months: TOTAL J £

2 Financial Details

Part 9 Income: Income from state benefits (including state pension and child benefit)

2.18 Details of all state benefits that you are currently receiving.

Name of benefit	Amount paid	Frequency of payment	Estimated income for the next 12 months

Estimated TOTAL benefit income for the next 12 months: TOTAL K | £

17

2 Financial Details   Part 10   Income: Any other income

2.19 Details of any other income not disclosed above.

   INCLUDE:

Any source including a Pension (excluding State Pension), and Pension Protection Fund (PPF) compensation
- from which income has been received during the last 12 months (even if it has now ceased)
- from which income is likely to be received during the next 12 months

You are reminded of your obligation to give full disclosure of your financial circumstances

Nature of income	Paid gross or net	Income received in the last financial year	Estimated income for the next 12 months

Estimated TOTAL other income for the next 12 months: TOTAL L   £

2 Financial Details   Summaries

2.20 Summary of your capital (Parts 1 to 5).

Description	Reference of the section on this statement	Value
Current value of your interest in the family home	A	
Current value of your interest in all other property	B	
Current value of your interest in personal assets	C	0.00
Current value of your liabilities	D	0.00
Current value of your interest in business assets	E	
Current value of your pension and PPF compensation assets	F	
Current value of all your other assets	G	

TOTAL value of your assets (Totals A to G less D): £ 0.00

2.21 Summary of your estimated income for the next 12 months (Parts 6 to 10).

Description	Reference of the section on this statement	Value
Estimated net total of income from employment	H	
Estimated net total of income from self-employment or partnership	I	
Estimated net total of investment income	J	
Estimated state benefit receipts	K	
Estimated net total of all other income	L	

Estimated TOTAL income for the next 12 months (Totals H to L): £ 0.00

19

3 Financial Requirements   Part 1 Income needs

3.1 Income needs for yourself and for any children living with you or provided for by you. ALL figures should be annual, monthly or weekly (state which). You *must not* use a combination of these periods. State your current income needs and, if these are likely to change in the near future, explain the anticipated change and give an estimate of the future cost.

The income needs below are: (delete those not applicable)	Weekly	Monthly	Annual
I anticipate my income needs are going to change because			

3.1.1 Income needs for yourself.

INCLUDE:
- All income needs for yourself
- Income needs for any children living with you or provided for by you only if these form part of your total income needs (e.g. housing, fuel, car expenses, holidays, etc)

Item	Current cost	Estimated future cost
SUB-TOTAL your income needs	£	

3.1.2 Income needs for children living with you or provided for by you.

INCLUDE:
- Only those income needs that are different to those of your household shown above

Item	Current cost	Estimated future cost
SUB-TOTAL children's income needs:	£	
TOTAL of ALL income needs:	£	0.00

20

3 Financial Requirements   Part 2 Capital needs

3.2 Set out below the reasonable future capital needs for yourself and for any children living with you or provided for by you.

3.2.1 Capital needs for yourself.

INCLUDE:

- All capital needs for yourself
- Capital needs for any children living with you or provided for by you only if these form part of your total capital needs (e.g. housing, car, etc.)

Item	Cost

SUB-TOTAL your capital needs:	£

3.2.2 Capital needs for children living with you or provided for by you.

INCLUDE:

- Only those capital needs that are different to those of your household shown above

Item	Cost

SUB-TOTAL your children's capital needs	£
TOTAL of ALL capital needs:	£ 0.00

4 Other Information

4.1 Details of any significant changes in your assets or income.

At both sections 4.1.1 and 4.1.2, INCLUDE:
- ALL assets held both within and outside England and Wales
- The disposal of any asset

4.1.1 Significant changes in assets or income during the LAST 12 months.

4.1.2 Significant changes in assets or income likely to occur during the NEXT 12 months.

4.2 Brief details of the standard of living enjoyed by you and your spouse/civil partner during the marriage/civil partnership.

4.3 Are there any particular contributions to the family property and assets or outgoings, or to family life, or the welfare of the family that have been made by you, your partner or anyone else that you think should be taken into account? If there are any such items, briefly describe the contribution and state the amount, when it was made and by whom.
INCLUDE:
- Contributions already made
- Contributions that will be made in the foreseeable future

4.4 Bad behaviour or conduct by the other party will only be taken into account in very exceptional circumstances when deciding how assets should be shared after divorce/dissolution. If you feel it should be taken into account in your case, identify the nature of the behaviour or conduct below.

4.5 Give details of any other circumstances that you consider could significantly affect the extent of the financial provision to be made by or for you or any child of the family.
INCLUDE (the following list is not exhaustive):
- Earning capacity
- Disability
- Inheritance prospects
- Redundancy
- Retirement
- Any agreement made between you and your spouse/civil partner before or after your marriage/civil partnership stating whether or not you rely upon the agreement giving your reasons
- Any plans to marry, form a civil partnership or live with a new partner
- Any contingent liabilities

23

4.6 If you have subsequently married or formed a civil partnership (or intend to) or are living with another person (or intend to), give brief details, so far as they are known to you, of his or her income, assets and liabilities.

Annual Income		Assets and Liabilities	
Nature of income	Value (if known, state whether gross or net)	Item	Value (if known)
Total income: £		Total assets/liabilities: £	

5 Order Sought

5.1 If you are able at this stage, specify what kind of orders you are asking the court to make. Even if you cannot be specific at this stage, if you are able to do so, indicate:

a) If the family home is still owned, whether you are asking for it to be transferred to yourself or your spouse/civil partner or whether you are saying it should be sold

```


```

b) Whether you consider this is a case for continuing spousal maintenance/maintenance for your civil partner or whether you see the case as being appropriate for a 'clean break' *(A 'clean break' means a settlement or order which provides amongst other things, that neither you nor your spouse/civil partner will have any further claim against the income or capital of the other party. A 'clean break' does not terminate the responsibility of a parent to a child.)*

```


```

c) Whether you are seeking a
   i) pension sharing order
   ii) pension attachment order
   iii) pension compensation sharing order
   iv) pension compensation attachment order

```


```

d) If you are seeking a transfer or settlement of any property or assets, identify the property or assets in question

```



```

5.2 If you are seeking a variation of an ante-nuptial or post-nuptial settlement or a relevant settlement made during, or in anticipation of, a civil partnership, identify the settlement, by whom it was made, its trustees and beneficiaries and state why you allege it is a settlement which the court can vary.

```




```

5.3 If you are seeking an avoidance of disposition order, or if you have already applied for such an order, identify the property to which the disposition relates and the person or body in whose favour the disposition is alleged to have been made.

```




```

Sworn confirmation of the information

I, [   ] Enter your full name

of [   ] Enter your full residential address

The above named ☐ Applicant
☐ Respondent

☐ make oath
☐ affirm

and confirm that the information given above is a full, frank, clear and accurate disclosure of my financial and other relevant circumstances.

SWORN / AFFIRMED at [   ]

in the County of [   ]

on [D D / M M / Y Y Y Y]

[   ]

Before me, [   ]

☐ A Commissioner for Oaths
☐ Officer of the Court appointed by the Judge to take Affidavits

Address all communications to the Court Manager of the Court and quote the case number.
If you do not quote this number, your correspondence may be returned.

Schedule of Documents to accompany Form E

The following list shows the documents you must attach to your Form E if applicable. You may attach other documents where it is necessary to explain or clarify any of the information that you give in the Form E.

Form E paragraph	Document	Please tick		
		Attached	Not applicable	To follow
1.14	**Application to vary an order:** if applicable, attach a copy of the relevant order.	☐	☐	☐
2.1	**Matrimonial home valuation:** a copy of any valuation relating to the matrimonial home that has been obtained in the last six months.	☐	☐	☐
2.1	**Matrimonial home mortgage(s):** a recent mortgage statement in respect of each mortgage on the matrimonial home confirming the amount outstanding.	☐	☐	☐
2.2	**Any other property:** a copy of any valuation relating to each other property disclosed that has been obtained in the last six months.	☐	☐	☐
2.2	**Any other property:** a recent mortgage statement in respect of each mortgage on each other property disclosed confirming the amount outstanding.	☐	☐	☐
2.3	**Personal bank, building society and National Savings accounts:** copies of statements for the last 12 months for each account that has been held in the last twelve months, either in your own name or in which you have or have had any interest.	☐	☐	☐
2.4	**Other investments:** the latest statement or dividend counterfoil relating to each investment as disclosed in paragraph 2.4.	☐	☐	☐
2.5	**Life insurance (including endowment) policies:** a surrender valuation for each policy that has a surrender value as disclosed under paragraph 2.5.	☐	☐	☐
2.11	**Business interests:** a copy of the business accounts for the last two financial years for each business interest disclosed.	☐	☐	☐
2.11	**Business interests:** any documentation that is available to confirm the estimate of the current value of the business, for example, a letter from an accountant or formal valuation if that has been obtained.	☐	☐	☐
2.13	**Pension and PPF compensation:** a recent statement showing the cash equivalent (CE) provided by the trustees or managers of each pension arrangement or valuation of each PPF entitlement provided by the PPF Board that you have disclosed (or, in the case of the additional state pension, a valuation of these rights). If not yet available, attach a copy of the letter sent to the pension company, administrators or the PPF Board requesting the information.	☐	☐	☐
2.15	**Employment income:** your P60 for the last financial year in respect of each employment that you have.	☐	☐	☐
2.15	**Employment income:** your last three payslips in respect of each employment that you have.	☐	☐	☐
2.15	**Employment income:** your last form P11D if you have been issued with one.	☐	☐	☐
2.16	**Self-employment or partnership income:** a copy of your last tax assessment or if that is not available, a letter from your accountant confirming your tax liability.	☐	☐	☐
2.16	**Self-employment or partnership income:** if net income from the last financial year and the estimated income for the next twelve months is significantly different, a copy of the management accounts for the period since your last accounts.	☐	☐	☐
State relevant Form E paragraph	Description of other documents attached:	☐	☐	☐

FORM E1

	Financial Statement for a financial remedy (other than a financial order or financial relief after an overseas divorce or dissolution etc) in the county or High Court

Name of court	Case No.
Name of Applicant	
Name of Respondent	

(please tick the appropriate boxes)

This is the Financial Statement of the

☐ Applicant
☐ Respondent

in this application

This form should only be completed if you are applying for a financial remedy other than a financial order or financial relief after an overseas divorce or dissolution etc. in the county or high court.

If you are applying for a financial order or financial relief after an overseas divorce or dissolution etc. in the county court you should complete Form E

If you are applying for a financial remedy in the magistrate's court you should complete Form E2.

Please fill in this form fully and accurately. Where any box is not applicable, write 'N/A'.

You have a duty to the court to give a full, frank and clear disclosure of all your financial and other relevant circumstances.

A failure to give full and accurate disclosure may result in any order the court makes being set aside.

If you are found to have been deliberately untruthful, criminal proceedings may be brought against you for fraud under the Fraud Act 2006.

The information given in this form must be confirmed by an affidavit. Proceedings for perjury may be brought against a person who makes or causes to be made, a false statement in a document confirmed by an affidavit.

You must attach documents to the form where they are specifically sought and you may attach other documents where it is necessary to explain or clarify any of the information that you give.

If there is not enough room on the form for any particular piece of information, you may continue on an attached sheet of paper.

If you are in doubt about how to complete any part of this form you should seek legal advice.

This statement is filed by

Name and address of solicitor

1. General information

1.1 Full name

1.2 Date of birth `D D / M M / Y Y Y Y`

1.3 Are you married/in a civil partnership? ☐ Yes ☐ No

1.4 If you are not married or in a civil partnership are you living with a partner? ☐ Yes ☐ No

1.5 Your present residence and the occupants of it and on what terms you occupy it (e.g. tenant, owner-occupier).

Address	Occupants	Terms of occupation

1.6 Children living with you

Names	Date of birth
	`D D / M M / Y Y Y Y`
	`D D / M M / Y Y Y Y`
	`D D / M M / Y Y Y Y`
	`D D / M M / Y Y Y Y`
	`D D / M M / Y Y Y Y`
	`D D / M M / Y Y Y Y`

1.7 Children not living with you

Names	Date of birth
	`D D / M M / Y Y Y Y`
	`D D / M M / Y Y Y Y`
	`D D / M M / Y Y Y Y`
	`D D / M M / Y Y Y Y`
	`D D / M M / Y Y Y Y`
	`D D / M M / Y Y Y Y`
Amount of any maintenance being paid	£

1.8   Other dependents
      (Give details – including whether you have these responsibilities on a permanent basis).

Names	Details

1.9   Details of the state of health of yourself and the children if you think this should be taken into account.

Yourself	Children

1.10 Details of the present and proposed future educational arrangements for the children.

Present arrangements	Future arrangements

1.11 Details of any child support maintenance calculation or any maintenance order or agreement made in respect of any children of the family. If no calculation, order or agreement has been made, give an estimate of the liability of the non-resident parent in respect of the children of the family under the Child Support Act 1991.

1.12 Details of any other court cases between you and your spouse/civil partner, whether in relation to money, property, children or anything else.

Case No.	Court	Type of proceedings

2. Employment

2.1   I am   ☐ employed (complete 2.2)

☐ self employed (complete 2.3)

☐ unemployed (go to 3.)

☐ a pensioner (go to 3.)

2.2 Details of earned income from employment. Complete one page for each employment.

Documentation required for attachment to this section:
a) P60 for the last financial year (you should have received this from your employer shortly after the last 5th April)
b) Your last three payslips
c) Your last Form P11D if you have been issued with one

Name and address of your employer	
Job title and brief details of the type of work you do	
Hours worked per week in this employment	
How long have you been with this employer?	
Explain the basis of your income i.e. state whether it is based on an annual salary or an hourly rate of pay and whether it includes commissions or bonuses	
Gross income for the last financial year as shown on your P60Net income for the last financial year i.e. gross income less income tax and national insurance	
Average net income for the last three months i.e. total income less income tax and national insurance divided by three	
Briefly explain any other entries on the attached payslips other than basic income, income tax and national insurance	
If the payslips attached for the last three months are not an accurate reflection of your normal income briefly explain why	
Details and value of any bonuses or other occasional payments that you receive from this employment not otherwise already shown, including the basis upon which they are paid	
Details and value of any benefits in kind, perks or other remuneration received from this employer in the last year (e.g. provision of a car, payment of travel, accommodation, meal expenses, etc.)	
Your estimate of your net income from this employment for the next 12 months.	
Estimated TOTAL of ALL net earned income from employment for the next 12 months: Total A	£

2.3 *Income from self-employment or partnership*

Complete this section giving details of your income from your business. Complete one page for each business.

Documentation required for attachment to this section:

a) Copies of your business accounts for the last 2 years

b) A copy of your last tax assessment or, if that is not available, a letter from your accountant confirming your tax liability

c) If net income from the last financial year and estimated net income for the next 12 months is significantly different, a copy of management accounts for the period since your last account

Name of the business	
Date to which your last accounts were completed	
Your share of gross business profit from the last completed accounts	
Income tax and national insurance payable on your share of gross business profit above	
Net income for that year (using the two figures directly above, gross business profit less income tax and national insurance payable)	
Details and value of any benefits in kind, perks or other remuneration received from this business in the last year e.g. provision of a car, payment of travel, accommodation, meal expenses, etc.	
Amount of any regular monthly or other drawings that you take from this business	
If the estimated figure directly below is different from the net income as at the end date of the last completed accounts, briefly explain the reason(s)	
Your estimate of your net annual income for the next 12 months	

Estimated TOTAL of ALL net income from self-employment or partnership for the next 12 months: Total B   £

3. Other income

3.1 Details of income from investments (e.g. dividends, interest or rental income) received in the last financial year (the year ended last 5th April), and your estimate of your income for the current financial year. Indicate whether the income was paid gross or net of income tax. You are not required to calculate any tax payable that may arise.

Nature of income and the asset from which it derived	Paid gross or net	Income received in the last financial year	Estimated income for the next 12 months
Estimated TOTAL investment income for the next 12 months: Total C			£

3.2 Details of all state benefits (including state pension and child benefit) that you are currently receiving.

Name of benefit	Amount paid	Frequency of payment	Estimated income for the next 12 months
Estimated TOTAL investment income for the next 12 months: Total D			£

3.3 Details of any other income not disclosed above.
INCLUDE:

Any source including a Pension (excluding State Pension), and Pension Protection Fund (PPF) compensation
- from which income has been received during the last 12 months (even if it has now ceased)
- from which income is likely to be received during the next 12 months

You are reminded of your obligation to give full disclosure of your financial circumstances.

Nature of income	Paid gross or net	Income received in the last financial year	Estimated income for the next 12 months
Estimated TOTAL other income for the next 12 months: Total E			£

4. Capital

4.1 Details of your interest in property, land or buildings. Complete one page for each property you have an interest in.

Documentation required for attachment to this section:
a) A copy of any valuation of the property obtained within the last six months. If you cannot provide this document, please give your own realistic estimate of the current market value
b) A recent mortgage statement confirming the sum outstanding on each mortgage

Property name and address	
Land Registry title number	
Mortgage company name(s) and address(es) and account number(s)	
Type of mortgage	
Details of who owns the property and the extent of your legal and beneficial interest in it (i.e. state if it is owned by you solely or jointly owned with your spouse/civil partner or with others)	
If you consider that the legal ownership as recorded at the Land Registry does not reflect the true position, state why	
Current market value of the property	
Balance outstanding on any mortgage(s)	
If a sale at this stage would result in penalties payable under the mortgage, state amount	
Estimate the costs of sale of the property	
Total equity in the property (i.e. market value less outstanding mortgage(s), penalties if any and the costs of sale)	

TOTAL value of your interest in ALL other property: Total F £

4.2 Details of all personal bank, building society and National Savings Accounts that you hold or have held at any time in the last twelve months and which are or were either in your own name or in which you have or have had any interest. This applies whether any such account is in credit or in debit. For joint accounts give your interest and the name of the other account holder. If the account is overdrawn, show a minus figure.

> Documentation required for attachment to this section:
> For each account listed, all statements covering the last 12 months.

Name of bank or building society, including branch name	Type of account (e.g. current)	Account number	Name of other account holder (if applicable)	Balance at the date of this statement	Total current value of your interest

TOTAL value of your interest in ALL accounts: (G1) £

4.3 Details of all investments, including shares, PEPs, ISAs, TESSAs, National Savings Investments (other than already shown above), bonds, stocks, unit trusts, investment trusts, gilts and other quoted securities that you hold or have an interest in. (Do not include dividend income as this will be dealt with separately later on.)

> Documentation required for attachment to this section:
> Latest statement or dividend counterfoil relating to each investment.

Name	Type of Investment	Size of holding	Current value	Name of any other account holder (if applicable)	Total current value of your interest

TOTAL value of your interest in ALL holdings: (G2) £

9

4.4 Details of all life insurance policies including endowment policies that you hold or have an interest in. Include those that do not have a surrender value. Complete one page for each policy.

Documentation required for attachment to this section:
A surrender valuation of each policy that has a surrender value.

Name of company	
Policy type	
Policy number	
If policy is assigned, state in whose favour and amount of charge	
Name of any other owner and the extent of your interest in the policy	
Maturity date (if applicable)	D D / M M / Y Y Y Y
Current surrender value (if applicable)	
If policy includes life insurance, the amount of the insurance and the name of the person whose life is insured	
Total current surrender value of your interest in this policy	
TOTAL value of your interest in ALL policies: (G3)	£
Add together the totals of G1 to G3 to give TOTAL G	£

10

4.5   Give details of any other assets not listed above.

INCLUDE (the following list is not exhaustive):

- Any personal or business assets not yet disclosed
- Any monies owed to you
- Any cash sums held in excess of £500
- Any other personal belonging individually worth more than £500
- Trust interests (including interests under a discretionary trust), stating your estimate of the value of the interest and when it is likely to become realisable. If you say it will never be realisable, or has no value, give your reasons
- Any asset that is likely to be received in the foreseeable future
- Any asset held on your behalf by a third party
- Any asset not disclosed elsewhere on this form even if held outside England and Wales
- You are reminded of your obligation to disclose all your financial assets and interests of ANY nature.

Type of asset	Value	Total NET value of your interest
TOTAL value of ALL your other assets: Total H	£	

4.6   Details of any liabilities you have.

EXCLUDE liabilities already shown such as:

Mortgages

Any overdrawn bank, building society or National Savings accounts

INCLUDE:

Money owed on credit cards and store cards

Bank loans

Hire purchase agreements

List all credit and store cards held including those with a nil or positive balance. Where the liability is not solely your own, give the name(s) of the other account holder(s) and the amount of your share of the liability.

Liability	Name(s) of other account holder(s) (if applicable)	Total liability	Total current value of your interest in the liability
TOTAL value of your interest in ALL liabilities: Total I		£	

11

5. Income needs
(Do not include any payments made by other members of the household out of their own income)

5.1 I have regular expenses as follows:
(do not include payments on any arrears)

	Amounts are per ☐ week ☐ month
Mortgage	
Rent	
Council Tax	
Gas	
Electricity	
Water charges	
TV rental/licence	
HP repayments	
Mail order	
Housekeeping, food, school meals	
Travelling expenses	
Children's clothing and pocket money	
Maintenance Payments	
Car Expenses	
Insurance – House	
Insurance – Other (please give details)	
Others	
Total payments:	£

5.2 Income needs for children living with you or provided for by you.
INCLUDE:
• Only those income needs that are different to those of your household shown above

Item	Current cost	Estimated future cost
SUB-TOTAL children's income needs:		£
TOTAL of ALL income needs:		£

12

6. Financial resources of child(ren)

Income	Property	Other
TOTAL:	TOTAL:	TOTAL:

7. Financial Details *Summaries*

7.1 Summary of your estimated income for the next 12 months (Parts 2 to 3).

Description	Reference of the section on this statement	Value
Estimated net total of income from employment	A	
Estimated net total of income from self-employment or partnership	B	
Estimated net total of investment income	C	
Estimated state benefit receipts	D	
Estimated net total of all other income	E	
Estimated TOTAL income for the next 12 months (Totals A to E):		£

7.2 Summary of your capital (Part 4).

Description	Reference of the section on this statement	Value
Current value of your interest in property	F	
Current value of personal assets	G	
Current value of all your other assets	H	
Current value of your liabilities	I	
TOTAL value of your assets (Totals F to H minus I):		£

13

Sworn confirmation of the information

I, [   ]   Enter your full name

of [   ]   Enter your full residential address

The above named ☐ Applicant
                 ☐ Respondent

☐ make oath
☐ affirm

and confirm that the information given above is a full, frank, clear and accurate disclosure of my financial and other relevant circumstances.

SWORN / AFFIRMED at [   ]

in the County of [   ]

on [D | D |/| M | M |/| Y | Y | Y | Y]

[   ]

Before me, [   ]

☐ A Commissioner for Oaths
☐ Officer of the Court appointed by the Judge to take Affidavits

Address all communications to the Court Manager of the Court and quote the case number.
If you do not quote this number, your correspondence may be returned.

14

Schedule of Documents to accompany Form E1

The following list shows the documents you must attach to your Form E1 if applicable. You may attach other documents where it is necessary to explain or clarify any of the information that you give in the Form E1.

Form E1 paragraph	Document	Please tick		
		Attached	Not applicable	To follow
2.2	**Employment income:** your P60 for the last financial year in respect of each employment that you have.	☐	☐	☐
2.2	**Employment income:** your last three payslips in respect of each employment that you have.	☐	☐	☐
2.2	**Employment income:** your last form P11D if you have been issued with one.	☐	☐	☐
2.3	**Self-employment or partnership income:** a copy of your last tax assessment or if that is not available, a letter from your accountant confirming your tax liability and business accounts for the last 2 years.	☐	☐	☐
2.3	**Self-employment or partnership income:** if net income from the last financial year and the estimated income for the next twelve months is significantly different, a copy of the management accounts for the period since your last accounts.	☐	☐	☐
4.1	a copy of any valuation relating to each other property disclosed that has been obtained in the last six months.	☐	☐	☐
4.1	a recent mortgage statement in respect of each mortgage on each other property disclosed confirming the amount outstanding.	☐	☐	☐
4.2	**Personal bank, building society and National Savings accounts:** copies of statements for the last 12 months for each account that has been held in the last twelve months, either in your own name or in which you have or have had any interest.	☐	☐	☐
4.3	**Other investments:** the latest statement or dividend counterfoil relating to each investment as disclosed in paragraph 4.3.	☐	☐	☐
4.4	**Life insurance (including endowment) policies:** a surrender valuation for each policy that has a surrender value as disclosed under paragraph 4.4.	☐	☐	☐
State relevant Form E1 paragraph	Description of other documents attached:			

15

FORM E2

Financial Statement for a financial remedy in the magistrates' court	Name of court	Case No.
	Name of Applicant	
	Name of Respondent	

(please tick the appropriate boxes)

This is the Financial Statement of the

- ☐ Applicant
- ☐ Respondent
- ☐ Child

in this application

This form should only be completed if you are applying for a financial remedy in the magistrates court.

If you are applying for a financial order or financial relief after an overseas divorce or dissolution etc. in the county court you should complete Form E.

If you are applying for a financial remedy other than a financial order or financial relief after an overseas divorce or dissolution etc. in the county court you should complete Form E1.

Please fill in this form fully and accurately. Where any box is not applicable, write 'N/A'.

You have a duty to the court to give a full, frank and clear disclosure of all your financial and other relevant circumstances.

A failure to give full and accurate disclosure may result in any order the court makes being set aside.

If you are found to have been deliberately untruthful, criminal proceedings may be brought against you for fraud under the Fraud Act 2006.

The information given in this form must be confirmed by an affidavit. Proceedings for perjury may be brought against a person who makes or causes to be made, a false statement in a document confirmed by an affidavit.

You must attach the documents listed in the Schedule to the form where applicable and you may attach other documents where it is necessary to explain or clarify any of the information that you give.

If there is not enough room on the form for any particular piece of information, you may continue on an attached sheet of paper.

If you are in doubt about how to complete any part of this form you should seek legal advice.

This statement is filed by

Name and address of solicitor

1. Personal details

First names	
Surname	
Marital status	
Date of birth	D D / M M / Y Y Y Y
Address	

Postcode | | | | | | | |

2. Dependents (People you support financially)

Children living with you

Names	Date of birth
	D D / M M / Y Y Y Y
	D D / M M / Y Y Y Y
	D D / M M / Y Y Y Y
	D D / M M / Y Y Y Y
	D D / M M / Y Y Y Y
	D D / M M / Y Y Y Y

Children not living with you

Names	Date of birth
	D D / M M / Y Y Y Y
	D D / M M / Y Y Y Y
	D D / M M / Y Y Y Y
	D D / M M / Y Y Y Y
	D D / M M / Y Y Y Y
	D D / M M / Y Y Y Y

Amount of any maintenance being paid £

Other dependents

(give details – including whether you have these responsibilities on a permanent basis)

Names	Details

3. Employment

I am ☐ employed as a

☐ self employed as a

☐ unemployed

☐ a pensioner

| My employer is: | Name | |
| Address | | |

Postcode ☐☐☐ ☐☐☐

Employment other than main job

Self employment annual turnover

☐ I am not in arrears with my national insurance contributions, income tax and VAT

☐ I am in arrears and I owe £

Give details of contracts and other work in hand

Give details of any sums due in respect of work done

4. Bank accounts and savings

☐ I have no bank building society or savings accounts

☐ I have ☐ bank or building society accounts:

Name of accounts	Average balance over last six months

I have [   ] savings accounts:

Name of account(s)	Amount in account (£)

5. Property

I live in ☐ my own property   ☐ privately rented property

☐ lodgings   ☐ other, please state

☐ jointly owned property

☐ council property/ housing association

Value of (jointly) owned property   £

When filling in sections 6, 7 and 9, please give amounts on a weekly or monthly basis.
***Do not** mix weekly and monthly figures.*

6. Income

	Amount are per ☐ **week** (£) ☐ **month** (£)
My usual take home pay (including overtime, commission and bonus pay)	
Income from employment	
Income from Self employment	
Income Support	
Child benefit(s)	
Other state benefit(s)	
My pension(s)	
Others living in my home give me	
Other income (please give details)	
Total	£

4

7. Expenses

Do not include any payments made by other members of the household out of their own income

I have regular expenses as follows:
(do not include payments on any arrears)

	Amount are per ☐ **week** (£) ☐ **month** (£)
Mortgage	
Rent	
Council Tax	
Gas	
Electricity	
Water charges	
TV rental/licence	
HP repayments	
Mail order	
Housekeeping, food, school meals	
Travelling expenses	
Children's clothing and pocket money	
Maintenance Payments	
Car Expenses	
Insurance – House	
Insurance – other (please give details)	
Others (but do not include credit dept payments or court orders)	
Total payments	£

8. Court Oders

Please include fines, compensation etc.

Court	Case number	Amount outstanding	Payment per month
		Total	£

5

9. Money you owe on essential bills

Please state the amount of any arrears owing and the amount of any payments you make towards these arrears.

	Amount are per ☐ **week** (£) ☐ **month** (£)	Amount are per ☐ **week** (£) ☐ **month** (£)
	Total amount outstanding	Amount of payment
Rent		
Mortgage		
Council Tax		
Water Rates		
Fuel Debts (Gas Electricity Other)		
Maintenance arrears		
Total priority debts		
Total	£	£

10. Other commitments

Give details of any payments on credit cards, other loans, storecards, loans from family etc.

Type of payment	Total amount outstanding	Amount of payment
Total	£	£

11. Child(ren)'s resources

	Income	Property	Other
Totals	£	£	£

6

Sworn confirmation of the information

I, [   ] Enter your full name

of [   ] Enter your full residential address

The above named ☐ Applicant
☐ Respondent

☐ make oath
☐ affirm

and confirm that the information given above is a full, frank, clear and accurate disclosure of my financial and other relevant circumstances.

SWORN / AFFIRMED
at [   ]

in the County of [   ]

on [D D / M M / Y Y Y Y]

[   ]

Before me, [   ]

☐ A Commissioner for Oaths
☐ Officer of the Court appointed by the Judge to take Affidavits

---

Address all communications to the Court Manager of the Court and quote the case number.
If you do not quote this number, your correspondence may be returned.

Schedule of Documents to accompany Form E2

The following list shows the documents you must attach to your Form E2 if applicable. You may attach other documents where it is necessary to explain or clarify any of the information that you give in the Form E2.

Form E2 paragraph	Document	Please tick		
		Attached	Not applicable	To follow
4	**Personal bank, building society and National Savings accounts:** copies of statements for the last 6 months for each account that has been held in the last twelve months, either in your own name or in which you have or have had any interest.	☐	☐	☐
6	**Employment income:** your P60 for the last financial year in respect of each employment that you have.	☐	☐	☐
6	**Employment income:** your last three payslips in respect of each employment that you have.	☐	☐	☐
6	**Employment income:** your last form P11D if you have been issued with one.	☐	☐	☐
6	**Self-employment or partnership income:** a copy of your last tax assessment or if that is not available, a letter from your accountant confirming your tax liability.	☐	☐	☐
State relevant Form E2 paragraph	Description of other documents attached:	☐	☐	☐

FORM F

**Notice of allegation in
proceedings for a
financial remedy**

To be completed by the relevant party	
Name of court	Case No.
Name of Applicant	
Name of Respondent	

The following statement has been filed in proceedings for a financial remedy:

Signed _____   Dated `D D / M M / Y Y Y Y`

(Applicant) (Respondent)
(Solicitor for the (Applicant)(Respondent))

If you wish to be heard on any matter affecting you in these proceedings you may intervene
by applying to the Court for directions regarding:

- the filing and service of pleadings
- the conduct of further proceedings

You must apply for directions **within seven days** after you receive this Notice. The period of
seven days includes the day you receive it.

FORM G

<table>
<tr><td rowspan="2">Notice of Response
To First
Appointment</td><td colspan="2">In the</td></tr>
<tr><td>Case No.
Always quote this number</td><td></td></tr>
<tr><td></td><td>Applicant's Solicitor's
reference</td><td></td></tr>
<tr><td></td><td>Respondent's

Solicitor's reference</td><td></td></tr>
</table>

Take Notice that

At the First Appointment which will be heard on [hearing date]

at [hearing time]

the [Applicant/Respondent] [will/will not] be in a position to proceed on that

occasion with a Financial Dispute Resolution appointment for the following reasons:-

[Text]

Dated:[Date]

Form G – Notice of Response to First Appointment

FORM H

Estimate of costs (financial remedy)

of
_____

(name of party)

the ☐ Applicant
☐ Respondent

To be completed by the relevant party	
Name of court	Case No.
Name of Applicant	
Name of Respondent	

Estimate of costs relating to a financial remedy application for hearing on: ☐ ☐ / ☐ ☐ / ☐ ☐ ☐ ☐

Please Note: it is a requirement of the rules to provide full costs information to the court

(Do not include here costs incurred in respect of other aspects of the case, for example, the divorce or civil partnership proceedings, children matters, injunctions, etc.)

Summary of costs estimate

	Prescribed rates for publicly funded services £	Indemnity rate £
Grand Total (Box 7 + Box 14)	0.00	0.00
State what has been paid towards the grand total above.		
Amount of any contributions paid by the funded client towards their publicly funded services.		

Signature of solicitor (or party, if not represented) _____

Dated ☐ ☐ / ☐ ☐ / ☐ ☐ ☐ ☐

Name of firm of solicitors _____

Reference _____

continued over the page ➪

1

Section A:

Costs incurred in the financial remedy proceedings **prior** to issue of Form A

Part 1

		Prescribed rates for publicly funded services £	Indemnity rate £
1.	Financial remedy solicitors' costs (including VAT) incurred by any previous solicitors.		
2.	Financial remedy solicitors' costs (including VAT) incurred by the current solicitors.		
3.	Disbursements (including VAT, if appropriate) incurred by any previous solicitors.		
4.	Disbursements (including VAT, if appropriate) incurred by current solicitors.		
5.	All counsel's fees (including VAT).		
	Sub-Total	0.00	0.00

Part 2

6.	Add any private client costs previously incurred (in publicly funded cases only).		
7.	**Total of Section A**	**0.00**	**0.00**

Section B:

Costs incurred in the financial remedy proceedings **after** issue of Form A

Part 3

		Prescribed rates for publicly funded services £	Indemnity rate £
8.	Financial remedy solicitors' costs (including VAT) incurred by any previous solicitors.		
9.	Financial remedy solicitors' costs (including VAT and costs of the current hearing) incurred by the current solicitors.		
10.	Disbursements (including VAT, if appropriate) incurred by any previous solicitors.		
11.	Disbursements (including VAT, if appropriate) incurred by current solicitors.		
12.	All counsel's fees (including VAT).		
	Sub-Total	0.00	0.00

Part 4

13.	Add any private client costs previously incurred (in publicly funded cases only).		
14.	**Total of Section B**	**0.00**	**0.00**

FORM H1

Statement of costs (financial remedy)

of

(name of party)

the ☐ Applicant

☐ Respondent

To be completed by the relevant party	
Name of court	Case No.
Name of Applicant	
Name of Respondent	

Statement of costs relating to the financial remedy application for hearing on: ☐D☐D☐/☐M☐M☐/☐Y☐Y☐Y☐Y☐

Please Note: it is a requirement of the rules to provide full costs information to the court

(Do not include here costs incurred in respect of other aspects of the case, for example, the divorce or civil partnership proceedings, children matters, injunctions, etc.)

Description of fee earner:

(a) Name:	Status:	Hourly rate claimed: £
(b) Name:	Status:	Hourly rate claimed: £
(c) Name:	Status:	Hourly rate claimed: £
(d) Name:	Status:	Hourly rate claimed: £

Summary of costs statement

	Prescribed rates for publicly funded services £	Indemnity rate £
Total Section A (Box 7)		
Total Section B (Box 14)		
Total Section C (Box 21)		
Total Section D (Box 25)		
Total Section E (Box 26) (if completed)		
Grand Total (A+B+C+D+E)		
State what has been paid towards the grand total above.		
Amount of any contributions paid by the funded client towards their publicly funded services.		

Signature of solicitor (or party, if not represented)		Dated	☐D☐D☐/☐M☐M☐/☐Y☐Y☐Y☐Y☐
Name of firm of solicitors		Reference	

Form **H1** Statement of costs (financial remedy) (04.11)   © Crown Copyright 2011

1

Section A:

Costs incurred in the financial remedy proceedings **prior** to issue of Form A.

Part 1

		Prescribed rates for publicly funded services £	Indemnity rate £
1.	Financial remedy solicitors' costs (including VAT) incurred by any previous solicitors.		
2.	Financial remedy solicitors' costs (including VAT) incurred by the current solicitors.		
3.	Disbursements (including VAT, if appropriate) incurred by any previous solicitors.		
4.	Disbursements (including VAT, if appropriate) incurred by current solicitors.		
5.	All counsel's fees (including VAT).		
	Sub-Total		

Part 2

6.	Add any private client costs previously incurred (in publicly funded cases only).		
7.	**Total of Section A**		

Section B:

Costs incurred in the financial remedy proceedings **after** issue of Form A up to and including FDR appointment (or, if none, the date of the last Form H).

Part 3

		Prescribed rates for publicly funded services £	Indemnity rate £
8.	Financial remedy solicitors' costs (including VAT) incurred by any previous solicitors.		
9.	Financial remedy solicitors' costs (including VAT and costs of the current hearing) incurred by the current solicitors.		
10.	Disbursements (including VAT, if appropriate) incurred by any previous solicitors.		
11.	Disbursements (including VAT, if appropriate) incurred by current solicitors.		
12.	All counsel's fees (including VAT).		
	Sub-Total		

Part 4

13.	Add any private client costs previously incurred (in publicly funded cases only).		
14.	**Total of Section B**		

Section C:

Costs incurred in the financial remedy proceedings **after** FDR appointment (or, if none, the date of the last Form H) up to the date of this form.

Part 5

	Prescribed rates for publicly funded services £	Indemnity rate £
15. Financial remedy solicitors' costs (including VAT) incurred by any previous solicitors.		
16. Financial remedy solicitors' costs (including VAT) incurred by the current solicitors.		
17. Disbursements (including VAT, if appropriate) incurred by any previous solicitors.		
18. Disbursements (including VAT, if appropriate) incurred by current solicitors.		
19. All counsel's fees (including VAT). (Counsel's fees for final hearing should not be included here, but given in Section D.)		
Sub-Total		

Part 6

20. Add any private client costs previously incurred (in publicly funded cases only).		
21. **Total of Section C**		

Section D:

Estimate of costs expected and incurred in the financial remedy proceedings **after** the date of this form up to the end of the final hearing.

Part 7

	Prescribed rates for publicly funded services £	Indemnity rate £
22. Financial remedy solicitors' costs (including VAT).		
23. Disbursements (including VAT, if appropriate).		
24. All Counsel's fees (including VAT). (All counsel's fees expected to be incurred for final hearing should be included here.)		
25. **Total of Section D**		

continued over the page ⇨

Section E:

Estimate of costs to be incurred in implementing proposed order for the financial remedy.

(Note: Include only those costs which it is known or anticipated will be incurred in giving effect to the order.
If the work to be carried out is only conveyancing, the prescribed rates for public funding services do not apply.)

Part 8

	Prescribed rates for publicly funded services £	Indemnity rate £
26. **Total of Section E** (Total estimated costs of implementing proposed order)		

FORM I

Notice of request for periodical payments order at same rate as order for maintenance pending outcome of proceedings

Name of court	Case No.
Name of Applicant	
Name of Respondent	

Take notice that

On [   ] 20 [   ]
the Applicant obtained an Order for you to pay maintenance pending outcome of proceedings at the
rate of £   .

The Applicant having applied in his/her petition (answer) for a Periodical Payments Order for
himself/herself has requested the Court to make such an Order at the same rate as above.

What to do if you object to this Order being made

If you object to the making of such a Periodical Payments Order, you must notify the District Judge
and the Applicant/Respondent of your objections within 14 days of this notice being served on you.
If you do not do so, the District Judge may make an Order without notifying you further.

FORM P

Pension Inquiry Form

Information needed when a Pension Sharing Order or Pension Attachment Order may be made

Insert details of pension scheme here	
To:	
of:	
Reference No:	

A. To be completed by Pension Scheme member or policy holder:

1. Pension scheme member or policy holder's details:

Name

Address (including postcode)

Postcode

Reference

2. Solicitors details:

Name

Address (including postcode)

Postcode

Reference

Telephone

3. Address to which the form should be sent once completed if different from 2 above:

Address (including postcode)

Postcode

Signature

of Pension Scheme member or policy holder

(The scheme member's signature is necessary to authorise the release of the requested information, unless a court order requiring the information is attached to this form.)

B. To be completed by the pension arrangement

This section deals with information required to be provided under the Pensions on Divorce etc (Provision of Information) Regulations 2000 S.I.1048/2000, Regulations 2 and 3 and Chapter 8 of Part 9 to the Family Procedure Rules 2010. If a request for a Cash Equivalent Value has been made, the pension arrangement has 3 months to provide the information or 6 weeks if notified that the information is needed in connection with matrimonial or civil partnership proceedings, or such shorter time as notified by the court. Otherwise, the information should be provided within one month or such shorter time as notified by the court. The valuation referred to in paragraph 1(a) below must have been made not more than 12 months before the date fixed for the first appointment.

If this information has already been prepared in a standard form please send this instead.

1. (a) Please confirm that you have already provided a valuation of the member's pension rights to the scheme member or to the Court. ☐ Yes ☐ No

   (b) If the answer to (a) is No, details of the CEV quotation should be attached and the date on which it was calculated.

2. Provide a statement summarising the way in which the valuation referred to above has been or will be calculated.

3. State the pension benefits included in the valuation referred to in B1 above.

4. (a) Does the person responsible for the pension arrangement offer scheme membership to the person entitled to a pension credit? ☐ Yes ☐ No

   (b) If Yes, does this depend on Employer and/or trustee approval? ☐ Yes ☐ No

5. If the answer to 4(a) is Yes, what benefits are available to the person with the pension credit?

6. **Charging Policy**
   - Does the arrangement charge for providing information or implementing a pension sharing order? ☐ Yes ☐ No

   If Yes, please:
   - provide a list of charges
   - indicate when these must be paid, and
   - whether they can be paid directly from benefits held in the scheme or policy, or the pension credit.

2

C. To be completed by the pension arrangement

This information is required to be provided by the pension arrangement under the Pension on Divorce (Provision of Information) Regulations 2000 S.I. 1048, Regulation 4 within 21 days of being notified that a pension sharing order may be made. If such notification has not already been given, please treat this document as notification that such an order may be made. Alternatively the Court may specify a date by which this information should be provided.

If this information has already been prepared in a standard form please send this instead.

1. The full name of the pension arrangement and address to which a pension sharing order should be sent.

   Postcode

2. In the case of an occupational pension scheme only, is the scheme winding up?   ☐ Yes   ☐ No

   If Yes:
   - when did the winding up commence, and
   - give the name and address of the trustees who are dealing with the winding up.

3. In the case of an occupational pension scheme only, assuming that a calculation of the member's CEV was carried out on the day the pension scheme received notification that a pension sharing order may be made, would that CEV be reduced?   ☐ Yes   ☐ No

4. As far as you are aware, are the member's rights under the pension scheme subject to any of the following:
   - a pension sharing order   ☐ Yes   ☐ No
   - a pension attachment order made under section 23 of the Matrimonial Causes Act 1973 (England and Wales), section 12A(2) or (3) of the Family Law (Scotland) Act 1985 or under Article 25 of the Matrimonial Causes (Northern Ireland) Order 1978   ☐ Yes   ☐ No
   - a pension attachment order made under Part 1 of Schedule 5 to the Civil Partnership Act 2004 (England and Wales), section 12A(2) or (3) of the Family Law (Scotland) Act 1985 or under Part 1 of Schedule 15 to the Civil Partnership Act 2004 (Northern Ireland)   ☐ Yes   ☐ No
   - a forfeiture order   ☐ Yes   ☐ No
   - a bankruptcy order   ☐ Yes   ☐ No
   - an award of sequestration on a member's estate or the making of the appointment on his estate of a judicial factor under section 41 of the Solicitors (Scotland) Act 1980.   ☐ Yes   ☐ No

5. Do the member's rights include rights which are not shareable by virtue of regulation 2 of the Pension Sharing (Valuation) Regulations 2000?   ☐ Yes   ☐ No

   If Yes, please provide details.

6. Does the pension arrangement propose to levy additional charges specified in Regulation 6 of the Pensions on Divorce (Charging) Regulations 2000? ☐ Yes ☐ No

   If Yes, please provide the scale of the additional charges likely to made.

7. Is the scheme member a trustee of the pension scheme? ☐ Yes ☐ No

8. If a pension sharing order is made, will the person responsible for the pension arrangement require information regarding the scheme member's state of health before implementing the pension sharing order? ☐ Yes ☐ No

9. Does the person responsible for the pension sharing arrangement require any further information other than that contained in regulation 5 of the Pensions on Divorce etc. (Provision of Information Regulations) 2000, before implementing any Pension Sharing Order? ☐ Yes ☐ No

   If Yes, specify what.

D. To be completed by the pension arrangement

The following information should be provided if the scheme member requests it or the Court orders it pursuant to its powers under the Pensions on Divorce etc (Provision of Information) Regulations 2000, S.I. 1048/2000. Please note that pension arrangements may make an additional charge for providing this information.

1. Disregarding any future service or premiums that might be paid and future inflation, what is the largest lump sum payment that the member would be entitled to take if s/he were to retire at a normal retirement age?

2. What is the earliest date on which the member has the right to take benefits, excluding retirement on grounds of ill health? `D D / M M / Y Y Y Y`

3. Are spouse's or civil partner's benefits payable? ☐ Yes ☐ No

4. What lump sum would be payable on death at the date of completion of this form?

5. What proportion of the member's pension would be payable as of right to the spouse or civil partner of the member if the member were to die:

   (a) before retirement, and

   (b) after retirement, disregarding any future service or premiums that might be paid and future inflation?

6. Is the pension in payment, drawdown or deferment? ☐ Yes ☐ No

   If Yes, which?

7. Please provide a copy of the scheme booklet.

Dated `    /    /        `

4

FORM P1

Pension Sharing Annex under [section 24B of the Matrimonial Causes Act 1973] [paragraph 15 of Schedule 5 to the Civil Partnership Act 2004]	In the	
		*[County Court] *[Principal Registry of the Family Division]
	Case No. (Always quote this)	
	Transferor's Solicitor's reference	
	Transferee's Solicitor's reference	

Between _____ **(Petitioner)**

and _____ **(Respondent)**

Take Notice that:

On _____ the court   *(delete as appropriate)

- made a pension sharing order under Part IV of the Welfare Reform and Pensions Act 1999.

- [varied] [discharged] an order which included provision for pension sharing under Part IV of the Welfare Reform and Pensions Act 1999 dated D D / M M / Y Y Y Y .

This annex to the order provides the person responsible for the pension arrangement with the information required by virtue of rules of court:

A. Transferor's details

(i) The full name by which the Transferor is known:

(ii) All names by which the Transferor has been known:

(iii) The Transferor's date of birth: D D / M M / Y Y Y Y

(iv) The Transferor's address:

(v) The Transferor's National Insurance Number:

B. Transferee's Details

(i) The full name by which the Transferee is known:

(ii) All names by which the Transferee has been known:

(iii) The Transferee's date of birth:

     `D D / M M / Y Y Y Y`

(iv) The Transferee's address:

(v) The Transferee's National Insurance Number:

(vi) If the Transferee is also a member of the pension scheme from which the credit is derived, or a beneficiary of the same scheme because of survivor's benefits, the membership number:

C. Details of the Transferor's Pension Arrangement

(i) Name of the arrangement:

(ii) Name and address of the person responsible for the pension arrangement:

(iii) Reference Number:

(iv) If appropriate, such other details to enable the pension arrangement to be identified:

(v) The specified percentage of the member's CEV to be transferred:

         _ . _ %

D. Pension Sharing Charges

It is directed that: (*delete as appropriate)

*The pension sharing charges be apportioned between the parties as follows:

or

*The pension sharing charges be paid in full by the Transferor.

E. Have you filed Form D81 (Statement of Information for a Consent Order for a financial remedy)?

    ☐ Yes   ☐ No

If 'Yes' delete the text opposite.

The parties certify that:

(i) they have received the information required by Regulation 4 of the Pensions on Divorce etc (Provisions of Information) Regulations 2000;

(ii) that information is attached on Form P (Pension Inquiry Form); and

(iii) it appears from that information that there is power to make an order including provision under [section 24B of the Matrimonial Causes Act 1973] [paragraph 15 of Schedule 5 to the Civil Partnership Act 2004].

2

F.   In cases where the Transferee has a choice of an   ☐ Internal transfer   ☐ External transfer
internal or external transfer, if the Transferee has
indicated a preference, indicate what this is.

G.   **In the case of external transfer only
(recommended but optional information)**

(i) The name of the qualifying arrangement which
has agreed to accept the pension credit:

(ii) The address of the qualifying arrangement:

(iii) If known, the Transferee's membership or
policy number in the qualifying arrangement and
reference number of the new provider:

(iv) The name, or title, business address, phone
and fax numbers and email address of the person
who may be contacted in respect of the discharge
of liability for the pension credit on behalf of the
Transferee:
(This may be an Independent Financial Advisor, for
example, if one is advising the Transferee or the new
pension scheme itself.)

(v) Please attach a copy of the letter from the   ☐
qualifying arrangement indicating its willingness to
accept the pension credit

Please complete boxes H to J where applicable

H.   Where the credit is derived from an occupational   ☐ Yes   ☐ No
scheme which is being wound up, has the
Transferee indicated whether he wishes to
transfer his pension credit rights to a qualifying
arrangement?

I.   Where the pension arrangement has requested   ☐ Yes   ☐ No
details of the Transferor's health, has that
information been provided?

J.   Where the pension arrangement has requested   ☐ Yes   ☐ No
further information, has that information been
provided?

Note: Until the information requested in A, B, (and as far as applicable G, H, I and J) is provided the pension sharing
order cannot be implemented although it may be made. Even if all the information requested has been provided, further
information may be required before implementation can begin. If so, reasons why implementation cannot begin should
be sent by the pension arrangement to the Transferor and Transferee within 21 days of receipt of the pension sharing
order and this annex.

THIS ORDER TAKES EFFECT FROM the later of

a. the date on which the Decree Absolute of Divorce or Nullity of marriage is granted, or the Final Order of Dissolution or Nullity of civil partnership is made;

b. 28 days from the date of this order or, where the court has specified a period for filing an appeal notice, 7 days after the end of that period;

c. where an appeal has been lodged, the effective date of the order determining that appeal.

To the person responsible for the pension arrangement:

*(delete as appropriate)

*1. Take notice that you must discharge your liability within the period of 4 months beginning with the later of:
  - the day on which this order takes effect; or
  - the first day on which you are in receipt of –
  a. the pension sharing order including this annex (and where appropriate any attachments);
  b. in a matrimonial cause, a copy of the decree of divorce or nullity of marriage and a copy of the certificate that the decree has been made absolute;
  c. in a civil partnership cause, a copy of the final order of dissolution or order of nullity of civil partnership and a copy of the certificate that the order has been made final;
  d. the information specified in paragraphs A, B and C of this annex and, where applicable, paragraphs G to J of this annex; and
  e. payment of all outstanding charges requested by the pension scheme.

*2. The court directs that the implementation period for discharging your liability should be determined by regulations made under section 34(4) or 41(2)(a) of the Welfare Reform and Pensions Act 1999, in that:

FORM P2

	In the
Pension Attachment Annex under [section 25B or 25C of the Matrimonial Causes Act 1973] [paragraph 25 or 26 of Schedule 5 to the Civil Partnership Act 2004]	*[County Court]* *[Principal Registry of the Family Division]*
	Case No. (Always quote this)
	Applicant's Solicitor's reference
	Respondent's Solicitor's reference

Between _____ (Petitioner)

and _____ (Respondent)

Take Notice that:

On _____ the court   *(delete as appropriate)

- made an order including provision under [section [25B][25C]* of the Matrimonial Causes Act 1973]* [paragraph [25][26]* or Schedule 5 to the Civil Partnership Act 2004]*.

- [varied] [discharged] an order which included provision under [section [25B][25C]* of the Matrimonial Causes Act 1973] [paragraph [25][26] of Schedule 5 to the Civil Partnership Act 2004]* and dated [D D /M M /Y Y Y Y]

This annex to the order provides the person responsible for the pension arrangement with the information required by virtue of rules of court:

1. Name of the party with the pension rights:

2. Name of the other party:

3. The National Insurance Number of the party with pension rights:

4. Details of the Pension Arrangement:
    (i) Name and address of the person responsible for the pension arrangement:

    (ii) Policy Reference Number:

    (iii) *if appropriate, such other details to enable the pension arrangement to be identified:*

5A. **(i) To be completed where a Periodical Payments Order is made under s.25B of the Matrimonial Causes Act 1973.**

The specified percentage of any payment due to the party with the pension rights that is to be paid for the benefit of the other party: _ . _ %

(ii) To be completed where the court orders that the party with pension rights commutes a percentage of his pension to a tax free lump sum on retirement under s.25B of the Matrimonial Causes Act 1973.

(a) the specified percentage of the maximum lump sum available that is to be commuted: _ . _ %

(b) the specified percentage of the commuted sum which is to be paid to the spouse or the former spouse of the party with pension rights: _ . _ %

(iii) To be completed where the court orders, under s.25C of the Matrimonial Causes Act 1973, that all or part of a lump sum payable to the party with pension rights in respect of his death be paid to the other party.

(a) the percentage of the lump sum to be paid by the person responsible for the pension arrangement to the other party: _ . _ %

(b) the percentage of the lump sum payable (in accordance with a nomination by the party with pension rights) to the other party: _ . _ %

(c) the percentage of the lump sum to be paid by the person responsible for the pension arrangement for the benefit of the other party: _ . _ %

5B. **(i) To be completed where a Periodical Payments Order is made under paragraph 25 of Schedule 5 to the Civil Partnership Act 2004.**

The specified percentage of any payment due to the civil partner with the pension rights that is to be paid for the benefit of the other civil partner: _ . _ %

(ii) To be completed where the court orders that the civil partner with pension rights commutes a percentage of his pension to a tax free lump sum on retirement under paragraph 25 of Schedule 5 to the Civil Partnership Act 2004.

(a) the specified percentage of the maximum lump sum available that is to be commuted: _ . _ %

(b) the specified percentage of the commuted sum which is to be paid to the civil partner or the former civil partner of the civil partner with pension rights: _ . _ %

(iii) To be completed where the court orders, under paragraph 26 of Schedule 5 to the Civil Partnership Act 2004, that all or part of a lump sum payable to the civil partner with pension rights in respect of his death be paid to the other civil partner.

(a) the percentage of the lump sum to be paid by the person responsible for the pension arrangement to the other civil partner: __ . __ %

(b) the percentage of the lump sum payable (in accordance with a nomination by the civil partner with pension rights) to the other civil partner: __ . __ %

(c) the percentage of the lump sum to be paid by the person responsible for the pension arrangement for the benefit of the other civil partner: __ . __ %

To the person responsible for the pension arrangement:
*(delete if this information has already been provided to the person responsible for the pension arrangement)

1.   *You are required to serve any notice under the Divorce etc. (Pensions) Regulations 2000 or the Dissolution etc. (Pensions) Regulations 2005 on the other party at the following address:

2.   *You are required to make any payments due under the pension arrangement to the other party at the following address:

3.   *If the address at 2. above is that of a bank, building society or the Department of National Savings the following details will enable you to make payment into the account of the other party (e.g. Account Name, Number, Bank/Building Society/etc. Sort code):

Note: Where the order to which this annex applies was made by consent the following section should also be completed.

The court also confirms: *(delete as appropriate)

- *That notice has been served on the person responsible for the pension arrangement and that no objection has been received.

- *That notice has been served on the person responsible for the pension arrangement and that the court has considered any objection received.

PENSIONS ON DIVORCE ETC (PROVISION OF INFORMATION) REGULATIONS 2000

SI 2000/1048

1 Citation, commencement and interpretation

(1) These Regulations may be cited as the Pensions on Divorce etc (Provision of Information) Regulations 2000 and shall come into force on 1st December 2000.

(2) In these Regulations –

'the 1993 Act' means the Pension Schemes Act 1993;
'the 1995 Act' means the Pensions Act 1995;
'the 1999 Act' means the Welfare Reform and Pensions Act 1999;
'the Charging Regulations' means the Pensions on Divorce etc (Charging) Regulations 2000;
'the Implementation and Discharge of Liability Regulations' means the Pension Sharing (Implementation and Discharge of Liability) Regulations 2000;
'the Valuation Regulations' means the Pension Sharing (Valuation) Regulations 2000;
'active member' has the meaning given by section 124(1) of the 1995 Act;
'day' means any day other than –
    (a)   Christmas Day or Good Friday; or
    (b)   a bank holiday, that is to say, a day which is, or is to be observed as, a bank holiday or a holiday under Schedule 1 to the Banking and Financial Dealings Act 1971;

'deferred member' has the meaning given by section 124(1) of the 1995 Act;
'implementation period' has the meaning given by section 34(1) of the 1999 Act;
'member' means a person who has rights to future benefits, or has rights to benefits payable, under a pension arrangement;
'money purchase benefits' has the meaning given by section 181(1) of the 1993 Act;
'normal benefit age' has the meaning given by section 101B of the 1993 Act;
'normal pension age' has the meaning given in section 180 of the 1993 Act (normal pension age);
'notice of discharge of liability' means a notice issued to the member and his former spouse or former civil partner by the person responsible for a pension arrangement when that person has discharged his liability in respect of a pension credit in accordance with Schedule 5 to the 1999 Act;
'notice of implementation' means a notice issued by the person responsible for a pension arrangement to the member and his former spouse or former civil partner at the beginning of the implementation period notifying them of the day on which the implementation period for the pension credit begins;

'occupational pension scheme' has the meaning given by section 1 of the 1993 Act;

'the party with pension rights' and 'the other party' have the meanings given by section 25D(3) of the Matrimonial Causes Act ;

'pension arrangement' has the meaning given in section 46(1) of the 1999 Act;

'pension credit' means a credit under section 29(1)(b) of the 1999 Act;

'pension credit benefit' means the benefits payable under a pension arrangement or a qualifying arrangement to or in respect of a person by virtue of rights under the arrangement in question which are attributable (directly or indirectly) to a pension credit;

'pension credit rights' means rights to future benefits under a pension arrangement or a qualifying arrangement which are attributable (directly or indirectly) to a pension credit;

'pension sharing order or provision' means an order or provision which is mentioned in section 28(1) of the 1999 Act;

'pensionable service' has the meaning given by section 124(1) of the 1995 Act;

'person responsible for a pension arrangement' has the meaning given by section 46(2) of the 1999 Act;

'personal pension scheme' has the meaning given by section 1 of the 1993 Act;

'qualifying arrangement' has the meaning given by paragraph 6 of Schedule 5 to the 1999 Act;

'retirement annuity contract' means a contract or scheme which is to be treated as becoming a registered pension scheme under 153(9) of the Finance Act 2004 in accordance with paragraph 1(1)(f) of Schedule 36 to that Act;

'salary related occupational pension scheme' has the meaning given by regulation 1A of the Transfer Values Regulations;

'transfer day' has the meaning given by section 29(8) of the 1999 Act;

'transferee' has the meaning given by section 29(8) of the 1999 Act;

'transferor' has the meaning given by section 29(8) of the 1999 Act;

'the Transfer Values Regulations' means the Occupational Pension Schemes (Transfer Values) Regulations 1996;

'trustees or managers' has the meaning given by section 46(1) of the 1999 Act.

Amendments—SI 2000/2691; SI 2005/2877; SI 2006/744; SI 2007/60; SI 2008/1050; SI 2009/615.

2 Basic information about pensions and divorce or dissolution of a civil partnership

(1) The requirements imposed on a person responsible for a pension arrangement for the purposes of section 23(1)(a) of the 1999 Act (supply of pension information in connection with divorce etc.) are that he shall furnish –

(a) on request from a member, the information referred to in paragraphs (2) and (3)(b) to (f);

(b)   on request from the spouse or civil partner of a member, the information referred to in paragraph (3); or

(c)   pursuant to an order of the court, the information referred to in paragraph (2), (3) or (4),

to the member, the spouse or civil partner of the member, or, as the case may be, to the court.

(2) The information in this paragraph is a valuation of pension rights or benefits accrued under that member's pension arrangement.

(3) The information in this paragraph is –

(a)   a statement that on request from the member, or pursuant to an order of the court, a valuation of pension rights or benefits accrued under that member's pension arrangement, will be provided to the member, or, as the case may be, to the court;

(b)   a statement summarising the way in which the valuation referred to in paragraph (2) and sub-paragraph (a) is calculated;

(c)   the pension benefits which are included in a valuation referred to in paragraph (2) and sub-paragraph (a);

(d)   whether the person responsible for the pension arrangement offers membership to a person entitled to a pension credit, and if so, the types of benefits available to pension credit members under that arrangement;

(e)   whether the person responsible for the pension arrangements intends to discharge his liability for a pension credit other than by offering membership to a person entitled to a pension credit; and

(f)   the schedule of charges which the person responsible for the pension arrangement will levy in accordance with regulation 2(2) of the Charging Regulations (general requirements as to charges).

(4) The information in this paragraph is any other information relevant to any power with respect to the matters specified in section 23(1)(a) of the 1999 Act and which is not specified in Schedule 1 or 2 to the Occupational Pension Schemes (Disclosure of Information) Regulations 1996 (basic information about the scheme and information to be made available to individuals), or in Schedule 1 or 2 to the Personal Pension Schemes (Disclosure of Information) Regulations 1987 (basic information about the scheme and information to be made available to individuals), in a case where either of those Regulations applies.

(5) Where the member's request for, or the court order for the provision of, information includes a request for, or an order for the provision of, a valuation under paragraph (2), the person responsible for the pension arrangement shall furnish all the information requested, or ordered, to the member –

(a)   within 3 months beginning with the date the person responsible for the pension arrangement receives that request or order for the provision of the information;

(b)   within 6 weeks beginning with the date the person responsible for the pension arrangement receives the request, or order, for the provision of the information, if the member has notified that person on the date of the request or order that the information is needed in connection with proceedings commenced under any of the provisions referred to in section 23(1)(a) of the 1999 Act; or

(c) within such shorter period specified by the court in an order requiring the person responsible for the pension arrangement to provide a valuation in accordance with paragraph (2).

(6) Where –

(a) the member's request for, or the court order for the provision of, information does not include a request or an order for a valuation under paragraph (2); or

(b) the member's spouse or civil partner requests the information specified in paragraph (3),

the person responsible for the pension arrangement shall furnish that information to the member, his spouse civil partner, or the court, as the case may be, within one month beginning with the date that person responsible for the pension arrangement receives the request for, or the court order for the provision of, the information.

(7) At the same time as furnishing the information referred to in paragraph (1), the person responsible for a pension arrangement may furnish the information specified in regulation 4(2) (provision of information in response to a notification that a pension sharing order or provision may be made).

Amendments—SI 2005/2877.

3 Information about pensions and divorce and dissolution of a civil partnership: valuation of pension benefits

(1) Where an application for financial relief under any of the provisions referred to in section 23(a)(i), (ia), (iii) or (iv) of the 1999 Act (supply of pension information in connection with domestic and overseas divorce etc in England and Wales and corresponding Northern Ireland powers) has been made or is in contemplation, the valuation of benefits under a pension arrangement shall be calculated and verified for the purposes of regulation 2 of these Regulations in accordance with –

(a) paragraph (3), if the person with pension rights is a deferred member of an occupational pension scheme;

(b) paragraph (4), if the person with pension rights is an active member of an occupational pension scheme;

(c) paragraphs (5) and (6), if –
    (i) the person with pension rights is a member of a personal pension scheme; or
    (ii) those pension rights are contained in a retirement annuity contract; or

(d) paragraphs (7) and (8), if –
    (i) the pension of the person with pension rights is in payment;

(ii)   the rights of the person with pension rights are contained in an annuity contract other than a retirement annuity contract; or

(iii)   the rights of the person with pension rights are contained in a deferred annuity contract other than a retirement annuity contract; or

(iv)   the pension of the person with pension rights is not in payment and the person has attained normal pension age.

(2) Where an application for financial provision under any of the provisions referred to in section 23(1)(a)(ii) of the 1999 Act (corresponding Scottish powers) has been made, or is in contemplation, the valuation of benefits under a pension arrangement shall be calculated and verified for the purposes of regulation 2 of these Regulations in accordance with regulation 3 of the Divorce etc (Pensions) (Scotland) Regulations 2000 (valuation).

(3) Where the person with pension rights is a deferred member of an occupational pension scheme, the value of the benefits which he has under that scheme shall be taken to be –

(a)   in the case of an occupational pension scheme other than a salary related scheme, the cash equivalent to which he acquired a right under section 94(1)(a) of the 1993 Act (right to cash equivalent) on the termination of his pensionable service, calculated on the assumption that he has made an application under section 95 of that Act (ways of taking right to cash equivalent) on the date on which the request for the valuation was received; or

(b)   in the case of a salary related occupational pension scheme, the guaranteed cash equivalent to which he would have acquired a right under section 94(1)(aa) of the 1993 Act if he had made an application under section 95(1) of that Act, calculated on the assumption that he has made such an application on the date on which the request for the valuation was received.

(4) Where the person with pension rights is an active member of an occupational pension scheme, the valuation of the benefits which he has accrued under that scheme shall be calculated and verified –

(a)   on the assumption that the member had made a request for an estimate of the cash equivalent that would be available to him were his pensionable service to terminate on the date on which the request for the valuation was received; and

(b)   in accordance with regulation 11 of, and Schedule 1 to, the Transfer Values Regulations (disclosure).

(5) Where the person with pension rights is a member of a personal pension scheme, or those rights are contained in a retirement annuity contract, the value of the benefits which he has under that scheme or contract shall be taken to be the cash equivalent to which he would have acquired a right under section 94(1)(b) of the 1993 Act, if he had made an application under section 95(1) of that Act on the date on which the request for the valuation was received.

(6) In relation to a personal pension scheme which is comprised in a retirement annuity contract made before 4th January 1988, paragraph (5) shall apply as if such a scheme were not excluded from the scope of Chapter IV of Part IV of the 1993 Act by section 93(1)(b) of that Act (scope of Chapter IV).

(7) Cash equivalents are to be calculated and verified in accordance with regulations 7 to 7C and 7E(1) to (3) of the Transfer Values Regulations as appropriate.

(8) But when calculating and verifying a cash equivalent in accordance with those regulations –

- (a) references to 'trustees' must be read as references to 'person responsible for the pension arrangement';
- (b) where the person with pension rights is a pensioner member on the date on which the request for the valuation is received, the value of his pension must be calculated and verified in accordance with regulations 7 to 7E of the Transfer Values Regulations as appropriate;
- (c) where the person is over normal pension age but not in receipt of a pension –
    - (i) the value of his pension must be calculated and verified in accordance with regulations 7 to 7E of the Transfer Values Regulations as appropriate; and
    - (ii) the person responsible for the pension arrangement must assume that the pension came into payment on the date on which the request for the valuation was received; and
- (d) the date by reference to which the cash equivalent is to be calculated and verified is to be the date on which the request for the valuation was received.

(10) Where paragraph (3), (4) or (7) has effect by reference to provisions of Chapter IV of Part IV of the 1993 Act, section 93(1)(a)(i) of that Act (scope of Chapter IV) shall apply to those provisions as if the words 'at least one year' had been omitted from section 93(1)(a)(i).

Amendments—SI 2005/2877; SI 2007/60; SI 2008/1050.

4 Provision of information in response to a notification that a pension sharing order or provision may be made

(1) A person responsible for a pension arrangement shall furnish the information specified in paragraph (2) to the member or to the court, as the case may be –

- (a) within 21 days beginning with the date that the person responsible for the pension arrangement received the notification that a pension sharing order or provision may be made; or
- (b) if the court has specified a date which is outside the 21 days referred to in sub-paragraph (a), by that date.

(2) The information referred to in paragraph (1) is –

(a) the full name of the pension arrangement and address to which any order or provision referred to in section 28(1) of the 1999 Act (activation of pension sharing) should be sent;

(b) in the case of an occupational pension scheme, whether the scheme is winding up, and, if so, –

    (i) the date on which the winding up commenced; and

    (ii) the name and address of the trustees who are dealing with the winding up;

(c) in the case of an occupational pension scheme, whether a cash equivalent of the member's pension rights, if calculated on the date the notification referred to in paragraph (1)(a) was received by the trustees or managers of that scheme, would be reduced in accordance with the provisions of paragraphs 2, 3 and 12 of Schedule 1A to the Transfer Values Regulations (reductions in initial cash equivalents);

(d) whether the person responsible for the pension arrangement is aware that the member's rights under the pension arrangement are subject to any, and if so, to specify which, of the following –

    (i) any order or provision specified in section 28(1) of the 1999 Act;

    (ii) an order under section 23 of the Matrimonial Causes Act 1973 (financial provision orders in connection with divorce etc.), so far as it includes provision made by virtue of section 25B or 25C of that Act (powers to include provisions about pensions);

    (iii) an order under section 12A(2) or (3) of the Family Law (Scotland) Act 1985 (powers in relation to pensions lump sums when making a capital sum order) which relates to benefits or future benefits to which the member is entitled under the pension arrangement;

    (iv) an order under Article 25 of the Matrimonial Causes (Northern Ireland) Order 1978, so far as it includes provision made by virtue of Article 27B or 27C of that Order (Northern Ireland powers corresponding to those mentioned in paragraph (2)(d)(ii));

    (v) a forfeiture order;

    (vi) a bankruptcy order;

    (vii) an award of sequestration on a member's estate or the making of the appointment on his estate of a judicial factor under section 41 of the Solicitors (Scotland) Act 1980 (appointment of judicial factor);

(e) whether the member's rights under the pension arrangement include rights specified in regulation 2 of the Valuation Regulations (rights under a pension arrangement which are not shareable);

(f) if the person responsible for the pension arrangement has not at an earlier stage provided the following information, whether that person requires the charges specified in regulation 3 (charges recoverable in respect of the provision of basic information), 5 (charges in respect of pension sharing activity), or 6 (additional amounts recoverable in respect of pension sharing activity) of the Charging Regulations to be paid before the commencement of the implementation period, and if so, –

    (i)   whether that person requires those charges to be paid in full; or

    (ii) the proportion of those charges which he requires to be paid;

(g)   whether the person responsible for the pension arrangement may levy additional charges specified in regulation 6 of the Charging Regulations, and if so, the scale of the additional charges which are likely to be made;

(h)   whether the member is a trustee of the pension arrangement;

(i)   whether the person responsible for the pension arrangement may request information about the member's state of health from the member if a pension sharing order or provision were to be made; and

(j)   whether the person responsible for the pension arrangement requires information additional to that specified in regulation 5 (information required by the person responsible for the pension arrangement before the implementation period may begin) in order to implement the pension sharing order or provision.

Amendments—SI 2000/2691; SI 2003/1727; SI 2008/1050.

5 Information required by the person responsible for the pension arrangement before the implementation period may begin

The information prescribed for the purposes of section 34(1)(b) of the 1999 Act (information relating to the transferor and the transferee which the person responsible for the pension arrangement must receive) is –

(a)   in relation to the transferor –

    (i)   all names by which the transferor has been known;

    (ii) date of birth;

    (iii) address;

    (iv) National Insurance number;

    (v) the name of the pension arrangement to which the pension sharing order or provision relates; and

    (vi) the transferor's membership or policy number in that pension arrangement;

(b)   in relation to the transferee –

    (i)   all names by which the transferee has been known;

    (ii) date of birth;

    (iii) address;

    (iv) National Insurance number; and

    (v) if the transferee is a member of the pension arrangement from which the pension credit is derived, his membership or policy number in that pension arrangement;

(c)   where the transferee has given his consent in accordance with paragraph 1(3)(c), 3(3)(c) or 4(2)(c) of Schedule 5 to the 1999 Act (mode of discharge of liability for a pension credit) to the payment of the pension credit to the person responsible for a qualifying arrangement –

(i)   the full name of that qualifying arrangement;

(ii)   its address;

(iii)   if known, the transferee's membership number or policy number in that arrangement; and

(iv)   the name or title, business address, business telephone number, and, where available, the business facsimile number and electronic mail address of a person who may be contacted in respect of the discharge of liability for the pension credit;

(d)   where the rights from which the pension credit is derived are held in an occupational pension scheme which is being wound up, whether the transferee has given an indication whether he wishes to transfer his pension credit rights which may have been reduced in accordance with the provisions of regulation 16(1) of the Implementation and Discharge of Liability Regulations (adjustments to the amount of the pension credit – occupational pension schemes which are underfunded on the valuation day) to a qualifying arrangement; and

(e)   any information requested by the person responsible for the pension arrangement in accordance with regulation 4(2)(i) or (k).

6 Provision of information after the death of the person entitled to the pension credit before liability in respect of the pension credit has been discharged

(1) Where the person entitled to the pension credit dies before the person responsible for the pension arrangement has discharged his liability in respect of the pension credit, the person responsible for the pension arrangement shall, within 21 days of the date of receipt of the notification of the death of the person entitled to the pension credit, notify in writing any person whom the person responsible for the pension arrangement considers should be notified of the matters specified in paragraph (2).

(2) The matters specified in this paragraph are –

(a)   how the person responsible for the pension arrangement intends to discharge his liability in respect of the pension credit;

(b)   whether the person responsible for the pension arrangement intends to recover charges from the person nominated to receive pension credit benefits, in accordance with regulations 2 to 9 of the Charging Regulations, and if so, a copy of the schedule of charges issued to the parties to pension sharing in accordance with regulation 2(2)(b) of the Charging Regulations (general requirements as to charges); and

(c)   a list of any further information which the person responsible for the pension arrangement requires in order to discharge his liability in respect of the pension credit.

Amendments—SI 2000/2691.

7 Provision of information after receiving a pension sharing order or provision

(1) A person responsible for a pension arrangement who is in receipt of a pension sharing order or provision relating to that arrangement shall provide in writing to the transferor and transferee, or, where regulation 6(1) applies, to the

person other than the person entitled to the pension credit referred to in regulation 6 of the Implementation and Discharge of Liability Regulations (discharge of liability in respect of a pension credit following the death of the person entitled to the pension credit), as the case may be –

(a)   a notice in accordance with the provisions of regulation 7(1) of the Charging Regulations (charges in respect of pension sharing activity – postponement of implementation period);

(b)   a list of information relating to the transferor or the transferee, or, where regulation 6(1) applies, the person other than the person entitled to the pension credit referred to in regulation 6 of the Implementation and Discharge of Liability Regulations, as the case may be, which –

(i)   has been requested in accordance with regulation 4(2)(i) and (k), or, where appropriate, 6(2)(c), or should have been provided in accordance with regulation 5;

(ii)   the person responsible for the pension arrangement considers he needs in order to begin to implement the pension sharing order or provision; and

(iii) remains outstanding;

(c)   a notice of implementation; or

(d)   a statement by the person responsible for the pension arrangement explaining why he is unable to implement the pension sharing order or agreement.

(2) The information specified in paragraph (1) shall be furnished in accordance with that paragraph within 21 days beginning with –

(a)   in the case of sub-paragraph (a), (b) or (d) of that paragraph, the day on which the person responsible for the pension arrangement receives the pension sharing order or provision; or

(b)   in the case of sub-paragraph (c) of that paragraph, the later of the days specified in section 34(1)(a) and (b) of the 1999 Act (implementation period).

8 Provision of information after the implementation of a pension sharing order or provision

(1) The person responsible for the pension arrangement shall issue a notice of discharge of liability to the transferor and the transferee, or, as the case may be, the person entitled to the pension credit by virtue of regulation 6 of the Implementation and Discharge of Liability Regulations no later than the end of the period of 21 days beginning with the day on which the discharge of liability in respect of the pension credit is completed.

(2) In the case of a transferor whose pension is not in payment, the notice of discharge of liability shall include the following details –

(a)   the value of the transferor's accrued rights as determined by reference to the cash equivalent value of those rights calculated and verified in accordance with regulation 3 of the Valuation Regulations (calculation and verification of cash equivalents for the purposes of the creation of pension debits and credits);

(b)   the value of the pension debit;

(c)   any amount deducted from the value of the pension rights in accordance with regulation 9(2)(c) of the Charging Regulations (charges in respect of pension sharing activity – method of recovery);

(d)   the value of the transferor's rights after the amounts referred to in sub-paragraphs (b) and (c) have been deducted; and

(e)   the transfer day.

(3) In the case of a transferor whose pension is in payment, the notice of discharge of liability shall include the following details –

(a)   the value of the transferor's benefits under the pension arrangement as determined by reference to the cash equivalent value of those rights calculated and verified in accordance with regulation 3 of the Valuation Regulations;

(b)   the value of the pension debit;

(c)   the amount of the pension which was in payment before liability in respect of the pension credit was discharged;

(d)   the amount of pension which is payable following the deduction of the pension debit from the transferor's pension benefits;

(e)   the transfer day;

(f)   if the person responsible for the pension arrangement intends to recover charges, the amount of any unpaid charges –

(i)   not prohibited by regulation 2 of the Charging Regulations (general requirements as to charges); and

(ii)   specified in regulations 3 and 6 of those Regulations;

(g)   how the person responsible for the pension arrangement will recover the charges referred to in sub-paragraph (f), including –

(i)   whether the method of recovery specified in regulation 9(2)(d) of the Charging Regulations will be used;

(ii)   the date when payment of those charges in whole or in part is required; and

(iii)   the sum which will be payable by the transferor, or which will be deducted from his pension benefits, on that date.

(4) In the case of a transferee –

(a)   whose pension is not in payment; and

(b)   who will become a member of the pension arrangement from which the pension credit rights were derived,

the notice of discharge of liability to the transferee shall include the following details –

(i)   the value of the pension credit;

(ii)   any amount deducted from the value of the pension credit in accordance with regulation 9(2)(b) of the Charging Regulations;

(iii)   the value of the pension credit after the amount referred to in sub-paragraph (b)(ii) has been deducted;

    (iv)   the transfer day;

    (v)   any periodical charges the person responsible for the pension arrangement intends to make, including how and when those charges will be recovered from the transferee; and

    (vi) information concerning membership of the pension arrangement which is relevant to the transferee as a pension credit member.

(5) In the case of a transferee who is transferring his pension credit rights out of the pension arrangement from which those rights were derived, the notice of discharge of liability to the transferee shall include the following details –

    (a)   the value of the pension credit;

    (b)   any amount deducted from the value of the pension credit in accordance with regulation 9(2)(b) of the Charging Regulations;

    (c)   the value of the pension credit after the amount referred to in sub-paragraph (b) has been deducted;

    (d)   the transfer day; and

    (e)   details of the pension arrangement, including its name, address, reference number, telephone number, and, where available, the business facsimile number and electronic mail address, to which the pension credit has been transferred.

(6) In the case of a transferee, who has reached normal benefit age on the transfer day, and in respect of whose pension credit liability has been discharged in accordance with paragraph 1(2), 2(2), 3(2) or 4(4) of Schedule 5 to the 1999 Act (pension credits: mode of discharge – funded pension schemes, unfunded public service pension schemes, other unfunded pension schemes, or other pension arrangements), the notice of discharge of liability to the transferee shall include the following details –

    (a)   the amount of pension credit benefit which is to be paid to the transferee;

    (b)   the date when the pension credit benefit is to be paid to the transferee;

    (c)   the transfer day;

    (d)   if the person responsible for the pension arrangement intends to recover charges, the amount of any unpaid charges –

        (i)   not prohibited by regulation 2 of the Charging Regulations; and

        (ii)   specified in regulations 3 and 6 of those Regulations; and

    (e)   how the person responsible for the pension arrangement will recover the charges referred to in sub-paragraph (d), including –

        (i)   whether the method of recovery specified in regulation 9(2)(e) of the Charging Regulations will be used;

        (ii)   the date when payment of those charges in whole or in part is required; and

        (iii) the sum which will be payable by the transferee, or which will be deducted from his pension credit benefits, on that date.

(7) In the case of a person entitled to the pension credit by virtue of regulation 6 of the Implementation and Discharge of Liability Regulations, the notice of discharge of liability shall include the following details –

(a) the value of the pension credit rights as determined in accordance with regulation 10 of the Implementation and Discharge of Liability Regulations (calculation of the value of appropriate rights);

(b) any amount deducted from the value of the pension credit in accordance with regulation 9(2)(b) of the Charging Regulations;

(c) the value of the pension credit;

(d) the transfer day; and

(e) any periodical charges the person responsible for the pension arrangement intends to make, including how and when those charges will be recovered from the payments made to the person entitled to the pension credit by virtue of regulation 6 of the Implementation and Discharge of Liability Regulations.

9 Penalties

Where any trustee or manager of an occupational pension scheme fails, without reasonable excuse, to comply with any requirement imposed under regulation 6, 7 or 8, the Regulatory Authority may by notice in writing require that trustee or manager to pay within 28 days from the date of its imposition, a penalty which shall not exceed –

(a) £200 in the case of an individual, and

(b) £1,000 in any other case.

Amendment—SI 2009/615.

10 Provision of information after receipt of an earmarking order

(1) The person responsible for the pension arrangement shall, within 21 days beginning with the day that he receives –

(a) an order under section 23 of the Matrimonial Causes Act 1973, so far as it includes provision made by virtue of section 25B or 25C of that Act (powers to include provision about pensions);

(b) an order under section 12A(2) or (3) of the Family Law (Scotland) Act 1985; or

(c) an order under Article 25 of the Matrimonial Causes (Northern Ireland) Order 1978, so far as it includes provision made by virtue of Article 27B or 27C of that Order (Northern Ireland powers corresponding to those mentioned in sub-paragraph (a)),

issue to the party with pension rights and the other party a notice which includes the information specified in paragraphs (2) and (5), or (3), (4) and (5), as the case may be.

(2) Where an order referred to in paragraph (1)(a), (b) or (c) is made in respect of the pension rights or benefits of a party with pension rights whose pension is not in payment, the notice issued by the person responsible for a pension arrangement to the party with pension rights and the other party shall include a list of the circumstances in respect of any changes of which the party with pension rights or the other party must notify the person responsible for the pension arrangement.

(3) Where an order referred to in paragraph (1)(a) or (c) is made in respect of the pension rights or benefits of a party with pension rights whose pension is in payment, the notice issued by the person responsible for a pension arrangement to the party with pension rights and the other party shall include –

(a)　the value of the pension rights or benefits of the party with pension rights;

(b)　the amount of the pension of the party with pension rights after the order has been implemented;

(c)　the first date when a payment pursuant to the order is to be made; and

(d)　a list of the circumstances, in respect of any changes of which the party with pension rights or the other party must notify the person responsible for the pension arrangement.

(4) Where an order referred to in paragraph (1)(a) or (c) is made in respect of the pension rights of a party with pension rights whose pension is in payment, the notice issued by the person responsible for a pension arrangement to the party with pension rights shall, in addition to the items specified in paragraph (3), include –

(a)　the amount of the pension of the party with pension rights which is currently in payment; and

(b)　the amount of pension which will be payable to the party with pension rights after the order has been implemented.

(5) Where an order referred to in paragraph (1)(a), (b) or (c) is made the notice issued by the person responsible for a pension arrangement to the party with pension rights and the other party shall include –

(a)　the amount of any charges which remain unpaid by –

　　(i)　the party with pension rights; or

　　(ii)　the other party,

in respect of the provision by the person responsible for the pension arrangement of information about pensions and divorce or dissolution of a civil partnership pursuant to regulation 3 of the Charging Regulations, and in respect of complying with an order referred to in paragraph (1)(a), (b) or (c); and

(b)　information as to the manner in which the person responsible for the pension arrangement will recover the charges referred to in sub-paragraph (a), including –

　　(i)　the date when payment of those charges in whole or in part is required;

　　(ii)　the sum which will be payable by the party with pension rights or the other party, as the case may be; and

　　(iii)　whether the sum will be deducted from payments of pension to the party with pension rights, or, as the case may be, from payments to be made to the other party pursuant to an order referred to in paragraph (1)(a), (b) or (c).

Amendments—SI 2005/2877.

PENSION SHARING (VALUATION) REGULATIONS 2000

SI 2000/1052

1 Citation, commencement and interpretation

(1) These Regulations may be cited as the Pension Sharing (Valuation) Regulations 2000 and shall come into force on 1 December 2000.

(2) In these Regulations –

'the 1993 Act' means the Pension Schemes Act 1993;
'the 1995 Act' means the Pensions Act 1995;
'the 1999 Act' means the Welfare Reform and Pensions Act 1999;
'the 2004 Act' means the Pensions Act 2004;
'employer' has the meaning given by section 181(1) of the 1993 Act;
'initial cash equivalent' means the amount calculated in accordance with regulation 7(1)(a) of the Transfer Values Regulations;
'occupational pension scheme' has the meaning given by section 1 of the 1993 Act;
'pension arrangement' has the meaning given by section 46(1) of the 1999 Act;
'relevant arrangement' has the meaning given by section 29(8) of the 1999 Act;
'scheme' means an occupational pension scheme;
transfer credits' has the meaning given by section 181(1) of the 1993 Act;
'transfer day' has the meaning given by section 29(8) of the 1999 Act;
'transferor' has the meaning given by section 29(8) of the 1999 Act;
'the Transfer Values Regulations' means the Occupational Pension Schemes (Transfer Values) Regulations 1996;
'trustees or managers' has the meaning given by section 46(1) of the 1999 Act;
'valuation day' has the meaning given by section 29(7) of the 1999 Act.

Amendments—SI 2000/2691; SI 2003/1727; SI 2005/3377; SI 2006/744; SI 2007/60; SI 2008/1050.

2 Rights under a pension arrangement which are not shareable

(1) Rights under a pension arrangement which are not shareable are –

    (a) subject to paragraph (2), any rights accrued between 1961 and 1975 which relate to contracted-out equivalent pension benefit within the meaning of section 57 of the National Insurance Act 1965 (equivalent pension benefits, etc);

    (b) any rights in respect of which a person is in receipt of –

        (i) a pension;

        (ii) an annuity;

(iii)   payments under an interim arrangement within the meaning of section 28(1A) of the 1993 Act (ways of giving effect to protected rights); or

(iv)   dependants' income withdrawal within the meaning of paragraph 21 of Schedule 28 to the Finance Act 2004 (dependants' income withdrawal).

by virtue of being the widow, widower, surviving civil partner or other dependant of a deceased person with pension rights under a pension arrangement; and

(c)   any rights which will result in the payment of a benefit which is to be provided solely by reason of the –

(i)   disablement, or

(ii)   death,

due to an accident suffered by a person occurring during his pensionable service.

(2) Paragraph (1)(a) applies only when those rights are the only rights held by a person under a pension arrangement.

Amendments—SI 2005/2877; SI 2006/744.

3 Calculation and verification of cash equivalents for the purposes of the creation of pension debits and credits

For the purposes of section 29 of the 1999 Act (creation of pension debits and credits), cash equivalents may be calculated and verified –

(a)   where the relevant arrangement is an occupational pension scheme in accordance with regulations 4; or

(b)   in any other case, in accordance with regulations 5 and 7.

Amendments—SI 2010/499.

4 Manner of calculation and verification of cash equivalents: occupational pension schemes

(1) Subject to this regulation, cash equivalents for members of occupational pension schemes are to be calculated and verified in accordance with regulations 7 to 7E of the Transfer Values Regulations.

(2) Reductions to initial cash equivalents can only be made in accordance with regulation 7D of, and paragraphs 1 to 6 and 12 to 14 of Schedule 1A to, those Regulations.

(3) The reduction referred to in paragraph 2 of Schedule 1A to the Transfer Values Regulations must not be applied to a case where liability in respect of a pension credit is to be discharged in accordance with –

(a)   paragraph 1(2) of Schedule 5 to the 1999 Act (pension credits: mode of discharge – funded pension schemes); or

(b)   paragraph 1(3) of that Schedule, in a case where regulation 7(2) of the Pension Sharing (Implementation and Discharge of Liability) Regulations 2000 (funded pension schemes) applies.

(4) When calculating and verifying the cash equivalent, the Transfer Values Regulations are to be read as if—

(a)   in regulation 1(2) (interpretation), there were inserted at the appropriate alphabetical places—

'normal pension age' has the meaning given by section 180 of the 1993 Act (normal pension age);';
'occupational pension scheme' has the meaning given by section 1 of the 1993 Act (categories of pension schemes);';
'transfer day' has the meaning given by section 29(8) of the Welfare Reform and Pensions Act 1999 (creation of pension debits and credits);';
'valuation day' has the meaning given by section 29(7) of the Welfare Reform and Pensions Act 1999;';

(b)   in regulation 7(1) (manner of calculation and verification of cash equivalents – general provisions), for 'paragraphs (4) and (7)' there were substituted 'paragraphs (4), (7) and (8) to (11)';

(c)   after regulation 7(7), there were inserted –

'(8) Where the person with pension rights is a deferred member of an occupational pension scheme on the transfer day, the value of the benefits which he has accrued under that scheme must be taken to be—

    (a)   in the case of an occupational pension scheme other than a salary related scheme, the cash equivalent to which he acquired a right under section 94(1)(a) of the 1993 Act (right to cash equivalent) on the termination of his pensionable service, calculated and verified on the assumption that he has made an application under section 95(1) of that Act (ways of taking right to cash equivalent); or

    (b)   in the case of a salary related occupational pension scheme, the guaranteed cash equivalent to which he would have acquired a right under section 94(1)(aa) of the 1993 Act if he had made an application under section 95(1) of that Act.

(9) Where the person with pension rights is an active member of an occupational pension scheme on the transfer day, the value of the benefits which he has accrued under that scheme must be calculated and verified on the assumption that the member had made a request for an estimate of the cash equivalent that would be available to him were his pensionable service to terminate on the transfer day.

(10) Where the person with pension rights is a pensioner member of an occupational pension scheme on the transfer day, the value of his pension must be calculated and verified in accordance with this regulation and regulations 7A to 7C and 7E(1) to (3) as appropriate.

(11) Where the person with pension rights attains, or is over, normal pension age and is not in receipt of a pension—

    (a)   the pension must be calculated and verified in accordance with this regulation and regulations 7A to 7C and 7E(1) to (3) as appropriate; and

(b) the trustees must assume that the member's pension comes into payment on the 'transfer day';

(d) in regulation 7A(2), the reference to 'guarantee date' was a reference to 'valuation day'; and

(e) in paragraph 12 of Schedule 1A, the reference to 'guarantee date' was a reference to 'valuation day'.

Amendments—Substituted by SI 2008/1050.

5 Manner of calculation and verification of cash equivalents: other relevant arrangements

(1) Subject to this regulation, cash equivalents for members of a relevant arrangement other than an occupational pension scheme are to be calculated and verified in accordance with regulations 7 to 7E of the Transfer Values Regulations.

(2) When calculating and verifying the cash equivalent, the Transfer Value Regulations are to be read as if –

(a) in regulation 1(2) –

(i) for the definition of 'trustees' there were substituted –
'trustees' means the person responsible for the relevant arrangement;'; and

(ii) there were inserted at the appropriate alphabetical places

'personal pension scheme' has the meaning given by section 1 of the 1993 Act (categories of pension scheme);';
'transfer day' has the meaning given by section 29(8) of the Welfare Reform and Pensions Act 1999 (creation of pension debits and credits);';

(b) in regulation 7(1) (manner of calculation and verification of cash equivalents – general provisions), for 'paragraphs (4) and (7)' there were substituted 'paragraphs (4), (7) and (8)'; and

(c) after regulation 7(7), there were inserted –

'(8) Where the person with pension rights is a member of a personal pension scheme, or those rights are contained in a retirement annuity contract, the value of the benefits which he has accrued under that scheme or contract on the transfer day must be taken to be the cash equivalent to which he would have acquired a right under section 94(1)(b) of the 1993 Act (right to cash equivalent), if he had made an application under section 95(1) of that Act (ways of taking right to cash equivalent) on the date on which the request for the valuation was received.'.

(3) In relation to a personal pension scheme which is comprised in a retirement annuity contract made before 4th January 1988, this regulation applies as if such a scheme were not excluded from the scope of Chapter IV of Part IV of the 1993 Act by section 93(1)(b) of that Act (scope of Chapter IV);

(c) regulation 7 (other relevant arrangements: reduction of cash equivalents) becomes paragraph (1) of regulation 7; and

(d) in regulation 7, after paragraph (1) insert –

'(2) This regulation does not apply to occupational pension schemes.'.

Amendments—Substituted by SI 2008/1050.

6 ...

Amendments—Substituted by SI 2008/1050.

7 Other relevant arrangements: reduction of cash equivalents

(1) Where all or any of the benefits to which a cash equivalent relates have been surrendered, commuted or forfeited before the date on which the person responsible for the relevant arrangement discharges his liability for the pension credit in accordance with the provisions of Schedule 5 to the 1999 Act, the cash equivalent of the benefits so surrendered, commuted or forfeited shall be reduced in proportion to the reduction in the total value of the benefits.

(2) This regulation does not apply to occupational pension schemes.

Amendments—SI 2008/1050.

DIVORCE ETC (PENSIONS) REGULATIONS 2000

SI 2000/1123

1 Citation, commencement and transitional provisions

(1) These Regulations may be cited as the Divorce etc (Pensions) Regulations 2000 and shall come into force on 1st December 2000.

(2) These Regulations shall apply to any proceedings for divorce, judicial separation or nullity of marriage commenced on or after 1st December 2000, and any such proceedings commenced before that date shall be treated as if these Regulations had not come into force.

2 Interpretation

In these Regulations –

(a) a reference to a section by number alone means the section so numbered in the Matrimonial Causes Act 1973;
(b) 'the 1984 Act' means the Matrimonial and Family Proceedings Act 1984;
(c) expressions defined in sections 21A and 25D(3) have the meanings assigned by those sections;
(d) every reference to a rule by number alone means the rule so numbered in the Family Procedure Rules 2010.

Amendments—SI 2011/1045.

3 Valuation

(1) For the purposes of the court's functions in connection with the exercise of any of its powers under Part II of the Matrimonial Causes Act 1973, benefits under a pension arrangement shall be calculated and verified in the manner set out in regulation 3 of the Pensions on Divorce etc (Provision of Information) Regulations 2000, and –

    (a)   the benefits shall be valued as at a date to be specified by the court (being not earlier than one year before the date of the petition and not later than the date on which the court is exercising its power);

    (b)   in determining that value the court may have regard to information furnished by the person responsible for the pension arrangement pursuant to any of the provisions set out in paragraph (2); and

    (c)   in specifying a date under sub-paragraph (a) above the court may have regard to the date specified in any information furnished as mentioned in sub-paragraph (b) above.

(2) The relevant provisions for the purposes of paragraph (1)(b) above are –

    (a)   the Pensions on Divorce etc (Provision of Information) Regulations 2000;

    (b)   regulation 5 of and Schedule 2 to the Occupational Pension Schemes (Disclosure of Information) Regulations 1996 and regulation 11 of and Schedule 1 to the Occupational Pension Schemes (Transfer Value) Regulations 1996;

    (c)   section 93A or 94(1)(a) or (aa) of the Pension Schemes Act 1993;

    (d)   section 94(1)(b) of the Pension Schemes Act 1993 or paragraph 2(a) (or, where applicable, 2(b)) of Schedule 2 to the Personal Pension Schemes (Disclosure of Information) Regulations 1987.

4 Pension attachment: notices

(1) This regulation applies in the circumstances set out in section 25D(1)(a) (transfers of pension rights).

(2) Where this regulation applies, the person responsible for the first arrangement shall give notice in accordance with the following paragraphs of this regulation to –

    (a)   the person responsible for the new arrangement, and

    (b)   the other party.

(3) The notice to the person responsible for the new arrangement shall include copies of the following documents –

    (a)   every order made under section 23 imposing any requirement on the person responsible for the first arrangement in relation to the rights transferred;

    (b)   any order varying such an order;

    (c)   all information or particulars which the other party has been required to supply under any provision of rule 9.33 or 9.34 for the purpose of enabling the person responsible for the first arrangement –

     (i)   to provide information, documents or representations to the court to enable it to decide what if any requirement should be imposed on that person; or

     (ii)   to comply with any order imposing such a requirement;

(d)   any notice given by the other party to the person responsible for the first arrangement under regulation 6;

(e)   where the pension rights under the first arrangement were derived wholly or partly from rights held under a previous pension arrangement, any notice given to the person responsible for the previous arrangement under paragraph (2) of this regulation on the occasion of that acquisition of rights.

(4) The notice to the other party shall contain the following particulars –

(a)   the fact that the pension rights have been transferred;

(b)   the date on which the transfer takes effect;

(c)   the name and address of the person responsible for the new arrangement;

(d)   the fact that the order made under section 23 is to have effect as if it had been made in respect of the person responsible for the new arrangement.

(5) Both notices shall be given –

(a)   within the period provided by section 99 of the Pension Schemes Act 1993 for the person responsible for the first arrangement to carry out what the member requires; and

(b)   before the expiry of 21 days after the person responsible for the first arrangement has made all required payments to the person responsible for the new arrangement.

Amendments—SI 2011/1045.

5 Pension attachment: reduction in benefits

(1) This regulation applies where –

(a)   an order under section 23 or under section 17 of the 1984 Act has been made by virtue of section 25B or 25C imposing any requirement on the person responsible for a pension arrangement;

(b)   an event has occurred which is likely to result in a significant reduction in the benefits payable under the arrangement, other than –

     (i)   the transfer from the arrangement of all the rights of the party with pension rights in the circumstances set out in section 25D(1)(a), or

     (ii)   a reduction in the value of assets held for the purposes of the arrangement by reason of a change in interest rates or other market conditions.

(2) Where this regulation applies, the person responsible for the arrangement shall, within 14 days of the occurrence of the event mentioned in paragraph (1)(b), give notice to the other party of –

    (a)   that event;

    (b)   the likely extent of the reduction in the benefits payable under the arrangement.

(3) Where the event mentioned in paragraph (1)(b) consists of a transfer of some but not all of the rights of the party with pension rights from the arrangement, the person responsible for the first arrangement shall, within 14 days of the transfer, give notice to the other party of the name and address of the person responsible for any pension arrangement under which the party with pension rights has acquired rights as a result of that event.

6 Pension attachment: change of circumstances

(1) This regulation applies where –

    (a)   an order under section 23 or under section 17 of the 1984 Act has been made by virtue of section 25B or 25C imposing any requirement on the person responsible for a pension arrangement; and

    (b)   any of the events set out in paragraph (2) has occurred.

(2) Those events are –

    (a)   any of the particulars supplied by the other party under rule 9.33 or 9.34 for any purpose mentioned in regulation 4(3)(c) has ceased to be accurate; or

    (b)   by reason of the remarriage of the other party, or his having formed a subsequent civil partnership, or otherwise, the order has ceased to have effect.

(3) Where this regulation applies, the other party shall, within 14 days of the event, give notice of it to the person responsible for the pension arrangement.

(4) Where, because of the inaccuracy of the particulars supplied by the other party under rule 9.33 or 9.34 or because the other party has failed to give notice of their having ceased to be accurate, it is not reasonably practicable for the person responsible for the pension arrangement to make a payment to the other party as required by the order –

    (a)   it may instead make that payment to the party with pension rights, and

    (b)   it shall then be discharged of liability to the other party to the extent of that payment.

(5) Where an event set out in paragraph (2)(b) has occurred and, because the other party has failed to give notice in accordance with paragraph (3), the person responsible for the pension arrangement makes a payment to the other party as required by the order –

    (a)   its liability to the party with pension rights shall be discharged to the extent of that payment, and

    (b)   the other party shall, within 14 days of the payment being made, make a payment to the party with pension rights to the extent of that payment.

Amendments—SI 2005/2114; SI 2011/1045.

7 Pension attachment: transfer of rights

(1) This regulation applies where –

(a) a transfer of rights has taken place in the circumstances set out in section 25D(1)(a);

(b) notice has been given in accordance with regulation 4(2)(a) and (b);

(c) any of the events set out in regulation 6(2) has occurred; and

(d) the other party has not, before receiving notice under regulation 4(2)(b), given notice of that event to the person responsible for the first arrangement under regulation 6(3).

(2) Where this regulation applies, the other party shall, within 14 days of the event, give notice of it to the person responsible for the new arrangement.

(3) Where, because of the inaccuracy of the particulars supplied by the other party under rule 9.33 or 9.34 for any purpose mentioned in regulation 4(3)(c) or because the other party has failed to give notice of their having ceased to be accurate, it is not reasonably practicable for the person responsible for the new arrangement to make a payment to the other party as required by the order –

(a) it may instead make that payment to the party with pension rights, and

(b) it shall then be discharged of liability to the other party to the extent of that payment.

(4) Subject to paragraph (5), where this regulation applies and the other party, within one year from the transfer, gives to the person responsible for the first arrangement notice of the event set out in regulation 6(2) in purported compliance with regulation 7(2), the person responsible for the first arrangement shall –

(a) send that notice to the person responsible for the new arrangement, and

(b) give the other party a second notice under regulation 4(2)(b);

and the other party shall be deemed to have given notice under regulation 7(2) to the person responsible for the new arrangement.

(5) Upon complying with paragraph (4) above, the person responsible for the first arrangement shall be discharged from any further obligation under regulation 4 or 7(4), whether in relation to the event in question or any further event set out in regulation 6(2) which may be notified to it by the other party.

Amendments—SI 2011/1045.

8 Service

A notice under regulation 4, 5, 6 or 7 may be sent by fax or by ordinary first class post to the last known address of the intended recipient and shall be deemed to have been received on the seventh day after the day on which it was sent.

9 Pension sharing order not to take effect pending appeal

(1) No pension sharing order under section 24B or variation of a pension sharing order under section 31 shall take effect earlier than 7 days after the end of the period for filing notice of appeal against the order.

(2) The filing of a notice of appeal within the time allowed for doing so prevents the order taking effect before the appeal has been dealt with.

10 Revocation

The Divorce etc (Pensions) Regulations 1996 and the Divorce etc (Pensions) (Amendment) Regulations 1997 are revoked.

INDEX

References are to paragraph numbers.